AMERICAN HORIZONS

AMERICAN HORIZONS

U.S. HISTORY IN A GLOBAL CONTEXT

Third Edition

Volume I · To 1877

Michael Schaller
University of Arizona

Janette Thomas Greenwood
Clark University

Andrew Kirk
University of Nevada, Las Vegas

Sarah J. Purcell
Grinnell College

Aaron Sheehan-Dean
Louisiana State University

Christina Snyder
The Pennsylvania State University

with contributions by:
Robert Schulzinger
University of Colorado, Boulder

John Bezís-Selfa
Wheaton College

New York Oxford
OXFORD UNIVERSITY PRESS

Oxford University Press is a department of the University of Oxford. It furthers the
University's objective of excellence in research, scholarship, and education by publishing worldwide.
Oxford is a registered trade mark of Oxford University Press in the UK and certain other countries.

Published in the United States of America by Oxford University Press
198 Madison Avenue, New York, NY 10016, United States of America.

For titles covered by Section 112 of the US Higher Education
Opportunity Act, please visit www.oup.com/us/he for the latest
information about pricing and alternate formats.

Library of Congress Cataloging-in-Publication Data

CIP data on file with Library of Congress
ISBN: 9780190659486

11 10 9 8 7 6 5 4
Printed in Mexico by Quad / Mexico.

DEDICATION

To all our students.
The individual authors would also like to dedicate this book to the following people.
Michael Schaller: *to GS, N, G, & D*
Janette Thomas Greenwood: *to M, E, & S*
Andrew Kirk: *to L, H, & Q*
Sarah J. Purcell: *to H, E, & M*
Aaron Sheehan-Dean: *to M, L, & A*
Christina Snyder: *to JFL*

⊘BRIEF CONTENTS

CONTENTS

CHAPTER 5

Battling for Souls, Minds, and the Heart of North America, 1730–1763 · 155

CHAPTER 6

Empire and Resistance, 1763–1776 · 195

CHAPTER 7

A Revolutionary Nation, 1776–1789 · 227

CHAPTER 8

A New Nation Facing a Revolutionary World, 1789–1815 · 261

CHAPTER 11

New Boundaries, New Roles, 1820–1856 · 363

MAPS

PREFACE

American Horizons offers students in American history courses the opportunity to put that story in a global context.

For more than 500 years, North America has been part of a global network centered on the exchange of peoples, goods, and ideas. Human migrations—sometimes freely, sometimes forced—have continued over the centuries, along with the evolution of commerce in commodities as varied as tobacco, sugar, and computer chips. Europeans and Africans came or were brought to the continent, where they met, traded with, fought among, and intermarried with Native peoples. Some of these migrants stayed, whereas others returned to their home countries. Still others came and went periodically. This initial circulation of people across the oceans foreshadowed the continuous movement of people, goods, and ideas that made the United States. Such forces have shaped American history, both dividing and unifying the nation. American "horizons" truly stretch beyond our nation's borders, embracing the trading networks established during and after the colonial era as well as the digital social networks connecting people globally today.

American Horizons tells the story of the United States by exploring this exchange on a global scale and placing it at the center of that story. By doing so, we provide a different perspective on the history of the United States, one that we hope broadens the horizons of those who read our work and are ever mindful of the global forces that increasingly and profoundly shape our lives. At the same time, *American Horizons* considers those ways in which U.S. influence reshaped the lives and experiences of people of other nations.

U.S. history is increasingly perceived, interpreted, and taught as part of a global historical experience. The mutual influence of change—of global forces entering the United States and of American ideas, goods, and people moving out through the world—has been a consistent feature since the 16th century. Although most Americans today are aware that their influence is felt abroad and are increasingly aware of the influence of events abroad on their own lives, they tend to think of these as recent developments. In fact, those earliest exchanges of beliefs and products some 500 years ago established a pattern of interaction that continues today.

We have written a narrative that encourages readers to consider the variety of pressures that spurred historical change. Some of these pressures arose within America, and some came from outside. In the 1820s, the global market for whale oil shaped labor conditions throughout New England. At the same time, the American political system was transformed by the unique inheritance of the American Revolution and the relative abundance of land in North America. In the 1940s and 1950s, the federal government designed a unique set of policies to help World War II veterans readjust to civilian life, whereas the civil rights movement unfolded within a global context of decolonization in Africa and Asia. Topics such as these help readers consider the relationship between local and global forces that shaped American history.

American Horizons presents an opportunity to view the nation's history as more than a mere sequence of events for students to memorize. Although adhering to the familiar chronological organization of this course, our narrative style and structure provide the flexibility of shifting emphasis from time to time to the global aspects of American history. Although the story of the United States is always at the center, that story is told through the movement of people, goods, and ideas into, within, or out of the United States.

How did the United States emerge from a diverse set of colonies? How did colonists interact with Native American nations? How did the United States become a major player on the world stage of nations? What qualities make the United States unique? What does the United States share with other nations and empires? History includes many story lines that contribute to this narrative. *American Horizons* is the story of where this nation came from and how its people have been shaped by their own values as well as their interactions with the rest of the world. It recognizes that many of the significant events in American history had causes and consequences connected to developments elsewhere and presents those events accordingly. *American Horizons* depicts this intersection of story lines from many nations that influenced, and were influenced by, the United States of America.

As readers engage with the text, we encourage them to think explicitly about what makes history. What matters? What forces or events shaped how people lived their lives?

The Development Story

The six coauthors of this book specialize in a variety of time periods and methodologies. Based on our research and teaching, we all share the idea that the nation's history can best be understood by examining how, from the precolonial era forward, the American experience reflected the interaction of many nations, peoples, and events. We present this idea in a format that integrates traditional narrative history with the enhanced perspective of five centuries of global interaction.

About the Third Edition

This new edition of *American Horizons* is comprehensive yet concise enough for instructors who prefer a more economical option for their students without forgoing the primary advantages of a traditional, longer text. This has been achieved without sacrificing the kinds of features, images, tables, maps, and figures expected in this course.

HALLMARK FEATURES

- Each chapter begins with a compelling story at the core of the chapter theme.
- **Global Passages** boxes feature a unique story illustrating America's connection to the world.
- A rich graphics program of maps and figures helps students explore essential chapter themes.
- Timelines highlighting significant happenings in North America *and* the rest of the world, presented in parallel, provide students with a global context for American events.

- **America in the World** maps at the end of each chapter visually summarize the key themes of exchange (of peoples, goods, and ideas between America and other nations) discussed in each chapter.
- **Key Terms and People** lists at the end of each chapter help students recall the important people and events of that chapter.
- Throughout the chapters, **Study Questions** test students' memory and understanding of the chapter content. Chapter-ending **Review Questions** ask students to think critically and analyze what they have learned.

New to the Third Edition

NEW COAUTHOR

The *American Horizons* team welcomes new coauthor Christina Snyder, Professor of History at The Pennsylvania State University to the third edition. Christina was responsible for revising Chapters 1–5 and brings her knowledge of colonialism, race, slavery, and Native North America to this edition.

NEW GLOBAL PASSAGES BOXES

For the third edition, the following Global Passages boxes have been refreshed with new examples of key global connections.

- Chapter 1: Chocolate
- Chapter 5: The Deerskin Trade and Indian Consumers
- Chapter 7: Phillis Wheatley, Revolutionary Transatlantic Poet
- Chapter 13: Making Boundaries
- Chapter 14: A Global War for Democracy

NEW AND REVISED CHAPTER CONTENT

Chapter 1

- New chapter opener discussion of the Lady of Cofitachequi and her encounter with Hernando de Soto and the Spanish army.
- Inclusion of a new section on the origins and arrival of the "first Americans" in the Americas.
- Addition of a new section on hunting, gathering, and farming and how Native societies developed specialized economies according to regional climates and geographies.
- Inclusion of a new section on trade and how the exchange of products contributed to the growth of Native cities.
- Addition of a new section on how climatic changes led to resource degradation, migration, and the de-urbanization of Native societies prior to the arrival of Christopher Columbus.
- Revised section on European expansion highlighting Leif Ericson as the first European to lead a transatlantic expedition, followed by a discussion of factors that encouraged exploration beyond the European continent.
- Inclusion of a new section highlighting the effects of the Columbian exchange, with a focus on violence, disease, and cultural exchange.

Chapter 2

- Expanded discussion of Indian reactions to Franciscan missions and conversion efforts.
- Expanded coverage of how trade and access to European goods affected Indians.
- Revised discussion of conflicts between colonists and Indians, with a focus on the Pequot War.

Chapter 3

- Revised and expanded discussion of the devastating effect of smallpox on Indian populations and how the subsequent "Beaver Wars" reshaped eastern North America and contributed to the Indian slave trade.

Chapter 4

- New chapter opener discussion of the Natchez War of 1729–1731.
- New section that highlights how the growth of colonies, the expansion of trade, and the resulting economic revolution shifted power dynamics among Native Americans.
- Revised coverage of French Louisiana's alliances with Indian nations and how the colony's shift to plantation agriculture affected such alliances.
- Revised and expanded discussion of South Carolina's role in the Indian slave trade and how the Yamasee War reshaped Native American politics.

Chapter 5

- New section on settler colonialism and how displacement affected eastern Indians.
- Expanded discussion of Indian awakenings to include coverage of the Native spiritual leader Neolin and his effort to promote Indian unity.

Chapter 6

- Inclusion of a new section on Lord Dunmore's Proclamation.

Chapter 8

- New chapter opener on "Toussaint's Clause," American legislation that aided Saint-Domingue's independence movement (Haitian Revolution).

Chapter 9

- Revised discussion of Native Americans and civilization policy.

Chapter 12

- New chapter opener on abolitionists Sarah and Angelina Grimké.
- Expanded discussion of women's efforts to obtain economic autonomy as a part of the women's rights movement.
- A new section, "Love and Sex in the Age of Reform," that discusses sexual habits generally and homosexuality in 19th-century America.
- Expanded discussion of Walt Whitman's work that addresses allusions to homosexuality in his poetry.

Chapter 15

- Expanded discussion of the pursuit of women's suffrage in the 1870s.

Additional Learning Resources

Oxford University Press offers a complete and authoritative package of learning resources for students and instructors.

Reading American Horizons, **Third Edition:** This two-volume primary source collection (ISBN for volume I: 9780190698034; ISBN for volume II: 9780190698041), expertly edited by the authors of *American Horizons,* provides a diverse set of documents (both textual and visual) that situate U.S. history in a global context. The more than 200 documents—25 of which are new to this edition—cover political, social, and cultural history. Each document includes a headnote and discussion questions. A significant discount is provided when *Reading American Horizons* is packaged with *American Horizons.* Contact your Oxford University Press sales representative for details.

Dashboard (www.oup.com/us/dashboard): Simple, informative, and mobile, Dashboard is an online learning and assessment platform tailored to your textbook that delivers a simple, informative, and mobile experience for professors and students. It offers quality content and tools to track student progress in an intuitive, web-based learning environment; features a streamlined interface that connects students and instructors with the most important course functions; and simplifies the learning experience to save time and put student progress first.

Dashboard for *American Horizons,* third edition, includes:

- An embedded e-book that integrates multimedia content, providing a dynamic learning space for both students and instructors

  Each chapter includes:

  📷 image analysis

  ✋ map analysis, interactive timelines, and quizzes

  🔊 audio flashcards

  📄 document analysis

  Many chapters also include ▷ video analysis

- The complete set of questions from the test bank that provide, for each chapter, multiple-choice, short-answer, true-or-false, and fill-in-the-blank and essay questions

  For more information about Dashboard, contact your Oxford University Press sales representative.

Ancillary Resource Center (ARC): This online resource center (https://arc2.oup-arc.com/), available to adopters of *American Horizons*, includes:

- **Oxford University Press's Video and Image Library:** Designed to engage students and stimulate class discussion, the video library consists of 40 videos. Each video was custom-produced by Oxford University Press and runs between two to three minutes, with topics that range from "The Life and Death of John Brown" to "The Disco Wars." The Image Library includes over 2,000 images, organized by period, topic, and region. To see a demo video and sample PowerPoint module, contact your Oxford University Press sales representative or go to https://arc2.oup-arc.com/access/us-history-image-and-video-library.
- **Instructor's Resource Manual:** Includes, for each chapter, a detailed chapter outline, suggested lecture topics, learning objectives, quizzes, tests, sample syllabi, in-class discussion questions, and suggested Web resources.
- **PowerPoints and Computerized Test Bank:** Includes PowerPoint slides and JPEG and PDF files for all the maps and photos in the text. The computerized test bank includes:
  - **Quizzes** (two per chapter, 25 multiple-choice questions each)
  - **Tests** (two per chapter, offering 10 identification/matching, 10 multiple-choice, 5 short-answer, and 2 essay questions)

Course Cartridges: Complete Course Management cartridges are also available to qualified adopters.

Student Companion Website: The open-access companion website for *American Horizons* (www.oup.com/us/schaller) helps students review what they have learned from the textbook as well as explore other resources online. Resources include the following:

- **Note-taking guides** help students focus their attention in class.
- **Multiple-choice and identification quizzes** *different* from those found in the Instructor's Manual/Test Bank) allow students to assess their knowledge of a topic before a test.
- **Interactive flashcards** using key terms and people listed at the end of each chapter help students remember who's who and what's what.
- **Weblinks** encourage students to explore topics of interest.
- **Author videos** allow students to listen to the authors discuss the content of each chapter.

Other Oxford Titles of Interest for the U.S. History Classroom

Oxford University Press publishes a vast array of titles in American history. The following is just a small selection of books that pair particularly well with *American Horizons*. Any of the books in these series can be packaged with *American Horizons* at a significant discount to students. Please contact your Oxford University Press sales representative for specific pricing information or for additional packaging suggestions. Please visit www.oup.com/us for a full listing of Oxford titles.

New Narratives in American History

At Oxford University Press, we believe that good history begins with a good story. Each volume in this series features a compelling tale that draws on a sustained narrative to illuminate a greater historical theme or controversy. Then, in a thoughtful afterword, the authors place their narratives within larger historical contexts, discuss their sources and narrative strategies, and describe their personal involvement with the work. Intensely personal and highly relevant, these succinct texts are innovative teaching tools that provide a springboard for incisive class discussion as they immerse students in a particular historical moment.

- *Escaping Salem: The Other Witch Hunt of 1692*, by Richard Godbeer
- *Sleuthing the Alamo: Davy Crockett's Last Stand and Other Mysteries of the Texas Revolution*, by James E. Crisp
- *In Search of the Promised Land: A Slave Family in the Old South,* by John Hope Franklin and Loren Schweninger
- *The Making of a Confederate: Walter Lenoir's Civil War*, by William L. Barney
- *"They Say": Ida B. Wells and the Reconstruction of Race*, by James West Davidson
- *Wild Men: Ishi and Kroeber in the Wilderness of Modern America*, by Douglas Cazaux Sackman
- *The Gentle Subversive: Rachel Carson, Silent Spring, and the Rise of the Environmental Movement*, by Mark Hamilton Lytle
- *"To Everything There Is a Season": Pete Seeger and the Power of Song*, by Allan Winkler
- *Tales from a Revolution: Bacon's Rebellion and the Transformation of Colonial America*, by James D. Rice

Critical Historical Encounters

The volumes in this Oxford University Press book series focus on major critical encounters in the American experience. The word "critical" refers to formative, vital, transforming events and actions that have had a major impact in shaping the ever-changing contours of life in the United States. "Encounter" indicates a confrontation or clash, oftentimes but not always contentious in character, but always full of profound historical meaning and consequence. The Critical Historical Encounters series emphasizes formative episodes in America's contested history. Each volume contains two fundamental ingredients: a carefully written narrative of the encounter and the consequences, both immediate and long-term, of that moment of conflict in America's contested history.

- *For Ourselves and Our Posterity: The Preamble to the Federal Constitution in American History*, by Peter Charles Hoffer
- *Marching Across the Color Line: A. Philip Randolph and Civil Rights in the World War II Era*, by David Welky
- *Pennsylvania Hall: A "Legal Lynching" in the Shadow of the Liberty Bell,* by Beverly Tomek
- *The Battle of Ole Miss: Civil Rights v. States' Rights*, by Frank Lambert
- *The Making of a Patriot: Benjamin Franklin at the Cockpit*, by Sheila L. Skemp
- *The Jerry Rescue*, by Angela F. Murphy

Acknowledgments

A book as detailed as this draws on the talents and support of many individuals. Our first thanks must certainly go to our families for their support and patience during the development of this textbook. We would also like to acknowledge the team at Oxford University Press for their support in making this book a reality. Thanks go first to our editor, Charles Cavaliere, who encouraged and challenged us at every step of the process. Publisher John Challice supported the project at an early stage and spurred us to think broadly about how we envisioned it. We appreciate the able assistance of development manager Thom Holmes and development editor Maegan Sherlock. Editorial assistant Rowan Wixted was especially helpful in wrangling the art program for the book. We thank the Oxford production team, led by manager Lisa Grzan and production editor Micheline Frederick, for their encouragement and help in generating this book and shaping its final form. The interior and cover design were created by art director Michele Laseau. The innovative map program was created by International Mapping.

Manuscript Reviewers

We have greatly benefited from the perceptive comments and suggestions of the many talented scholars and instructors who reviewed *American Horizons*. Their insight and suggestions contributed immensely to the published work.

Reviewers of the Third Edition

Nicole Anslover
Indiana University Northwest

Joseph Bagley
Georgia Perimeter College

Robert Caputi
Erie Community College

Donald C. Elder III
Eastern New Mexico University

A. James Fuller
University of Indianapolis

R. Scott Huffard, Jr.
Lees-McRae College

Richard Hughes
Illinois State University

Hannah Kim
University of Delaware

Mark A. Mengerink
Lamar University

Deirdre P. O'Shea
University of Central Florida

Matthew Pehl
Augustana College

Steven D. Reschly
Truman State University

Beth Slutsky
California State University, Sacramento

Brandon Wolfe-Hunnicutt
California State University, Stanislaus

Reviewers of the Second Edition

Ian J. Aebel
Virginia State University

Cynthia Counsil
Florida State College at Jacksonville

Brittany Fremion
Central Michigan University

Larry Grubbs
Georgia State University

Thomas Humphrey
Cleveland State University

Christopher Jones
College of William and Mary

Bill Mauzey
Metropolitan Community College

Karen Miller
Oakland University

Jeremy Neely
Missouri State University

Chad Parke
University of Louisiana Lafayette

Mary Ellen Rowe
University of Central Missouri

Diane C. Vecchio
Furman University

Felicia Viator
San Francisco State University

Reviewers of the First Edition

Stanley Arnold
Northern Illinois University

Shelby M. Balik
Metropolitan State College of Denver
University of Colorado

Eirlys M. Barker
Thomas Nelson Community College

Toby Bates
University of Mississippi

Carol Bender
Saddleback College

Wendy Benningfield
Campbellsville University

Katherine Benton-Cohen
Georgetown University

Angela Boswell
Henderson State University

Robert Bouwman
North Georgia College & State
University

Jessica Brannon-Wranosky
Texas A&M University–Commerce

Blanche Brick
Blinn College

Howard Brick
University of Michigan

Margaret M. Caffrey
University of Memphis

Jacqueline B. Carr
University of Vermont

Dominic Carrillo
Grossmont College

Brian Casserly
Bellevue College

Cheryll Ann Cody
Houston Community College–Southwest
College

Elizabeth Collins
Triton College

Edward M. Cook, Jr.
University of Chicago

Cynthia Gardner Counsil
Florida State College–Jacksonville

C. David Dalton
College of the Ozarks

David Dzurec
University of Scranton

Brian J. Els
University of Portland

Kevin Eoff
Palo Verde College

Richard M. Filipink
Western Illinois University

Joshua Fulton
Moraine Valley Community College

David Garvin
Highland Community College

Glen Gendzel
San José State University

Tiffany Gill
University of Texas–Austin

Aram Goudsouzian
University of Memphis

Larry Gragg
Missouri University of Science and Technology

Jean W. Griffith
Fort Scott Community College;
Labette Community College

Mark Grimsley
Ohio State University

Elisa M. Guernsey
Monroe Community College

Aaron Gulyas
Mott Community College

Michael R. Hall
Armstrong Atlantic State University

David E. Hamilton
University of Kentucky

Peggy J. Hardman
Eastern New Mexico University

Kristin Hargrove
Grossmont College

Claudrena N. Harold
University of Virginia

Edward Hashima
American River College

Robin Henry
Wichita State University

John Herron
University of Missouri–Kansas City

L. Edward Hicks
Faulkner University

Matt Hinckley
Richland College

D. Sandy Hoover
East Texas Baptist University

Jerry Hopkins
East Texas Baptist University

Kelly Hopkins
University of Houston

Kenneth W. Howell
Prairie View A&M University

Raymond Pierre Hylton
Virginia Union University

Bryan M. Jack
Winston-Salem State University

Brenda Jackson-Abernathy
Belmont University

Volker Janssen
California State University–Fullerton

Lawrence W. Kennedy
University of Scranton

William Kerrigan
Muskingum University

Andrew E. Kersten
University of Wisconsin

Todd Kerstetter
Texas Christian University

Patricia Knol
Triton College

Jeffrey Kosiorek
Hendrix College

Peter Kuryla
Belmont University

Peggy Lambert
Lone Star College–Kingwood

Alan Lehmann
Blinn College

Carolyn Herbst Lewis
Louisiana State University

Christopher J. Mauceri
Farmingdale State College of New York

Derrick McKisick
Fairfield University

Marian Mollin
Virginia Tech

Linda Mollno
Cal Poly Pomona

Michelle Morgan
Missouri State University

Susan Rhoades Neel
Utah State University

Caryn E. Neumann
Miami University

Jeffrey Nichols
Westminster College

Christopher H. Owen
Northeastern State University

Jeffrey Pilz
North Iowa Area Community College

Amy M. Porter
Georgia Southwestern State University

William E. Price
Kennesaw State University

Emily Rader
El Camino College

Matthew Redinger
Montana State University–Billings

Yolanda Romero
North Lake College

Jessica Roney
Ohio University

Walter L. Sargent
University of Maine–Farmington

Robert Francis Saxe
Rhodes College

Jerry G. Sheppard
Mount Olive College

Robert Sherwood
Georgia Military College

Terry L. Shoptaugh
Minnesota State University–Moorhead

Jason H. Silverman
Winthrop University

Nico Slate
Carnegie Mellon University

Jodie Steeley
Merced Community College

Jennifer A. Stollman
Fort Lewis College

James S. Taw
Valdosta State University

Connie Brown Thomason
Louisiana Delta Community College

Kurt Troutman
Muskegon Community College

Stanley J. Underdal
San José State University

David Voelker
University of Wisconsin–Green Bay

Charles Waite
University of Texas–Pan American

R. Stuart Wallace
NHTI-Concord's Community College
University of New Hampshire–Manchester

Pamela West
Jefferson State Community College

William Benton Whisenhunt
College of DuPage

Louis Williams
St. Louis Community College Forest Park

Scott M. Williams
Weatherford College

Mary Montgomery Wolf
University of Georgia

Bill Wood
University of Arkansas Community College–Batesville

Melyssa Wrisley
Broome Community College

Charles Young
Umpqua Community College

Nancy L. Zens
Central Oregon Community College

ABOUT THE AUTHORS

Michael Schaller (Ph.D., University of Michigan, 1974) is Regents Professor of History at the University of Arizona, where he has taught since 1974. His areas of specialization include U.S. international and East Asian relations and the resurgence of conservatism in late 20th-century America. Among his publications are *Altered States: The United States and Japan Since the Occupation* (Oxford University Press, 1997), *The U.S. and China into the 21st Century* (Oxford University Press, 2002), *Right Turn: American Life in the Reagan-Bush Era* (Oxford University Press, 2007), and *Ronald Reagan* (Oxford University Press, 2011).

Janette Thomas Greenwood is Professor of History at Clark University (Ph.D., University of Virginia) and specializes in African American history and history of the U.S. South. Books include *The Gilded Age: A History in Documents* (Oxford University Press, 2000), *Bittersweet Legacy: The Black and White "Better Classes" in Charlotte, 1850–1910* (University of North Carolina Press, 1994), and *First Fruits of Freedom: The Migration of Former Slaves and Their Search for Equality in Worcester, Massachusetts, 1862–1900* (University of North Carolina Press, 2010).

Andrew Kirk is Professor and Chair of History at University of Nevada, Las Vegas (Ph.D., University of New Mexico) and specializes in the history of the U.S. West and environmental history. Books include *Collecting Nature: The American Environmental Movement and the Conservation Library* (University Press of Kansas, 2001), *Counterculture Green: The Whole Earth Catalog and American Environmentalism* (University Press of Kansas, 2007), and *Doom Towns: The People and Landscapes of Atomic Testing* (Oxford University Press, 2017).

Sarah J. Purcell is L. F. Parker Professor of History at Grinnell College (Ph.D., Brown University) and she specializes in the early national period, antebellum United States, popular culture, politics, gender, and military history. Books include *Sealed with Blood: War, Sacrifice, and Memory in Revolutionary America* (University of Pennsylvania Press, 2002), *The Early National Period* (Facts on File, 2004), and *The Encyclopedia of Battles in North America, 1517–1916* (Facts on File, 2000).

Aaron Sheehan-Dean is the Fred C. Frey Professor at Louisiana State University (Ph.D., University of Virginia) and specializes in antebellum United States and the U.S. Civil War. Books include *Why Confederates Fought: Family and Nation in Civil War Virginia* (University of North Carolina Press, 2007), *The View from the Ground: Experiences of Civil War Soldiers* (University Press of Kentucky, 2006), and *Concise Historical Atlas of the U.S. Civil War* (Oxford University Press, 2008).

Christina Snyder is the McCabe Greer Professor of History, The Pennsylvania State University. She researches colonialism, race, and slavery, with a focus on Native North America from the pre-contact era through the 19th century. Snyder is the author of the award-winning book *Slavery in Indian Country: The Changing Face of Captivity in Early America* (Harvard University Press, 2010). Her most recent book is *Great Crossings: Indians, Settlers, and Slaves in the Age of Jackson* (Oxford University Press, 2017). At Indiana University, Snyder offers courses in Native American studies and U.S. history.

AMERICAN HORIZONS

This engraving from the 1500s of an elite Timucuan woman and her entourage gives us an idea of how the Lady of Cofitachequi may have appeared to Hernando de Soto and his army.

The Origins of the Atlantic World

The Lady of Cofitachequi had anticipated the arrival of the Spanish army. For days, her warriors had been gathering intelligence about the bearded strangers who had bumbled around the forests and swamps bordering her region, apparently lost, yelling at one another, violent among themselves and worse toward Indians who crossed their path. On May 1, 1540, Hernando de Soto and his army finally arrived and set up camp.

While she had never met men such as these, the **Lady of Cofitachequi** was a master of foreign diplomacy, having dealt with many other chiefs. Covering much of present-day South Carolina, her own chiefdom stretched from the Atlantic coast to the foothills of the Appalachian Mountains. The Lady governed tens of thousands of subjects, who cultivated rich cornfields, giving her a portion of every harvest as tribute. Recently, some had been unruly, but the Lady, backed by her own army, retained power.

When greeting the Spaniards, the Lady of Cofitachequi demonstrated the wealth and power of her chiefdom. She dressed in pearls and a finely woven white shawl. A group of favored subjects carried her on a litter to the river's edge, then placed her in a canoe and rowed out to greet the newcomers. Once ashore, the Lady sat on a chair brought by her subjects and then surveyed the strangers. There were over 600 of them, mostly male, and they were obviously warriors. Seeking to impress, they stood in formation, flew their banners, and brandished a shocking number of weapons. Even their dogs wore armor.

But the Lady saw their weakness, too. Clad in chain mail, they sweated miserably, and most looked lean and hungry.

The Lady could have taken advantage of the newcomers' vulnerability by sending her army to attack them, but she chose peace instead. Following Native protocols, the Lady, through a chain of interpreters, proposed an alliance. She gave the Spanish leaders many gifts, including pearls and dressed deerskins, and fed the entire army from her corn granaries. The Lady took de Soto and his officers on a tour of her chiefdom, and, after visiting her ancestral temple, one of the Spaniards exclaimed that it "was among the grandest and most wonderful of all the things that he had seen in the New World." In return for her generosity, the Lady of Cofitachequi hoped that de Soto would reciprocate, perhaps offering military support to subdue her rebellious subjects.

While Hernando de Soto and other Europeans thought of North America as the "New World," it was actually Indians' Old World. For millennia, Indigenous peoples had shaped America's cultural and physical landscape. The European invasion of America happened slowly, and Europeans did not immediately dominate Native Americans. Many early European expeditions like de Soto's failed, while Cofitachequi's chiefdom endured for generations. Native leaders like the Lady of Cofitachequi drew on both time-honored strategies and new information to deal with life in a changing world. Still, Hernando de Soto laid the groundwork for later invasions and inaugurated a violent epoch that would transform North America.

⊘ NORTH AMERICA TO 1500

North America has an ancient and complex history. By 11,000 BCE, Native Americans had settled the entire continent. Over the course of millennia, they adapted to climatic shifts, environmental stress, population increase, social upheaval, and cultural change. Contrary to popular belief, precolonial North America was not a virgin wilderness, but rather a place profoundly shaped by its Native inhabitants. Exploiting locally available resources, Native Americans established viable economies and created specialized products for long-distance exchange. Trade routes crisscrossed the continent, and some extended into Mesoamerica and the Caribbean. Among the most important of these exchange items was maize, or corn, a Mesoamerican plant that fueled population booms in the Southwest and much of eastern North America. In the centuries before colonization, Native societies depended heavily on farming, though the continent was extremely diverse, home to city dwellers, fishermen, hunters, and gatherers.

The First Americans

Modern humans, *Homo sapiens sapiens*, originated in Africa between 100,000 and 200,000 years ago and later migrated to other continents. The date of human arrival in the Americas is the subject of ongoing research and a hotly contested topic. Archaeological evidence indicates that Native Americans descend from peoples of northeastern Asia. These first settlers probably came by both land and sea. Most archaeological research has focused on the land bridge that once connected Siberia to Alaska. During the last Ice Age, massive ice sheets blocked water, exposing Beringia (the land underneath the Bering Sea) and other portions of the continental shelf. The first Americans probably followed herds of big game across Beringia and into North America. A newer theory suggests that some also arrived in boats. Advocates of this theory argue that peoples of northeastern Asia had already developed maritime technology to fish and hunt large sea mammals. Using boats, they hopped from one rich beachhead to the next, traveling east, then south down the Alaskan coastline.

The first Americans likely arrived by multiple routes in several waves. The oldest sites date reliably to 13,000 BCE, but some archaeologists argue that settlement was even more ancient. Most Natives' ancestors probably arrived by 11,000 BCE, though archaeological and linguistic data suggest that two major groups came later: Na-Dene speakers between 6,000 and 8,000 BCE, and Inuits and Aleuts around 3,000 BCE.

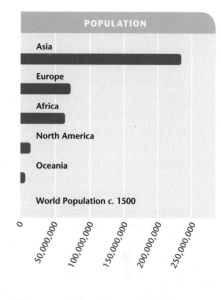

Native American oral traditions also speak to their origins. Confirming their ancient American roots, many Native peoples identify a specific, sacred place from which they originated. Those who believe in the literal truth of their origin stories often doubt archaeological theories. However, Pawnee scholar Roger Echo-Hawk has argued that Native oral traditions often confirm and even enhance archaeological findings. According to Echo-Hawk, migration figures prominently in many origin stories. The Haudenosaunees (Iroquois), Arikaras, and Cherokees all remember that their ancestors met daunting expanses of ice and water. Ojibwas say that they, along with Ottawas and Potawatomis, descend from one people who lived near the "Great Salt Sea" in northeastern North America before moving to the Great Lakes, where they parted ways to become three distinct nations.

Increasingly, interdisciplinary research like that of Roger Echo-Hawk is building bridges between academics and Native American nations. The **Native American Graves Protection and Repatriation Act (NAGPRA)**, passed by the U.S. Congress in 1990, requires universities and museums to share information about human remains as well as sacred and culturally significant items with descendant communities, who may also arrange for repatriation. In practice, NAGPRA demands ethical research and encourages archaeologists and Native nations to undertake collaborative, mutually beneficial projects.

Hunters, Gatherers, and Farmers

There are few ancient American sites, so it is difficult to make broad generalizations about them. Paleoindian culture, which emerged around 11,000 BCE, is the oldest widespread cultural tradition that archaeologists can identify. By that time, the ice sheets that once covered much of North America had retreated, and Native peoples settled across the continent. Mobile and efficient, they carried stone toolkits, including the era's most distinctive artifact, the Clovis point, which is a lancelet-shaped, fluted spear point. Paleoindian peoples used Clovis points to hunt big game, including mastodon, mammoth, giant bison, and caribou. They also migrated seasonally, gathering nuts,

Clovis points

berries, and wild plants to supplement their diets. Paleoindians usually lived in small bands, but they occasionally camped in larger groups, perhaps to trade or celebrate religious festivals.

Native societies changed profoundly around 8,000 BCE, when the Ice Age ended and many big game animals became extinct. Departing from Paleoindian culture, which had been fairly similar across the continent, Native Americans created specialized economies to fit regional climates and geographies. Some still based their economies on gathering and hunting, though they targeted different animals. Inuits of the Arctic and Subarctic used sophisticated technology, including waterproof boats and sealskin parkas, to hunt sea mammals in an extreme environment. The peoples of the Pacific Northwest, too, were seafarers, hunting whale and seal, but they also fished in fresh water. Salmon, in particular, was such a rich food source that northwestern peoples developed dense populations and permanent villages. Native Floridians were also settled fishermen, and they developed the continent's first cemeteries, which suggest that they laid claim to a specific territory. Some other Native peoples remained more mobile, following a regular migration schedule that allowed them to exploit seasonally available resources. Native Californians hunted small game like rabbits and deer and ate a wide range of fish, shellfish, nuts, and fruit. Plains peoples occasionally staged large communal hunts for bison, but they relied more heavily on deer and smaller game. Even in the deserts of the Great Basin, Native peoples made a living by gathering acorns and snaring small game.

Like Native Americans elsewhere, people of the Southwest and Eastern Woodlands hunted and gathered, but they also began to experiment with agriculture. Caring for domesticated plants required a change in lifestyle. Although many community

MIWOK ACORN GRANARIES, CALIFORNIA, 1870s Miwoks interlaced branches and grass to build structures like these to store acorns. They and many other California peoples harvested acorns, a staple of their diets, from oak groves that they maintained. These Indians' skillful use of California's varied ecologies enabled them to become some of North America's densest populations.

members continued to journey abroad for seasonal hunts, others stayed behind in permanent villages, which proliferated during this era. Oral traditions suggest that women were the first Native farmers. They probably played a leading role in gathering and, over time, began to cultivate desirable plants, watering, weeding, and even transplanting them. By 3,000 BCE, farmers of the Eastern Woodlands had domesticated squash. Over time, they added sunflowers, chenopodium, and marsh elder. Some of the new cultigens were not eaten. One of the oldest Native domesticated plants is tobacco (*Nicotiana rustica*). Strong and harsh, quite different from the Caribbean variety introduced during the colonial era, this North American variety of tobacco was probably smoked only during ceremonies. Bottle gourds, after being hollowed out and dried, made excellent containers. Pottery also emerged as a symbol of this lifestyle change, first appearing in the Savannah River valley around 2,500 BCE, used for storing the fruits of the harvest.

Trade and the Rise of Native Cities

As Native Americans developed specialized economies, they began to exchange products over vast distances and created transcontinental trade routes. Among the most widely traded products were busycon conch shells from the Gulf coast, copper from Lake Superior, and galena (lead sulfide) from the Midwest. Some Native traders engaged in hemispheric trade, traveling outside what is now the United States. The Calusas of Florida, for example, built double-hulled canoes and sailed to what is now the Bahamas and Cuba. Another key route linked the Southwest to Mesoamerica, a center of innovation that contributed to southwestern foodways, religion, and architecture.

One of the most important products in global economic history—corn—was first developed in present-day Mexico and arrived in the Southwest around 2,000 BCE. Initially, corn was used sparingly, perhaps only in ceremonial contexts. By 1,500 BCE, however, Native peoples of the Southwest—likely assisted by Uto-Aztecan-speaking immigrants from Mesoamerica—began to cultivate corn on a large scale. Over the centuries, Native farmers developed new varieties of corn suited to specific regional climates. Around 700 CE, southwestern peoples created eight-rowed flint corn, which matured in as little as 90 days and grew well in many North American regions. This variety was adapted by Native farmers across the Southwest, Plains, and Eastern Woodlands, and soon comprised much of the diet in those regions. An incredibly productive plant, corn produced almost twice as many calories per acre as wheat, the favored European staple.

New farming practices and climate change led to population growth. Although corn displaced some of the older cultigens, Native farmers retained squash, which is high in vitamin C, and they also added another Mesoamerican plant, beans, to their diet around 700 CE. Together, these "three sisters" provided a full range of amino acids and a healthful diet. Crops flourished during the Medieval Warm Period (900–1300 CE), which resulted in warmer temperatures and higher than average rainfall. Plentiful harvests supported demographic booms and the first Native American cities.

Two urban cultures, called Hohokam and Anasazi by archaeologists, arose in the Southwest. Both groups owed their success to irrigation systems. The Hohokam began to build canals to divert river water to their fields around 800 CE. Over the next

HOPI BOWL This ceramic bowl, likely made by Hopi Indians between 1300 and 1400 CE, features macaws. These birds, which came from central Mexico, were one of the many trade items that linked the American Southwest and Mesoamerica.

four centuries, they created thousands of miles of canals that supported a population of tens of thousands. The modern-day city of Phoenix has a canal system that was virtually superimposed on the one the Hohokam constructed. Another key element of Hohokam architecture—one imported from their Mesoamerican homeland—was the ball court. At the center of every town, ball courts served many purposes. During games, crowds gathered to socialize and mingle. On market days, traders and farmers sold their wares in stalls around the court. Archaeologists speculate that the ball game may have even served a political role, providing a nonviolent outlet for factions to compete.

As the Hohokam made more of modern-day Arizona bloom, the Anasazi developed a commercial hub known as Chaco Canyon, in what is now New Mexico. In 1100 CE, Chaco Canyon included over 300 apartments and 12 massive structures called "great houses." The largest of these, Pueblo Bonito, contained 700 rooms arranged in four stories, plus dozens of ceremonial structures called kivas. Several thousand people once lived in this core area, and Chaco anchored a network of at least 70 communities that stretched over 25,000 square miles, linked by a vast network of orderly roads. Chaco residents specialized in making turquoise, which they exchanged for shells from the Gulf of California and copper bells, macaws, and feathers from Mesoamerica.

Meanwhile, Mississippian culture arose in the Southeast and Mississippi valley. Between 750 and 950 CE, corn agriculture intensified and the population boomed. Native polities changed, shifting from loosely integrated tribal communities to more hierarchical institutions called chiefdoms. Chiefdoms were multivillage, regional polities dominated by hereditary chiefs who ruled from a capital town. Many resided atop platform mounds, which are distinctive architectural features of Mississippian culture. Controlling a network of satellite villages, farmsteads, and hunting grounds, chiefs ruled populations ranging from a few thousand to tens of thousands, but some of the most prominent leaders (including the Lady of Cofitachequi) gained control over other chiefdoms and claimed vast territories.

The largest and most influential chiefdom was headquartered at **Cahokia**, just east of modern-day St. Louis at the confluence of the Mississippi and Missouri rivers. Peaking around 1100 CE, the capital city had a population of perhaps 15,000, and its suburban sprawl included at least 20,000 to 30,000 additional residents. At the time, Cahokia

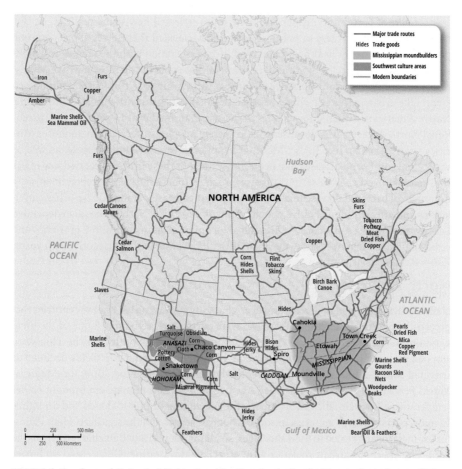

MAP 1.1 Trade and Selected Urbanized Indian Societies in North America, c. 700 to c. 1450 This map shows major trade routes and the goods transported along them c. 1450. Overlaid are the areas in the Southwest where the Anasazi and Hohokam settled and areas in the Mississippi River valley in which Mississippian societies flourished between roughly 900 and 1450 CE. Modern political boundaries are included to provide orientation.

was by far the largest city north of Mexico, and its population exceeded that of London, England. No North American city surpassed Cahokia until 1760, when Philadelphia became an international trading center. Cahokia was a planned city that included a "woodhenge" used to time the agricultural cycle, many plazas for sport and ceremony, and over 100 mounds, which varied in design and purpose. Some were rounded burial mounds, while others were platform mounds inhabited by elites or used for ceremonies. The largest, now called Monks' Mound, contains over 21 million cubic feet of earth, making it among the largest man-made earthworks on Earth, outstripping even the pyramids at Giza. No other Mississippian society rivaled Cahokia in size, but other Native cities emulated its layout and architecture. Cahokia was also a major center of trade and art, shaping **Mississippian societies** as distant as Etowah, near modern-day Atlanta; Moundville in central Alabama; and Town Creek in North Carolina (Map 1.1).

Cahokia

Centers of power and influence, Native cities reflected new social realities. As certain lineages gained access to political power, they elevated themselves above common people, enjoying better health and nutrition, close association with the sacred, and high-status burials. New archaeological data confirm that some of the most massive Mississippian mounds were built in a decade or less, which suggests that elites commanded labor. Like urban places elsewhere, Native cities also struggled with public health. While Native Americans suffered lower rates of disease than medieval Europeans did, precolonial North America was not disease-free. Native peoples suffered from zoonoses (diseases from animals), like Rocky Mountain spotted fever and Lyme disease, as well as water- and soil-borne diseases like hepatitis A. Most of these illnesses carried low infection rates. However, more serious diseases, such as tuberculosis and treponematosis, a nonvenereal bacterial disease related to syphilis, spread easily among dense urban populations and affected many Native people in towns and cities. Native cities also depended heavily on a single crop—corn. While elites stockpiled corn in communal granaries and redistributed it when necessary, they had difficulty dealing with consecutive lean years.

North America on the Eve of Colonization

Native Americans lived in diverse and ever-changing communities, but the centuries that preceded Christopher Columbus's arrival were particularly dynamic. Some of the great agricultural societies overtaxed their environments. In the Southwest, the Hohokam stopped building ball courts after 1150 and villagers dispersed. Crop yields declined as irrigated soils became saltier and increasingly poisonous. Around 1300, the Medieval Warm Period ended and the Little Ice Age began. This new climate era brought colder temperatures, less rainfall, and erratic weather, including dramatic floods and droughts. In many parts of North America, resources became scarce. On the southern High Plains, for example, droughts led to food shortages, so Plains people raided Pueblo farmers to the west. The effects on urban societies were especially devastating. Cities could no longer support dense populations, so most people left, dispersing into smaller settlements. By 1400, the Hohokam had abandoned their towns and combined with nearby peoples. One branch became known as Tohono O'odham ("Desert People"), while the other was called Akimel O'odham ("River People"). Meanwhile, many Anasazi descendants had migrated out of Chaco Canyon and other major sites and into the region's major river valleys, where they settled into small towns built of adobe, located in defensible places. If less grand than the cities of old, these towns were also more egalitarian, with greater social equality and more open religious participation. These peoples were diverse, belonging to more than 60 autonomous towns, but the Spanish later dubbed them all "Pueblos."

The Little Ice Age also transformed eastern North America. Competition over resources resulted in increased warfare. Mississippians fortified their capitals, adding—for the first time—bastions with watchtowers, and southeastern art often depicted warriors, valorizing their feats. In this time of hunger and heightened violence, many Mississippian capitals, including Cahokia, were abandoned after invaders breached their city walls. Others, like Moundville, hosted smaller populations but remained important religious sites. Meanwhile, peoples of the Northeast sought to overcome warfare and political instability. Around 1400, five nations of Iroquoian-speaking peoples—the Mohawk, Oneida, Onondaga, Cayuga, and Seneca—made peace and joined to form the Great League of Peace. They call themselves *Haudenosaunee*, meaning "People of the Longhouse," though most outsiders call them "Iroquois."

WOMAN POUNDING CORN INTO MEAL, 1657 This image of a Huron woman at work in front of a longhouse comes from a map drawn by an Italian Jesuit who lived among Huron in the 1640s. It illustrates the centrality of women, their labor, and their roles in Native agricultural societies.

Meanwhile, migration reshaped central Mexico. New arrivals, who called themselves *Mexica*, fled south from their ancestral homeland Aztlán (hence the name "Aztecs," by which Mexica are often known), finding refuge on an island in Lake Texcoco. There, around 1325, the Mexica founded their capital Tenochtitlán. By the early 1400s, Mexica warriors had made Tenochtitlán a formidable power. Mexica were ruled by *tlatoani*, which literally translates as "the one who speaks," but whom the Europeans called "emperors." Under Itzcoatl and Moctezuma I, the Mexica became Mesoamerica's dominant power in the 1460s. They collected tribute from millions, many of whom, like Mexica, spoke Nahuatl. Tenochtitlán soon had over 100,000 residents and a skyline dominated by two massive pyramids, one devoted to the Mesoamerican rain god Tlaloc, and the other to Mexica patron deity Huitzilopochtli. The Mexica fought battles to seize captives who were sacrificed to Huitzilopochtli to ensure that the sun would again rise and to keep death at bay. Demands for tribute and captives created many enemies for Mexica and stiffened the resolve of city-states like Tlaxcala to remain independent.

 Tenochtitlán

Columbus invaded North America during a particularly vulnerable period, in which Native societies were readjusting to global climatic changes that, on a more tangible, human level, had resulted in drought, famine, war, regime changes, mass migrations, and de-urbanization. Native Americans were resilient, however, and they adapted to life in a changing world. Population estimates are difficult to ascertain, but, in 1491, it is likely that 5–10 million Native Americans lived north of present-day Mexico. Speaking over 300 different languages, they lived in thousands of vibrant polities across the continent (Map 1.2).

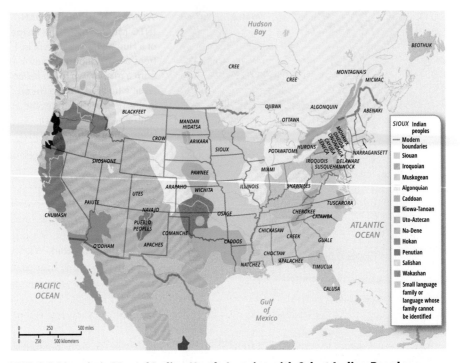

MAP 1.2 Linguistic Map of Indian North America with Select Indian Peoples Included North America's Indians spoke over 300 different languages when Europeans first arrived. Shown here are the continent's major language families (meaning a group of related languages, not all of which were mutually intelligible), along with locations for a number of Indian peoples, both of which reflect the time when Europeans first made sustained contact with peoples in that region.

STUDY QUESTIONS FOR NORTH AMERICA TO 1500

quiz

1. How would you characterize North America before 1492?
2. In what ways did climate and agriculture change Indian life and politics?

EARLY COLONIALISM, 1000–1513

The first Europeans to invade North America were Vikings, whose short-lived settlement in Newfoundland left little impact. By the 1400s, other western Europeans had developed technologies that enabled them to cross the Atlantic and return home. The Spanish and Portuguese discovered new sources of wealth and new allies in sub-Saharan Africa and Asia. They initiated trade in enslaved Africans that encouraged the spread of plantation agriculture to new Iberian (Spanish and Portuguese) colonies off Africa's coast. Spanish mariners brought and extended that new **Atlantic world** to the Americas in 1492, an act that had the most immediate impact on people of the Caribbean island of Española.

European Expansion Across the Atlantic

The first European to spearhead a transatlantic expedition was not Christopher Columbus, but rather a Norseman named Leif Ericson. Originally from Scandinavia, the Norse were experienced mariners who perfected the longship, which facilitated their expansion across the North Atlantic. By the 10th century, Vikings had colonized parts of England, Iceland, and Greenland. Leif Ericson, the son of a chieftain, pushed even farther west, founding Vinland around 1000. The first European settlement in the Americas, Vinland was located in northern Newfoundland at the site now called L'Anse aux Meadows. As the Norse colonized Vinland and explored nearby regions, they encountered Indigenous people, probably Algonquian-speaking Beothuks and perhaps Inuit as well. According to oral traditions, Vikings and Natives held at least one council meeting, but they also fought. On one occasion, Vikings found several sleeping fishermen and killed them. As foreign relations with Indigenous people soured, Vikings faced declining food stores. Trying to replicate their traditional diet, Vikings attempted to grow wheat and raise cattle, but the environment proved too cold. Within a generation, Vikings abandoned Vinland and sailed eastward. The first European settlement in America had failed. Because Vikings developed poor relations with local Natives, they could not—or would not—adopt local foods and technologies that might have sustained the colony. Centuries passed before other Europeans attempted to colonize North America.

Europe, like North America, transformed during the Little Ice Age. Beginning around 1315, Europe's weather grew colder and more erratic, resulting in poor harvests. Soon thereafter, trading vessels from Asia brought the bubonic plague, devastating populations already weakened from famine. By 1352, the plague, also known as the Black Death, had killed as many as one in three people and destabilized European society, which for centuries had been structured by feudalism. Under the feudal system, the vast majority of Europeans were vassals tied to the estate of a lord. A vassal owed his lord a portion of his harvest and labor, while a lord and his knights were obligated to protect vassals. High death rates during the Black Death, however, led to labor shortages, enabling vassals to bargain for more resources and greater freedom of movement. Many common people chose to leave the countryside and move to booming cities. Like Native American cities, European cities were centers of trade. But European merchants differed from Native traders in that they controlled large concentrations of capital and aggressively sought to extend overseas trade. Western Europe was then a cultural backwater, a relatively poor region on the fringe of a prosperous Mediterranean world. Ottomans and Venetians controlled access to luxury goods—gold and ivory from sub-Saharan Africa and silks, gems, and spices from Asia. Envious Europeans sought to circumvent the Mediterranean middlemen who brought them luxury goods and deal directly with Africans and East and South Asians.

Meanwhile, as common people gained mobility and local lords lost power, Europeans vested greater authority in centralized monarchies and began to develop national identities. European kings jockeyed for power, leading their people into war with rival nations. Monarchs in England, France, Portugal, and Spain sought revenue to fund armies and consolidate power over nobles. Despite their national differences, Europeans were overwhelmingly Christian, and, during the Crusades, multiple kingdoms united to fight Islamic powers. As the colonial era dawned, many factors—economic ambition, militarism, political rivalries, and a shared Christian identity—drove western Europeans to venture beyond the world that they knew.

By 1450, Europeans had the technology to sustain long-distance maritime commerce. Iberian and Genoese shipyards produced a new kind of ship, the caravel. Caravels combined the strength and durability required of vessels that plied the stormy waters off northern Europe with the speed and maneuverability of those that operated in the relatively calm Mediterranean. They could sail in protected coastal waters or on the open ocean. On board, compasses aided navigation and hourglasses permitted rough calculations of velocity. **Astrolabes** and quadrants helped to determine latitude. They also employed classical knowledge. A Latin translation of Ptolemy's *Geography* appeared in 1406. It summarized the Greek world's understanding of geography circa 100 CE and offered guidance on how to represent Earth's spherical shape on a flat map. Subsequent editions added maps created during the 1400s.

Meanwhile, ideas coursed more rapidly thanks to Europeans' adaptation of two Chinese inventions. One was a technique for making paper. Arabs introduced it to Spain, and it diffused slowly to most of Europe in the early 1400s. The other was block printing, inspired by a Chinese technique whereby characters carved into wood were

Map of the known world by Martellus, ca. 1489

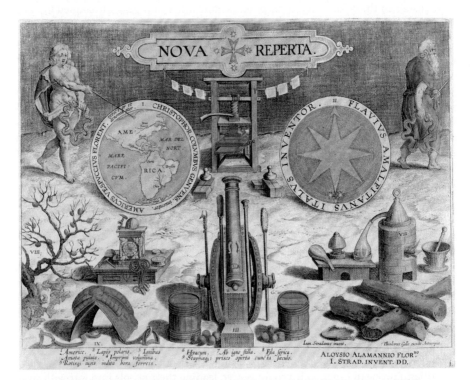

NOVA REPERTA This image, from *Nova Reperta*, a book published in Antwerp in 1600, illustrates how Europeans identified their "discovery" of the Americas with technologies that they had modified and mastered. At the center, a cannon, flanked by shot and barrels of gunpowder, takes aim at a printing press.

dipped in ink and pressed onto paper. In the 1450s, German artisans brought together moveable metal typecasts of each letter of the alphabet, ink, and a machine to press inked type against paper. The printing press revolutionized access to information. Scholars could refer to standardized texts rather than inaccurate transcriptions made by hand. Books became cheaper and more widely available. As of 1500, Europe's printers had turned out some six million books, probably more than had appeared in the previous 1,000 years.

In the 1450s, Europeans also developed techniques of warfare to support expansion. They obtained gunpowder from China by 1250 and about 70 years later used it to propel missiles. In 1400, Europeans were producing firearms, especially artillery, used for sieges. By 1500, soldiers carried arquebuses, the ancestor of the musket, into battle, although their primitive design made them inaccurate. Surging metal production met the demand for more weaponry. Improvements in mining and to blast furnaces enabled Europeans to make five times more iron in 1530 than in 1460. Much of it was forged into steel and beaten into pikes and swords, which remained indispensable in combat.

Christian kingdoms of the Iberian Peninsula spearheaded western European expansion during the 1400s. Those that formed modern-day Spain had entered the final stage of a centuries-long process of evicting Islamic emirates from Iberia. Their *reconquista* (reconquest) combined religious, economic, and political goals. Christians saw themselves as crusaders who were reclaiming Iberia for their faith. Monarchs could not afford to mount military campaigns themselves, so they licensed private entrepreneurs who shared the spoils of conquest. Those who succeeded received *encomiendas*—grants of land that they had conquered. **Isabel of Castile**'s marriage to **Ferdinand of Aragon** in 1469 united two principal Christian kingdoms; 13 years later, Christian forces launched the conquest of Granada, Iberia's last emirate. The conflict drew volunteers from all over Europe. In January 1492, the last Muslim settlement capitulated. The victorious Christians, seeking religious conformity, soon decreed that Muslims and Jews should accept baptism or leave Spain in a matter of months.

Meanwhile, the Portuguese gazed south and west. Unlike Spain, England, or France, Portugal was a united kingdom at peace with its neighbors for most of the 1400s. It was also relatively poor with a long coastline that drew thousands of Portuguese to the sea. Located near northwest Africa and thrust far out into the Atlantic, Portugal was poised to use the ocean to link the two continents.

Iberians, Africans, and the Creation of an Eastern Atlantic World

Europeans and Africans created an eastern Atlantic world over the course of the 15th century, largely by connecting western Africa directly to the outside world. That laid a foundation for the conquest and colonization of the Americas and for the enslavement of millions of Africans.

Portugal's expansion into Africa began in 1415 with the conquest of Ceuta, a Muslim city in Morocco. Portuguese mariners soon began to map Africa's northwest coast by inching south, trading with or raiding whomever they encountered, and returning home to report on their exploits and split the profits. Their efforts, sponsored

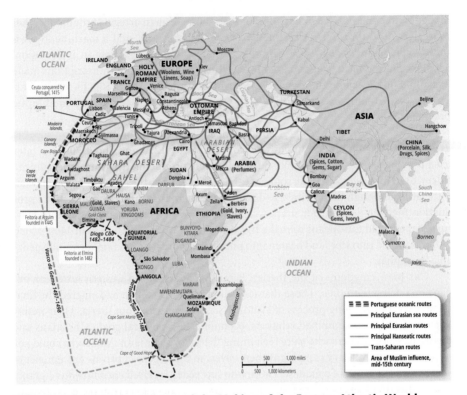

MAP 1.3 Global Trade, Africa, and the Making of the Eastern Atlantic World, 15th Century The Mediterranean Basin linked Europe to Africa and Asia for thousands of years through a combination of oceanic and overland routes. Portuguese seafaring along Africa's Atlantic coast during the 15th century brought West Africa into maritime global trade networks and launched the Atlantic slave trade.

The West African gold trade, from the Catalan Atlas

by Prince Henry, the younger son of King John I, had three linked objectives. One was to challenge Muslim powers in North Africa. Another was to make direct contact and ally with the Christian kingdom of Ethiopia, which had begun to send emissaries to Europe in the early 1400s. Europeans hoped for a Christian African-European alliance against a common Muslim foe. The third objective, gold, mattered most to the Portuguese. North African Muslims controlled the flow of West African gold across the Sahara and into the Mediterranean. The Portuguese wanted to divert that stream into their pockets by trading directly with West Africans. They established their first *feitoria* (fortified trading post) at Arguim in 1445. In 1482, the Portuguese built a feitoria at Elmina, on Africa's Gold Coast, because of its proximity to mines (Map 1.3). To obtain African cooperation and consent, the Portuguese employed locals to operate them and paid rent to their rulers.

Portuguese mariners launched the **Atlantic slave trade**. The first cargo of enslaved people shipped directly from Africa arrived in Portugal in 1441. At first, the Portuguese raided for slaves, but they soon found it easier and more profitable to buy slaves from African captors. Slavery was already common in West and West Central Africa when the Portuguese arrived. Slaves were the only form of private, revenue-producing property that legal systems widely recognized. Those condemned to slavery in Africa were usually criminals, war captives, or debtors. They did not inherit their status, nor did they pass it on to their children.

Africans were also already engaging in long-distance slave trading. Thousands were driven across the Sahara or transported up the Red Sea to North Africa and the Middle East annually between 800 and 1600. In Europe, the Ottoman conquest of Constantinople, today's Istanbul, in 1453 made it harder for Europeans to purchase Slavs (hence the word "slave") from the Black Sea, a key source of enslaved labor to northern and western Europe for centuries. So, these countries began to purchase African slaves available through the Mediterranean slave markets.

At first, relatively few entered the Atlantic slave trade—about 800 a year during the 1450s and 1460s and over 2,000 by the 1490s. By 1550, however, Africans comprised about 10 percent of Lisbon's population, a reflection of Portuguese dominance of the Atlantic slave trade until the late 1500s.

The Atlantic slave trade affected how Europeans viewed Africans. By the late 1400s, Christian Europeans seldom enslaved one another, mainly for religious reasons. Muslims who ruled Iberia had distinguished between slaves on the basis of skin color: they considered darker-skinned people from sub-Saharan Africa inferior and most suitable for enslavement. Christian Iberians came to hold similar views of sub-Saharan Africans, partly because they also associated dark-skinned Africans with Muslims, whom they condemned as infidels. Demographic changes in the slave trade during the 1400s reinforced such beliefs. Ottoman control of the eastern Mediterranean and the Atlantic slave trade meant that dark-skinned Africans soon became the majority of Christian Europe's slaves, leading more Europeans to associate black skin with servility. Prejudice based on skin color arose before Europeans reached the Americas.

As the Atlantic slave trade began, Iberians were already colonizing islands off Africa's northwest coast. The most significant of these were the Canary Islands and Madeira. The islands' Indigenous people, Guanches, probably descended from Berbers of North Africa. In 1402, Iberians began to colonize the lands of the Guanche, who became targets of slaving raids and fell victim to diseases to which they had no acquired immunity. There were virtually no Guanches left by the 1490s.

Meanwhile, Portuguese colonists established sugar plantations off northwest Africa's coast on the Madeira Islands. Europeans first encountered cultivation of sugar cane in the Middle East during the Crusades. For the next few centuries, Cyprus and Sicily supplied European markets with sugar from plantations staffed by enslaved Slavs, Tatars, and Mediterranean captives. Genoese merchants brought sugar-making technology from Sicily to Iberia, and by the 1450s Sicilians ran sugar mills on Madeira. Genoese merchants financed many of them and had the sugar hauled back to Europe. By 1500, about 2,000 slaves, mostly Africans, toiled on Madeira's plantations. They became one of western Europe's main sources of sugar, along with Spanish plantations on the Canaries.

The imperative to spread Christianity helped to propel and justify Portuguese expansion into Africa. Papal decrees issued between 1442 and 1456 granted Portugal the right to colonize islands off Africa's coast and monopolize trade between West Africa and Europe. In exchange, Portugal agreed to establish Catholic missions in Africa. One

PORTUGUESE INFLUENCE IN WEST AFRICA This brass casting, probably made by an African artist at the royal court of Benin in the late 1500s or early 1600s, illustrates exchange between Europeans and West Africans. It depicts a Portuguese mercenary fighting for the oba (king) of Benin. He carries a firearm, which the Portuguese introduced to the region.

decree permitted Portuguese to buy African captives if doing so meant that they might become converts.

The Portuguese saw missionaries as a way to forge diplomatic and commercial ties in Africa, a view that African rulers sometimes shared. To them, conversion offered a way to gain a powerful ally and bolster their own authority. In 1491, Portuguese soldiers helped the Kongolese king, Nzinga a Nkuwu, put down a rebellion, and on Christmas Day, he and his family were baptized. For the next 15 years, Kongolese fought over who should rule them. In 1506, the victor, Afonso, committed Kongo to an alliance with the Portuguese. His son Henrique studied in Portugal, became a priest in 1518, and was appointed the first sub-Saharan African bishop two years later. Thousands of Kongolese accepted baptism and gradually infused Christianity with their traditions.

By the time the Kongolese had begun to Africanize Western Christianity, the Portuguese were about to open a direct water route to the Indian Ocean. In 1487, Bartolomeu Dias rounded the Cape of Good Hope and entered the Indian Ocean. Eleven years later, an Arab pilot guided Vasco da Gama across the Indian Ocean to India. Da Gama returned to Lisbon with spices. King Manoel fired off a letter to Ferdinand and Isabel trumpeting da Gama's achievement and pledging to force Muslim merchants to relinquish control of the Indian Ocean's spice trade to Portugal.

The Portuguese never made good on Manoel's boast, but they did dominate the eastern water route to Asia for over a century. A chain of feitorias down Africa's Atlantic coast, their cannon facing the ocean, backed Portugal's claim. But the Portuguese could not monopolize knowledge of winds and currents gleaned from thousands of voyages to Africa, Madeira, and the Canaries, and this knowledge suggested that one might reach Asia by crossing the Atlantic.

Columbus Invades the Caribbean

Christopher Columbus, who had traveled widely across the eastern Atlantic, sought to extend Europe's dominion. Born in Genoa around 1450, Columbus likely began his maritime career in the early 1470s. He soon moved to Lisbon, drawn by opportunities offered by the city's Genoese merchants. He had ties to Portugal's royal court and supervised the colonization of one of the Madeira Islands. By the early 1480s, Columbus had visited Ireland, Iceland, Madeira, the Canaries, and Elmina.

Columbus also studied geography, sold books, and made maps. He pored over Ptolemy's *Geography*, which postulated that one could sail across the Atlantic to Asia. Ptolemy, however, thought the distance between the continents was so great that no

SEVILLE This view of Seville, attributed to Alonso Sánchez Coello and painted in the late 1550s, captures the city's status as Spain's main gateway to the Americas. In the foreground, an expedition prepares to set off for the Americas.

ship or crew could reach Asia and return. Access to the royal court alerted Columbus to a more optimistic alternative. In 1474, the Florentine cosmographer Paolo dal Pazzo Toscanelli had written the king of Portugal to claim that 5,000 miles separated the Canaries and China—still a great distance but one that sounded more feasible.

Columbus needed financial and legal backing to get to Asia. He tried and failed to interest John II of Portugal, so Columbus moved to Spain in 1485. He spent the next seven years lobbying Ferdinand and Isabel for support. They had reasons to expand their influence into the Atlantic: the ongoing conquest of the Canaries, competition with Portugal, and a need for new sources of gold. Ferdinand and Isabel approved Columbus's proposal shortly after the conquest of Granada and put up more than half the money for the voyage. The monarchs also granted him noble status and the offices of admiral, viceroy, and governor-general. Columbus had to provide one-quarter of the financing, most of which he borrowed from Italian merchants.

With three ships and 90 men under his command, Columbus departed Spain in early August 1492. After a stop in the Canaries, trade winds propelled them west. In mid-October, the crew made landfall on an island in the Bahamas. The Lucayan Taínos who lived there called it "Guanahaní." Columbus, thinking he had landed near the Indian Ocean's eastern edge, called them "Indians." His account of their first encounter stressed how little clothing the Taínos wore. Europeans of Columbus's time used clothing as a benchmark to judge individuals' social status and the level of civilization that a society had attained. Columbus also interpreted Taínos' lack of clothing as a sign of their innocence. Their willingness to trade whatever they

Columbus and the Taínos as depicted in a 1494 woodcut

had for glass beads, coins, and copper bells was another. Both suggested to Columbus that Taínos might make suitable converts and good workers. He took seven people from Guanahaní to serve as guides and interpreters. The three ships then sailed south in search of Asian ports as well as gold and other commodities that would sell in Europe. Along the way they overtook a Taíno in a canoe who was carrying a string of glass beads and some small coins. News of the strangers and items that they had brought were circulating through Indigenous information networks just four days after they arrived.

After exploring Cuba, Columbus reached an island that the Taínos called Quisqueya. He renamed it "La Isla Española"—the Spanish island, now Haiti and the Dominican Republic. On Española, the visitors met Taínos who seemed more like themselves. The ancestors of these Natives had migrated from South America over a thousand years earlier. These Taínos wore gold jewelry and lived in villages of up to 2,000 people governed by chiefs called caciques. They subsisted mainly on what they grew in conucos—plots that they had slashed and burned from the forest. Their major crop was cassava (or yucca), from which they made bread. One of the Taínos' two main deities was Yúcahu, god of cassava and of the sea. Taíno gods took physical form as zemis—carved idols that occupied places of honor in villages and homes. Taínos had a profound impact on how Europeans viewed the Americas and Indians. Many Arawak (the Taíno language) words entered Spanish and English, including "canoe" and "hammock." The word "Taíno" means "good" or "noble" in Arawak. Taínos used it to distinguish themselves from Caribs, who inhabited much of the Caribbean. Taínos told Columbus that Caribs were a vicious, warlike people who ate their enemies. Columbus was inclined to accept how the Taínos portrayed their foes, largely because it enabled him and the Spanish to pose as Taíno protectors, seek alliances with caciques, and claim that the Spanish were the Taínos' rightful rulers. Columbus later had a violent encounter with Caribs, which in his mind reinforced what the Taínos told him. An account of Columbus's first voyage distinguished between "good noble" Indians and violent "savage" ones. It circulated widely in Europe and molded European perceptions of Indians, including the belief that many were "cannibals"—a corruption of the word "Carib."

Columbus touted Española as a paradise. It had gold and a large population that farmed and lived in villages. After spending a few weeks along the island's north coast, Columbus loaded two ships with gold, chilies, tobacco, a canoe, a hammock, and seven Taínos. He left 39 men behind, sailed north, and discovered winds that blew east. Columbus reached Spain in March 1493 and headed to Barcelona to brief Ferdinand and Isabel and display the Taínos. He arrived to learn that a published account of his trip had beaten him there by two weeks. By December, versions of the story were being sold in Paris, Florence, and Rome. Some debated what Columbus had found. A few thought he had reached the Antilles, islands where legend had it that Christian Iberians fleeing Muslim rule had taken refuge centuries earlier. Columbus insisted that he had reached Asia and that Japan and China could not be far beyond. Pope Alexander VI believed that he had found people who required evangelization and proclaimed Spain's sovereignty over the lands Columbus had visited. This sat poorly with the Portuguese. In 1494, Spain and Portugal signed the **Treaty of Tordesillas**, by which they divided the world between them. The Americas, excepting Brazil, ended up on the Spanish side of the line (Map 1.4).

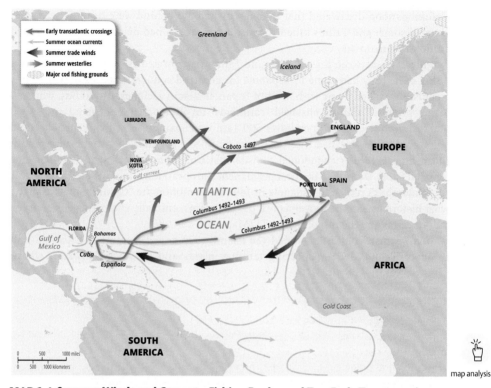

MAP 1.4 Summer Winds and Currents, Fishing Banks, and Two Early Transoceanic Crossings of the North Atlantic Mariners who sailed the Atlantic needed a good understanding of the ocean's winds and currents to navigate it successfully. Note the major cod fishing grounds where cold and warm currents collided.

An Italian named **Giovanni Caboto** was visiting Spain when Columbus returned. Like Columbus, he had lobbied the monarchs of Portugal and Spain to sponsor a voyage to Asia. Caboto moved to England and settled in Bristol, a home port for fishermen who sailed beyond Iceland. He obtained the backing of Henry VII and crossed the ocean in 1497. After exploring the coasts of Labrador and Newfoundland, Caboto returned with stories of seas full of fish and of a land that must be near Asia. The following year, Caboto embarked with five vessels laden with goods to trade. Only one made it home, without Caboto. English interest in western ventures dimmed for nearly a century. Caboto had publicized the marine resources of Newfoundland and Canada, places that soon formed the northwestern edge of the Atlantic world. But the Caribbean, especially Española, attracted more attention from powerful and ambitious Europeans.

Violence, Disease, and Cultural Exchange

In November 1493, Columbus returned to Española with about 1,500 men. He hoped to create a colony built around a feitoria, with colonists as company employees.

Columbus soon discovered that the men he had left behind were dead. Disease had claimed some, and Taínos killed the rest because they had demanded gold or raped Taíno women.

Relations between the colonists and Taínos deteriorated as Columbus lost control of his men. They had come to Española for gold and conquest, not a salary. In 1495, colonists provoked a war with most of Española's main caciques. Columbus, who had earlier proposed trading enslaved "cannibals" for livestock to Ferdinand and Isabel and had been rejected, shipped over 500 Taínos to Spain to show that Española could be profitable. He justified their enslavement on the grounds that they had rebelled. Meanwhile, colonists abandoned the site that Columbus had chosen. In 1496, they founded Santo Domingo, the first permanent European town in the Americas.

Columbus's return to Española in 1493 set in motion the "**Columbian exchange**," what historians call the movement of people, plants, animals, and pathogens between the Americas and the rest of the world (Map 1.5).

As Spanish colonists claimed the island, they hoped to remake Española into a "Spanish land" by transporting familiar plants and livestock. However, wheat,

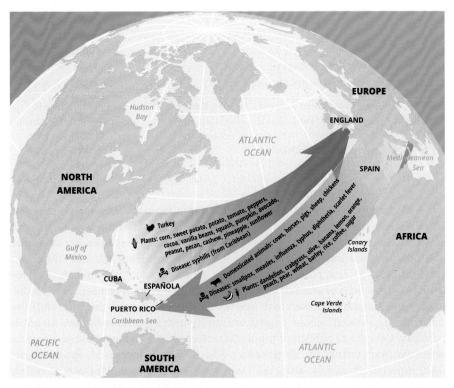

MAP 1.5 The Columbian Exchange Columbus's second voyage established a permanent exchange of plants, animals, and microbes between the Americas and the rest of the world. In some cases, it took centuries for Europeans, Africans, and Asians to adopt American crops. The impact of Eurasian microbes on American Indians was devastating, especially when combined with colonial violence.

chickpeas, grapes, olives, and sheep, staples of the Mediterranean diet, fared poorly in Caribbean heat and humidity. Because they could not subsist on locally grown grains of European origin, Española's colonists relied heavily on cassava, a starchy root popular among Native peoples of the Caribbean and South America. By 1496, Spanish authorities were demanding cassava of Taínos as tribute. Farmers of the Americas introduced the rest of the world to other new crops, including potatoes, tomatoes, cacao (or cocoa), peanuts, tobacco, and chili peppers. The most important food product of the Columbian exchange was corn, which is still the most widely grown crop in the Americas as well as a major food and fuel source globally.

Europeans domesticated more animals than did Native Americans. In 1493, Columbus brought cattle and pigs to Española, where colonists turned them loose to forage. Because Española had no natural predators, pigs and cattle soon overran the island, destroying native plants and diminishing the island's biodiversity. By 1508, authorities sought to protect the native farms that fed Española by permitting hunters to kill feral swine. Enslaved West Africans, Spaniards, and Indians herded, slaughtered, and skinned the animals. Spaniards depended on African and Indian slaves to cultivate another European introduction, sugar, which soon became Española's most profitable export.

Sex accelerated the Columbian exchange. Because no European women accompanied Columbus's second expedition, Taíno women became Spanish men's sexual partners. Some of the Spaniards contracted a mutated strain of treponematosis, syphilis, a disease previously unknown in Europe and the only American disease to plague Europeans in the wake of contact. The nature of these early sexual encounters varied: many Taíno were raped, while others formed long-term relationships with Spaniards. A 1514 census of prominent Spanish colonists indicates that 37 percent had Native wives, although the majority of Spanish colonists did not marry Taíno women. At first, many fathers recognized the children that resulted from such unions, and most colonists considered them Spanish. But by the 1530s, the Spanish had begun to consider them a separate and subordinate group whom they called *mestizos*.

Colonists also introduced Taínos to new diseases. Many of these diseases were common in Europe, where regular exposure produced antibodies that afforded Europeans some immunity to subsequent epidemics. However, because Native Americans had never been exposed to European diseases, they lacked acquired immunity. Moreover, colonists made war, took slaves, and raided Native food stores, all of which enhanced Indigenous mortality. Pigs from Columbus's second voyage probably brought influenza to the Americas. Gold mining overworked Taínos and crowded them together. The Taíno population declined, and the Spanish responded by forcing Taínos into fewer but larger settlements so that they could be counted, taxed, put to work, and converted to Christianity more easily. These became death traps. Smallpox, the most devastating European pathogen, first reached the Americas in January 1519, devastating communities throughout the Caribbean and Mesoamerica. Cycles of disease and violence decimated the Native population of Española, which stood at 400,000 in 1492 but plummeted to only 500 in 1548.

Spaniards stormed the Caribbean in search of new conquests, riches, and slaves. Between 1508 and 1513, they raided Cuba, the Bahamas, Puerto Rico, and Jamaica,

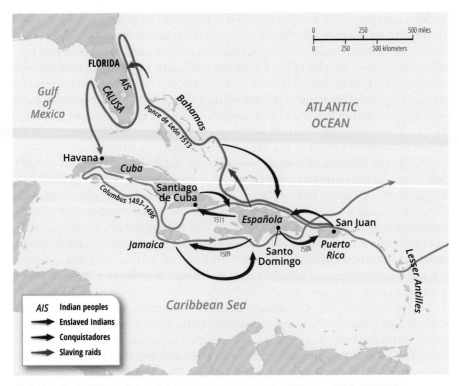

MAP 1.6 Española and Spanish Conquests in the Caribbean, 1493–1515 The depopulation of Española's Taínos caused by microbes that the Spanish brought and by Spanish abuses spurred conquistadores and slave raiders to invade nearby islands, a process that led the Spanish to Florida in 1513.

taking Indian slaves who were forced to work on encomiendas in Española. These raids spread disease and destabilized Indigenous societies throughout the region (Map 1.6).

The depopulation of much of the Caribbean spurred a missionary-led campaign to end the worst abuses of the conquest. In 1511, the friar Antonio de Montesinos enraged Santo Domingo's elite by delivering a sermon in which he threatened that God would punish them for their cruelty toward Indians. In response, King Ferdinand hired a jurist to draft the **Requerimiento**, a declaration addressed to Indian peoples. Each time a conquistador encountered a new group, he was supposed to read and, if possible, translate the Requerimiento. The declaration commanded Indians to submit to Spanish rule and Catholicism. To those who resisted, the Requerimiento promised consequences: "We will come upon you and make war upon you everywhere and in every way that we can and . . . will take from you your bodies, your wives, and your children and make them slaves, and as slaves shall sell them and dispose of them however their Majesties may command." Thus, the Requerimiento created a legal justification for Indian enslavement. A Montesinos disciple, **Bartolomé de las Casas**, a priest and former Cuban encomendero, criticized the Requerimiento and other Indian policies. He focused his ire on colonists and conquistadors but never questioned Spain's right to rule in the Americas.

Bartolomé de las Casas, *A Short Account of the Destruction of the Indies* (1542)

The decimation of the Taíno and missionaries' efforts to stem it facilitated the extension of African slavery and plantation agriculture to the Americas. The first enslaved Africans arrived in Española in 1502. Fourteen years later, las Casas proposed enslaved Africans as an alternative to Indian labor on humanitarian grounds, a position that he later bitterly regretted. That year, a colonist built Española's first functional mill to crush sugar cane, extract the juice, and boil it down to make sugar. During the 1520s, Española witnessed the first sugar boom in the Americas. At first, most who toiled in the cane fields were enslaved Indians, with artisans from the Canaries, Italy, and Portugal supervising the mills. By the late 1520s, enslaved Africans had mostly replaced Indians on plantations. As of 1540, 15,000 slaves had been sent to Española and the island had an African majority—some of whom had escaped slavery to found the first free black communities in the Americas. Española remained an important source of sugar to Europe until the 1580s, when sugar production boomed in Brazil.

Engraving showing African slaves working in the mines of Española (1595)

The devastation of the Greater Antilles led conquistadors to look to the American mainland. The Caribbean served as the gateway for invasions of Central America, Mexico, and Florida. An expedition from Española seeking gold and slaves in Panama became the first group of Europeans to set eyes on the Pacific Ocean in 1513. Meanwhile, Juan Ponce de León, who led the conquest of Puerto Rico, made the first recorded European visit to Florida. Florida's Ais and Calusa Indians assumed that he led a group of slavers and repelled the expedition. In 1521, Ponce de León returned to conquer and colonize Florida. The Calusa again turned the invaders back. Ponce de León died in Cuba, wounded by a Calusa arrowhead. The Atlantic world, however, represented mainly by Europeans seeking precious metals, passages to Asia, Indians to enslave, and lands to conquer, had reached North America.

STUDY QUESTIONS FOR EARLY COLONIALISM, 1000–1513

1. What factors led Spain to colonize the Americas?
2. Why did Native peoples of Española face such high mortality rates after the colonial invasion?

quiz

◉ THE INVASION OF NORTH AMERICA, 1513–1565

Knowledge that the Americas had wealthy Indigenous empires and that the world's oceans are connected intensified European interest in North America. Mariners mapped the continent's coasts as Spanish-led expeditions invaded its interior in search of Indian empires to conquer and pillage. Europeans soon realized that there were few riches to be had easily in North America. Nevertheless, the continent became a stage for European imperial rivalries and religious conflicts that led the Spanish to establish the first colony in what would become the United States.

The Fall of Mexica

In September 1519, **Hernán Cortés**, leader of a Spanish expedition to Mexico, persuaded the leaders of Tlaxcala to join him against the Mexica. Scholars have long sought to explain how fewer than a thousand Spaniards could have toppled a mighty empire of millions. Most agree that three factors were paramount: Indian allies, technology, and disease.

Cortés could not have prevailed without Indian allies such as Tlaxcalans or his translator and advisor, **Malintzín.** Cortés acquired Malintzín and 19 other enslaved women from the Chontal Maya in 1519. They were baptized, renamed, divided among Spanish soldiers, and forced to act as concubines. Malintzín was a Nahua (speaker of Nahuatl, the language of the Mexica and millions of others in central Mexico) who probably grew up in a noble's household. Her knowledge of Nahua culture and politics helped to win allies against Mexica. Bernal Díaz, a soldier in Cortés's expedition, wrote of Malintzín, "After Our Lord God, it was she who caused New Spain (what the Spanish renamed Mexico after the conquest) to be won."

Malintzín knew that Mexica demands for tribute and captives had alienated many Nahua peoples, including Tlaxcalans. When the Spanish arrived, Tlaxcala clung to independence, surrounded by city-states allied with or subject to Mexica. One Tlaxcalan faction fought the Spanish and lost badly. Thereafter, Tlaxcalans presented themselves as Spain's most loyal allies. Several thousand escorted Cortés when he entered Tenochtitlán in 1519. They suffered the brunt of the casualties when Mexica reclaimed the city the following year. The Spanish found sanctuary in Tlaxcala and used it as a base to recruit more allies. In 1521, tens of thousands of Tlaxcalans, along with warriors from other Nahua city-states, joined 900 Spaniards in besieging Tenochtitlán and taking the city two months later.

"The Capture of Tenochtitlán"

Technology played a key role in the conquest. Horses afforded the Spanish advantages in speed, mobility, and height. They proved especially effective when those who rode them wielded swords and wore armor. Nahua memories of the conquest stressed two forms of technology. One was metal, especially steel blades and armor. The other was the ability of the Spanish to summon help from lands overseas. Ironically, the Spanish maritime network benefited Cortés even when his superiors did not intend it to. Cortés disobeyed the orders of the Spanish governor of Cuba when he chose to embark on the conquest of Mexica. In 1520, the governor sent Pánfilo de Narváez and several hundred men to force Cortés to surrender. Cortés persuaded most to defect by promising them a share of the spoils of Tenochtitlán. The Cuban governor's failed plan to control Cortés inadvertently helped him to succeed. When Narváez retreated to Cuba, having lost an eye in battle, the defectors reinforced Cortés's army.

Narváez's reinforcements also brought smallpox to Mexico. Unfamiliar with the disease, the people of Tenochtitlán called it *huey zuahtal,* or "big rash." The Mexica had never been exposed to the disease, so they lacked acquired immunity. Their immunity was further compromised by the long Spanish siege of Tenochtitlán, where disease spread quickly among the dense, hungry population. One Spanish solider recalled that by the time his army stormed Tenochtitlán, "the streets, squares, houses, and courts were filled with bodies, so that it was almost impossible to pass." The largest Indian city in the Americas had fallen.

The most important Nahua allies of the Spanish, Malintzín and the Tlaxcalans, retained their ties to the conquerors after the fall of Tenochtitlán. Not long after the

Mexica surrendered, Malintzín gave birth to Martín Cortés, Hernán's son. She later married another Spaniard, with whom she had a daughter, Maria. In 1535, Charles V granted Tlaxcala special rights as a reward for helping to conquer Tenochtitlán, Guatemala, and western Mexico. Tlaxcalans were to answer directly to Spanish monarchs and no other authority. They also continued to act as co-conquerors of the Americas. Tlaxcalans claimed that they accompanied **Francisco de Coronado** to New Mexico in 1540 and participated in a failed Spanish colony in southeastern North America in the early 1560s. Malintzín, Tlaxcalans, and other Indians were crucial in remaking Mexico into New Spain.

Malintzín and Cortés from the *Lienzo de Tlaxcala* (1552)

Efforts to convert Mexico's Indians into Christians also helped to create New Spain. Twelve **Franciscans** arrived in Mexico from Española in 1524. The friars followed strict vows of poverty and viewed Europe as corrupt and sinful. They saw in Mexico a chance to recreate the original Christian communities. Once they had preached the gospel in every language, "The Twelve" believed, Jesus would return to earth, determine who was saved and who was damned, and bring on the end of the world. The eagerness with which Indians sought baptism, sometimes by thousands at a time, seemed to confirm their vision. To convert more Indians, Franciscans and other missionaries burned most of the histories that Nahuas and Maya had written before the conquest and had most of their temples demolished. Franciscans studied Indian languages and wrote detailed accounts of Indian cultures and histories in hopes of facilitating conversion of Indians. They developed a Romanized alphabet for Nahuatl that many Indians quickly mastered. A monk, Peter of Ghent, helped to write the first instruction manual in Nahuatl. Another, Bernardino de Sahagún, in 1547 directed Nahuas to gather information about Mexico before and during the conquest. The result was the Florentine Codex. Compiled mainly from Nahua interviews, it is invaluable to scholars who study Mexico. Over time, Franciscans' zeal faded, partly because most Indian converts blended their Indigenous beliefs and rituals with Christianity. Their successors looked for other Indians to convert. A few decades later, they believed that they had found them in Florida and New Mexico, where Franciscans followed the conversion strategies they had learned in Mexico.

Spanish-Nahuatl dictionary, printed in Mexico in 1571

The conquest of Mexico also triggered more Spanish invasions. In 1532, 160 men led by Francisco Pizarro intervened in a civil war over who should rule the Inca Empire based in modern-day Peru. The intruders took one claimant to the throne, Atahualpa, hostage and ransomed him for enough gold and treasure to fill the room in which they imprisoned him. Pizarro's men melted down the ornaments and artwork that they extorted into nearly 20 tons of gold and silver before murdering Atahualpa. The Spanish had decapitated the Inca Empire. Still, it took 40 more years and the help of Indian allies to conquer it. From the Spanish perspective, Mexico and Peru yielded the best of treasures, precious metals. Mexico and Peru became the hubs of the Spanish Empire and the main destinations for Spanish immigrants for centuries.

Early Encounters

Cortés's success in Mexico inspired other conquistadors, who dreamed of finding and conquering other wealthy Indian empires or discovering a quicker route to Asia. Between the early 1520s and the early 1540s, explorers in the service of Spain and

Chocolate

Chocolate originated in the tropical rainforests of Mesoamerica, where Indigenous people have cultivated cacao for thousands of years. The cacao tree is unusual in that its flowers grow directly on the trunk and older limbs. When Native people picked the flowers' pods, they found a sweet pulp and bitter beans inside. At first, they ate the pulp and threw the beans away. Over time, however, they experimented with the cacao beans and, by 1150 BCE, made a fermented beverage with them. A few hundred years later, they had perfected a frothy, nonalcoholic version of hot chocolate made with ground cacao beans, water, and spices like achiote and chili.

Aztecs called this beverage *xocoatl*, the origin of our word "chocolate." They and other Mesoamerican people revered chocolate, offering it to the gods. Among mortals, consumption of chocolate was largely restricted to elites and priests. Chocolate figured prominently in several religious rituals, and it still plays a role at Zapotec weddings, where a groom gives it to his new bride. Even in the precolonial era, cacao beans were a highly valuable commodity, and some Mesoamericans, including Mayans, used them as a currency.

During the early colonial era, Europeans tried to avoid Indigenous foods. At that time Europeans took the axiom "You are what you eat" quite literally. They feared that eating American foods would compromise their European identity. Gradually—often by necessity—Europeans started incorporating more American foods into their diets. The first Europeans to try chocolate were Spaniards, who complained that it was too bitter. To compensate, the Spanish added sugar, a crop that they had recently introduced to the Americas. Sweetened hot chocolate proved tremendously popular among wealthy families in New Spain.

Starting in the late 1500s, chocolate became a major export commodity. Spain led production, but soon other imperial powers developed chocolate plantations in the Caribbean. A labor-intensive crop, chocolate was produced by growing numbers of

France mapped the coasts. Soldiers and entrepreneurs tried to establish outposts in the Southeast and Northeast. Meanwhile, three Spanish-led expeditions invaded the interior. Indians rebuffed every incursion.

Europeans first charted the Gulf of Mexico and then began to map the Eastern Seaboard. Most sought a channel to the Pacific, a possible North American counterpart to the one that Ferdinand Magellan's fleet had used to pass through South America in 1520 and to circumnavigate the globe two years later, a journey that proved that the oceans are connected. Meanwhile, the small fleet of Juan Rodríguez Cabrillo, veteran of the conquests of Cuba and Mexico, hugged the California coast in the early 1540s (Map 1.7). The voyages exposed more Indians to Europeans, as traders or as captors, laying a foundation for more intensive migration and exchange. This contact also furnished Indians with information to resist European invasions.

CACAO GOD This Mayan depiction of the cacao god reflects the religious importance of the drink for Mesoamerican peoples. The god's body also reveals a unique characteristic of the cacao plant—note how pods sprout directly from the trunk.

Native American and African slaves. When chocolate hit the European market, it was initially expensive, largely a luxury item for European courtiers. Although Europeans disassociated chocolate from religious rituals, they, like Mesoamericans, believed that it had powerful properties. The storied Venetian writer Casanova asserted that chocolate was the best aphrodisiac. In the Caribbean, where chocolate was cheaper and more abundant, many Europeans consumed drinking chocolate on a daily basis. According to Hans Sloane, a doctor in Jamaica, "Chocolate is given to young Children here, almost the first Meat they take except the Mothers Milk." Chocolate remained too expensive for most British North Americans until 1765, when the first chocolate factory opened in Massachusetts. Today, Americans, along with millions of people across the world, enjoy chocolate as an everyday luxury.

- Why did Europeans initially fear chocolate and other American foods? Why do you think they overcame this anxiety?
- How has the meaning behind chocolate consumption changed over time?

Meanwhile, three groups of conquistadors pushed into the interior of the Southeast and Southwest. The leader of the first, Pánfilo de Narváez, lost Mexico to Cortés in 1520. Eight years later, Narváez hoped to find gold and glory in Florida. Hernando de Soto, who commanded the second, was an officer to Pizarro. From 1539 to 1543, his expedition traversed the Southeast, encountering dozens of Native chiefdoms and powerful leaders like the Lady of Cofitachequi. Francisco de Coronado headed the third expedition, which followed a model established by the conquest of Mexico. Most of the nearly 2,000 men whom Coronado led into the Southwest and onto the Great Plains were Mexican Indians.

None of the expeditions found riches or a powerful empire. Because the Indian governments of North America were less centralized than those of the Mexica or Incas, the Spanish could not target and overthrow a single leader. Moreover, Indians did not

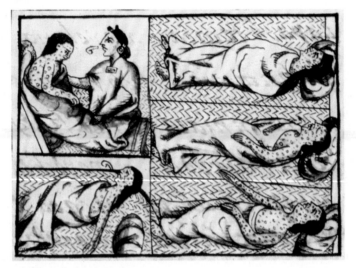

THE DEVASTATION OF DISEASE The first smallpox epidemic in the Americas devastated Mesoamerica between 1519 and 1521. This image, drawn by a Nahua (Aztec) man, shows the progression of the disease.

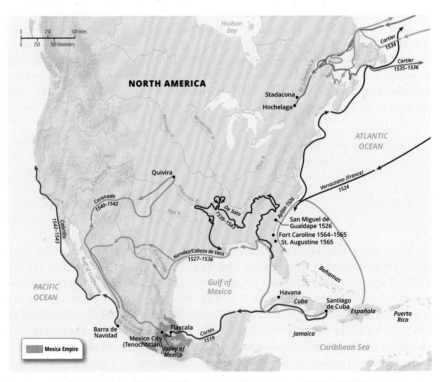

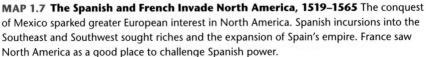

MAP 1.7 The Spanish and French Invade North America, 1519–1565 The conquest of Mexico sparked greater European interest in North America. Spanish incursions into the Southeast and Southwest sought riches and the expansion of Spain's empire. France saw North America as a good place to challenge Spanish power.

ally en masse with the Spanish as Nahuas had against Mexica. Instead, the invaders quickly exhausted whatever welcome they received. De Soto's men extorted huge quantities of corn and enslaved hundreds of Indians to shoulder their gear and booty as they plundered the Southeast. Coronado's army took food from Pueblos who had little to spare.

Indian resistance ensured that such incursions failed. News of the invaders traveled far and fast. Long before Pánfilo de Narváez arrived, the people of Apalachee (who lived near what is now Tallahassee) learned that the Spaniards had been trekking for months through Florida's swamps and were now starving. Rather than allowing the invaders access to their corn granaries, the Apalachee chiefdom drove them back to the sea. Attempting escape, the survivors built rafts, but most died of thirst or exposure while floating in the Gulf of Mexico. Some washed ashore on the Texas coast, where the Karankawa Indians enslaved them. After years of captivity, only 4 men out of the original 300 were still alive; they managed to walk to Mexico City, arriving eight years after their initial departure.

Indians repeatedly deflected invaders, often toward their enemies, with tales that the gold and riches they sought were somewhere else. The greedy Spanish took the bait and invariably got lost, far from reinforcements. Indians controlled the flow of information because the Spanish had to depend on Native guides and interpreters. Coronado's men met an enslaved Indian whom they called El Turco (The Turk) at Pecos Pueblo. He spoke Nahuatl (as did many Indians who marched with Coronado) and a Plains Indian sign language. El Turco promised to lead the expedition to Quivira, a town on the Great Plains, where the Spanish would find what they wanted. Quivira turned out to be a modest Wichita village. El Turco admitted that Pueblos had asked him to guide the invaders to a place where they and their horses would get lost and starve. Coronado had him garroted. The expedition, adrift on the Plains, spent months trudging back to New Mexico. Coronado retreated to Mexico, leaving behind some Indians and two friars whom Pueblos soon killed.

Indians also scuttled two initiatives to colonize North America between 1526 and 1543. Francisco de Chicora, an Indian seized on the southeast Atlantic coast by Spanish slavers, was instrumental in the rise and demise of the first European settlement in mainland North America. After his capture, Francisco accompanied Nicolás Vázquez de Ayllón, an Española lawyer and sugar planter, to Spain. There, he spun stories of his homeland, claiming that it rivaled Spain's richest regions and produced Mediterranean crops like olives, almonds, and figs. These stories captivated Ayllón and the royal court, who, falling into Francisco's trap, commanded the Indian to guide them back to his rich kingdom. In 1526, Ayllón, Francisco, and 600 colonists, including the friar Antonio de Montesinos and some African slaves, landed in South Carolina. Francisco deserted, as did the other Indians Ayllón brought as interpreters. The colonists moved to present-day Georgia and founded **San Miguel de Gualdape**, the first European settlement in today's mainland United States. They arrived in October, too late to plant. Disease and cold killed Ayllón and many others as the survivors split into factions. Only 150 returned to Española.

A similar fate befell the first French effort to colonize North America. In 1534, **Jacques Cartier** entered the Gulf of St. Lawrence seeking precious metals, gems, and a passage to the Pacific. He encountered Iroquoian speakers from the village of Stadacona. Cartier took two of the Indians, Domagaya and Taignoagny, back to France to learn French. He returned the following year, sailed up the St. Lawrence River, and returned the two men to Stadacona. The villagers, hoping to monopolize access to French goods, tried to dissuade Cartier from proceeding upriver. Cartier ignored them and proceeded to Hochelaga, a village on the site of present-day Montreal. Iced in until April 1536, several French died of scurvy before Domagaya showed them how to brew a tea from cedar bark and needles that contained the vitamin C that they needed. Five years later, Cartier led colonists to Canada, where they erected a fort. By 1543, the French had left after suffering harsh winters and two more bouts with scurvy. It added insult to injury that samples that Cartier had carried to France and touted as gold and diamonds turned out to be worthless. "Faux comme des diamants du Canada" (as false as Canadian diamonds) soon became a French expression to describe something without value.

Indians turned back European invasions at a profound cost. The French returned to Stadacona and Hochelaga in the late 1500s to find them abandoned. Disease and warfare had forced their residents to flee. De Soto's expedition accelerated the decline of Mississippian chiefdoms. Spaniards returned to the Southeast interior in the 1560s to find most towns deserted. Historians debate why this happened. Some contend that de Soto's army, especially the pigs that they brought along to eat, spread diseases that killed thousands. Others argue that the invasion disrupted Indian societies by slaughtering thousands, causing food shortages that were exacerbated by a cooling climate, and undermining the chiefs' authority. By the early 1700s, the Mississippian chiefdoms had fallen, but the Mississippians' ancestors banded together to form large nations that contested European claims to their region.

Religious Reformation and European Rivalries

In the 1550s, European rivalries in the Americas became entrenched in religious conflict. It began in 1517 when a monk named **Martin Luther** nailed his *Ninety-Five Theses* to the door of a church in Germany. He challenged the propriety and ability of church officials to confer forgiveness of sins and salvation on others. Only personal faith, Luther argued, could save one's soul. Those who concurred came to be known as Protestants for their protests against the Catholic Church's authority.

Protestantism was part of a broader reform movement that swept Christianity in western Europe in the 1500s. All reformers, Protestant or Catholic, held that church members should be more pious and know basic Christian doctrine. They agreed that Christians should reject folk beliefs that reformers considered pagan superstition or even satanic. Most demanded that government enforce religious conformity. Protestants denied the authority of the pope and the Catholic Church on the grounds that both were corrupt and violated God's will. They believed that the Bible should be accorded more authority and that its verses should be made more accessible by translating them from Latin into languages such as English or German. Defying Catholic doctrine, Luther asserted that faith mattered more than deeds for salvation. This left ample room for Protestants to disagree. They differed, sometimes violently, on matters such as infant baptism; the degree to which they should reject Catholic ritual, iconography, and theology; how they should govern their churches; and what was the proper relationship between church and state.

Religious groups that arose during the western European Reformation played a key role in conflicts over the Americas. One was the Catholic Reformation, which created new organizations to win converts, renewed insistence on religious orthodoxy, and bolstered Spanish determination to uphold Catholicism. In 1540, Ignatius Loyola, a Basque priest, founded the **Jesuits (Society of Jesus)**. One of their main goals was to make new converts overseas and in Europe. By 1550, they operated in India and Brazil. Jesuits also sought to spread Catholic doctrine by founding and operating schools. Meanwhile, the Spanish proclaimed themselves Catholicism's staunchest defenders and Protestantism's worst enemy.

Jesuit
missionaries

A second group that played a major role in the Americas were the Calvinists, products of the Protestant Reformation. In 1534, Parliament passed the **Act of Supremacy**, which abolished papal authority over England and made King **Henry VIII** head of the **Church of England (Anglican Church)**. Henry's Protestant daughter **Elizabeth I** established a policy of religious moderation that satisfied most English but alienated a minority who sought to purge England of all vestiges of Catholicism. Critics labeled these more extreme Protestants "puritans." **Puritans** followed the teachings of **John Calvin**, a theologian based in Geneva. He argued that God had already determined who would be saved or damned. People might recognize God's elect by their professions of faith that God had saved them and by their conduct. Calvin thought that a body composed of ministers and elders should oversee church affairs and that local officials should uphold religious orthodoxy. By 1560, **Calvinism** had spread to England, Scotland, the Netherlands, Germany, and France, where its followers were known as **Huguenots**.

Although both Catholic, France and Spain fought a series of wars starting in the 1520s. French kings authorized private vessels to seize Spanish ships and sell their cargoes. Such **privateers**, many of them Huguenots, began to prowl the Caribbean in the 1530s, capturing ships laden with gold and silver and raiding Spanish settlements. When peace came, some privateers continued to operate without official license as corsairs or pirates. Spain responded in the 1540s by starting to provide military escorts for vessels traveling to and from the Caribbean. The toll on Spanish America and on Spain's coffers was immense. Between 1556 and 1561, French privateers and pirates made off with more than half of the royal revenues from Spanish America.

As Huguenots attacked Spanish shipping, bloodier religious violence in France encouraged them to seek refuge. Admiral Gaspard de Coligny, a Huguenot who financed privateers, directed the founding of a colony in Brazil in 1555. Factionalism and poor relations with Indians sapped the outpost, located near today's Rio de Janeiro. The Portuguese destroyed it five years later. Florida seemed a good alternative. It was relatively safe, and most Spain-bound ships rode the Florida current up the peninsula's coast. Florida could be an ideal base for French who sought to get rich and wound Catholicism's most militant champion.

The Founding of Florida

By the early 1560s, ocean currents, religion, and piracy had made the Florida peninsula a global crossroads. Florida Indians had endured countless Spanish slaving raids and four Spanish colonization ventures. Ais and Calusa Indians had also absorbed hundreds of people who were left behind or whose ships had run aground or sunk and salvaged the wrecks, trading the gold and other items that they recovered with other Indians.

interactive timeline

TIMELINE ANCIENT TIMES–1565

AMERICA	YEAR	THE WORLD
Hunters and fishermen from East Asia enter Alaska and settle North America	c. 13,000–11,000 BCE	Global temperatures rise, causing rising sea levels and flooding that diminish resources but contribute to fishing in Japan and Southeast Asia
	10,000 BCE	Africa and Europe are largely populated by hunter-gatherers
Na-Dene speakers cross Bering Sea into Alaska	c. 8,000–6,000 BCE	Conditions become suitable for farming communities to grow and spread in Asia
Peoples in central Mexico begin to cultivate ancestor of corn	c. 7,000 BCE	Farming communities appear in Europe
Aleut and Inuit ancestors begin to arrive in Alaska First domesticated crops in North America	c. 3,000 BCE	Egyptian communities build irrigation channels centered around the Nile, leading to establishment of the First Dynasty
Southwestern peoples begin to cultivate corn on a large scale	c. 1500 BCE	
Bow and arrow spread throughout North America	c. 700 CE	
Anasazi culture peaks in Southwest Mississippian chiefdoms emerge in Mississippi River valley and in Southeast	c. 900–1300	Medieval Warm Period occurs European economy grows, thanks to increased population, increasing capitalization, and developing markets
Cahokia reaches its zenith	c. 1100–1200	
Drought plagues Indian peoples in Mississippi valley, Plains, and Southwest	c. 1200–1300	Mongol Empire, founded by Temujin, expands westward
	c. 1200–1400	
Drought and raids compel Anasazi to abandon towns in Southwest	c. 1300	
Cahokia abandoned	1300s	Plague peaks in Europe
Iroquois Great League of Peace and Huron Confederacy founded	c. 1400	
	1415–1469	Portuguese forces capture Ceuta in North Africa Portuguese mariners launch Atlantic slave trade Papal decrees authorize Portuguese conquests in Africa and Atlantic slave trade Marriage of Isabel and Ferdinand
	1487	Bartolomeu Dias navigates past Cape of Good Hope
Apr Christopher Columbus contracts with Ferdinand and Isabel to sail west across Atlantic **Aug** Columbus's expedition departs Spain **Oct** Columbus's expedition makes landfall in Bahamas	1492	**Jan** Muslim forces surrender Granada, completing Iberian Christians' reconquest of the peninsula
Jan Columbus departs Española for Spain **Mar** Columbus returns to Spain **Nov** Columbus returns to Española and introduces cattle, pigs, and sugar cane to the Americas	1493	
	1494	Treaty of Tordesillas divides most of world into territories claimed by Spain or Portugal
Santo Domingo, first permanent European settlement in the Americas, founded on Española	1496	

AMERICA	YEAR	THE WORLD
Giovanni Caboto explores Newfoundland on behalf of England	1497	
	1498	Portuguese mariner Vasco da Gama arrives in India
Enslaved Africans arrive in Española European women arrive in Americas	1502	
	1508–1513	Spanish conquer Puerto Rico, Jamaica, the Bahamas, and Cuba
Spanish slaving raids depopulate Bahamas and likely start targeting Florida	1509–1513	
Juan Ponce de León leads first recorded European visit to Florida	1513	
	1517	Martin Luther releases *Ninety-Five Theses* against church indulgences; Protestant Reformation begins
	1519–1522	Voyage originally led by Ferdinand Magellan circumnavigates globe
Jan First recorded smallpox epidemic reaches the Americas **Feb** Spanish expedition led by Hernán Cortés reaches Yucatán Peninsula **Oct** Spanish-Nahua forces enter Tenochtitlán	1519	
Jul Spanish-Nahua forces conquer Tenochtitlán	1521	
First Franciscan missionaries arrive in Mexico	1524	
Spanish colonists found and abandon San Miguel de Gualdape in Georgia	1526	
Spanish expedition becomes first European group to enter interior of what is today the United States	1528–1536	
	1532	Spanish expedition launches conquest of Peru
Spanish expedition led by Hernando de Soto invades southeastern North America	1539–1543	
Spanish expedition invades southwestern North America and southern Great Plains	1540–1542	
Spanish expedition led by Juan Cabrillo explores California's coast	1542–1543	
	1540–1558	Spanish begin to exploit silver deposits in Mexico and Bolivia "Elizabethan Settlement" brings religious peace to England
French privateers and pirates step up attacks on Spanish shipping in Caribbean	1550s to early 1560s	
French attempt to establish colonies in southeastern North America	1562–1565	
	1564	William Shakespeare born in England, 1564
Sep Spanish forces defeat French and found St. Augustine, Florida	1565	

Soon Florida became the first European battleground for North America and the first permanent European outpost in the mainland United States.

In 1562, the French admiral Coligny sent Huguenot captain Jean Ribault and 150 men, mostly Huguenots, to North America to establish a colony. Ribault quickly returned to France, where a religious war had just erupted. He fled to England, where he proposed a joint Anglo-French venture to found a Protestant colony in Florida. The men Ribault left behind built a fort in present-day South Carolina. They soon alienated their Guale Indian hosts, and most abandoned the colony. In 1564, another Huguenot fleet under the command of René de Laudonnière arrived with 300 colonists, including Jacques Le Moyne, who had been hired to paint illustrations of Florida to promote the colony in France. They erected Fort Caroline near present-day Jacksonville. At that time, the region was dominated by Timucua Indians, who spoke 9 or 10 different dialects and lived in 35 independent chiefdoms. Initially, the French welcomed an alliance with Saturiwa, chief of the eastern Timucua, who fed the French garrison. Laudonnière, however, decided to switch French allegiance, allying with a more powerful chief named Outina. According to a French colonist, Outina treated them "like other Indians." Outina demanded that the French fight alongside his forces in a series of battles against rivals. Military losses mounted, supplies dwindled, and many French deserted. Colonists saw that Timucuas had silver and gold and assumed that these precious metals came from nearby mines. Many left to find them, unaware that Timucuas had taken these riches from European shipwrecks. Fort Caroline was on the brink of collapse when John Hawkins, an English pirate, slave trader, and smuggler, showed up in 1565 with provisions and a boat. Ribault's French fleet brought reinforcements a few weeks later.

The Spanish monitored developments in Florida. Pedro Menéndez de Avilés, who had escorted several fleets across the Atlantic, battled French privateers and corsairs, and knew eastern North America's coastline well, thought that the future of the Spanish Empire hung in the balance. If the French had a base in Florida, Menéndez argued, pirates could attack the Spanish at will. Worse, Menéndez warned **Philip II of Spain**, French colonists were forging alliances with Florida Indians and might convince African slaves in Cuba and Española to rebel. Philip appointed Menéndez governor of Florida and subsidized his expedition of 800 soldiers, mariners, and colonists.

They landed near a Timucuan village on the feast day of Saint Augustine and renamed the town in his honor. Chief Saturiwa, seizing an opportunity to repay the French for their betrayal, allied with the Spanish, providing Menéndez with supplies as well as extensive information about Fort Caroline. This intelligence proved crucial as the Spanish seized Fort Caroline and found most of the members of Ribault's fleet. Menéndez executed most of the French on grounds that they were pirates and Protestant heretics. He spared women, children, and Catholics. Laudonnière and Le Moyne escaped. In the 1580s, each published an account that perpetuated the myth that eastern North America contained precious metals, animating English readers who dreamed of riches like those the Spanish enjoyed.

The founding of **St. Augustine** signaled that Europeans and Africans were in North America to stay. The colonial history of what would become the mainland United States had begun, more than 70 years after Spaniards and Taínos first met in the Bahamas.

Early map of Spanish Florida

STUDY QUESTIONS FOR THE INVASION OF NORTH AMERICA, 1513–1565

1. What explains the conquest of Mexica?

2. How did Native North Americans frustrate early Spanish attempts at colonization?

3. How did religious changes in Europe and piracy lead to the founding of St. Augustine?

quiz

Summary

- In the millennia before the European invasion, Indians in North America settled the entire continent, transformed its landscape, and created hundreds of diverse societies capable of adapting to political, social, and environmental change.
- In the 1400s, Europeans and Africans created networks that accelerated the flow of people, goods, and ideas between them and enabled Europeans to colonize the Caribbean and establish a foothold in the Americas by the 1510s.
- In the 1520s, new conquests and new knowledge spurred Europeans to explore North America's coasts and invade its interior, efforts that Indians successfully resisted until the 1560s, when imperial rivalries and religious conflicts led Spain to begin colonizing Florida.

Key Terms and People

audio
flashcards

Act of Supremacy 33

astrolabes 14

Atlantic slave trade 16

Atlantic world 12

Caboto, Giovanni 21

Cahokia 8

Calvin, John 33

Calvinism 33

Cartier, Jacques 31

Church of England (Anglican Church) 33

Columbian exchange 22

Columbus, Christopher 18

Coronado, Francisco de 27

Cortés, Hernán 26

Elizabeth I 33

encomiendas 15

feitoria 16

Ferdinand of Aragon 15

Franciscans 27

Henry VIII 33

Huguenots 33

Isabel of Castile 15

Jesuits (Society of Jesus) 33

Lady of Cofitachequi 3

las Casas, Bartolomé de 24

Luther, Martin 32

Malintzín 26

Mississippian societies 9

Native American Graves Protection and Repatriation Act (NAGPRA) 5

Philip II of Spain 36

privateer 33

Protestantism 32

Puritans 33

reconquista 15

Requerimiento 24

St. Augustine, Florida 36

San Miguel de Gualdape 31

Treaty of Tordesillas 20

Reviewing Chapter 1

1. Compare and contrast North America and Europe before 1492.
2. What factors led Europeans to colonize the Americas?
3. Europeans had conquered Mexico, Central America, and much of South America by 1565, but they had conquered none of North America north of Mexico. Why?

Further Reading

Abulafia, David. *The Discovery of Man: Atlantic Encounters in the Age of Columbus*. New Haven, CT, and London: Yale University Press, 2008. An excellent synthesis that places the European "discovery" of the Americas within the context of the formation of the Atlantic world.

Kelton, Paul. *Epidemics and Enslavement: Biological Catastrophe in the Native Southeast, 1492–1715*. Lincoln: University of Nebraska Press, 2007. Examines disease before and after the Columbian exchange, arguing that colonial warfare and slaving—not just germs—devastated Native populations.

Northrup, David. *Africa's Discovery of Europe, 1450–1850*. New York: Oxford University Press, 2002. A concise overview of relations between Europeans and Africans that emphasizes African perspectives and motives.

Norton, Marcy. *Sacred Gifts, Profane Pleasures: A History of Tobacco and Chocolate in the Atlantic World*. Ithaca, NY: Cornell University Press, 2008. An insightful analysis of how two of the most important products of the Columbian exchange reshaped Europe and the Americas.

Pauketat, Timothy R. *Cahokia: Ancient America's Great City on the Mississippi*. New York: Viking, 2009. Brings together the latest historical and archaeological scholarship on the premiere example of a Mississippian chiefdom in one compact and readable package.

Reséndez, Andrés. *A Land So Strange: The Epic Journey of Cabeza de Vaca: The Extraordinary Tale of a Shipwrecked Spaniard Who Walked Across America in the Sixteenth Century*. New York: Basic Books, 2007. A beautifully written account of Cabeza de Vaca's journey that strives to capture Indian as well as Spanish perspectives on a North America that was about to change drastically as a result of Spanish incursions.

Townsend, Camilla. *Malintizin's Choices: An Indian Woman in the Conquest of Mexico*. Albuquerque: University of New Mexico Press, 2006. A sensitive account of Malintzín and her world that explains how and why so many Nahuas chose to join Cortés in attacking Mexica, an act that enabled the Spanish to conquer Mexico.

America in the World
GOODS, IDEAS, PEOPLE

CHAPTER 1: The Origins of the Atlantic World, Ancient Times to 1565

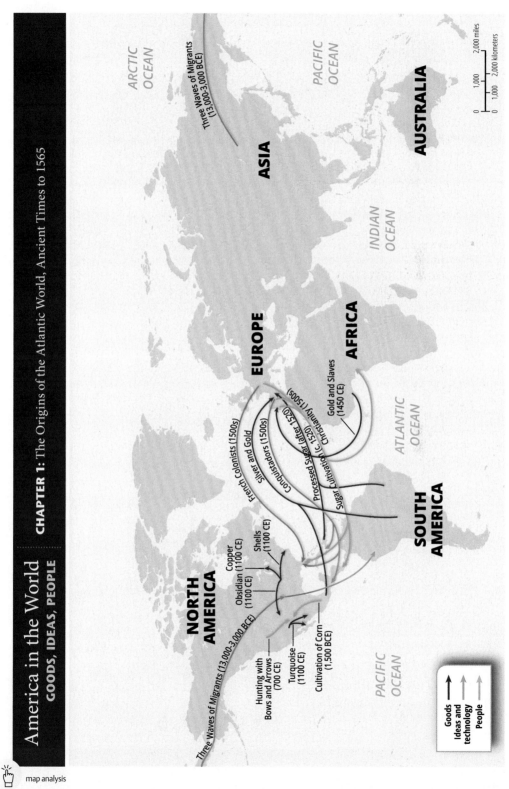

map analysis

Their green

Corne newly

Their sitting at meate

The place of solemne prayer.

Those wherin the Tombe of their Herounds standeth.

SECOTON.

Village of Secotan, located in what is now North Carolina, by John White.

Colonists on the Margins

I n 1616, the **Virginia Company of London** found itself in dire financial straits. Nine years had elapsed since **Jamestown's** founding and the firm had yet to turn a profit. Reports from Virginia of hard winters, starving colonists, and frequent hostilities with Powhatans, the people who dominated eastern Virginia, scared off investors. The company badly needed good publicity, which was fortuitously provided by the visit of an Indian noblewoman named Matoaka, her English husband, their infant son, and an Indian priest to London.

Matoaka was better known by one of her nicknames, **Pocahontas**, or "playful one." She was the daughter of Wahunsenacawh, who took the title **Powhatan** when he became paramount chief. Powhatan ruled Tsenacomoco (the Algonquian term for eastern Virginia), a region that included about 30 different groups with a total of at least 15,000 people. The Virginia Company touted Pocahontas as a "princess," though Powhatans did not see it that way. They also highlighted Pocahontas's baptism, trying to assure nervous investors that the English could convert Native Americans into Anglicized Christian subjects. The visit was important to the Virginia Company's well-being, so the hosts had every reason to make the Indians' stay in London as pleasant as possible.

Instead, the English deeply offended their Indian guests by repeatedly deviating from protocols that Powhatans normally followed with their allies. Pocahontas reprimanded **John Smith**, a former colonist who initiated relations between Jamestown and Tsenacomoco and who Pocahontas believed should have known better: "You did promise Powhatan what was yours should be his, and he the like to you." She addressed Smith as "father," using the language of kinship to indicate that they were allies. Pocahontas reminded Smith, "You had also called him [Powhatan] father, being in his land a stranger, and by the same reason so must I do you." Smith had failed to treat Powhatan and Pocahontas as kin, and the English king, too, showed disrespect. Uttamatomakkin, the Indian priest, exploded when Smith told him that he had just met **James I**. A paramount chief would have offered him a gift as a symbol of their alliance. James had not. "You gave Powhatan a white Dog, which Powhatan fed as himself," he scolded Smith, "but your King gave me nothing, and I am better than your white Dog."

The English obeyed their own social and cultural norms, especially in England. Smith, a commoner, could not allow a princess to call him "father." His English peers and social superiors would find that unseemly and presumptuous. Smith might have explained to Uttamatomakkin that a king outranked everyone in his realm. Subjects normally paid him tribute, and James certainly considered Pocahontas and Uttamatomakkin his subjects.

Still, the Virginia Company reaped good publicity from their visit. Pocahontas, however, fell ill, died, and was buried in England in 1617. Her husband **John Rolfe** returned to Virginia, leaving their son Thomas behind for his kin to raise and educate. Uttamatomakkin also sailed home to tell a grieving Powhatan what he had learned from his visit. Meanwhile, thousands of English poured into Tsenacomoco, most of them to burn the woods and plant tobacco amidst the ashes and charred stumps. Soon hundreds would die at the hands of Powhatan warriors.

Europeans like John Smith and the Virginia Company projected an image of confidence and strength, but in reality their early settlements were precarious and depended heavily on Native hosts and allies. Intermarriage and trade with Native people might bring prosperity, while misunderstandings and arrogance wrought violence. Clinging to the edge of an Indian continent, early settlers pursued different colonial strategies. After several failed expeditions by conquistadors, the Spanish instituted missions, using conversion to create North America's first permanent European colonies. The French also evangelized Indians, but their major economic endeavor in the early colonial era was the fur trade, an enterprise that relied heavily on Indian collaboration. English and Dutch colonists expended far less effort on making Christians of Indians and far more on expelling them and resettling their lands. These colonial strategies resulted in differing relationships with Native peoples, whose receptions of the newcomers varied. Willingly or not, Native people became drawn into the global economy as colonialism linked North American networks to those that extended across the Atlantic. By the early 1640s, Europeans' ability to draw on overseas ties had enabled their colonies to take root despite often fierce Indian resistance.

⬇ IMPERIAL INROADS AND THE EXPANSION OF TRADE, 1565–1607

The colonization of what became the United States began as Latin America expanded north. Spanish soldiers and friars struggled to colonize Florida and expand Mexico by conquering New Mexico. An unlikely rival, England, emerged as Spain's main

European adversary in North America. Meanwhile, European fishermen flooded northeastern North America with goods that intensified competition among Indians and began to transform their cultures.

Spain Stakes Claim to Florida

After founding St. Augustine and defeating the French, Pedro Menéndez had an ambitious vision for Florida. The Spanish, supported by a network of coastal garrisons, could protect sea lanes and salvage shipwrecks more easily. The governor hoped that Indians, awed by Spanish might, would become allies and subjects. In 1566, Menéndez married a Calusa chief's sister. Baptized as Doña Antonia, she accompanied Menéndez to Havana. Jesuit missionaries arrived that same year to cement Hispanic-Indian alliances by converting Florida Indians and sending chiefs' sons and nephews to Havana to be schooled alongside sons of prominent Cuban colonists. Menéndez also planned a road between his capital, Santa Elena, founded in today's Georgia in 1566, and the mines of the Zacatecas in Mexico so that the Spanish Empire could move silver overland and bypass the pirate-infested Caribbean.

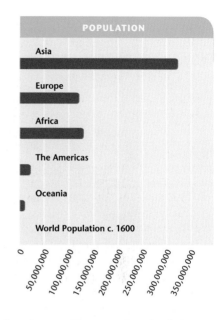

Little of his vision became reality. Menéndez ran out of money and lost interest in Florida once he became governor of Cuba in 1567. He had also badly underestimated the distance between Georgia and Mexico. Two expeditions headed west to launch his far-fetched plan. They built small garrisons along the way, but Indians destroyed every one, killing or capturing the Spanish soldiers who had manned them.

Indian resistance and European attacks nearly finished off Florida too. Timucua and French soldiers teamed up to destroy one Spanish fort. Santa Elena and St. Augustine, the last outposts standing by 1574, barely weathered repeated Indian attacks. Thirteen years later, the Spanish abandoned Santa Elena and retreated to a St. Augustine reeling from an English raid led by the English privateer Francis Drake. Enslaved Africans owned by **Philip II**, king of Spain, assisted recovery efforts, which included construction of a stone fort like those the Spanish were building in their major Caribbean ports to protect them from their European foes. In 1600, St. Augustine had only 500 residents, all of whom subsisted on food shipped from Havana or supplied by Florida Indians. More than half were officers, soldiers, or mariners. Officers and imperial officials had Spanish wives. Soldiers and sailors wed Indian women, including Doña Maria Meléndez, a female chief.

Franciscan friars pursued Indian converts outside St. Augustine. They replaced the Jesuits in 1573, the same year that Philip II issued the **Royal Orders for New Discoveries**. He decreed that missionaries should play the principal role in exploring, pacifying, and colonizing new territories. Philip also mandated that baptized Indians should live on missions and be hispanized—in other words, learn to speak Spanish, keep livestock, cultivate European crops, and use European tools to master European crafts.

FRANCIS DRAKE SACKS ST. AUGUSTINE, 1586 War between Spain and England in the 1580s accelerated English attacks on Spanish-American colonies. St. Augustine, besieged by English forces, is at the upper left, while more English ships lurk in the Atlantic. Drake, then en route to Roanoke, had raided Santo Domingo and Cartagena before attacking St. Augustine.

Franciscans began to intensify their efforts in 1595, focusing on northern Florida and the Georgia coast.

Indian reactions varied. Timucuas, who had already formed military alliances with the Spanish, saw missions as an opportunity to gain access to political and economic networks that stretched across the Atlantic world. Timucuan chiefs, who benefited from better access to European goods, encouraged the establishment of missions. However, Guales, who lived in the coastal region of what is now Georgia, rebelled. The Franciscans banned polygamy, a traditional marriage pattern for Guale elites, as well as other important practices, and restricted Guale movement. Guales destroyed the missions and killed or captured all the friars. The Spanish and their Timucua allies compelled some chiefs to surrender in 1600. Within four years, a new mission opened and Guales were forced to pay tribute to the Spanish by sending corn and laborers to St. Augustine.

New Spain into the Southwest

As Florida's Indians dealt with missionaries, Pueblo Indians in what is today New Mexico faced a series of Spanish-led invasions. Franciscans sought souls, while colonists drawn north from central Mexico by silver strikes in and around Zacatecas sought riches. In 1581, a small group of friars and soldiers arrived and renamed the region New Mexico. Pueblos soon killed the missionaries. Indians endured three more Spanish incursions before an expedition led by **Juan de Oñate** arrived in 1598.

Visions of riches and glory in Mexico motivated Oñate to conquer New Mexico. Pueblos were still nursing the wounds that they had endured from previous Spanish-led invasions, so they decided to receive Oñate peacefully.

image analysis

INDIAN PICTOGRAPH OF SPANIARDS ON HORSEBACK Indians drew this image on the walls of Cañón del Muerto. Note how prominently the artist(s) displayed horses and the lances that their riders wielded. The figure in black with a white cross is probably a missionary.

Spanish soldiers, frustrated that New Mexico had few of the riches that Mexico did, plotted mutiny. Pueblos offered them scarce food and clothing as gifts. When the soldiers did not get what they wanted, they extorted, raped, and murdered. Acoma's residents fought back, killing 11 Spanish soldiers. Oñate's men slaughtered 800 Acomas, including 300 women and children, and enslaved 500 women and children. Every Acoma between 12 and 25 years old was sentenced to 20 years' servitude. Children under age 12 became servants to monasteries or Spanish households. Every Acoma man over age 25 had one foot cut off. Such brutality dissuaded most Pueblos from challenging Spanish authority for decades. In 1998, someone commemorated the conquest's 400th anniversary by severing the right foot from Oñate's statue in Santa Fé.

New Mexico served as a base for Spanish expeditions in the region. Oñate journeyed to the southern Great Plains and found little there that interested him. Three expeditions searched for the Pacific. The last, in 1604–1605, found it by marching through Arizona and following the Colorado River to the Gulf of California.

Oñate wanted to reach the Pacific in part because the Spanish were considering a California outpost to facilitate trade with East Asia and ward off European rivals. In 1565, Spanish mariners discovered a route from the Philippines to Acapulco. The journey took four to five months, so mariners needed a port to stop for repairs and provisions. The Mexican-Filipino trade was lucrative. Mexican silver bought Chinese silks and porcelain in Manila. Francis Drake's raids along the Pacific coast in 1579 and the English capture of an Acapulco-bound ship off Baja California in 1587 stoked Spanish interest in California. Sebastián Vizcaíno explored its coast in 1602–1603, inadvertently sailed past San Francisco Bay, and concluded that Monterey Bay would best harbor a Spanish port. But New Spain's viceroy decided that a California base would lure English

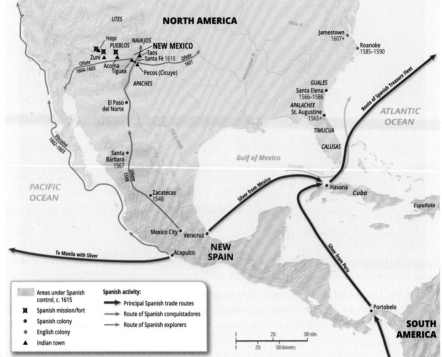

map analysis

MAP 2.1 European Invasions of the Southwest and Southeast, 1565 to c. 1610 Florida and New Mexico were the first European outposts in North America. European colonization of what is today the United States began from the Caribbean and Mexico and was oriented toward those regions. Note the location of Roanoke, chosen largely to give English privateers better access to Spanish ships that left the Caribbean laden with gold, silver, and other riches.

and French smugglers to a remote place that they would otherwise ignore. As a result, Spain showed little interest in California until the 1760s (Map 2.1).

Franciscan lobbying prevented Spain from abandoning New Mexico. Friars' enthusiastic accounts claimed that 7,000 Pueblos had already converted and that more sought baptism. New Mexico remained a poor remote satellite of Mexico that drew few Spanish immigrants. As in Florida, friars were at the forefront of colonization as they dispersed to found missions among Indians.

England Enters Eastern North America

Three European powers contested Spanish claims to North America and the Caribbean during the last quarter of the 16th century: France, the Netherlands, and England. The French and Dutch were wealthier and better able to finance colonizing ventures than the English but faced religious and political strife at home. Seven civil wars between Catholics and Huguenots (French Calvinist Protestants) unsettled France between 1562 and 1580. France did not enjoy peace until 1598, when Henry IV became king and granted limited toleration to Huguenots with the **Edict of Nantes**. The Dutch, under direct Spanish rule since 1519, rebelled in the 1570s, an effort led by Calvinists. The two sides did not negotiate a ceasefire until 1608.

By contrast, England enjoyed relative political stability that helped it to emerge as Spain's main rival in the West Indies and North America. Elizabeth I's moderate policies ended domestic religious strife and enabled the English to focus on other challenges. England's population nearly doubled from three million to around five million between 1500 and 1650, but its economy could not create enough jobs to keep pace. To make matters worse, prominent landlords fenced off **commons** (lands previously open to all residents) to graze sheep and grow grain. This concentrated more land in the hands of the wealthy, while increasing poverty and hunger among poorer people.

Meanwhile, some English merchants pursued new markets by obtaining licenses for monopolies on commerce with eastern Europe, the Mediterranean, or Asia. The Muscovy Company formed in 1555 to operate in Russia. Its success encouraged the creation of the Levant Company to trade with the Middle East in 1582 and the East India Company, chartered in 1600. These **joint-stock companies** offered a model for financing colonial ventures. Investors bought shares and hoped to earn dividends. Joint-stock companies later owned and directed English colonies in Virginia, Plymouth, and Massachusetts Bay. Many who invested in the Virginia Company also held shares in the East India Company and the Levant Company.

England's renewed interest in the Americas focused first on the Caribbean and on diverting the Spanish Empire's wealth into English hands. Englishman John Hawkins tried to enter the lucrative slave trade, dominated by Spanish merchants. He led three expeditions from West Africa to the Caribbean to smuggle enslaved Africans to Spanish colonists in the 1560s. The last ended in 1568 when Spanish vessels destroyed two of Hawkins's ships. The English largely abandoned the Atlantic slave trade until the 1640s and instead focused on seizing Spanish ships and raiding Spanish colonies. Francis Drake became famous in 1573 for capturing a Spanish silver fleet in Panama. Eight years later, Elizabeth knighted Drake after he raided Spanish ports in the Pacific and circumnavigated the globe. When England and Spain went to war in 1585, Elizabeth licensed privateers (privately owned armed ships) to attack Spanish vessels and divide the spoils. Over 200 English privateering vessels prowled the Caribbean between 1585 and 1603. Privateers boosted the English economy; the goods that they seized accounted for up to 10 percent of England's imports during the 1590s. After James I became king of England in 1603, he made peace with Spain and temporarily halted privateering.

Some English touted colonization as a way to oppose Spain and Catholicism and solve many of England's social and economic problems. In the 1570s, English forces conquered more of Catholic Ireland, which soon lured thousands of land-hungry English colonists and investors such as **Walter Raleigh** who hoped to profit from their labor. The translation and publication in 1583 of Bartolomé de las Casas's writings fueled belief in a **"Black Legend"** of the Spanish conquest in which Spaniards indiscriminately slaughtered Indians, tyrannized them, and imposed Catholic "superstition" on them. Raleigh, an explorer and confidant of Elizabeth, cited las Casas often and claimed that the English would deliver Indians from Spanish and Catholic "tyranny" and convert them into grateful subjects and Protestants.

Privateering and opposition to Spain led to England's first sustained attempt to colonize North America. Investors wanted a coastal base a safe distance from St. Augustine so that privateers could sail the Caribbean most of the year. To that end,

Raleigh sent an expedition to present-day North Carolina in 1584. The explorers recommended Roanoke on the Outer Banks and brought home two Indian men, **Manteo** and Wanchese, to learn English. They taught the scientist **Thomas Harriot** to speak Carolina Algonquian. The following year, Raleigh sent a hundred men, including Harriot and the painter **John White**, to study the area and its peoples. The English stopped in Española to buy livestock and set sail for Roanoke. Their flagship ran aground and seawater ruined their food supply. The English pressed Roanoke Indians for food, but they had little to spare. Convinced that Roanokes would attack, the colonists struck first, killing Roanoke chief Wingina and then displaying his severed head. Drake arrived in 1586, having just torched St. Augustine in hopes of preventing a Spanish attack on Roanoke. Panicked colonists swarmed aboard his ships. Drake made room for them by stranding hundreds of Africans and Indians he had picked up in the Caribbean.

Watercolor by John White showing mother and child (1585)

Raleigh did not give up on the colony, sending a second group composed mostly of families in 1587. Eleanor Dare, daughter of painter and governor John White, gave birth to Virginia, the first English child born in North America. Meanwhile, Manteo accepted baptism and White named him lord of Roanoke. Envisioning that colonists would govern the area's Indians through Manteo, White returned to England. Harriot's report of his 1585 visit, illustrated with engravings of White's paintings, was published in 1588 to drum up support for the Roanoke colony in England. The report circulated widely. It profoundly shaped English views of Algonquians and of North America. War with Spain kept the English from returning to Roanoke until 1590. They found the colony abandoned and a post with the word "CROATOAN" (probably the name of the island where Manteo's people lived) carved into it. The "lost" colonists likely became Indian adoptees who lived in eastern North Carolina or moved north to the Chesapeake Bay. Meanwhile, most English interest in colonization stayed focused on Ireland, which attracted far more English migrants than North America did until the 1640s.

The events at Roanoke and English interpretations of them established key patterns in English colonization of the Americas. The display of Wingina's severed head belied Raleigh's assertion that the English would be kinder and gentler colonists than the Spanish. But the English presentation of themselves as more humane than the Spanish took root. It still shapes how many in the United States view the nation's colonial past and distinguish it from Latin America's.

The Fur Trade in the Northeast

Long before St. Augustine's founding, Indians in eastern Canada had regular contact with Europeans fishing offshore for cod. By the 1530s, Europeans were hunting whales, processing the carcasses onshore. By 1580, as many as 20,000 Europeans were journeying across the North Atlantic and back each year. More ships sailed between Europe and Canada than between Spain and its American colonies during the late 1500s. Europeans traded glass beads, metal tools, kettles, and woolen cloth to Indians for small quantities of furs. The imports circulated among Indians via established routes that stretched hundreds of miles inland.

In the early 1580s, French merchants began to specialize in acquiring beaver pelts from the St. Lawrence valley. They sought to meet growing demand in Europe for felted beaver hats. Indian men were happy to bring more pelts; they found beaver less taxing to hunt than other fur-bearing animals. The **fur trade**, like the fishing and whaling industries that gave rise to it, ensured that the St. Lawrence River remained the main gateway for European goods into North America well into the 1600s (Map 2.2).

BEAVER HUNTING   This illustration shows the various ways that Indians hunted beaver and some of the animal's habits, including the construction of dams. Beaver pelts were New France's chief export. Trade in them was key to relations between European colonists, their descendants, and Indians in northern North America well into the 1800s.

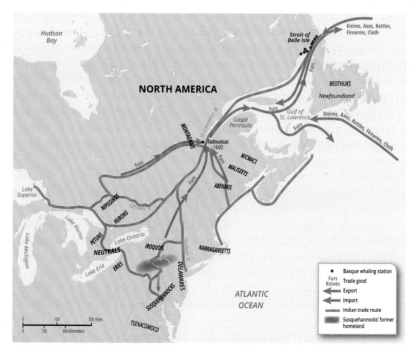

MAP 2.2 Trade in the Indian Northeast, c. 1580–1607 The St. Lawrence River valley and the Indian trade routes that ran through it helped to make the region the chief entry point for European goods into North America. The Huron Confederacy, located at the intersection of many trade routes, had a relatively easy time acquiring imports, while the Iroquois League's peoples, whose lands lay outside those routes, initially had far more difficulty.

The imports initially reinforced traditional Indian beliefs and practices. Before 1600, relatively few Indians had steady access to such goods, so they seldom used or viewed them in ways that Europeans did. Instead, Indians incorporated imports into their world on their own terms. Most brass or copper kettles were broken apart and repurposed. Chiefs replaced shell gorgets (necklaces with large pendants covering the throat) with metal ones. Like shell, European metal signified distant trade connections that conferred political and even spiritual power. Native leaders enhanced their authority by giving trade goods to their people. By the early 1600s, copper, brass, and iron goods as well as glass beads accompanied many Indian people to their graves.

The fur
trade

Over time, Indians with direct and steady access to European goods increasingly used them as their manufacturers intended. The imports made life easier, especially for women. Steel axes simplified gathering firewood, and metal kettles were more durable and versatile than ceramic or wooden ones. Refashioning woolen cloth into traditionally styled garments took less work than it did to dress skins and furs. In fact, throughout the colonial era, the items most frequently traded to Indians were clothing; Native people appreciated the vibrant colors and diverse materials produced by European manufacturers. Incorporating select European clothes into preexisting wardrobes, Native peoples used these exotic, long-distance exchange items to express status.

Trade brought opportunity as well as risk. Competition for European trade alliances heightened violence among Native rivals. The Northeast's two major Iroquoian-speaking confederacies, the Iroquois (Seneca, Cayuga, Onondaga, Oneida, and Mohawk) League and the Huron Confederacy, both sought to secure better access to trade routes. By the 1570s, Mohawks and Oneidas were at war with Montagnais and northeastern Algonquians, who controlled the trade in European manufactured goods and therefore had superior weapons. Brass arrowheads outperformed stone-tipped ones. They were lighter, easier to aim, and penetrated wooden armor. Iroquois warriors adapted as best they could by shedding their wooden armor and raiding in small parties to minimize casualties. But as late as 1610, Iroquois still fought with stone-tipped hatchets, spears, and arrowheads and found themselves on the losing end of a regional arms race.

Europeans also introduced Indians to firearms. The earliest guns, arquebuses, were brought to North America by conquistadors and early French explorers like Champlain. The arquebus was heavy, inaccurate, and inoperable in wet conditions. In many ways, Native bows were superior weapons. By the early 1600s, however, Flemish gunsmiths had invented the flintlock rifle, which was more accurate and lighter than the arquebus with a longer range than the Native bow. Additionally, the flintlock's flash, smoke, and loud discharge inspired psychological terror, making it an ideal weapon of war. Indian groups with privileged access to firearms automatically gained a tremendous advantage over their bow-and-arrow neighbors. In a time of heightened violence, firearms made warfare more deadly.

European imports became indispensable. The Micmacs, who lived in what is now Maine and southern Canada, had once maintained a diversified economy, taking advantage of seasonal resources within their territory. After they allied with the French, however, Micmacs became hunting specialists, devoting more of their time to trapping beaver for the European market and very little to food production. To feed themselves,

Micmacs warred against tribes to the south and took their corn, using European fire-arms to dominate Native neighbors. This strategy worked for a time, but within a few decades beaver became scarce in Micmac territory and the French made new Native alliances, leaving the Micmacs short on food and other supplies and surrounded by newly armed rivals. Indians who relied heavily on European trade—especially those who specialized in a single export commodity—became vulnerable to the caprices of a global marketplace.

STUDY QUESTIONS FOR IMPERIAL INROADS AND THE EXPANSION OF TRADE, 1565–1607

1. In what ways did the Spanish colonization of Florida and New Mexico differ? In what ways did Indian responses to Spanish colonization differ in Florida and New Mexico?

2. By what means and for what reasons did England become Spain's chief rival in North America?

3. What impact did the fur trade and trade goods have on Indians in the Northeast?

quiz

EUROPEAN ISLANDS IN A NATIVE AMERICAN OCEAN, 1607–1625

Indians from the St. Lawrence River to the Chesapeake Bay cautiously welcomed the thousands of strangers who arrived between the 1600s and 1620s and began to occupy their lands. A minority of them spoke French or Dutch, came in small numbers, and devoted themselves to trading with their neighbors. The vast majority of the foreigners spoke English and staked claim to large quantities of land, which they soon divided among themselves and began to farm. Most of these disembarked in Tsenacomoco along the estuaries of the Chesapeake Bay. The rest landed in Massachusetts Bay in territory claimed by Wampanoags. All the newcomers depended on Native-grown corn and knowledge to survive their first years in North America. They traded with Indians to make their colonies financially viable. But the English decided rather quickly that they needed the locals less than they needed their land. Their refusal to collaborate with Indians led to wars with the Tsenacomoco and tension along the shores of Massachusetts Bay (Map 2.3).

Tsenacomoco and Virginia

In May 1607, 144 English colonists founded Jamestown on a marshy triangle of land that jutted into the James River. The location offered protection from Indian land attacks and Spanish sea attacks. The Virginia Company of London's royal charter gave it exclusive rights to colonize from New England south to Virginia. Its directors and investors hoped to turn a quick profit. But the hardships of establishing a new colony

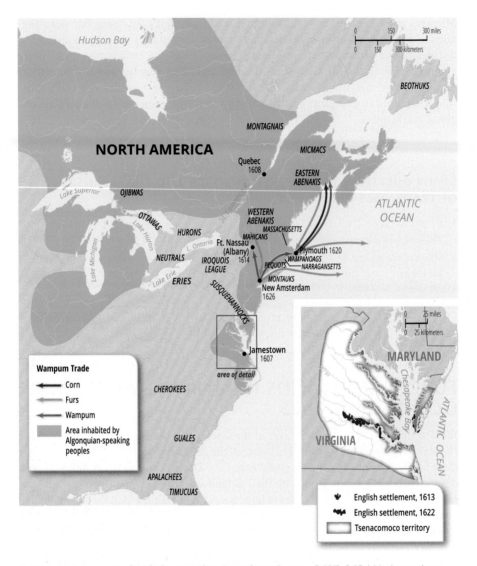

MAP 2.3 European Islands in a Native American Ocean, 1607–1626 Native nations surrounded the European outposts at Quebec, New Netherland, Plymouth, and Virginia; sustained them; and sometimes threatened them.

and the lack of gold or silver dimmed English hopes. Hunger, disease, and cold claimed all but 38 Jamestown residents by the spring of 1608.

Peoples of Tsenacomoco watched warily as they tried to determine the strangers' motives. Tsenacomoco had expanded over the previous four decades under the leadership of Powhatan. As paramount chief, he had used diplomacy, marriage, intimidation, and warfare to gain the allegiance of other tribes and collect tribute from them. By the time the English strangers arrived, Tsenacomoco included almost all Algonquian speakers who lived in Virginia's tidewater region.

Powhatan decided to incorporate Jamestown into Tsenacomoco. In December 1607, warriors seized John Smith, one of the colony's leaders, and delivered him to Powhatan. Powhatan's nine-year-old daughter Pocahontas helped to stage Smith's mock execution. Smith claimed that Pocahontas demonstrated her love by throwing herself on top of him. In reality, the event was an adoption ritual intended to symbolize the death of Smith's former identity and his rebirth as a subordinate chief subject to Powhatan. This is why, many years later, Pocahontas used the language of kinship when addressing John Smith.

Smith either did not understand or refused to accept the role. Neither did his superiors in the Virginia Company, who believed that Tsenacomoco was subject to Virginia and James I and not the other way around. In 1608, Christopher Newport arrived from England with orders to make Powhatan James's vassal. Powhatan saw no reason to submit. After all, his people vastly outnumbered the English, who subsisted almost entirely on corn Powhatan had given them. After John Smith departed in October 1609, relations between the two groups broke down and the First Anglo-Powhatan War began. As casualties mounted, Powhatan refused to feed the unruly English. When Smith left, there were 490 colonists. When Thomas Gates arrived as governor in May 1610, only 60 remained.

John Smith, excerpt from *The Generall Historie of Virginia* (1624)

Pocahontas helped Powhatan monitor events in Jamestown by acting as his emissary and keeping lines of communication open. In 1613, colonists took her hostage. John Rolfe, a prominent immigrant, fell in love with her, and the following year, Pocahontas, who was then only 16, married Rolfe and was baptized as Rebecca. The marriage ended the first war between Tsenacomoco and Virginia. A tense peace bought the colony some time.

Meanwhile, officials on both sides of the Atlantic concluded that only drastic action could save the colony and the Virginia Company. In 1612, the firm tried to lure more investors by putting governance in stockholders' hands. It also added the island of Bermuda to its jurisdiction. In Virginia, reforms focused on breaking English dependence on Indians. Gates and his successor, Thomas Dale, both military men, put Jamestown under martial law. Dale tried to make Jamestown more self-sufficient by renting land to former company servants in exchange for one month of service and some of the corn that they harvested. Meanwhile the company's defenders in England pleaded for patience. It would take time to turn a profit.

The Virginia Company never earned one, even though colonists learned to cultivate tobacco, a valuable export crop that enabled Virginia to survive. Instead of cultivating North America's indigenous tobacco (*Nicotiana rustica*), which is harsh and strong, John Rolfe imported a milder, sweeter Caribbean variety (*Nicotiana tabacum*) in 1611. Within a few years, the English learned how to cure tobacco and began to export it. First commercialized by Virginians, the Caribbean variety of tobacco quickly became popular throughout the Atlantic world and now dominates the global market.

Virginia colonists also adapted English labor systems to meet their needs. In England, families or magistrates regularly bound adolescents and young adults by a practice known as **indentured servitude**. Young servants might learn a skill and cease to be financial burdens on kin or on England's poor relief system. In Virginia, indentured servants, most of them men between 18 and 26 years old, agreed to serve from three to seven years in exchange for passage overseas. They mainly did the hard work of

INDENTURE OF RICHARD LOWTHER, 1627 By this indenture (contract), Lowther agreed to serve a Virginia plantation owner for four years, after which he was to receive 50 acres of land. Lowther differed from most English indentured servants who went to the Americas in that he signed his indenture, an indication that he was probably literate.

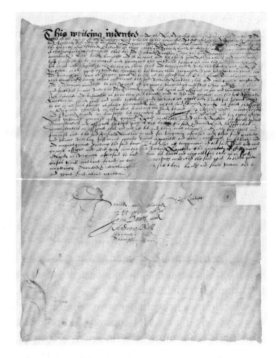

growing, harvesting, and curing tobacco. They could be bought and sold against their will. The Virginia Company encouraged immigration and the colony's expansion in 1617 by promising 50 acres of land for every free adult who went to Virginia and another 50 for each servant imported.

Two years later, company officials sent 90 young women to become planters' wives. They hoped that married men would stay rather than return to England. Persuading English women to emigrate proved a challenge. A shortage of labor and the tobacco boom compelled English women, be they servants or wives, to work in the fields, an arrangement that fit Native gender norms but violated those of the English.

The need for labor also led Virginia colonists to enslave Indians and Africans. In Jamestown's early, lean years, colonists raided Indian corn granaries, leading to the First Anglo-Powhatan War (1609–1614). The English considered slavery a legitimate fate for their Powhatan prisoners of war, who became the colony's first slaves. Virginia's entrance into the Atlantic slave trade came several years later. In 1619, an English privateer raided a Portuguese slave ship called the *São João Batista*, capturing over 20 Africans. They were originally enslaved during a military campaign spearheaded by the Portuguese governor of Angola and his Imbangala allies, who took advantage of a dynastic dispute in the Kingdom of Ndongo to extend Portuguese power into the interior and enrich themselves in the process. When these Africans arrived in Virginia in August of 1619, the colony had no clear policies about imported slaves. Some masters considered Africans and Indians to be indentured servants whom they would free after completing a set term. Other colonists thought that slavery should be a lifelong condition. Over the next several decades, Virginians would develop clearer laws regarding slavery.

In the late 1610s, Virginia Company officials decided to let colonists own land and govern themselves. The right to own land drew tens of thousands of men, mostly indentured servants, to Virginia over the next several decades. Land was increasingly scarce in England. To English men, land ownership brought respect, economic independence, and political rights such as serving on a jury, voting, and holding office. In 1619, the Virginia Company established English America's first representative assembly, the **House of Burgesses**. The firm also replaced martial law with English **common law**, setting in motion the development of county courts. The fields that they cleared for tobacco plantations steadily encroached on Tsenacomoco.

This alarmed Powhatan's kinsman and successor Opechcancanough, who made plans to push back the Virginians. In March 1622, Tsenacomoco warriors stormed Virginia, killing more than one in four colonists. The English counterattacked brutally, but the war dragged on for 10 years.

The war finished off the Virginia Company, which had never earned a profit and faced charges that its mismanagement had cost thousands of English lives. About 1,200 colonists lived in Virginia in 1622, just one-third of the number of immigrants who had arrived in the previous three years. Most succumbed to disease. In 1624, James I revoked the bankrupt company's charter and put Virginia under royal rule. Virginians' aggression toward the Powhatans had nearly led to their colony's demise. But thickening ties to the Atlantic world and England, sustained mainly by European demand for tobacco, ultimately saved Virginia. Although the Virginia Company failed, its policies, which empowered colonists to own land, form militias, and elect representatives to govern themselves, offered other English colonies a blueprint to follow.

New France, New Netherland, New Indian Northeast

As English immigrants struggled to turn Tsenacomoco into Virginia, the French and Dutch claimed the St. Lawrence and Hudson River valleys, respectively. In 1603, Pierre de Gua received a 10-year monopoly on the Acadia and St. Lawrence fur trade. His associate **Samuel de Champlain** charted the coast from Nova Scotia to Cape Cod for France, established alliances with Micmacs and Abenakis, and learned of growing English interest in the cod-rich coastal waters of New England. In 1608, Champlain founded what became Quebec City. Built on the site of the abandoned Iroquoian town Stadacona, the new French village controlled water access inland. But New France's immediate future looked dim. Only 8 of 28 colonists survived their first Canadian winter.

Samuel de Champlain's map of the northeast coast of North America (1607)

Indians who forged ties to New France for their own purposes saved the colony. In 1609, Montagnais and other Algonquian speakers teamed up with Hurons to persuade Champlain to help them attack Mohawks, a member of the Iroquois League. Champlain brought his arquebus, an early musket, which, like other firearms of the time, was wildly inaccurate. With some lucky shooting, Champlain managed to kill three Mohawks. The rest fled, having never seen firearms. Six years later, Champlain joined Huron and Algonquian warriors as they invaded Iroquois League territory, cementing an alliance with the Huron Confederacy, a longtime Iroquois League foe. Hurons became the principal Indian middlemen in New France's fur trade, gathering pelts from peoples to their north and west and taking them to Quebec. They and other Indian allies sustained New France's economy.

Champlain lobbied for more support from France, but internal political turmoil and the Thirty Years' War left France with little money and few people to spare. The Catholic Church proved more receptive. In 1615, four French Récollet priests arrived, followed a decade later by Jesuit missionaries. An English attack the following year forced Champlain to surrender Quebec and send the Jesuits home. They returned when England ceded Quebec to France.

By then, Dutch entrepreneurs had established a colony on the Hudson. In 1609, Henry Hudson, an English captain hired by the Dutch East India Company, sailed upriver in search of a water route to Asia, trading with Indians along the way. Five years later, the Dutch founded a trading post, Fort Nassau, now Albany, New York, on Mahican land. Fort Nassau's residents emulated the French by allying with their neighbors. In 1615, they joined a Mohawk-Mahican raid on Susquehannocks. By the early 1620s, the Dutch had expanded their commercial network to both sides of Long Island Sound and the Delaware valley.

They did so by catering to Indian beliefs and needs. The Dutch learned of wampum's spiritual and material value to the Northeast's Indians. Wampum manufacturing, simplified by imported iron tools that reshaped shells into beads and bored holes through them, soon spread to Narragansett Bay and Long Island Sound. Algonquian women incorporated gathering shells and fashioning them into wampum into their winter routines. Pequots and Narragansetts, two peoples well positioned to make wampum, emerged as southern New England's main powers, partly because wampum soon became currency among Indians in the Northeast. English and Dutch merchants used it to lure the business of Indians, particularly those who sold pelts to the French. Meanwhile, Mohawks feared that they might get cut off from the imports that enabled them to fight off their enemies. In 1624, they forced Mahicans to move, linking Iroquois lands to New Netherland.

Like New France, New Netherland at first was a satellite of its Indian neighbors. In 1621, Dutch officials awarded the **Dutch West India Company (DWIC)** a monopoly on commerce between the Americas, West Africa, and the Netherlands and charged it to establish colonies. The firm focused mainly on the Caribbean and South America. It sent no colonists to New Netherland until 1624. Two years later, the company purchased Manhattan from Indians and founded its local headquarters, New Amsterdam, on the island to coordinate commerce with Indians. New Netherland remained a low priority for the DWIC. In 1630, it had just 300 colonists.

Pilgrims and Northeastern Natives

In 1620–1621, Indians watched English immigrants weather their first New England winter. The 102 newcomers called themselves "Pilgrims." Delayed by storms and blown well north of their intended destination—Virginia—they sighted Cape Cod in November. Pilgrims spent a month searching for a suitable site, which they named Plymouth. Some aboard the *Mayflower* argued that the location of their new home nullified the royal charter under which they were to settle. They questioned who should govern them. Their leaders responded with the Mayflower Compact, an agreement that all free adult male passengers signed. They promised to obey laws enforced by the officials whom they chose. The Pilgrims arrived too late to plant and failed to bring enough to eat. They devoured corn that Indians had buried, but only half of them survived the winter.

Plymouth's leaders were religious dissidents from England who had just spent 12 years in the Netherlands. They followed principles articulated by the reformer John Field, who argued that the Church of England was too Catholic. It did not allow believers to choose their own leaders or even whether they wished to belong to the Church of England at all. Puritans believed that Anglican clergy dishonored God by preventing the faithful from disciplining and excluding those who did not believe or practice what the church preached. The Pilgrims who founded Plymouth believed that they could save themselves only by leaving the Anglican Church. Pilgrims enjoyed freedom of worship in the Netherlands but worried that their children would become Dutch or marginalized if they stayed there.

Meanwhile, an epidemic devastated the Algonquian-speaking peoples who lived near Massachusetts Bay. Fishermen from England and Virginia frequented their waters in the 1600s and 1610s in pursuit of cod. They introduced an unknown disease between 1616 and 1618 that killed up to 90 percent of the peoples who lived nearby. Massasoit, chief of the decimated Pokanoket Wampanoags, had to submit to the Narragansetts and pay them tribute. **Tisquantum**, often known as Squanto, paid a higher price. In 1614, an English captain seized him and tried to sell him into slavery in Spain. Tisquantum escaped and somehow made his way to London and Newfoundland. He arrived home in 1619, only to find that disease had killed most of his people, the Patuxet.

▷

Squanto: Helping Indian or World Traveler?

Massasoit, like Powhatan before him, initially believed that he could incorporate the newcomers into his world. In 1621, Plymouth and Massasoit's Wampanoags signed a peace treaty. The Wampanoags supplied Plymouth with corn and, in return, hoped that friendship with Plymouth would allow them to escape Narragansett control by securing a powerful ally and better access to imported goods. Meanwhile, Pilgrims envisioned that Plymouth would become southeastern New England's most powerful village, with Massasoit collecting tribute from nearby groups as Plymouth shipped beaver pelts to England to pay off company investors. Tisquantum would live in Plymouth and serve as the Pilgrims' guide and interpreter.

Tensions rose as colonists and Indians interpreted the agreement differently. Tisquantum aimed to reconstitute the Patuxet under his leadership by stoking English mistrust of Massasoit, who soon learned that Plymouth's leaders viewed him and his people as subjects. By the summer of 1621, colony officials had prohibited Wampanoag social visits and allowed only Massasoit or his designated representative to enter Plymouth. Word of the Second Anglo-Powhatan War led Plymouth colonists to fear a massive conspiracy between Tsenacomoco and New England Algonquian peoples against all English. They embarked on building a fort and sent armed expeditions to nearby villages to extort corn and intimidate their residents. Plymouth sought to break its dependence on Indian-grown corn, so the colonists instituted a new system inspired, in part, by Native agricultural practices. Each family received a parcel to plant, although the land remained company property. Colonists grew corn mostly, with women and children performing much of the field labor. Within two years, Plymouth fed itself and had corn left over.

Angela's Ordeal, the Atlantic Slave Trade, and the Creation of African North American Cultures

In 1620, an African woman named Angela arrived in Jamestown. Her Christian name indicates that Angela was baptized. Like Angela, most Africans brought to North America before 1660 came from West Central Africa. They spoke one of two closely related Bantu languages, Kikongo or Kimbundu. Many probably knew some Portuguese too. Most had been baptized, and many considered themselves Christian.

Angela had been captured during a Portuguese-Imbangala war against the Kingdom of Ndongo in Angola. She and about 350 others boarded the *São João Bautista*, one of the Portuguese-registered vessels that ferried the vast majority of Africans to the Americas until 1650. Nearly 700,000 enslaved Africans crossed the Atlantic between 1600 and 1650. More than three-quarters of them departed West Central Africa as Angela did, but most West Central Africans who left between 1616 and 1625 were taken to Brazil or Central America. Angela's intended destination was Mexico. But two privateers, each commanded by an English captain, intercepted the *São João Bautista* in the Gulf of Mexico. The privateers seized Angela and over 50 others, divided them, and sailed for Virginia. The *White Lion* arrived first and sold 20 people in Jamestown.

Until 1670, fewer than 5 percent of Virginians were Africans. Angela's background and experience matched those of the first Africans shipped to English and Dutch North America before 1660. Most came as a result of English or Dutch piracy on Spanish shipping (Portugal and Spain were united under Spanish rule between 1581 and 1640). English ships transported fewer than 2,000 Africans across the Atlantic in any decade until the 1640s, when sugar cultivation boomed on Barbados.

No one bid on Angela, who landed in Virginia in February 1620. She became one of William Pierce's four "servants" and probably spent most of her time tending to livestock. Angela joined 32 African Virginians and about 900 other colonists. Among them were Antonio and Isabel, who by 1625 had their son William baptized. A generation later they were free and had become the Johnsons, the most prosperous African American family in English North America, one that owned slaves who grew tobacco.

The surplus of corn strengthened the colony's position strategically and financially. In 1625, its merchants began to exchange corn for beaver pelts with Maine's Kennebec Abenaki. Plymouth also joined the Dutch-Algonquian wampum network.

Still, Plymouth never prospered. In 1627, colonists bought out English shareholders and divided the livestock and land among male heads of household. They built a relatively obscure society of a few thousand small farmers who scratched out a living on poor soil. But the English had put down roots in New England, and subsequent waves of migration would soon overwhelm the Native population and bring additional conflict as well as new diseases.

In 1667, their son John bought 44 acres and named the estate "Angola" to honor his parents' origins.

About one-quarter of the Africans whose names appear in Virginia's public records between 1635 and 1650 had Iberian names such as Antonio, Manuel, or Maria. Before 1640, most lived and worked alongside at least five other Africans. We do not know when Angela died or if she ever became free. We do know that Angela and other Africans shared much in common that helped them to weather their bondage and sometimes escape it during the first decades of Afro-Virginian history.

- In what ways did the struggle between England and Spain for supremacy in the Americas shape Angela's ordeal and English participation in the Atlantic slave trade?
- In what ways did shared origins in West Central Africa likely shape the lives of Angela and other Africans in early Virginia?

BAPTISM   West Central African leaders often saw baptism as a tool of diplomacy. Here Njinga Mbandi, sister and representative of King Ngola Mbandi of Ndongo, receives baptism during a visit to Angola's Portuguese governor that aimed to end the wars that decimated Ndongo and enslaved thousands of West Central Africans, including Angela.

STUDY QUESTIONS FOR EUROPEAN ISLANDS IN A NATIVE AMERICAN OCEAN, 1607–1625

1. In what ways did Indians influence the development of European colonies in eastern North America between 1607 and 1625?

2. The stories of Pocahontas and the Pilgrims are two founding myths of the United States. Does viewing their stories from Native perspectives change your understanding of them? Explain.

quiz

⊖ SEEKING GOD, SEIZING LAND, REAPING CONFLICT, 1625 TO C. 1640

As small European outposts grew in three corners of the continent, new patterns emerged and old ones became entrenched. The French and Spanish anxiously noted the growth of English and Dutch settlements but had difficulty attracting their own settlers, so they intensified trade and missionization among Indians. They hoped that Indian allies and converts would help maintain their imperial claims. Meanwhile, political and religious turmoil in England and western Europe encouraged thousands to seek refuge in New Netherland and in the new English colonies in New England and Maryland. Thousands more flooded into Virginia to plant tobacco and seek land. New arrivals who hoped to create a harmonious and prosperous society in New England multiplied rapidly but quickly divided into factions. The English colonies, booming from heavy immigration, prized Indian land over Indian alliances. Colonial expansion intensified pressure on Indians from New England south to the Chesapeake Bay, resulting in a series of wars.

Missionaries and Indians in New France and New Mexico

In the late 1620s and early 1630s, Catholic missionaries brought new zeal to their efforts to evangelize Indians in New France and New Mexico. Jesuits served as New France's principal emissaries to Native allies and the colony's most vocal promoters in France. Meanwhile, Franciscans preached to new groups of Indians on New Mexico's borders while sparring with governors over who should have more power over colonists and Native groups. Missionaries studied the cultures of Indians whom they evangelized. However, New France's Jesuits proved more willing to meet converts part way than New Mexico's Franciscans.

Jesuits embarked on two related tasks when they returned to New France in 1632. One was to establish missions among Montagnais and Hurons. The other was to promote their work, seek financial support for it, and recruit colonists. They sought to achieve these goals by gathering reports from Jesuits in New France and publishing them in France. Historians call these narratives, compiled and distributed annually between 1632 and 1673, the *Jesuit Relations*. Many study them closely for their detailed if heavily biased observations of the Indians whose souls Jesuits aspired to save.

📄 Selections from *The Jesuit Relations*

Jesuits focused on Hurons, who were easier to reach most of the year because they lived and farmed in large villages. Most Indians who traded with the Hurons spoke their language, so Jesuits who learned it could preach to Huron allies as well. Two-thirds of the pelts that New France exported between 1616 and 1629 passed through Huron hands. Trade with the French shored up Huron power, particularly against the Iroquois League. That was why Huron leaders decided to accept Jesuit missions when Champlain renegotiated the colony's alliance with them in 1633.

Jesuits found Hurons to be grudging hosts, partly because the priests often behaved like rude and annoying guests. At first, the Jesuits demanded that converts become culturally French. They expected Indians to renounce their faith in dreams as revelations of the future and become monogamous. To Hurons, Jesuits, with their short hair and beards, looked beastly, smelled bad, could neither hunt nor fight, and butchered their language. Christian concepts such as sin or eternal punishment after

PORTRAIT OF FATHER PAUL LE JEUNE, FROM ENGRAVING FROM RENÉ LOCHON, 1665 Le Jeune served as Jesuit superior in New France from 1632 to 1639. He noted that Montagnais audiences laughed at him because "I pronounce the Indian as a German pronounces French" but were impressed that he could interpret dreams. Le Jeune edited the first 11 editions of the *Jesuit Relations*.

death did not exist in Huron religion. Hurons prized ties of kinship above all others, so they found the promise of a heaven that excluded non-Christian kin repellent. Jesuits' practice of baptizing dying infants and children led many Hurons to conclude that the priests were sorcerers.

Despite these conflicts, the Huron valued their alliance with France and spared Jesuit lives. Hurons also admired many Jesuit qualities. Unlike other French men, the priests cared little about land, pelts, or sex with Indian women. Viewing their mission as a chance to become martyrs for bringing the gospel of Christ to North America, Jesuits often showed a warrior's stoic courage in the face of captivity, torture, and death. Native people also noted that Jesuits possessed some immunity to disease.

Epidemics and Jesuits' increasing willingness to compromise with converts saved their missions. A smallpox outbreak in 1640 pushed over 1,000 Hurons to seek baptism. Many hoped that the sacrament would heal or spare them. Jesuits soon tried to build on beliefs that Catholics and Hurons shared, such as the power of prayer and the immortality of souls. They created prayer books and catechisms in the Huron language and employed Huron translators to explain doctrine. Priests encouraged converts to substitute crucifixes, medallions, and rosaries for the stone amulets that Hurons traditionally wore. Relatively few Hurons identified themselves as Christians; only 500 did so in 1646. But Jesuits established a foothold in Huron territory, sealing the alliance between that confederation and New France and making themselves targets for Iroquois warriors.

As Jesuits prepared to return to New France, Franciscans in New Mexico expressed a renewed sense of optimism. Eight friars arrived in 1629 and promptly founded missions among the Acoma, Zuni, and Hopi Indians. The head of New Mexico's missions, Fray **Alonso de Benavides**, eagerly anticipated the conversion of Apaches and Navajos who lived just outside Pueblo territory. In 1630, Benavides published a report in Madrid that boasted that friars had baptized 86,000 Indians in New Mexico.

Benavides celebrated that thousands of Pueblos lived within New Mexico's missions but misinterpreted why many did. Life outside the missions was hard. Spanish officials often seized corn from Pueblos who did not live on missions, disrupting trade with Indians who supplied bison and other game in exchange for Pueblo corn. Missions offered cattle, pigs, and sheep for butchering as well as some protection from Apache raids and Spanish governors.

These benefits came at a price. Mission Indians endured campaigns to remake them into hispanized Christians. Friars confiscated and destroyed their religious symbols and built crosses over **kivas**—the sacred underground structures in which Pueblos participated in religious ceremonies. Friars also undermined systems of Pueblo authority. By supplying livestock and meat to baptized Indians, they usurped the role of Pueblo hunting chiefs. Franciscans targeted free and enslaved Indian children for baptism and catechization. They incorporated some into their households as adopted children, though, in practice, many of these adoptees were treated as servants. They inverted Pueblos' gendered division of labor to match Hispanic norms by compelling men to build homes and women to weave. Pueblo peoples were traditionally **matrilineal** (meaning that they inherited social identity and property through the female line), but Pueblo women lost their exclusive rights to land, seeds, and children to men wherever missions took root.

By the early 1640s, Pueblos found themselves besieged by Apaches. The Spanish had introduced horses to Pueblo peoples, who began to trade them to the Apaches in 1601. Horses facilitated Apache raids and reinforced Apache ways by making them more mobile and facilitating their hunts. Growing herds of Apache horses exhausted pastures, forcing Apaches to move more often, strengthening each band's autonomy, and encouraging more raids on Pueblos and colonists. Meanwhile, the Diné, whom the Spanish at first called "Apaches Navaju," traded and raided for sheep as well as horses. Raising sheep and weaving wool soon became central to Navajo culture and the foundation of the Navajo economy.

Indians also raided New Mexico to avenge kin captured and enslaved by Spanish-led incursions. Governor Luis de Rosas saw Indian slavery as a way to profit from his office. Some slaves worked in colonists' households, others in Rosas's textile factory in Santa Fé to make blankets to trade to Plains peoples. The rest were sold to Mexican mines. In 1638, Rosas attacked Plains Apaches, killing 100 and enslaving as many. A raid on Utes the following year yielded 80 more slaves. Apaches retaliated by raiding the lightly defended colony. Between 1639 and 1640, they destroyed stores of corn, leaving the disease-ravaged Pueblos weaker and hungrier. About 80,000 Pueblos lived in 150 towns in 1598. By 1640, fewer than half as many inhabited just 43 towns.

Migration and the Expansion of Dutch and English North America

Heavy immigration between the mid-1620s and 1640 caused the New Netherland and English colonies in the Chesapeake, New England, and the Caribbean to grow rapidly. Demand for labor in North America and the West Indies, recruitment by company officials, and events in Europe and the South Atlantic rim channeled migrants across the Atlantic. Political and religious conflict in England prompted the creation of two new mainland colonies, Massachusetts Bay in 1629 and Maryland in 1634, founded to provide a haven for Puritans and Catholics, respectively. The new colonies attracted thousands of migrants who helped to anchor English claims to North America.

By contrast, the DWIC did relatively little to promote New Netherland to prospective colonists. The firm's directors considered the Hudson River valley a northern outpost of a global Dutch empire that by the early 1640s linked New Netherland to South and Southeast Asia, northeastern Brazil, Angola, and the West Indies. Nearly all offered more lucrative opportunities than New Netherland. In addition, few Dutch had reason to leave Holland, where they enjoyed a prosperous economy, low unemployment, and religious toleration.

As a result, New Netherland became a Dutch colony composed mostly of people who were not Dutch. In 1629, the DWIC copied what the Virginia Company had done in the 1610s to boost immigration. Directors encouraged private investment by offering patroonships, large land grants along the Hudson, to those who brought at least 50 immigrants with them. Rensselaerswyck, the most successful patroonship, attracted English, Norwegian, and German migrants during the 1630s. In 1638, however, a group opposed to company rule left New Netherland, settled near what later became Philadelphia, and recruited colonists from Sweden. Susquehannock Indians made an alliance with them, offering military protection in exchange for trade goods. In 1640, the DWIC issued a **Charter of Freedoms and Exemptions**. It granted 200 acres to whoever brought five adults to New Netherland, and it promised prospective colonists religious freedom and local self-governance, guarantees that lured English Puritans from Massachusetts to eastern Long Island. New Netherland became the most ethnically and religiously diverse colony yet seen in North America. In 1644, the French Jesuit Isaac Jogues visited New Amsterdam and heard 18 languages spoken on its streets.

1639 map of New Amsterdam

New Netherland also grew because African bondage took root there sooner than in English North America. Africans and their American-born children comprised 30 percent of New Amsterdam's 100 residents in 1638 and 20 percent of nearly 2,000 in 1664. The DWIC's ties to Africa, Brazil, and the Caribbean and its demand for labor, largely to build and maintain fortifications and conduct commerce, drove the growth of the African population. In 1648, the DWIC ended its monopoly over the African slave trade to and from New Netherland but remained the colony's largest importer and buyer of enslaved Africans.

New Amsterdam's Africans created the first urban African American community north of St. Augustine. Like their peers in Virginia, New Amsterdam's Africans shared similar origins and experiences. In 1644, 11 men petitioned company director **Willem Kieft** for their freedom. He permitted them to work for themselves and live where they wished but required that the men pay the DWIC and bind themselves and their children to serve the company. Such "half-freedom" exemplified the discrimination that New Amsterdam's Africans confronted. But, in time, many Africans and African Americans earned real freedom. By 1664, one in five in New Netherland had done so. Africans in New Amsterdam also participated in church life, accounting for 28 percent of marriages in New Amsterdam's Dutch Reformed Church between 1639 and 1652. Almost one in three people baptized in the 1640s was African.

Although DWIC reforms enabled New Netherland's population to increase rapidly, the Dutch failed to keep pace with the English. The number of people who lived in New Netherland nearly doubled between 1638 and 1643 to 2,000. By 1664, the colony had 10,000 residents. But Virginia had 40,000 and New England 50,000.

Between 1560 and 1640, emigrants departed England, Wales, and Scotland in droves. Most went to Ireland. However, migration to America soared during the 1630s. Thousands went to five recently founded colonies in the Caribbean: St. Christopher, Barbados, Nevis, Providence Island, and Antigua. Thousands more left for the tobacco fields of Maryland and Virginia. Meanwhile, 13,000 headed for New England in the most concentrated and targeted movement of people across the Atlantic and into North America yet. The wave of immigrants during the 1630s swelled the population of English North America and the Caribbean from 9,500 in 1630 to 54,000 ten years later. English colonists vastly outnumbered their French, Dutch, and Spanish counterparts from then on, giving England a huge advantage over its European rivals in North America.

Most English immigrants to Virginia and Maryland were young single men. Landless and unemployed, they initially sought economic opportunities in London and other cities but most were disappointed. Tobacco planters, who desperately needed labor, lured such men to the colonies. One in four died of malaria or another disease within a year of landing in the Chesapeake, but those who survived their American servitude stood a good chance of becoming landowners. About half the men who left London for Maryland or Virginia in 1635 managed to acquire land and move up the social ladder. During this period, relatively few white women chose to emigrate, so those who did could be choosier about whom they wished to marry. Those who outlived their husbands owned a large share of land in the Chesapeake colonies and often attracted many suitors.

Meanwhile, an array of forces pushed people out of England and drew them to Puritan New England colonies in America. A worsening economy in eastern England in the 1620s made migration look more attractive. **Charles I**'s decision to suspend Parliament in 1629 cut off the main avenue for peaceful expression of dissent. Some Puritan leaders and London merchants organized the **Massachusetts Bay Company** in 1629 and recruited emigrants by promising them the opportunity to create godly communities in America. Some 3,000 people fled for New England in 1635 after William Laud became Archbishop of Canterbury, Anglicanism's second highest-ranking official after the monarch, and persecuted Puritan reformers.

Those who moved to New England prospered and multiplied. Almost all adult English men there owned land during the 1600s. Many kept moving until they found a town with religious views that agreed with their own and with enough land for themselves and their heirs. The number of colonists in New England grew by 66 percent during the 1640s, almost entirely through births, largely because women and children comprised a large share of migrants during the 1630s. White women in New England on average gave birth to eight children (compared to seven in England), and more of them reached adulthood. The majority of American-born children knew their grandparents; most people lived past age 60, a rarity for that period. Such rapid population growth made it harder to achieve the social harmony that Puritans sought to create in America, but it allowed them to usurp resources claimed by neighboring Native nations.

Dissent in the "City upon a Hill"

In 1630, Massachusetts Bay Colony's first governor, **John Winthrop**, articulated the principles on which he and his fellow Puritans would build a new society. He reminded them that they had entered into a **covenant** with God that required them to translate their faith into actions that obeyed God's will as revealed in the Bible. If colonists stayed united and honored their word to God and one another, they would set the standard for others to follow. "We shall be as a city upon a hill," Winthrop exhorted; "the eyes of all people are upon us." But if colonists violated the covenant, they would invite divine wrath on themselves and "open the mouths of enemies to speak evil of the ways of God." God, Winthrop argued, had charged them to create a new and godly England in America for the whole world, especially England, to see and emulate.

John Winthrop, "A Model of Christian Charity" (1630)

Winthrop drew deeply from Calvinist beliefs. His shipmates thought that each congregation should decide how it should operate and who should belong to it. Church members should be those whom God had designated for salvation, those who truly believed in God and acted accordingly. The Church of England made no such distinction. It presumed that all English were members because Anglicanism was the realm's official faith. Winthrop and most who accompanied him argued that they could still reform the Anglican Church from within but had to move to New England to do so. There the faithful could honor their covenant with God by purging their churches and communities of sin.

To sustain their "city upon a hill," Massachusetts Bay Puritans tried to ensure that only God's elect were church members and that God's elect held political power. To accomplish the first goal, they developed a "**conversion test**" in the 1630s. Prospective members had to appear before those already deemed elect, testify to their relationship with God, and offer proof that God had saved them. Members judged whether candidates had received saving grace and merited full admission to their congregation. Men who were not church members were barred from voting or holding office, a form of exclusion adopted nowhere else. Other Puritans did adopt the conversion test, which spread from Massachusetts Bay through New England and then to England.

Religious convictions also led Massachusetts Bay Puritans to create a well-educated society. All believers merited direct access to God's will as written in the Bible, so they needed to know how to read. Persecution of Puritans in England meant that New Englanders could not travel there for schooling, and so they had to educate themselves in America. In 1636, reformers founded Harvard College to educate colonists' sons and train ministers. Harvard operated Anglo America's first printing press, which rolled off its first publication in 1639. Three years later, Massachusetts Bay magistrates required that parents teach children to read. By 1647, six towns had started grammar schools, and a new law mandated that every community with more than 100 households have one. A college, a printing press, and an educated public positioned New England Puritans to generate ideas and broadcast them to the Anglo-Atlantic world.

Reforms inspired by Puritanism also reshaped marriage and family life. Puritans in North America made marriage, a sacrament within the Church of England, a civil ceremony. That made it easier for couples to divorce, although few did. Courts regularly addressed domestic violence, whether complaints were generated by victims or neighbors, and prosecuted male offenders. Authorities also granted parents more power over children. In 1647, Massachusetts Bay became the first place in the Anglo-Atlantic world to give parents power over whom their adult children could marry. New laws empowered fathers and husbands most of all.

As Massachusetts Bay's founders labored to make a model English society, they also proclaimed that they would convert Indians and live alongside them peacefully. "Come over and help us" declared the Indian depicted on the colony's seal. A campaign to convert Indians did not begin until the mid-1640s. Before then, Puritans imagined that they would set examples that would encourage their Indian neighbors to become Christian and adopt English ways, including English gender norms. In 1634, William Wood published *New England's Prospect* to encourage more Puritans to sail to New England. He cast Indian men as lazy tyrants who did little but hunt as they "forced" women to grow corn, trap lobsters, and build houses—all "man's" work in English eyes. English women, Wood thought, offered good role models for Native women. Meanwhile, John Winthrop argued that Indians did not deserve their lands because they did not exploit them fully. He drew from an emerging body of international law to assert that Indian New England was *vacuum domicilium*—empty of "settlement." English who farmed, grazed livestock, and claimed land as personal property had a far more legitimate claim, Winthrop insisted.

To Winthrop's chagrin, fellow colonist **Roger Williams** challenged the governor's view of Indians. Williams arrived in 1631 and quickly moved to Plymouth, where most shared his belief that Puritans should separate from the Anglican Church. Williams forged ties to Wampanoags and Narragansetts and began to learn their dialects of Algonquian. He returned to Massachusetts Bay after authoring a tract that argued that the patent Charles I had given the Massachusetts Bay Company did not entitle colonists to Native land. Indians rightfully owned their land and could cede it only voluntarily. Massachusetts Bay leaders condemned Williams and had his work burned. Williams threw fuel on the fire. He even wrote Charles I to criticize the patent that he had issued to Massachusetts Bay. The colony's officials responded by banishing Williams in 1636. He moved to Narragansett Bay, founding Providence on land that Narragansetts granted him.

There Williams established the principle of separation of church and state in English America. Use of government power to compel conformity of belief, Williams argued, corrupted religion. Authorities instead should allow what Williams called "soul liberty," the freedom to believe and worship as one wished. Williams practiced what he preached by cofounding the Americas' first Baptist church in 1639. He also maintained close ties to Indians, who protected Providence and collaborated with him on an Algonquian-English dictionary. Providence became the first of four English towns, each founded by Massachusetts Bay exiles, that joined to form Rhode Island in 1644.

Anne Hutchinson was, after Williams, Rhode Island's second most notorious resident. She was 43 when she sailed to Boston with her husband and 11 children and was admitted to a congregation. Hutchinson soon began to hold meetings for women at her home at which she reviewed the sermons of John Cotton, her spiritual mentor in England and a Boston minister. Before long, Hutchinson, her adversaries charged, was preaching her own views and insisting that good works had no bearing on salvation or on others' knowledge of it. Her enemies, Winthrop among them, abhorred her alleged emphasis on faith alone as evidence of salvation. It challenged how Massachusetts Bay Puritans determined church membership and who should exercise political power. By developing her own theology and preaching it, Hutchinson had also claimed a public role that magistrates thought belonged to men alone. Hutchinson was tried in court and exiled. She recanted her views before heading for Rhode Island. Dozens followed her there.

Puritans' tendency to resolve disputes through exile or migration accelerated colonial New England's expansion in the 1630s. The founders of Hartford, Connecticut, considered the criteria for church membership in Massachusetts Bay too restrictive and thought that its congregations had too much power over government. By contrast, the founders of New Haven Colony left Massachusetts Bay because they considered its union of church and state too loose and permissive. They constructed a theocracy in which ministers made the rules. Rhode Island, Hartford, and New Haven were all fruits of the tension between individual conscience and conformity within Puritanism. Their creation put even more pressure on Native Americans (Map 2.4).

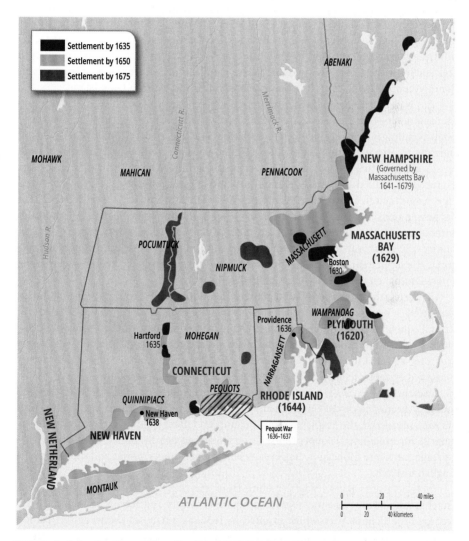

MAP 2.4 Colonization of New England, 1635–1675 Religious dissent among Puritans and their habit of migrating as families accelerated English invasions of lands that belonged to Indian peoples. Connecticut, New Haven Colony, and Rhode Island, all colonies founded by dissenters who had left Massachusetts Bay, expanded rapidly after 1635, a process enabled partly by the Pequot War.

Early Wars Between Colonists and Indians

Wars, triggered mainly by Euro-American demand for land, erupted between colonists and Native peoples in New Netherland, New England, and Virginia between 1636 and 1644. Each threatened the existence of Native peoples who lived on the borders of English and Dutch North America.

New Netherland generally enjoyed amicable relations with Munsee-speaking peoples of the lower Hudson valley until Willem Kieft arrived in 1638 to oversee Dutch West India Company operations. He aggressively acquired land north and east of Manhattan. Colonists who resettled those areas turned cattle and pigs loose to forage and devour crops that Munsee women planted. Kieft fanned Munsee resentment by demanding tribute to bolster New Amsterdam's defenses. Indians, provoked by the Dutch militia, attacked Staten Island in 1641. The war raged for four years, forcing colonists to seek shelter within New Amsterdam. Native people, too, fled from the violence, abandoning their settlements in the lower Hudson valley and western Long Island.

As war raged around Manhattan, another conflict engulfed Virginia and Tsenacomoco—the Third Anglo-Powhatan War. The colony's expansion, driven by English immigrants and their desire for more land for tobacco, provoked Powhatan warriors to attack in 1644. They killed 500 colonists. Virginia militiamen retaliated by storming Native villages and massacring their inhabitants. Two years later, they captured and killed the elderly paramount chief, Opechcancanough. Officials forced Opechcancanough's successor Necotowance to sign a peace treaty that declared that his people were English subjects. Indians could no longer enter English communities without passes. Necotowance and those under his authority had to return guns, African captives, and runaway Indian servants. Thomas Rolfe, Pocahontas's son, fought for Virginia. His service earned him an appointment to run a fort in Chickahominy territory, a position that enabled him to acquire hundreds of acres.

In the Northeast, tensions flared between the Pequots and their European and Indian neighbors. When the Dutch tried to establish free trade at a new post on the Connecticut River, Pequots balked. Pequots, seeking to retain their dominance of the wampum trade, blocked other tribes and were soon at war with Narragansetts and Mohegans. The Dutch, too, retaliated by killing the influential Pequot sachem Tatobem. Pequots were further weakened by a major smallpox epidemic that lasted from 1633 to 1634.

Meanwhile, English colonization accelerated and expanded. In 1636, settlers founded the new colony of Connecticut within Pequot territory. After two English traders were murdered, the English blamed Pequots and demanded that they hand over the culprits for execution. Pequots refused and turned to nearby Indian nations for help. Narragansetts and Mohegans, however, resented the Pequots' power and sided with the English instead.

Massachusetts Bay's leaders, reeling from the conflict that swirled about Anne Hutchinson, saw war as a way to unite a fractious society and acquire more land. They regarded the **Pequot War**, which erupted in 1636, as a holy war between civilization and savagery and showed no mercy to their enemy. The war's bloodiest chapter came in May 1637, when an English-Narragansett-Mohegan force surrounded a Pequot village on Mystic River in Connecticut populated mostly by noncombatants—women, children, and elderly men. The Indian allies set fire to the village, and the English shot whoever fled. They killed about 300 men and 700 women and children. Over the next

SILVER BADGE GIVEN TO "KING OF THE MACHOTICK INDIANS," VIRGINIA, c. 1662–1677 The 1646 treaty between Tsenacomoco and Virginia required Indians to wear a striped coat to enter English territory. In 1662, Virginia required Indians to carry metal passports. Chiefs needed a silver badge like this one presented to the chief of the Machodoc. Other Indians had to use copper badges.

several months, English and Native forces broke Pequot resistance, executing many Pequot men.

A few hundred Pequots escaped and eventually gained a reservation, but most survivors became captives and were divided among the victors. Narragansetts and Mohegans adopted or executed some; colonists retained some as domestic servants or sold them into slavery in Bermuda and the Caribbean. In exchange, New England received enslaved Africans. In 1641, Massachusetts Bay became the first English North American colony to explicitly legalize slavery.

English and Native peoples drew different lessons from the war. Most immigrants rejoiced; it opened more land and demonstrated English might. Despite the fact that most of the region's Indians had fought on their side, the English came to fear and demonize their Native neighbors. Governor William Bradford argued that the English must "look at the Pequots, and all other Indians as a common enemy."

Indians responded in a variety of ways. In 1638, Quinnipiacs, outnumbered by residents of New Haven Colony, agreed to surrender most of their land and confine themselves to a reservation. No outsiders could visit without the permission of New Haven authorities. In return, Quinnipiacs received promises of protection, the right to hunt and fish off the reservation as long as they did not bother colonists, and some coats and tools. The Mohegans, led by **Uncas**, concluded that it was better to side with the English than fight them. Narragansetts found the new balance of power disturbing. They had expected the war to confirm them as southern New England's largest power. Instead, the English claimed land, influence, and Pequot captives that Narragansetts considered rightfully theirs. The English treated the Narragansetts as subjects.

interactive timeline

TIMELINE 1555–1646

AMERICA	YEAR	THE WORLD
	1555	English merchants found Muscovy Company to trade with Russia
Spanish mariners discover route from Philippines to North America	**1565**	
	1568	**May** Eighty Years' War begins
	1573	Philip II of Spain issues Royal Orders for New Discoveries
French merchants establish trade in beaver pelts with Indians in Canada	**1580s**	
English launch colony at Roanoke	**1585**	
Sir Francis Drake attacks and destroys St. Augustine	**1586**	
English abandon Roanoke colony	**1587**	
Guales rebel against Spanish in the Southeast	**1597–1601**	
Spanish forces colonize New Mexico	**1598**	Edict of Nantes grants tolerance to France's Huguenots
Apaches begin to acquire horses from Pueblo peoples	**1601**	
Sebastián Vizcaíno explores and maps coast of California	**1602–1603**	
May Employees of Virginia Company found Jamestown **Dec** Powhatan warriors take John Smith captive	**1607**	
Spanish officials decide to remain in Florida and New Mexico **Jul** French colonists found Quebec	**1608**	
First Anglo–Powhatan War	**1609–1614**	
French colonists ally with the Montagnais and Huron against the Mohawks Henry Hudson sails up river that bears his name and founds New Netherland	**1609**	**Apr** Treaty of Antwerp introduces Twelve Years' Truce in Eighty Years' War between the Netherlands and Spain
Santa Fé, New Mexico, founded	**1610**	
Virginia planters begin to export tobacco	**1614**	
Bermudans purchase first unfree Africans brought to English America	**1616**	**Apr** William Shakespeare dies
Epidemic devastates Indians of coastal New England	**1616–1618**	
Virginia Company permits colonists to own land	**1618**	Thirty Years' War begins in Europe
Virginia planters purchase the first unfree Africans shipped to mainland English North America Virginia Company permits colonists to establish first representative assembly in English North America	**1619**	
Nov Adult male Pilgrims sign Mayflower Compact **Dec** Pilgrims found Plymouth Colony	**1620**	
Dutch West India Company founded and charged to govern New Netherland	**1621**	
Second Anglo-Powhatan War	**1622–1632**	

AMERICA	YEAR	THE WORLD
Dutch merchants create wampum industry	**1622**	
James I puts Virginia under direct royal rule Colonization of St. Christopher, first permanent English colony in the West Indies, begins	**1624**	
Jesuits arrive in New France	**1625**	
New Amsterdam (now New York City) founded	**1626**	
English begin to colonize Barbados	**1627**	
English begin to colonize Nevis	**1628**	
English Puritans found Massachusetts Bay Colony	**1629**	**Oct** Plague arrives in Milan, Italy; one of the last major European outbreaks
More than 13,000 English emigrate to New England in "Great Migration"	**1630–1642**	
Providence Island Company forms and begins to plan colonization of Providence Island in Caribbean	**1630**	
Jesuit Relations begins publication English begin to colonize Antigua	**1632**	
French–Huron alliance renegotiated to require Jesuit missions within Huron Confederacy	**1633**	
Maryland founded	**1634**	
Connecticut founded	**1635**	Sakoku Edict issued, locking Japan's borders to Japanese and Europeans, restricting Catholicism, and limiting trade
Roger Williams banished from Massachusetts Bay and founds Providence, Rhode Island Suffrage in Massachusetts Bay restricted to adult male church members Harvard College founded	**1636**	
Pequot War in New England	**1636–1637**	
New Haven Colony founded	**1637**	
Anne Hutchinson banished from Massachusetts Bay	**1638**	
Printing press at Harvard, English America's first, begins operating	**1639**	
Dutch West India Company issues Charter of Freedoms and Exemptions for New Netherland	**1640**	
Massachusetts Bay becomes first English North American colony to recognize slavery as a legal institution	**1641**	Epidemic in China spreads along Grand Canal; kills up to 90% of population in some towns
Miantonomi attempts to organize Indian alliance against New England	**1641–1643**	
Kieft's War rages in New Netherland	**1641–1645**	
United Colonies of New England forms	**1643**	
Third Anglo-Powhatan War	**1644–1646**	

The Narragansett chief **Miantonomi** was particularly offended. By the early 1640s, he had concluded that the English had become too powerful and threatened all the region's Native nations, so he began to recruit Native peoples throughout the Northeast to ally against the foreigners. In 1642, Miantonomi urged that Montauks should see themselves as nearly all English saw them, as *Indians* first and foremost, who shared more in common with each other than they did with the newcomers. He explained, "We must be one as they are, otherwise we shall be all gone shortly."

Miantonomi's words fell mostly on deaf ears among the Indian peoples he had hoped to reach, but colonists paid rapt attention. In 1643, Massachusetts Bay, Plymouth, Connecticut, and New Haven formed the **United Colonies of New England** for their mutual defense. Its commissioners urged Uncas to capture Miantonomi, who was killed while in Mohegan custody later that year. Uncas had played, and would continue to play, a role similar to that which Massasoit filled for Plymouth in the 1620s. To most Mohegans, that seemed the best way to meet the challenges they faced. Some Narragansetts chose a different path. They teamed up with Rhode Islanders, excluded from the United Colonies, to take their case straight to Charles I. In a 1644 letter, Canonicus and Pessacus, Miantonomi's uncle and brother, respectively, requested protection from English colonists as his loyal subjects and as their equals. Charles, then facing a rebellion from Puritans on both sides of the Atlantic, ignored the petition. Still, like Miantonomi's proposition, it was a novel way in which Indians attempted to regain control over a world that three generations earlier had been entirely theirs.

Excerpts from the Narragansett Act of Submission to Charles I (1644)

STUDY QUESTIONS FOR SEEKING GOD, SEIZING LAND, REAPING CONFLICT, 1625 TO C. 1640

quiz

1. England's North American colonies grew more rapidly than New Netherland or New France. Why? What impact did such rapid growth have on Indians?
2. What factors led to early colonial conflicts between Europeans and Indians?

Summary

- The Spanish Empire initiated the colonial era of what became the mainland United States by clinging to Florida and New Mexico, using the mission system to gain Indian allies and converts.
- French colonization began in Canada, focusing on evangelism but also the fur trade, which drew Native Americans into the global economy as both producers and consumers.
- The English and Dutch founded colonies on the Atlantic coast. These agricultural societies demanded vast amounts of land, which resulted in a series of wars with Native Americans.
- Europeans' desire for labor and valuable export commodities led them to enslave increasing numbers of African and Native American slaves; these slave trades contributed to the growth of European colonies while destabilizing African and Native polities.

Key Terms and People

audio
flashcards

Reviewing Chapter 2

1. Compare and contrast European colonial strategies in North America.
2. In what ways did religion influence events in North America between 1565 and 1640?
3. How did incorporation into the global economy impact North America and its peoples?

Further Reading

Brewer, Holly. *By Birth or Consent: Children, Law, and the Anglo-American Revolution in Authority*. Chapel Hill: University of North Carolina Press, 2005. A fascinating account that accords a central role to Puritans in the shaping of modern Anglo-American concepts of rights, be they children's, spouses', or parents' rights.

Dubcovsky, Alejandra. *Informed Power: Communication in the Early American South*. Cambridge, MA: Harvard University Press, 2016. Traces how Africans, Europeans, and Native Americans created information networks as well as how that communication influenced alliance making, warfare, and power.

Games, Alison. *Migration and the Origins of the English Atlantic World*. Cambridge, MA: Harvard University Press, 1999. Tracks English men and women who migrated through London in the 1630s to North America and the Caribbean and examines how they fared in their new homes.

Kupperman, Karen Ordahl. *The Jamestown Project*. Cambridge, MA: Belknap Press of Harvard University Press, 2007. A comprehensive history published on the 400th anniversary of the founding of Jamestown that argues that early Virginia provided a successful model to the English for how to colonize the Americas.

Sleeper-Smith, Susan. *Indian Women and French Men: Rethinking Cultural Encounter in the Western Great Lakes*. Amherst: University of Massachusetts Press, 2001. Focusing on gender, this important study explores Native relationships with French missionaries and fur traders.

Townsend, Camilla. *Pocahontas and the Powhatan Dilemma*. New York: Hill and Wang, 2004. A sensitive account of Pocahontas and her world that clearly spells out the challenges that English colonization posed for her and for Tsenacomoco's residents.

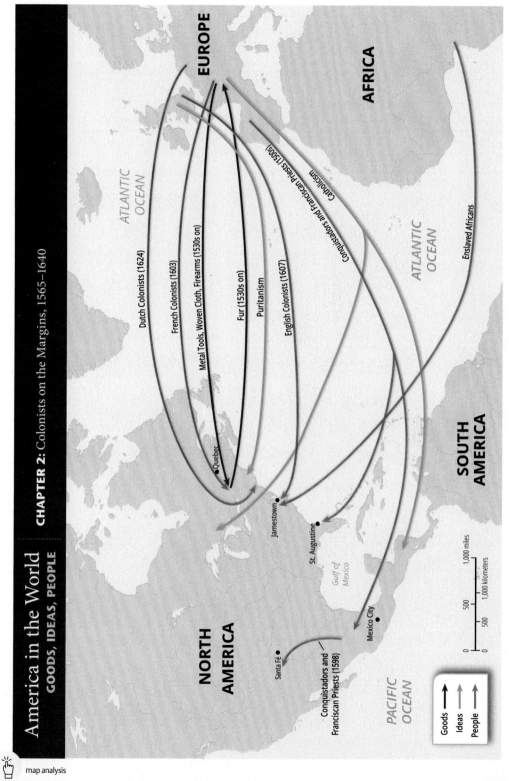

America in the World
GOODS, IDEAS, PEOPLE

CHAPTER 2: Colonists on the Margins, 1565–1640

map analysis

EUROPE

AFRICA

NORTH AMERICA

SOUTH AMERICA

ATLANTIC OCEAN

ATLANTIC OCEAN

PACIFIC OCEAN

Gulf of Mexico

Quebec

Jamestown

St. Augustine

Mexico City

Santa Fé

Dutch Colonists (1624)

French Colonists (1603)

Metal Tools, Woven Cloth, Firearms (1530s on)

Fur (1530s on)

Puritanism

English Colonists (1607)

Conquistadors and Franciscan Priests (1500s)

Catholicism

Enslaved Africans

Conquistadors and Franciscan Priests (1598)

Goods

Ideas

People

0   500   1,000 miles

0   500   1,000 kilometers

RUN away from the subscriber, living in *King's-Town,* *Queen Ann's* county, *Maryland,* an *Irish* servant woman, named *Martha Carr,* about 24 years of age, of a fresh complexion, is supposed to have had on when she went away, a red stuff gown and petticoat, but her dress is uncertain, as she carried other clothes with her. She is thought to have gone off with a couple of sailors, deserted from the ship *Randolph,* Captain *Price,* lying at *Chester* town, K___ county. Whoever takes up said woman, and confines her in any gaol, so that her master may have her again, shall have *Twenty Shillings* reward, and all reasonable charges, paid by JOHN BIRSTALL.

Queen Ann's, Jan. 24, 1768.

N. B. Said servant was in *New-Castle* gaol a long time, and left it about nineteen months ago.

A runaway servant ad from 1768, written by the runaway's master, describes the woman's clothing and general appearance.

CHAPTER 3

Forging Tighter Bonds

1640–1700

"Who is the father?" the midwife demanded of Anne Orthwood, an indentured servant who was in the throes of labor in the summer of 1664. The young woman identified him as John Kendall, one of Virginia's most prominent men and her former master. Orthwood gave birth to twins before suffering an agonizing death, probably from an infection she contracted during childbirth. One baby died. The other, Jasper, faced a hard life. John Kendall denied he was the father. County officials agreed but did not want taxpayers to foot the bill for raising Jasper, so they found Kendall legally responsible for his son's care. Kendall soon bound Jasper out to a friend who owned a nearby plantation. For the next 22 years, Jasper worked as an indentured servant. In 1686, he sued for his freedom, won, and then disappeared from local records.

Anne Orthwood's path to an early grave and Jasper's passage from servitude to freedom were products of economic and social changes taking place in Virginia between the 1660s and 1680s. Anne was born into poverty and a fatherless home in Bristol, England. In 1662, she joined a torrent of nearly 30,000 English streaming to Virginia and Maryland during the 1650s and 1660s to work as servants. Their labor, and that of a slowly increasing population of enslaved Africans, more than doubled Virginia's tobacco exports during the 1660s. Meanwhile, masters tightened their grip on servants and slaves. In 1662, Virginia lawmakers empowered them to punish female servants like Anne who became pregnant and deprived masters of their services.

Had Anne survived, she would have faced the prospect of several lashes and at least two more years of servitude. Hard labor and harsh laws gave indentured servitude a bad image in England and fueled the resentment of servants and ex-servants in Virginia. In 1672, legislators addressed these concerns by enacting a law that emancipated male bastards at age 21, three years sooner than the standards set by English poor law. Jasper's lawsuit was a direct result. Despite his master's protests that English poor law entitled him to Jasper's services until he turned 24, Anne's son based his claim on the 1672 Virginia law that his mother's former master had helped to write. But the change in the law did not improve Virginia's reputation overseas or calm sullen servants and ex-servants. Immigration from England slowed. Servants, ex-servants, and slaves joined a rebellion that nearly toppled the colony's government. Masters responded by buying more slaves and fewer indentured servants to tend their tobacco.

North America's colonies and neighboring Indian societies weathered many crises between 1640 and the 1690s. The resolution to these crises redrew the continent's political map, developed the economies of some English colonies, rooted African slavery in North American soil, checked Spanish power, and turned the English and French empires into North America's dominant European powers. Indians still controlled most of North America. But colonists, be they free, in servitude, or enslaved, claimed and colonized more of the continent, due largely to their tighter bonds to the world overseas.

UNCIVIL WARS, 1640–1660

Death and violence gripped North America and the Anglo-Atlantic world in the 1640s and 1650s. Epidemics ravaged the Iroquois and Great Lakes peoples, fueling an increasingly destructive cycle of warfare. A civil war in England echoed in English North America, prompting religious, social, and economic upheaval that in turn led New England to diversify its economy and forge stronger ties to the Caribbean, where planters established English America's first society built on plantation slavery. Meanwhile, the Spanish expanded mission systems in Florida and New Mexico, brutally crushing Indian rebellions.

Smallpox and War Plague the Great Lakes

In the 1630s, thousands of Dutch and English colonists arrived in the Northeast, many carrying the smallpox virus. A major epidemic struck in 1633, followed by another six years later. The virus felled Indians of all ages but killed a disproportionate number of people between the ages of 15 and 40, those who usually did most of the farming, hunting, and caring for children, the sick, and the elderly. By the early 1640s, epidemics had probably killed more than half the population of Iroquois, reducing it to around 10,000. Disease continued to ravage the Iroquois League and its Indian neighbors over the next 30 years.

Seeking to reclaim power in the face of devastating loss, the Iroquois launched a series of attacks that reshaped eastern North America. These attacks, which began in the 1620s and lasted for 70 years, are sometimes collectively referred to as the "**Beaver Wars**" because trade was a motivating factor. By 1628, Iroquois warriors had defeated the Mahicans and gained direct access to Dutch merchants in Albany. Within a decade, however, the Iroquois found that they had little to trade. Iroquois had overhunted beaver in their own territory, and, in any case, Dutch traders preferred thicker beaver pelts from farther north. Iroquois, who now relied on European trade for firearms, clothing, tools, and other necessities, sought to expand their territory and economic power by conquering their neighbors.

The Beaver Wars peaked in 1648–1657, as the Iroquois League devastated the Huron Confederacy. Hurons (also known as Wendats or Wyandottes) benefited from a long-term French alliance, but Jesuit missionaries barred non-Christian Hurons from purchasing guns. This policy contributed to a wave of conversions, but, by the 1640s, the Hurons were vastly outgunned by the Iroquois. In the spring of 1649, Iroquois warriors destroyed several Huron towns, killing over 700 and taking hundreds

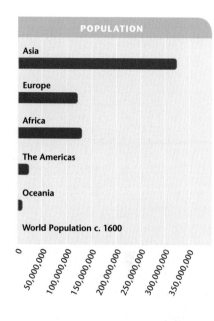

of others captive. Over the next several years, Iroquois warriors pursued Huron survivors, who had dispersed to form small communities within neighboring Indian nations.

The fur trade played a role in the Beaver Wars, but the Iroquois's paramount concern was their declining population. The Iroquois had long captured their enemies in war and then divided them according to age and gender. Men taken prisoner, deemed least likely to accept life in captivity, were often ritually killed, which allowed captors to assuage their grief and avenge the loss of loved ones. The captive demonstrated his manhood by meeting his excruciating death stoically. But the Iroquois deemed women and children more likely to assimilate, and so they preserved these captives—and even some men—using adoption rituals to incorporate them into Iroquois society. Such adoption rituals were widespread across Native North America and probably ancient, but, as the Iroquois faced demographic collapse from epidemic diseases, they adopted unprecedented numbers of captives. By 1657, one Jesuit missionary claimed that "more Foreigners than natives of the country" lived in Iroquoia.

For a time, captive adoption bolstered the Iroquois population, but cycles of violence and disease led to additional Iroquois mortality and devastating consequences for their neighbors. During the long Beaver Wars, the Iroquois dispersed or displaced most nearby nations: Hurons, Petuns, and many Algonquian-speaking peoples fled west; Abenakis retreated east; some Christians traveled to French missions farther north; and the Erie and Susquehannocks moved south. Within a few decades, warfare and disease had transformed a vast swath of North America (Map 3.1).

English Civil Wars and the Remaking of English America

Across the Atlantic, the English divided into those who believed that Charles I was their supreme leader and those who insisted that **Parliament** should have the ultimate political and religious authority. In 1642, the factions took up arms against each other, triggering the English Civil War. Most Puritans sided with Parliamentarians, who in 1649 tried Charles, beheaded him, and proclaimed that England had become a commonwealth. Four years later, the Puritan general **Oliver Cromwell**, commander of the

IROQUOIS French drawing of an Iroquois (probably Seneca) tree bark carving depicting a battle during the Beaver Wars. Each member of the war party drew the totem animal of his clan, holding a weapon. The three upside-down figures at center right indicate that the warriors killed two men and one woman. At bottom left, one warrior carries two scalps, while the other watches over a captive.

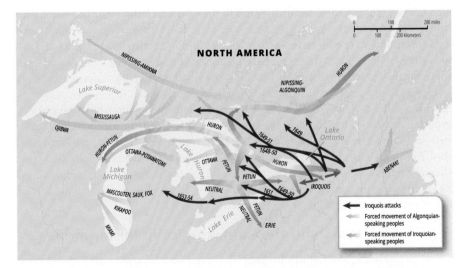

MAP 3.1 Iroquois Mourning Wars and the Dispersal of Great Lakes and New England Peoples, 1648–1657 The Iroquois League's mourning wars took their greatest toll on nearby Indian peoples between 1648 and 1657. This map shows peoples claimed or dispersed by Iroquois attacks and where those who escaped Iroquois raids sought refuge. Refugees who headed for Quebec were usually Christian converts.

New Model Army, staged a military coup and named himself Lord Protector. Cromwell died in 1658 after trying to appoint his son to succeed him. By then, the English had tired of political instability. Charles I's son and heir, **Charles II**, rose to the throne in 1660, an event that restored the English monarchy.

Leaders of six colonies, including Maryland and Virginia, responded to news of Charles's execution by declaring allegiance to his son. Barbados and Virginia, then the only colonies under direct royal rule, offered refuge to royalists fleeing England. In 1652, a Commonwealth fleet forced Virginia governor **William Berkeley** to accept England's new rulers before its commander removed him from office.

In New England, England's Civil War brought religious, social, and economic upheaval. When the war began, New England's orthodox leaders rejoiced that their vision of a godly society might be transplanted to England. Reformers in England initially sought an alternative to Anglicanism. In the early 1640s, many thought that New England might offer one, a prospect that delighted Massachusetts Bay leaders. London printers published over 20 favorable works about New England between 1641 and 1643, most written by colonists. Virtually all recommended some aspect of New England's religious life to English readers. In 1644, Roger Williams and others countered, publishing accounts in London that claimed that all New England colonies except Rhode Island regularly persecuted religious dissenters. In 1649, developments across the Atlantic dashed Puritan hopes when Cromwell formally recognized the Church of England as the official state religion.

The English Civil War also precipitated New England's first concerted effort to convert Indians, largely to improve the region's reputation overseas. Puritans in England founded the Society for the Propagation of the Gospel in New England, which was later called the **New England Company**. Cromwell's New Model Army was initially one of the society's largest benefactors. The missionary **John Eliot** led the campaign to

JOHN ELIOT, 1659 Eliot led the campaign to convert Indians in New England. He began to organize "praying towns," separate communities for Christian Indians, during the 1650s and later translated the Bible into the Massachusetts dialect of Algonquian. Eliot also lobbied vociferously against the Indian slave trade during King Philip's War.

evangelize Indians. He founded separate towns for baptized Indians in the 1650s and, with the help of Native translators, published a catechism and the Bible in Algonquian in the early 1660s.

Events in England also helped give rise to colonial North America's first witch scare. As many as 200,000 people in Europe, at least three-fourths of them women, were accused of witchcraft during the 1500s and 1600s. Approximately 60,000 people were executed. Witch hunts peaked in England in the mid-1640s, particularly in East Anglia, the birthplace of many New Englanders. Connecticut prosecuted and executed its first witch in 1647. Massachusetts Bay authorities convicted and hanged Margaret Jones, a midwife, a year later. In all, 79 New England colonists, 61 of them women, were accused of witchcraft; 33 were tried, and 15 were executed between 1647 and 1663. John Winthrop, Jr., son of Massachusetts Bay's first governor, was instrumental in ending New England's first witch hunt.

Some accused witches belonged to a new egalitarian sect that originated in England during the Civil War. Its members called themselves the **Society of Friends**. Their enemies knew them as "**Quakers**" because their bodies "quaked" when they encountered God. Friends preached that people would find little of God's will in biblical verses, ministers' sermons, or formal services. Instead, God had given everyone an "inner light"—an innate ability to determine what God wanted for them and for the world. Friends preached and practiced pacifism, did not remove their hats on meeting someone who outranked them socially, and addressed superiors in familiar terms using "thee" or "thou" rather than the formal "you." They also created separate and autonomous governing structures for men and women and permitted women such as Mary Dyer to preach and serve as missionaries.

Such beliefs and practices brought Quakers persecution on both sides of the Atlantic, especially in New England. Their often confrontational tactics alienated ministers and magistrates. Massachusetts Bay officials executed four Quakers between 1659 and 1661, Mary Dyer among them. Quakers publicized such persecution as they lobbied English authorities to revoke New England colonies' charters.

The English Civil War created even bigger headaches for New England's leaders, slowing immigration to New England and thus provoking a full-blown economic depression. New England ran a large trade deficit with English merchants. The savings of thousands of English immigrants had streamed funds into the New England economy, but the war halted the stream of immigrants into New England. When the immigrants stopped coming in the early 1640s, so did the money.

Colonists had to find other ways to earn income and produce some of what they could no longer afford to import. English immigrants to New England were among the Atlantic world's best-educated people, and many had skills to process what the region's fields, forests, and seas offered. Massachusetts Bay boasted North America's first integrated ironworks, featuring one of only a dozen rolling and slitting mills in operation in the Atlantic world in the early 1650s. The ironworks soon expired in a flurry of bankruptcies and lawsuits. Other efforts to exploit New England's natural resources enjoyed more success. Axe-wielding men cut into massive forests, furnishing local and Caribbean carpenters with wood. The English Civil War sharply reduced the number of English vessels that fished off New England's coast, so crews of colonists filled the breach. They caught and salted cod, packing the fish in locally crafted barrels. New England–made ships ferried the fishermen into the sea and back.

THE QVAKERS MEETING

THE QUAKERS MEETING The Society of Friends offended many English for several reasons, significant among them their willingness to permit women to speak during church services. This mezzotint, produced in the late 1600s, intended to satirize Quakers by showing them in a meeting as a woman stands on a box and preaches to them.

The English Civil War also accelerated the development of New England's shipbuilding industry. By the early 1640s, New England–built ships, sailed by colonists, were taking salted fish, salt pork, horses, and timber to Spain, Portugal, and the West Indies. Three decades later, Massachusetts residents had built and owned over 700 ships of at least six tons. New England shipyards soon employed thousands exporting vessels to England. Thousands more found work sailing the Atlantic or pulling cod from it.

New Englanders clashed over the Atlantic slave trade. In 1646, a ship arrived in Boston from West Africa carrying the first enslaved Africans whom mainland English colonists brought across the Atlantic. Authorities charged the captain with kidnapping and repatriated his victims at public expense. Rhode Island responded to the Atlantic slave trade by outlawing lifelong slavery in 1652. The bill's authors noted, "There is a common course practiced among English men" to buy Africans so that "they may have them for service or slaves forever." Antislavery views, however, did not prevail. By the

1670s, Boston merchants were buying small numbers of enslaved people in Madagascar and selling them in the Caribbean and North America.

Necessity compelled New England to lay the foundation of a diverse economy. Heavy immigration was the region's economic lifeline in the 1630s. A generation later, colonists' trade with other North American colonies, Europe, and the West Indies sustained them. To John Winthrop, such ties seemed heaven sent. Just as Massachusetts Bay seemed about to go bankrupt, "it pleased the Lord to open to us a Trade with Barbados."

Planters and Slaves of the Caribbean

In 1627, English colonists splashed ashore on Barbados. Thirteen years later, Barbados, just 144 square miles, had as many English as Virginia. By 1680, it was England's wealthiest and most populous colony, with 60,000 people. The vast majority were enslaved Africans who toiled and died in the sugar cane fields that blanketed the island.

At first, it looked as if Barbados might become a smaller version of Virginia, a place where English grew tobacco on small farms staffed with white indentured servants. The wealthy island looked more alluring to young English men than New England or the Chesapeake. Two features soon distinguished Barbados from Virginia. First, in 1636, the governor declared that all Africans and Indians brought to the island were to be considered slaves unless they had a contract that said otherwise. Planters began to grow export crops other than tobacco and earn higher profits from them. These included cotton and indigo, the source of a brilliant blue dye. The new crops enabled planters to buy more laborers, expand their estates, and experiment with cultivating sugar cane. Their success made them look like good credit risks to London merchants, who issued planters loans to purchase more land, enslaved Africans, and the expensive machinery that processed cane into sugar. Barbados soon replaced Brazil as the Americas' biggest supplier of sugar to Europe.

The sugar boom tied Barbados and New England together. The English quickly deforested Barbados as they cleared land for cane fields and sent lumber to mills, where enslaved people boiled cane juice down to sugar. Seeking a new source of building material and fuel, Barbadians eagerly acquired lumber from New England. Additionally, New England's fields, meadows, and coasts fed Barbadian workers and allowed most of them to produce sugar and little else. The more land and labor devoted to cane, the less remained for growing food on Barbados.

The sugar boom of the 1640s accelerated the rise of slavery and the decline of indentured servitude on Barbados. The more that planters demanded cane, the worse Barbados looked to English servants. Almost no one with better options would choose to work on a sugar plantation. Cane leaves cut skin, and the fields were hot, dirty places, full of rats and snakes. The rollers that squeezed juice from cane trapped and crushed fingers, arms, and heads. Servants, many of them Irish prisoners of war, rebelled in 1647, making enslaved African labor look more desirable to planters. In England, members of Parliament criticized the treatment of English servants in Barbados, increasing the planters' interest in and reliance on enslaved labor. By this time, the Caribbean's Native population had been devastated by disease, warfare, and slave raiding, so Caribbean planters acquired increasing numbers of slaves from Africa (Table 3.1).

Table 3.1 Estimated Numbers of Enslaved Africans Transported by Each Nation and/or Colony, 1601–1775

The Barbados sugar boom of the 1640s made England a major participant in the Atlantic slave trade. From 1651 until the American Revolution in 1775, ships registered to owners in England or Britain carried more Africans than those of any other European or American power.

YEARS	SPAIN	PORTUGAL/ BRAZIL (C)	ENGLAND/ BRITAIN	NETHERLANDS	BRITISH NORTH AMERICA (C)	FRANCE	DENMARK	TOTALS
1601–1625	83,496	267,519	0	1,829	0	0	0	352,843
1626–1650	44,313	201,609	33,695	31,729	824	1,827	1,053	315,050
1651–1675	12,601	244,793	122,367	100,526	0	7,125	653	488,064
1676–1700	5,860	297,272	272,200	85,847	3,327	29,484	25,685	719,674
1701–1725	0	474,447	410,597	73,816	3,277	120,939	5,833	1,088,909
1726–1750	0	536,696	554,042	83,095	34,004	259,095	4,793	1,471,725
1751–1775	4,239	528,693	832,047	132,330	84,580	325,918	17,508	1,925,314
Totals	150,509	2,551,028	2,224,947	509,172	126,012	744,387	55,525	6,361,580

Note: Places that were colonies between 1601 and 1775 are designated with (c).

Barbados legislators sought tighter control of enslaved people by enacting English America's first slave code in 1661. The code prescribed different treatment and different levels of protection before the law for enslaved Africans and white servants. It deputized free white men to police slaves' movements and encouraged them to whip those found without a pass from their masters. The **Barbados slave code** became one of the most influential pieces of legislation in the Anglo-Atlantic world. Many English colonies duplicated portions of it. Four, including South Carolina and Georgia, copied it completely.

Excerpts from the Barbados Slave Code (1661)

The sugar boom made England a major participant in the Atlantic slave trade. By 1684, enslaved Africans outnumbered whites more than two to one in Barbados. Most Africans met an early grave. West Indian planters estimated that a young enslaved African male might survive only seven years. Few had families; planters preferred to buy young men because they considered them better workers. They also calculated that it was cheaper to import people than to ensure that those whom they had already enslaved lived longer and healthier lives. Only the Atlantic slave trade sustained the black majority on Barbados and elsewhere in the English West Indies (Figure 3.1).

TWO ENSLAVED AFRICAN FUGITIVES FLEE A WHITE PURSUER The image illustrates a map that accompanied a history of Barbados written by Richard Ligon, who visited there in the late 1640s. In 1661, Barbados enacted English America's first slave code, much of which addressed the capture and punishment of runaways.

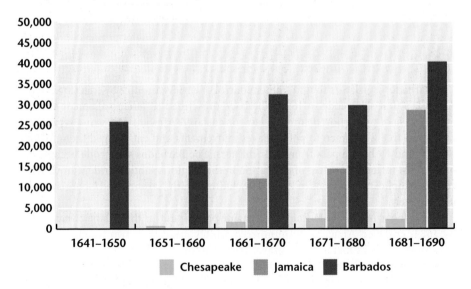

FIGURE 3.1 Enslaved Africans disembarked in the Chesapeake colonies, Barbados, and Jamaica (estimated), 1641–1690 More enslaved Africans by far went to the English Caribbean than to English colonies in mainland North America. Over 20 times as many went to Barbados as to Virginia and Maryland between 1641 and 1690, partly because so many were overworked in the island's cane fields and died young.

Missionaries and Indians in the Southeast and Southwest

As the English colonies established roots in North America and the Caribbean, Spanish mission spread in Florida and New Mexico. In 1633, Spanish friars added Apalachee Indians in the Florida Panhandle to their extensive network of missions. Their initiative answered a long-standing invitation from Apalachee chiefs who thought that better relations with the Spanish would bring them more power, prestige, and better access to imports. Fourteen years later, however, unconverted Apalachee and their Chisca allies set seven missions ablaze and drove the Spanish out. About 30 Spanish soldiers and 500 Timucua warriors recruited from missions retaliated, forcing Apalachee to surrender. They handed over those who the Spanish believed had led the rebellion. Some were hanged; the rest were sentenced to toil in St. Augustine. Florida's governor also demanded that Apalachee chiefs send laborers to the Spanish town, just as Timucua and Guales did.

Apalachees integrated into Florida's economy with tragic results. In 1655, an epidemic followed the road that linked Apalachee, Timucua, and St. Augustine, spread largely by Indians forced to transport goods or work in the Spanish town. It devastated Apalachee towns already reeling from Spanish demands for tribute and labor. By midcentury, the Apalachee population had plummeted from 30,000 to 10,000. Multiple villages of Guales and Timucua were consolidated into just one mission village for each people, neither of which could fill St. Augustine's appetite for labor any longer.

Many Timucua could take no more. In 1656, following rumors of an English raid, Timucua chiefs refused the governor's order to muster warriors and march to St. Augustine's defense. Lucas Menéndez, a Timucua chief who nursed grievances against the governor, refused to go. He persuaded some of his peers to attack Spanish colonists. They killed or drove off most colonists but spared the friars who ran the missions. Unlike Guale insurgents in 1597 or the Apalachee in 1647, Timucua chiefs accepted missions as integral to their world. They communicated with letters written in a Timucuan alphabet that friars had taught them. Executions and sentences of forced labor in St. Augustine ended the **Timucua Revolt**. The Timucua were forced to resettle into isolated missions strewn along the road between Apalachee and St. Augustine. Spanish Florida, with few colonists, hoped that these Timucuan outposts would help protect their colony from imperial rivals and nearby Indian nations.

Bilingual catechism in Spanish and Timucuan

The Timucua Revolt exposed a long-standing conflict between political and religious officials in Florida. Governor Diego de Rebolledo ridiculed missionaries' efforts to reform Indian cultures. The Timucua Revolt, however, confirmed friars' claims that Governor Rebolledo's policies abused Indians. In 1658, friars had Rebolledo summoned to Spain to stand trial for his treatment of Indians. Meanwhile, the missions stabilized. By 1675, 11,000 Indians—mostly Apalachees—lived in missions. Florida's mission system and the friars would never be more powerful.

Tensions between friars, officials, and Indians also roiled New Mexican politics. Small revolts in Taos in 1639 and in Tewa villages in 1650 temporarily allied church and state, as did rumors of a conspiracy between Pueblos and Indians of northern Mexico. However, cultural and linguistic differences made it hard for the diverse Pueblos to unite, and the revolts were soon suppressed. Rebels were hanged or sold into slavery. Some sought refuge among Apaches and helped to organize raids on the colony.

The ceasefire between Franciscan friars and governors ended in the late 1650s. The new governor, Bernardo López de Mendizábal, thought the friars had too much power. He outlawed the use of involuntary Indian labor at missions. Friars charged that the governor undermined them by siding with village chiefs and medicine men and encouraging polygamy and ceremonial dances. Reacting to a drought that began in 1660, Pueblos revived ritualistic dances to make the rains return, rituals that friars labeled devil worship. Franciscans had Mendizábal arrested and taken in chains to Mexico City. They did the same to his successor, securing their dominance over New Mexico.

STUDY QUESTIONS FOR UNCIVIL WARS, 1640–1660

1. What impact did the English Civil War have on North America and the West Indies?

2. In what ways and for what reasons did Indian life change between 1640 and 1660?

quiz

⊘ NEW IMPERIAL ORDERS, 1660–1680

The 1660s heralded a new order for colonial English and French North America. New monarchs launched reforms and waged wars intended to forge integrated empires from scattered North American and Caribbean colonies. Conquest brought a large, diverse, and established population of colonists who were not English under English rule for the first time. Meanwhile, political and social changes in the Chesapeake and a new Barbadian colony in Carolina rooted plantation slavery in North America.

The English Colonial Empire and the Conquest of New Netherland

In 1660, English America learned that England again had a king. Charles II restored his father's ally William Berkeley to the governorship of Virginia. Massachusetts Bay feared retribution for having supported the defeated side in the English Civil War but still took months to proclaim the new monarch. Charles's reign brought enduring changes for colonists and Indians. By the time Charles II died in 1685, English entrepreneurs had founded four new colonies, and imperial officials had reorganized three others. New Netherland entered England's empire by conquest, making it the first Anglo-American society in which authorities governed large numbers of settled Europeans who were not English. All colonists faced an empire that sought to tighten oversight of their internal affairs and their commerce overseas (Figure 3.2).

Under Charles II, England established the **Navigation Acts** (Table 3.2), a series of laws that began to go into effect in 1651. The Navigation Acts permitted free trade within England's colonial empire but restricted commerce with people outside it. English merchants applauded them, but the reaction among colonists was mixed. On the positive side, the laws guaranteed markets for their goods and services. Nevertheless, colonial planters and merchants chafed at the regulations. Planters thought the laws deprived them of markets by levying duties on tobacco and sugar and by

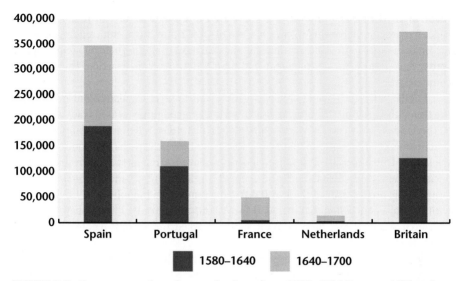

FIGURE 3.2 European emigration to the Americas, 1580–1700 Between 1580 and 1700, England sent more Europeans to the Americas than any of its rivals. Nearly half the European immigrants to the Americas between 1640 and 1700 were English. The majority of English went to mainland North America, where the populations of English colonies dwarfed those of European rivals.

Table 3.2 Navigation Acts

As English authorities began to see colonies as a key source of wealth, they increasingly regulated American colonists' commerce with Atlantic markets. Here are some of the most important laws, known as the Navigation Acts.

YEAR LEGISLATION PASSED	KEY PROVISIONS AND OUTCOMES
1651	All goods sent to England from America, Africa, or Asia must be carried in vessels owned and staffed by English men or English colonists Dutch merchants barred from English colonies Provokes First Anglo-Dutch War
1660	Only vessels owned by English men and operated by crews that were at least three-quarters English may dock in colonial ports Stipulates list of "enumerated goods," including sugar and tobacco, which have to be shipped to England before they can be taken elsewhere
1663	Most non-English goods headed for English colonies must first be shipped through England and taxed there
1673	Colonists required to pay duties on enumerated goods shipped to England Customs agents appointed and stationed in every colony to collect duties
1696	Extends system of vice-admiralty courts from England to colonies to clamp down on smuggling and enforce Navigation Acts

requiring that those commodities be unloaded in England before proceeding to European markets. Merchants in the colonies objected that European imports destined for English North America also had to pass through England before being shipped across the Atlantic, an arrangement that they believed unfairly favored their English counterparts.

The Navigation Act (1651)

English officials looked to the Navigation Acts to sever English colonists' thickening ties with Dutch merchants. Massachusetts Bay grudgingly ceased trade with New Netherland during the **First Anglo-Dutch War** (1652–1654) but quickly resumed it when peace came, even though the first Navigation Act of 1651 clearly barred commerce with the Dutch. Dutch merchants also transported enslaved Africans to English colonies, especially when the English Civil War disrupted Anglo-Atlantic trade. In 1663, Charles II awarded the predecessor of the **Royal African Company** a monopoly on English trade with Africa, a concession that included the Atlantic slave trade. The company's attacks on Dutch shipping and forts in West Africa sparked the **Second Anglo-Dutch War** (1664–1667).

In North America, that war began when a small English fleet won New Amsterdam's surrender without firing a shot. The city and New Netherland became New York in August 1664, taking on the title of King Charles II's brother **James, Duke of York**. Commander Richard Nicolls knew that it would be difficult to control such a diverse colony, so he promised Dutch colonists a New York that would resemble New Netherland. The **Articles of Capitulation** granted Dutch residents religious liberty, freedom from military conscription, property rights, the ability to leave New York within 18 months, and free trade and freedom of movement within the English Empire. The Articles also allowed the Dutch to continue following their inheritance customs.

England's grip on New York was tenuous. In 1673, a Dutch fleet delighted most Dutch and many English residents by retaking the colony. Dutch authorities seized property of English officials and merchants. A peace treaty returned the colony to England a year later, but the English were alarmed at New York's quick capitulation to the Dutch. Much of New York's "Dutch" majority, in fact, strove to become more "Dutch" in the wake of English conquest. The Dutch Reformed Church assumed a more prominent role in New York than it had in New Netherland. Another way for Dutch colonists to assert a Dutch identity was to continue to divide their estates in Dutch ways. This gave Dutch women more power than English women had. Dutch inheritance law permitted women to keep property that they brought to a marriage and divided estates equally between sons and daughters. These practices eroded gradually during the early 1700s.

Growing English domination of New York's public life during the 1680s alienated many Dutch and widened political divisions. An English minority seized the agenda in New York's first representative assembly in 1683. Three years later, all government bodies, including those of towns, followed English norms. Dutch who lived upriver resented the growing power of Manhattan's wealthy Anglo-Dutch merchants. So did most of the city's artisans, Dutch and English, who saw a small number of well-connected men conspiring with officials to issue regulations that threatened their livelihood. Dutch who considered the Dutch Reformed Church the bulwark of Dutch identity expressed dismay at English officials' growing influence over clergy. In 1689, this brew of class and ethnic tensions boiled over as political instability wracked the Anglo-Atlantic world and war erupted with France.

Quebec and the Expansion of French America

In 1665, as New Yorkers adjusted to their first year of English rule, a regiment of some 1,000 French troops landed in Quebec. The arrival of North America's first standing army doubled the number of men in New France. Louis XIV's minister **Jean-Baptiste Colbert** considered the regiment crucial to his plan to reform France's empire. He, like his English rivals, believed in **mercantilism**: an economic system in which colonies existed mainly to provide raw materials and to serve as protected markets for finished goods. To accomplish these goals, Colbert aimed to repopulate Canada, increase royal control over New France, diversify the colony's economy, and better integrate it into French-Atlantic trade networks.

First, the French had to curb Iroquois raids. Except for Mohawks, all Iroquois nations favored peace with New France, partly because England's conquest of New Netherland curtailed their supply of firearms. In 1666, seeking Mohawk capitulation, the French launched their final invasion of Mohawk country, looting and torching dozens of longhouses and two years' worth of food stores.

After securing a tense peace, French officials focused on recruiting settlers to New France. Colbert noted how colonization with families seemed to enhance English power, and he wanted to emulate it. Seeking a gender balance in New France, where white men greatly outnumbered white women, Colbert directed officials to recruit more young women. He hoped that these women would marry, have many children, and enhance New France's low settler population.

Wars in Europe and budgetary constraints stopped the flow of immigrants by the mid-1670s. However, New France's population had already reached 10,000 and continued to grow, mostly through rising birth rates rather than immigration. In New France, women gave birth to more children than women in France did, and more of their children survived to adulthood. France's population barely grew during the 1700s, whereas New France's practically doubled every generation.

Aside from more native-born French Canadians, New France attained few of Colbert's goals. He sought a New France that would serve the French economy as New England did the English. Instead, New France developed into a modest colony of landlords, tenants, and peasants that still depended on furs to pay for imports. Colbert envisioned that Canadian-built ships would ferry fish, provisions, and timber to France's Caribbean colonies and return with sugar, rum, and molasses. However, New England outcompeted New France in the French West Indies. Its merchants provided more goods more cheaply as well as access to a far bigger colonial market.

As a consequence of its treaty with the Iroquois, New France gained greater trade access inland. The French King **Louis XIV** gave Robert Cavalier de La Salle permission to sail down the Mississippi and establish trading posts along the way. He reached the river's mouth in 1682, claimed the area for France, and named it Louisiana after Louis XIV. The **Hudson's Bay Company,** which had formed in England in 1670, competed with the French. The English, who offered more goods at better prices than the French, attracted Cree Indians, who brought pelts to Hudson's Bay outposts. A struggle soon began between England and France for control of the fur trade in interior North America. Although Indian nations still controlled the interior, the English and French made inroads with trade and military posts. For decades, whoever best met Indian needs held the upper hand.

Servitude and Slavery in the Chesapeake

During the second half of the 1600s, Maryland and Virginia also experienced drastic changes. Both colonies originally relied on indentured servants as a source of labor. By the early 1680s, the Chesapeake resembled Barbados. It too had become a society dependent on slavery and founded on the principle of white supremacy.

Plantation slavery and racial consciousness emerged gradually and together in the Chesapeake. The profitability of tobacco encouraged English immigration and the expansion of plantations further inland. During the Third Anglo-Powhatan War, Powhatans failed in their attempt to push back settlers, who now vastly outnumbered them. In the peace treaty that concluded the war, the English demanded that Indian children serve as hostage-servants in Virginia households. The General Assembly defined these children as indentured servants, but many Indians protested that their children were later sold on the slave market. Throughout the 17th and 18th centuries, Virginia lawmakers tried to regulate or even outlaw Indian slavery, but colonists continued to buy and sell Indian slaves.

The legal status of people of African descent remained ambiguous into the 1660s. Many were considered indentured servants. A few gained freedom, owned land, and even held slaves. A 1668 law, however, compelled free black women to pay a tax, compounding the burden on struggling black families (Table 3.3).

While Virginia lawmakers associated Indian captives with servitude, they increasingly pushed Africans into slavery. They laid one cornerstone in 1662 by declaring that a child's legal status should follow that of the mother. This broke with English law and gender norms, under which a child inherited legal status from the father. Worse, it made slavery heritable and, in the masters' eyes, remade enslaved women into commodities valued for their production and reproduction. This encouraged masters to abuse enslaved women sexually, and it emasculated enslaved fathers. Legislators laid another cornerstone in 1667 by resolving that slaves who had been baptized and had converted to Christianity did not have legal grounds to sue for freedom.

Although masters enjoyed new powers, they did not immediately purchase many more slaves. In 1670, the 2,000 enslaved Virginians formed 5 percent of the colony's population. Many had not come directly from Africa but rather from the West Indies, where planters traded slaves for grain and meat (Map 3.2). Still, around 6,000 Africans arrived in the Chesapeake Bay between 1660 and 1690.

The gradual expansion of African slavery in the Chesapeake was tied to changes in indentured servitude and to the region's reputation in England. In the late 1650s and early 1660s, the number of servants who came to Virginia, three-quarters of them men, surged as their prospects declined in Barbados (Figure 3.3). But soon Chesapeake planters had trouble finding servants at a price that they were willing to pay. Improving job prospects in England kept many at home, as did reports of what awaited servants across the ocean. As with Barbados, news from the Chesapeake likened servitude to slavery. A critic in the 1670s insisted that masters tyrannized servants "as Turks do over Galley-slaves."

Women and men experienced servitude differently. Recruiters told women in England weighing whether to cross the Atlantic that they would not have to work in the tobacco fields and that they could pick a husband in a society teeming with eligible bachelors. The first claim was usually a lie, though the second claim carried some truth. Female servants could find suitors, but they had to beware of men who might lure them

Excerpts from acts of the Virginia General Assembly concerning slaves and servants (1662, 1667, 1705)

Table 3.3 Selected Key Legal Developments Concerning Slavery and Race in English America, 1635–1696

Slavery and racism emerged gradually and together in English America during the 17th century. Here are some of the key legal milestones in that process, one in which Barbados played a key role.

YEAR	COLONY	KEY PROVISIONS
1635	Barbados	Governor declares that all Africans and Indians brought to the island are to be considered slaves unless they have a contract that says otherwise
1641	Massachusetts Bay	Legalizes slavery within the colony
1643	Virginia	Women of African descent and all men made subject to tithe to support Church of England
1661	Barbados	First comprehensive slave code in English America, setting model for other colonies to follow
1661	Virginia	Indentured servants who run away with slaves must serve time that slave missed as well as time that they missed
1662	Virginia	Child's legal status to follow that of the mother rather than the father
1664	Maryland	Slavery defined as a lifelong legal condition
1665	New York	New English Assembly, composed largely of migrants from New England, recognizes slavery as lifelong condition
1667	Virginia	Denies that baptism provides legal grounds to sue for freedom
1670	Virginia	Indians taken captive outside colony and imported to serve for life; those captured within colony to serve 12 years (if children) or until age 30
1679	New York	Enslavement of Indians prohibited
1680	Virginia	Enslaved blacks barred from carrying arms, gathering (particularly for feasts and burials), or leaving plantations without a pass from their master
1691	Virginia	Whites barred from marrying blacks, mulattos, or Indians; children born of unions between English women and black men to become servants; mothers to pay fine, become servants, or have their servitude extended Masters owed compensation if their runaway slaves are killed while being captured Freed people ordered to leave colony
1692	Virginia	Special courts created for trying slaves accused of crimes
1696	South Carolina	First comprehensive slave code established, modeled after that of Barbados, in English North America

to bed with promises of marriage and then leave them to deal with the consequences of pregnancy. Making matters worse, a 1662 Virginia law made female servants, who were frequent targets of sexual advances, solely responsible for compensating masters for time lost by pregnancy and labor. That could add at least two years to their servitude. If a servant mother died and the father dodged responsibility for paternity, her

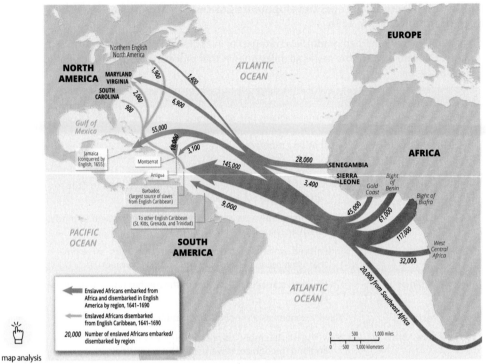

map analysis

MAP 3.2 **The Atlantic Slave Trade and English America, 1641–1690** Nearly one enslaved African in four died while crossing the Atlantic to English America between 1641 and 1690. Over half of those who survived the journey landed in Barbados. That island and others in the English Caribbean sent at least 5,000 enslaved Africans to England's mainland North American colonies.

child had to become an indentured servant. This is the fate that befell Anne and Jasper Orthwood, whose story introduced this chapter.

Before the 1660s, young English men in the Chesapeake had reason to fear that they would not survive their servitude. But they also knew that they stood a good chance of owning land, even if it might not be the best land. By the mid-1670s, however, wealthy planters, many of them close associates of Governor Berkeley, had claimed most good land with easy access to the Chesapeake Bay. Ex-servants and sons of small planters could work either as tenants or as hired hands—or move to the colony's borders and risk Indian attacks.

Other tensions divided Virginians. Women's criticism of their neighbors often prompted their husbands to come to blows, so Virginia legislators tried to silence such women by sentencing them to a ducking, a centuries-old English punishment normally meted out to wives considered unruly. Offending women were marched to a pond or river, tied to a stool, and thrust underwater. In addition, small planters were angered by a tax hike that Governor Berkeley earmarked to bolster coastal defenses against Dutch attack. The small planters were already pressed by a long-term decline in tobacco prices.

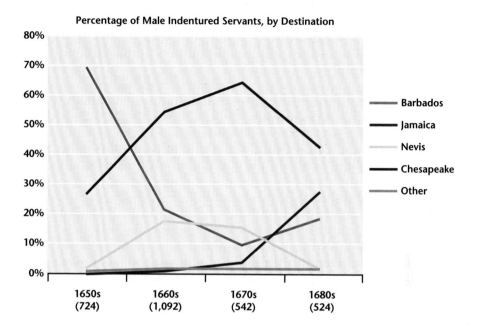

Percentage of Male Indentured Servants, by Destination

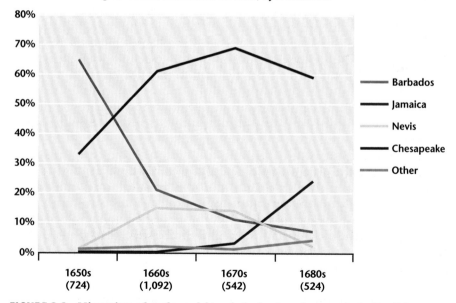

Percentage of Female Indentured Servants, by Destination

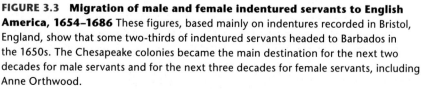

FIGURE 3.3 Migration of male and female indentured servants to English America, 1654–1686 These figures, based mainly on indentures recorded in Bristol, England, show that some two-thirds of indentured servants headed to Barbados in the 1650s. The Chesapeake colonies became the main destination for the next two decades for male servants and for the next three decades for female servants, including Anne Orthwood.

Governor Berkeley also made powerful enemies, none more prominent than **Nathaniel Bacon**. The English aristocrat arrived in 1674, certain that his high birth entitled him to high office. Berkeley agreed, appointing Bacon to his council, but the two men clashed. Governor Berkeley, who had not allowed Virginians to elect representatives since 1662, ruled in alliance with a small cadre of rich planters, whom he favored with choice land grants. Bacon took charge of a faction that opposed Berkeley, arguing that power should be shared more broadly.

Bacon gained support as war erupted between colonists, most of whom wanted Indian land. In July 1675, Doeg Indians who lived in Maryland attempted to collect a debt from a Virginia colonist, sparking a confrontation that claimed lives on both sides. Chesapeake militia leaders blamed Susquehannocks for sheltering Doegs. The Susquehannocks were themselves refugees, pushed south by Iroquois raids, who had resettled in Maryland at the invitation of its government. Virginia militiamen murdered Susquehannock chiefs and besieged their town. Susquehannocks retaliated by raiding Virginia in early 1676. Governor Berkeley responded in a measured way, condemning the militias while advocating punitive raids on Susquehannocks. The governor knew that war was engulfing New England and feared that a broader anti-English alliance of Indians would threaten colonies from Massachusetts to Virginia.

Nathaniel Bacon, "Manifesto Concerning the Present Troubles in Virginia" (1676)

Bacon's solution, however, was far more popular among white Virginians—target all Indians. In May, Governor Berkeley declared Bacon a rebel and organized elections. The governor's forces captured Bacon, but the newly elected burgesses asked that Berkeley pardon him. The governor did so, reseating Bacon on the council but refusing to authorize Bacon to attack the Indians. Bacon's followers took up arms and drove Berkeley from Jamestown, an event known as **Bacon's Rebellion**. The governor's supporters soon regained the upper hand. Bacon, desperate to save himself, promised freedom to the servants and slaves of Berkeley loyalists. About 250 slaves joined white servants and ex-servants to storm and torch Jamestown as Berkeley fled for his life. Charles II authorized Berkeley to offer freedom to servants and slaves who sided with him. The governor declined, calculating that it would alienate planters. Some of his allies thought otherwise. One persuaded hundreds of servants and slaves to surrender by promising them freedom, a ruse that effectively ended the rebellion.

Bacon's Rebellion remade Virginia's borders and its politics. Susquehannocks straggled north, where many submitted to the Iroquois. Charles II appointed a commission to investigate matters in Virginia. It concluded that high taxes, vulnerability to Indian attack, government corruption, and concentration of land ownership had sparked the uprising. The king, increasingly dependent on revenues raised from duties on tobacco, needed a stable Virginia, so he dismissed Berkeley. The war and growing English involvement in Indian diplomacy diminished the threat of Indian attacks while pressuring Native nations to cede more land. Meanwhile, a steep tax cut in 1686 stabilized provincial politics.

The rebellion accelerated the entrenchment of racism and slavery. Planters fretted that economic inequity divided whites, so increasing numbers of planters opted to purchase enslaved Africans rather than indentured servants. Consequently, Virginia's black population grew to 5,000 by 1698 so that slaves comprised at least half the colony's unfree workers. New laws passed between 1680 and 1691 hardened racial distinctions and empowered masters and officials to exert more control over slaves and free blacks. In 1691, Virginia prohibited interracial marriage, punished white women for giving birth to interracial children, and required anyone who was freed to leave the colony within six months or the person who freed them would be fined. Unlike Barbados, Maryland and Virginia retained a white majority. They formed the northern edge of a rim of societies based on African slavery that extended south to Carolina, the Caribbean, and Brazil.

The Creation of South Carolina

When Charles I was executed in the English Civil War, Sir John Colleton, one of his greatest supporters, fled England to become a Barbados planter. In 1663, Charles II rewarded his loyalty by granting the exclusive right to colonize land between Virginia and Florida to a group that Colleton headed. The planter and his partners named the colony "Carolina" to honor the king.

Carolina's proprietors envisioned that colonists would pay them to use their land and live peacefully alongside Indians. They promised land grants for each immigrant who paid for his passage as well as religious toleration and a representative assembly. Most colonists came from Barbados, and many brought slaves with them. Barbados profoundly influenced the development of the new colony. Barbadians founded Carolina's first permanent colonial settlement in 1670 and comprised most of the 1,300 people of European descent who moved to South Carolina over the next two decades. Land drew most, whether they were sons of prominent planters who feared that their status would erode if they stayed on Barbados or young men, craftsmen, or small planters who decided that they would never succeed there. Barbadians helped to craft Carolina's slave code in 1696. They also oriented Carolina's economy toward the West Indies, which needed food and labor. Initially, free and enslaved Carolinians reared cattle and pigs and grew corn and peas, while the colony's Indian allies supplied the colony with Native slaves. Some of these Native slaves were exported to the Caribbean, while others served alongside Africans on the colony's first plantations.

Carolina's first major Indian allies were the Westos. Victims of the Beaver Wars, the Westos moved south in the 1650s. Their experience with the Iroquois convinced Westos of the need to dominate trade with colonists. The Westos first allied with Virginia, then South Carolina. In 1674, Carolina diplomat Henry Woodward reported that Westos welcomed him into their village and showed him "ye effigies of a bever, a man, on horseback & guns, intimating thereby as I suppose, their desire for friendship, & comerse wth us." Their village, Woodward noted, was well stocked with firearms, ammunition, European cloth, and other trade goods. They had procured these items by trading beaver pelts, deerskins, and Indian slaves. In fact, to seal their new alliance with Carolina, the Westos gave Woodward an Indian boy whom they had captured in Virginia. This boy, nameless in the records, was the first of thousands of Indian slaves forced to Carolina.

English colonists reported that other Indians were "afraid of ye very foot step of a Westoe." Newcomers who lacked Native allies in the region, the Westos raided Native groups from the Atlantic coast to the Appalachian Mountains and beyond. At that time, few southern Indians owned firearms. The most vulnerable were Florida's mission Indians because Spain refused to trade guns to its Indian allies. Westo raids devastated Indian missions among the Timucua, Mocama, Guale, and Yamasee Indians. Some of these victims sought greater Spanish military protection, while others became convinced that they, too, needed an English trade alliance.

The Indian slave trade spread violence throughout the South and created conflict within Carolina. Seeking easier access to Florida missions, the Westos moved to the Savannah River, just south of Carolina. Carolinians, however, came to fear their well-armed and powerful Native neighbors. From 1680 to 1682, Carolina waged a brutal war against the Westos, killing most of the men and selling women and children as slaves. Carolina's Lords Proprietors, a group of eight English nobles who ruled the colony from afar, denounced the Westo War, fearing that conflicts with Indian neighbors would destabilize the colony. The proprietors declared that only Indians captured in "just wars" could be enslaved, but their agents in Carolina did not enforce this policy. Carolina had already come to depend on Indian slaves as laborers on growing plantations and valuable export commodities. In the wake of the Westo War, Carolina sought out other Native allies to act as middlemen in the Indian slave trade. Desperate to catch up in a regional arms race, several Native groups agreed. Among them were the Yamasees, who abandoned their Spanish mission to settle closer to Carolina.

Metacom and the Battle for New England

Most New England colonists dreaded the news of Charles II's coronation. Many had supported the losing side of the English Civil War and now feared repercussions. England revoked New Haven's charter and subjected its residents to Connecticut's authority in 1664. Massachusetts Bay, too, endured a wave of assaults on its legal right to exist. Quakers launched many of them, as did colonists in New Hampshire and Maine who did not want Massachusetts to govern them. Indians also petitioned Charles II as loyal subjects who deserved protection from disloyal colonists headquartered in Boston.

Political uncertainty fed a growing sense of crisis in New England in the 1660s and 1670s. Some took defeat in the English Civil War as a sign that they had lost God's favor. Worse might befall them, they feared, as the generation that had founded New England began to die off. Were they worthy, they wondered, of the founders' legacy? A growing number of ministers told them, in sermons called jeremiads, that they were not and never would be unless they changed their ways and honored God as their parents had.

Meanwhile, some New England colonists seized opportunities to forge new ties to England. In 1661, John Winthrop, Jr., became a charter member of the **Royal Society**, a group that advocated scientific inquiry. Its founders believed that people glorified God and bolstered faith by studying the natural world. Cotton Mather, a leading Boston minister, became a Royal Society fellow.

Colonists such as Winthrop and Mather sent specimens to London, corresponded with other fellows, and published in the society's journal. They subscribed to Royal Society journals and lent them to others. Winthrop donated New England's first telescope to Harvard, where others used it to observe comets in the 1680s. Their work informed the thought of Isaac Newton.

Some of these self-proclaimed scientists considered themselves experts on Indians and used transatlantic scientific networks to develop theories about race. While in London, Winthrop reported to the Royal Society on how to grow and use corn. Winthrop and his American peers claimed that their engagement with science demonstrated their superiority to "superstitious" Indians, who, they claimed, were incapable of such intellectual work. This reassured colonists who feared that life or birth in America made them seem inferior in the eyes of English across the Atlantic.

Native peoples in southern New England feared the rising power and mounting racism of their English neighbors. They had become the minority, forced to accommodate immigrants who had arrived only a generation earlier. As Miantonomi had warned in the early 1640s, Native people had to modify their ways to survive. Economic and environmental changes left them no choice. In 1661, a mint opened in Boston; within a year, most New England colonists had stopped using wampum as currency and showed little interest in other Indian trade goods. Southern New England Indians increasingly found that they could pay their debts only with land. The more land they sold, the less they had for hunting and fishing. Multiplying herds of English-owned cattle and pigs threatened to overrun what land remained in Indian hands. The livestock ate many of the same plants as deer; trampled Native gardens; and devoured Indian plots of corn, beans, and squash. Indians who faced famine countered such invasions by filing suits in colonial courts or by killing and eating the invading animals.

Native peoples eventually decided to selectively adopt English ways and began keeping pigs. Colonists, however, refused to share public grazing lands with Indians. In 1669, Portsmouth, Rhode Island, officials forced Massasoit's son, the Wampanoag sachem **Metacom** (whom they called **Philip**), to remove his pigs from "Hog Island." Two years later, Plymouth demanded that Metacom and the Wampanoags formally submit to colonial rule.

Metacom responded by organizing an Indian alliance to confront the English. An Indian spy, John Sassamon, informed Plymouth governor John Winslow of Metacom's plans. After Sassamon's lifeless body was discovered in a frozen pond, a Plymouth jury hastily tried and hanged three Wampanoags. This marked the first time that English colonists interfered in judging a crime that should have been handled by tribal authorities. Determined to maintain their sovereignty, a diverse coalition of Indians—mostly Wampanoags, Narragansetts, and Nipmucs—took up arms against colonists in **King Philip's War** (1675–1677). The English, however, retained key Indian allies including the Massachusetts, Mohegans, and Pequots.

One of the deadliest conflicts in American history, King Philip's War claimed 2,500 English (about 5 percent of the colonial population) and at least 5,000 Natives (40 percent of New England's Indian population). Indian attacks terrified colonists and destroyed 25 English towns. Massachusetts Bay leaders made plans to evacuate most of the colony and shelter colonists behind a ring of wooden ramparts a few miles from Boston.

Indians, regardless of which side they chose, suffered most from the war. English-led attacks compelled most to flee inland and keep moving, leaving them hungry and vulnerable to cold and disease. New York's governor persuaded Mohawks to side with the

MEDALLION PRESENTED TO CHRISTIAN INDIAN SOLDIERS SERVING WITH MASSACHUSETTS FORCES DURING KING PHILIP'S WAR, 1676 Christian Indians helped New England win King Philip's War and secure the release of captured colonists. Massachusetts Bay officials gave this medallion to Christian Indian soldiers for their service (to quote the inscription on the back of the medallion) "in the present Warr [*sic*] with the Heathen Natives of this Land."

Global Catholicism, Indian Christianity, and Catherine/Kateri Tekakwitha

A young Mohawk woman died in April 1680. Father Claude Chauchetière called her Catherine, her baptismal name. His superior Pierre Cholenec gave Catherine last rites and claimed that he saw her pockmarked face clear after she died. Both men wrote a biography of Catherine. Chauchetière advised ill French colonists to pray for her help. Catherine soon won a regional following. Three hundred years later, the "Mohawk saint" had an international one consisting largely of Catholic clergy and American Indians. Pope John Paul II beatified Catherine in 1980, the first step on the path toward sainthood.

In 1656, an Algonquin captive living in the Mohawk village Gandaouagué gave birth to Tekakwitha. Smallpox scarred the girl's face when she was six and killed her mother and brother. When war with New France broke out, the village residents fled. Peace required that they accept Jesuits. One baptized Tekakwitha on Easter Sunday in 1676, giving her the name of Catherine. She moved to Kahnawake, a village peopled mostly by Christian Mohawks located near Montreal. Kin awaited her there. Tekakwitha joined other devout women who practiced celibacy and inflicted pain on themselves. She became the group leader shortly before she died at the age of 24.

Jesuits viewed Catherine and her peers as women who had almost ceased to be Indian, but Catherine and her peers likely saw themselves as Catholic and Iroquoian. Baptism, a ritual in which one assumed a new identity to join a community, had Iroquoian analogs. So did abstaining from sex, burning or whipping oneself, and plunging into an icy pond. Jesuits interpreted these as acts of penance for sins. Tekakwitha and her circle could have seen them as preparation for possible torment, in this world or the next, and as a means to spiritual transcendence.

Chauchetière promoted Catherine's power to work miracles rather than her melding of Catholic and Indian beliefs. Tekakwitha's remains were exhumed in 1684 and buried in a mission chapel to accommodate pilgrims, almost all of whom were French Canadians. Chauchetière's biography of Catherine collected dust in France for nearly two centuries.

A campaign to beatify Catherine Tekakwitha began in the 1880s in the United States with strong support from Catholic bishops who believed that her beatification might counter rampant anti-Catholic prejudice by showing that Catholicism was "native" to American soil. The number of publications devoted to Tekakwitha's life surged over the next century. In 1939, a group of white missionaries founded the Tekakwitha Conference in Montana to promote her beatification.

English, deny Metacom's pleas for help, and raid his allies. Both sides considered Christian Indians suspect. Massachusetts Bay soldiers rounded up and exiled most to a bleak island in Boston Harbor, where many died or were enslaved illegally. Other Christian Indians negotiated the release of English captives or fought alongside colonists. One shot Metacom in August 1676. English captain Benjamin Church took Metacom's severed head

KATERI TEKAKWITHA This bronze statue of Kateri Tekakwitha by Estella Loretto, a Jemez Pueblo sculptor, stands in front of the Cathedral Basilica of St. Francis of Assisi in Santa Fé. Unveiled in 2002 to mark the cathedral structure's 150th anniversary, it testifies to the devotion for Kateri Tekakwitha in New Mexico, particularly among Indians. A Vatican tribunal's investigation has found that her intercession miraculously saved the life of a hospitalized Lummi Indian boy in Washington state named Jake Finkbonner, prompting Pope Benedict XVI to declare Kateri eligible for canonization. She became a saint in 2012.

Meanwhile, Tekakwitha earned a following among Indian Catholics, who took control of the Tekakwitha Conference in the 1970s. Indian devotees revere Kateri Tekakwitha as someone who was fully Catholic and fully Indian. In 2012, Pope Benedict XVI officially declared her a saint. In life, **Catherine/Kateri Tekakwitha** journeyed between upstate New York and Quebec. In death, her example has circled the world.

- In what ways have Catholic clergy and Indians viewed the life of Tekakwitha since her death? In what ways have those portraits differed? What might account for such differences?
- Tekakwitha and Pocahontas chose to participate in colonial societies that profoundly altered their worlds. Are their lives, and the choices that they made, comparable? Explain.

back to Plymouth and displayed it atop a post. Metacom's wife and their nine-year-old son were sold as slaves in Bermuda. Hundreds of other Indian prisoners of war were enslaved in New England or exported to slave markets in Virginia and the Caribbean. Many of those who escaped captivity became refugees or struggled to remain autonomous peoples surrounded by colonists who chipped away at their sovereign rights and territory.

Excerpt
from Mary
Rowlandson,
*The
Sovereignty
and
Goodness of
God* (1682)

Metacom's death did not end the war. Warriors in northern New England continued to raid New Hampshire and Maine. The attacks revived traumatic memories for colonists, who unleashed a torrent of published works about King Philip's War that were read on both sides of the Atlantic. One, by **Mary Rowlandson**, a minister's wife whom Indians had captured, was published in Massachusetts and London in 1682. It became the second best-selling book in New England after the Bible. Rowlandson interpreted her ordeal and that of colonists as an act of God and an example of His saving grace. Like the Pequot War and Bacon's Rebellion, King Philip's War heightened anti-Indian racism. Meanwhile, English officials saw the war as proof that they needed tighter reins on colonists.

STUDY QUESTIONS FOR NEW IMPERIAL ORDERS, 1660–1680

quiz

1. Wars between colonists and Indians erupted across eastern North America in the 1660s and 1670s. Why? Did the conflicts share one underlying cause, or did each have distinct origins? Explain.

2. How was slavery established in Virginia, Barbados, and South Carolina?

3. Why did royal power increase within the English and French colonial empires during the 1660s? What impact did royal reforms have on North America?

⊘ VICTORIOUS PUEBLOS, A NEW MID-ATLANTIC, AND "GLORIOUS" REVOLUTIONS, 1680 TO THE 1690S

The 1680s brought revolutions to the Spanish Southwest and the Anglo-Atlantic world that resulted in civil wars, social turmoil, and imperial conflicts throughout North America. Pueblo Indians united to drive the Spanish from New Mexico but then divided over what they should do afterward. New English colonies emerged in the mid-Atlantic, each committed to religious freedom that attracted thousands of immigrants from other parts of English America, the British Isles, and western Europe. The overthrow of another English king in 1688 triggered revolts in three colonies and the first of many wars between England, France, and Indians for control of eastern North America.

The Pueblo War for Independence

On an August evening in 1680, Pueblo messengers departed Taos. **Popé**, a medicine man whom Spanish friars had recently whipped for practicing "idolatry," had dispatched them to alert other towns that a planned uprising would begin in two days. The Pueblos were diverse, dwelling in more than two dozen independent towns and speaking at least six different languages, but they united against Spanish rule. As their rebellion began, Indian warriors slaughtered horses and mules to constrict colonists' mobility before storming missions and Spanish towns. Within two weeks, 1,400 colonists, with 500 Indian slaves in tow, had abandoned New Mexico, leaving behind hundreds of dead, including over 20 friars. Pueblos had waged the most successful war for independence in North American history to date (Map 3.3).

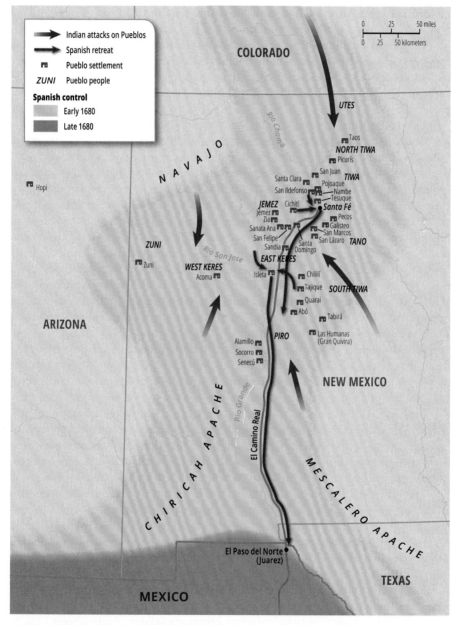

MAP 3.3 Pueblo War for Independence The Pueblo War for Independence, organized largely by Popé of Taos Pueblo, drove the Spanish out of New Mexico in 1680. Colonists sought refuge in El Paso del Norte (today's Ciudad Juárez, Mexico). They did not return for a dozen years.

A number of factors prompted the war. Approximately 100,000 Indians lived in New Mexico when the Spanish conquered the region in 1598. By 1680, only 17,000 remained. The Southwest had endured a severe drought for two decades. Navajo and Apache raids in the 1670s worsened food shortages. Spanish demands for tribute became even more onerous in such trying times. Some Spanish colonists raped Pueblo women. In 1675, the Spanish cracked down on Pueblo rituals, especially those that beseeched **katsinas**—ancestral god spirits—to bring rain, fertility, and prosperity. That may well have been the final provocation.

Popé considered the Pueblo gods the war's real leaders and himself their instrument. Popé claimed the gods had punished Pueblos for having adopted the ways of their foreign oppressors. Only when Pueblos returned to their preconquest beliefs would they regain the favor of katsinas and other gods who would restore an era of peace and prosperity.

That idyllic time, however, did not return. Most Pueblos wanted the Spanish gone but disagreed on what should happen once they left. Many men celebrated the end of monogamy, one of the friars' most hated impositions, by seeking a different or an additional wife. Pueblos restored kivas to reenact their creation, while many destroyed churches, crosses, and images of Jesus Christ and the Virgin Mary. Popé's allies rejected their Christian names for Native ones and punished those who spoke Spanish or invoked Jesus or Mary. The most zealous sought to reject what the Spanish had brought, regardless of its usefulness. They demanded that Spanish tools be cast aside and broken and that Indians plant only corn and beans as their ancestors had and "burn the seeds which the Spaniards sowed." For many Pueblos, this went too far. Spanish tools had become integral to their lives. So had peaches, beef, and pork. They had used European plants and animals for generations and now saw them as "native" to their New Mexico. So were Jesus and the Virgin Mary, whom many had incorporated into the pantheon that created and sustained their ancestors.

Such differences fed conflicts that erupted almost as soon as the Spanish fled. The drought and Apache raids continued as violence broke out within some towns between supporters and opponents of Popé's reforms. Warriors stormed granaries of neighboring communities, and nearly all Pueblo towns fell victim to Ute raids.

Popé died in 1692, just as the Spanish were launching their reconquest of New Mexico. They feared that growing French interest in Texas and Louisiana threatened Spanish control of northern Mexico and the silver that flowed from that region. New Mexico's new governor, Diego de Vargas, also believed that Pueblo victory had sustained a wave of Indian rebellions across northern Mexico and inspired new ones.

Many Pueblos had decided that they preferred a future alongside Spaniards. According to some Pueblo accounts, a delegation representing several towns invited the Spanish to return. After Vargas reached Santa Fé, friars baptized over 100 Pueblo children born after 1680. Many Pueblo leaders asked Vargas to stand as godfather to their children to gain his protection. Popé's successor Luis Tupatú initiated peace talks. Tupatú's peace faction allowed the Spanish back into Pueblo lands but demanded greater autonomy. Thereafter, the Spanish stopped demanding forced labor from free Indians and decreased taxes. The Franciscan friars returned, but Pueblos barred them from traditional religious ceremonies. Some Pueblos went back to church, while others returned to kivas; many Pueblos did both, practicing the Catholic faith as well as traditional ways.

Some Pueblos disagreed with Tupatú and pledged to continue the fight. Vargas toured nearly two dozen rebel towns, bullying most into submission. After returning to El Paso, he mustered several hundred men, most of them New Mexico refugees, and returned to Santa Fé in late 1693. Vargas found the town in enemy hands. It took the Spanish and their Pueblo allies two days to take it. Vargas had dozens executed, enslaved 400 women and children, and parceled them out to colonists. It took nine more months to conquer most of the towns that refused to accept Spanish rule. In 1696, a Pueblo raid killed over 25 colonists and friars. Vargas forced Indian allies to attack holdout towns and compel those in hiding to surrender, finally bringing the **Pueblo War for Independence** to an end. Hundreds of Pueblos fled, seeking shelter among Hopis and Navajos.

Excerpts from the Pueblo War of Independence

Royal Charters for New Jersey and Pennsylvania

As Pueblos gained control of New Mexico, Delawares (also known as Lenni Lenapes) watched thousands of Europeans stream into their lands. England staked claim to the area by conquering New Netherland, which gave Charles II more opportunities to reward supporters. In 1664, he granted title to land between the Hudson and Delaware rivers to two Carolina proprietors, John Berkeley and George Carteret, who named their venture New Jersey. Twelve years later, Berkeley sold his share to a London-based group of Quakers, an act that split the colony into East and West Jersey. **William Penn**, one of England's most famous Quakers, was the son of an English admiral and a royal advisor. Charles repaid a debt to the deceased father and sought to rid England of the dissenting son by granting land west of the Delaware to Penn. He named it Pennsylvania. New Jersey and Pennsylvania roughly followed models set by New Netherland and Carolina, with proprietors promising European immigrants religious freedom. In 1665, New Jersey's original proprietors also promised them a representative assembly and free trade within the English Empire, all of which attracted English from New England and eastern Long Island. Quakers and Baptists saw New Jersey as a place to worship freely. So did the ultraorthodox Puritans who despised them. Migrants from New Haven, unable to live with its merger with Connecticut, founded Newark in 1666. Soon Barbadians came, some with as many as 30 enslaved Africans. East Jersey's proprietors recruited hundreds of Scots after taking on Scottish partners in 1683. Each group of free immigrants settled among their own, creating an ethnic and religious quilt that barely cohered politically. The only issue that united the 7,000 Europeans who lived in East Jersey in 1700 was hatred of **quitrents**, an annual fee that proprietors demanded for use of land that colonists had cleared, built on, and believed should be entirely theirs (Map 3.4).

The Quaker proprietors of West Jersey and Pennsylvania persistently recruited immigrants. In 1682, about 2,000 Quakers landed in Pennsylvania, followed by another 6,000 over the next three years. By 1700, Pennsylvania had 18,000 colonists who hailed from all over the British Isles and central Europe. Penn had pamphlets printed in German and Dutch to advertise Pennsylvania's religious freedom, cheap land, and low taxes. Much of the colony's rapid population growth owed to American-born children, for many immigrants came as families. As in East Jersey, they usually settled near others who spoke and prayed as they did.

William Penn extols the virtues of Pennsylvania (1681)

A new model city, Philadelphia, linked Pennsylvania to the Atlantic world. Founded in 1682, the town had 2,000 residents by 1700. Penn hoped that Philadelphia

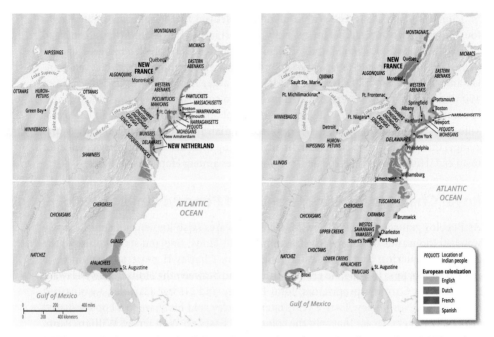

MAP 3.4 Missions and Colonial Settlements in Eastern North America, 1660 and 1700 The English conquest of New Netherland in 1664 and the founding of colonies in New Jersey, Pennsylvania, Delaware, and the Carolinas enabled the English to stake claim to colonize much of the eastern coast of North America from Maine to South Carolina by 1700.

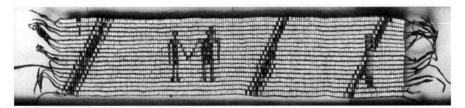

WAMPUM BELT GIVEN TO WILLIAM PENN It is believed that Delawares (also known as Lenni Lenape) gave this wampum belt to Penn to represent, record, and commemorate their treaty with him at Shackamixon (located in today's Philadelphia) in the early 1680s. Delawares often invoked the memory of Penn when they negotiated with Pennsylvania authorities during the colonial era.

would avert the fate of London, where fire and plague spread easily among the dense population. He oriented the city on a grid, with wide streets, room between low-rise homes to allow air to circulate and contain fires, and open space set aside for parks. The Philadelphia that emerged reflected little of his vision. Development sprawled along the Delaware River as merchants claimed valuable waterfront parcels. Land speculators and the artisans, shopkeepers, and indentured servants who streamed in made a dense urban environment of Penn's model city. So did merchants' ties to ports throughout the

English Atlantic, which spurred more immigration and anchored a growing trade in flour and other provisions to the West Indies.

Links to the West Indies helped slavery take root in Pennsylvania, even as some there expressed opposition to slavery. In 1688, a group of four Germantown Quakers petitioned the local Quaker meeting to end the colony's participation in the Atlantic slave trade and bar slavery within it. Slavery, they insisted, made Pennsylvania Quakers look like hypocrites, handed ammunition to their critics overseas, and discouraged European immigration. Quakers sent Pennsylvania's first antislavery statement to the Germantown Meeting, which forwarded it to a superior meeting; neither took a definitive stance. By 1700, some 3,000 Pennsylvanians, one in six, were enslaved and of African descent.

Pennsylvania's leaders cultivated amicable relations with Indians. This owed partly to Quaker principles of pacifism and justice. Penn negotiated land concessions with Delaware leaders personally, learned their language, and bought land from them on terms that they found agreeable. The Delawares saw such transactions as a way to maintain ties to Pennsylvania's rulers, whose support they needed to counter Iroquois influence. Penn achieved mythic status for Indians. They invoked his memory as they negotiated with Penn's successors and tried to hold them to the lofty example that they claimed he had set.

English North America's "Glorious" Revolutions

In the 1680s, political turmoil engulfed Europe once again and sent shockwaves across the Atlantic. When Charles II died in 1685, his brother James II became king of England. The next three years brought bitter disputes between James and Parliament over whose authority was supreme and over the king's embrace of Catholicism. When James suspended Parliament, his opponents feared the king would ally with France's Louis XIV to impose Catholicism and deprive them of liberty and property. Louis's persecution of Protestants fanned such fears. Over 100,000 Huguenots fled France. Many sought refuge in England, while over 2,000 journeyed to Massachusetts, New York, and South Carolina.

The Huguenots' ordeal incensed James's enemies in England. In 1688, they asked Prince William of Orange, the Dutch husband of James's Protestant daughter Mary, to intervene. A few months later he did, backed by an army of 15,000. William invaded less to save English liberties than to save the Netherlands from an English–French alliance. Parliament declared the throne vacant after James fled to France and then invited William and Mary to occupy it. The victors trumpeted James's abdication as a peaceful and bloodless "**Glorious Revolution**" that preserved English liberty, even though mob attacks and pitched battles claimed thousands of lives in England, Scotland, and Ireland over the next two years.

Colonists had reasons to bid James good riddance. He had hit planters' pockets by raising duties on sugar and tobacco, which had made those goods more expensive and decreased demand for them. He had created the **Dominion of New England** in 1685, modeling it on the Spanish system. The Dominion united eight contiguous colonies, from New England to New Jersey, under one governor, Edmond Andros, who dissolved representative assemblies; reduced town meetings to once a year; jailed dissidents; enforced the Navigation Acts; and barred Puritan congregations

interactive timeline

TIMELINE 1640–1693

AMERICA	YEAR	THE WORLD
Sugar boom begins on Barbados	1640s	
Puritan migration to New England halts	1642	English Civil War erupts
First colonial ship carrying enslaved Africans to North America docks in Boston	1646	
Apalachee rebellion in Florida	1647	
Iroquois attacks destroy Huron Confederacy Predecessor of New England Company founded to promote conversion of New England Indians	1649	Charles I beheaded; England becomes a commonwealth
First Navigation Act to regulate commerce of English colonies	1651	
First Anglo-Dutch War	1652–1654	
Rhode Island outlaws lifelong slavery for Europeans and Africans	1652	
Timucua rebel in Florida	1656	
	1660	Monarchy restored to England with crowning of Charles II
Barbados legislators create colonial English America's first comprehensive slave code Royal Society of London founded and colonists admitted as members	1661	
Virginia lawmakers decide that children should inherit their legal status from mothers rather than fathers	1662	
Proprietors receive English royal charter to Carolina Antecedent of Royal African Company granted monopoly to ship enslaved Africans	1663	
Second Anglo-Dutch War	1664–1667	
Aug English forces conquer New Netherland and rename it New York	1664	
Sep French raid on Mohawk country	1666	**Sep** Great Fire of London destroys over 13,000 buildings and properties
Jun Mohawks join rest of Five Nations in peace treaty with New France	1667	
Fundamental Constitutions of Carolina written	1669	
First permanent English settlement in South Carolina Hudson's Bay Company Founded	1670	

from using taxes to pay ministers. Most unsettling of all, the Dominion jeopardized land titles and required that their holders pay a quitrent on land that they had once owned outright.

Colonists in Massachusetts Bay, New York, and Maryland responded to news of the Glorious Revolution with violence. In April 1689, around 2,000 armed militiamen descended on Boston. Andros, guarded by 14 soldiers, surrendered. He and his closest advisors spent 10 months in prison before colonists sent them to England. In May, New York militias mutinied, forcing the lieutenant governor into exile. In Maryland, a group

AMERICA	YEAR	THE WORLD
Third Anglo-Dutch War	1672–1674	
Jul New York captured by Dutch and renamed New Netherland	1673	
Oct Dutch return New York to English control	1674	
Jun King Philip's War begins in southern New England **Jul** Doeg Indian raid into Virginia sparks Bacon's Rebellion **Sep** King Philip's War spreads to northern New England	1675	
Aug King Philip's War ends in southern New England **Oct** Bacon's Rebellion ends	1676	Beginning of Russo-Turkish War
Apr English colonies and Iroquois League establish Covenant Chain **Aug** King Philip's War ends in northern New England	1677	
Aug Pueblo War for Independence drives Spanish from New Mexico	1680	
Charles II grants Pennsylvania to William Penn	1681	
Mary Rowlandson's captivity narrative published Philadelphia founded Robert Cavalier de La Salle arrives at mouth of Mississippi River, claims watershed for France, and renames area Louisiana	1682	
Dominion of New England established	1685	James II crowned king of England
	1688	William and Mary crowned king and queen of England "Glorious Revolution" in England James II forced to abdicate throne
Revolts inspired by "Glorious Revolution" overthrow governments of Massachusetts Bay, New York, and Maryland **Apr** Dominion of New England terminated	1689	
King William's War	1689–1697	
Massachusetts granted new royal charter	1691	
Jan Salem witch crisis begins **Aug** Spanish forces begin to reconquer New Mexico	1692	
May Salem witch crisis ends **Nov** Spanish complete reconquest of New Mexico and end Pueblo War for Independence	1693	

called the Protestant Associators demanded that the governor and his council proclaim William and Mary as monarchs of England. They refused, so the Associators overthrew the governor and council and put them under house arrest.

Ironically, colonists helped to strengthen royal authority. Maryland and Massachusetts both accepted governors appointed by the English monarch. Massachusetts's 1691 royal charter also curbed religion's influence over politics. Property holding replaced church membership as one key qualification to vote. The Glorious Revolution tightened the political bond between England and its colonies.

North America's Hundred Years' War Begins

William and Mary's coronation triggered war in Europe and North America. In 1690, rebels in New York and New England sought to demonstrate loyalty to their monarchs and defend Protestantism by planning an invasion of Canada, an initiative that ended in fiasco and mutual recrimination. Canadian Mohawks and Abenakis, backed by the French, raided New York and northern New England, torching English towns and taking captives as colonists barricaded themselves behind ramparts. **King William's War** (1689–1697) marked New England's second devastating conflict in a generation. It struck when many were unsure of who had the right to govern them or on what terms. Massachusetts Bay still lacked a charter, so its rulers had no clear legal sanction to act.

The conflict sparked one of the last witch scares in the northern Atlantic world. In Salem, the terror of Abenaki attacks and uncertainty over who was in charge fed a panic that resulted in the execution of 20 and the accusation of nearly 200 on charges of witchcraft. The scare began in 1692 when Betty, the nine-year-old daughter of minister Samuel Parris, developed pains for which no doctor could find a physical cause. Tituba, an enslaved Arawak Indian from Guyana whom Parris purchased in Barbados and brought to New England, tried to end Betty's suffering by baking a cake that contained the girl's urine and feeding it to a dog. Popular belief held that the dog, whose form the witch had taken, would name the witch. Tituba was among the first women arrested. Her testimony convinced investigators that there were indeed witches in Salem who had made a pact with Satan. That, they thought, could explain the Abenaki raids and the symptoms that afflicted people, particularly young females, who implicated others, mostly women. Magistrates stopped prosecuting when a growing number of the accused were prominent figures rather than socially marginal ones—and when they began to doubt the evidence presented to them. Tituba eventually recanted her confession and was sold to someone who paid her jail fees.

Depositions from the Salem Witch Trials (1692)

King William's War had far bigger repercussions for Indians. It widened divisions within the Iroquois League. While most Iroquois were English allies, Mohawks were split—some favored the English, while others sought closer ties to the French. Pro-English Mohawk joined English invasions of Canada. These invasions were unsuccessful, but French forces guided by their Mohawk allies invaded Iroquoia, torched three towns, and headed north with 300 captives. Meanwhile, New France's governor encouraged Hurons, Petuns, and other victims of the Beaver Wars to avenge the Iroquois raids that in the 1640s and 1650s had forced them from their homelands. Besieged Iroquois leaders concluded that the English would never honor their promises of assistance and looked to negotiate peace with New France. King William's War ended in 1697 for colonists. It raged four more years for most Indians and devastated the Iroquois population. Thereafter, Iroquois diplomats strove for neutrality in the conflicts between the two European empires that claimed parts of the Northeast.

For the Boston minister Cotton Mather, King William's War gave New England a new sense of purpose. He considered the region a shield that defended the English world and Protestantism against France and Catholicism. For English and French colonists, the war made their corner of the world seem more important. The war tightened bonds between North America and the European monarchs at the dawn of the 18th century.

STUDY QUESTIONS FOR VICTORIOUS PUEBLOS, A NEW MID-ATLANTIC, AND "GLORIOUS" REVOLUTIONS, 1680 TO THE 1690S

1. What impact did the Glorious Revolution have on North America?
2. New York, New Jersey, Pennsylvania, and Carolina all became part of the English empire as a result of Charles II's coronation. Did these colonies have anything else in common? Please support your answer with specific examples.

quiz

Summary

- Through immigration, war, and the expansion of slavery, English colonies expanded in size and power relative to other colonies. The conquest of New Netherland and the founding of South Carolina opened more land to English settlement, while New England gained economic power by forging trade ties to Barbados, English America's largest slaveholding society.
- Colonial demand for animal pelts, slaves, conversion, and land unleashed new pressures in Indian country. Violence increased as Iroquois raids devastated their Indian neighbors and several other groups, seeking to regain power in a changing world, targeted colonists.
- Political instability in Europe and North America and colonial warfare with Indians led English and French imperial officials to seek tighter control over North American colonies. Spanish power was challenged by a successful Pueblo revolt in the Southwest and a crumbling mission system in the Southeast.

Key Terms and People

audio
flashcards

Articles of Capitulation 90
Bacon, Nathaniel 96
Bacon's Rebellion 96
Barbados slave code 85
Beaver Wars 78
Berkeley, William 81
Catherine/Kateri Tekakwitha 101
Charles II 81
Colbert, Jean-Baptiste 91
Cromwell, Oliver 79
Dominion of New England 107
Eliot, John 81
First Anglo-Dutch War 90
Glorious Revolution 107
Hudson's Bay Company 91
James, Duke of York (James II) 90
katsinas 104
King Philip's War 99

King William's War 110
Louis XIV 91
mercantilism 91
Metacom/Philip 99
Navigation Acts 88
New England Company 81
Parliament 79
Penn, William 105
Popé 102
Pueblo War for
    Independence 105
quitrents 105
Rowlandson, Mary 102
Royal African Company 90
Royal Society 98
Second Anglo-Dutch War 90
Society of Friends/Quakers 82
Timucua Revolt 87

Reviewing Chapter 3

1. How did global trade and transatlantic politics shape North America from the mid to late 17th century?
2. Was the Pueblo War for Independence a unique event in the history of colonial North America up to the 1690s? If so, why? If not, why not?
3. In what ways did patterns of migration to, from, and within North America change between 1640 and the 1690s? How did changing demography impact the continent?

Further Reading

Greer, Allan. *Mohawk Saint: Catherine Tekakwitha and the Jesuits*. New York: Oxford University Press, 2005. A superb account of Tekakwitha, Iroquois conversion to Christianity, and the challenges that she and other Mohawks faced during the mid to late 17th century.

Knaut, Andrew L. *The Pueblo Revolt of 1680: Conquest and Resistance in Seventeenth-Century New Mexico*. Norman: University of Oklahoma Press, 1995. A clear and concise account of the origins and legacies of the Pueblo War for Independence.

Menard, Russell R. *Sweet Negotiations: Sugar, Slavery, and Plantation Agriculture in Early Barbados*. Charlottesville and London: University of Virginia Press, 2006. An excellent explanation of the causes and consequences of the Barbados sugar boom.

Pagan, John Ruston. *Anne Orthwood's Bastard: Sex and Law in Early Virginia*. New York: Oxford University Press, 2003. A carefully crafted study of gender, indentured servitude, and the rise of an "American" body of legal thought in mid-17th-century Virginia.

Pestana, Carla Gardina. *The English Atlantic in an Age of Revolution, 1640–1661*. Cambridge, MA, and London: Harvard University Press, 2004. Presents the English Civil War as a transatlantic event that profoundly remade the English Empire.

Pulsipher, Jenny Hale. *Subjects unto the Same King: Indians, English, and the Contest for Authority in Colonial New England*. Philadelphia: University of Pennsylvania Press, 2005. Explores English–Native relations and their relationship to English imperial politics during the 17th century.

America in the World
GOODS, IDEAS, PEOPLE

CHAPTER 3: Forging Tighter Bonds, 1640–1700

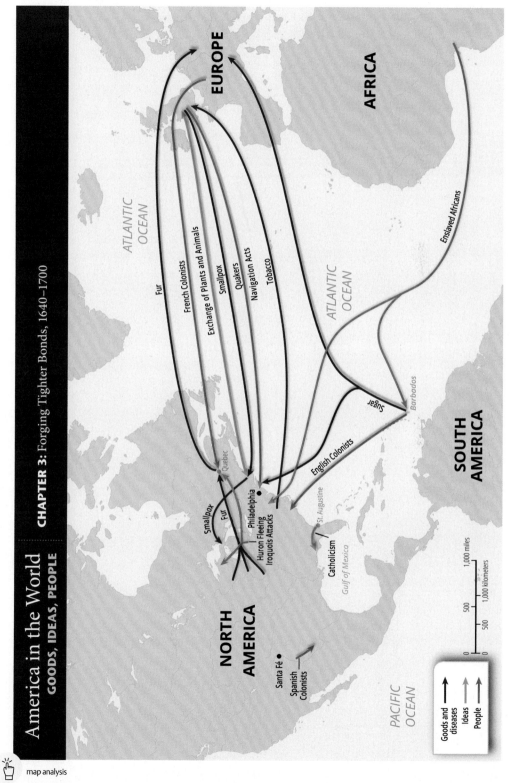

EUROPE

AFRICA

ATLANTIC OCEAN

Fur
French Colonists
Exchange of Plants and Animals
Smallpox
Quakers
Navigation Acts
Tobacco

Enslaved Africans

ATLANTIC OCEAN

Barbados

Sugar

English Colonists

SOUTH AMERICA

Quebec

Smallpox

Fur

Philadelphia

Huron Fleeing
Iroquois Attacks

St. Augustine

Catholicism

Gulf of Mexico

NORTH AMERICA

Santa Fé

Spanish Colonists

PACIFIC OCEAN

Goods and diseases
Ideas
People

0   500   1,000 miles
0   500   1,000 kilometers

map analysis

Tee Yee Neen Ho Ga Row (Hendrick Tejonihokarawa).

Accelerating the Pace of Change

c. 1690–1730

O n November 28, 1729, a group of Natchez Indians arrived at Fort Rosalie bearing corn, meat, and other gifts. The French commandant, Sieur de Chepart, felt grati-fied. Chepart was part of a wave of French settlers moving up the Mississippi valley to start plantations on rich Natchez farmland. A recent arrival, Chepart found that much of the best land was already taken, so he demanded that the Natchez give him one of their main towns, White Apple. Chepart declared that the people of White Apple must leave im-mediately, but the town council offered him a cut of the harvest if he would allow them to stay long enough for their crops to mature. When the Natchez arrived at Fort Rosalie, Chepart thought that they were holding up their end of the bargain, submitting to his demand.

But Chepart was mistaken. Once the Natchez were inside Fort Rosalie's gate, the assembled warriors dem-onstrated that they brought their arms not in prepara-tion for a hunt, as they had initially claimed, but rather to violently sever their relationship to the French. That day, Natchez warriors killed at least 229 colonists and captured 50 white women and children and over 300 African slaves. A few weeks later, two other Indian na-tions of the lower Mississippi valley, the Koroas and Yazoos, launched a similar surprise attack at Fort Pierre. Thus began the **Natchez War** of 1729–1731.

The conflict was rooted in the changing power dy-namics of the region. In 1699, the French claimed the mouth of the Mississippi by building a fort at Biloxi. By 1718, the French had added settlements at Mobile and New Orleans, but less than 400 French resided in the entire region. Indians were dominant, and the most powerful nation was the Natchez, who proudly main-tained their Mississippian traditions of mound building and chiefly rule. In the decade before the Natchez War, however, the colonial population of Louisiana skyrock-eted to 5,300. Most of the new arrivals were slaves from

Senegambia. The growth of plantations disturbed the Natchez, who, during the Natchez War, urged their African captives to rise up with them and fight the French.

Governor Étienne Périer feared that an African-Indian uprising would destroy French Louisiana. Seeking to divide the groups and instill fear among neighboring Indians, Périer deployed a company of free black militia to destroy the tiny Chaouachas Nation, which had not been involved in the Natchez War. Périer also sought to renew the French alliance with the Choctaws to the east. At that time, the Choctaw Nation had a much larger population than any nearby group—including the French—and they saw the Natchez War as an opportunity to extend their influence in the lower Mississippi valley.

The Choctaw alliance proved decisive, helping the French defeat the Natchez, Koroas, and Yazoos in 1731. The war destroyed the Natchez Nation—nearly 1,000 died. Some managed to escape to larger southeastern Indian nations like the Chickasaws and Creeks, but most of the survivors were taken as slaves by the French and then deported to Saint-Domingue to toil on sugar plantations.

The Natchez War reflected broader trends that were transforming North America. The growth of plantation agriculture accelerated the slave trade and produced racially divisive laws and policies. Settlers increasingly sought Indian land. Native responses varied: some declared war, while others redoubled efforts at alliance. Indians from vulnerable or displaced groups often sought inclusion in large Native nations that still dominated the interior of North America.

NATCHEZ INDIANS, C. 1725 Antoine Simon Le Page du Pratz, a French planter who lived among the Natchez, drew this sketch a few years before the Natchez War. It shows Natchez subjects carrying their leading chief, the Great Sun. This display of prestige and power was rooted in Mississippian ceremonialism, which was maintained by the Natchez into the 1700s.

⬦TRADE AND POWER

Between the 1690s and 1730, the growth of colonies and the expansion of trade shifted power dynamics among Native Americans. Native nations fought for access to horses and guns. Through trade, some nations managed to stabilize their populations and maintain or enhance their economic, political, and military power. However, competition over trade and the resources that fueled it also promoted violence among Indians from the Rockies east to the Appalachians, stoking an Indian slave trade that moved captives across the continent and altered Indian politics. The founding of new colonies in Texas and Louisiana accelerated these developments, empowering some neighboring Indian peoples at the expense of others and extending European claims into the interior.

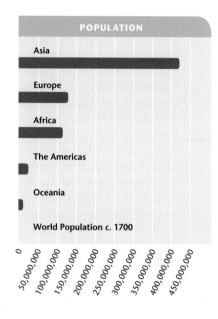

An Economic Revolution on the Plains

Colonialism unleashed a maelstrom of violence but also created opportunities that Native people sought to exploit. Before the arrival of Europeans, most Native people on the Plains made their living through farming. Bison hunting, which required communal hunts to drive herds from cliffs, was difficult and dangerous. But, by the early 1700s, Native peoples of the interior had acquired guns from French and British traders via the Mississippi valley and horses from Spanish and Pueblo settlements in the Southwest. While many Plains peoples still farmed, the availability of horses and guns transformed bison hunting into an attractive and lucrative lifestyle. Ailing from European incursions in the East and West, increasing numbers of Native Americans moved onto the Plains and revised their economies to focus on hunting bison, herding horses, and trade.

Among the arrivals were the Siouan-speaking Osages, who probably came from the Ohio valley and then settled in the Missouri and Osage valleys of what is now Missouri. They farmed but maintained a dispersed settlement pattern, which helped prevent the spread of European diseases. By the late 1690s, Osages had gained access to French trade goods through neighboring Illinois Indians. Seeking direct trade, Osage leaders welcomed French traders into their towns; many of these French traders married Osage women from prominent families. Once Osages secured privileged access to French trade, they blocked other tribes, dominating the region between the Mississippi valley and the eastern Plains. Bolstered by their large population—about 10,000—and superior arms, the Osage expelled many of their neighbors, including Wichitas and a portion of the Hasinai Confederacy. In fact, the Osages grew so powerful that they restricted colonial movement within the region and dictated trade terms to Europeans. Seeking alliance, the French and Spanish participated in Native diplomatic rituals that acknowledged Osage power.

Farther west, Comanches came to dominate the southern Plains. Their ancestors came from the Great Basin but moved to the northern Plains in the 1500s. For a time, colonialism had little impact on them, but a devastating epidemic struck in the late 1600s. The tribe splintered, and one faction—the Comanches—moved to the southern Plains. At that time, as a result of the Pueblo War for Independence, Indians gained unprecedented access to Spanish horses, which they began to trade among themselves. Comanches immediately recognized the potential of the horse. These "magic dogs," as Comanches initially called them, enabled warriors to travel eastward to trade with their Wichita allies for French guns and other goods. Taking advantage of their environment, Comanches grazed their growing herds on abundant prairie grass. They bred their own horses—hardy African Barbs originally from arid North Africa—and added to their herds through trade and raiding. By the 1760s, Comanches had displaced another powerful Native group, the Apaches, and built what one historian has called a "Comanche Empire" that encompassed a quarter of a million miles. No Native or European power seriously challenged Comanche dominance until the mid-1800s (Map 4.1).

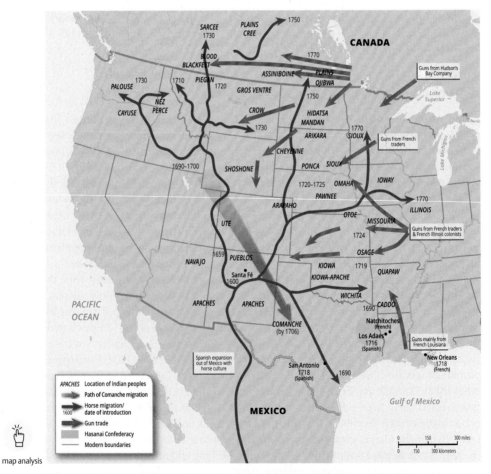

map analysis

MAP 4.1 Horses and Guns Enter the Great Plains, c. 1600 to c. 1770 Horses entered Indian country from the Southwest via Spanish colonists. Meanwhile, French traders from Louisiana and New France played a crucial role in introducing firearms to Plains peoples.

APACHE PICTOGRAPH, RATTLESNAKE CANYON, TEXAS Comanche raids forced many Apaches to seek shelter in Spanish missions, where they came under friars' supervision. Resentful Apaches who fled the missions painted the mission church as a friar whose upraised arms suggest church towers and whose hands are crosses. Note the arrow piercing the friar's body.

Farther north, Teton and Yanktonais Sioux gradually entered the Great Plains from Minnesota in the late 1600s, partly to hunt bison, but mainly to hunt beaver to trade to the French for firearms and other imports. As these Sioux depleted local stocks of beaver, they headed west, displacing less well-armed peoples such as the Omaha, Cheyenne, Missouri, and Iowa. By the 1740s, agricultural peoples along the Missouri River had impeded their expansion. However, the mobility that horses afforded the Sioux enabled them to dodge smallpox epidemics that devastated agricultural villagers. By the time Lewis and Clark arrived in 1804, the Sioux dominated the northern Great Plains.

While the trade in horses and guns enhanced the power of some Indian nations, it came at a cost. Rising powers weakened Native neighbors—sometimes even colonial neighbors—blocking their access to trade goods or forcing them to move. Conflict produced wars that became increasingly deadly thanks to firearms. Victors often sold captives to their Indian or European allies. Pawnee villages in Nebraska served as way stations for captives from the southwest and northern Plains. So many captives came from this region that French and Spanish colonists called any enslaved Indian who came to them from the Plains "Panis" (Pawnee) well into the 1700s. Some ended up in the Great Lakes or South Carolina. Others went to New Mexico or the Caribbean. Comanches sold some prisoners of war, including Indians and Mexicans, but they retained thousands of others, whom they put to work tending their horse herds or processing bison hides. The expansion of the global economy into the Plains increased violence among Native peoples and contributed to a continental Indian slave trade.

Accommodation in Tejas and the Southwest

In 1685, the French began to construct a fort near the Gulf coast. Spanish officials fretted that their French rivals might win over Indian customers and imperil Mexican silver mines and Spanish commerce in the Gulf. In the early 1690s, the French challenge and the Pueblo War for Independence spurred the Spanish to establish a mission and *presidio* (a fort) within the Hasinai Confederacy, a group of Caddoan-speaking towns in eastern Texas and western Louisiana. The Spanish knew the Hasinai as "the Tejas," the Caddo word for "ally." They anticipated success, as "Tejas" people seemed to worship one God and were skillful farmers who, in the words of the Spanish, had "civilization and government like the Mexican Indians."

By 1693, Hasinai had forced the Spanish to leave, largely because the newcomers would not follow Hasinai gender norms. Hasinai delegations to other peoples normally included women and children to convey peaceful intentions. The Spanish party that founded Texas was composed entirely of men, but it marched under a banner that depicted the Virgin Mary, symbolic leader of the Spanish campaign to evangelize Texas. Hasinai interpreted the strangers' display of a woman's image as a sign of peace. But Spanish soldiers soon began to assault Hasinai women, so they threw the Spanish out. The Spanish were unlike the French men who had arrived a decade earlier. The French had come alone rather than in heavily armed groups, and they had married Hasinai women who afforded them membership in a society organized around matrilineal clans. Failure to obey Hasinai ways and an inability to meet Hasinai demand for imported goods curbed Spanish influence.

In 1716, however, the Hasinai permitted the Spanish to construct a presidio and missions at a new outpost, Los Adaes. Hasinai people welcomed the Spanish as long as they behaved well and provided an alternative source of goods. Spanish officials tried to honor Hasinai values by recruiting families to settle in Los Adaes but found few takers. Celibate friars baffled Hasinai. Hasinai men relied on their wives, society's farmers, to provide food for the family as well as visitors. Without wives or other female kin, the priests could not feed themselves and thus drained Hasinai resources. Missionaries failed to convert a single Hasinai, so they abandoned the mission. Some Spanish colonists, however, remained behind, marrying Native women and adopting many aspects of Hasinai culture. The Hasinai and their Spanish kin prospered by supplying Louisiana with livestock and their Indian neighbors with French goods, particularly firearms.

Mission
Nuestra
Señora de
la Purísima
Concepción
de Acuña
(1716)

The Spanish also entered south Texas. In 1718, they founded missions and a presidio at San Antonio de Béjar, today's San Antonio. The small village attracted diverse bands of Indians from the lower Rio Grande valley who, like the Spanish, sought protection from Plains Apaches. Apache raids on San Antonio were so frequent that local officials begged for more colonists to help defend it. Their pleas fell on deaf ears until 1731, when 55 colonists arrived, increasing San Antonio's Hispanic population to 300 and Texas's to 500.

San Antonio remained a tiny Hispanic outpost surrounded by powerful Indian nations. Plains Apaches settled in river valleys where they could farm and pasture horses, making them tempting targets for Comanches and Utes. Apaches raided San Antonio to replace horses and to avenge colonists' enslavement of hundreds of their kin captured by Utes and Comanches or taken in Spanish-Pueblo raids.

Slaving raids also had a profound impact on Navajos. Navajos had offered refuge to hundreds of Pueblos who fled the Spanish. Pueblo refugees shared their weaving skills with Navajos. Soon, the Navajo economy depended on raising sheep and weaving wool into blankets and textiles. Navajos sometimes raided New Mexico for sheep. Retaliatory Spanish-Pueblo incursions between 1705 and 1709 took Navajo captives and forced Navajos to leave Spanish livestock alone.

Growing Navajo dependence on sheep had profound environmental and social consequences. By the 1720s, sheep had overgrazed canyons in northwestern New Mexico, which prompted Navajo people to move west in search of fresher pastures. Raising sheep also threatened to divide Navajo society into those who owned large flocks and those who did not. Rustling outsiders' flocks offered a way for poorer men to acquire sheep and ease tensions among the Navajos. So did new rituals. The Blessingway, which today forms the basis for Navajo ceremonialism, most likely emerged during the 1750s. It emphasizes reciprocity and gift giving, with the wealthier assuming responsibility for care of the less fortunate.

During this period, colonists and Pueblos in New Mexico found ways to compromise. After the reconquest, Pueblos accepted Spanish rule, helped to defend the colony, and joined in Spanish raids in exchange for more autonomy and Spanish protection from Indian foes. Governors still required Pueblo men to construct public buildings, maintain irrigation systems, and work Spanish officials' fields, while Pueblo women performed domestic labor, ground wheat and corn, and baked bread. But Indian leaders of each town determined who should serve when. Pueblo dignitaries and medicine men, not missionaries, chose town leaders, and friars intervened less frequently in Pueblo society. Hispanics and Pueblos had settled into an uneasy alliance, largely as a consequence of the Pueblo War for Independence and their mutual dependence in the face of Apache and Comanche raids.

Indians, the French, and the Making of Louisiana

In the 1690s, a decade after La Salle claimed Louisiana, the French sought to strengthen their influence in the mid-continent. They hoped to counter rising British power in the East and confine the Spanish to the Southwest while securing a route from New France to French colonies in the Caribbean. Within a few decades, the French had founded a string of small settlements along the Gulf coast near the mouth of the Mississippi River: Mobile, Biloxi, and New Orleans.

Initially, Louisiana's small colonial population relied heavily on its Native neighbors. The lower Mississippi valley was then dominated by many small Indian nations—the French called them "petites nations"—including the Bayagoulas, Chitimachas, Koroas, Ofogoulas, and Tensas. At first, the tiny French colonial population meant that Louisiana, too, was a "petite nation." Unable to feed themselves or mount an army, the French gratefully entered into an alliance network that connected many of the petites nations. In exchange for food, furs, and military protection, Louisiana gave the petites nations access to European trade goods, including firearms, which helped them combat slave raiders and other enemies.

By the 1720s, however, Louisiana's colonizing strategy had shifted. Louisiana's population grew tenfold, to over 5,000, mostly due to the forced migration of African slaves and French convicts. Louisiana's economy also moved away from the New France model, which emphasized trade with Indians, and toward plantation agriculture. In the lower Mississippi valley, the French started to grow tobacco, hoping to emulate British success in the Chesapeake. Farther up the Mississippi, French farmers settled among the Illinois Indians. Some moved to the ancient Native city of Cahokia and grew wheat in the shadow of Mississippian mounds. They, like other French farmers in the Illinois country, helped feed growing French colonies in the lower Mississippi valley and the

image
analysis

INDIANS AND AFRICANS ON A NEW ORLEANS LEVEE, 1730s An enslaved Fox woman, barrels of liquor, and bundles of deerskins occupy the foreground. An enslaved African boy and an Attakapa hunter stand to the right. He holds a calumet (peace pipe), used in Indian diplomatic rituals throughout the region. The scene illustrates Louisiana's dependence on Indians and Africans.

Caribbean. By 1731, French Illinois was exporting more than 100,000 pounds of flour, which, as one official exclaimed, was "as fine as any in France."

Agriculture, unlike the fur trade, did not require alliances with Native Americans. In fact, as the French expanded their farms, they demanded more and more land from their former allies. This conflict became most pronounced in the lower Mississippi valley, where the growth of plantations led to the Natchez War of 1729–1731. The Koroas and Yazoos sided with the Natchez, while several other petites nations remained allied to the French. However, the region's most powerful polity—European or Indian—was the Choctaw Nation.

A nation of about 20,000, Choctaws were by far the biggest group in the region and could field the largest army. An alliance with the French enabled Choctaws to secure firearms to combat their English-armed enemies, the Chickasaws. Moreover, the Choctaw Nation, well to the east of Louisiana, was not disrupted by Louisiana's agricultural expansion. Choctaw warriors turned the tide of the Natchez War, but Choctaw military strength intimidated the French. Louisiana's governor, exasperated by his dependence on Indians, requested more troops so that he could enhance French power in the region. Instead he lost his job. **Louis XV**, fed up with bad news from Louisiana, took control of the colony in 1731 and then mostly ignored it. Imperial neglect and a sharp decline in immigration ensured that the colonial population of French Louisiana remained small. In the decades after the Natchez War, the French revived alliances with the remaining petites nations while relying on the Choctaws for military protection.

Slaving Raids, Expansion, and War in the Carolinas

To the east, people from Virginia and European immigrants moved deeper into Carolina, establishing small farms and new settlements. In 1710, the colony was divided into North Carolina and South Carolina. Although South Carolina did not depend on Indians as much as Louisiana did, the colony needed them to supply two exports: deerskins and slaves. Indian hunters provided deerskins, which Europeans used for leather. Indian warriors captured people and traded them to the English colonists in Carolina, who shipped most of them to New England and the West Indies. Some enslaved Indians had trudged from as far as the northern Plains and the Southwest, but most came from southeastern peoples allied with France or Spain whom English-allied warriors had seized.

Slaving raids engulfed the Indian Southeast, spreading disease to populations weakened by warfare and displacement. Dozens of South Carolina soldiers accompanied thousands of Indians, most of them Creek, in a wave of attacks on Apalachee missions in northern Florida. They killed hundreds, enslaved thousands, and reduced Florida's missions to ashes between 1702 and 1706 (Map 4.2). Five years later, Tuscarora

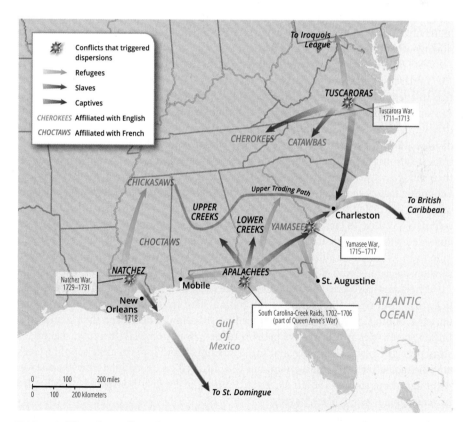

MAP 4.2 War, the Indian Slave Trade, and the Dispersal of Southeastern Indians, c. 1700–1730 Epidemics, demand for Indian slaves, and English and French invasions of Indian lands devastated the Southeast's Indian peoples. This map charts the movements of four peoples—Apalachees, Tuscaroras, Yamasees, and Natchez—dispersed by conflicts with European colonists and Indians affiliated with them.

people retaliated for slaving raids and colonists' encroachment on their lands by attacking farms and towns in North Carolina. South Carolina troops joined Catawba, Yamasee, and Cherokee forces that killed or enslaved about 1,000 Tuscaroras and won the **Tuscarora War** (1711–1715).

Peoples who suffered slaving raids often split apart. Some Tuscaroras stayed in North Carolina after the war ended. About 2,000 others fled northeast; they found shelter alongside fellow Iroquoian speakers, becoming the sixth nation of the Iroquois League. Some mission Apalachees relocated near St. Augustine for protection. Others sought refuge among other Indians in present-day Georgia and Alabama. Some Indians fled deep into Florida, with Indian slave raiders in hot pursuit. In 1711, nearly 300 Florida Indians boarded ships for Cuba, which offered them refuge.

South Carolina's leading role in the Indian slave trade tarnished its relationship with neighboring Indian nations. So many Indians left Charleston in chains that the port exported more slaves than it imported until 1715. Many also remained in South Carolina, where, by 1710, 25 percent of white households owned at least one Indian slave. Many southeastern nations felt cheated by traveling English traders licensed by the colony. Yamasees were particularly resentful. They had been allies to South Carolina for three decades, but by the early 1710s, they were deeply indebted to English merchants. Some traders became abusive, enslaving Yamasees to satisfy debts and committing other crimes like rape and battery.

In 1715, Indian grievances against South Carolina turned violent. On April 15, Yamasees sparked the **Yamasee War** (1715–1717) by killing South Carolina's Indian agent Thomas Nairne. Nearby nations, including the Creeks, Savannahs, and Apalachees, joined the Yamasees, and together they destroyed dozens of plantations, driving most of South Carolina's population to huddle in fortified Charleston. More distant allies of the Yamasees—Choctaws, Cherokees, and Catawbas—severed their trade relationships with South Carolina by killing most English traders residing in their villages. South Carolina's leaders begged for help from Virginia and Indian allies. Economic factors led Cherokees to reconsider their position and, ultimately, side with colonists, a decision that brought Cherokees into conflict with Creeks. In exchange for colonists' promise to emancipate their kin, some Tuscaroras and other Carolina Indians sided with the English. The English–Indian alliance won the war but not before it killed 1 in 16 South Carolina colonists and hundreds of Native warriors. Many Yamasee survivors were enslaved, and the rest fled to Florida.

Watercolor showing Choctaws, 1730

The Yamasees were defeated, but they succeeded in reforming English trade practices that resulted in the decline of the Indian slave trade. Fearful of another Indian uprising, South Carolina and many other English colonies decreased their demand for Indian slaves. Meanwhile, Native peoples turned away from slave trading, seeking instead peaceful forms of alliance making. The English and Indians alike sought to reestablish trade after the Yamasee War, but they focused on deerskins rather than slaves. Although thousands of Indian slaves still served in English households, the English increasingly turned to black slavery.

The Yamasee War reshaped Native American politics by accelerating nation building. Decades of war, slaving, and disease had destroyed the Mississippian chiefdoms that once dominated the Southeast. Groups of survivors, seeking to retain power in the face of colonial encroachment, formed diverse nations that were multi-ethnic and multilingual. Some, like the Chickasaws and Catawbas, had a population in the low thousands, but others, including the Cherokee, Choctaw, and Creek, were much larger than neighboring colonies. Native nations used their power to negotiate favorable treaties and trade deals. In the aftermath of the Yamasee War, the Creek Nation, for example, pursued a policy of neutrality, refusing to participate in colonial wars while maintaining diplomatic and economic ties with the English of Carolina, the French of Louisiana, and the Spanish of Florida. By pursuing multilateral strategies, nations like the Creeks were able to stabilize their populations and enhance their political power.

Iroquois Hegemony and Concessions in the Northeast

Indian politics in the Northeast and Great Lakes also managed to stabilize, thanks largely to two treaties signed by Iroquois leaders, known together as the "**Grand Settlement of 1701.**" In one, Iroquois people, decimated by King William's War, agreed to cease hostilities with Great Lakes peoples and exchange captives with them. The French guaranteed the Iroquois hunting and trading rights west to Detroit, which the French founded in 1701. Through the other treaty, Iroquois retained the right to trade at Albany. The Iroquois League also promised to remain neutral in future Anglo-French wars.

Conflict over trade with Great Lakes peoples and conflict within the Iroquois League nearly unraveled the "Grand Settlement." The French had hoped that they would be able to monitor relations between Iroquois on the one hand and on the other Ottawa, Potawatomi, Wyandot, and Ojibwa, thousands of whom accepted a French invitation to resettle near Detroit. This brought these French allies closer to sources of British goods, such as coarse woolen cloth, blankets, and kettles, which tended to be cheaper, more abundant, and better suited to Indian tastes than similar French imports. The most direct path to those British goods was through Iroquois territory, and in 1707 Iroquois leaders granted Great Lakes Indians permission to travel to Albany. As trade dried up at Montreal, the French intervened in the Iroquois League's internal affairs, enraging a large faction of Mohawks.

Those Mohawks decided to take sides in **Queen Anne's War** (1702–1713). This conflict originated in Europe as a dynastic dispute, pitting Austria, Holland, and Britain against France and Spain. In North America, however, Indian people like the Mohawks joined the fight to further their own political and economic goals. In 1709, Mohawks agreed to join an invasion of Canada that British officials later canceled. The following year, three Mohawks and a Mahican traveled to London, where the "Four Indian Kings" (as the London press called them) met Queen Anne to lobby for a British invasion of Canada. Their efforts initially bore fruit. In 1711, Britain sent more than 5,000 troops across the Atlantic, the largest British military force yet to reach the Americas, to join New England and New York militiamen in an attack on New France. A storm off the coast of Canada ran nine ships aground, claiming over 700 lives and prompting the British to scuttle the mission.

By 1717, the Iroquois had agreed that neutrality was their best course. Tuscaroras driven north by British colonists helped to maintain that consensus, especially after the Iroquois admitted them to their league in 1722. Iroquois forces directed their wars for captives at peoples such as Catawbas and Cherokees and negotiated with British colonies to ensure that their warriors could travel freely to and from the Southeast.

Meanwhile, the French struggled to keep the Iroquois from taking sides in wars in the Great Lakes that involved their Indian allies. Peoples friendly to the French sought to drive a wedge between the Iroquois-allied Fox and the French, fearing that a French–Fox alliance would deprive them of trade goods. It helped their cause that New France had legalized Indian slavery in 1709 to meet colonists' growing demand for labor. Skillful diplomacy and "gifts" of Fox slaves persuaded the French to side against Fox in three wars (1712–1716, 1723–1725, and 1728–1735). Fox peoples numbered several thousand when the **Fox Wars** began but only a few hundred when the wars ended. The rest escaped to Iowa or were killed, adopted by their enemies, or enslaved by the French. Some Fox slaves deemed too dangerous were sent to the West Indies. The war chief Kiala and his wife (captors did not record her name) were auctioned in Martinique in 1734. No planter would bid on them for fear that they might incite a rebellion among African slaves, so the couple was deported to South America.

Peace between the Northeast's three main powers—British, French, and Iroquois—displaced weaker Indians. By 1722, Pennsylvania officials had accepted Iroquois claims that they spoke for Delawares and Shawnees. The arrangement enhanced Iroquois power, partly because it provided the league's peoples with an alternative source of British goods. But Delawares and Shawnees had their lands in eastern Pennsylvania sold out from under them. They headed west, where they began to upset the region's delicate balance of power in the 1740s.

The stability that Iroquois people carved out came at a high cost. They alienated some Indian allies while depending on Europeans for trade goods. In the 1720s, the Iroquois permitted the French and British to construct rival forts and trading posts near Lake Ontario. These diverted western Indians' trade and flooded Iroquois villages with cheap alcohol, eliciting requests that the sale of rum be banned west of Albany. "You may find graves upon graves along the Lake," said one protester in 1730, all "occasioned by Selling Rum to Our Brethren." Meanwhile, New York encroached on Mohawk country. The colonization of Iroquoia, the Northeast's preeminent Indian power for generations, had begun.

STUDY QUESTIONS **FOR TRADE AND POWER**

quiz

1. In what ways did horses and guns change life for Indians on the Plains and in the Southwest?

2. What impact did the Indian slave trade have on North America?

3. What was the Great Settlement of 1701? How did it reshape northeastern North America?

⊘ MIGRATION, RELIGION, AND EMPIRES

Indians' grip on eastern North America weakened in part because tens of thousands of enslaved Africans and European immigrants flooded in. As slavery grew, white colonists developed increasingly racist attitudes and laws. Meanwhile, European immigration, along with increasing transatlantic ties among Protestants who sought American converts and a more powerful British Empire, bound North America more tightly to the Atlantic world.

The Africanization of North America

Colonial North America expanded rapidly in the early 1700s, largely as a result of forced African migration through the slave trade. More Africans landed in North America in the first decade of the 18th century than had done so between 1565 and 1690. They represented some of the nearly 70,000 enslaved Africans who together comprised the majority of immigrants to North America between 1691 and 1730.

The intensification of the Atlantic slave trade destabilized African politics and coincided with major economic changes in Africa. In 1704, a popular Christian movement erupted in West Central Africa that sought to end years of civil war between competitors for the throne of Kongo. The movement temporarily halted the flow of thousands of captives into the Atlantic slave trade. However, King Pedro eventually captured the throne and sold most of the members of the movement into slavery. Meanwhile, gold production tailed off near the Gold Coast in the late 1600s. Warring states in the region needed to pay for firearms and gunpowder to equip armies, so the streams of captives were sent to the coast. The Gold Coast exported over 330,000 people between 1690 and 1730.

Excerpt from Jean Barbot, A Description of Coasts of North and South Guinea (1732)

Most captives suffered alienation long before boarding a slave ship. Separated from kin and village, captives were viewed as conquered peoples as they traveled to the coast. There European traders imprisoned them in "slave castles," sometimes for months. Captives then endured a long voyage across the Atlantic, shackled together and confined below deck. About one in five did not survive it. Merchants and captains, especially of British ships, gradually improved survival rates over time, though they were driven more by a desire for greater profit than for humanitarian reasons.

North American colonies remained a relatively small market for the Atlantic's vast and rapidly growing slave trade (Map 4.3). Most enslaved Africans were shipped to the Caribbean or Brazil. North American colonists purchased only 5 percent of the Africans exported to the Americas and 10 percent of those carried in British ships. Enslaved people came to North America from all parts of Africa, but those who landed in North America between 1691 and 1730 departed from ports in Senegambia or the Bight of Biafra.

Although more than two-thirds of the Africans shipped to North America between 1691 and 1730 arrived in Virginia or Maryland, the market for them extended to all the British and French colonies. South Carolina and Louisiana began to import Africans in large numbers in the 1720s. Over 3,000 enslaved Africans disembarked in northern British colonies between 1691 and 1730, including hundreds who arrived in New York from Madagascar in the 1690s. Another 6,000 arrived in New England, New York, and Pennsylvania via the West Indies (Figure 4.1).

Expanded cultivation of tobacco stoked North American demand for enslaved labor. Tobacco exports from Maryland and Virginia to Britain nearly tripled between 1705 and 1730. Louisiana imported thousands of Africans between 1717 and 1731, as planters tried and failed to make the colony a tobacco exporter that could compete with the Chesapeake and Brazil.

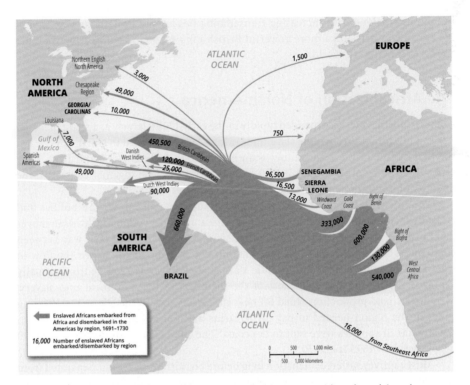

MAP 4.3 The Atlantic Slave Trade, 1691–1730 This map provides a broad American perspective on the Atlantic slave trade. About 69,000 enslaved Africans landed in North America between 1691 and 1730, about twice as many as between 1641 and 1690. More than half arrived in the 1720s. But over 95 percent went elsewhere in the Americas, mostly to the Caribbean or Brazil.

Meanwhile, the expansion of rice cultivation made South Carolina a major destination for enslaved Africans. Carolina planters began to grow the crop in the 1690s, and by the 1720s, the knowledge, skill, and labor of thousands of recently arrived Africans had enabled South Carolina to export millions of pounds of rice a year.

Regional differences shaped Africans' lives in North America. Slaves did not comprise 20 percent of Virginians until 1710. Chesapeake planters bought so many Africans from different parts of the continent that it was hard for slaves to find a common language other than English. The presence of more American-born slaves meant that there were more enslaved black women in the Chesapeake than anywhere else in North America, so relatively more enslaved men could find partners and start families. By contrast, South Carolina and Louisiana had African majorities by the 1720s. Most who arrived in both colonies during that decade came from Senegambia, increasing the odds that they would meet someone who spoke their language or shared their memories of home.

For many Africans, North American slavery brought profound social isolation and an early grave. Colonists considered Africans dangerous and brutish, partly because they did not speak or understand English or French. As many as one in four succumbed

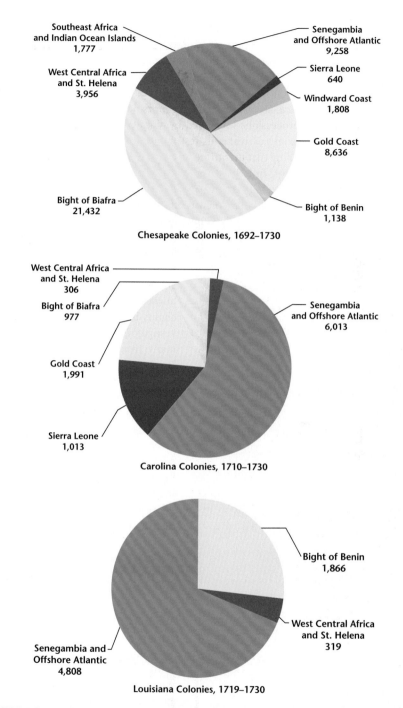

FIGURE 4.1 **Regional origins of enslaved Africans disembarked in regions of North America (estimated), 1692–1730** Enslaved Africans sent from ports in the Bight of Biafra composed nearly half of those brought directly to the Chesapeake colonies between the 1690s and 1730, while those who left Africa from Senegambia comprised the majority of those sent directly from Africa to South Carolina and Louisiana.

to disease and died within a year of arrival. Africans combated alienation by adapting beliefs and practices of their homelands, many of which centered around honoring their dead. For most Africans, death initiated the soul's journey from the material world to the realm of spirits and ancestors. Those who died without kin risked becoming ghosts doomed to haunt the living. Only a proper funeral ensured that the soul reached its final destination and found peace, so friends and neighbors acted as kin to the deceased. They sponsored funeral processions—followed by singing, dancing, drumming, and feasting—to celebrate the soul's arrival at its resting place. These rituals alarmed colonists. Virginia officials, fearing that nighttime funerals would enable slaves to conspire, tried to ban them in the 1680s. In 1699, slaves in Philadelphia protested that their long days of work did not allow them to finish burials before sunset. Still, Africans continued to maintain their traditions and honor their dead. Tobacco pipes often accompanied those buried in Virginia during the early 1700s, a practice common in West Africa.

Some Africans violently resisted enslavement. In 1712, some four dozen slaves set fire to a building in New York City and attacked the whites who came to extinguish the blaze, killing nine and injuring several more. Officials hanged 20 slaves, burned 3 at the stake, and hoisted 1 in chains until he starved to death. Investigators concluded that the rebels, many from the Gold Coast, sought "to destroy all the White[s] in order to obtain their freedom." The rebels prepared for battle as if they had been in Africa by binding one another to secrecy "by Sucking the blood of each Others hands," while some rubbed a powder on their clothing in the belief that it would make them invulnerable.

Meanwhile, Virginia masters had nightmares of slave conspiracies. They claimed to have uncovered six between 1709 and 1731. In 1729, a dozen runaways tried to create a sanctuary for themselves. Governor William Gooch ordered it destroyed to save Virginia from "a design which might have proved as dangerous" to whites "as is that of the Negroes in the Mountains of Jamaica." Gooch likened the runaways to Jamaican **Maroons**, participants in a form of resistance long common in the Caribbean and Brazil.

Many British colonists, alarmed by the rapidly growing numbers of Africans among them, tried to restrict

JAMAICAN DRUM Sir Hans Sloane obtained this drum in Jamaica while visiting there in the early 1700s and noted that it had come from Virginia. Someone brought the drum from Africa to Virginia, where enslaved Africans likely used it for funeral rites that helped them forge a sense of kinship and community.

the Atlantic slave trade. In Boston, Judge **Samuel Sewall** and merchant **John Saffin** debated the slave trade in the early 1700s. Sewall charged that the Atlantic slave trade was immoral and that it endangered whites because Africans took the place of "Men that might make Husbands for our Daughters" and would "remain in our Body Politick as a kind of extravasat [alien] Blood." Saffin countered with Anglo-America's first militant defense of the Atlantic slave trade and slavery. The Bible and the Atlantic world provided examples, he insisted, which indicated that God had decreed that some were to rule while others were "to be born Slaves, and so to remain during their lives." Pennsylvania lawmakers responded to the 1712 New York revolt by imposing a tax on each imported slave. Eleven years later, Virginia legislators imposed a duty on imported Africans to pay for a militia that would protect against possible slave rebellions.

The "Naturalization" of Slavery and Racism

The tens of thousands of enslaved people brought to North America between the 1690s and 1730 accelerated the growth of slavery in the British colonies and Louisiana. So did the births of thousands of children to enslaved women. Meanwhile, British colonists and French imperial officials, alarmed by a rapidly growing black population, enacted laws that codified slavery and enshrined racism throughout North America.

African and African American women in the Chesapeake reared the first large generation to be born into slavery in North America. In the early 1700s, an American-born slave woman usually conceived her first child by the time she was 19. She could expect to give birth to nine children, six of whom might survive past age four. By the 1730s, the Chesapeake colonies were home to the first enslaved population composed mostly of native-born people of African descent.

Chesapeake masters' desire to cut costs helps to explain why they promoted the growth of slave families. The Chesapeake Bay was farther from Africa than any other major market for enslaved Africans, which increased what Chesapeake masters paid for those brought directly from Africa. An enslaved African faced a high chance of dying soon after arrival and had to learn basic English to understand commands. Anglo-American masters also believed that American-born slaves were more intelligent, better suited for skilled labor, and less likely to rebel than Africans. In 1724, Hugh Jones, an Anglican clergyman in Virginia, contrasted Africans with American-born slaves who "talk good English, and affect our language, habits, and customs." Maryland and Virginia planters also encouraged the formation of slave families by buying more African women during the 1720s.

The growth of slavery spurred the creation of slave codes throughout colonial North America. In 1726, Pennsylvania became the last British colony founded during the 1600s to pass a comprehensive slave code. Meanwhile, Louisiana colonists mostly ignored North America's first imperially mandated slave code issued in 1685. In 1724, Louis XV explicitly extended the **Code Noir** to cover the French West Indies to Louisiana. The Louisiana Code Noir directed masters to provide slaves with a minimum amount of food and clothing as well as access to religious instruction. Slaves were to be baptized and married; married slaves had the right to stay together. Virtually all these provisions went unenforced. Free people of color had more success claiming rights under the Code Noir. The Code Noir afforded free people of color many rights that free whites enjoyed, including the right to petition officials and testify in court. They quickly used such rights to get a discriminatory tax abolished. But the 1724 Code Noir also discriminated against free people of color by banning interracial marriages and imposing fines on parents of mixed-race children. French officials hoped to ensure that Louisiana would not become like the French Caribbean, where a growing population of mixed-race people stoked racial anxiety in Europe.

The Code Noir was part of another wave that swept North America in the 1690s and early 1700s—the desire to draw a clear color line. Discouraging private **manumissions** was one way to limit the ranks of free blacks. By 1729, every northern British colony had made slaveholders financially responsible for freeing their slaves by requiring them to post bonds to ensure that freed people would not become a burden on taxpayers.

The new laws discouraged manumissions and made life harder for free blacks. The slave codes of New York and New Jersey prohibited former slaves from owning real estate. Pennsylvania's slave code empowered local officials to sentence free black "loiterers" to at least one year's service and make indentured servants of children born to free black women. Virginia and South Carolina disenfranchised black men in the 1720s and Virginia reimposed a tax on free black women. The colony's governor thought that lawmakers should "fix a perpetual Brand" on free blacks because he saw them as troublemakers who might try to emancipate others.

Prohibitions on interracial sex were crucial to guarding the color line. In 1705, Massachusetts outlawed marriage between people of African and European descent. That same year, Virginia's slave code decreed that unwed white mothers of biracial children should pay a fine or serve a five-year indenture, whereas free whites who chose to wed a black partner were to be fined and spend six months in prison. North Carolina criminalized interracial sex for white women in 1715. A Pennsylvania law passed in 1700 made black male rape of a white woman a capital offense, but there was no penalty for raping a black woman.

The press reinforced the color line. In 1718, *The Boston News-Letter* published a story in which a white vigilante in Connecticut sliced off the genitalia of a black man who the vigilante claimed was about to rape a white woman. The paper's editors celebrated his deed, which they thought sent an unmistakable message to "all Negroes meddling with any White Woman." Collectively, new racial laws and attitudes sought to promote white supremacy, divide interracial families, discourage manumissions, and minimize rights for free people of color.

European Immigrants and Imperial Expansion

In contrast to Africans, most Europeans who came to North America between 1690 and 1730 did so voluntarily, with the vast majority going to British colonies. Stronger commercial, personal, and institutional ties between British North America, Britain, and German-speaking Europe helped to determine who went where and when they arrived; so did political changes, including the **Acts of Union**, which created the United Kingdom by merging the kingdoms and parliaments of England and Scotland in 1707.

The Acts of Union opened the British Empire fully to Scots. A Scot in New York, Samuel Vetch, touted the expansion of British North America as a way to knit the new

United Kingdom together. He led a transatlantic campaign that advocated using British soldiers to conquer Canada and colonizing Nova Scotia with Scots. Soldiers from New England and Britain succeeded in taking Nova Scotia for the British Empire during Queen Anne's War, but most of it remained in the hands of French Acadians and Micmac Indians for decades. The 1,300 Scots who landed in North America between 1710 and 1730 mostly settled elsewhere, but they had a greater impact on British colonies than their numbers would suggest (Table 4.1). Many royal governors were Scots. Scottish doctors trained at the University of Edinburgh dominated the ranks of elite physicians in British North America and linked the colonies to scientific networks in Britain and Europe.

Immigrants from southern Ireland and Ulster (northern Ireland) comprised a much larger stream of people to North America between 1690 and 1730. Most migrants from southern Ireland came as indentured servants and landed in the Chesapeake colonies or Pennsylvania. Ulsterite migration was largely a byproduct of that region's linen trade. The **Linen Act of 1705** encouraged the export of Irish linen to North America. In turn, linen manufacturing in northern Ireland boosted demand for flaxseed (the source of linen) that New England and Pennsylvania farmers grew. Overdependence on linen, rent increases, and crop failures between 1718 and 1729 prompted thousands of Ulsterites to set sail to North America (Table 4.1). The linen–flaxseed trade provided a way to get there. Emigrants boarded ships that had come to Ireland with bulky cargoes of flaxseed and were returning to the colonies with lighter and more compact linen. Passages were relatively inexpensive, so most Ulster migrants could pay their own way and travel as families. Most Ulsterites settled in Pennsylvania.

Table 4.1 Estimated European Migration to British North America by Ethnic Group and Compared to Enslaved African Migration, 1700–1729

Over two-thirds of migrants who arrived in English/British North America between 1700 and the 1720s were enslaved Africans. The vast majority of European immigrants were not English, the first time that had happened in the history of English/British colonization of the Americas.

DECADE	GERMANS	ULSTER IRISH	SOUTHERN IRISH	SCOTS	ENGLISH	WELSH	OTHER	AFRICANS	TOTAL
1700–1709	100	600	800	200	400	300	100	12,900	15,400
1710–1719	3,700	1,200	1,700	500	1,300	900	200	10,500	20,000
1720–1729	2,300	2,100	3,000	800	2,200	1,500	200	30,500	42,600
TOTALS	6,100	3,900	5,500	1,500	3,900	2,700	500	53,900	78,000

Note: "Germans" refers to German speakers, not to people who came from what is today Germany. "Africans" refers to people brought via the Atlantic slave trade from Africa who disembarked in British North America. "British North America" does not include Nova Scotia or the Caribbean.

Meanwhile, thousands of Germans headed for North America. They came in three waves. The first arrived between 1683 and 1709, mainly to escape religious persecution. They came from many parts of German-speaking northern and central Europe and sailed for Philadelphia, drawn by William Penn's promises of religious freedom, pamphlets published in German, or letters from kin or from fellow believers who had already emigrated. The second wave of German immigration occurred between 1709 and 1714 and hailed mainly from what is today southwest Germany, an area ravaged by Queen Anne's War. Most migrated to New York or North Carolina as participants in large planned colonization ventures. The third wave was the largest. Triggered primarily by overpopulation and land scarcity, it also originated mainly in southwest Germany and lasted from 1717 until 1775. Like Ulsterites, most Germans settled in Pennsylvania, while a small number went to Louisiana in the 1720s.

British colonists had mixed reactions to the Ulsterite and German immigrants. In New England, the minister **Cotton Mather** at first celebrated Ulsterite immigration as a way to bolster local defenses against French and Indian foes. He soon changed his mind, however, declaring that the Presbyterian newcomers had "most indecently and ingratefully given much disturbance to the peace of our churches." In Pennsylvania, James Logan, provincial secretary in the late 1720s, worried that the Irish might soon "make themselves Proprietors of the Province," whereas the Germans might ensure that "these colonies will in time be lost to the Crown." Sometimes such sentiments turned violent. In 1729, a Boston mob prevented a ship of Ulster immigrants from landing, charging that the "confounded Irish will eat us all up."

Although most Europeans chose to sail to North America, thousands came against their will. The Spanish, British, and French empires sent convicts to work in their colonies. Many of the hundreds who went to Florida in the early 1700s had been prisoners in Spanish and Mexican jails. They manned the fort that guarded St. Augustine. English officials sentenced Scottish and Irish rebels to servitude in North America or the West Indies on various occasions during the 1600s. A similar fate befell some 500 Scots who in 1715 participated in the **Jacobite Rebellion** against the crowning of **George I**. The governor of South Carolina purchased some and sent them to fight the Yamasee War.

Worries about surging crime led Parliament to make colonial servitude a tool of Britain's criminal justice system. The **Transportation Act of 1718** mandated exile to North America for terms ranging from seven years to life for those convicted of crimes ranging from theft to receipt of stolen goods to capital felonies. Most convicts sent to North America had committed property crimes. A few were violent offenders. At least 3,000 had come from Britain and Ireland by 1730, the first of 50,000 to be transported to North America before 1775.

Convicts played a significant role in the colonization of Louisiana. Most Europeans who went to Louisiana before 1763 arrived between 1717 and 1721 and were prisoners or indentured servants, bound to serve the Company of the Indies for three years. In 1720, inmates at a Paris prison rioted and 50 destined for North American bondage escaped. Louis XV soon declared that there would be no more forced deportations to Louisiana. Few chose to go to Louisiana, where disease and, to a lesser extent, warfare quickly claimed many lives. In 1726, Louisiana census takers counted 2,300 Europeans, including 300 indentured servants. Five years later, there were 2,000. Immigration to French Louisiana, like that to New France in the 1660s

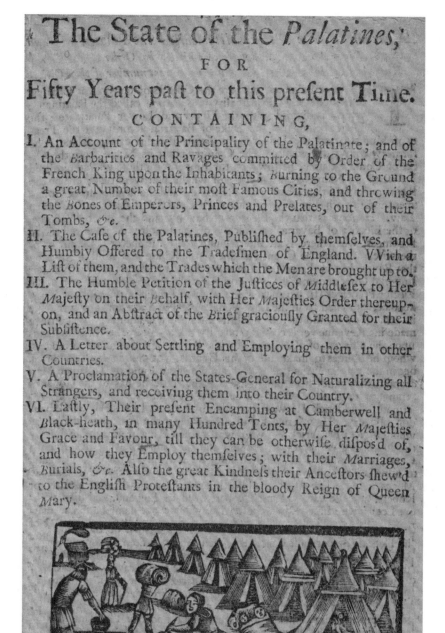

The State of the *Palatines,*

FOR

Fifty Years paſt to this preſent Time.

CONTAINING,

I. An Account of the Principality of the Palatinate; and of the Barbarities and Ravages committed by Order of the French King upon the Inhabitants; Burning to the Ground a great Number of their moſt Famous Cities, and throwing the Bones of Emperors, Princes and Prelates, out of their Tombs, &c.

II. The Caſe of the Palatines, Publiſhed by themſelves, and Humbly Offered to the Tradeſmen of England. With a Liſt of them, and the Trades which the Men are brought up to.

III. The Humble Petition of the Juſtices of *Middleſex* to Her *Majeſty* on their Behalf, with Her *Majeſties* Order thereupon, and an Abſtract of the Brief graciouſly Granted for their Subſiſtence.

IV. A Letter about Settling and Employing them in other Countries.

V. A Proclamation of the States-General for Naturalizing all Strangers, and receiving them into their Country.

VI. Laſtly, Their preſent Encamping at Camberwell and Black-heath, in many Hundred Tents, by Her *Majeſties* Grace and Favour, till they can be otherwiſe diſpos'd of, and how they Employ themſelves; with their Marriages, Burials, &c. Alſo the great Kindneſs their Anceſtors ſhew'd to the Engliſh Proteſtants in the bloody Reign of Queen *Mary.*

PALATINE REFUGEE CAMP IN LONDON, 1709 Some 15,000 Germans fled war-torn areas of the Rhine valley for London, lured by rumors that they would be resettled and granted land in North America. Many ended up in refugee camps like this one located near London, from which they were transported to North Carolina and upstate New York.

and 1670s, was brief and concentrated. Europeans did not return in significant numbers until Spain took charge of the colony in the 1760s.

European immigration left a profound mark on North America. It helped France cling to the middle of the continent. It pushed the boundaries of British North America outward as Ulsterite and German immigrants settled new lands. It also reinforced British colonists' ties to an Atlantic Protestant network that had mobilized partly to counter what it perceived as a global Catholic threat.

Pietism and Atlantic Protestantism

In 1710, Cotton Mather, New England's most prominent minister, published *A Discourse Concerning Faith and Fervency*. It was one of his contributions to **Pietism**, a Protestant movement that linked North America, Britain, the Netherlands, and central Europe. Pietists promoted the personal piety of believers and the evangelization of all, including American Indians and enslaved Africans.

Pietism drew from many sources. These included English Puritanism, Anglicanism, and Dutch Calvinism. Pietists affiliated with Germany's University of Halle and the Church of England played crucial roles in spreading Pietism's principles overseas. Halle faculty influenced many German and Dutch pastors in New York, New Jersey, and Pennsylvania. Meanwhile, Anglican reformers in London founded the **Society for the Propagation of the Gospel in Foreign Parts (SPG)** in 1701. It focused on sending missionaries to North America and the West Indies.

Seal of the Society for the Propagation of the Gospel in Foreign Parts

The SPG devoted much of its attention to enslaved Africans. But SPG missionaries persuaded few masters that conversion would make for more obedient slaves. Pietists like Francis Le Jau in South Carolina usually blamed planters for their lack of success, claiming that they unduly limited access to slave audiences. But SPG advocates did not realize or did not acknowledge that their own message often discouraged Africans from converting. Le Jau required slaves seeking baptism to swear that they were not doing so to press masters to free them. Converts also had to promise to abandon **polygamy**, a marriage pattern found in many parts of West Africa. Missionaries also requested that enslaved converts devote part of each Sunday to attending services, the day they customarily had for themselves and one that they often spent trying to grow more food.

Some Anglicans confirmed masters' worries about the risks of evangelizing slaves. In 1729, James Blair, a Virginia clergyman, noted that some slaves converted because they believed that "Christianity will help them to their freedom." The following year, some slaves who were questioned concerning a rumored slave rebellion cited their conversion as justification. A few also claimed that George II had "ordered all those slaves free that were Christians." They linked conversion to Christianity and royal authority to their yearning for freedom.

Puritan and SPG missionaries evangelized Africans and African Americans in northern cities. In 1693, Cotton Mather founded the Society of Negroes in Boston. Mather invited slaves, with masters' permission, to meet at his home every Sunday, where he preached against drunkenness, stealing, and disobedience. Mather further promoted evangelization of slaves by publishing *The Negro Christianized* in 1706. Meanwhile, Elias Neau, an SPG missionary to New York City, operated a school that attracted as many as 1 in 10 black New Yorkers. Few were able to attend regularly, but still they kept the catechism books that they had been given, hoping to learn to read.

The visit of the "Four Indian Kings" to London encouraged English Pietists to pay more attention to Indians. A mission to a Mohawk village enjoyed modest success before the SPG shut it down in 1719. Indian disinterest ensured that other SPG missions fared as poorly or worse. The same was true for most New England ministers who worked under the auspices of the New England Company.

Pietists were responding to French Jesuits' efforts among Abenaki groups in Maine. New England, they contended, was a key front in the battle to preserve British and Protestant liberty from French and Catholic tyranny. That struggle, British North Americans believed, also bound them more tightly to the British Empire and to the monarchs who headed it.

Imperial Authority and Colonial Resistance

Starting in the late 1600s, royal supervision of colonial British North America intensified, as did imperial efforts to regulate its economy. Colonists tried to skirt rules that they deemed contrary to their interests and promoted those that they thought served them well. In the process, their ties to their monarchs, the British Empire, and the Atlantic world grew stronger.

Royal authority played a bigger role in British colonists' lives in many ways. Monarchs began to appoint governors for New Jersey, Nova Scotia, South Carolina, and North Carolina between 1702 and 1729, bringing 9 of the 13 British mainland colonies under royal rule. By the 1720s, many colonists' homes contained mass-produced images of British royalty. Celebrations of royal holidays dotted the calendars of major port towns, which by 1740 staged at least six such events a year, including royal birthdays and coronation anniversaries. The most raucous was November 5th, Pope's or Guy Fawkes Day. It commemorated the discovery of a Catholic plot to blow up Parliament. **Pope's Day** processions featuring the display (and sometimes burning) of papal effigies were common in port towns by the late 1690s. In 1702, Bostonians added an effigy of **"the Pretender"**—the Catholic Stuart who claimed the British throne during the 1715 Jacobite Rebellion—to the festivities. This practice spread throughout British North America. Colonists' enthusiasm for such rituals expressed their growing desire to be recognized as Britons who were loyal subjects and partners in a global battle against what they saw as a Catholic menace.

As British colonists celebrated their monarchs, imperial officials claimed more power over their commerce. In 1696, William III created the **Board of Trade**, an advisory council charged to oversee colonial matters. The creation of this board testified to the colonies' growing significance to England's economy. In 1700–1701, colonists in British North America and the West Indies comprised just over 10 percent of the market for goods England exported and produced almost 20 percent of the value of goods it imported. The Board of Trade implemented a series of **Navigation Acts** to tighten regulations on colonial trade and established **vice-admiralty courts** in the colonies to enforce the law.

Between 1700 and 1730, the Royal Navy and the vice-admiralty courts waged a war on piracy that colonists increasingly supported. Pirates had long found shelter in colonial ports as good customers who often paid in scarce silver or gold. However, the end of Queen Anne's War sparked a growth of piracy. As the Royal Navy was demobilized, mariners' wages were cut and thousands lost their jobs. Many turned to piracy. As many as 5,000 pirates operated between 1716 and 1726. They increasingly targeted ships belonging to colonial merchants. Such ventures could be lucrative, but they were also dangerous. In 1700, Parliament passed the first effective empire-wide law to combat piracy. It mandated the death penalty for those convicted of piracy or for aiding and abetting pirates.

Some pirates, driven from the Bahamas, sought sanctuary in North Carolina. Their leaders included Edward Teach, better known as Blackbeard. In 1718, a fleet of British, Virginia, and South Carolina vessels killed Teach and captured many of his associates, who were tried, convicted, and hanged. A similar fate befell hundreds more as colonial officials, naval officers, and vice-admiralty judges throughout North America tightened the noose on piracy, at times stringing up the condemned by the dozen. By the late 1720s, the British Empire had won the war on piracy, making the Atlantic safer for commerce that its leaders considered legitimate.

Securing raw materials for the Royal Navy that defeated the pirates also proved to be a challenge. As Britain's forests receded from overcutting, its shipbuilders became dependent on timber and naval stores (tar, pitch, and turpentine—used mainly to preserve and waterproof ships) from Sweden and Russia. The Navy especially needed timber for ship masts. Vast forests of white pine in Maine and New Hampshire seemed the solution to their problem. By 1717, North America made over half of England's tar and pitch. A series of laws enacted between 1691 and 1729 barred New England lumbermen and mill owners from cutting down and exporting

HANGING OF MAJOR STEDE BONNET Bonnet was a Barbadian planter who turned to piracy in 1717, preying on shipping along the Atlantic coast of North America and in the Caribbean. Captured along the North Carolina coast, he was convicted by Charleston's vice-admiralty courts and executed in 1718.

mature white pines that the Royal Navy wanted to reserve for its masts. Colonists, often aided by corrupt officials, dodged the regulations. In 1734, gunshots and a mob turned away one official eager to uphold the law in New Hampshire. The Royal Navy had better luck at encouraging colonists to make naval stores by offering them financial incentives.

The challenges facing imperial officials illustrate key developments in the relationship between Britain and its North American colonies. Colonists could defy or ignore laws that they found onerous, often with the complicity of those charged to enforce them. Historians have called this arrangement "**salutary neglect**" and claim that it characterized the colonial–imperial relationship into the 1760s. Colonists also kept tabs on events in Britain and forged ties to prominent figures there. Although North Americans never wielded as much influence in London as their West Indian counterparts did, they often steered policies and politics to suit their purposes.

Factions of colonists enlisted contacts in London to fight local political battles, often targeting royal governors. One campaign centered around Edward Hyde, Viscount Cornbury, governor of New York and New Jersey. Cornbury's efforts to consolidate imperial authority and strengthen the Church of England won him enemies on both sides of the Atlantic: prominent colonists, members of the Whig Party in England, and English Protestants who were not Anglicans. Colonists accused Cornbury of corruption, charges that gained traction in London as the power of Cornbury's Tory (the party that opposed the Whigs) allies waned. Between 1707 and 1709, three colonists asserted, probably falsely, that Cornbury had often appeared in public in New York dressed in women's clothing. He was removed from office, his reputation in England in tatters.

Colonists' transatlantic lobbying undermined many royal governors. Because high rates of land ownership enabled them to vote, male colonists in North America exercised more political power than their British counterparts. Colonists elected assemblies composed of wealthy men who jealously guarded their powers to tax and budget and frequently deprived governors of funds. Such bodies increasingly viewed themselves as mini-Parliaments obliged to defend and preserve what they understood to be British liberties against what they deemed arbitrary executive power. Colonists professed adoration for kings and queens, but they often showed contempt for those whom monarchs appointed to govern them.

GOSSIP MONGERS Putative portrait of Edward Hyde, Viscount Cornbury. Cornbury, who served as governor of New York, acquired many enemies there. Some spread rumors in England that Cornbury wore women's clothing publicly. This portrait was painted in England, probably in the early 1700s, and is most likely of a woman. Decades later, people in England began to claim that it was of Cornbury.

New York, Madagascar, and Indian Ocean Piracy

Around 1680, pirates began to leave the Caribbean, their base for over a century, to dodge naval patrols. They set out in search of easier pickings. By 1690, a base in Madagascar gave them easy access to the Red Sea and Indian Ocean. Pirates often targeted a fleet that sailed between India and Mocha, an Arabian Peninsula port on the Red Sea that exported coffee.

New Yorkers helped to establish European piracy in the Indian Ocean. Like other North American port cities, New York welcomed pirates, who needed food, clothing, alcohol, and ship repairs and paid for them with scarce gold and silver. During the 1680s, New York merchants had learned that they could reap even bigger profits by shipping supplies to the Indian Ocean and charging pirates for the convenience.

Economic and political changes intensified New York's ties to the Indian Ocean piracy in the early 1690s. King William's War disrupted New York's economy, and the high unemployment that followed tempted some mariners to turn or return to piracy. After the colony's new governor, Benjamin Fletcher, took office in 1692, he granted pirates refuge, often using his official powers to designate them "privateers" and line his own pockets. Fletcher's council consisted largely of merchants who traded with pirates. One councilor, Frederick Philipse, employed an agent in Madagascar who sold clothing, naval stores, firearms, ammunition, and liquor to pirates and local rulers. The local rulers handed war captives over to pirates, who sold them to Philipse's agent along with gold, silver, spices, and Indian textiles they had stolen. Rum sold in Madagascar for up to 30 times what it cost in New York, while slaves could be bought in Madagascar for a

STUDY QUESTIONS FOR MIGRATION, RELIGION, AND EMPIRES

quiz

1. In what ways and by what means did slavery and racism expand in North America during the early 1700s? In what ways did enslaved Africans adjust to their new lives in North America?

2. What impact did Pietism and growing royal authority have on British North America?

◉ LAYING FOUNDATIONS IN BRITISH NORTH AMERICA

Unprecedented levels of involuntary immigration and stronger ties to transatlantic networks transformed colonial North America. Colonial British North America's economy grew and diversified, financing the emergence of a native-born elite that could fraction of the price on Africa's Atlantic coast. Philipse shipped hundreds of Madagascar slaves to New York during the 1690s.

Events in the Indian Ocean, London, and New York severed New Yorkers' ties to Madagascar. Pirate attacks on ships belonging to subjects of India's Mughal Empire created a crisis for the **East India Company (EIC)** and England. Mughals imprisoned company employees and threatened to throw the EIC out. Meanwhile, Parliament passed the East India Act in 1698 to cement the firm's monopoly on English commerce in the Indian Ocean. London officials also cracked down on piracy by recalling Fletcher. His replacement, the Earl of Bellomont, denounced piracy as "not only injurious to the Honour of his Majesty, and the English Nation, but also highly prejudicial to the Trade of England." Bellomont ordered that illicit cargoes be confiscated. Some local officials defied him by helping to smuggle illegal goods into town. Philipse sent a ship to Delaware Bay to meet a vessel arriving from Madagascar. It offloaded most of the contraband and headed to Hamburg to sell it. Philipse tried to sneak East Indian cargo into New York, but officials confiscated it. He was removed from the council. Philipse died in 1702, leaving over 90,000 acres of land, city real estate, slaves, and a small fleet, a fortune built largely on trade with pirates.

Two important precedents had been set: ties between colonial merchants and pirates could be cut, and imperial officials had demonstrated that they would act on the EIC's behalf against colonists' interests. In the 1770s, that became a major issue for colonists who drank tea provided by the EIC.

- Why did New Yorkers help to establish European piracy in the Indian Ocean? Why did English officials seek to sever their ties to Indian Ocean pirates in the 1690s?
- What relationship did the campaign to cut New York's ties to Indian Ocean pirates have to the British Empire's broader war on piracy during the 1700s?

more easily imitate its English peers because of improvements in shipping and communication that kept colonists abreast of events across the Atlantic and within the colonies.

An Industrious Revolution

By 1730, colonists in British North America had laid a foundation for the economic development of what would become the United States in response to overseas and domestic markets. Households diversified the range of goods that they produced and services that they provided. Their Anglo-American version of a transatlantic "**industrious revolution**" enabled colonial British North America to take significant steps toward industrialization and created market-oriented societies that relied more heavily on enslaved labor and devalued the voices and skills of white women (Map 4.4).

The English Civil War had forced New England colonists to pursue a wider variety of ways to earn a living to narrow the region's trade deficit. Most continued to scratch out a living on small farms, while others fished or cut timber for export. Migration to

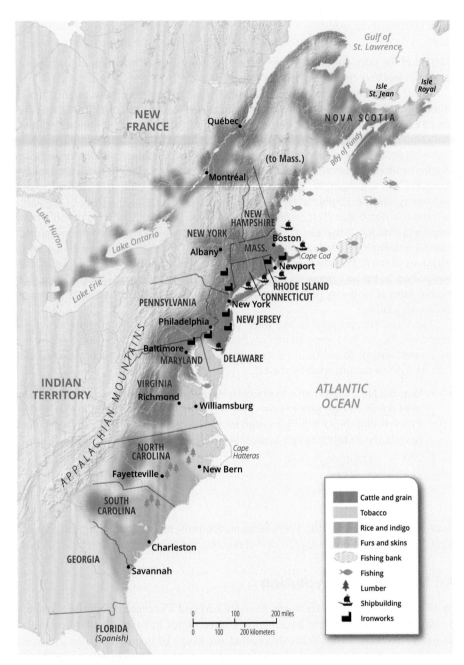

MAP 4.4 The Economy of British North America, c. 1750 The industrious revolution of the late 1600s and early 1700s made British North America a major supplier of ships, iron, rice, and naval stores to Atlantic markets and rapidly expanded grain and meat exports, much of which went to the Caribbean, Spain, or Portugal.

areas recently conquered from or ceded by Indians enabled New England to accommodate a growing and mostly native-born population—86,000 strong by 1690, and over
200,000 by 1730. Expansion enabled the majority of these households to be economically independent.

New Englanders responded by working harder and diversifying their labor. This
was particularly true in coastal or densely populated areas. Fishermen journeyed farther out to sea to catch more cod, which they processed on board rather than returning
immediately to port. Whalers began to pursue their prey into the deep ocean. Meanwhile, more young men left home in hopes of becoming financially independent sooner.
Some toiled on neighbors' farms, while others took up a trade such as blacksmithing,
tanning, or shoemaking. Women and girls who churned butter, grew vegetables, and
operated a growing number of spinning wheels in rural New England often secured a
household's place in an expanding market economy.

Two developments marked the commercialization of New England's economy. One
was use of paper money, introduced to ease the scarcity of coin. Massachusetts first
issued paper money in 1690 as an emergency measure to finance wartime spending. By
1712, its government had declared that paper could be used to pay private debts. Prominent Boston merchants and their creditors in England were incensed. They feared that
debtors would repay loans, pegged to the value of silver or gold, with paper that would
become worthless. Officials tried to blunt such objections by issuing paper money
backed by mortgages on land. Paper money soon became one of the most controversial
issues in colonial politics.

The other key development was the growth of manufacturing. Shipbuilding soared
during the late 1600s and early 1700s in port cities and towns. The imperial wars that
ravaged New England's borders fed demand for ships throughout the Anglo-Atlantic.
Shipbuilding further diversified the region's economy and knit it more tightly together.
Shipyards created work for loggers and millworkers as well as for carpenters, joiners,
and caulkers who crafted vessels and kept them seaworthy. Investors bought shares in
ships, local firms insured them, and thousands of local men sailed them. By the early
1700s, New England shipbuilders competed with peers in New York and Philadelphia.
Colonists built the vessels that plied the Atlantic Seaboard, linking the mainland to the
West Indies. By the Revolution, one-third of the ships known to the insurer Lloyd's of
London had been launched from North America.

The Chesapeake colonies' economy initially relied heavily on tobacco. However,
overproduction and war lowered the value of tobacco between 1680 and 1720. To stay
afloat, planters and farmers diversified their products, cultivating more wheat and raising more livestock. Abundant rivers and bigger grain harvests encouraged investment
in water-powered mills to grind grain into flour. Clusters of mills gave rise to new towns
such as Norfolk and Baltimore.

Diversification brought an early form of industrialization. By the 1720s, planters
and English investors were operating iron furnaces and forges near the shores of the
Chesapeake Bay. Ironworks demanded enormous amounts of land, capital, and labor.
The iron business attracted planters in part because it could employ indentured servants and slaves all year round. American-made iron served as ballast on ships that
carried tobacco to Britain and could substitute for imported Swedish iron there. Colonial ironmasters soon discovered that they had a bigger market locally than overseas.
By 1750, the center of iron manufacturing had shifted north to Pennsylvania. By the

Revolution, British North America made one-seventh of the world's raw iron and was its third-largest producer, an accomplishment that owed largely to thousands of slaves who staffed ironworks.

Enslaved labor played an indispensable role in the development of British North America's economy. Slaves enabled the expansion of tobacco production in the Chesapeake and the exponential increase in rice production in South Carolina. By the 1730s, enslaved men, almost all American born, filled many skilled positions in ironworks in the Chesapeake. They were part of a growing contingent of enslaved tradesmen on plantations and in port cities as planters and urban artisans looked to cut costs. The labor and expertise of enslaved craftsmen enriched masters, strengthened slavery, and helped it to expand. Such opportunities sharpened inequality among slaves, as trades remained virtually off-limits to African-born men and to women.

Meanwhile, white women found themselves increasingly cast to the sidelines of the economy and the legal system. The diffusion of paper money and growing use of promissory notes as paper money facilitated the marginalization of women. English common law allowed only property holders to sign promissory notes. Yet women rarely owned property, as their husbands were recognized as sole owners of all marital property. Women's legal participation declined, and their voices carried less weight in court. Fewer wives helped to draw up wills, and fewer widows administered husbands' estates.

The expansion and diversification of British North America's economy also widened the gap between rich and poor. Most of the benefits ended up in the hands of those best positioned to profit from Atlantic ties: urban merchants and large planters. They used their growing fortunes to distinguish themselves from other colonists.

A Creole Elite Pursues Gentility

Starting around 1660, England's merchants began to build stylish townhouses in cities, while its gentry, lesser aristocrats, remodeled country houses or built new ones according to the latest fashions. New standards of beauty, speech, dress, body carriage, and personal conduct arose. Three decades later, British North America's wealthiest strove to be genteel, modeling themselves on their English counterparts, and by the early 1700s, an American-born elite had adopted and adapted transatlantic norms of gentility. By the Revolution, colonists who wished to be considered gentlemen and ladies—prominent merchants and planters, clergy, professionals, judges, and officials—were expected to follow the rules of "polite society."

Three developments heralded gentility's arrival in British North America and helped to disseminate it. One was the courtesy book. Intended principally for children and adolescents, courtesy books instructed readers on codes of conduct. These books admonished children to mind their table manners and stay clean when they played. They sought to inculcate deference to social rank, control over one's body, and regard for others' feelings. "Polite" people were gracious, elegant, and restrained individuals who did not offend or embarrass others.

Another sign of gentility was drinking tea, which the East India Company (EIC) purchased in China and shipped to Britain. Around 1690, women of means in England began to gather in the parlors of urban townhouses and country estates to converse and drink tea. Etiquette required that hostesses buy a teapot, containers for sugar and cream, tongs, teaspoons, cups, and saucers as well as tea and sugar. By the 1720s, white women of means in the colonies had made "tea tables" the principal vehicle for spreading ideas about manners and taste.

The mansion house also hastened and symbolized the rise of gentility in North America. The Virginia mansions differed from the homes they replaced in many ways. They contained several rooms and were two stories rather than one. The first floor was principally for entertaining guests. It provided the stage for wealthy planters to host dinners and dances that displayed their gentility. Mansions were designed to conceal the labor that sustained their privileged inhabitants. Kitchens and laundries, operated mainly by enslaved women and supervised by planters' wives, were moved to separate buildings. Erected on bluffs and surrounded by landscaped gardens, the mansions trumpeted their owners' wealth and power.

The Wren Building, Williamsburg, Virginia (1695)

Colonial mansions reflected a more assertive and native-born Chesapeake elite. By the 1690s a clear majority of the region's prominent families were American born. They consolidated their power through intermarriage over the next few decades. Elites laid out new capitals at Annapolis in the 1690s and Williamsburg a decade later, housing the institutions of provincial government in stately brick buildings. In 1693, they chartered the College of William and Mary, British North America's second institution of higher education.

Improved Communications

In 1690, a prominent English immigrant complained of Virginia, "We are here at the end of the World, and Europe may be turned topsy turvy ere we can hear a Word of it." Forty years later, fewer in British North America would have shared his frustration. Improved communication had accelerated and broadened the flow of information across the Atlantic and throughout British North America.

Heavier maritime traffic disseminated news more quickly and conveniently. The number of ships that traveled between England, North America, and the West Indies increased sharply, with the total number entering Boston harbor nearly tripling between 1688 and 1730. Intercolonial coastal trade grew even more spectacularly. The number of vessels docking in Boston from other British North American ports multiplied eight times between the late 1680s and the late 1720s.

Overland travel was much slower and more expensive, but colonists as well as the British government took steps to improve it. Mail began to move more rapidly overland after colonists launched a delivery service between Boston and New York in 1673. The service expanded in the 1690s to all of New England and Philadelphia, but it was so expensive that relatively few could afford to use it. Britain, however, crafted new policies designed to improve communication infrastructure in the colonies. Especially important was the Postal Act of 1711, which created a unified mail system that linked North America to England, Ireland, and Scotland.

Printed information reached more people as colonists began to publish their own newspapers. In 1704, *The Boston News-Letter* became British North America's first established newspaper. Its publisher, John Campbell, was Boston's postmaster, which enabled him to get the paper to rural subscribers and boost demand for postal services. Campbell modeled his paper after *The London Gazette*, copying its format, publication schedule, and much of its content, while adding shipping lists, reports from meetings with provincial officials, and news gathered from mariners and correspondents in other colonies. *The News-Letter* provided little local coverage, focusing mainly on foreign news that interested merchants. Campbell soon had competitors in Boston, Philadelphia, New York, and other major cities.

Colonial newspapers became a forum for debating matters of local interest as publishers began to vie for readers. The *Courant* immediately took sides in the biggest controversy raging in Boston—whether residents should be inoculated against

PRINTED AUTHORITY This is the first issue of *The Boston News-Letter*, the first newspaper to be published continuously in British North America. The phrase "Published by Authority" indicates that the paper served as an official organ of the Massachusetts government. This issue was just two pages, one sheet printed on both sides.

smallpox after an epidemic had struck the city. Cotton Mather learned of inoculation, practiced in the Ottoman Empire and Africa, from his slave Onesimus, who showed Mather his scar and described the procedure to him. Mather advocated inoculation to Boston's physicians, nearly all of whom countered that deliberately exposing people to smallpox would fan the epidemic. The *Courant* sided with them and poked fun at ministers like Mather: "Who like faithful Shepherds take care of their *Flocks*, / By teaching and practising what's Orthodox, / Pray hard against *Sickness*, yet preach up the POX!" The *Courant* persuaded Boston officials to halt inoculation, but *Courant* publisher James Franklin made powerful enemies who had him arrested in 1723 after he refused to obey an order to clear future issues of the paper with Massachusetts officials before publishing them. James's younger brother Benjamin began to publish the *Courant* later that year. The paper folded in 1726, but not before demonstrating that there was a market for local political controversy and that newspapers could fill it.

Colonial newsprint connected colonists to one another. In 1706, *The Boston News-Letter* trumpeted that a servant and a slave who had fled Maine had been captured in South Carolina, thanks to an ad placed in the newspaper months earlier. After 1725, masters from as far away as Virginia advertised for runaways in the *Boston Gazette*. Newspapers became a common means by which masters tried to

THE COFFEEHOUS MOB, FROM EDWARD WARD, *VULGUS BRITANNICUS; OR, THE BRITISH HUDIBRAS* (1710) Coffeehouses were public spaces where men shared information, did business, and discussed politics. Note the newspapers and pamphlets on the table in the foreground. Some, including this image's creator, thought that coffeehouses enabled "vulgar" people, like the patron who is hurling his coffee at another, to spread gossip and disorder.

interactive timeline

TIMELINE 1676–1731

AMERICA	YEAR	THE WORLD
First coffeehouse in English North America opens in Boston	**1676**	
Hasinai Confederacy ejects Spanish soldiers and missionaries who staked claim to Texas	**1690–1693**	
Massachusetts Bay Colony issues paper money	**1690**	
College of William and Mary founded	**1693**	
	1694	University of Halle founded in Germany
England creates Board of Trade to monitor colonial affairs	**1696**	
Vice-admiralty courts created to enforce England's Navigation Acts in American colonies		
Anglicans found Society for Promoting Christian Knowledge (SPCK)	**1698**	
Monopoly of Royal African Company on English Atlantic slave trade ends		
French begin to colonize Louisiana by building fort at Biloxi	**1699**	
Bostonian Samuel Sewall condemns slave trade as immoral in *The Selling of Joseph*	**1700**	Parliament mandates death penalty for piracy or for aiding and abetting pirates
Church of England creates Society for the Propagation of the Gospel in Foreign Parts (SPG)	**1701**	
Iroquois reach "Grand Settlement" with English and French empires and France's Indian allies		
Jul Detroit founded		
Boston merchant John Saffin responds to Sewall with militant defense of Atlantic slave trade and slavery		
	1702–1713	Queen Anne's War erupts, pitting Austria, Holland, and Britain against France and Spain
English and Indian raids virtually destroy Spanish Florida's mission system	**1702–1706**	
The Boston News-Letter becomes first continuously published newspaper in British North America	**1704**	
Linen Act permits export of Irish linen to English North America	**1705**	
Comanches complete migration from Great Basin to southern Plains	**1706**	
	1707	Acts of Union join kingdoms of England and Wales and Scotland to form United Kingdom
Indian slavery legalized in New France	**1709**	

stop people whom they claimed as property from fleeing for their freedom. Newspapers also reported on events in other colonies. The *American Weekly Mercury* monitored Boston's smallpox controversy and alerted readers to efforts to shutter the *Courant*. Colonial newspapers still focused on news from Britain and Europe, gleaned mainly from London papers, but their attention to affairs elsewhere

AMERICA	YEAR	THE WORLD
German war refugees arrive in British North America	1709–1714	
Four Indian "kings" visit London to lobby for a British invasion of New France British forces capture Port Royal, Acadia	1710	
Tuscarora War in North Carolina	1711–1715	
British scuttle invasion of Quebec	1711	
First Fox War	1712–1716	
Slave rebellion in New York City North Carolina separates from South Carolina and becomes royal colony	1712	
Treaty of Utrecht ends Queen Anne's War; British Empire wins claim to Gibraltar, Hudson Bay, Nova Scotia, St. Kitts, and Newfoundland	1713	
	1714	George, Elector of Hanover, crowned George I of the United Kingdom
	1715	Jacobites in Scotland rebel against crowning of George I
Yamasee War in South Carolina, curbing that colony's Indian slave trade	1715–1717	
Transportation Act approves exile of British convicts to North America as servants First wave of Ulster emigration to North America begins New Orleans founded San Antonio de Béjar founded, establishing a permanent Spanish settlement in Texas	1718	
Rice cultivation booms in South Carolina, increasing demand for enslaved Africans	1720s	
Tuscaroras admitted to Iroquois League	1722	
Second Fox War	1723–1725	
Louis XV modifies Code Noir and extends it to Louisiana	1724	
Third Fox War	1728–1735	
First wave of Ulster immigration to North America ends	1729	
Natchez War in Louisiana	1729–1731	
Louis XV assumes control of Louisiana from Company of the Indies	1731	

in British North America made colonists more aware of one another and set the stage for coverage of intercolonial events such as the religious revivals of the 1730s and 1740s.

The growth of social and commercial enterprises also helped to circulate ideas. The most common was the tavern, the number of which increased sharply during the late

1600s and early 1700s. By the 1720s, there was one licensed tavern for every 100 residents of Boston, New York, and Philadelphia. People gathered in taverns to share news as well as to drink and eat.

Meanwhile, coffeehouses sprang up in colonial cities. The first coffeehouse in the colonies opened in Boston in 1676, and by 1724, every major port city in British North America had at least one. Coffeehouses were places for men to do business and to get the latest information on local and global events. Leaders of Philadelphia's government began to meet in a coffeehouse in 1703, partly because its owner, unlike his peers elsewhere in the colonies, refused to sell wine or ale. Philadelphia also posted official municipal notices there. The Exchange Coffee House, opened in 1729, quickly became the hub of New York's real estate market. Others went to coffeehouses and taverns to read newspapers or listen to others read them aloud.

Coffeehouses were also places to receive mail from overseas, but security was a problem. In 1718, Boston's postmaster warned that letters deposited in coffeehouse mailbags might be "Opened, Imbezled or Detained." He requested that captains of ships headed for Britain collect mail at the post office. The communications revolution had brought the Atlantic world closer together and made British North American colonists more engaged participants in it.

STUDY QUESTIONS FOR LAYING FOUNDATIONS IN BRITISH NORTH AMERICA

quiz

1. How and why did British North Americans diversify their economies? What were the consequences of commercialization and diversification?

2. In what ways did ideas and practices in England influence society and culture in British North America?

Summary

- Horses, guns, and other imported goods diffused more widely among Indians. Some Native nations capitalized on the opportunity, dominating Indian and even European neighbors, but trade also stoked conflict among Indians and escalated the Indian slave trade.
- Unprecedented levels of African and European immigration, a growing transatlantic Protestant network, and a mightier British Empire expanded the borders of colonial North America, entrenched slavery and racism throughout eastern North America, and bound British colonists more tightly to the Atlantic world.
- British North America's economy grew and diversified, helping a native-born elite to form and encouraging the development of communication networks that accelerated and expanded the flow of ideas within the Anglo-Atlantic world.

Key Terms and People

audio
flashcards

Reviewing Chapter 4

1. By 1730, global networks had penetrated the North American interior, bringing new goods and peoples to those regions. How did this transformation reshape power relations? Were differences uniform across North America, or did they vary from one region to the next?
2. In what ways did North Americans adjust to growing imperial influence between 1690 and 1730? What role did the flow of ideas across the Atlantic play in determining how colonists in British North America saw themselves and their relationship to the British colonial empire?

Further Reading

Anishanslin, Zara. *Portrait of a Woman in Silk: Hidden Histories of the British Atlantic World*. New Haven, CT: Yale University Press, 2016. Focuses on a fascinating set of producers and consumers, exploring how goods linked the Atlantic world but also provided a forum for a multiplicity of views about the British Empire.

Barr, Juliana. *Peace Came in the Form of a Woman: Indians and Spaniards in the Texas Borderlands*. Chapel Hill and London: University of North Carolina Press, 2007. An excellent account of Spanish–Indian relations in 18th-century Texas in which Indians compelled colonists to conform to their ways of diplomacy.

DuVal, Kathleen. *The Native Ground: Indians and Colonists in the Heart of the Continent*. Philadelphia: University of Pennsylvania Press, 2006. Focusing on the greater Arkansas valley, DuVal demonstrates how Native peoples like the Osage used trade, war, and diplomacy to enhance their power in the face of European colonialism.

Gallay, Alan. *The Indian Slave Trade: The Rise of the English Empire in the American South, 1670–1717*. New Haven, CT: Yale University Press, 2002. An exploration of the Indian slave trade's impact on southeastern North America's Indians and on English colonization and imperial expansion.

Hämäläinen, Pekka. *The Comanche Empire*. New Haven, CT: Yale University Press, 2008. An engrossing account of the Comanches' rise to dominate the southern Plains.

McConville, Brendan. *The King's Three Faces: The Rise and Fall of Royal America, 1688–1776*. Chapel Hill and London: University of North Carolina Press, 2006. An iconoclastic view of British North American politics that argues that colonists regarded British monarchs highly until just before the American Revolution.

Richter, Daniel K. *The Ordeal of the Longhouse: The Peoples of the Iroquois League in the Era of European Colonization*. Chapel Hill: University of North Carolina Press, 1992. A masterful account of how the Iroquois resisted and adapted to colonization over the course of two centuries.

Smallwood, Stephanie E. *Saltwater Slavery: A Middle Passage from Africa to American Diaspora*. Cambridge, MA: Harvard University Press, 2007. A sensitive and haunting portrait of the Atlantic slave trade focused on trying to fathom its meaning and the meaning of enslavement to those who endured it.

America in the World
GOODS, IDEAS, PEOPLE

CHAPTER 4: Accelerating the Pace of Change, c. 1690 to 1730

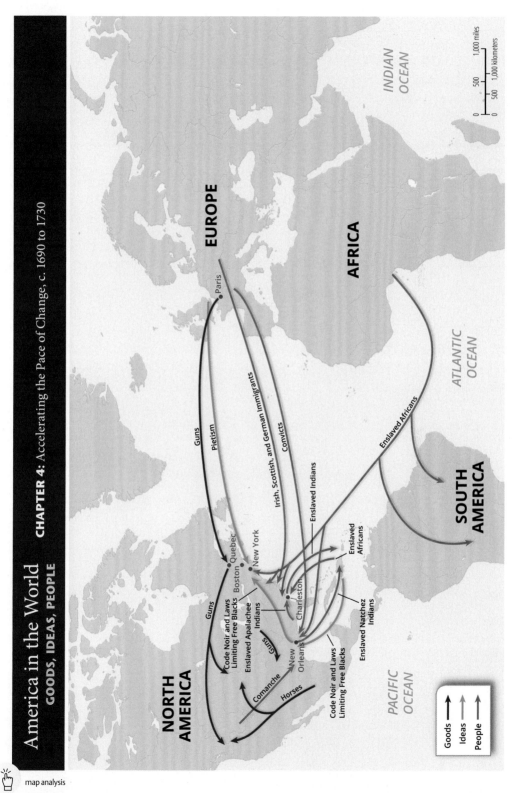

map analysis

Portrait of George Whitefield by John Wollaston, oil on canvas, c. 1742.

Battling for Souls, Minds, and the Heart of North America

I n August 1763, 50 people boarded a ship in St. Augustine, Florida, heading to Havana, Cuba. Most had come to Spanish Florida after escaping slavery in South Carolina or Georgia or had parents who did. Now Britain claimed Florida as spoils of its victory over Spain and France in the Seven Years' War. Fearing enslavement if they stayed, Captain Francisco Menéndez and his neighbors in Gracia Real de Santa Teresa de Mose (the first free black town in what is today the United States) again sought liberty by fleeing south.

Few on board knew better than Menéndez how precarious freedom could be. Born in Africa in 1703 and later enslaved, he won his freedom at age 35 by serving in the Spanish military. In 1740, Menéndez commanded a contingent of free black soldiers who helped to save St. Augustine from British forces. Believing that his deeds in battle merited a royal commission and a salary from King Philip V, Menéndez resolved to go to Spain to make his case in person. He became a privateer to pay his way across the Atlantic but never made it to Spain. In 1741, a Boston-based privateer captured and tortured Menéndez. The ship's captain renamed Menéndez "Don Blass" and took him to the Bahamas, where the British vice-admiralty court condemned him to slavery. Somehow Menéndez regained his freedom, for by 1759 he again led the militia of Gracia Real de Santa Teresa de Mose.

The aftermath of the Seven Years' War forced Menéndez to move again to preserve his freedom. In Cuba, he and his family tried to settle in San Agustín de la Nueva Florida, a new town created near Havana for 84 Florida families. Spanish authorities gave each household land, provisions, tools, and an enslaved African. Most Floridians soon abandoned the struggling town. Menéndez and his family returned to Havana.

Francisco Menéndez navigated many of the dra-
matic changes that profoundly altered North America and the Atlantic world between 1730 and 1763. Rapid expansion of British North America, largely through the immigration of enslaved Africans like Menéndez, fed

conflicts with Indian nations and rival European empires. Menéndez won his freedom in one of these wars but lost it in the next. Meanwhile, as British colonists' demand for imported goods grew and they began participating in more rigorous intellectual and religious networks, a war for control of eastern North America broke out. Following victory, Britain claimed all of North America east of the Mississippi. Some, like Menéndez, fled to preserve their freedom. Those who remained behind lived in a world increasingly shaped by British policy and British goods.

IMMIGRANTS AND INDIANS

African and European immigration to British North America surged between 1730 and 1775, elevating tensions within colonies that absorbed tens of thousands of newcomers. Settlers, who included immigrants and American-born colonists, sought greater opportunities and headed west. In doing so, they displaced Indians, upsetting a precarious balance of power in eastern North America. Settlers' growing farms, plantations, ranches, and other economic endeavors led to greater demand for slave labor.

The Arrival of Immigrants in Chains

The population of colonial British North America soared from 900,000 in 1730 to 2.5 million 45 years later. Immigrants directly accounted for 40 percent of that growth.

POTTER FAMILY OF MATUNUCK, RHODE ISLAND, c. 1740 Here the Potter family of southern Rhode Island poses with an enslaved boy who is serving them tea, linking their aspirations to gentility with slavery. Rhode Island's enslaved population grew more than six times between 1720 and 1750, due mostly to local merchants' growing participation in the Atlantic slave trade.

By the American Revolution, most people in British North America were immigrants or first-generation colonists.

Most who came to North America between 1730 and 1775 arrived in chains. Over 200,000 came from Africa (Figure 5.1). Enslaved Africans outnumbered European immigrants in every decade except the 1750s.

Most enslaved Africans entered North America through South Carolina or Virginia, but demand for enslaved labor in South Carolina plummeted during the 1740s as wars raged in the Atlantic and rice prices collapsed. It picked up again in the 1760s, when thousands landed in Charleston and were taken to Georgia, where slavery had been recently legalized.

The number of slaves in northern British colonies increased sharply. The black population of New York, New Jersey, Pennsylvania, and Delaware tripled, and that of New England more than doubled between 1730 and 1770. Few enslaved northerners arrived directly from Africa prior to 1740 but instead had lived in the Caribbean or in another mainland colony (Map 5.1).

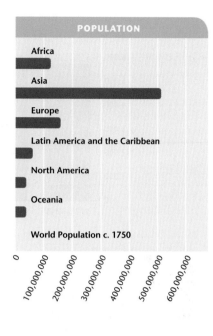

Slavery in northern colonies differed markedly from slavery in the South. Unlike slaves in the South, most of whom lived and worked on plantations, most northern slaves lived in or near a city, particularly Boston, New York, Philadelphia, or Newport. During the 1740s, one Bostonian in nine was enslaved, as was one New Yorker in five. In 1760, enslaved men, many of them owned by artisans, comprised 20 percent of Philadelphia workingmen. One Rhode Island household in seven owned at least one slave in 1774; some owned as many as 20. Most enslaved northerners were men and lived with at most one other slave, making it harder to establish families or an autonomous culture. Still, black New Englanders, free and enslaved, were staging annual Election Days to choose a "king" or "governor" by the 1750s. Their peers in New York and New Jersey did likewise. Whites in Salem, Massachusetts, complained in 1758: "Great disorder usually exists here on Election days by negroes assembling together, beating drums, using powder and having guns and swords." Africans in the Caribbean and Brazil had long staged similar events.

The growth of slavery in northern colonies owed partly to colonists' greater participation in the Atlantic slave trade. In the 1730s, Rhode Island merchants began to invest heavily in shipping and selling Africans (Figure 5.2). Four decades later, they controlled 70 percent of British North America's colonial slave trade, and their vessels had transported nearly 60,000 Africans across the Atlantic. Rhode Islanders' ability to supply New England rum to suit African tastes prompted Gold Coast merchants to seek their business. Once they had secured their human cargoes, more than two in three Rhode Island–based crews set sail for the Caribbean. Rhode Island dominated North American participation in the Atlantic slave trade until 1808, when the United States outlawed it.

Tens of thousands of British and Irish convicts also came to North America against their will after 1730. They made up the majority of English immigrants to North

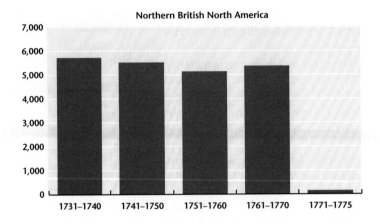

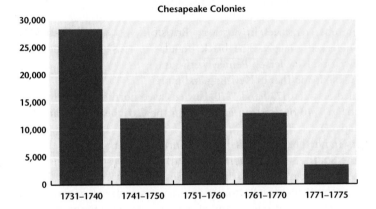

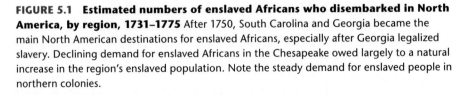

FIGURE 5.1 Estimated numbers of enslaved Africans who disembarked in North America, by region, 1731–1775 After 1750, South Carolina and Georgia became the main North American destinations for enslaved Africans, especially after Georgia legalized slavery. Declining demand for enslaved Africans in the Chesapeake owed largely to a natural increase in the region's enslaved population. Note the steady demand for enslaved people in northern colonies.

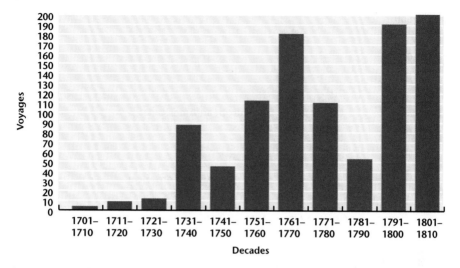

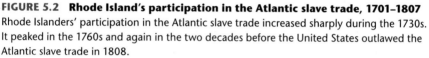

FIGURE 5.2 Rhode Island's participation in the Atlantic slave trade, 1701–1807
Rhode Islanders' participation in the Atlantic slave trade increased sharply during the 1730s.
It peaked in the 1760s and again in the two decades before the United States outlawed the
Atlantic slave trade in 1808.

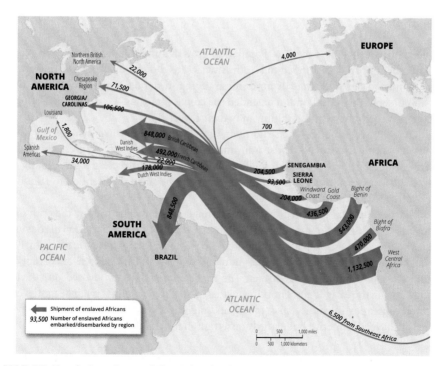

MAP 5.1 North America and the Atlantic Slave Trade, 1731–1775 Demand for
enslaved Africans continued to surge throughout the Americas after 1730. Nearly three times
as many enslaved Africans landed in mainland North America between 1731 and 1775 as
in the previous 40 years, with most landing in South Carolina or Georgia rather than the
Chesapeake colonies.

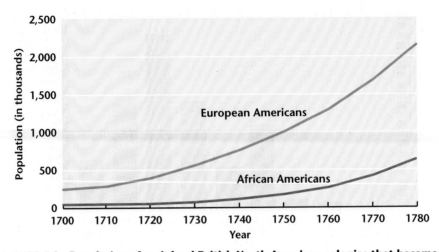

FIGURE 5.3 Population of mainland British North American colonies that became part of the United States, 1700–1780 Between 1700 and 1750, the population of British North America more than doubled, and it doubled again by the American Revolution, by which time one in five colonists was African or African American. Natural increase rather than immigration directly accounted for most of this rapid population growth.

America between 1700 and 1776. Population growth and rising crime rates increased the number of convicts shipped to North America, as did more severe laws in England that mandated servitude in exile for crimes ranging from poaching to perjury. In 1731, a pamphlet published in London defended the convict trade as "Draining the Nation of its offensive Rubbish without taking away their Lives."

Over 90 percent of convicts did their time in the Chesapeake, where they toiled alongside slaves in tobacco fields, iron mines, and charcoal pits. Planters considered them cheap labor: in the 1760s, a male convict cost two-thirds less than a young enslaved African man. But buying convicts was risky because they tended to run away more often than other servants or slaves.

Not all colonists welcomed the arrival of England's convicts. Among the critics was **Benjamin Franklin**, who campaigned vociferously against the transportation of convicted felons to the colonies. "What good mother," he wrote in the *London Chronicle* in 1759, "would introduce thieves and criminals into the company of her children, to corrupt and disgrace them?" Franklin's newspaper, *The Pennsylvania Gazette*, focused on convicts' crimes during the early 1750s. Franklin once suggested that colonists retaliate for the convict trade by exporting rattlesnakes to England, signing the essay "Americanus." He spoke to a British North America built largely on a transatlantic trade in people in chains.

The Impact of Irish and German Immigration

Ireland was the second largest source of immigrants to British North America between 1730 and 1775, with over half arriving after 1750 (Table 5.1). Most Irish who migrated

Table 5.1 Estimated European Migration to British North America by Ethnic Group and Compared to Atlantic Slave Trade, 1730–1775

Enslaved Africans comprised the majority of migrants to British North America during the 1730s, and they were the largest group of migrants entering the colonies in each decade thereafter. Most of the nearly 30,000 Germans to enter British North America during the 1750s arrived shortly before the Seven Years' War began.

DECADE	GERMANS	ULSTER IRISH	SOUTHERN IRISH	SCOTS	ENGLISH	WELSH	OTHER	AFRICANS	TOTAL
1730–1739	13,000	4,400	7,400	2,000	4,900	3,200	800	60,700	96,400
1740–1749	16,600	9,200	9,100	3,100	7,500	4,900	1,100	21,600	73,100
1750–1759	29,100	14,200	8,100	3,700	8,800	5,800	1,200	38,200	109,100
1760–1769	14,500	21,200	8,500	10,000	11,900	7,800	1,600	51,600	127,100
1770–1775	5,200	13,200	3,900	15,000	7,100	4,600	700	31,000	80,700
Total	78,400	62,200	37,000	33,800	40,200	26,300	5,400	203,100	486,400

Note: "Germans" refers to German speakers, not to people who came from what is today Germany. "Africans" refers to people brought via the Atlantic slave trade who disembarked in British North America. "British North America" does not include Nova Scotia or the Caribbean.

between 1730 and 1763 were young, single, male indentured servants. Crop failures and slumping demand for linen in 1739 sparked a wave of immigration to North America over the next two years. The promise of better opportunities, particularly land ownership, led thousands more young men to follow. Between 1763 and the Revolution, immigration patterns shifted: most of those who left Ireland during that time were families from Ulster (northern Ireland) who had enough money to pay their own way across the Atlantic (Map 5.2).

Most Irish immigrants landed in Philadelphia or in New Castle, Delaware, where demand for indentured servants was high. Commercial ties linked those ports to Ireland. By 1750, Irish merchants in Philadelphia were exporting wheat and flour to Ireland and importing linens, flaxseed, and servants. Most ex-servants who concluded their terms headed for Pennsylvania's and New Jersey's frontiers, where land was cheaper. Ulsterites, later known in North America as Scots Irish, who had paid their own way went west immediately. After 1750, more of them landed in Pennsylvania and trekked south to western Maryland, Virginia's Shenandoah valley, Piedmont North Carolina, and South Carolina's Upcountry. Thousands followed the Great Wagon Road, on which construction began in 1730, from Philadelphia to the southern backcountry.

Letter from a Scot-Irish immigrant to his brother (1767)

Along the way, the Irish encountered thousands of Germans. Absolutist princes, high taxes, compulsory labor, and scarcity of land pushed over 70,000 Germans, mainly from the Palatinate (the region bordering the Rhine River), to North America between 1730 and 1775. The prospect of land ownership, lower taxes, and religious freedom lured them across the Atlantic in numbers that alarmed German authorities. German archives contain many unfavorable letters and reports from North

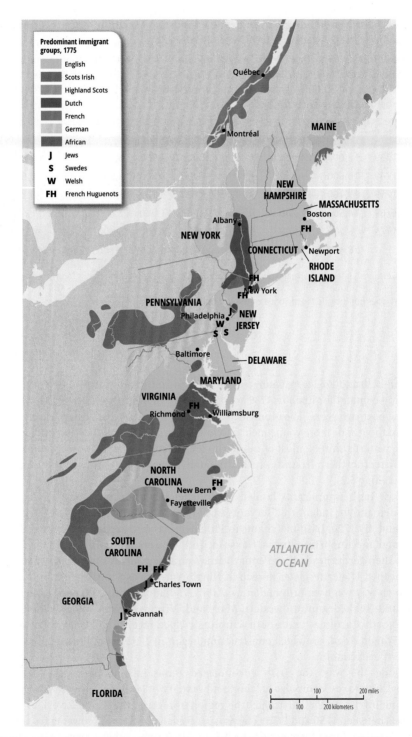

map analysis

MAP 5.2 Race, Ethnicity, and the Colonization of British North America, c. 1775 European immigration and the Atlantic slave trade made an ethnic and racial mosaic of colonial British North America. The colonies were even more diverse than this map suggests, for it shows the largest group in each area, which often was not the majority. Most Scots arrived after the Seven Years' War.

America because local officials preserved and used them to dissuade migrants from going there. In 1768, Joseph II, emperor of Austria, tried unsuccessfully to curb emigration by ordering that no one from his empire could relocate there.

Most Germans landed in Philadelphia, where nearly 35,000 docked between 1749 and 1754. Before the 1750s, most German immigrants had come as families. Many had kin who wrote them about North America and helped them adjust to their new lives. After the 1750s, most German immigrants were single men who became "**redemptioners,**" indentured servants who paid for their passage across the Atlantic by selling their services when they landed. In 1775, 1 in 10 colonists spoke German, as did 1 in 3 Pennsylvanians.

The influx of Germans alarmed many colonists, particularly Franklin. He referred to them as "Palatine Boors" who threatened to make Pennsylvania "become a Colony of *Aliens,* who will shortly be so numerous as to Germanize us instead of our Anglifying them, and will never adopt our Language or Customs, any more than they can acquire our Complexion." Such views, printed in London in 1755, came back to haunt Franklin.

"PALATINE BOORS" German printers in Pennsylvania made a point of broadcasting Benjamin Franklin's insulting "Palatine Boors" comment and translating it into German during charged elections in the mid-1760s. Here is an example from a German-language newspaper published in Philadelphia in 1764.

That was partly because Germans comprised over 90 percent of naturalized British subjects in the mainland colonies. The **Plantation Act of 1740** made it easier for non-Catholic aliens to become citizens. After residing for at least seven years in British North America, such immigrants were required to receive communion in a Protestant church, swear allegiance to George II, and pay two shillings—an amount that an average laborer could earn in a day. The law also permitted Jews in the colonies to naturalize by excusing them from the religious requirement, a provision that in 1753 prompted Jews in England to lobby unsuccessfully for the same right.

Political controversies in Pennsylvania and the English- and German-language press spurred thousands of Germans to become naturalized British subjects. Most German voters traditionally supported the Assembly Party, which kept taxes low; did not demand military service of them or their sons; and opposed the colony's proprietor, Thomas Penn, who sought to increase rents and land prices. In 1755, Christopher Saur published essays in his newspaper *Pennsylvanische Berichte* and in his annual almanac in which he likened Penn to the feudal lords who exploited Germans. Ten years later, over 2,600 Germans applied for naturalization just before an election that turned on whether Pennsylvania should be governed by the king or the Penns. The Penns had recently made it easier to own land. Many new German voters and a sizable number of more established Germans, appalled by what Franklin had written about Germans in the 1750s, sided with the Penns. Franklin and others in the Assembly Party lost their elections and left the colony's assembly.

Heavy immigration accelerated the expansion of British North America and sparked debates on who could be considered British and who belonged in the colonies. The labor of thousands of enslaved Africans accelerated the growth of Virginia and Georgia and extended plantation agriculture to new areas. Meanwhile, thousands of German and Irish immigrants flooded into Pennsylvania and spilled into Indian territories.

Slave Resistance and the Creation of Georgia

In 1733, a group of English entrepreneurs led by **James Oglethorpe** founded Georgia. The colony's trustees hoped to offer sanctuary to Europe's persecuted Protestants and free British debtors from prison. They also aspired to convert Indians, particularly those allied with the British. In addition, the trustees envisioned Georgia as a buffer between South Carolina, where the majority of the population was enslaved, and Florida, where hundreds who fled enslavement sought freedom among the Spanish and their Indian allies. Therefore, in 1735, Oglethorpe and the trustees outlawed slavery. Banning slavery, they hoped, would also redeem former convicts through the hard work of establishing a new society that would be more egalitarian than England.

Georgia's ban took shape as slaves fled south from the Carolinas. Seeking sanctuary, the first Carolina runaways had reached Florida back in the 1680s. Spain's King Charles II reasoned that such runaways would weaken British colonies while bolstering the small population of Spanish Florida. In 1693, Charles II granted freedom to all slaves who ran away from English colonies if they converted to Catholicism and supported the Spanish Empire. Word spread among enslaved communities, and dozens successfully escaped. In 1738, Florida's governor licensed Gracia Real Santa Teresa de Mose, a town near St. Augustine composed largely of people who had escaped slavery in South

Carolina. The men of Mose, led by Francisco Menéndez, formed a militia to defend St. Augustine. The governor and Mose residents followed a precedent set in the Caribbean in the late 1500s in which Spanish officials allowed blacks who had escaped slavery to form towns in exchange for assurances that residents would defend the Spanish.

In 1739, offers of sanctuary in Florida helped to spark the **Stono Rebellion** in South Carolina, the largest and bloodiest slave revolt in colonial British North American history. The group of slaves who led the revolt had recently arrived from Kongo, were baptized Catholics, and likely had military experience in Africa. Rebels burned homes and killed over 20 whites as they headed for Florida. It took whites a month to restore order. In 1740, legislators passed a more draconian slave code in hopes of preventing further revolts and tried to limit how many Africans entered South Carolina by levying a duty on each slave imported.

 An account of the Stono Rebellion (1739)

The Stono Rebellion was part of a wave of slave revolts and conspiracies that rocked the West Indies and eastern North America between 1733 and 1741. The first revolt occurred in the Danish Virgin Islands. Akwamu slaves from Africa's Gold Coast took control of the island of St. John, where they hoped to establish a kingdom and enslave everyone who was not Akwamu. Three years later, Gold Coast slaves conspired to stage a similar revolt in Antigua. In 1739, Jamaica's **Maroons**, fugitives from slavery and their descendants, forced the British to sign peace treaties. Finally, rumors that slaves had plotted with foreign agents to commit arson, kill whites, and turn New York over to Spain shook the city in 1741. Officials interrogated nearly 200 people, banished more than 70, and executed 4 whites and 30 slaves.

War between the British and Spanish empires influenced events in South Carolina and New York. Parliament declared war on Spain in 1739, ostensibly to defend British commerce and mariners. The Spanish coast guard had boarded an English vessel and severed the ear of its captain, Robert Jenkins, which was displayed in Parliament.

MEDAL OF ST. CHRISTOPHER, FLORIDA Archaeologists found this at the site of Gracia Real de Santa Teresa de Mose. St. Christopher, patron saint of travelers and of Havana, Cuba, is carrying Jesus over water. Africans' beliefs that they would return to Africa after death may have encouraged Mose residents to identify with St. Christopher.

The **War of Jenkins' Ear** (1739–1742) had two main American theaters—the Caribbean and southeastern North America—and was the first conflict in which large numbers of British colonists left North America to fight. British officers recruited 3,500 volunteers from New Hampshire to North Carolina to help besiege Cartagena, Colombia, where hundreds died of disease. The survivors sailed to Guantánamo Bay, Cuba, to regroup and prepare to storm Santiago, where the British hoped to establish a colony. Disease claimed most. Few colonists returned from Cuba.

Meanwhile, British and Spanish forces, along with thousands of Indians, faced off in the Southeast. Troops under Oglethorpe's command failed to take St. Augustine, thanks partly to Mose's militia. The Spanish and their Indian allies invaded Georgia and were driven back to Florida. Georgia had shielded South Carolina from Florida, while Spain's policy of sheltering fugitives from British slavery had shored up Florida's defenses.

The War of Jenkins' Ear led to many changes. It cut South Carolina off from Spain and the Mediterranean, key markets for rice. This precipitated a recession that encouraged planters to diversify their crops. Many experimented with indigo, which yielded a blue dye that British textile firms imported from the Spanish and French Caribbean. An imperial bounty (bonus) on indigo initiated in 1749 helped to make it South Carolina's second most valuable export. After peace with the Spanish Empire was restored, many South Carolina planters moved to Georgia. They argued strenuously that the region's climate and malarial swamps necessitated the exploitation of Africans, who, they claimed, were naturally suited to withstand both better than whites. In 1750, Georgia's trustees legalized slavery.

Settler Colonialism and Eastern Indians

After 1730, massive European immigration created a crisis for many eastern Indians. The majority of these newcomers practiced **settler colonialism**. Instead of engaging with Indians through missions or the fur trade, they hoped to push Native Americans out and resettle the land themselves. Settler colonialism forced some eastern peoples into exile. Farther removed from the East Coast, interior Native nations absorbed refugees and developed strategies to retain their power and territory.

Few Indians suffered more from displacement by immigrants than Delawares (also called Lenni Lenapes). Natives of the Hudson and Delaware valleys, Delawares had maintained peaceful relations with their neighboring colony Pennsylvania, thanks in part to friendly relations with William Penn. Decades later, Pennsylvania's population boomed, threatening Delaware lands. After Penn's death, his heirs produced an old treaty between Pennsylvania and the Delawares that they claimed gave the colony the right to purchase a section of land—as far as a man could walk in a day and a half—near the junction of the Delaware and Lehigh Rivers. Delaware leaders thought that the treaty was probably forged, but they agreed. Seeking to maintain peace, Delawares figured that this "Walking Purchase" would not be substantial. However, provincial secretary James Logan hired the colony's three fastest runners and cleared a trail through the forest. The fastest runner made it 70 miles, forcing the Delawares to cede their entire homeland. The Delawares protested, but the Iroquois League, citing their claim to speak for the region's Indians, supported Pennsylvania. The Walking Purchase of 1737 underwrote Pennsylvania's expansion westward. Meanwhile, Delawares were forced into diaspora. Most resettled in the Ohio valley alongside Shawnees who had also been pushed west (Map 5.3).

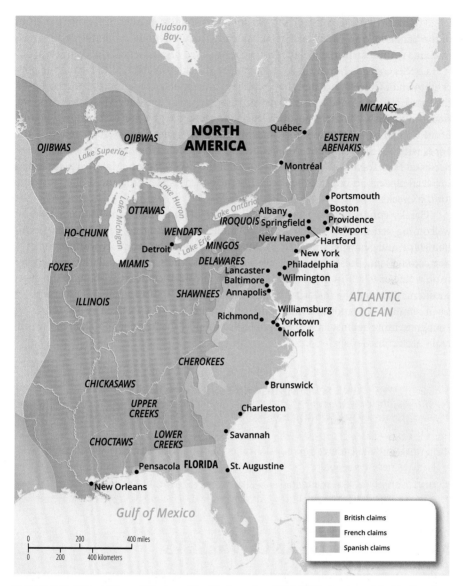

MAP 5.3 Political Map of Eastern North America, Mid-18th Century Most Indians in the Ohio valley who chose to take sides between the French and British preferred the French. British colonization, focused on control of land and exclusion of Indian peoples, expanded rapidly between 1700 and 1740, particularly in Pennsylvania and Virginia. Note the westward exodus of Delawares and Shawnees from Pennsylvania.

Farther south, Indian nations also confronted expanding British colonies. In 1733 and 1736, Georgia signed treaties with the Creek Nation promising to confine colonial settlement to the coastal region. By the 1750s, however, Georgians had violated those agreements, settling 70 miles over the treaty line. Conflicts over land and hunting rights led to fights between Creeks and settlers and, occasionally, murder. Since the conclusion of the Yamasee War, Creek leaders had tried to maintain good economic and political relations with their British neighbors, so they worked toward a peaceful solution.

Creeks engaged in multilateral diplomacy abroad. Malatchi, a chief from the powerful town of Coweta, insisted that imperial governments recognize the sovereignty of the Creek Nation. Aided by his relative Coosaponakeesa (or Mary Musgrove), who was fluent in English, Malatchi pushed Georgia to recognize the precise territorial bounds of the Creek Nation. At the same time, Malatchi and other Creek leaders renewed alliances with the Spanish of St. Augustine and the French, who, with Creek permission, occupied Fort Toulouse in the western part of the Creek Nation. Malatchi played these imperial powers off one another, securing the best possible trade and diplomatic deals for the Creeks.

Creeks enhanced their power in the eyes of Europeans and Indians alike by welcoming refugees into their nation. Among these refugees were Natchez fleeing Louisiana and Shawnees pushed out of the Northeast by Iroquois warfare and settler colonialism. Bolstered by Native immigrants, the Creek population rebounded from a low of 9,000 in 1700 to 20,000 in the late 18th century. Although Muscogee speakers remained the majority, the Creek Nation was multilingual and diverse. Each town retained a great deal of autonomy, but, as one visitor reported, Creeks were "wise enough to unite against a common enemy, to support the interest and glory of the general Creek confederacy."

STUDY QUESTIONS FOR IMMIGRANTS AND INDIANS

quiz

1. In what ways did unfree and free immigration alter North America between 1730 and the 1760s?

2. In what ways did European immigration affect Indian societies and Indian politics? How did Native Americans adapt?

3. How did settler colonialism differ from other forms of colonialism?

⊗ MINDS, SOULS, AND WALLETS

In the 1730s, colonists in British North America began to participate in new ways in transatlantic intellectual, commercial, and religious networks. The most educated of them embraced and practiced science, while thousands flocked to sermons delivered by people who brought evangelical Christianity to both sides of the Atlantic and converted thousands of blacks and Indians. Nearly everyone in eastern North America eagerly purchased British imports as stronger ties to transatlantic and continental networks transformed how colonists and Indians thought of themselves and of their relationships to the rest of the world.

North Americans Engage the Enlightenment

After 1730, colonists became fully engaged in the ideas of the Enlightenment. This philosophical movement attracted intellectuals in Britain, continental Europe, and the Americas; celebrated the use of reason as the key to progress; and disseminated knowledge via international communication networks. Enlightenment participants saw themselves as part of a collective effort to improve humanity. They tried to determine a system of universal laws that governed nature and the development of human societies. Most viewed science as critical to discovering and understanding such laws, and most considered arbitrary authority, whether wielded by clergy or monarchs, an impediment to progress that must be challenged.

Expansion of the newspaper industry kept colonists informed on distant developments. The number of newspapers published in British North America rose from 5 to 22 between 1728 and 1760. By the early 1740s, a number of changes had occurred in the newspaper business. Printers began to produce them in southern colonies, which helped to reinforce their role as brokers for the purchase of servants and slaves as well as for the return of runaways. Colonists began to accept newspapers as legitimate vehicles for political dissent. Coverage of religious revivals and wars alerted readers to events in neighboring colonies and led many to identify more closely with one another and the British colonial empire.

The creation of more colonial colleges also facilitated the exchange of ideas. Clergy founded five between 1746 and 1766. They are today the University of Pennsylvania, Columbia, Princeton, Rutgers, and Brown. Most were established to train ministers, but all offered a secular and practical curriculum to students of all Christian denominations. The colleges trained a growing number of American-born doctors, lawyers, and merchants.

KING GEORGE'S WAR To British colonists, the most significant event of King George's War occurred when colonial soldiers besieged and captured the French fortress and town of Louisbourg in Canada. Newspapers like this issue of *The Pennsylvania Gazette* kept readers in the colonies abreast of developments at Louisbourg.

Beyond the walls of the colonies' colleges, libraries brought ideas swirling about the Atlantic world to colonists. In 1731, Franklin and other members of the Junto, a mutual aid society, formed the Library Company of Philadelphia, which lent books to members. By the 1750s, many towns had lending libraries. Many of the books patrons checked out offered self-improvement: advice on how to become a better farmer, public speaker, or bookkeeper. Histories filled library shelves. An increasing number of them addressed North America's past and were written by colonists. Like newspapers, such histories revealed and nurtured colonists' growing consciousness of ties that bound them to one another and to the British Empire.

Novels, the most popular type of books borrowed from colonial libraries, also encouraged readers to think of themselves as part of an Anglo-Atlantic world. Relatively few colonists read them before 1740. Most early novels targeted an urban female audience, which was rather small in the colonies until the mid-1700s. Such works focused on women's marriage and career choices in an emerging commercial society in which families afforded daughters less guidance or protection, above all from grasping, lustful, or deceitful suitors. Some novelists, including Samuel Richardson, offered moral instruction. In 1742, his most popular work, *Pamela: Or, Virtue Rewarded*, was the first novel to be published in North America, two years after it appeared in Britain. It told the story of a servant girl who resists her employer's efforts to seduce her. Her virtue so impresses him that he asks her to marry him. *Pamela* evoked negative reactions from some female readers, but most seem to have identified with Pamela for having honored her parents' wishes and her principles while attracting a husband.

Meanwhile, more British North Americans became ambitious and noteworthy scientists. They continued the practice, begun in the 1660s, of providing firsthand accounts of local plants and animals and shipping specimens overseas. John Bartram and his son William toured eastern North America, gathered many of its plants into a botanical garden, and published accounts of their travels. Cadwallader Colden studied botany, maintained a horticultural garden, and furnished European contacts with seeds and seedlings. His daughter Jane inherited the garden, made hundreds of detailed observations of American plants, and became the Anglo-Atlantic's first widely acclaimed female botanist.

Benjamin Franklin was the 18th century's most famous American-born person in Europe, principally because of his scientific research. In 1747, Franklin left management of his print shop to others to concentrate on science and politics. He focused on electricity, long considered little more than a curiosity. Franklin had read Isaac Newton's works and attended a lecture in Boston given by an Edinburgh doctor who used demonstrations of electricity to wow audiences. Franklin designed experiments that led to inventions like the lightning rod, proving that scientific experiments could yield practical benefits. He also developed a set of general laws that seemed to govern how electricity worked and did so under controlled conditions resembling those in nature. His discovery prompted British philosopher Joseph Priestley to compare Franklin to Isaac Newton, which helped Franklin get elected to the Royal Society of London in 1756.

Benjamin Franklin, "A Proposal for Promoting Useful Knowledge Among the British Plantation in America" (1743)

Franklin's reception overseas as a first-rate scientist who also was an American made him an exception. European scientists generally saw their American peers as suppliers of specimens and firsthand observations of North American nature but did not think them capable of ascertaining laws that governed the universe. Such disdain led some colonial scholars to assert that as Americans, they were best qualified to explain and depict American flora and fauna. They began to speak of the emergence of a distinctly "American

Philosophy," discussions that led Franklin and John Bartram to organize North America's first intercolonial scientific society in Philadelphia in 1743. Twenty-six years later, it merged with a rival to become the **American Philosophical Society (APS)**, with Franklin as president. In 1771, the APS launched *Transactions*, a journal modeled on the Royal Society's most famous publication. Franklin sent copies of the first volume to Britain to trumpet British North America's latest and most erudite entry to the world of ideas.

Becoming a Consumer Society

Most British North Americans did not read *Transactions* or frequent libraries, but almost everyone bought the British goods that filled shops. By the 1750s, most white families proudly displayed British-made ceramic teapots and teacups, china, and silverware in their homes. "Our Beds, our Tables and our Bodies are covered" with British-made cloth, commented one colonial pamphlet of that decade. In 1773, North Americans bought 26 percent of manufactured goods exported from Britain, almost five times as much as in 1700. British industry and Anglo-Atlantic shipping networks offered colonists an unprecedented number and variety of goods. Their expanding choices as consumers led colonists to redefine their relationships to one another and to the British Empire (Map 5.4).

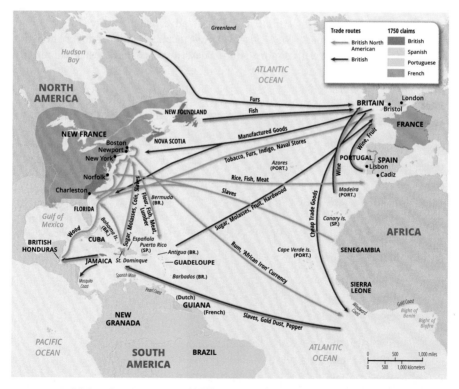

MAP 5.4 British Atlantic Trade, c. 1750 By 1750, British North America was integral to British Atlantic commerce. Colonists' trade with Spain, Portugal, and the Caribbean helped them foot the bill for the manufactured goods that they imported from Britain.

Drinking tea, a sign of refinement and gentility to British on both sides of the Atlantic, helped usher in the consumer revolution. One writer asserted in 1734 that New Yorkers had to "have their tea tho their families want bread." Indians drank tea, too, and some purchased tea sets made of Chinese porcelain. In 1750, a Seneca chief hosted two missionaries who were surprised to be served on a well-set tea table.

In the 1740s, representatives (factors) of mercantile houses headquartered in Glasgow began to set up shop in Virginia to compete with large planters for the business of small farmers, producers of two-thirds of the colony's tobacco. Small planters sold tobacco at the "Scotch stores," selected from a wide variety of goods, and bought on long-term credit. This decreased the influence of planter elites, who had long controlled their access to Atlantic markets. Colonial merchants and shopkeepers spurred demand by extending credit to customers. "Credit is to Trade, what the Blood is to the Body," a debtor wrote from a Newport jail in 1754. In the major port cities of New England and the mid-Atlantic, wholesale merchants imported goods and shipped many of them to retailers in the countryside. The retailers bought on credit and sold the imported goods on credit to their rural customers, who paid their debts with what they made, grew, or raised. Retailers had those products hauled or shipped to wholesalers in the major port cities, who in turn sold many of them to the West Indies or southern Europe for specie or bills of exchange to pay creditors in Britain. Ships built by colonists and raw materials such as whale oil or naval stores such as tar or pitch also helped colonial merchants balance their accounts with British merchants.

Marketing via newsprint stimulated sales as advertising featured more prominently in colonial newspapers. The 1750s saw a huge increase in the number of items advertised in newspapers as well as more detailed descriptions of goods that had recently

SUSANNA TRUAX Here Susanna Truax poses at ease with imported possessions. Her striped dress is made of British cloth. On the table behind her are a teapot, a full teacup on a saucer, and a bowl with sugar cubes, all testament to her participation in colonial Anglo-America's consumer revolution.

image analysis

reached warehouses in Boston, New York, Philadelphia, and Charleston. By the 1760s, newspapers devoted as much or more space to ads as they did to news.

Ads in newspapers indicate that British North America was becoming one interconnected market. Colonists could buy the same goods almost everywhere at the same time. Archaeological studies reveal that colonists who shared a socioeconomic bracket bought virtually the same goods wherever they lived. A growing network of small coastal vessels carried imports from merchants in northern cities to small ports in the South.

African Americans also bought imports. Enslaved men who lived in or near Charleston, especially tradesmen, often sold their time and expertise to whites. Enslaved ironworkers in the Chesapeake had access to the overwork system, under which they earned the market rate in cash or credit for work that exceeded their daily or weekly quotas. By 1750, most Lowcountry South Carolina plantations had implemented the **task system**. Like the overwork system, the task system assigned enslaved adults a daily or weekly work quota. Once they met it, they could tend their own gardens, raise chickens, or weave baskets. Gardens, in which slaves often grew African crops such as sesame or okra, offered a bigger and more varied diet than what masters provided, and slaves could sell what they made or grew. Their earnings enabled them to buy hats or cloth for new garments. Such attire displayed the fruits of their labor and distinguished them from slaves who wore the standard clothing that masters distributed.

Slaves had unequal access to opportunities to earn income. Those who had marketable skills, worked for an industrial enterprise, or lived in or near a city enjoyed advantages that most who worked the fields or lived in more remote areas did not. Slaves who labored under the **gang system**, commonly used to tend tobacco, had less autonomy than those who worked under the task system. Men accounted for the vast majority of slaves with training in skilled trades and had more chances than women did to earn money. But enslaved women dominated public markets in Charleston and Savannah, where they sold produce and handicrafts, replicating a gendered division of labor long common in Africa and the Caribbean.

Authorities failed to stymie the rise of an autonomous slave economy. Artisans feared that the hiring of enslaved men would threaten their livelihood, and other whites insisted that hiring of slaves was a security risk. In 1740, just after the Stono Rebellion, such arguments prevailed as South Carolina legislators prohibited slaves from hiring themselves out and fined those who hired them. Eleven years later, however, Charleston officials acknowledged that such laws were unrealistic. Instead, they required licenses for enslaved men who worked as porters, laborers, fishermen, or craftsmen and set rates to eliminate bargaining between slaves and employers. Still, the employment of slaves bothered some masters, one of whom complained in the *South Carolina Gazette* that his slave Cuffee often hired "himself out without my knowledge, whereby I am defrauded of his wages."

South Carolina authorities also worried about the role that slaves, particularly women, played in public markets. The slave code of 1740 permitted slaves to attend the Charleston public market on masters' behalf, provided that they carried tickets listing what they were to buy or sell. Slaves and masters soon agreed that slaves could hawk masters' produce and use part of the earnings to buy goods, resell them to other slaves when they returned home, and keep the profits. A market clerk claimed in 1741 that the "insolent abusive Manner" of slave marketers left him "afraid to say or do Anything in the Market." A petition submitted six years later complained that slaves who ran market stalls bought items that they resold to city residents, enabling them to evade "the government of their masters." Many masters fretted that economic autonomy afforded slaves too much power but permitted it anyway. They enjoyed lower provisioning costs and encouraged slaves to be more industrious, while allowing few to earn enough to buy their or their children's freedom.

This anxiety about slaves' economic activities was part of a larger discussion in which wealthier colonists, mostly men, insisted that consumerism had led to moral and social decline. The poor (black or white), women, and youth no longer knew their place, and no one could be sure who was who. A commentator complained in 1765 that one could no longer use clothing to distinguish between those "of great Fortune, and People of ordinary Rank." Conspicuous consumption, many charged, tempted all to live beyond their means.

Women took a disproportionate share of the blame for the ills of the consumer revolution. Two ironmasters complained in 1761 that they had to pay high wages and keep their ironworks' store well stocked because ironworkers' wives required "a great deal of finery. They cannot do without tea, coffee, chocolate, and loaf sugar." Some women hurled the blame back at men. In 1746, one noted in a Boston newspaper that male readers had called tea "a Female Luxury." She retorted that her male friends were as "great *Tea-Sots* as any of us."

North America's growing significance to Britain led imperial officials to seek more control over the colonial economy. Between 1732 and 1764, Parliament enacted laws that tightened regulations on colonial manufacturing and restricted what British North Americans could export or import, particularly from the French and Dutch Caribbean (Table 5.2). Meanwhile, British lawmakers and imperial officials constricted colonists'

Table 5.2 Key Laws Regulating British North America's Manufacturing, Trade, and Monetary Supply, 1732–1764

Imperial officials marked British North America's growing importance to Britain as a market for British goods and as a potential competitor for British manufacturers by crafting new regulations in the mid-1700s. Many colonists resented these laws, a sentiment that fed their resistance to imperial reforms in the wake of the Seven Years' War.

NAME OF LEGISLATION	YEAR PASSED	KEY PROVISIONS
Hat Act	1732	Barred colonists from producing beaver felt hats for export to other British colonies to protect British manufacturers
Molasses Act	1733	Imposed prohibitively high duty on sugar and molasses imported to British North America from French and Dutch Caribbean to protect British West Indies planters
Iron Act	1750	Barred colonists from building more rolling or slitting mills, which made hoops, tire iron, and nails that colonists usually imported from Britain
Currency Act	1751	Prohibited colonial governments from issuing more paper money, except in cases of emergency
Sugar Act	1764	Modified regulations issued under Molasses Act and bolstered their enforcement First overt tax raised by Parliament in British America Yielded more revenue than any imperial tax levied on British America prior to American Revolution
Currency Act	1764	Outlawed printing of paper money in colonies

ability to set their own monetary policies, measures that delighted merchants and other lenders in England.

Some colonists thought that such regulations signaled that Britain discounted their importance to the empire. In 1751, Franklin responded to the Iron Act by asserting that colonists' growing consumption of British goods should lead imperial officials to see them as fellow Britons who were partners in forging the empire's future. Seven years later, Franklin explicitly connected consumer choice and personal liberty. He asked, "Would you not say that you are free, have a Right to dress as you please, and that such an Edict . . . would be a Breach of your Privileges, and such a Government tyrannical?" In the 1760s and 1770s, thousands of colonists linked liberty and consumer choice by boycotting British imports to protest imperial reforms that they considered tyrannical.

Benjamin Franklin, "Observations Concerning the Increase of Mankind, Peopling of Countries, Etc." (1751)

Revivals and the Rise of Evangelical Christianity

In 1741, Hannah Heaton, a 20-year-old Connecticut woman, attended a sermon. Years later, she recalled how it had transformed her life: "It seemed to me I was a sinking down in to hell. I thot the floor I stood on gave way and I was just a going but then I began to resign and as I resigned my distress began to go off till I was perfectly easy quiet and calm. . . . It seemed as if I had a new soul & body both." Heaton had participated in the revivals that gripped most of British North America in the 1730s and 1740s and flared again in the South during the 1750s and 1760s.

Heaton remembered a time when religion became more important to residents of British North America. Church membership grew rapidly between 1730 and 1776. The number of church buildings tripled between 1740 and 1780. Ministers filled churches and preachers lured thousands to outdoors sermons with emotional messages of damnation and redemption delivered in simple and direct language that anyone could understand. The preachers brought evangelical Christianity to North America. They sought converts by stressing personal piety and the relative equality of all believers before God and one another. Most discounted adherence to ritual and reason and denied that formal education and theological training were the best claim to spiritual authority. Expression of such beliefs opened deep divisions within colonial Christianity and led colonists to identify more closely with fellow believers in other colonies and across the Atlantic.

In many ways, Hannah Heaton's spiritual awakening and that of thousands of other colonists was a legacy of Pietism, which celebrated the exchange of ideas and techniques across ethnic, national, and denominational lines and promoted the evangelization (the conversion to Christianity) of Africans and Indians. The **United Brethren** knitted these strands of Pietism together. Revived in Germany in 1727 on the estates of Count Nicolaus Ludwig von Zinzendorf, the Brethren, better known as **Moravians**, sought to create closed, economically autonomous, sex-segregated communities in which Christian liturgical rituals and piety infused daily life. In 1735, James Oglethorpe invited Moravians to Georgia, where they established a school to evangelize Indians. Five years later, the Moravians left after Georgia officials requested that they violate their pacifist beliefs by taking up arms in the War of Jenkins' Ear. They moved to Pennsylvania, founding Bethlehem and Nazareth. Persecution in Germany during the 1740s displaced thousands of Moravians, many of whom found refuge in 1753 in North Carolina.

GLOBAL PASSAGES

The Deerskin Trade and Indian Consumers

During the colonial era, Native Americans were drawn into a global economy that reshaped their lives. Among the most highly valued Indian products were animal pelts, and Native Americans of the Southeast specialized in deerskins. Indian men were highly accomplished hunters. For thousands of years, Native communities had used deer meat as a major food source, bone and sinew for tools, and hides for clothing. European newcomers also prized deer, mostly for the dressed skins that could be easily exported.

In the first half of the 18th century, a cattle plague forced English ports to ban European cattle hides, and the resulting leather shortage increased the demand for American deerskins. Like cattle hides, deerskins provided versatile leather used for book-binding, gloves, saddlebags, and breeches worn by the likes of George Washington. Native communities eagerly met this rising European demand. In the aftermath of the Yamasee War (1715–1717), many Native Americans refused to participate in the Indian slave trade and looked for other economic opportunities. Therefore, Native communities amplified production; men hunted, while women processed the hides. Exports from Charleston, the region's largest port, skyrocketed from about 54,000 deerskins in 1700 to 150,000 by 1750.

Deerskins played a major role in the economy. Trading posts commonly set prices in deerskins: in colonial Louisiana, for example, 4 skins bought an axe and 20 skins bought a gun. Unscrupulous merchants preferred to sell alcohol, and they flooded Indian towns with a cheap Caribbean rum called tafia. Alcohol addiction increased, and many Indians became indebted to Euro-American traders. However, not everyone

They played a key role in the development of Anglo-Atlantic Christianity by pioneering evangelizing techniques and sharing them with British and colonial **revivalists**.

Jonathan Edwards, "Sinners in the Hands of an Angry God" (1741)

Colonists filled leading roles in the transatlantic awakening, none more so than **Jonathan Edwards**, a Massachusetts minister. He merged Pietism with an emotional style of preaching and brought both to orthodox New England Puritanism. Edwards's charged sermons sparked a revival, an outpouring of religious enthusiasm, in the Connecticut River valley in the 1730s. Edwards demanded that listeners repent and practice what they professed or face eternal damnation. Edwards broadcast news of his labors to an Anglo-Atlantic audience. Word of his deeds spread to Britain, prompting **George Whitefield**, an Anglican pastor, to tour British North America. Whitefield was probably the first transatlantic celebrity. He followed the Welsh model, a form of itinerant field preaching that drew huge socially mixed crowds, sometimes numbering in the tens of thousands. His tour itself garnered an unprecedented level of coverage of colonial events in North American newspapers (Map 5.5).

In part, public interest was so great because revivalists generated enormous controversy. Critics directed fire at the revivalists' enthusiasm and disdain for authority.

suffered. Some Indians profited, and a number of Native men and women became traders in their own right. A Creek man known as the Boatswain of Apalachicola developed a profitable business exporting deerskins to Savannah, Georgia, and used the proceeds to build a plantation where his slaves served guests venison on dishes produced in China. Participation in global trade heightened wealth disparities among Native Americans; some became successful planters and traders, while others lost everything.

The deerskin trade was so central to southern culture that it reshaped gender roles. As farmers, women had long been the backbone of Native economies, but as the deerskin trade increased, men's role as hunters became more important. Women transitioned from being producers to helpmates, an economic shift that may have compromised their power in other arenas of life.

By the late 18th century, the deerskin trade was in decline. European markets were glutted, making the deerskin trade less profitable for merchants. Meanwhile, hunters had difficulty locating deer, which had disappeared from many southern forests. The deer population would not rebound until the 20th century. Still, Native Americans sought to participate in global trade, for they had come to depend on European manufactured goods like textiles, firearms, and tools. Indian men still associated masculinity with the world of animals, so many former deer hunters became cattle ranchers. As maize agriculture resumed its importance, women recovered a measure of economic power. Women also sought new opportunities, selling food to colonial settlements and growing cotton, which they spun and wove for export.

- How and why did the deerskin trade reshape Native American life?
- How did environmental factors in both Europe and North America impact trade?

Revivalists sparked conflicts between established ministers and itinerants, touring preachers who did not oversee a congregation. One faction within each denomination cast revivalism as irrational, too egalitarian, and too disrespectful of trained ministers. In 1738, North American Presbyterians divided after a ruling that required a university degree to become licensed as a minister. Defenders of the policy, mainly older clergymen born in Ulster, became known as the "Old Side." Their opponents, the "New Side" ministers, were younger than Old Siders and were mostly born in North America. Meanwhile, New England Congregationalists split into "Old Lights" and "New Lights." In 1742, Old Light supporters in Connecticut targeted itinerants by passing a law that declared that "any *Foreigner* or *Stranger*" who preached without permission from settled ministers was to be considered "a *vagrant*" and banished from the colony. In the 1740s and early 1750s, German Lutheran and Reformed ministers in Europe and North America targeted Moravians, largely because their preaching and attentive ministry attracted Germans in New Jersey and Pennsylvania who had no Lutheran or Reformed pastor to serve them. Such campaigns sometimes led to violence against Moravian missionaries.

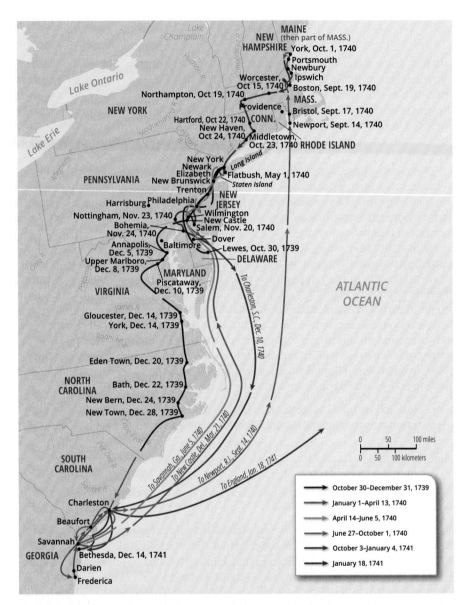

MAP 5.5 George Whitefield's First American Tour, 1739–1741 Whitefield preached to huge audiences in every English colony, some of which he visited multiple times. He died in 1770, having completed 15 preaching tours of Scotland, 3 of Ireland, and 7 of North America. But his first American tour was by far his most famous.

Moravians also drew fire because they disobeyed gender norms. Hundreds of Moravian women in Germany and North America served as eldresses, teachers who instructed women and men, overseers, deaconesses, or itinerant missionaries. The "choir system" by which Moravian communities segregated the sexes, including some married couples, allowed women autonomy and challenged the model of the male-dominated nuclear family. Moravian hymns and imagery attributed some feminine characteristics to Christ. Moravian theology spoke of the Holy Spirit as "Mother."

Other revivalists also empowered women. Women's voices echoed loudly in New Light congregations that formed in New England during Baptist revivals in the 1730s and 1740s as well as in many Baptist churches in Pennsylvania. Women disciplined others for sexual misconduct, theft, and improper preaching. Women's votes helped to select some ministers, choose deacons, and admit new members, a practice last seen in England during the English Civil War. As evangelical congregations took root, however, women's influence within them ebbed. Male Baptists disenfranchised women as part of a broader retreat from sexual egalitarianism within their communities.

Even so, the ideals of the awakening and evangelical Christianity promoted egalitarianism and skepticism toward established authority. Baptists, **Methodists,** and Presbyterians who evangelized Virginia in the 1760s and 1770s challenged the notion of a hierarchical, official, taxpayer-supported religion to which all must at least theoretically belong. Their efforts shaped James Madison's and Thomas Jefferson's views concerning the separation of church and state. Evangelicals helped to reconceive the relationship of the individual society so that people could decide for themselves to which community they wished to belong. Finally, revivalists drew Africans, African Americans, and Indians to Christianity.

African, African American, and Indian Awakenings

Many black Americans and Indians proved receptive to evangelical Protestantism, largely because preachers reached out to them with messages that they found attractive. Moravians were the first evangelicals in the Americas to target Africans and African Americans for conversion, establishing their first mission in the Danish Virgin Islands in 1732. Moravian outreach to Africans and African Americans spread from the Virgin Islands to the British West Indies, Pennsylvania, and New Jersey. Moravians were practically the only evangelicals permitted to proselytize among British West Indies slaves until the 1780s. They preached racial equality among believers but submission to masters, some of whom were Moravian church officials.

Like Moravians, George Whitefield considered enslaved Africans and African Americans his spiritual equals, and he exhorted masters to practice what he preached. In 1740, Whitefield convinced the South Carolina planter Jonathan Bryan to build a school for black students. Bryan and his kin soon led a local movement to evangelize slaves. In 1743, they helped to found the Stoney Creek Independent Presbyterian Church, where enslaved women were the majority of those admitted to full communion by the 1760s. Like Moravians, Whitefield reconciled himself to slavery. He advocated its legalization in Georgia and later became a slave owner. That did not diminish Whitefield's importance to some black converts. His death in 1770 moved Phillis Wheatley to publish her first poem, which circulated through the colonies via newsprint.

Excerpt from George Whitefield's diary (1740)

A number of factors encouraged more slaves and free blacks to convert to Christianity. Charismatic sermons and services lured black audiences and kept them as congregants. So did the willingness of evangelicals, especially Baptists and Methodists, to permit blacks, be they enslaved or free, to preach and become leaders.

Demographic changes helped to spread evangelical Christianity among Africans and African Americans. The growing numbers of American-born, English-speaking slaves lowered linguistic and cultural barriers to conversion. These slaves became the majority among blacks in Maryland and Virginia by 1730 and in South Carolina during the 1740s. By the American Revolution, just 1 in 3 enslaved people in South Carolina and fewer than 1 in 10 in Virginia was African. By the 1740s, cabins for families had replaced dormitory-style group or communal quarters, giving slaves more privacy to worship as they wished.

Similarities between evangelical and African rituals and worldviews attracted black converts. The beliefs and practices of Methodists and Separate Baptists resembled those of many West Africans. Baptism was akin to West and West Central African initiation rituals associated with the symbolic death and rebirth of initiates in which a ritual bath marked rebirth and preceded return to ordinary life. African beliefs that the world would return to an idyllic past found confirmation in Separate Baptists' and Methodists' acceptance of all converts as spiritual equals.

Separate Baptist preachers from New England, led by Shubal Stearns, arrived in Virginia in the 1750s. They preached redemption for all, welcomed blacks, and at first allowed women to serve as elders and deaconesses. This earned them the scorn of Regular Baptists. Two Stearns followers founded North America's first African Baptist church, which was reconstituted in 1772 under four black ministers.

Native peoples of eastern North America also experienced religious awakenings. Moravians established five mission towns for Indians between the 1740s and 1760s, the most significant of them in Pennsylvania. They baptized hundreds of Mahicans and Delawares, particularly women and children. Moravian women's participation in evangelization encouraged such conversions, as did similarities between Moravian and Indian beliefs. Moravians and Indians believed that dreams offered revelation and required careful interpretation. Moravians associated the shedding of blood with spiritual power. Indians believed that menstruating women were powerful and had to be isolated from their families and barred from preparing food or taking part in community ceremonies. Indian women were also attracted to Moravians' portrayal of the Holy Spirit as Mother. Mahican and Delaware Moravians afforded their male kin better access to colonial networks and served to bridge Christian and non-Christian Indian communities.

Excerpt from the auto-biography of a Mahican missionary (1768)

Meanwhile, missionaries and itinerants won Indian converts in New England. In 1753, Eleazar Wheelock, a New Light Congregational minister, founded a free school in Connecticut for Indian children who, he envisioned, would become agents of spiritual and cultural transformation among their peoples. Another New Light minister, James Davenport, converted many Narragansetts in the 1740s. Narragansetts soon built a separate church in which they practiced a form of Christianity that resembled their traditional beliefs. It emphasized visions rather than scripture and was guided by Native ministers.

Race shaped Native peoples' reception of new religious messages. Narragansett Christians in part reacted to discrimination that Indians confronted in New England. By the mid-1700s, most Old Lights and Anglicans had black and Indian worshippers sit in separate pews or galleries. Within seven years of its founding, Dartmouth College's white students drove out Indian pupils.

While many Native Americans embraced Christianity, the most popular Indian spiritual movement of the era was not Christian. The movement was led by **Neolin**, who preached to multitribal audiences in the Ohio valley. Neolin's people, the Delaware, had been forced into the Ohio valley by the Walking Purchase. Along with other Delaware prophets, Neolin used this experience to craft a **nativist** message. Encouraging Indians to put aside their tribal differences, he urged Indian unity as well as a rejection of European influence. In 1761, Neolin encouraged all Indians to "learn to live without any Trade or Connections with the White people." Two years later, Delaware councils resolved to train boys in traditional ways of warfare and adopt a ritual diet that included an herbal tea that induced vomiting to cleanse them of the "White people's ways and Nature."

Neolin's message was a radical one, for Native peoples traditionally identified with their kin group and political community, not with broader racial identity. Some Native communities rejected Neolin's message, but others—particularly those who had experienced settler colonialism—embraced it. Neolin's most famous follower, Pontiac, would use nativism to forge a multitribal alliance that countered British influence in the West. By the 1750s, the Ohio valley had become a battleground, home to a multitude of Native nations and the focal point of the struggle between the British and French for supremacy in North America.

STUDY QUESTIONS FOR MINDS, SOULS, AND WALLETS

1. What impact did the circulation of goods and ideas have on British North America? In what ways did the flow of goods and ideas shape how colonists related to one another and to the British Empire?

2. What was the relationship between spiritual awakening and the movement of goods and ideas in North America between 1730 and 1763? Did the relationship between such awakening and the flow of goods and ideas change depending on whether one was white, black, or Indian? Explain.

quiz

NORTH AMERICA AND THE FRENCH AND INDIAN WAR, 1754–1763

In 1754, skirmishes between British colonists, the French, and Indians in western Pennsylvania erupted into a world war. North America became the focus of British and French aims and the cause of war between the two colonial empires. The conflict, often known as the **French and Indian War** in the United States and the **Seven Years' War** in Europe, transformed North America politically and socially. Victory made Britain eastern North America's dominant power and sparked new tensions between imperial officials, colonists, and Indians.

The Struggle for the Ohio Valley

In the 1740s, the delicate balance of power between the British and French, Iroquois, and Indians of the Great Lakes that had long kept the peace in the Ohio valley tottered. Immigration to British North America and colonial expansion pushed Indians, mostly

Delawares and Shawnees, into the Ohio valley and beyond the reach of Iroquois. In 1744, the Iroquois League ceded claims to the Ohio valley to Virginia with the Treaty of Lancaster. By early 1745, Virginia had granted over 300,000 acres to a group of land speculators composed mainly of well-connected planters who soon called themselves the **Ohio Company of Virginia**. After King George's War ended, the Ohio Company sent surveyors to map the area and traders to sell to Indians. They found plenty of takers; the British offered a wider array of goods at better prices than the French.

French officials responded by staking their claim to the Ohio valley. The Ohio River and its northern tributaries linked Quebec, Illinois, and Louisiana, so British control of the region would effectively cut French North America in two. In 1749, a French expedition planted lead plates bearing the fleur-de-lis, the symbol of Louis XV, along the Ohio River in a bid to stake claim to the area. The French also had more effective ways to assert influence. One was a staple of French and Indian diplomacy: distributing subsidized trade goods to recruit Indian allies from the Great Lakes to attack British-allied Indians. Another was new: build a chain of forts to halt British encroachment. Soldiers completed the last and most important of these, Fort Duquesne, the site of today's Pittsburgh, in 1754.

Construction of French forts provoked panic among British colonists and imperial officials. In June 1754, representatives of seven colonies and of the Iroquois League met at Albany in a bid to keep the Iroquois from siding with the French. The **Albany Congress** dissuaded Iroquois officials from becoming French allies but did little to unite colonial governments that prized their autonomy. A few months earlier, Virginia's government had appointed the young planter and surveyor **George Washington** to command 200 men and build Fort Necessity. The fort was meant to shadow Fort Duquesne and block the way to Maryland and Virginia. Washington had little military experience and had been put in charge of poorly trained soldiers and an underfunded operation.

He also proved to be a poor diplomat to Indians, most of who were inclined to stay out of the conflict or side with the French because the British had thousands of land-hungry colonists and seemed to pose the greater threat. With little Native support, George Washington's Virginia troops were defeated at Fort Necessity by a much larger French and Indian force. The humiliated survivors trudged east as French soldiers torched what remained of British claims in the Ohio valley. The war for the heart of eastern North America had begun.

The War in North America and in Europe

For three years, the war went badly for Britain and its colonies. Word of Washington's defeat prompted officials in London to send two regiments of British soldiers under the command of Edward Braddock. Braddock and his army, accompanied by Washington and colonial militiamen, headed for Fort Duquesne. Braddock's incompetent diplomacy, combined with British policies that transferred Native land to colonists, drove most Indians to the French. In July 1755, the British approached the Monongahela River, marching down a narrow road in orderly columns. Their French, French Canadian, and Indian foes, concealed behind trees or rocks, attacked from all sides. The British colonists sensibly aped their enemy's tactics or fled. Braddock and the British regulars did neither. Their European tactical training equated standing one's ground with valor and courage. It got nearly 1,000 of them killed or wounded at the

Monongahela, including Braddock, whose body the survivors buried as they retreated. Only one field aide, Washington, escaped the battle unscathed. The debacle exposed Pennsylvania, Maryland, and Virginia to Native raids, triggering political turmoil in Pennsylvania as victims and fearful colonists clamored for protection.

George Washington describes the Battle of the Mononga-hela (1755)

The battle at the Monongahela underscored French dependency on Native military might. So did subsequent defeats inflicted on British and provincial troops in New York, a key battleground. Only one British official, William Johnson, appointed in 1755 to the newly created post of Indian superintendent for the northern colonies, managed to recruit Indian allies and persuade them to fight. Johnson was married to a Mohawk woman, so he could call on Mohawks for help. They answered his pleas once before following an Iroquois League recommendation to stay out of the war.

By 1758, three developments had turned the tide in the British Empire's favor. First, the French lost most of their Indian allies. A year earlier, nearly 2,000 Indians, including about 1,000 from the Great Lakes and farther west, helped to besiege Fort William Henry. The commander of French forces, the **Marquis de Montcalm,** negotiated the surrender of the British and provincial garrison and promised it safe passage to a nearby British fort. Montcalm behaved as if he were fighting in Europe and dealing with a defeated foe. His Indian allies, denied even the weapons that their enemy had handed over, reminded him that he was in America by killing nearly 200 provincial soldiers and camp followers and taking away hundreds. Great Lakes warriors did not heed French requests for help in large numbers again, particularly as the French proved increasingly unable to supply them with the firearms and other goods that they needed (Map 5.6).

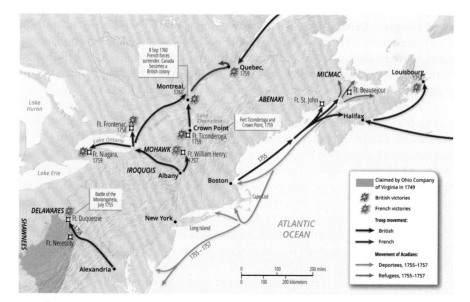

MAP 5.6 The Seven Years' War in Northeastern North America, 1754–1760 Together, the Ohio valley, upstate New York, and Canada comprised the bloodiest battleground of the Seven Years' War in North America. Shown here are the principal battles discussed in the text and when they occurred as well as the routes that Acadian deportees and refugees took after the British invasion in 1755.

Meanwhile, new British leaders plotted a different course. In 1757, **William Pitt** assumed charge of war policy as anxiety gripped Britain. The war had recently spread to Europe. Pitt authorized large payments to Hanover and Prussia, financed by British taxpayers, which would enable them to continue fighting. The Royal Navy, the world's mightiest, would raid French ports; disrupt France's oceanic supply lines; and seize its outposts in Africa, India, and North America. Pitt hoped to tie down French forces in Europe and force France to sacrifice its colonies and the revenue they generated. By the time Pitt resigned in 1761, his plan had succeeded brilliantly. His successors, however, were left to determine how to pay for it.

Finally, British victory in North America came largely because tens of thousands of colonists took up arms. In 1758, they comprised almost half of the nearly 50,000 men whom British commanders sent into battle. Provincial leaders from the colonies recruited most in a matter of months.

The British military advantage in North America arose from differences in how the English and French had colonized North America since the early 1600s. Massive immigration, high birth rates, and intensive resettlement of Indian lands gave the British a much larger potential fighting force in North America than the French. The French model of colonization—minimal and sporadic immigration, with extensive territorial claims backed by Indian alliances—could not match that of the British, who fielded twice as many troops in North America than the French. France counted on Native allies to make up the difference. Once most Indians abandoned the war, British victory was a matter of time.

In 1758, Anglo-Americans won four key victories, three through combat and one through Indian diplomacy. The British took Louisbourg, key to France's naval defense of Canada, in July. A few weeks later, a force composed mainly of colonists captured Fort Frontenac, the key supply post to French forts and Indian allies to the west. An agreement concluded at the Treaty of Easton in October secured peace with Ohio Indians, above all Delawares, in exchange for promises to bar colonization of their lands. With their supply lines cut and most Indian allies gone, French soldiers blew up Fort Duquesne. Anglo-Americans built a replacement and named it Fort Pitt.

French and Canadian forces retreated to Canada to await an Anglo-American invasion. It arrived in the summer of 1759, when troops commanded by **James Wolfe** besieged the city of Quebec. In September, they scaled the cliffs that guarded the city and engaged Montcalm's army. Within a day, the Anglo-Americans had won, although Wolfe and Montcalm died in battle. In April 1760, French forces surrounded Quebec, but British reinforcements soon broke the siege and effectively completed the conquest of Canada by taking Montreal in September. The war between European and Euro-American combatants in North America had ended.

The war between Britain, colonists, and Indians dragged on. In the Southeast, most Creeks chose to remain neutral. Abuse at the hands of British traders, British colonial violence, and incursions onto Cherokee lands had led Cherokees to side with the French in 1759. Colonists and British soldiers invaded Cherokee country two years later, burned 15 villages, and forced Cherokee leaders to cede land and acknowledge British territorial claims.

By then, the war outside Europe had shifted to the West Indies and Asia. The British captured Guadeloupe in 1759 and Martinique three years later. Only Saint-Domingue,

BENJAMIN WEST, THE *DEATH OF GENERAL WOLFE*, 1770 West, a Pennsylvanian, painted this 11 years after British forces captured Quebec. It is highly allegorical; only the officer clutching the flag could have been with Wolfe when he died. British colonists found West's work compelling. They purchased thousands of copies, an indication of their eagerness to identify as Britons.

the wealthiest plantation colony in the Americas, and Guyana remained of France's once-vast American empire. Between 1759 and 1761, the British East India Company won battles in India. In 1762, Spain entered the war on France's side. Britain retaliated by conquering Havana and Manila, capital of the Philippines.

In February 1763, Europeans agreed to end hostilities among themselves under the terms of the **Treaty of Paris**. The British emerged as the dominant European power in North America and the West Indies and seemed on their way to becoming the world's mightiest empire.

Britain Gains Control of Eastern North America

The French and Indian War redrew political boundaries in North America. France surrendered North America, swapping Canada for the return of Guadeloupe. France had lured the Spanish into the war by agreeing to cede Louisiana to them. The Treaty of Paris awarded control of that colony to Spain, which traded Florida to the British to regain control of Havana. The British Empire claimed almost all of North America east of the Mississippi, though, in reality, Indian nations still dominated the area west of the Appalachians.

1774 map showing political divisions of North America after the French and Indian War.

West of the Mississippi, the new European division of North America changed little. In 1764, Spanish officials founded St. Louis to bolster their claim to the region, reap more profits from Indian trade, and clamp down on the Indian slave trade. Competition from British and French Canadian traders offered Indians of the upper Mississippi and Missouri River valleys better access to trade goods.

Most Indians who lived between the Mississippi and the Appalachians confronted a new challenge. They could no longer play two strong European rivals against one another as many had for decades. Worse, the more populous empire, the one that grew through intensive resettlement of Indian lands, had won, and its colonists wanted their land. Many eastern Indians, figuring that they could either accept British rule and gradually cede their lands or take up arms, decided to fight. Their success prompted the British to issue a decree in October 1763 that barred colonists from crossing the Appalachians, a decision that only widened divisions between imperial officials and colonists.

The French and Indian War elevated tensions between colonists and the empire for which they had proudly fought. To most British officials, the war's prosecution and steep costs demonstrated that they needed more control over colonial affairs, including tighter regulation of commerce. For colonists, particularly veterans, the war offered an often unsettling view of the British Empire. Rates of service were high; at least one-third of service-eligible men in Massachusetts, for example, fought in the French and Indian War. Their wartime experiences led many to think of themselves as a people distinct from the British officers who barked orders at them and the British regulars who marched alongside them. New England soldiers often saw British commanders as despots too eager to use the whip to maintain authority and British regulars as debauched sinners whose wickedness might cause New Englanders to lose God's favor in a war that they considered an epic struggle against Catholicism. This did not, however, make colonial veterans incipient revolutionaries. For years, their service made them identify more strongly as Britons and subjects of George III. But it also gave them perspectives and skills that some later drew on to resist imperial policies that they believed threatened their British liberties.

The war's prosecution also widened divisions among colonists. In 1756, many Quakers withdrew from Pennsylvania politics to protest the government's decision to support the war and dodge accusations that Quaker legislators had not budgeted enough to defend the colony adequately. Some left politics as part of a broader campaign for Quaker spiritual renewal, which required that Quakers renounce activities that compromised their core values.

A few Quaker reformers, particularly **John Woolman** and **Anthony Benezet**, targeted slavery. Woolman denounced slaveholding as a violation of Quaker values, while Benezet denounced the Atlantic slave trade as immoral. Benezet pointed out that while many colonists critiqued Indians for taking captives during the French and Indian War, colonists' demand for slaves drove human trafficking on a much greater scale in Africa. In 1758, the Philadelphia Yearly Meeting addressed these concerns, deciding that Quaker monthly meetings should punish buyers and sellers of slaves. Meanwhile, Benezet recommended in 1771 that Britain outlaw the Atlantic slave trade. Benezet's writings, and the relationships that he formed with activists in Britain, exported a campaign to abolish the Atlantic slave trade to the world's largest trafficker in enslaved Africans.

The French and Indian War permanently displaced tens of thousands of people. In 1755, New England and British soldiers stormed Nova Scotia. They aimed to secure what had for nearly 40 years been a British colony by deporting **Acadians**, who the British feared were a security risk because they were Catholic, spoke French, and often had kin ties to Micmac families. By year's end British soldiers had removed nearly 7,000 Acadians, torching their homes and fields and destroying the dikes that protected them from flooding during high tides. Some Acadians evaded British custody and sought shelter among Micmacs or Abenakis, while others moved to French Canada (Map 5.7).

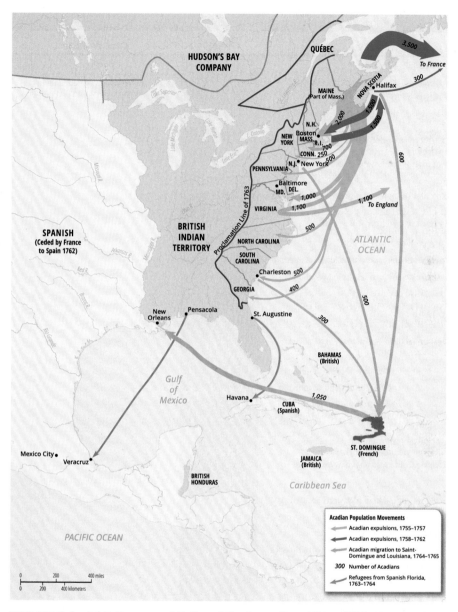

MAP 5.7 Colonial Refugees and Exiles of the Seven Years' War, 1755–1765 British victories in the Seven Years' War forced thousands of colonists to leave their homes. This map shows imperial claims in North America as well as the movement of deportees and refugees. Thousands of Acadians began to relocate to Louisiana in 1765, while Floridians of Hispanic, African, and Indian descent fled British Florida for Cuba or Mexico.

British officials sent Acadians to 9 of the other 13 mainland colonies. Colonies that accepted Acadians scattered them across hundreds of townships, thinking that this would prevent them from aiding the French and compel them to assimilate. Most Acadians preferred to leave British America if they could not return to Nova Scotia. A few

interactive timeline

TIMELINE 1727–1765

AMERICA	YEAR	THE WORLD
Junto founded in Philadelphia	1727	
First subscription library in British North America founded in Philadelphia	1731	**Mar** Treaty of Vienna signed, ending Anglo–French alliance and beginning Anglo–Austrian alliance
Parliament passes Hat Act	1732	
James Oglethorpe founds Georgia as colony to reform English debtors Parliament passes Molasses Act, placing duties on molasses imported to British colonies from French Caribbean **Nov** Gold Coast slaves rebel and seize most of St. John, Danish Virgin Islands	1733	
Jonathan Edwards leads religious revival in Massachusetts	1734–1735	
John Peter Zenger acquitted of seditious libel in New York, establishing precedent for press freedom	1735	
Slave conspiracy in Antigua results in execution of 88 slaves	1736	
Pennsylvania's proprietor makes "Walking Purchase" from Delawares	1737	**Sep** The *News Letter*, oldest English-language newspaper still in publication, founded in Ireland
Gracia Real de Santa Teresa de Mose, a free black town, founded in Florida	1738	
Sep Stono Rebellion in South Carolina	1739	
War of Jenkins' Ear between British and Spanish empires	1739–1742	
Evangelist George Whitefield completes first tour of British North America	1739–1741	
Parliament passes Plantation Act, streamlining naturalization in British American colonies South Carolina legislators enact new slave code	1740	
	1740–1741	Irish famine kills 10% of population
Suspected slave conspirators tried and executed in New York City Moravians arrive in Pennsylvania and establish settlements at Bethlehem and Nazareth	1741	
Pamela, first novel published in British North America	1742	
Precursor to American Philosophical Society founded in Philadelphia	1743	
King George's War between British and French empires	1744–1748	
Massachusetts troops capture Louisbourg, Canada, from French	1745	
College of New Jersey (later Princeton) founded	1746	

hundred Acadian men made it home, where they repaired dikes and reclaimed flooded lands for some of the thousands of New Englanders who moved to Nova Scotia during the 1760s. The next best option was to go to France or a French colony. Over 1,000 Acadians sailed to Saint-Domingue, resettled there by the French government. Nearly

AMERICA	YEAR	THE WORLD
End of King George's War spurs German emigrants from Rhineland to North America	**1749–1754**	
Parliament passes Iron Act Georgia's trustees legalize slavery in colony	**1750**	Little Ice Age, a cool period covering several centuries, reaches its peak
Reverend Eleazar Wheelock admits Indians to Dartmouth College's Connecticut predecessor	**1753**	
Jun–Jul Albany Congress reaches treaty with Iroquois League and discusses potential union of British mainland colonies **Jul** French and Indian War begins, triggered by combat in western Pennsylvania between Virginia militia commanded by George Washington and French–Indian alliance	**1754**	
Jul British and provincial forces under command of General Edward Braddock defeated at Battle of Monongahela **Oct** Nearly 7,000 Acadians deported from Nova Scotia to British mainland colonies	**1755**	
	1756	Britain officially declares war on France
Prime Minister William Pitt revamps British war strategy **Aug** French forces capture Fort William Henry but alienate Indian allies	**1757**	British rule formally begins in India
May–Jul British and provincial forces besiege and capture Fort Louisbourg **Aug** British forces capture Fort Frontenac **Oct** Treaty of Easton makes peace between British authorities and Ohio Indians **Nov** French forces blow up Fort Duquesne to prevent British capture of it	**1758**	
Jun–Sep British forces under the command of General James Wolfe besiege and conquer city of Quebec	**1759**	
Sep British forces capture Montreal, effectively ending war between British and French in North America	**1760**	**Oct** George II dies; his grandson George III becomes king of Britain
Spain declares war on British Empire; British forces capture Havana	**1762**	
Feb Treaty of Paris ends Seven Years' War: France cedes Louisiana to Spain; Spain cedes Florida to Britain; France cedes Canada, most of North America between Appalachians and Mississippi River, and four Caribbean islands to Britain **May** Multitribal alliance led by Pontiac (Ottawa) attacks Detroit to prevent British resettlement of Ohio valley and Great Lakes region **Oct** George III issues royal proclamation barring colonists from settling west of Appalachians	**1763**	
Acadians begin to move to Louisiana	**1765**	

half of them left for Louisiana, where French officials remained in charge until 1766. There they began to call themselves Cajuns.

As Acadians dreamed of an American refuge, thousands of Floridians sailed away. British officials told free residents of Spanish Florida that they could stay and accept

EXILE OF THE ACADIANS FROM GRAND PRÉ.

EXILE OF THE ACADIANS FROM GRAND PRÉ This image depicts the mid-18th-century British expulsion of the Acadians from Grand Pré, their main settlement in Nova Scotia. Sympathy for the tragedy of the Acadians' forced migration out of British Canada was revived nearly 100 years after it took place when Henry Wadsworth Longfellow published his poem "Evangeline," which depicted it. This British 19th-century engraving adopts Longfellow's view of the expulsion as a sentimental tragedy.

assurances of freedom of religion and respect for their property rights or sell what they owned and leave. Most left. Nearly 3,000 headed to Cuba between August 1763 and January 1764. They included Francisco Menéndez, his neighbors, and hundreds of Canary Islanders and Catalan soldiers who had recently arrived to defend Florida from the British. Hundreds of south Florida Indians also went to Cuba, whereas Floridians who fled Pensacola sought refuge in Mexico. Most were Spanish soldiers and their families. Others were Christian Yamasees, almost half of whom died en route before resettling in a separate town. Most refused to return when Spain regained control of Florida in the aftermath of the American Revolution.

STUDY QUESTIONS **FOR NORTH AMERICA AND THE FRENCH AND INDIAN WAR, 1754–1763**

quiz

1. What explains French success early in the French and Indian War? What explains the British Empire's ultimate victory in the conflict?

2. What new divisions did the French and Indian War create in North America? Why did some of those divisions result in the movement of thousands from or within North America?

Summary

- Record levels of free and unfree immigration accelerated population growth in British North America and fostered political and cultural tensions within the colonies while creating upheaval among eastern Indians.
- African Americans, Indians, and whites all became vital consumers of imported goods and important participants in Atlantic intellectual and religious networks in ways that changed their understanding of who they were.
- The French and Indian War resulted in a British victory that altered North America's political map, creating new divisions within North America and forcing thousands to leave.

Key Terms and People

Acadians 186
Albany Congress 182
American Philosophical Society
    (APS) 171
Benezet, Anthony 186
Edwards, Jonathan 176
Franklin, Benjamin 160
French and Indian War (Seven
    Years' War) 181
gang system 173
Maroons 165
Marquis de Montcalm 183
Methodists 179
Moravians (United Brethren) 175
nativist 181
Neolin 180

Oglethorpe, James 164
Ohio Company of Virginia 182
Pitt, William 184
Plantation Act of 1740 164
redemptioners 163
revivalists 176
settler colonialism 166
Stono Rebellion 165
task system 173
Treaty of Paris 185
War of Jenkins' Ear 166
Washington, George 182
Whitefield, George 176
Wolfe, James 184
Woolman, John 186

audio
flashcards

Reviewing Chapter 5

1. How did Native Americans respond to increasing pressure from British settler colonialism? What strategies did they use to try to reclaim power?
2. How did the global circulation of people, goods, and ideas reshape North America from 1730 to 1763? Explain your answer using specific examples from this chapter.
3. British North Americans considered themselves more British in 1763, even though they had never been more American. Why?

Further Reading

Braund, Kathryn E. Holland. *Deerskins & Duffels: The Creek Indian Trade with Anglo-America, 1685–1815*, 2nd ed. Lincoln: University of Nebraska Press, 2008. Explores how the deerskin trade reshaped Native American life in the Southeast.

Faragher, John Mack. *A Great and Noble Scheme: The Tragic Story of the Expulsion of the French Acadians from Their American Homeland*. New York: W. W. Norton, 2005. An evocative overview of Acadian removal and of what happened to Acadians after they were expelled from their homeland.

Hartigan-O'Connor, Ellen. *The Ties That Buy: Women and Commerce in Revolutionary America*. Philadelphia: University of Pennsylvania Press, 2009. Focusing on white and black women, this book explores the consumer revolution and other changes in the American marketplace from roughly 1750 to 1820.

Landers, Jane. *Black Society in Spanish Florida*. Urbana and Chicago: University of Illinois Press, 1999. Sharply contrasts slavery and freedom in Florida while under Spanish rule with slavery and freedom in the English colonies and in the states that bordered Florida.

Merritt, Jane T. *At the Crossroads: Indians and Empires on a Mid-Atlantic Frontier, 1700–1763*. Chapel Hill and London: University of North Carolina Press, 2003. Examines intercultural relations between Indians and European colonists in Pennsylvania in ways that are sensitive to gender as it explains why some Indians converted to Christianity while others rejected it.

Parrish, Susan Scott. *American Curiosity: Cultures of Natural History in the Colonial British Atlantic World*. Chapel Hill and London: University of North Carolina Press, 2006. Explores and explains how British colonists' participation in scientific investigation of the natural world reinforced racist thought and helped to create an American identity.

Waldstreicher, David. *Runaway America: Benjamin Franklin, Slavery, and the American Revolution*. New York: Hill and Wang, 2004. A concise and engagingly written account of Franklin and the evolution of his views on slavery, focused on his activities as an entrepreneur and politician.

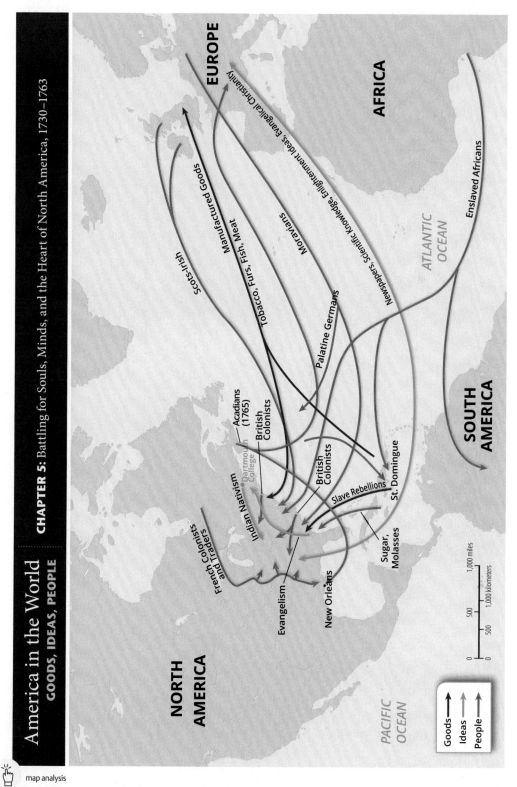

America in the World
GOODS, IDEAS, PEOPLE

CHAPTER 5: Battling for Souls, Minds, and the Heart of North America, 1730–1763

NORTH AMERICA

EUROPE

AFRICA

SOUTH AMERICA

ATLANTIC OCEAN

PACIFIC OCEAN

Scots-Irish

Manufactured Goods

Tobacco, Furs, Fish, Meat

Moravians

Newspapers, Scientific Knowledge, Enlightenment Ideas, Evangelical Christianity

Palatine Germans

Enslaved Africans

Acadians (1765)

Dartmouth College

British Colonists

British Colonists

St. Domingue

Slave Rebellions

Indian Nativism

French Colonists and Traders

Evangelism

New Orleans

Sugar, Molasses

Goods
Ideas
People

0   500   1,000 miles
0   500   1,000 kilometers

map analysis

The Death of General Montgomery in the Attack on Quebec, December 31, 1775, by John Trumbull, oil on canvas, 1786.

Empire and Resistance

1763–1776

On December 31, 1775, American major general **Richard Montgomery** was killed while leading a failed invasion of Quebec by Continental Army soldiers. Montgomery attacked the Canadian capital city in a last-ditch effort to salvage an invasion that had stalled during a tough winter. The Continental Congress had hoped to force concessions from the British government by invading Canadian colonies. Instead, Montgomery died, and his fellow commander Benedict Arnold led a miserable retreat back to New England.

Montgomery was immediately hailed as a hero and martyr to the American cause of liberty. The Continental Congress authorized a huge public funeral in Philadelphia and built a monument to his memory. Ten years later Montgomery had become the subject of many other commemorations. American artist John Trumbull painted a heroic image of Montgomery's death that directly referenced a famous painting of the idolized British general James Wolfe, who had died in an attack on Quebec in the French and Indian War and been immortalized by painter Benjamin West. Even in fighting the British, Americans looked to British examples to define images of heroism.

Richard Montgomery was born into an aristocratic Dublin family, attended Trinity College, and joined the British army in time to fight against the French in Canada during the French and Indian War. He rose through the ranks from 1757 to 1763, serving in Canada, New York, Barbados, Martinique, and Cuba. By the end of the war, he was a respected captain in the British army, one of the men who enforced the British Empire with military power.

After the war, Montgomery befriended several members of Parliament in England who disagreed with their government's efforts to tax the American colonies. Growing disgruntled with the military hierarchy,

195

Montgomery moved to New York in 1773, where he married Janet Livingston, a member of one of the colony's wealthiest families. Montgomery was elected to the New York legislature, where he voiced opposition to British crackdowns on the colonies. Montgomery was a natural choice to be appointed a commander when the Continental Army formed in June 1775. When Montgomery was killed in Quebec, this time fighting *against* the British army, he was one of the most experienced and promising military commanders in the American army.

As an American hero who until recently had been a British army officer, Richard Montgomery was in many ways the perfect symbol of how resistance began to undermine the British Empire in North America between 1763 and 1775. Many American colonists had strong ties to Britain or had recently immigrated, and they mostly considered themselves obedient subjects of the British crown at the end of the French and Indian War. Yet the series of British taxes and government restrictions imposed on the colonies after the war convinced many Americans that the time had come to throw off imperial control. British military presence in North America heightened the tension.

Between 1763 and 1776, both the British and Spanish empires sought increased control over their North American subjects. North Americans, many of whom like Montgomery had cast off old identities to feel more "American," challenged European control. Spain was able to maintain control and spread its empire, but in the British case, a cycle of protest and reaction would lead to a full-scale war and to the United States of America declaring its independence.

⊘ ENGLISH AND SPANISH IMPERIAL REFORM

As the French and Indian War ended in 1763, two newly crowned kings consolidated power in Europe. Charles III was crowned in Spain in 1759, while George III became king of Britain in 1760. Both kings won substantial new colonial territory from France in the war and substantial financial burdens along with it. Besides an estimated £140 million in war debt, it cost Britain about £300,000 per year to defend the North American territories. British and Spanish officials both began attempting to recover some costs from the profits of the colonies themselves as well as trying to calm internal conflicts. The new policies unleashed many unintended consequences in North America. Spanish royal officials consolidated their control over New Spain and managed to expand their territory despite some colonist resistance. Canadian and Caribbean colonies remained loyal to the British crown, in part because some were granted direct parliamentary representation, but many American colonists resisted imperial reforms and became rebellious.

Transatlantic Trade as an Engine of Conflict

Each region of the British colonies had its own economic character, but trade was central to all of them. New England shipbuilding and lumber equipped the navy that policed much of the rest of the British Empire and provided barrels for the rum trade, and New England fishermen fed Europe with 240 million pounds of cod and mackerel each year. The mid-Atlantic colonies added iron production, fur trading, and ship-building to their trade in agricultural products, and Quaker and Jewish merchants relying on transatlantic religious and kinship networks grew especially prosperous. Maryland and Virginia produced tobacco, a staple crop since the 17th century that made up more than 25 percent of all American exports by the 1770s, while the

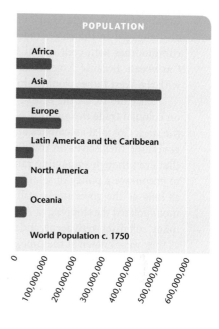

POPULATION

Africa

Asia

Europe

Latin America and the Caribbean

North America

Oceania

World Population c. 1750

0 100,000,000 200,000,000 300,000,000 400,000,000 500,000,000 600,000,000

PORTRAIT OF GEORGE III
George III assumed the throne of Great Britain in 1760, and he reigned as king longer than any previous British monarch, until 1820. The beginning of George III's reign was marked by the British defeat of the French in the Seven Years' War, but his keen regard for royal privilege was soon tested by the American Revolution.

Carolinas and Georgia contributed pine tar, indigo, and rice. Merchants in every colony also engaged in the slave trade. Britain sought to monopolize the trade of colonial commodities with continental Europe and with Spanish and French colonies in the Caribbean. Because Americans imported 30 percent more than they exported, trade with the West Indies would help finance trade deficits elsewhere.

Since the 1650s, the British Parliament had imposed a series of controls and taxes on colonial trade through the **Navigation Acts**. But officials had not strictly enforced the laws. Colonial assemblies and merchants had by the 1760s become accustomed to governing themselves on trade matters. Trade in the British colonies was so lucrative that even though smuggling ran rampant, the government enjoyed sufficient revenue to encourage a policy of salutary neglect (ignoring infractions of the Navigation Acts as long as the government still made hefty profits). The British government largely monopolized the shipping of American trade goods to Europe and the West Indies, and many colonists were deeply indebted to English and Scottish wholesalers (or "factors," as they were known at the time). The colonial population doubled from one million in 1750 to two million in 1770, and Great Britain made good money both importing from and exporting to that growing population.

As transatlantic trade grew, so did North American cities. By 1775, Boston, New York, Newport, Philadelphia, and Charleston held more than 9,000 people, and each was a fast-growing commercial center. These cities, and a host of smaller ones, housed the legal, political, and financial institutions that facilitated imperial trade. In cities, colonists of different religions, income levels, and backgrounds lived close together. Boston, Philadelphia, and New York all experienced a sharp growth in poverty during the 1750s and 1760s. Urban trade and the close contact between people from different ends of the social spectrum (from slaves to artisans to merchants to imperial officials) would help to make colonial cities centers of political mobilization in the 1770s (Map 6.1).

A view of Boston in 1770

The debts incurred by the British in the Seven Years' War caused British officials to renew their interest in North American trade when George Grenville became prime minister, first lord of the treasury, and chancellor of the exchequer in April 1763. Grenville enacted a series of policies that touched off colonial resistance. Grenville sought to lower the domestic tax burden in England by raising revenues from the colonies. He moved to enforce and expand trade regulations and invested new power in colonial customs officials, who were supposed to collect duties under the 1733 Molasses Act, which often went unpaid. By 1764, colonial exports to Britain had reached £1.5 million annually, and Grenville hoped to increase the government's share.

Grenville's Program

Grenville moved the Sugar Act through Parliament in 1764. It was a clever piece of legislation designed to raise revenue through strict enforcement of trade taxes on the American colonies, even as it lowered many previous trade duties. The Sugar Act increased taxes not only on sugar but also on coffee, coconuts, whale fins, silk, and animal hides. The act also forbade American colonists from importing rum from any non-British source. Many colonists smuggled molasses from Spanish and French Caribbean islands to avoid paying taxes, and smuggled goods were often much cheaper than legal ones. Grenville established a new vice-admiralty court at Halifax, Nova Scotia, to seize any ships caught smuggling goods between the British American colonies and

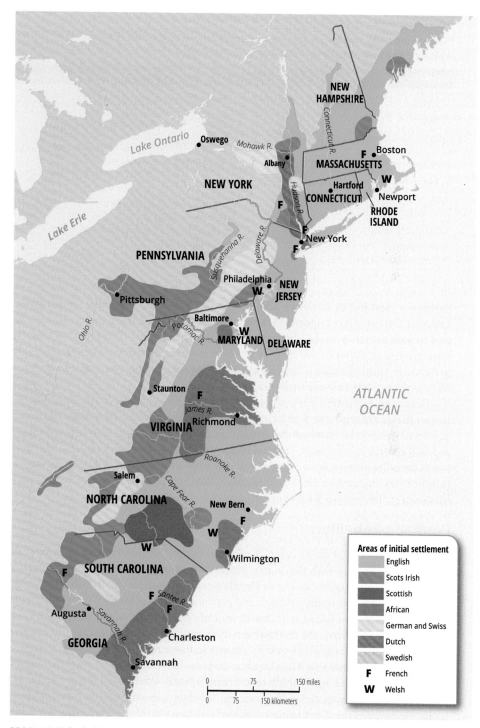

MAP 6.1 Ethnic Diversity The British colonies in North America were marked by an unusually high level of ethnic and racial diversity.

Table 6.1 Imperial Taxes in the 1760s and 1770s

Parliament passed a series of taxes on the North American colonies that sparked resistance and helped to propel the American Revolution.

YEAR	LEGISLATION
1764	Sugar Act
1765	Stamp Act
1766	Declaratory Act
1767	Townshend Revenue Acts
1773	Tea Act
1774	Coercive or Intolerable Acts Boston Port Bill Massachusetts Government Act Quartering Act Quebec Act

the French West Indies. Grenville also expanded restrictions on colonial paper money. The 1764 Currency Act required that both British trade merchants and trade taxes be paid in hard currency backed by precious metals. The colony of Virginia had tried to evade paying £250,000 in war debt by printing more paper money. These restrictions particularly affected tobacco farmers in the Chesapeake region who had run up huge debts with the Scottish trade firms (Table 6.1).

Grenville's legislation allowed for some expansion in colonial trade, including increases in rice exports from South Carolina to Latin America and New England timber exports to Ireland and Portugal. But stricter tax enforcement raised fears of overarching imperial control among many colonial residents. Elected assemblies in New York and North Carolina protested the Sugar Act on the basis that they had not been allowed to vote for taxes imposed on them by Parliament. But their protests were merely mild precursors of stiffer resistance yet to come.

Pontiac's Rebellion

As it tightened control on its colonial subjects, the British government took an even harder line in dealing with the Indian peoples who surrounded its colonies. Indians stretching from northern Canada to Florida were dismayed by the British triumph in 1763. Many had better trade, political, and personal relationships with the French than the British. They also feared that British officials and settlers would seize additional land. Sir Jeffrey Amherst, the commander-in-chief of the British forces in the imperial war who exercised particular brutality against Indians, remained in charge as governor general of British North America after 1763. Amherst imposed new restrictions on Indian fur traders and aggressively seized Seneca lands. **Pontiac**, an Ottawa chief, interpreted Delaware prophet **Neolin**'s message of indigenous spiritual revival in military terms. He declared that the Creator mandated resistance to "those who come to trouble your lands,—drive them out, make war upon them."

Pontiac did just that in the spring of 1763. He gathered multitribal forces from groups of Ohio valley and Great Lakes Indians who wished to keep British settlers from the land between the Allegheny Mountains and the Mississippi River and to drive British military forces back east of the Alleghenies. Beginning in May, Pontiac assaulted Detroit while his allied Potawatomi, Miami, Huron, Mingo, Ojibwa, and Shawnee forces attacked 11 different British forts and a number of settler communities. British Superintendent of Indian Affairs Sir William Johnson estimated the Indian population of the area to be as low as 50,000. Nonetheless, the 3,500 warriors allied to Pontiac were well matched against a roughly equal number of British troops. Pontiac's forces captured most of the forts they attacked, but by fall their food and ammunition had run low—and many were afflicted with smallpox, in part spread by British troops who intentionally traded infected blankets.

In October 1763, London tried to deal with the rising violence by sending reinforcements. King George III accommodated Indian demands by issuing the **Proclamation of 1763**, which prohibited almost all settlement west of the Appalachian Mountains and restricted land sales to the east (Map 6.2). Britain also sought to license traders, who would be required to behave more favorably toward Indian suppliers and customers. But many British settlers simply ignored the Proclamation and continued to settle in western territories occupied by Indians. Pontiac and many of his supporters concluded a peace agreement with the British in 1766, while thousands of settlers poured into their territories by the mid-1770s.

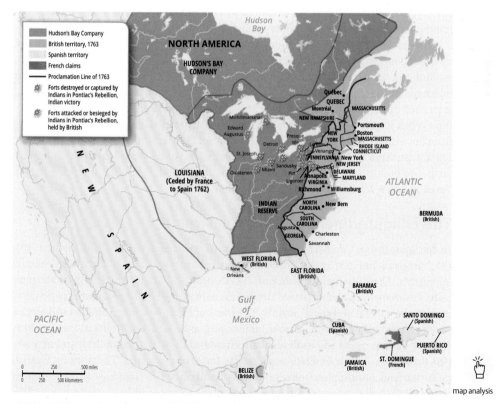

map analysis

MAP 6.2 North America in 1763 This map shows the line drawn in the Proclamation of 1763 and depicts the major clashes during Pontiac's Rebellion.

Bourbon Reforms

The Spanish government was more successful at centralizing control and reforming its empire in North America after 1763. In the peace of 1763 that settled the global war for empire, Spain acquired the French territory west of the Mississippi River and the city of New Orleans but traded possession of Florida to Britain in exchange for Havana, Cuba, which the British had occupied in 1762. Charles III (a member of the Bourbon dynasty that took control of the Spanish crown in the 1710s) and a group of reforming bureaucrats influenced by ideas of the Iberian Enlightenment sought to rebuild centralized control over North and South America. The Bourbon Reforms (as their actions came to be called) also aimed to increase Spanish revenues and control over institutions of the Catholic Church.

Charles III appointed José de Gálvez (after whom Galveston, Texas, is named) as minister of the Indies, and Gálvez immediately sought to reduce the authority of Creole families who governed the mixed-race and indigenous populations in Spanish America. He claimed they were "too bound by ties of family and faction in the New World" to govern well. Gálvez and other officials tried to reform almost every area of imperial life: administrative, economic, and religious. Gálvez traveled to Cuba and Mexico to impose new regulations that raised greater revenue from trade customs, mining, and Indian tribute payments. In 1765, the Spanish crown broke up colonial trade monopolies long enjoyed by Seville and Cádiz merchants and increased taxes on merchants allowed into colonial markets. Gálvez installed Spanish salaried officials to collect taxes directly and imposed a state-sponsored monopoly on tobacco trading.

Several groups resisted the Bourbon Reforms. In addition to unrest among Indians, slaves, and mixed-race peasant farmers, imperial officials had to keep Creole elites from striking against royal authority. Jesuits, Catholic friars who had played a large role for hundreds of years in establishing the Spanish Empire, now saw their economic and even their spiritual power challenged by Charles's royal decrees and colonial inspectors. When Jesuits resisted the Bourbon Reforms, Charles III expelled the 2,200 Jesuits from Spanish America in 1767. This expulsion set the stage for the reemergence of the Franciscan order in North America. The Franciscans would spread the Spanish Empire farther by building a system of missions in California and expanding their missions in Texas and New Mexico in the decades to follow.

The Enlightenment and Colonial Identity

As the Spanish and English empires in North America underwent reforms in the 1760s, the European Enlightenment influenced both European leaders and their colonial opponents. The Enlightenment began in 17th-century France and Britain as an intellectual movement that emphasized the powers of reason, observation, and experience to explain the natural and social worlds. The ideas of Enlightenment thinkers influenced social and economic reform, science, philosophy, and social and political theory. Principles of human rights and individualism circulated in books, pamphlets, and newspapers throughout North America, especially in the British colonies. The works of English politician and philosopher **John Locke**, especially his *Two Treatises on Government* (1690), argued that governments must protect the rights of individuals to pursue life, liberty, and property. Scottish writers Francis Hutcheson and David Hume emphasized the potential of individuals to pursue moral progress, especially in a commercial age.

The French writers who most influenced British North Americans were Voltaire and Montesquieu; the latter's *Spirit of the Laws* (1748) became a well-read guide on how to create a republic, a representative government with separation of powers.

Most British American colonists in 1763 saw themselves as part of the empire of British liberty, a view enhanced by Enlightenment principles. They believed that the British government was a bastion of liberty and property rights, and they revered the powerful check that Parliament could provide on royal authority in the British system of mixed government. But whereas Enlightenment ideals strengthened some allegiance to empire, they also exposed the colonies' economic and political dependence, leading some to oppose Great Britain. American colonists became fascinated with British writers who extolled more radical forms of republican government, such as Algernon Sidney, John Trenchard, and Thomas Gordon. Their republican ideas influenced colonists who viewed parliamentary and royal crackdowns as threats to liberty. Spanish Bourbon reformers were influenced by Montesquieu and by Spanish Enlightenment thinkers to apply rationalist principles to their reform efforts, but the Jesuits who opposed them cited more traditional Catholic doctrines in defense of church power.

Excerpt from John Locke, *Two Treatises on Government* (1690)

Americans who opposed British taxes during the imperial crisis called themselves **Whigs** after the opposition political party in England that stood against excesses of centralized royal power. Learned Americans, interested in pursuing and promoting enlightened scientific knowledge, founded the American Philosophical Society in Philadelphia in 1769. **Benjamin Franklin**, David Rittenhouse, and John Bartram, three of its founders, were also internationally known scientists who belonged to the most important British scientific society, the Royal Society of London. But Franklin and several other founders of the American Philosophical Society would soon become leaders of colonial resistance to Britain.

STUDY QUESTIONS FOR ENGLISH AND SPANISH IMPERIAL REFORM

1. In what ways were British and Spanish colonial reforms similar or different?

2. Why did Pontiac's Rebellion help lead to the Proclamation of 1763?

quiz

STAMP ACT AND RESISTANCE

When the British Parliament and Prime Minister Grenville imposed direct taxes on American colonists in 1764 and 1765, they galvanized colonial protest movements. Americans were used to taxing themselves, and they objected to change. The 1765 **Stamp Act**, which taxed paper products and documents, inaugurated a new era of resistance in the British colonies. Maryland lawyer Daniel Dulany urged fellow colonists during the Stamp Act crisis: "Instead of moping . . . and whining to excite compassion; in such a situation we ought with spirit, and vigour, and alacrity, to bid defiance to tyranny, by exposing its impotence." Men and women of various social classes across British North America heeded his call to defiance, and Parliament faced a resistance movement more widespread and coordinated than any it had seen before.

Parliamentary Action

In the months leading up to the Stamp Act's passage in March 1765, eight colonial assemblies sent petitions to Parliament in protest. But Grenville was determined to raise funds and to assert imperial authority. The Stamp Act assessed, for the first time, a unified tax that would fall on all British colonists across boundary lines. Grenville argued before Parliament that Americans were "virtually" represented in that body.

The Stamp Act taxed paper, shipping and legal documents, playing cards, dice, newspapers, pamphlets, almanacs, and calendars. Although the tax was approximately 30 percent lower than similar taxes within Great Britain, the amount mattered little to those who objected to what they saw as a change in parliamentary authority, from the regulation of trade to direct taxation. To enforce the taxes, the British government appointed stamp "distributors" in each colony, chosen from among the colonial population to collect the taxes.

Protest and Repeal

When word of the Stamp Act reached the colonies, the Virginia House of Burgesses adopted resolutions of protest proposed by **Patrick Henry**. Virginia's royal governor, Francis Fauquier, dissolved the assembly rather than let protest grow. The stamp distributors provided a target for colonial resistance to the Stamp Act. In August 1765, after Andrew Oliver, the brother-in-law of Massachusetts Royal Lieutenant Governor Thomas Hutchinson, agreed to become the stamp distributor in that colony, a crowd in Boston hanged him in effigy from what became known as the "liberty tree." A crowd led by a poor shoemaker, Seven Years' War veteran **Ebenezer MacIntosh**, then attacked Oliver's office and his house. The following day, Oliver resigned his post as stamp tax collector. Similar actions followed across the colonies over the next few months.

Crowd violence against British authority spread. In Boston, residents attacked officials of the royal admiralty courts and destroyed the house of Lieutenant Governor Hutchinson. Despite their traditional lack of shared political interests, both rich and poor people joined the protests, which worried colonial officials. A group of well-off Bostonian craftsmen calling themselves "The Loyal Nine" organized many actions in Massachusetts, while in Newport, Rhode Island, John Webber, a young transient, led the protests of local merchants. Groups of Stamp Act protesters soon began calling themselves "**Sons of Liberty**." The Sons of Liberty coordinated crowd actions, petitions, pamphlets, and consumer boycotts and spread awareness of colonial protests between colonies. One of the leaders of the Boston Sons of Liberty, **Samuel Adams**, claimed that British subjects would have pursued the same strategies if they saw "their essential Unalienable Rights . . . invaded by Parliament."

James Otis, "The Rights of the British Colonies Asserted and Proved" (1764)

In addition to popular protest, first the Virginia House of Burgesses and then other colonial assemblies passed legislation opposing the Stamp Act. The Massachusetts legislature called on other colonies to appoint delegates to a meeting in New York in October 1765. Twenty-seven delegates from nine colonies met for two weeks and passed a series of resolutions insisting that although colonial subjects owed allegiance to king and Parliament, they were "entitled to all the inherent rights and liberties of his natural born subjects within the kingdom of Great-Britain." The Stamp Act Congress also protested in petitions to the British against taxation without representation while acknowledging obedience to the government. Ultimately, the actions of the Stamp Act Congress held no legal force, but they demonstrated an unprecedented level of cooperation among colonies and a strong resolution to resist taxation.

STAMP ACT Publisher William Bradford put this image on the front page of his *Pennsylvania Journal and Weekly Advertiser* newspaper on October 24, 1765, as part of the protest against the tax provisions of the Stamp Act. The act required all printed material, including newspapers, to affix a "stamp" certifying that the proper taxes had been paid to British officials. Bradford's menacing skull-and-crossbones image reinforced the message that some colonists would be willing to resist the tax strenuously, even violently.

SAMUEL ADAMS Adams was a member of the Boston Town Meeting and the Massachusetts House of Representatives when he began to coordinate protests against increased British taxation and colonial control in the 1760s. Credited as one of the founders of the Sons of Liberty, Adams circulated letters to other colonies calling for solidarity and protest against British authority. He became a member of the Continental Congress and later served as governor of Massachusetts in the 1790s.

In the midst of the Stamp Act protests, George III replaced Grenville as prime minister, appointing the Marquis of Rockingham in July 1765. Rockingham, who aligned himself with the Whig Party in Parliament, faced the immediate challenge of how to quell the unrest. The commander of British military forces in the colonies, General **Thomas Gage**, told the government that he lacked the time, resources, and troops to subdue the opposition, as such a wide range of the populace seemed to be involved. In addition to resisting the Stamp Act through crowd action and legislative protest, colonists in British America also began to organize boycotts of British trade goods. Their efforts increased fears among British merchants that an economic downturn might worsen. Rockingham faced a difficult choice in Parliament, especially after Whig leader **William Pitt** declared that Parliament had no right to tax the unrepresented colonists. Rockingham realized that enforcement of the tax had become impossible. On March 1, 1766, Parliament repealed the Stamp Act.

Empire and Authority

Although Parliament repealed the Stamp Act, Britain retained its authority to tax the colonies. The debate over repeal prompted discussion in both Parliament and the colonies about the nature and limits of British sovereignty. But even parliamentarians friendly to the colonists' tax resistance, such as Pitt, were not willing to concede ultimate authority. Worried that repeal of the Stamp Act would send the wrong message to Americans, Parliament passed the Declaratory Act. This new act reasserted the British right to control the colonies and pass laws "in all cases whatsoever," a phrase that echoed a declaratory act used to emphasize English control of Ireland in 1719. British commentators also stressed that the king's royal authority united all subjects of the crown throughout the empire, and most Americans agreed in 1766. Even protestor John Dickinson wrote that Americans admired their "excellent prince" in whose "good dispositions they could confide."

Benjamin Franklin's account of the Paxton Boys' attack on the Conestoga Indians (1764)

Apart from the Stamp Act, tensions inside the colonies provoked conflicts over imperial authority. In several colonies, conflict between eastern and western inhabitants over land rights, political representation, and Indian policy caused trouble for imperial officials. Pontiac's War had increased tensions, particularly in Pennsylvania. In 1763 and 1764, a group of armed men in western Pennsylvania calling themselves the "Paxton Boys" attacked Susquehannock Indians (also known as Conestoga) who had been guaranteed protection by the crown and by the royal government in Philadelphia. Benjamin Franklin negotiated a compromise when 600 armed westerners marched on the capital to protest the Paxton Boys' indictment. As a result, the Pennsylvania assembly granted the western part of the colony greater representation, which proved that armed protest could gain political representation. In the following years, groups of armed "regulators," farmers from western North Carolina, marched against imperial officials who had tried to enforce taxes and legal judgments against them. Regulators destroyed the houses of North Carolina's royal governor William Tryon and Superior Court judge Richard Henderson.

This kind of unrest led Parliament to pass the first Quartering Act in 1765, authorizing British military forces to be permanently housed in the colonies—at the expense of colonists. In the midst of their resistance to the Stamp Act, many colonists refused to comply with the requirement to house and feed British troops. Colonists resented British troops. The Sons of Liberty in Charleston, South Carolina, argued in newspapers that they were willing and able to keep the peace themselves—even as they resisted imperial authority.

CONSUMER RESISTANCE

Britain was expanding as a consumer society by the mid-18th century, and many American colonists wanted to emulate the British taste in clothing, furniture, and housing. Tied to the British Empire through education, trade, and reverence for English liberty, Americans also found themselves enmeshed in a common world of goods and the credit relationships that enabled their circulation. Ironically, this developing consumer society in the colonies also provided a powerful new strategy of resistance during the rising tensions of imperial conflict after 1765. During the 1760s, the American population grew by an astonishing 40 percent, and, between 1700 and 1770, the per capita American expenditure on British goods grew by 20 percent. These growth trends meant that American consumers held enormous economic clout. When they began collectively to exercise that clout to protest British control and taxation, they helped accelerate an imperial crisis.

Townshend Duties

In June 1767, the British Parliament passed a new series of taxes that emphasized its resolve to legislate for the colonies "in all cases whatsoever," as the Declaratory Act stated. The annual cost of keeping troops in North America had reached £700,000 (over $134 million today). Despite the fact that the Whig faction in charge of the British government was more sympathetic to American objections to "internal" taxation, they still sought to increase government revenue through a series of new taxes on trade. Chancellor of the Exchequer Charles Townshend ushered a series of taxes through Parliament known as the **Townshend Acts**, or "Townshend duties." These taxes hit a variety of commodities central to the transatlantic colonial trade: tea, paper, lead, glass, and paint. The acts also continued a previous tax on molasses, the essential product used to manufacture rum, although at a lower rate.

Along with the new taxes, Parliament continued to press for stricter enforcement of trade duties. The British Treasury Department created an American Board of Customs in Boston staffed by royal appointees. Vice-admiralty courts were established at Boston, Philadelphia, and Charleston and granted the authority to try smugglers without any local jury. The British government also centralized oversight of the colonies and instructed colonial governors to impose control over elected colonial assemblies. The presence of British troops in major American cities, under the terms of the 1765 Quartering Act, emphasized that military power might be used to enhance this new imperial control, and Parliament further authorized soldiers to be forcibly housed in private homes. When the New York assembly refused to enforce the Quartering Act, Parliament passed a restraining act that suspended its legislative authority until it complied. When considering the bill to discipline New York, Charles Townshend told Parliament, "The superiority of the mother country can at no time be better exerted than now."

The Non-Importation Movement

Colonists who opposed British taxation immediately responded to the Townshend duties by renewing their collective action against the "superiority of the mother country." By October 1767, when news of the acts spread, men and women in Boston and elsewhere had started to discuss boycotting British imports. By the time the new taxes went into effect in November 1767, many American colonists had already pledged to avoid purchasing British goods and vowed to make do with their own homemade items and homespun cloth. By the spring of 1768, the non-importation movement had spread from Boston to New York, Philadelphia, Charleston, and other port cities. John Dickinson argued in his popular 1768 pamphlet series *Letters from a Farmer in Pennsylvania* that Parliament could regulate trade but that colonists would not submit to parliamentary taxation of any kind. Samuel Adams drafted a petition to King George III, passed by the Massachusetts legislature in January 1768 and subsequently endorsed by Virginia and other colonial assemblies, that protested "taxation without representation" and called for colonies to coordinate their resistance.

John Dickinson, excerpt from *Letters From A Farmer in Pennsylvania* (1768)

Britain largely ignored the protests by colonial assemblies throughout 1768, and so the non-importation movement spread. In 1769, groups in several colonies signed formal non-importation agreements, called "associations," and the Sons of Liberty and other organizations that had protested the Stamp Act reemerged. In New England and the middle colonies, merchants led the non-importation movement, while in the southern colonies associations of merchants, traders, politicians, and small farmers held meetings to endorse even broader boycotts. Several colonial governments—including the Boston Town Meeting and the Connecticut, New Jersey, and New York assemblies—passed resolutions supporting non-importation. Non-importation drastically reduced the trade of sugar into the North American colonies and increased hardship where sugar was produced in the West Indies, causing thousands of enslaved people to starve. But the British continued to ignore the boycotts.

Although broadly based, the non-importation movement fostered bitter disputes between those who supported Parliament and the boycotters. People caught selling or trying to buy British goods in major cities found themselves punished by angry crowds; several Boston newspapers even published violators' names on their front pages. Merchants who opposed the boycotts labeled the movement as the actions of "the deluded multitude." These merchants claimed that traders who subscribed to the non-importation agreements often violated them secretly to make higher profits. Elsewhere, wealthier Revolutionaries joined causes with the poor, although their political similarities could never totally cover over economic differences.

Men and Women: Tea and Politics

The non-importation movement brought men and women together politically as they opposed imperial authority. Boycotts invested political meaning in women's everyday activities of purchasing, preparing, and consuming commodities such as tea. Tea drinking had become an important part of many white women's social rituals by the mid-1700s, linking American women to the British importers who traded tea from India and China to North America. From the upper classes who drank tea out of silver pots and china cups around polished mahogany tea tables to poor women who used pottery cups and prized only a few cups of the expensive beverage per week, white women were associated with tea. As one Boston newspaper predicted in November 1767, "The cost of consuming foreign tea is very expensive in this colony. . . . [T]o lay an extensive tax on its consumption, would be very disagreeable to the Ladies."

In speeches and newspaper articles, male supporters of the non-importation movement appealed to women to participate in the boycotts, and several women also wrote to newspapers appealing for the "Daughters of Liberty" to act. Female shopkeepers were among those who signed public pledges not to sell imported British goods, and city women made a show of drinking only coffee or herbal tea. Other women conspicuously wore only homespun fabric and held spinning bees to raise supplies of homemade textiles. New England shopkeeper Elizabeth Murray urged a relative that it was everyone's "duty to stand up for so valuable a country & not be tax'd" by Parliament or forced to keep soldiers in North America.

By the end of 1769, the British government had realized that the Townshend duties had failed. The taxes had brought in less than £20,000, while British merchants had lost more than £700,000. Colonial merchants smuggled vast quantities of goods and traded with Dutch merchants willing to sell illegal tea. The new British ministry, headed by Lord North, decided in 1770 to repeal all the Townshend duties except for the tax on tea, which would continue "as a mark of the supremacy of Parliament." The non-importation movement quickly faded with the repeal of the other Townshend duties, but the legacy of political mobilization would live on.

TEA TABLES AND HOME DÉCOR This portrait of a Connecticut clockmaker shows how genteel furnishings provided the setting for socializing in elite American homes, where men and women drank tea from polished mahogany tea tables, like the one featured here. The clockmaker also displays an example of his work—a wooden clock—and many of his books. Portraits like this show how objects made in the colonies by master furniture makers could become important parts of American identities.

The Boston Massacre

While the Townshend duties were in place, harsh resistance to them in Boston particularly vexed the British government, which responded by sending British soldiers to keep order. Beginning on October 1, 1768, the first of 4,000 British soldiers arrived to police Boston, a city of just 15,000. The soldiers, stationed around the city in private residences, often clashed with local citizens—who feared the power of a standing army. Soldiers also competed for seasonal jobs with poor working people of Boston, many of whom were also active in the Whig resistance. Tensions heated up in February 1770 when a customs

image analysis

THE BOSTON MASSACRE Paul Revere published this propagandistic engraving of the Boston Massacre in 1770. It shows British soldiers shooting down unarmed civilians in front of the Boston Custom House, which Revere relabeled as "Butcher's Hall." Revere was one of the best engravers in Massachusetts, and his work helped to spread outrage.

official killed 11-year-old Christopher Seider, sparking mob action and a skirmish between Boston rope workers and British soldiers on March 3.

Tensions boiled over on March 5, 1770, in the incident that became known as the **Boston Massacre**. A crowd began to harass a British sentry, and when eight soldiers came to his aid, the crowd threw rocks and snowballs at them. The soldiers fired into the crowd. Five working men were killed, including a runaway slave named Crispus Attucks. Following the skirmish, British soldiers and customs collectors withdrew to the fortress of Castle William on an island in Boston Harbor. Public opinion against the British soldiers ran high, especially after silversmith **Paul Revere** published an inflammatory engraving of the incident depicting the British soldiers as cruel murderers. **John Adams** and **Josiah Quincy, Jr.**, Boston lawyers who were loyal to the Whig cause but believed in fair trials, helped to acquit the British commander, Captain Preston. Only two of the soldiers were found guilty of manslaughter, and they were lightly punished and released.

STUDY QUESTIONS FOR CONSUMER RESISTANCE

1. Why did North American colonists use non-importation as a resistance strategy against British taxation?

2. In what ways did protests mobilize elite white women and poorer men and women?

quiz

⊘RESISTANCE BECOMES REVOLUTION

Between 1770 and 1776, resistance to imperial change turned into a full-on revolution. After a short cooling-off period at the beginning of the 1770s, colonial protests threatened to turn violent. Eventually, that violence would be channeled into organized revolutionary warfare. How could the colonists fight a war with Britain and still remain part of the British Empire?

Boston Tea Party and Coercive Acts

Although the formal associations that organized boycotts during the non-importation movement faded away after 1770, the tax on tea remained, and many colonists continued to avoid drinking tea. Beginning in Boston, and then spreading to every colony, groups of men formed Committees of Correspondence to provide networks of communication between Whigs in different colonies. The committees were in place when Parliament passed the Tea Act in March 1773, granting the East India Company a monopoly on the North American tea trade. The monopoly lowered the price of tea, but it did not remove the tax, and it granted new powers to colonial customs officials and to the East India Company to appoint official tea merchants in each colony. This legislation reawakened popular protest, as Whigs quickly planned resistance against tea agents.

In several port cities, to avoid protests, government officials persuaded ship captains to leave port without unloading the East India Company tea. But in Boston in December 1773, Governor Thomas Hutchinson refused to allow the tea ships to leave Griffin's Wharf without unloading their cargo of tea. On December 16, Samuel

Adams and other Sons of Liberty organized a huge mass meeting in Old South Meeting House where they denounced the tea shipments as instruments of British tyranny. That evening, 30 to 60 men disguised as Mohawk Indians stormed the tea ships and dumped 90,000 pounds of tea into Boston harbor. The **Boston Tea Party** mobilized Bostonians and spread resistance to other colonies. Protestors burned a tea ship in Annapolis, Maryland; Princeton University students destroyed tea and effigies of Thomas Hutchinson; and new tea boycott associations formed—including one among the women of Edenton, North Carolina. One South Carolinian remarked that in Charleston, all ranks of individuals, "the gentleman and the mechanic, those of high and low life, the learned and illiterate," had been mobilized into political action.

The destruction of property in the tea protests shocked Parliament, which quickly sanctioned Massachusetts in a series of 1774 laws dubbed the **Coercive Acts**, or the "**Intolerable Acts**" by Whig colonists. Lord North told the House of Commons, "We are now to establish our authority, or give it up entirely"—and not even parliamentary representatives who favored the colonists' cause, such as Edmund Burke, would relent. The Coercive Acts closed the port of Boston and reorganized the Massachusetts government, altering its colonial charter to put more authority in the hands of royal appointees. The acts also imposed royal control over local courts, authorized troops to be forcibly billeted in private houses and buildings, and installed the British army commander Thomas Gage as the new colonial governor. In addition to these Coercive Acts, Parliament also passed the Quebec Act in 1774—which further frightened Protestant New Englanders by expanding royal control in Canada and endorsing official Catholicism.

THE DESTRUCTION OF THE TEA This engraving shows the Boston Tea Party, or the "destruction of the tea," as it was sometimes known in the 19th century. The depiction of the incident shows how the Tea Party has been a subject of popular imagination since the end of the 18th century. Although the protesters did disguise themselves as "Mohawk Indians," the effect was likely not as complete as depicted here.

Empire, Control, and the Language of Slavery

The Coercive Acts galvanized political opposition inside Massachusetts, and Whigs soon organized a new boycott movement. The crackdown on Massachusetts also energized Whigs in many other colonies who feared similar repressive action. Virginia legislator **Thomas Jefferson** wrote in a pamphlet, *A Summary View of the Rights of British America*, that the colonies held natural rights to free international trade and that only the king, not Parliament, held limited sovereignty over the colonies. Philadelphians began to call for a meeting to issue colonial petitions to the king—the highest and last authority who might redress their grievances. After Virginia's royal governor dissolved the House of Burgesses, the legislative body met illegally at a tavern in Williamsburg to endorse a new boycott and to call for a continental congress to coordinate protests.

Thomas Jefferson, *A Summary View of the Rights of British America* (1774)

When Jefferson argued that Parliament sought to subdue the colonies through "a series of oppressions," he expressed a vision of the British engaged in "a deliberate systematical plan of reducing us to slavery." Jefferson's use of the word "slavery" signaled the extreme fear that many colonists had of being deprived of their liberties. The term was used by a range of Americans who shared that fear. During the boycott movement, **Abigail Adams** referred to tea as "this weed of Slavery." Her husband, Massachusetts lawyer John Adams, wrote that England, "once the land of liberty—the school of patriots—the nurse of heroes, has become the land of slavery." This language of slavery indicated how deeply many Whigs had come to fear the British government and the perceived corruption of the British system.

American colonists were not blind to the irony of calling themselves "slaves" to the British government while many colonists actually owned African American slaves. In fact, they intentionally used the term "slavery" to indicate a subordinate, degraded position with which they were intimately familiar. Many of the leaders of the Revolutionary movement, especially in colonies such as Virginia where slavery was widespread, had social prestige because of inherited wealth based on slave ownership and labor. Virginian **George Washington** wrote during the controversy over the Coercive Acts, "The crisis is arrived when we must assert our rights or submit to every imposition, that can be heaped upon us, till custom and use shall make us as tame and abject slaves, as the blacks we rule over with such arbitrary sway." In every colony, African American slaves lived beside free men and women, and that reality made political "slavery" all the more fearsome as the British asserted their power.

Mobilization

Parliament had intended the Coercive Acts to cut off Massachusetts from the other colonies, to isolate radicals and stop their rebellion. Instead, the acts aroused sympathy for Massachusetts and prompted Whigs in far-flung colonies to unite more than ever before. In September 1774, representatives of 12 colonies (the royal governor prevented Georgia from sending representatives) met in a continental congress at Philadelphia. Jamaica and other Caribbean colonies opposed the Coercive Acts, but their assemblies took no action to join the Continental Congress, since Caribbean planters served in and had more direct access to Parliament than did their neighbors to the north. Many colonists loyal to the British government questioned the authority of the **First Continental Congress** to speak for them. The Congress even discussed colonial independence, although very few delegates supported it. The First Continental Congress also charged committees in each colony to vigorously enforce boycotts; endorsed a declaration of rights and grievances on October 14, 1774; and then adjourned, hoping that their appeal to the king would check parliamentary authority.

But an angry King George urged Parliament to impose even more control on the colonies to break what he deemed "disobedience to the law." Committees in all 13 British North American colonies organized for public defense. In Boston, Thomas Gage's troops all but shut down the city. In the surrounding small towns and countryside, Whig men and women began to stockpile weapons, manufacture bullets, commandeer royal caches of gunpowder, and practice military drills. Local militias in Massachusetts and Connecticut went on alert to respond quickly (as **minutemen**) to possible British military action after Gage's forces captured a powder cache in Charlestown in September 1774. Virginia Governor John Murray, Earl of Dunmore, told crown officials that committees in every township violently enforced boycotts and that Whig military companies had organized to protect them. In the early months of 1775, Edmund Burke and other sympathetic members of Parliament tried unsuccessfully to get the British government to make concessions to the colonists.

Edmund Burke, excerpts from "Conciliation with the Colonies" (1775)

War Begins

Early in 1775, General Gage decided to crack down on Concord, Massachusetts, where the dissolved colonial assembly met illegally and where he suspected colonists had a large stockpile of weapons and gunpowder. On the evening of April 18, 1775, Gage assembled 700 of his 3,500 redcoats (as British soldiers were nicknamed) on Boston Common and readied them to be transported into the countryside. Whig activists Paul Revere and William Dawes rode out of Boston to warn the militiamen at Concord and nearby Lexington to ready themselves and to warn radical leaders Samuel Adams and John Hancock to leave Lexington, where they were hiding from arrest. In the early morning of April 19, Captain John Parker's company of militia skirmished with British soldiers led by Major John Pitcairn on Lexington green. Eight militiamen were killed in the opening battle of the Revolutionary War.

Later that morning, five miles away in Concord, the local militia, now reinforced by other men from the surrounding countryside, engaged British regulars in a larger battle at the North Bridge. After the battle, the British soldiers made their way back to Boston along the winding 16-mile rural road. They came under fire from the woods, as hundreds of Massachusetts militia troops sniped at the regulars. Gage's troops holed up in Boston, awaiting reinforcements, as more than 10,000 colonial militia forces surrounded the city over the next month. Colonists up and down the Eastern Seaboard celebrated resistance to the British army. Peter Timothy, the secretary of the Charleston, South Carolina, Committee of Correspondence, wrote in his newspaper that the "ever-memorable" battles on April 19, 1775, would mark "a grand epoch in the History of Mankind. . . . An Epoch, that in all Probability will mark the Declension of the British Empire!"

The Second Continental Congress convened on May 10, 1775, just one day after **Ethan Allen**, with assistance from men commanded by Benedict Arnold, had captured the British Fort Ticonderoga. As the British planned their next move, the Continental Congress set about organizing the Continental Army, and on June 15 they chose as its commander George Washington, whose genteel Virginia heritage and military experience made him stand out among the delegates. Even before Washington could assume command, the **Battle of Bunker Hill** took place on June 17. Major General William Howe, who had arrived in Boston with reinforcements, ordered an attack on the heights at Charlestown, across the Charles River from Boston. The Americans fortified Breed's Hill, which they misidentified as Bunker Hill, and met the better-equipped regulars who streamed up the hill in three waves of attack to try and capture the heights. Although the colonial forces retreated to end the battle, they claimed victory in proving they could hold up against greater numbers of well-trained soldiers. The British also suffered their heaviest casualty rate of the entire war: of 2,500 soldiers, 228 died and 826 were wounded.

Death of General Warren at the Battle of Bunker Hill by John Trumbull (1786)

For the remainder of the year, the British remained in Boston plotting their next move as Washington and the Continental Congress worked to organize and equip the Continental Army. American commanders planned an invasion of Canada, intended to rouse Canadians against the British, who had very few troops stationed there. Two expeditions, one led by Philip Schuyler and Richard Montgomery, the other by Benedict Arnold, set out for Canada late in the year, but both ended in disaster. By January 1776, Montgomery had been killed and no groundswell of support had emerged for the American cause in Canada.

Lord Dunmore's Proclamation

In Virginia, by late December 1775, the war was beginning to take a different course. Royal Governor John Murray, Fourth Earl of Dunmore, had fought to contain the Revolutionary movement in that colony since he arrived in 1771. In 1774, Dunmore proved his pugnacious nature when he led military operations against Shawnee and Mingo Indian people in the west of the colony and forced Shawnee leader Cornstalk to withdraw across the Ohio River and to cede territory to expanding Virginian settlers. Dunmore insisted on crown power, whether fighting Native peoples or rebellious members of the Virginia House of Burgesses.

In November 1775, with the Revolutionary War underway, Revolutionaries fought with Dunmore over stores of gunpowder, and he responded by declaring martial law in Virginia. Following up on threats he had made several months earlier, Dunmore issued a proclamation that offered freedom to slaves and indentured servants who joined the British cause. Hundreds responded to Dunmore's proclamation, even as white slave-owning Revolutionaries were horrified. George Washington argued, "Dunmore should be instantly crushed." In December, Dunmore led a force of British regulars, escaped slaves, and loyalists in battle against a Virginia Continental Army regiment outside of Norfolk at Great Bridge. Dunmore's force was defeated, and he fled the colony. Some of the slaves who had joined his cause when he promised them freedom were executed, and others were sold back into bondage in the Caribbean. Still others joined the thousands of other enslaved African Americans who continued to fight on the British side in the war, seeking their freedom under royal protection.

Lord Dunmore's proclamation, November 7, 1775

STUDY QUESTIONS FOR RESISTANCE BECOMES REVOLUTION

1. How did Boston play a key role in the imperial crisis?

2. What British and North American actions caused colonial resistance to escalate into warfare?

quiz

Independence: Transatlantic Roots, Global Influence

The idea of political independence—that colonies could declare themselves to be a state separate from the colonial power—was an innovation in world politics in 1776. But the concept had roots in events and political philosophies that had taken shape in Europe in prior centuries. The Declaration of Independence would also have major global consequences, not the least in its influence on other independence movements, from 1776 until the present day.

The committee of the Continental Congress tasked with drafting the motion of independence in June 1776, led by Thomas Jefferson, was steeped in western European political theory and history. Jefferson was able to draw on both theory and practice in drafting the Declaration. Statements of sovereignty and autonomy stretching back to the Scottish Declaration of Arbroath in 1320 made it clear that self-determination could be a major factor in international relations.

The idea that a people who held valid grievances against their ruler could declare independence was influenced by several Enlightenment theories about what constituted a legitimate government. Thomas Jefferson drew on the ideas in John Locke's *Second Treatise of Government*, published in 1689 during the Glorious Revolution, the culmination of almost a century of fighting over who should occupy the British throne. Jefferson employed especially Locke's notion that monarchs and legislative bodies derive at least some of their authority from the consent of those who are governed, and he paraphrased some of Locke's justifications for how tyranny might force the "dissolution" of an unjust government. Jefferson was also influenced by ideas about natural rights and the obligations of moral necessity in essays published by Scottish judge and philosopher Henry Home, Lord Kames, in the mid-18th century. Independence itself was a strong component of national sovereignty as defined by Swiss legal expert Emer de Vattel in his 1758 *The Law of Nations*. Jefferson may also have been influenced by 16th-century Spanish Jesuit writings on the limits of kingship.

News of the Declaration of Independence spread unusually fast throughout Europe, with copies appearing in newspapers and translated pamphlets in Britain, Ireland,

◉ DECLARING INDEPENDENCE

With the Revolutionary War well underway, the British Empire in North America reached its breaking point. As the first six months of the Revolutionary War unfolded, the Second Continental Congress began to consider the possibility of declaring independence from Great Britain, even though colonies had never before tried such a bold maneuver. How would the British colonies conceive of their separation from Parliament and the crown? How would independent former colonies relate to the rest of the world? Would Spanish imperial reforms be met by similar resistance?

Holland, Austria, Denmark, Italy, Switzerland, and Poland by September 1776. Pamphlet copies also appeared in France, Spain, and Russia, whose rulers initially reacted cautiously even though they were supporting the American war effort against Britain. Translations of the Declaration also circulated around Latin America in the following decades, helping to influence Latin American independence movements from Mexico to Chile. Full translations did not appear in China and several other Asian countries until the 20th century, but English copies did circulate there.

As news of the Declaration spread, some Europeans resisted the notion that declaring independence was a legitimate political idea. This resistance intensified as Europe became embroiled in its own revolutionary conflicts by the end of the 18th century. As soon as news of the Declaration reached Britain, crown supporter John Lind wrote a scathing *Answer to the Declaration of the American Congress* that rejected the entire basis for the document. Some European translations of the Declaration, even in sympathetic countries such as Spain and Russia, downplayed the more radical implications of the document—toning down, for instance, the emphasis on the "pursuit of happiness" and natural and individual rights.

Even as the intellectual justifications of independence continued to be debated, the practical political strategy of declaring independence spread quickly in the decades after the American Revolution. By 1826, 20 other countries had declared their independence. Historian David Armitage, who has studied the global influence of the Declaration of Independence, notes that today "over half the countries of the world have their own declarations of independence." Armitage argues that countries as different as the Republic of Vietnam, Southern Rhodesia, Venezuela, and Liberia have all employed language similar to that of the U.S. Declaration in their own founding documents. Not all countries followed the U.S. model or justifications for independence, but the political tactic employed by the Continental Congress in 1776 has certainly influenced world history.

- Why was it so important for the Declaration of Independence to appeal to the broader world at large?
- In what ways do you think the Declaration of Independence has shaped global opinion of the United States?

The Venezuelan Declaration of Independence (1811)

The World's First Declaration of Independence

Through the first months of the Revolutionary War, many Whigs had continued to pledge allegiance to the king. They felt that royal authority would guard them against Parliament and that the empire need not be severed. In July 1775, the Continental Congress sent an **Olive Branch Petition** to George III asking him to settle the conflict, but, by spring 1776, Congress was fielding petitions from colonial committees and assemblies calling for independence. In March 1776, British forces evacuated Boston and retreated to Halifax to strategize and reinforce before planning a full-out

THE DECLARATION OF INDEPENDENCE The Continental Congress took a huge risk by issuing the Declaration of Independence in July 1776. No colony in the history of the world had ever declared its independence and asserted its right to become a nation. Success depended on the reaction of the rest of the world and on the ability of the Americans to win their Revolutionary War.

offensive against the Americans. In May, the City of London petitioned George III to approach his colonies peacefully, but the king responded that the colonists had "brought upon themselves" the trouble "by an unjustifiable resistance to the constitutional authority of this Kingdom." When the king rejected peace, even moderates like Philadelphia's Robert Morris conceded that a "declaration of Independency" was probably inevitable.

Virginia's delegation to the Continental Congress, headed by Richard Henry Lee, proposed a motion to declare independence from Great Britain on June 7, 1776. After debate over whether independence would bring aid from France and Spain, Congress delayed voting on the resolution until the beginning of July to give colonial committees and assemblies time to endorse the idea. A congressional subcommittee, which included John Adams and Thomas Jefferson, worked on the independence motion. Jefferson wrote the declaration, with some editing by Adams and Benjamin Franklin. The Continental Congress voted for independence on July 2, and the following day a large British fleet commanded by General William Howe bearing a rejuvenated British army force landed outside New York City.

The **Declaration of Independence**, issued by Congress on July 4, 1776, was the first document of its kind in world history. Many colonies, assemblies, and legislative bodies had in previous centuries put forth declarations concerning rights and privileges, and this document drew on historical precedents that defined British rights and liberty. But never before had a group of colonies listed its grievances, declared itself to be an independent state, and asserted its own sovereignty. The Declaration began with a sweeping statement about rights that put a new twist on the Enlightenment ideas of John Locke: "We hold these truths to be self-evident, that all Men are created equal, that

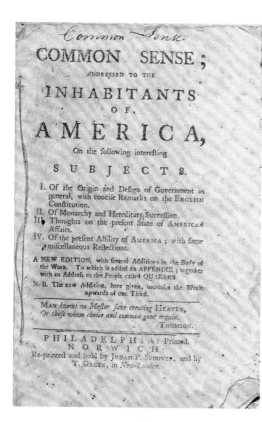

COMMON SENSE Thomas Paine was an English radical who had come to America in 1774, in part because he supported the American protests against Parliament. His immensely popular 1776 pamphlet *Common Sense* advocated independence and helped to gain public acceptance for that tactic among the patriot population. Paine also supported the American war effort with other pamphlets such as *The Crisis*. Later in the 1780s, he moved to France and became an important figure in the French Revolution.

they are endowed by their Creator with certain unalienable Rights, that among these are Life, Liberty and the Pursuit of Happiness." The Declaration focused heavily on perceived violations of rights committed by the king and royal officials—perhaps because most Whigs already felt a separation from Parliament.

The Declaration appealed to "the rest of mankind" to recognize that the United States was free and independent of Britain. **Thomas Paine**, the radical British writer who had immigrated and taken up the colonial cause, urged Americans in his popular pamphlet *Common Sense* at the beginning of 1776 to declare their independence to guarantee political relations and trade with "foreign Courts." The Declaration of Independence itself, however, would not be sufficient to guarantee the success of the United States. The Revolutionary War intensified and offered a military test for the new nation that would last several more years.

Thomas Paine, *Common Sense* (1776)

Spanish Imperial Consolidation

By contrast to the British Empire, Spanish officials were able to bring more of North America under control through the Bourbon Reforms.

José de Gálvez visited Mexico in the 1760s during his tour as inspector general of the Spanish colonies, and by the 1770s, many of his plans for California, New Mexico, and other areas of North America were bearing fruit. Franciscan friars Gaspar de Portolá,

interactive timeline

TIMELINE 1763–1776

AMERICA	YEAR	THE WORLD
Feb Treaty of Paris ends Seven Years' War **May** Pontiac's Rebellion begins when Ottawa forces lay siege to Fort Detroit **Oct** George III forbids settlement west of Appalachian Mountains **Nov** British reorganize governments of Quebec, Florida, and Grenada	**1763**	**Nov** Parliament accuses newspaper publisher John Wilkes of sedition
James Otis publishes pamphlet denying British right to tax colonies **Apr** Parliament revises Navigation Acts and passes Sugar Act **Apr** Currency Act curtails colonial paper money	**1764**	**Nov** Jesuit order is expelled from France **Nov** Japanese peasants riot to protest high taxes
Mar Parliament passes Stamp Act, which taxes legal documents, printed matter, and other paper goods **May** Quartering Act requires colonists to house and pay for British troops **May** Virginia House of Burgesses protests Stamp Act and urges other colonies to join **Oct** Stamp Act Congress meets in Philadelphia, issues "Declaration of Rights and Grievances"	**1765**	Scotsman James Watt invents the steam engine **Aug** Joseph II becomes Holy Roman Emperor, rules alongside his mother Maria Theresa
Mar Stamp Act is repealed, but Declaratory Act stresses that Parliament can tax colonies in "all cases whatsoever" **Jul** Treaty ends Pontiac's Rebellion	**1766**	Ali Bey rules Egypt and declares independence from Ottoman Empire
Mar Charles III expels Jesuits from New Spain for opposing his Bourbon Reform program **Jul** Parliament suspends New York legislature for disobeying Quartering Act **Nov** John Dickinson's *Letters from a Farmer in Pennsylvania* begin to appear in newspapers **Nov** Townshend duties tax a new range of colonial products	**1767**	**Mar** Charles III expels Jesuits from Spain, Parma, and Sicily
Jan Massachusetts legislature petitions George III to protest "taxation without representation"	**1768**	Ghurkas conquer Nepal *Encyclopedia Britannica* begins publication
May Virginia House of Burgesses resolves that Parliament may not tax the colony **Jul** Father Junípero Serra founds his first mission church at San Diego de Alcala	**1769**	China forces Burma to submit to its rule **Aug** Napoleon Bonaparte is born
Mar Five men are killed by British soldiers in "Boston Massacre" **Apr** Parliament withdraws all Townshend duties except for tax on tea	**1770**	The *London Evening Post* becomes first newspaper to reprint parliamentary business

Father Junípero Serra, and Fernando de Rivera y Moncada established a string of missions and presidio forts stretching from southern to northern California by 1774. Juan Bautista de Anza (later the colonial governor of New Mexico) opened a new land route from Mexico and brought an infusion of colonists and livestock to northern California. José de Gálvez put forth a plan in the 1760s to break the northern part of New Spain off from Mexico and bring it under direct crown control, and he got the chance to implement his plan when Charles III appointed him secretary of the Indies in January 1776.

Charles III issued a royal order on August 22, 1776, that created the Comandancia General of the Interior Provinces. The Spanish colonies north of Mexico were formed into a semiautonomous territory for military defense, trade, and crown administration. Teodoro de Croix, a French-born Spanish official who later served as viceroy of Peru, was appointed as the first governor of the Interior Provinces. Croix

AMERICA	YEAR	THE WORLD
Oct Boston Town Meeting urges Committees of Correspondence to form	**1772**	Russia and Prussia partition Poland
Apr Parliament passes Tea Act, seeking to bolster profits of the East India Company **Dec** 90,000 pounds of East India Company tea are thrown into Boston harbor at Boston Tea Party	**1773**	British East India Company becomes a government agency Civil war commences in Annam (now Vietnam) Jesuits expelled from Holy Roman Empire **May** Muhammad Bey assumes power in Egypt, rejoins Ottoman Empire
Mar Parliament closes port of Boston and suspends Massachusetts legislature **Sep** First Continental Congress meets in Philadelphia **Oct** Continental Congress forms a Continental Association to coordinate non-importation **Oct** Parliament passes Quebec Act	**1774**	**May** Louis XVI assumes throne of France **Aug** Jesuit order expelled from Poland
Mar Patrick Henry delivers "Give me liberty or give me death" speech in Virginia House of Burgesses **Apr** Revolutionary War begins at Battles of Lexington and Concord **May** American forces capture Fort Ticonderoga **May** Second Continental Congress meets in Philadelphia **Jun** Congress forms Continental Army and appoints George Washington as commander **Jun** Battle of Bunker Hill **Oct** Congress forms the Continental Navy **Nov** Governor of Virginia offers freedom to slaves who join against rebellious colonists **Nov** Richard Montgomery captures Montreal **Dec** Richard Montgomery killed in the unsuccessful American attack on Quebec	**1775**	
Jan Thomas Paine's *Common Sense* is published **Mar** British forces evacuate Boston **Jul 4** Congress issues Declaration of Independence, creating United States of America	**1776**	Spain opens Buenos Aires to free trade

was ordered to coordinate with the Spanish viceroy in Mexico City, but he exercised autonomous authority in many areas. Croix and Anza pursued aggressive policies against Native peoples, for example, playing Comanche and Apache peoples against one another, and sought to control the increasing number of Russian settlers entering Spanish territory. The organization of the Comandancia of the Interior Provinces helped the California mission system to spread, which extended crown control over more Indian people and territory. The Comandancia set in motion the development of northern Mexico as a semiautonomous region.

1768 map showing the frontiers of New Spain

Spain had been slower to take control over Louisiana after the French ceded it in 1763, and the first Spanish governor, Don Antonio de Ulloa, did not assume office in New Orleans until 1766. No one in the city's mix of French, German, Indian, and free and enslaved African settlers wanted to submit to Spanish authority—especially the

MISSION DOLORES   Father Junípero Serra founded the Misíon San Francisco de Asís (now known as Mission Dolores) in 1776 as part of the effort by the Franciscans to spread the Spanish mission system to the north in California from the 1760s to the 1780s.

city's elites, whose extensive trade and smuggling Ulloa tried to control. Prominent citizens of New Orleans, led by several French settlers, revolted in October 1768, demanded that Ulloa leave the colony, and tried to rejoin the French Empire. Spain sent a new governor, General Alexander O'Reilly, with 2,000 troops to put down the revolt. O'Reilly swiftly seized the protest leaders, tried them, confiscated their property, imprisoned many, and executed 12 men by firing squad. The Louisiana revolt was the largest in North America until that point, comprising the most aggressive imperial military crackdown in North America prior to 1774.

Spanish military force was effective at regaining civic control. Unlike the British, Spain maintained ultimate authority, and independence movements were postponed for several decades.

Ideology and Resistance

In the British colonies, the independence movement helped to solidify ideological changes that had been underway since the imperial crisis first began in 1763. Elite colonists who supported the Whig cause invoked Enlightenment political ideas, but ordinary men and women who participated in collective protest also believed in the importance of "liberty" and "representation." Committees passing resolutions and crowds rioting against tax collectors or boycott violators found that their place as consumers in the markets of the Atlantic world empowered their political views. Preachers such as Boston minister Jonathan Mayhew, politicians such as Virginian Richard Henry Lee, writers such as Thomas Paine, and average people like Massachusetts shoemaker George Robert Twelves Hewes all concluded in their own ways that violations of American "liberty" demanded resistance against the British.

Techniques of resistance in the 1760s and early 1770s—pamphlet writing, riots, destruction of property, crowd actions to enforce community standards, burning enemies in effigy, petitions—were all familiar to the British. Crowds in England and Ireland regularly used these methods throughout the first three-quarters of the 18th century to protest suppression of their political heroes, high food prices, taxes, and foreign policy changes. Tens of thousands of people in England petitioned the government and took to the streets between 1763 and 1774 to protest the persecution of radical printer John Wilkes, who had been denied his elected seat in Parliament. Cries of "Wilkes and Liberty!" could be heard in the streets of London and Middlesex, but also in Charleston, New York, and Boston—where the Sons of Liberty and other American protestors linked their own movement to the Wilkesite cause, especially after seven people were killed and scores wounded in May 1768 in what became known as the St. George's Field Massacre in London.

British American colonists fit into a transatlantic tradition of protest, but only they turned their efforts into a full-blown movement for political independence and a revolutionary war. In the move for independence, Whig Americans rejected not just the actions of the British government but British control altogether. They moved from hoping that the king would protect them from parliamentary control to rejecting the monarchy. They became Americans.

Taking Stock of Empire

In 1776, Spain was expanding its North American empire just as the British Empire in North America crumbled. New Spain stretched as far north as the presidio and Mission Dolores in San Francisco, and the Bourbon Reforms increased crown control over extensive territory north of Mexico. British imperial reforms had achieved the opposite result. After successive attempts to raise revenue from the colonies, and successive resistance in return, 13 British colonies declared independence from the British crown and formed the United States of America. Certainly not everyone in the British North American colonies supported independence, but the Whigs who supported the actions of the Continental Congress seemed to have the upper hand.

STUDY QUESTIONS FOR DECLARING INDEPENDENCE

1. On what grounds did the Declaration of Independence justify separation from Britain?
2. How did British colonial protests finally result in a revolutionary ideology by 1776?
3. How did the Spanish government consolidate control over increasing territory in North America in the mid-18th century?

quiz

Summary

- Both the British and Spanish governments sought centralized control over their North American colonies following the Seven Years' War, in part to raise revenue.
- The 1765 Stamp Act inaugurated an opposition movement in the British North American colonies and touched off a debate over Parliament's authority to tax the colonies.
- Between 1767 and 1770, American men and women politicized consumerism by fighting British taxation with non-importation.
- Between 1770 and 1776, British authorities cracked down on colonial resistance, especially in Massachusetts, and touched off a revolutionary war.
- In 1776, Congress declared independence from Great Britain and created the United States of America, and the Spanish imperial government created the Comandancia General of the Interior Provinces.

Key Terms and People

audio flashcards

Reviewing Chapter 6

1. How did the circulation of people, goods, and ideas between Europe and North America help lead to the American Revolution?
2. Compare the consequences of British and Spanish imperial reforms in the mid-1700s.

Further Reading

Armitage, David. *The Declaration of Independence: A Global History*. Cambridge, MA: Harvard University Press, 2007. This excellent, short book examines the global influences on the Declaration of Independence and how the Declaration has influenced other countries' independence movements ever since. The volume also contains copies of various declarations of independence from around the world from 1776 to 1993.

Elliott, J. H. *Empires of the Atlantic World: Britain and Spain in America, 1492–1830*. New Haven, CT: Yale University Press, 2006. This sweeping history contrasts the development of the British and Spanish colonies in North America over the course of more than 300 years. Elliott's book provides a good basis to compare how England and Spain dealt with resistance in the 1760s differently.

Fenn, Elizabeth. "Biological Warfare in Eighteenth-Century North America: Beyond Jeffrey Amherst." *Journal of American History* 86 (March 2000): 1,552–1,580. This important article examines the claims that British general Jeffrey Amherst intentionally traded smallpox-infected items with Pontiac's warriors and places the act in the context of other acts of germ warfare in the 18th century.

Taylor, Alan. *American Revolutions: A Continental History, 1750–1804*. New York: W. W. Norton, 2016. Taylor argues that the Revolution was a messy, violent contest for control in many different localities, fought despite deep colonial attachments to Great Britain. Taylor also covers the action in French and Spanish colonial America.

Young, Alfred F., Gary B. Nash, and Ray Raphael, eds. *Revolutionary Founders: Rebels, Radicals, and Reformers in the Making of the Nation*. New York: Alfred A. Knopf, 2011. Twenty-two biographical essays discuss ordinary men and women in the American Revolution considered "radical" for their work on behalf of liberty and equality.

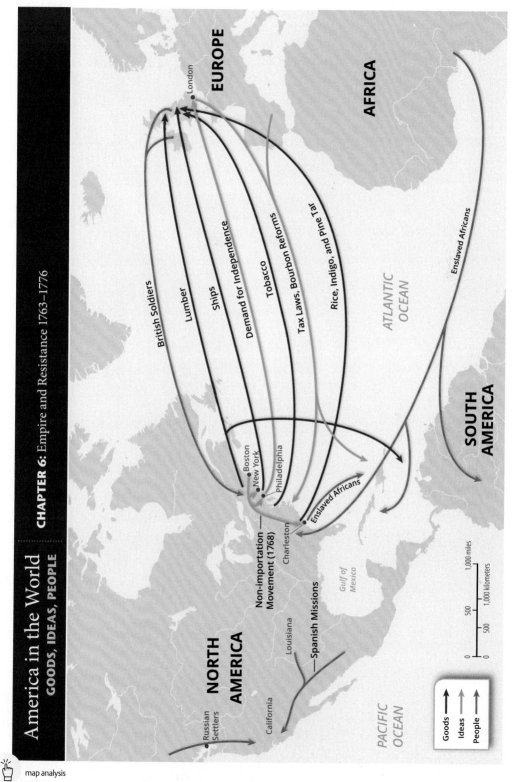

America in the World
GOODS, IDEAS, PEOPLE

CHAPTER 6: Empire and Resistance 1763–1776

EUROPE

London

AFRICA

British Soldiers

Lumber

Ships

Demand for Independence

Tobacco

Tax Laws, Bourbon Reforms

Rice, Indigo, and Pine Tar

ATLANTIC
OCEAN

Enslaved Africans

SOUTH
AMERICA

Boston

New York

Philadelphia

Non-importation
Movement (1768)

Charleston

Enslaved Africans

Gulf of
Mexico

NORTH
AMERICA

Louisiana

Spanish Missions

California

Russian
Settlers

PACIFIC
OCEAN

Goods
Ideas
People

0   500   1,000 miles
0   500   1,000 kilometers

map analysis

Benjamin Franklin This portrait of Benjamin Franklin, commissioned by the American Philosophical Society in 1789, depicts him as a learned man of science. Documents about and pieces of his invention—the lightning rod—lie on the table before him, as a bolt of lightning strikes outside his window. Franklin's scientific knowledge was one of the bases of his great international reputation.

A Revolutionary Nation

W hen Benjamin Franklin arrived in Paris on December 21, 1776, thousands turned out to catch a glimpse of him. Franklin was visiting to court French military and diplomatic assistance for the American fight against Great Britain, France's traditional enemy. Franklin hoped to convince the French to support the American Revolution because, as he declared, "'Tis a Common observation here that our Cause is the *Cause of all Mankind*; and that we are fighting for their liberty in defending our own." French king Louis XVI was not sure that he wanted to support the Americans in their Revolution; nor was he, as Europe's most absolutist king, convinced that French "liberty" was at stake. But Franklin's personal popularity grew so quickly by the beginning of 1777 that the French government could not ignore American diplomacy.

Franklin was the most famous American in Europe. His scientific publications had endeared him to French aristocrats and intellectuals. The Comte de Chaumont invited Franklin to live at his estate outside Paris, and fashionable aristocrats sought Franklin as a party guest. Franklin dressed simply and often wore a fur hat to project a rugged American image, and the French became obsessed with his appearance. Franklin's face appeared on paintings, engravings, statues, jewelry, candy boxes, dishes, and handkerchiefs. Franklin wrote his daughter, "Your father's face [is] as well known as that of the moon." Some fashionable Parisians even had their hair styled in a manner that imitated Franklin's. John Adams later wrote, "There was scarcely a peasant or a citizen, a valet de chambre, coachman or footman, a lady's chambermaid nor a scullion in the kitchen who was not familiar with Franklin's name."

Franklin left the United States for France just a few months after signing the Declaration of Independence and with the experience of having lived for almost

20 years in Britain, representing colonial interests to the British crown. Franklin hoped to win foreign assistance for the Revolutionary War even as France and other European powers waited to see whether Americans could win. Between 1776 and 1789, the United States relied on foreign help as it secured its independence from Great Britain and struggled to form a government. But Americans, like Franklin, also believed that their Revolution offered a new vision of liberty to the rest of the world.

THE REVOLUTION TAKES ROOT

Following the Declaration of Independence in 1776, the United States became a sovereign nation, and each of the 13 states also established new forms of Revolutionary government. The Declaration stated that it had become necessary for "one people to dissolve the political bands which have connected them with another," but, in reality, many Loyalists, Quakers, royal officials, and other American inhabitants did not cut ties to Britain or express allegiance to the new United States. The new nation would have to exert authority over these doubters, but it might never get that chance if it could not win the ongoing war with Great Britain. The United States faced five more years of warfare and the challenge of convincing the world that it was capable of governing itself and worthy of recognition. As the South Carolina legislator David Ramsay wrote, "Our enemies seemed confident of the impossibility of our union; our friends doubted it; and all indifferent persons . . . considered the expectation thereof as romantic." Against all this doubt, the American Revolution took deep root among most Americans.

Ideology and Transatlantic Politics

The American Revolutionaries expressed a set of political and social values that gave meaning to their actions. In their writings and in the state and national governments they established, patriots expressed an ideology of republicanism, which mixed classical Roman ideals with values from the European Enlightenment. The Declaration of Independence fused republican values with a Lockean emphasis on the property rights of free individuals when it termed "life, liberty, and the pursuit of happiness" as "unalienable rights."

American Revolutionaries rejected monarchy and established themselves as citizens of a representative republic. Republicanism emphasized liberty and guarded against tyrannical exercise of governmental power—such as the colonists perceived in the conflict with Britain leading up to the Revolutionary War. James Madison wrote after the Revolutionary War, "We may define a republic to be . . . a government which derives all its powers directly or indirectly from the body of the people." But republicanism meant more than just a form of government because it also implied much about how citizens should relate to one another and to the forms of power in society. Revolutionaries believed that for a voluntary republic to flourish, its citizens must show civic virtue, a care for the common good. Ideally, instead of being governed by hereditary aristocracy and patronage, as one Revolutionary put it, "all offices lie open to men of merit, of whatever rank or condition."

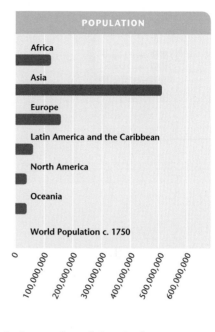

Because of their belief in republicanism, many American Revolutionaries also believed that the future worldwide cause of liberty and the happiness of "the great family of mankind" rested on the success of their movement. This belief in their own role in world history put some Revolutionaries in an awkward situation because they still had to gain European support for the war against Great Britain. John Adams, the Massachusetts politician who was sent to Europe as a diplomat and to negotiate foreign loans, firmly believed that America faced political danger in dealing with European monarchies. Adams desired good commercial and diplomatic relations with France, the Netherlands, and Spain, but he feared that "America has been the Sport of European Wars and Politicks long enough." Americans were in the paradoxical situation of needing help from European monarchs to win their own antimonarchical war—and thereby to guarantee the existence of their republic, which they believed could transform the world.

Trying Times: War Continues

Both British and American military commanders exercised caution in their approach to the Revolutionary War between 1776 and 1778. As a result, neither side gained a distinct strategic advantage. Each side won important battles, but neither was willing or able to inflict a crushing defeat on the other. As long as the Revolutionary spirit and independence movement survived, it would take a monumental British effort to make the United States lose the war. The Revolutionaries, although they enjoyed the support of about 70 percent of the white population in America, could not be assured of a victory either, especially if they could not convince other European nations to aid their cause (Map 7.1).

Briefly turning his attention south, British army commander **Sir William Howe** ordered his forces to evacuate Boston in March 1776. Nine British warships bearing seven regiments of soldiers, commanded by General **Lord Cornwallis**, arrived off the coast of South Carolina. There they joined Sir Henry Clinton's forces in an attack on Charleston that Revolutionaries narrowly rebuffed at the Battle of Sullivan's Island on June 28, 1776. British naval forces commanded by Admiral Sir Peter Parker sailed back north—headed for New York and Halifax.

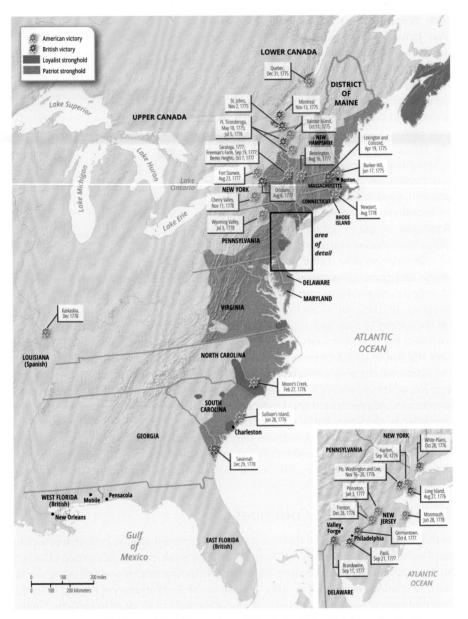

MAP 7.1 Major Revolutionary War Battles, 1775–1778 This map shows the locations of major battles in the first four years of the Revolutionary War and depicts areas of particular Loyalist and patriot strength.

In September 1776, William Howe and his brother Admiral **Sir Richard Howe** used their 32,000 British soldiers and German mercenary troops—dubbed "Hessians" by the Americans—to launch an attack against American commander General George Washington's forces at Long Island. Through the fall the Howes' forces defeated the American army and militia troops in a series of battles stretching from Brooklyn Heights to White Plains, New York. Although missing several chances to destroy the

Hessians
in the
American
Revolution

Americans, they managed to occupy New York City for the rest of the war. General Cornwallis's force chased Washington across New Jersey. Then, in the first week of December, Washington fled into Pennsylvania. Cornwallis left Hessian troops to watch the Americans across the Delaware, and returned to New York to go into winter quarters.

Thomas Paine correctly described the American military predicament when he declared in his pamphlet *The American Crisis* on December 19, 1776, "These are the times that try men's souls." Washington decided to cross the Delaware again and launch a surprise attack on the Hessian camp at Trenton, New Jersey, late on Christmas night. The unconventional attack was successful but also seemed to confirm that Washington was most successful when he avoided open European-style battles. Washington's victory at the Battle of Trenton, which he followed with a victory at the Battle of Princeton on January 3, 1777, represented two of his few early successes.

Thomas Paine, *The American Crisis* (1776)

General Washington had trouble taking advantage of the successes at Princeton and Trenton. American forces were plagued by spotty militia performance, expiring enlistments, and conflict with Loyalists, who took advantage of William Howe's offer to pardon any man who swore an oath to the crown or joined up with British military forces.

In the fall of 1777, Washington tried to defend the U.S. capital at Philadelphia, but Howe defeated him in a series of battles in and around Brandywine, Pennsylvania. Washington's force survived, but it was not clear whether American troops could beat the British in open battle. The British not only had the greater numbers of troops in most areas of the military conflict, but were also better trained and supplied. Congress fled Philadelphia, which Howe occupied in September. After losing a close contest at Germantown on October 4, Washington retreated and prepared to enter winter quarters at Valley Forge, Pennsylvania.

Farther north, the British government sent Major General John Burgoyne in early 1777 to Canada with another plan to invade New England and recapture Fort Ticonderoga. His mixed force of British, Hessian, Canadian militia, Loyalist, and Indian troops made slow progress after capturing Fort Ticonderoga at the beginning of July. American commander Major General **Horatio Gates** dealt Burgoyne's troops a blow at Freeman's Farm on the Hudson River in September. Gates won an even bigger battle at Saratoga, New York, on October 7, forcing Burgoyne to surrender his entire 6,000-man army to Gates, who had proved that American forces could inflict decisive defeat. Although most of his troops were held prisoner for the remainder of the war, "Gentleman

GENERAL WASHINGTON This portrait of George Washington, painted by Charles Willson Peale during the Revolutionary War (c. 1779–1781), depicts the physical confidence, stature, and commanding presence that helped establish his dominance as commander of the Continental Army.

Johnny" Burgoyne was released on parole, as befit an officer of the day, and he returned to Britain in disgrace. Victory in the Battle of Saratoga was one of the most significant moments in the entire Revolutionary War.

Alliance with France

The Battle of Saratoga was the turning point of the Revolutionary War because it helped to convince France to form an alliance with the United States. On December 4, 1777, Boston merchant Jonathan Loring Austin brought the news of Burgoyne's defeat at Saratoga to American diplomats Benjamin Franklin, Richard Henry Lee, and Silas Deane in France. The French foreign minister, the **Comte de Vergennes**, had authorized secret aid to the American Revolutionaries since May 1776. Sympathetic aristocrats and merchants sent money and supplies. The playwright Caron de Beaumarchais, for example, set up the trade company Hortalez & Cie. to secretly funnel aid to the United States. From 1776 onward, the French supplied over 90 percent of the gunpowder used by the American military. Vergennes wanted to ally with the United States, but he had not been able to build political support for the move. Now, the news of the decisive American victory at Saratoga gave Vergennes all he needed to support the United States openly against France's enemy, Great Britain. Spain continued to drag its feet, but the French moved forward with an alliance.

The French government granted the United States diplomatic recognition at the end of 1777. In February 1778, France and the United States signed a Treaty of Amity and Commerce and a Treaty of Alliance in which France promised "not to lay down their arms until the Independence of the United States shall have been formally or tacitly assured." Congress ratified both treaties on May 4, 1778, creating the first diplomatic alliance in American history. Vergennes was preparing for a possible Austro-Prussian war on the continent, so he hesitated to commit full French naval power to the fight in North America until 1780, but in April 1778, the Comte d'Estaing sailed for America with a fleet of 16 French warships and 4,000 troops. Early in 1778, George Washington despaired that the American military was in a "distressed, ruinous, and deplorable condition," and he feared defeat "if a remedy is not soon applied." Patriots hoped that French aid would bring just such a remedy.

STUDY QUESTIONS FOR THE REVOLUTION TAKES ROOT

1. In what ways did the Battle of Saratoga represent a turning point in the Revolutionary War?
2. Why did the American Revolutionaries seek and accept aid from European monarchies?

quiz

❂ THE STRUCTURE OF AUTHORITY

One cause of George Washington's despair over future prospects was the unstable organization of the American government and military—which French aid could only partially address. While trying to win a war, the United States had to build an effective governmental structure. The Second Continental Congress had directed the early operations of the war and had declared independence from Great Britain, but by the time it ratified the treaty with France, it still operated under no formal constitutional authority. It took the Congress more than 16 months to draft the **Articles of Confederation** and several more years for all the states to ratify it. In the meantime, Congress governed and states drafted constitutions. But questions of legitimacy remained. Although the Continental Army expressed clear allegiance to civilian congressional authority, it had its own internal difficulties—especially regarding supply and the coordination of army and militia forces and enlistments. How could the United States build a government strong enough to reassure foreign powers of its legitimacy? If government failed, even foreign aid might not be sufficient to win the war or to solidify the American Revolution.

State Governments

In May 1776, even before the Continental Congress adopted the Declaration of Independence, it instructed individual colonies to begin drafting state constitutions. Whigs, who had been governing in practice without constitutional authority in many colonies, and who had been directing war operations, decided to focus their energies on written constitutions that would define state power. In many cases, state constitutions as written documents (different from the unwritten British constitution) grew out of royal charters and other colonial decrees. Everywhere they defined power counter to the colonial organization of government. By the end of 1776, 11 of 13 states had drafted state constitutions, and Georgia and New York completed theirs the following year. Each state pursued economic policies, contracted debts, and pursued land claims with a minimum of coordination between them.

Every state established itself as a representative republic that derived sovereignty from the people, who would demonstrate their consent through voting. Each state established a balance between executive, legislative, and judicial powers, in keeping with the political idea of **separation of powers** articulated by the French Enlightenment philosopher the Baron de Montesquieu. Most states kept a judicial system similar to their colonial structures. Having cast off colonial governors who represented royal authority, however, most states limited the power of governors and established governor's councils appointed by the elected legislatures. Many states also implemented term limits for their governors. Almost every state established a two-house legislature, with a Roman-style senate that could brake any "excessively" democratic actions taken by the lower house.

Baron de Montesquieu, excerpts from *The Spirit of Laws* (1748)

Some states enlarged their legislatures to grant more representation to western areas that were filling up with settlers, and five states directly tied representation to population size, a very new concept. All but Massachusetts and Connecticut abolished established state religion, although most still required government officeholders to be Christian.

Despite similarities, some states were more democratic than others, varying the degrees of direct representation and restraint of government power in their constitutions. Pennsylvania had no governor at all and established a unicameral legislature with strict term limits that proportionally represented the population and was elected by all free men over 21 who paid taxes. By contrast, Maryland's Revolutionary planter elites defined a government in which only the lower house of the legislature was popularly elected, the governor held considerable power, and there were high property-holding qualifications for officeholders, who served long terms. In all the states, even the least democratic, new ranks of men such as artisans began to assume offices and responsibilities that would never have fallen to them in the hierarchical days of colonial government. However, African Americans, women (of all racial and ethnic groups), and poor white men were not permitted to vote, under the assumption that their interests were represented by their superiors—propertied white men.

Articles of Confederation

Soon after declaring independence, Congress realized the need to form a legitimate national government. A committee tasked with creating a national constitution drafted the Articles of Confederation in 1777, although deep disagreements among the states delayed full ratification. The Articles proposed a weak national government for "the United States of America." Most Americans closely identified with their separate states, and they were not ready for much in the way of national power, which they feared.

As North Carolina Congressman Thomas Burke wrote, "The United States ought to be as One Sovereign with respect to foreign Powers, in all things that relate to War or where the States have one Common Interest." The Articles limited centralized power and reserved decision making in most other areas to the states. Congress had no power to tax citizens of the states, which contributed to national financial problems. Congress controlled the military and the war-making power, but the Articles directly forbade sustaining a military force after the war. Each state exercised one vote under the Articles, and to change most national policies required 9 votes out of 13. Only a unanimous vote could change any provision of the actual Articles. Arguments over rival state claims to western lands held up the ratification of the Articles of Confederation until 1781. By then, Congress was almost bankrupt.

Military Organization

In republican theories of government, it was important to restrain military power and subordinate it to civilian authority. When the First Continental Congress created the Continental Army in June of 1775, it built in several weaknesses to prevent the military from assuming too much power in society. Americans distrusted standing armies and viewed militias, in the words of the Virginia constitution, as "the proper, natural, and safe defense of a free state." But militias could never be effective enough to win a war against the British military, so the United States had to create an army and a navy and fill their ranks.

Congress initially restricted enlistments in the Continental Army to one year, but after severe problems recruiting new men became apparent by 1777, Congress authorized three-year terms, began to pay cash enlistment bounties, and promised land grants to soldiers. By 1779, Congress allowed men to enlist for the duration of the war and paid bounties as high as $200. Continental officers at first recruited their own men, but after 1777, Congress imposed recruiting quotas on each state. Historians estimate the number of American men in arms during the Revolution at between 250,000 and 350,000, at least 10 percent of the total American population.

Volunteer state militias provided men to the Continental Army, but they also continued to fight in their own right throughout the war, partially as a republican restraint on excess military authority. Major General Charles Lee expressed a widespread republican belief when he declared that "a militia, animated by determination to preserve liberty, could become a formidable infantry." Although militia units were often less disciplined and organized in battle, they did contribute to troop strength and success, especially when

image
analysis

VALLEY FORGE This 19th-century lithograph depicts Generals Washington and Lafayette visiting the American camp at Valley Forge, where 12,000 men were facing near starvation, disease, and terribly cold weather in the winter of 1777–1778. Thousands died of pneumonia and typhoid fever, and thousands more were listed as "unfit for service."

the war turned south after 1778. Many men who enlisted in the Revolutionary military, especially at the beginning of the war, expressed a strong allegiance to the Revolutionary cause, but economic incentives also influenced the decision to join the Continental Army. The average soldier was in his late 20s. European officers serving with the Continental Army marveled at the success of common men, like shoemakers, who became American officers. But as a member of Congress, John Adams felt "wearied to Death with the Wrangles between military officers high and low. They Quarrell like Cats and Dogs."

The Continental Congress oversaw military affairs, but Congress also granted George Washington "full, ample, and complete" powers to direct the army as he saw fit. Both enlisted men and officers suffered from Congress' inability to guarantee adequate military supplies. Before Nathaniel Greene reorganized it in 1780, the quartermaster general's office was overwhelmed trying to provide supplies and coordinate transportation. Congress lacked funds, struggled to provide food and shoes to troops, and did not provide consistent uniforms until 1781. During the brutal winter of 1777–1778, one-quarter of the 12,000 American soldiers who wintered at Valley Forge, Pennsylvania, died, partly because of poor food and shelter. Some judged the winter encampment of 1780 at Morristown, New Jersey, to be even worse. Hard conditions made it even more remarkable that the mutiny of the Pennsylvania line in January 1780 marked one of the only large-scale troop revolts of the war. Army surgeon James Thacher wrote during that winter that "both the resources and the credit of our Congress appear to be almost exhausted." Congress printed large quantities of paper money, which quickly lost much of its value.

Diplomacy and International Finance

Aside from paper currency, foreign credit was the main engine of war finance. The United States sent a series of envoys to European countries, particularly Britain's rivals,

Phillis Wheatley, Revolutionary Transatlantic Poet

One of the most eloquent voices of the American Revolution belonged to **Phillis Wheatley**, a poet from Gambia who lived as a slave in Boston and who established her literary reputation in London. Wheatley was captured in Gambia as a child and endured the harsh middle passage Atlantic crossing before being sold as a slave in Boston to John and Susanna Wheatley in July 1761. John and Susanna Wheatley, who had connections among British aristocrats and religious reformers, subjected Phillis to less physical punishment than most slaves, and Susanna taught Phillis to read the Bible. Phillis also learned some classical Latin, and she quickly developed a talent for writing poetry, publishing her first poem in a newspaper before she was 13 years old.

Susanna Wheatley liked to show off Phillis's talent, inviting prominent Bostonians to come observe her "dark child from Africa" as a curiosity and to read the elegiac poems she composed. A 1770 elegy—or death tribute—that Phillis published in honor of the noted transatlantic Great Awakening preacher George Whitefield helped her achieve greater independence. The Countess of Huntingdon, one of Whitefield's patrons, invited Wheatley to London, where her first full book of poems was published in 1773 to wide acclaim. As a result, the Wheatley family freed Phillis in October 1773.

seeking recognition and funding. France, Spain, and the Netherlands extended aid with varying levels of enthusiasm. Prior to finalizing the Treaty of Alliance and the Treaty of Amity and Commerce with the United States, French citizens were already supplying financial and material aid to the war effort. Their support increased markedly after the 1778 agreements. The United States could not have continued the war without French assistance. The French lent the United States approximately $7 million and gave more than $2 million in outright gifts.

Other European countries also took an interest in the war, which German poet Christoph Wieland called "the greatest political event of the 1770s, and perhaps . . . of the entire century." The Spanish sent some help but largely held the United States at arm's length—in part because they did not wish to see colonial independence movements spread into Spanish America. Because of tensions in Europe, however, Spain declared war on Britain in April 1779. The Spanish governor of Louisiana and East Florida, Bernardo de Gálvez, captured several British forts along the Mississippi River and at Mobile and Pensacola, indirectly helping the American war effort. In January 1780, **John Jay** arrived in Madrid seeking diplomatic recognition, but the prediction by the French foreign minister that "Spain . . . will interest herself very little in the Americans" proved true. Despite promises to return West Florida to Spain after independence was secured, Spain never formally recognized American independence during the war—although the Spanish government did agree to open trade between the United States and Cuba and to loan the United States $170,000. The trade with Cuba was significant, given that it replaced much of the prohibited U.S. trade with the British West Indies and provided the United

Back in Boston, Phillis split from her former masters, who were Loyalists, as she embraced the patriot cause at the beginning of the American Revolution. She published a praise-filled poem, "To His Excellency General Washington," in 1775 and met the general in person the following year. Her ode to "Liberty and Peace," published at the end of the war, praised the United States as a "new-born *Rome*." As she supported the American cause, Wheatley also wrote poems and letters against the institution of slavery, emphasizing that enslaved people loved freedom and wanted it for themselves.

Wheatley wrote hundreds of poems during the Revolutionary War (some of which appeared in newspapers), although racism prevented her from ever publishing a book in the United States. She married free black laborer John Peters in 1778, but she died in 1784 shortly after giving birth to their third child (all of whom also died). While most of her Revolutionary War poems are lost, the ones that survive are so renowned that they have preserved her literary reputation. Defying the expectations of her age, the native African who became a literary sensation in England provided some of the strongest, most beautiful poetic inspiration for the American Revolution.

Phillis Wheatley, "To His Excellency, General Washington" (1775)

- In what ways might Phillis Wheatley have caused white Americans to question their assumptions about Africans and enslaved people?
- How did global movement influence Phillis Wheatley's life and work?

States access to hard currency. Cuba, whose large-scale sugar production was expanding under the Bourbon Reforms, also benefited from the U.S. trade goods—especially food to feed the growing number of slaves on the island.

When the British captured neutral ships from several countries trading with the United States in 1780, Russian empress **Catherine the Great** responded by forming the League of Armed Neutrality to protect neutral shipping, although Russia never formally recognized the United States during the Revolution. Sweden, Denmark, Portugal, the Netherlands, and Sicily all joined the League—tying up British naval resources and attempting to open further U.S. trade. Of these countries, the Dutch were the friendliest to the American cause, allowing a smuggled arms trade to the Revolutionaries even before 1777. A few months after all of the Dutch provinces and Prince William V formally recognized the United States, American envoy John Adams convinced Dutch bankers to loan the United States $2 million in July 1782.

European military officers who volunteered to fight with the Americans in the Revolutionary War brought with them connections to politicians and military establishments in Europe, personal financial resources, and military knowledge. Officers from continental Europe enhanced the cachet of the American military forces and increased international approval for the American Revolution. Benjamin Franklin and Silas Deane, American diplomats in France, actively recruited aristocratic Europeans to join the Continental Army.

Tadeusz Kosciuszko, a graduate of the Polish Royal School and the French school of engineering and artillery, was commissioned as a colonel in the Continental Army in

1776 and played a key role in designing the fortifications at West Point and entrenchments at Saratoga. Kosciuszko ended the war as a brigadier general. The Chevalier Louis Duportail, sent to the United States even before the French joined the cause, served most of the war as a brigadier general and chief of army engineers. Benjamin Franklin recruited **Friedrich Wilhelm von Steuben**, an impoverished former Prussian staff officer who was one of Washington's most effective aides. Less effective was Casimir Pulaski, a Pole who commanded American cavalry and later his own elite corps (the Pulaski Legion) as a brigadier general in the Continental Army.

The most famous French volunteer, **Major General Marie-Joseph-Paul-Yves-Roch-Gilbert du Motier, Marquis de Lafayette,** joined the American cause in 1777, when he was only 19 years old, along with his friend, the highly capable Johan de Kalb (who was also a French spy). Lafayette fought ably and played a major role in the defeat of Cornwallis at Yorktown in 1781.

STUDY QUESTIONS FOR THE STRUCTURE OF AUTHORITY

1. What difference did foreign aid make to the American Revolution?
2. How did the ideology of republicanism affect U.S. government and military authority during the American Revolution?

quiz

SECURING INDEPENDENCE

With the French as allies, American Revolutionaries had high expectations of winning the war, but the road ahead was not easy. The focus of the military conflict shifted to the seas and into the southern states. Bitter social divisions there helped to intensify the fighting. Loyalists held onto their British identities, even as they were forced to fight their neighbors or leave their homes. African Americans assessed how to maximize their own potential for freedom in the midst of wartime chaos. Indians tried to decide whether their future interests lay with the British or the United States. Nothing seemed easy during the last years of the Revolutionary War, but one thing was certain—the United States would cease to exist if it did not win the war.

War at Sea

The most immediate impact of French assistance came in the naval war. As early as the first year of the war, the United States established a navy and an ambitious shipbuilding program, with several states also fielding their own naval forces. Although the U.S. Navy succeeded in several small attacks, such as when Commander Esek Hopkins captured the British fort at Nassau, Bahamas, in November 1776, Americans could not hope to defeat the British navy—the strongest and best-equipped sea force in the world—which was blockading the northern U.S. coastline. Instead, the American navy and over 2,000 privateers harassed British war and commercial ships. Captain Nicholas Biddle, a former member of the Royal Navy, successfully raided British ships in the West Indies in 1777. Basing his U.S. naval operations in France, Captain John Paul Jones successfully raided

USS *BON HOMME RICHARD* John Paul Jones commanded the USS *Bon Homme Richard*, a warship loaned to the United States by France and named in honor of Benjamin Franklin's *Poor Richard's Almanac*. Jones battled the British ship HMS *Serapis* off the coast of Yorkshire, England, in September 1779, and his capture of the British naval vessel helped to convince the French to increase their support for the naval war against Britain.

the Scottish coastline and captured British prizes in the Irish Sea. Jones cemented his reputation in September 1779 when he defeated the British frigate *Serapis* in a thrilling battle, taking the ship as a prize after declaring, "I have not yet begun to fight!"

French entry into the war diverted British attention away from the fight in America and forced the British to commit ships to the English Channel, the Mediterranean, the Caribbean, and off the coast of India to defend their empire (Map 7.2). Sir William Clinton partly abandoned Philadelphia and the blockade of the U.S. coast in 1778, diverting 5,000 men to the sugar-rich West Indies, where he expected to engage the French. The French concentrated most of their force on the Caribbean islands that they had lost to the British in the Seven Years' War. The French admiral **Comte d'Estaing** arrived with his fleet in the summer of 1778, and, after botching an attack on British-controlled Newport, Rhode Island, he sailed for the West Indies. The British captured St. Lucia in December 1778, but the French captured and held the island of Grenada.

D'Estaing failed to oust the British from Savannah in September 1779—in part because he followed a French pattern of failing to coordinate well with U.S. ground forces. In 1780 and 1781, French naval assistance proved more effective. Commodore Ternay carried 5,500 French army troops under the Comte de Rochambeau to reinforce the Continental Army in July 1780, and in October 1781, the French admiral **Comte de Grasse** added his fleet to the fight at Yorktown.

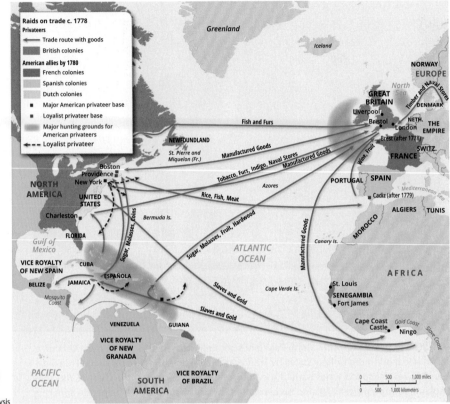

map analysis

MAP 7.2 The Caribbean During the Revolutionary War Much of the hottest naval warfare in the Revolutionary War took place around the Caribbean, where countries battled to control trade and tried to wrest control of islands away from one another.

War in the South

Britain's cabinet war ministers, led by **Lord George Germain**, shifted the focus of their ground efforts to the South in 1778. On March 8, 1778, British officials replaced Commander Sir William Howe with **Sir Henry Clinton**, whom they ordered to abandon Philadelphia to attack the Carolinas and Georgia. As Clinton tried to evacuate his army from Philadelphia back to New York, he ran up against George Washington's army. In winter quarters at Valley Forge, Washington's troops had suffered, but they had also been strengthened by the training and drill offered by the new inspector general of the army, the Baron von Steuben. U.S. and British forces clashed at Monmouth, New Jersey, on June 28, 1778, and, although Clinton's army escaped, only a poor performance from Washington's second-in-command Charles Lee kept the Americans from crushing the British army.

The South saw much of the worst fighting between patriots and Loyalists of the entire war. The British invaded Georgia and easily captured Savannah in December 1778. Support from Loyalists, thousands of runaway slaves, and some Cherokees helped subdue the patriot civilian population, and the British were able to recapture the Georgia state government. The patriot defeat in South Carolina was even more disastrous. The British sent forces over land to surround Charleston, and British generals Clinton and Cornwallis fought "storm, rain, hail, snow, and . . . waves" to sail to Charleston with additional troops. They bottled up American commander Major General Benjamin Lincoln in the city of Charleston, and after six weeks of siege and bitter fighting, Lincoln surrendered the city and his entire army on May 12, 1780. Clinton returned to New York, and he left Cornwallis in charge of putting down further resistance in South Carolina and pushing into North Carolina, with an eye toward eventually conquering Virginia. In the following months, the backcountry of South Carolina witnessed brutal clashes between Loyalist/British detachments and patriot militias. In 1780 British lieutenant colonel **Banastre Tarleton** acquired a bloody reputation by moving quickly between skirmishes, destroying property, and killing prisoners.

Without consulting General Washington, and against his wishes, Congress appointed Horatio Gates to command the Continental Army's Southern Department. Cornwallis crushed Gates at Camden, South Carolina, and his troops retreated in disarray. Gates himself rode as fast as he could all the way to Hillsboro, North Carolina. But the bitter defeat did little to change the course of the war, as rural skirmishes persisted and Cornwallis waited for an uprising of Loyalists. Instead, many white southerners began to support the Americans out of anger when the British shielded runaway slaves.

After Camden, Congress removed Gates from command and replaced him with Nathanael Greene, who was probably the finest strategist in the American military. Although his army was in poor shape, Greene took heart from the victory of American militia forces at Kings Mountain, South Carolina, on October 7. Greene recognized that he was unlikely to defeat Cornwallis in open battle, so he divided his army into four parts and kept British and Loyalist forces on the run through the Carolina backcountry. Greene and his able subcommander **Daniel Morgan**, who bested Tarleton at Cowpens in January 1781, engaged Cornwallis in three open battles that year at Guilford Courthouse, Hobkirk's Hill, and Eutaw Springs. The Americans lost all three battles, but they inflicted terrible damage on Cornwallis's combined forces. Greene wrote of the campaign, "We fight, get beat, rise and fight again." Greene's strategy inflicted some of the heaviest casualties of the war on Cornwallis, who moved into Virginia and marched toward Yorktown.

Loyalists: Resistance and Migration

The Loyalist population played a large role in the British war effort. Loyalists, dubbed "Tories" by the Revolutionaries, made up almost 20 percent of the total population of the United States. Loyalists expressed notions of "liberty" different from those put forth by the Revolutionaries, and they held onto British identity and obedience in the midst of conflict. Not all Loyalists agreed with one another beyond opposing independence. Several ethnic or religious minority groups who relied on crown protection remained loyal, although they did not constitute a majority in any state: Germans in the mid-Atlantic, Anglicans in New England, landholders in the Hudson valley, Scots Irish immigrants in the southern backcountry, and Dutch settlers in New Jersey. Although they aided the British military by providing supplies and even taking up arms against their neighbors, Loyalist opposition to the Revolution was not enough to enable the British to win the war.

Loyalist song, "The Rebels"

Estimates of the number of Loyalists who fled the United States for England, Canada, and the West Indies during and immediately after the war reach as high as 80,000, or 1 out of every 40 people in the United States. Many who emigrated were wealthy before the war, and Congress seized millions of dollars in Loyalists' property. An estimated additional 20,000 African American slaves ran away from their masters and sought British protection during the war, including some who emigrated to Canada, Nova Scotia, and Sierra Leone after the war. White and black Loyalists who resettled elsewhere in the British Empire sometimes helped to shore up imperial control, but some faced discrimination. Black emigrants to Canada achieved freedom, but other runaway slaves who joined the British were re-enslaved in the West Indies.

The post-revolutionary African American diaspora

Loyalists who resettled in England found they sometimes experienced what Samuel Curwen called an "uneasy abode in this country of aliens," but most found it even more difficult to return to their former homes—even after the war ended. **Benedict Arnold**, the Continental general who defected to the British side in 1780, became a scorned British military officer. Even groups who were merely ambivalent about the war and tried to remain neutral, such as the Pennsylvania Quakers whose religion forbade fighting, found it difficult to reintegrate into American society.

Indian Warfare

Indian populations in North America were also torn apart by the Revolutionary War. Many groups had barely finished navigating the tension-filled terrain created by the French loss in the Seven Years' War when the Declaration of Independence again placed them between rival powers. The United States sought Indian land even more aggressively than did Great Britain, but not all Indian peoples aligned themselves with the British. Religion, trade, political calculations, and personal relationships influenced Indian decisions, and divisions existed, even within tight-knit kinship groups. Some Native peoples also used the Revolution as an opportunity to try and advance their own regional interests, such as when **Joseph Brant** led Mohawk and other Iroquois troops against Pennsylvania and New York frontier settlers in the "Border War" of 1777–1779. Fighting between Iroquois and American settlers was particularly fierce in the Wyoming valley of Pennsylvania.

Oneida Declaration of Neutrality (1775)

Even Brant, who was a respected commander, could not unite the powerful Six Nations entirely in favor of the British. Some Oneida and Tuscarora peoples in New England joined the American army at Valley Forge. Oneida fighters played a decisive role in the American victory at the Battle of Oriskany in 1777, which destroyed their own village but set up the American victory at Saratoga. By the end of the war, most other Iroquois groups had joined Brant in his support for the British, especially after American major general John Sullivan pursued a scorched-earth campaign against them in New York in the summer of 1779. After the war, the British resettled Brant and his Iroquois allies in Canada.

The United States was not as generous to its Indian allies, notably pushing Delaware people into the arms of the British after failing to follow the terms of an alliance signed at Pittsburgh in 1778. Other Delawares were forced to abandon their lands in Ohio. Delaware warrior Buckongahelas lamented in 1781 that his people had been drawn into the Revolutionary War, "a family quarrel, in which I was not interested." Many Shawnee tried to remain neutral, but Shawnee warriors ended up fighting for the British in an attempt to hold onto Ohio lands. American troops attacked the Cherokee Nation in 1776, 1780, and 1781, and many Cherokees aligned themselves with Loyalist militias in the brutal fighting in the Carolinas and Georgia. No matter what side Indian nations chose, in the Revolution's aftermath they all confronted a new American power with a rapacious demand for land.

African Americans at War

Like Indians, not all African Americans adopted the same stance toward the Revolutionary War. But those who were able to fight—either on the American or the British side—often managed to change their social status as a result. African Americans constituted a small but significant percentage of Revolutionary War fighters on land and water, and in some battles—such as the 1778 battle at Monmouth, New Jersey—black men fought on both sides.

African American men served in the British infantry and navy, and many runaway slaves worked as spies and laborers for British forces. Some African Americans who were re-enslaved in the West Indies continued their military service by becoming part of the British West Indian regiments that fought in the Napoleonic Wars in the 1790s. For example, Harry, a slave who was transported to the Dutch island of St. Eustasius during the war, made a public reputation for himself as a Methodist preacher, although he continued to be enslaved.

Service in the American military presented a path to personal freedom, and many black men and women supported the patriot cause. Although George Washington initially banned blacks from the Continental Army, the need for troops forced him to abandon this policy within months, and in some areas, black men made up as much as 25 percent of American fighting forces. Many northern slaves enlisted, and their state governments sometimes purchased their freedom from their masters, whom they replaced in service. Some, such as the Concord, Massachusetts, slave Richard Hobby, joined the American military when their masters were absent. Even in southern states, some slaves and many free black men enlisted in the American army and militias. Both Massachusetts and Rhode Island set up separate black militia units, but for the most part, black and white men served together in integrated companies. Black men enhanced their personal freedom by joining the war effort, and their status as Revolutionary War veterans would also help the antislavery cause after the war.

Letters from John Laurens, Alexander Hamilton, and George Washington on the question of emancipating and arming of slaves (1778–79)

Peace and Shifting Empires

The final phase of the Revolutionary War began when British general Cornwallis entrenched his troops in Yorktown, Virginia, in August 1781. General Washington learned of Cornwallis's move and realized that Yorktown's position on the Chesapeake Bay made it vulnerable. He also learned that de Grasse's French squadron would soon arrive. So Washington boldly marched almost his entire army, accompanied by French forces under the Comte de Rochambeau, from New York to Virginia to link up with Greene. By the end of September, the American forces had surrounded Yorktown and laid siege to Cornwallis's force. For almost two weeks, the American and French forces pounded Cornwallis's men with artillery fire and pushed them back toward the Chesapeake coast with carefully executed skirmishes. Under increasing pressure, Cornwallis realized he had no escape, and on October 19, 1781, he had a subordinate, General Charles O'Hara, surrender his entire army (Map 7.3).

When British prime minister Lord North heard the news of Yorktown, he reportedly exclaimed, "Oh God! It is all over!" The British government decided to pursue peace. The new British prime minister Lord Shelburne sent merchant Richard Oswald to Paris

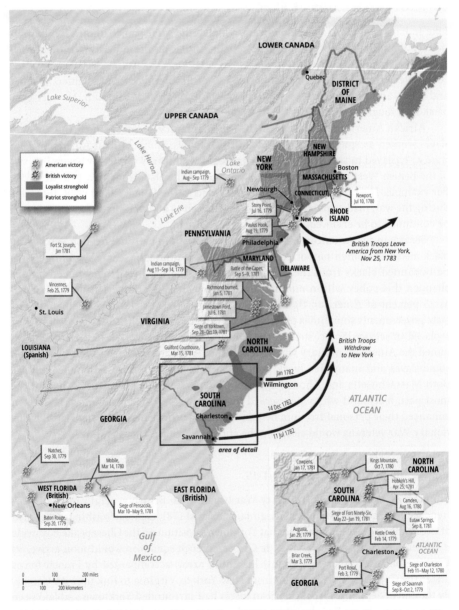

MAP 7.3 Major Revolutionary War Battles, 1779–1783 Although the Revolutionary War was mostly concluded after Cornwallis's surrender at Yorktown in 1781, skirmishing continued until the Treaty of Paris in 1783 ended the conflict.

BATTLE OF YORKTOWN This painting depicts the British surrender at the Battle of Yorktown in 1781, the last major campaign of the Revolutionary War. In the image, American general Benjamin Lincoln accepts the sword of surrender from British general Cornwallis's subordinate officer. Artist John Trumbull painted a larger version of this image inside the rotunda of the U.S. Capitol building.

at the beginning of 1782 to negotiate with Benjamin Franklin. They concluded a preliminary peace agreement in November 1782 without any input from French officials. French foreign minister Vergennes was impressed with the Americans' diplomacy, and he negotiated a separate peace with Britain and convinced the Spanish to do the same. The Netherlands also concluded a separate treaty. American negotiators Franklin, John Jay, John Adams, and **Henry Laurens** successfully played French and British interests against one another when they concluded negotiations with Britain and signed the final Treaty of Paris on September 3, 1783.

The terms of the Treaty of Paris favored the United States, largely because the British had decided to cut their losses. The treaty recognized American independence and established borders stretching from the Great Lakes down the Mississippi River to the 31st parallel. Britain granted American fishing rights off Nova Scotia, and Congress agreed to honor war debts, to restore confiscated Loyalist property, and to disallow retribution against British supporters. Britain's Native American allies were incensed that Britain had negotiated away land rights without consulting or involving them. The British and Americans agreed to free passage on the Mississippi, but the Spanish objected and blocked free trade on the river in 1784. In their separate negotiations, France, Spain, and Britain swapped possession of several Caribbean islands, and Britain traded control of East and West Florida to Spain in return for Gibraltar. Although the British dragged their feet enforcing parts of the Treaty of Paris, the agreement nonetheless concluded the first-ever successful colonial war of independence and guaranteed the existence of the United States of America.

STUDY QUESTIONS FOR SECURING INDEPENDENCE

quiz

1. How did divisions inside the United States shape the course of the Revolutionary War?

2. What were the immediate consequences of the Treaty of Paris?

RESTRUCTURING POLITICAL AND SOCIAL AUTHORITY

By winning the Revolutionary War, patriots gained the chance to make permanent their experiment with republican government. Now the national and state governments would have to solidify their efforts to govern for "the cause of all mankind." But Americans faced obstacles to the peaceful refashioning of society, and not everyone agreed on how to proceed. How could Loyalists be reintegrated into society? What consequences did republican liberty hold for subordinate people in society? Could the states govern harmoniously and share power with Congress? How would Americans pay the crushing debts incurred during the war? Would economic changes brought on by the war continue as the United States struggled to become successful in trade? Social and economic changes accompanied the shift in politics in the new nation, but nothing went smoothly.

Power in the States

During demobilization from the Revolutionary War, Congress and the states were still negotiating their power relationships. Under the Articles of Confederation, Congress coordinated national policy, but states exercised great power directly over their citizens. Several states, including Massachusetts, ratified less democratic constitutions in the 1780s. States gradually repealed laws against Loyalists, although many Loyalists, especially in northern states, never regained all the property they had lost in the war.

The states had to deal with political tensions unleashed by what John Jay called the "rage for emigrating to the western country," which sometimes worsened clashes between states. Western inhabitants, many of whom were veterans lured by land bounties or by land investment companies, demanded increased representation of western areas in state legislatures, which tended to overrepresent eastern elites. South Carolina, North Carolina, Georgia, and Virginia all moved their state capitals to towns that lay farther west, partly because of the shift in population. Hard-fought campaigns to separate Vermont, Kentucky, and Franklin (in modern-day Tennessee) into new states created political tensions, but none succeeded until after 1787. States also clashed with one another over rival land claims. Virginia peacefully ceded western territory to Congress in 1784, but border conflicts raged between Pennsylvania and Connecticut and between Pennsylvania and Virginia. New York and New Jersey engaged in an all-out trade war between 1783 and 1787.

The states' individual war debts and their shared national war debt made conflicts over land and representation even more difficult. Congress could not agree on how to finance these debts, but legislation in 1785 promised the states future repayment.

Robert Morris, who directed national finances until 1785, and his political allies wanted the states to grant Congress the power to tax, which would keep debt in national hands and enhance centralized power. But on a national level, the states could not even agree to grant Congress the power to impose a small impost tax. Southern states, especially Virginia, owed particularly large debts, which they might never be able to pay. By 1786, New York had become the first of several states to begin assuming national debts directly, which threatened to further weaken the national government.

Economic Change

A dizzying mix of economic opportunities and crises emerged in the postwar years. Devalued paper currency that Congress had printed during the war created inflation and conflicts between Congress and state governments that were required to pay war bills in hard currency after 1781. Congress had printed hundreds of millions of dollars' worth of bills of credit by 1778, but by 1781 they had lost 99 percent of their value. States also printed their own paper currency throughout the 1780s, causing further inflation. Prices declined after the war, but they did not return to their prewar level until 1789. State governments assessed property taxes and rival duties on trade goods. Congress defaulted on foreign and domestic loan payments after the war because it simply lacked funds.

The United States expanded foreign trade after the Revolution, but European powers still tried to restrict some international commerce. The war had opened new Caribbean and European trade routes. Now Britain closed its Caribbean island colonies to American trade, and both France and Spain left high duties in place on American–Caribbean trade. As a result, port cities such as Boston, Philadelphia, Newport, and Charleston faced slow recovery from the war, and their economies were depressed throughout the 1780s. The West Indies had become America's largest market for foodstuffs, and the crippling of that trade decreased farm income. Some U.S. exports to Europe and Latin America increased during these years, as the war

PAPER CURRENCY This Rhode Island bank note is just one example of the paper currency printed by various banks and states during and after the Revolution. The widespread exchange of state paper notes and paper certificates printed by private banks or land companies contributed to inflation and economic uncertainty during this period.

settlement allowed Americans to trade directly with those areas legally for the first time. A few merchants who gained special Spanish permission enriched themselves by trading flour and other products to Cuba. Tobacco, lumber, iron, and shipbuilding supplies remained popular, and corn and wheat also became highly prized American goods in Europe. Although the Treaty of Paris had guaranteed American fishing rights, Britain embargoed American fish, and France imposed high taxes. Americans continued to import far more than they exported, a fact that further exacerbated the shortage of hard currency.

Women and Revolution

Many women had participated in the Revolutionary War. As many as 20,000 accompanied the Continental Army as camp followers. These women, many of whom were related to soldiers, played vital roles cooking, doing laundry, and giving medical care to the troops. Other camp followers probably served direct military roles: bringing water to cool artillery pieces or even occasionally themselves firing weapons. The most notable example of a fighting woman was **Deborah Sampson Gannett**, who disguised herself as a man and twice enlisted in the Continental Army. After the war, Gannett went on a speaking tour and published a memoir about her experience, and her husband later received a federal widow's pension. Wealthier women organized by **Esther DeBerdt Reed** and **Sarah Franklin Bache** formed the Ladies' Association of Philadelphia, which raised funds and distributed clothing to needy soldiers in 1781.

Although American women had contributed mightily to the war effort, they had little direct political influence and no political power in the new republic. The Revolution did cause some shifts in white women's roles and gave them an important part to play in spreading republican values. Historians use the term "republican motherhood" to describe the social expectation that women would contribute to the republic by raising their children—especially their sons—to be good citizens. In a society that was struggling to define itself according to the civic virtue demanded of a liberated citizenship, women could also exert broader influence over society and culture in a way that had political consequences. As Delaware politician James Tilton put it, "The men possess the more ostensible powers of making and executing the laws, but the women, in every free country, have an absolute control of manners, and . . . in a republic, manners are of equal importance with laws." As the patriot women who had participated in the boycott movements before the Revolution had learned, women could also exert some degree of influence through their consumer choices.

Women's support for the patriot cause and their special role in spreading republican ideology did not translate into their inclusion in American politics. New Jersey allowed a small number of independent, property-holding women to vote for a time, but formal political participation was mostly a male privilege. Many states liberalized divorce laws following the Revolution to allow women to separate from abusive or runaway husbands, although **coverture** laws still meant that married women could not own property. Patriot women lost confiscated property if their husbands had been Loyalists because state laws did not recognize that they could possess separate political identities. The impact of republicanism and women's actions in the Revolutionary War opened up the possibility of women's actions being seen as politically significant, but decades elapsed before their direct political participation widened significantly.

Racial Ideology and Questioning Slavery

The Revolutionary notion that "all men are created equal" pushed antislavery efforts forward in many northern states. But slavery thrived elsewhere, and African Americans still faced constant racism and resistance to their full participation in American society.

Some black veterans, such as New Hampshire's Prince Whipple, used their Revolutionary military experience to argue on behalf of African American freedom. Whipple and other African American men petitioned the state legislature in 1779 to end slavery "for the sake of justice, liberty, and the rights of mankind." In 1783, New Hampshire adopted a state constitution that ended slavery in the state.

Before the Revolution, some Quakers and Mennonites had argued against the institution of slavery. After the war, Revolutionary ideology, black military heroism, and continued petitions by African Americans helped to expand the antislavery cause. Blacks generally lacked equal rights, but slavery was on the defensive. Vermont's state constitution became the first to outlaw slavery in 1777, and slaves who sued for their freedom under the Massachusetts 1780 constitution ended slavery there a few years later. Pennsylvania and several other northern states passed laws that gradually outlawed slavery by granting freedom to slaves once they reached a certain age.

Pennsylvania's abolition of slavery (1781)

BROTHER PRINCE HALL
WARRANTEE WORSHIPFUL MASTER AFRICAN LODGE 459 A. L. 5784, A. D. 1784
FOUNDER OF COLORED FRATERNITY OF FREE AND ACCEPTED MASONS.
BOSTON, MASS.

RAISED TO MASTER MASON

PRINCE HALL Although early biographical details of Prince Hall are hard to authenticate, he most likely was a former slave who served in the Massachusetts militia during the Revolutionary War. After the war, he became one of the most prominent free black men in Boston, where he worked to end slavery in Massachusetts and to better the lives of African Americans. He is depicted here in his role as the founder of the first black Masonic lodge in the United States, African Lodge No. 1 in Boston, an organization that also worked for black emancipation and betterment.

This gradual approach allowed the institution to linger into the 1820s in New York and New Jersey. In the states stretching south from Maryland, the institution of slavery survived and even intensified after the Revolution. Delaware, Maryland, and Virginia legislatures allowed individual slave owners to free their slaves for a time in the 1780s, but by the turn of the century, fear of slave rebellion ended that practice.

STUDY QUESTIONS FOR RESTRUCTURING POLITICAL AND SOCIAL AUTHORITY

quiz

1. In what ways did the Revolutionary War change the social roles of some women and African Americans?

2. Why was the economy in the post-Revolutionary United States so unstable?

⊘ A FEDERAL NATION

Many average Americans had fought for liberty in the Revolutionary War, but they were suffering in the postwar economic chaos. State and national governments faced troubles, but few people agreed on solutions: some favored a stronger central government, and others looked to the states for solutions. How could these two visions of government be satisfied by elite politicians who also wanted to control the democratic unrest that seemed to be bubbling up in the states? The creation of the U.S. Constitution was a victory for more centralized power, but the concept of **federalism** also ensured that the states would remain powerful. A new politics arose based on the concept of **popular sovereignty**, the notion that the people could consent to granting power to both state and federal governments without giving up their rights as the true source of authority in American society.

Debt and Discontent

The uncertain economic system in the United States following the Revolutionary War caused hardship and unrest. While governmental leaders worried that the Articles of Confederation provided too little national tax power, poor men and women felt simultaneously squeezed by heavy state taxation—poll taxes, land taxes, and taxes on certain occupations such as tavern keeping. The poor faced a variety of other economic challenges, starting with inflated prices. Both taxes and private debt payment often required hard currency, but many poor people had little access to anything other than devalued paper money or the direct trade of farm goods. Although excess paper money hurt them by causing inflation, the poor relied on it.

By 1785, as the number of people imprisoned for the inability to repay debts rose above 1,000 in each state, debtors from New Hampshire to Massachusetts to Virginia began to organize themselves to oppose state and county enforcement of debts. Taking lessons from the pre-Revolutionary political protest movements, debtors petitioned state legislatures for the redress of their grievances and to demand the reinstatement of paper currency. Debtors, many of whom lived in western counties that were underrepresented in state legislatures, were angry that their hard currency payments often went to land speculators who held state war bonds.

Some groups took stronger action and resorted to armed protests to close down county courts. One Connecticut lawyer worried about "contentions and civil discord in almost every state in the union." Armed individuals and groups tangled with sheriffs seeking to seize property from debtors in Virginia, Pennsylvania, Delaware, New Jersey, New York, and Massachusetts. The largest insurrection came when Revolutionary War veteran Daniel Shays organized protestors in western Massachusetts at the end of 1786 into an armed resistance movement. Denied the right to assemble to protest creditors and tax collectors, Shays threatened violence. In December 1786, the Shaysites shut down courts in Springfield, Massachusetts, and a month later they marched against the state arsenal in that city. Massachusetts governor Benjamin Lincoln called out the state militia to put down **Shays' Rebellion**, and Daniel Shays himself fled to Canada.

Lincoln also appealed to Congress for help in suppressing Shays' Rebellion. Although the rebellion ended before Congress responded, a number of national leaders seized the opportunity to call for enhancing the power of the national government. George Washington expressed agreement with his friend John Jay in 1786 when he said, "Our affairs are drawing rapidly to a crisis." Elites and politicians worried that popular uprisings like Shays' Rebellion could spread or get out of control. A small meeting in Annapolis, Maryland, in September 1786 solidified conversations among nationalists like James Madison and Alexander Hamilton, who thought the time had come to change the Articles of Confederation. The Annapolis Convention issued a call for all the states to send delegates to a new convention in Philadelphia the following summer.

Letter from Henry Knox to George Washington concerning Shay's Rebellion (1786)

Constitutional Convention

Instead of merely changing the Articles of Confederation, the Philadelphia Convention proposed an entirely new U.S. Constitution. It was perhaps not surprising that delegates to the Constitutional Convention moved beyond amending the Articles of Confederation because they largely came from the elite, creditor class of merchants, lawyers, and plantation owners who believed that the weakness of the national government and the popular unrest threatened social order. They also rose above those interests to create a political document that has become the longest-lasting written constitution for any government in the world. Every state but Rhode Island sent delegates to meet in Philadelphia in May 1787. Some of the most prominent leaders of the Revolution— George Washington, Benjamin Franklin, James Madison, and John Dickinson—came together to shape a new national government for the United States.

The convention elected George Washington presiding officer and agreed to meet in secret. Although the delegates tried hard to keep news of their deliberations from leaking out, we know much about what took place because of their written communications and the careful notes James Madison kept of their oral debates.

All of the proposals that the delegates debated fit within the conception of republicanism—the new national government would surely confirm the United States as a representative republic. The delegates clashed over how to balance regional and economic interests within that representation, and though they generally agreed that they needed to restrain volatile popular democracy, they did not agree on how to do that. In the first several days of debate, Edmund Randolph introduced James Madison's

Virginia Plan, which proposed a two-house national legislature chosen according to proportional representation (based on population), a judicial branch, and a president elected by the legislature. Madison strongly advocated for the Enlightenment idea of **balance of powers**, which would put authority in different branches of government, providing checks and balances against one another. Many states with small populations disliked Madison's plan, but it proved a useful starting point for debate—especially about the nature of Congress. William Paterson, a New Jersey delegate, proposed a rival New Jersey Plan that would keep more of the state power in the Articles of Confederation by retaining a unicameral legislature that would have equal state representation but greater financial power. On July 16, the delegates adopted what became known as "the Great Compromise" between the Virginia and New Jersey plans and decided to form a bicameral legislature: a House of Representatives with proportional representation, and a Senate with equal state representation. Creating this form for Congress allowed the convention to balance the interests of small and large states.

After the legislature was settled, other compromises followed. The delegates created the electoral college as a way to give power to the states and to restrain popular democracy. They also designated that the House of Representatives would stay quite small (as compared to the total population) in an effort to further insulate it from popular passions. Delegates to the convention largely tried to avoid the thorny issue of slavery, but they could not sidestep the institution altogether. After difficult debate, the delegates decided that three-fifths of slaves, or "other persons," as the final document phrased it, would be counted in the population for representation, although the convention never discussed direct citizenship rights or political status for the slaves themselves. The three-fifths compromise ensured that southern states, where most enslaved people lived, would exercise strong political influence in the first decades of the republic. Delegates also agreed to restrict Congress from outlawing the international slave trade until 1808. Many of the political structures and compromises at the convention—including the electoral college—attempted to deal with the fact that some states had large slave populations whereas others had outlawed the institution altogether, but the delegates largely managed to avoid openly discussing the ties between their politics and slavery.

Near the end of the convention, Virginian George Mason proposed the inclusion of a bill of rights, a written guarantee of civil liberties, within the Constitution. Many delegates, despite their desire for a more powerful central government, still feared too much national power infringing on the rights of individuals. Several state constitutions contained such guarantees, but most delegates did not think they were necessary. Even though they created a national government that was much more powerful—with the ability to tax and carry on foreign affairs—advocates believed that such power would only protect liberty, not threaten it. Several delegates, such as Marylander **Luther Martin**, were so upset by the exclusion of a bill of rights that they disavowed the work of the convention and opposed the Constitution. Three delegates refused to sign the final document. The Philadelphia Convention closed on September 17, 1787, and it remained to be seen whether such opposition would prevent the Constitution from being ratified.

Ratification

The new U.S. Constitution was ratified by specially elected conventions, not by the state legislatures, a majority of which would probably have rejected it. The Constitution

MERCY OTIS WARREN Warren was a sharp thinker and prominent resident of Boston who supported the Revolutionary cause by publishing, anonymously, poetry and plays during the war. After the war, she opposed the U.S. Constitution on the grounds that it created too much centralized government power. She continued to broadcast her Antifederalist opinions in her 1805 three-volume work, *History of the Rise, Progress, and Termination of the American Revolution.*

was set to go into effect when 9 of the 13 states ratified it. The Constitution's supporters, who dubbed themselves "Federalists," faced off against a very loose coalition of opponents, subsequently dubbed "Antifederalists." Federalist leaders, including Alexander Hamilton, John Jay, James Madison, and **John Marshall**, had impressive financing, coordination, and access to newspaper and pamphlet publishers. They also counted among their ranks the most famous national and international Revolutionaries: George Washington and Benjamin Franklin. The Federalists won converts in commercial cities and seaports and from creditors who favored strong government power. The Antifederalists—including Samuel Adams, Elbridge Gerry, Patrick Henry, George Mason, Richard Henry Lee, George Clinton, and Mercy Otis Warren—were much less organized and much warier of centralized power. Some Antifederalists objected to the lack of rights protection in the Constitution; others favored weak national power or direct democracy and agreed with Connecticut Antifederalist James Lincoln, who warned that if the Constitution were ratified, "you are at once rushing into an aristocratic government."

James Madison, *Federalist Number 10,* and anonymous, *Antifederalist Number 17*

Federalists displayed political skill as they easily won ratification in Delaware, Pennsylvania, and New Jersey by the end of 1787. Georgia and Connecticut each ratified the document in January 1788. In February, Massachusetts ratified the Constitution by a narrower margin, but only after proposing amendments and making Federalists promise to add a bill of rights later.

As the ratifying conventions continued, the newspaper and pamphlet war between the Federalists and Antifederalists intensified. Madison, Hamilton, and Jay anonymously published the "Federalist" essays, sometimes called the *"Federalist Papers,"* which offered wide-ranging arguments in favor of ratification. Their words, republished in books, pamphlets, and newspapers, helped to shape ratification politics

interactive timeline

TIMELINE 1776–1789

AMERICA	YEAR	THE WORLD
Jan Thomas Paine publishes *Common Sense* **Jun** Richard Henry Lee introduces first resolution of independence in Congress **Jul** Congress issues Declaration of Independence **Sep** British occupy New York City **Oct** Battle of White Plains, New York **Dec** Battle of Trenton, New Jersey	1776	Portugal unites South American colonies with Rio de Janeiro as capital
Aug Battle of Bennington **Sep** Battle of Brandywine, Pennsylvania **Sep** Congress flees Philadelphia **Sep** British occupy Philadelphia **Oct** Battle of Germantown, Pennsylvania **Oct** John Burgoyne surrenders his British army to Horatio Gates after losing Battle of Saratoga **Nov** Congress submits Articles of Confederation to the states **Dec** Continental Army enters winter quarters at Valley Forge, Pennsylvania	1777	British Parliament suspends Habeas Corpus Act Chinese missionaries introduce Catholicism to Korea Portugal gains South American territory from Spain
Feb Treaty of Alliance and a Treaty of Amity and Commerce between France and United States **Mar** France formally recognizes the United States **Jun** Battle of Monmouth, New Jersey **Jun** British evacuate Philadelphia **Dec** British seize control of Savannah, Georgia	1778	**Jun** France declares war on Great Britain **Jul** War of Bavarian Succession begins
Aug American forces defeat Iroquois leader Joseph Brant **Sep** John Paul Jones defeats the HMS *Serapis*	1779	British capture French African colony of Senegal and Gorée, key to slave trade Spain lays siege to Gibraltar **May** War of Bavarian Succession ends **Jun** Spain declares war on Great Britain but does not recognize the United States **Dec** Wars begin between Xhosa Bantu and Boers in southern Africa
Mar Spanish governor Gálvez captures Mobile from the British **May** British capture Charleston, South Carolina **Aug** Battle of Camden, South Carolina	1780	Peru rebels against Spain **Jul** Anti-Catholic Gordon riots in London **Nov** Britain declares war on the Netherlands
Jan Members of Pennsylvania line mutiny **Jan** Battle of Cowpens, South Carolina	1781	British seize Dutch colonies in western Sumatra

and became some of the most enduring political commentaries in American history. Madison, Hamilton, and Jay applied Enlightenment political theories to the U.S. context and argued that the Constitution was necessary. Madison, in particular, also took a new era of politics into account when he argued in Essays 10 and 51 that the Constitution could balance the behavior of self-interested Americans, who were not necessarily always guided by republican virtue.

By narrow margins, Maryland and South Carolina ratified the Constitution in the spring of 1788. When New Hampshire ratified it on June 21, 1788, the Constitution

AMERICA	YEAR	THE WORLD
Mar Battle of Guilford Courthouse, North Carolina **Sep** Battle of Eutaw Springs, South Carolina **Oct** Cornwallis surrenders his army to the United States **Dec** City of Los Angeles founded		
Apr The Netherlands recognizes the United States **May** Col. Lewis Nicola proposes George Washington become U.S. king	1782	Spain gains control of Florida
Jan France and Spain make peace with Britain Massachusetts Supreme Court declares slavery unconstitutional in that state **Mar** George Washington dispels Newburgh Conspiracy, rejects possible military coups **Sep** Treaty of Paris ends the Revolutionary War	1783	Spain re-establishes control of Peru **Jul** Britain forbids U.S. food exports to colonies in the West Indies France regains Senegal and Gorée
Jan Congress ratifies Treaty of Paris **Jun** Spain forbids American trade on Mississippi River **Aug** Russian permanent settlement in Alaska is founded	1784	**Aug** British Parliament passes India Act
Sep Annapolis Convention calls for amending the Articles of Confederation	1786	Lord Cornwallis becomes governor-general of India
Jan Shays' Rebellion is put down by Massachusetts militia **Feb** Congress calls for convention to amend Articles of Confederation **May** Constitutional Convention convenes in Philadelphia **Sep** Constitutional Convention closes **Oct** *Federalist Papers* first published **Dec** Delaware ratifies U.S. Constitution **Dec** Pennsylvania ratifies U.S. Constitution **Dec** New Jersey ratifies U.S. Constitution	1787	British assume control of Bahamas After Annam dynasty falls, France intervenes in central Vietnam
Jan Georgia ratifies U.S. Constitution **Jan** Connecticut ratifies U.S. Constitution **Feb** Massachusetts narrowly ratifies U.S. Constitution **Mar** Constitutional ratification fails in Rhode Island **Apr** Maryland ratifies U.S. Constitution **May** South Carolina ratifies U.S. Constitution **Jun** New Hampshire ratifies U.S. Constitution (technically fulfilling its ratification) **Jun** Virginia ratifies U.S. Constitution **Jun** New York ratifies U.S. Constitution (virtually guaranteeing it will succeed) **Aug** Constitutional ratification fails in North Carolina	1788	**Jan** Britain establishes penal settlements in Australia
Jan The U.S. Constitution takes effect	1789	

technically went into effect because nine states had completed the process. But it was unlikely that the new government would succeed without the support of the large and influential states of New York and Virginia. On June 23, Virginia gave its assent, delivering along with ratification 20 proposed amendments and support for a future bill of rights. On June 26, New York followed suit. North Carolina rejected ratification in August, only subsequently voting for ratification in November when it was clear the document would go into effect. Rhode Island, ever the dissenter, held out its ratification until May 1790 (Table 7.1).

Table 7.1 When the States Ratified the U.S. Constitution

DATE OF RATIFICATION	STATE
December 1787	Delaware New Jersey Pennsylvania
January 1788	Connecticut Georgia
February 1788	Massachusetts
April 1788	Maryland
May 1788	South Carolina
June 1788	New Hampshire Virginia
July 1788	New York
November 1789	North Carolina
May 1790	Rhode Island

At the conclusion of the Constitutional Convention in September 1787, Benjamin Franklin, less than a year away from his own death, rose to urge his fellow delegates to sign the new Constitution. He claimed that the document would "astonish our enemies, who are waiting with confidence to hear . . . that our states are on the point of separation." Franklin declared, "I consent, Sir, to this Constitution because I expect no better and because I am not sure that it is not the best. The opinions I have had of its errors, I sacrifice to the public good." That very notion of republican sacrifice for "the common good" had motivated many of those who fought in the Revolution. Conflicts during the war and developments in postwar society had proven that more struggle was necessary to find out whose version of "the public good" would reign in American government. And, as Franklin reminded the other convention delegates, much of the world would be watching to see if the United States of America could succeed.

STUDY QUESTIONS FOR A FEDERAL NATION

1. What factors led to the calling of the Constitutional Convention?

2. Why and how did Federalists and Antifederalists disagree so strongly over what form of government would protect liberty?

quiz

Summary

- The American Revolution centered around the best way to protect "liberty" and republican government, although not everyone in society agreed on how to do so.
- European help, especially from France, was essential to the American victory in the Revolutionary War, an international conflict.
- The ideology of republicanism built in some weaknesses to the American military, but forces performed surprisingly well against British troops and their allies.
- The Revolutionary War caused changes in the social roles and power of Native American groups, African Americans, and white women.
- During and after the Revolutionary War, financial and economic difficulties dramatized power struggles within the states and between the states and the U.S. national government.
- The U.S. Constitution created a new government based on ideas of federalism and popular sovereignty while at the same time seeking to restrain somewhat the forces of popular democracy.

Key Terms and People

audio
flashcards

Arnold, Benedict 242
Articles of Confederation 233
Bache, Sarah Franklin 248
balance of powers 252
Brant, Joseph 242
Catherine the Great 237
Clinton, Sir Henry 240
Cornwallis, Lord 229
coverture 248
de Grasse, Comte 239
d'Estaing, Comte 239
federalism 250
Federalist Papers 253
Gannett, Deborah Sampson 248
Gates, Horatio 231
Germain, Lord George 240
Howe, Sir Richard 230

Howe, Sir William 229
Jay, John 236
Lafayette, Marie Joseph Paul Yves Rock Gilbert du Motier, Marquis de 238
Laurens, Henry 245
Marshall, John 253
Martin, Luther 252
Morgan, Daniel 241
popular sovereignty 250
Reed, Esther DeBerdt 248
separation of powers 233
Shays' Rebellion 251
Steuben, Friedrich Wilhelm von 238
Tarleton, Banastre 241
Vergennes, Charles Gravier, Comte de 232
Wheatley, Phillis 236

Reviewing Chapter 7

1. How did the United States win independence from the world's most powerful empire?
2. Why did the United States win the Revolutionary War?
3. How did the circulation of people, goods, and ideas across the Atlantic Ocean complicate and contribute to the American victory in the Revolution?

Further Reading

Gould, Eliga H., and Peter S. Onuf, eds. *The American Revolution in the Atlantic World.* Baltimore: Johns Hopkins University Press, 2005. This volume of essays presents a look at the American Revolution in the context of Atlantic world history. It includes 15 essays on social, political, military, and cultural history stretching from the imperial crisis through the ratification of the Constitution.

Gray, Edward, and Jane Kamensky, eds. *The Oxford Handbook of the American Revolution.* New York: Oxford University Press, 2013. This collection features comprehensive articles by leading scholars that convey the latest scholarly opinion on the social, political, cultural, and military history of the Revolution.

Higginbotham, Don. *The War for American Independence.* Boston: Northeastern University Press, 1983. This book is the best one-volume military history of the American Revolution. It explains how the United States won the war, with European help, despite organizational and strategic disadvantages.

Holton, Woody. *Unruly Americans and the Origins of the American Constitution.* New York: Hill and Wang, 2007. Holton argues in this book that although the framers of the U.S. Constitution feared the middling and lower sort, the Constitution was nonetheless shaped by the desires and interests of people in the states who participated in the ratifying conventions. The conventions were much more democratic than the Constitutional Convention.

Jasanoff, Maya. *Liberty's Exiles: American Loyalists in the Revolutionary World.* New York: Alfred A. Knopf, 2011. Jasanoff's book traces the fate of white Loyalists, Indians, and African Americans who supported the British during the American Revolution as they were exiled to Britain and the British Empire, including Canada, Sierra Leone, India, and Australia.

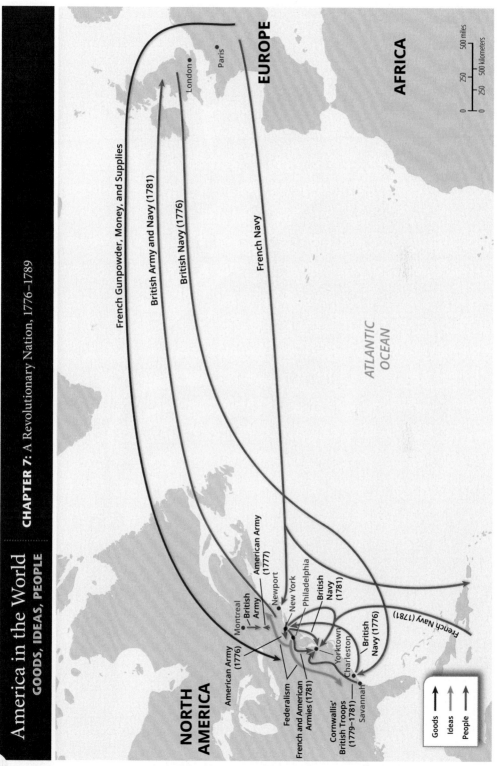

America in the World
GOODS, IDEAS, PEOPLE

CHAPTER 7: A Revolutionary Nation, 1776–1789

EUROPE

London
Paris

AFRICA

0   250   500 miles
0   250   500 kilometers

French Gunpowder, Money, and Supplies

British Army and Navy (1781)

British Navy (1776)

French Navy

ATLANTIC OCEAN

French Navy (1781)

NORTH AMERICA

Montreal
British Army
American Army (1777)
Newport
New York
Philadelphia
British Navy (1781)
American Army (1776)
Federalism
French and American Armies (1781)
Yorktown
Charleston
British Navy (1776)
Cornwallis' British Troops (1779–1781)
Savannah

Goods
Ideas
People

map analysis

General Toussaint Louverture (1743–1803).

A New Nation Facing a Revolutionary World

1789–1815

I n November 1798, **Toussaint Louverture**, the formerly enslaved black military leader of the French Caribbean colony of Saint-Domingue, wrote to U.S. president John Adams asking for help. Adams was embroiled in a "Quasi-War" with France that was snarling American trade and causing him trouble with rival politicians: fellow Federalist Alexander Hamilton, who wanted him to declare war on France, and Vice President Thomas Jefferson, whose supporters favored France. After Louverture's envoy in the United States visited Secretary of State Timothy Pickering in Philadelphia in December, Adams, a former Revolutionary himself, decided financial interest and a common revolutionary spirit meant the United States should help Louverture as he pushed for independence from France, despite the fact that the U.S. government would never have encouraged rebellious slaves within its own borders.

In January 1799, the U.S. Congress renewed legislation that halted U.S. trade with France and forbade U.S. ships to enter French ports, but a new clause allowed the president discretion to lift the trade restriction for any port where trade "may safely be renewed." Congressional debate openly acknowledged that this plank, dubbed "Toussaint's Clause," was intended to let Adams aid Louverture and his independence movement. Many southerners fought the legislation that Vice President Thomas Jefferson argued would make the United States susceptible to the influence of "Cannibals of the terrible republic"—meaning Saint-Dominguan rebellious slaves. Despite this, Toussaint's Clause passed with the support of some southern congressmen, whose wish for trade outpaced their fear of slave revolt.

President Adams signed the law on February 9, 1799, and sent war ships, trade goods, funding, and an official U.S. diplomat, Edward Stevens, to Saint-Domingue to support Louverture. The U.S. position toward Louverture would be reversed by Jefferson after he defeated Adams in the presidential election the following year, but for a time the U.S. supported the black rebel in a key phase of the Haitian Revolution.

Toussaint's Clause demonstrated how connected the new American nation continued to be to events in Europe and the Caribbean—where the French Revolution and Haitian Revolution were dramatically changing the political and social landscape. Even as U.S. citizens accustomed themselves to living under the terms of their new federal Constitution, revolutionary change in France and Saint-Domingue (soon to be Haiti) meant that Americans would have to be careful not to become ensnared in global turmoil.

THE UNITED STATES IN THE AGE OF THE FRENCH REVOLUTION

As Americans tried to implement their own government, they faced a new world changed by revolutions in both France and Haiti. Many Americans believed that the French Revolution grew out of a concept of American Revolutionary liberty, a familiar republicanism. But French radicalism and political conflict quickly increased after 1793, and the French revolutionary wars, especially with Great Britain, created a challenge for the new U.S. government. Against a backdrop of international turmoil, Americans fought their own ideological and political battles. As first president of the United States, George Washington wanted to remain neutral in the European wars, but such a position was not always easy. Conflicts in Europe helped to fuel the growth of the first U.S. political parties, which reflected deep disagreements among Americans about how their new government should work. In a revolutionary world, how would Americans manage their own political and social change?

The New Nation and the New Revolution

Initially, Americans believed that the 1789 French Revolution was linked to American Revolutionary ideals, especially as expressed in the Declaration of Independence. When the Estates General, the third estate of the French legislature, formed the National Assembly in June 1789 and street fighting escalated after the storming of the notorious Bastille prison in Paris in July, the American minister to France, Thomas Jefferson, looked on approvingly. At first, American friends such as the Marquis de Lafayette took a hand in shaping a new French government. King Louis XVI fled the capital, and in August, the Estates General issued the Declaration of the Rights of Man and of the Citizen, declaring, "Men are born and remain free and equal in rights." As Jefferson left France to take up his post as the first U.S. secretary of state, he thought that American liberty was taking root in Europe. Most Americans supported the French Revolution in its early stages. In towns and cities around the United States, Americans showed their enthusiasm by wearing French clothing, imitating French public festivals in honor of "Reason" and "Liberty," and celebrating French military victories.

Although the United States responded positively when France declared itself a republic in 1792, events soon weakened U.S. support. The execution of the royal family in 1793; the execution or imprisonment of leaders beloved by Americans, such as Lafayette; and France's bid to spread revolutionary republicanism through warfare soon divided U.S. opinion. During "the Terror" in France, hundreds judged to be political enemies of "the people" were executed by guillotine—which many Americans, like John Adams, viewed as far too radical. To many members of the American elite, the French seemed to endorse a dangerous excess of equality and democracy. But others, such as Jefferson himself, continued to view France as a new beacon of liberty.

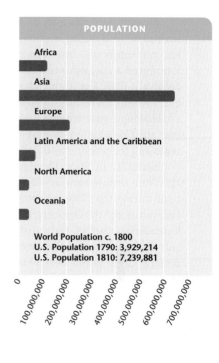

In an already contentious domestic political scene, Americans could not avoid conflict over the French Revolution and its social and political consequences. If the French based their revolution on American liberty, was the United States susceptible to the same kind of "Terror"? Would the French situation affirm or disrupt American politics? Would the French abolition of slavery in France's Caribbean colonies in 1794 affect the United States? Attorney General Edmund Randolph wrote to President Washington that he worried about the "ardour of some, to transplant French politics, as fresh fuel for our politics." Not all American political developments directly related to the French Revolution, but the backdrop of European change and uncertainty influenced Americans who worked to implement their federal government and to arrange their domestic politics.

Excerpts from Edmund Burke and Thomas Paine on the French Revolution (1790–91)

The Rise of Party Tensions

When the U.S. electoral college met for the first time in February 1789, it unanimously chose George Washington as president. His personal prestige and Revolutionary War heroism caused Americans to trust him with the expanded powers given to the federal government by the new Constitution. John Adams, the Massachusetts statesman and former U.S. minister to Great Britain, was elected the first vice president.

Despite the unanimity of support for Washington, the cabinet and Congress remained divided during his first term. Congress was dominated by merchants, lawyers, and gentlemen who had been strong supporters of the new Constitution. They soon introduced a slate of constitutional amendments, as promised during the ratification debates in 1788. The 10 amendments, known as the **Bill of Rights**, focused primarily on guaranteeing individual liberties and restraining Congress from inhibiting the press or establishing a state religion; they were ratified by the states in 1791. The old divisions over the Constitution, however, were soon overtaken by a new set of disagreements regarding the proper uses of federal power and attitudes toward Britain and France.

Secretary of State Thomas Jefferson and Secretary of the Treasury Alexander Hamilton opposed one another at almost every turn. They headed rival political factions during the 1790s, creating the first political parties in American history—the Federalists and the Democratic-Republicans—even though neither side believed in the legitimacy of parties. Federalists, led by the brilliant Hamilton, Washington's former aide-de-camp, favored the strong use of federal power, greater taxation, and keeping direct political power in the hands of educated elites. Federalists thought the United States should restore good relations with Great Britain, and Hamilton was among those political leaders most critical of the antiaristocratic "excesses" of the French Revolution. Democratic-Republicans, led by Jefferson and James Madison, favored the French and their democratic style. Jeffersonians argued that state governments should continue to check the power of the federal government. They rejected Hamilton's plans to encourage commerce and financial development. Jefferson believed farming to be the base of the ideal developing economy; in addition, he insisted, in contrast to Hamilton, that democratic politics should include the participation of nonelite white men, especially farmers and artisans (Table 8.1).

Federalists and Democratic-Republicans possessed different interpretations of the consequences of the American Revolution, clashing over notions of how government power ought to be used. The Federalists envisioned a version of American "liberty" that rested on traditional republican values and elite leadership, whereas the Democratic-Republicans generally favored a more personal notion of democratic "liberty." Each party also built up support among the populace, among voters and men and women who were unable to vote but still participated in public rituals that demonstrated their support for one side or another. When Bostonians celebrated George Washington's

Table 8.1 Political Parties in the 1790s

FEDERALIST PARTY	DEMOCRATIC-REPUBLICAN PARTY
Favored strong federal government	Favored limited federal power
Favored friendship with the British	Hostile to Great Britain
Opposed the French Revolution	Sympathetic to the French Revolution
Power base among merchants, property owners, urban workers in commercial enterprises	Power base among southern planters and northern farmers
Minority party after 1800	Majority party after 1800
Strongest region: New England	Supported by urban artisans and workingmen

birthday with parades, fireworks, and public celebrations, they attached themselves to the Federalist cause. When Philadelphians turned out for Independence Day celebrations that featured public readings of the Declaration of Independence and French-style festivals of "liberty," they openly supported Democratic-Republican politics.

One of the first issues that Hamilton's and Jefferson's supporters contended over—the assumption of state Revolutionary War debts by the federal government—also revealed the regional strength of each faction. Jefferson, James Madison, and other southerners opposed the assumption of state debts because they wanted to restrict centralized power and because many southern states had already paid back their creditors. Hamilton argued that the federal government had to pay the outstanding debts of large states such as Pennsylvania and New York to reassure foreign governments of the fiscal power of the United States. In the summer of 1790, the two sides compromised. Congress voted to assume the debts but pacified skeptical southerners by voting to locate the new federal capital city on the Potomac River in the District of Columbia, south of the previous capital in Philadelphia.

In 1790 and 1791, Hamilton's financial proposals drove the two political factions further apart. Hamilton wanted to encourage economic development by wielding federal power that the Democratic-Republicans opposed. He issued a *Report on Public Credit* arguing for financing public debt and proposing excise taxes. Hamilton also proposed the creation of a national bank, supported by federal funds and private shareholders. Although Jefferson and Madison argued that the bank was unconstitutional, Congress chartered it in February 1791. The Democratic-Republicans also opposed Hamilton's efforts to encourage domestic production of goods by imposing international tariffs and funding American economic enterprise.

Alexander Hamilton, "An Opinion on the Constitutionality of an Act to Establish a Bank" (1791)

Although neither the Federalists nor the Democratic-Republicans were yet organized as political parties, they were increasingly open about their mutual opposition. By 1792, each side patronized its own newspaper: **John Fenno** edited the Federalists' *Gazette of the United States* and **Philip Freneau** edited the *National Gazette* for the Democratic-Republicans. Neither side nominated official candidates in elections, but voters could choose allegiances because local candidates' sympathies were usually widely known, and many smaller newspapers openly supported one side or another.

Neutrality and Jay's Treaty

Amid infighting and opposition, President Washington tried to remain neutral regarding the two developing political parties, just as he wanted neutrality for the United States between Britain and France. By February 1793, however, he had grown increasingly concerned that the United States was getting too involved in France's new revolutionary wars. Even Jefferson wanted to keep the United States out of war, but he favored France and was keen to honor the 1778 alliance between the "sister republics." Hamilton, who Jefferson was convinced was a monarchist, believed that the alliance should be suspended.

In April 1793, the French government sent **Edmund Charles Genet** on a diplomatic mission to cement the 1778 alliance and to seek help in France's newly declared war on Great Britain, Spain, Austria, and Prussia. Genet hoped also to sign a new commercial treaty with the United States, to use the United States as a staging ground to outfit privateers, to expel Britain and Spain from Canada and Louisiana, and to recruit U.S. citizens for French military service.

As Genet traveled from South Carolina to the U.S. capital at Philadelphia, he defied American officials who wished him to keep a low profile because they were not ready to support the French government. He received an enthusiastic welcome, however, from crowds of men and women who demonstrated their support for the French Revolution by cheering, displaying French symbols, and attending banquets and balls in his honor.

President Washington issued a Proclamation of Neutrality in the European wars on April 22, just weeks after he had been inaugurated for his second term and only two weeks after Genet's arrival. The Proclamation of Neutrality aimed to keep open U.S. ships' trading rights with Britain, France, and their Caribbean colonies. Washington also hoped a neutral stance would allow the United States to secure its borders and avoid further hostilities in North America with Spain and with Indians allied to European powers.

Genet encouraged people to oppose Washington's Proclamation of Neutrality, and he hatched a secret plan in Georgia to mobilize backcountry Americans against the East Florida Spanish government, which had angered American settlers by shielding runaway slaves. Genet also outfitted and launched several American ships as French privateers.

Genet's fortunes changed when his political faction, the Girondins, fell from power in France in June 1793. By August 1793, Washington's politically divided cabinet had unanimously agreed to ask the French to recall Genet. Secretary of State Thomas Jefferson wrote diplomatic letters making the request while still trying to maintain the close U.S. relationship with France that he and his political allies prized. The Girondins' rivals, the Jacobins, agreed to recall Genet to help ensure that the United States would continue to export food to France (although Genet never returned to France under threat of execution).

The United States wanted to maintain trade relations with Britain and France but risked becoming a pawn between the two bigger European powers. The British government ordered the Royal Navy to seize any U.S. ship trading with the French in the Caribbean, and they took hundreds of American merchant vessels as prizes and began to kidnap American sailors and impress them into Royal Navy service. To stop this, Washington sent Chief Justice John Jay to London to negotiate a treaty with the British government, the terms of which Washington kept secret from the public for months. Thomas Jefferson resigned as secretary of state at the end of 1793, in part because he believed that Hamilton had influenced Washington to become pro-British.

When the Senate finally debated **Jay's Treaty** with Great Britain, which granted the United States trade rights on the Mississippi, in the British East Indies, and at western forts, French minister to the United States Pierre Adet, U.S. secretary of state Edmund Randolph, and several state legislatures all opposed it. They saw the treaty as a repudiation of America's Revolutionary commitment to France and a potential violation of neutrality. Opponents of the treaty charged that it was ragingly pro-British. Angry crowds of Americans with French and Democratic-Republican sympathies burned Jay in effigy. As the Senate narrowly ratified Jay's Treaty in June 1795, President Washington's popularity plummeted.

The Popular Politics of Rebellion

A series of events in 1794 also tested Washington's popularity and confirmed the intertwining of domestic politics and trade. Hamilton's 1791 excise taxes on distilled liquor threatened westerners, who could gain more profits by shipping spirits to urban markets than by shipping bulky corn or wheat. Farmers in Virginia, Kentucky, Maryland, North

Carolina, and South Carolina refused to pay the taxes. But Pennsylvanians mounted the hottest protest when, in July 1794, crowds attacked locally despised tax collector John Neville and burned his house. Within weeks, 6,000 protesters, including some members of the Pennsylvania militia, had gathered outside Pittsburgh and threatened more widespread violence against the whiskey tax.

The **Whiskey Rebellion** in western Pennsylvania prompted Washington to assert federal power using military force. Hamilton, who was increasingly close to Washington, led 15,000 federalized militia troops from other states into Pennsylvania in September. Troops avoided widespread violence but arrested several leaders of the rebellion. The use of federal military power against domestic protesters outraged Democratic-Republicans. President Washington, who blamed Democratic-Republicans for the unrest, suggested that radical pro-Jefferson political clubs, called Democratic-Republican societies, had encouraged protesters. Although these societies did not conspire against the government, Federalists and Democratic-Republicans disagreed about whether clubs that encouraged democratic politics and protest were dangerous or legitimate. The Whiskey Rebellion, and the controversy over Democratic-Republican societies, revealed deep disagreement over the proper exercise of federal power and the proper role of popular politics—especially against the backdrop of French popular upheaval. In 1794, some wondered if the Whiskey Rebellion and its suppression might be the beginning of an American version of the French "Terror." Indeed, the Whiskey Rebellion was one of the largest domestic uprisings in North American history before the Civil War, and President Washington put it down using unprecedented executive power.

Letter from Thomas Jefferson to James Madison on the Whiskey Rebellion (1794)

Indian Warfare and European Power

Federal power was also contested in western conflicts between settlers and Indians who were trying to navigate between increasingly aggressive U.S. citizens and traditional European enemies and allies. After 1789, the British kept seven forts south of Upper Canada, and they actively traded and negotiated with Miami, Shawnee, and other nations in the Ohio region who frequently clashed with U.S. settlers encroaching on their land. Settlers in western lands granted to Revolutionary War veterans also pressured Ohio-region Indian peoples.

The Washington administration sent the small U.S. Army, supplemented by western militia troops, to conquer the Ohio country in 1790 and in 1791. General Josiah Harmar attacked Miami Town, an Indian–British trade hub, in October 1790. Miami warrior **Little Turtle** surprised Harmar's force with superior numbers and tactics and inflicted a crushing defeat that cost Harmar his job. The following November, Little Turtle organized Miami, Shawnee, and other allied tribal forces, with British logistical support, to resist when **Arthur St. Clair**, governor of the Northwest Territory, led another attack on Miami Town. At the Wabash River, Little Turtle's forces killed more than 600 American soldiers and delivered one of the greatest-ever victories by Indians over the United States.

In 1794, Washington sent U.S. Army forces—this time headed by former Revolutionary War general **"Mad" Anthony Wayne**—to fight against the Shawnee and Miami Confederacy. Wayne commanded almost 4,000 army and militia troops, built strong forts, and exploited Indian disagreements. In August 1794, Wayne destroyed Indian villages, and he defeated what he called "the grand emporium of the hostile Indians of the West" at the Battle of Fallen Timbers. The following year he signed the Treaty of

Greenville with 12 Indian nations in the Northwest Territory, who were forced to grant U.S. settlers access to wide tracts of land. The Battle of Fallen Timbers was a watershed in Indian history, as it compelled many to accommodate U.S. demands and allowed the United States to extend its reach farther west. The British stayed out of the conflict temporarily but stood ready to exploit future tensions as settlement increased.

During the period of calm between the United States and Britain after Jay's Treaty and the Treaty of Greenville, the Spanish, weakened by their involvement in European wars, sought to reduce tensions with the United States. In 1795, they agreed to a new treaty. That summer in Madrid, U.S. diplomat Thomas Pinckney negotiated a highly favorable agreement with Prime Minister Don Manuel de Godoy, as Godoy sought to settle Spain's war with France. **Pinckney's Treaty**—also known as the Treaty of San Lorenzo—fully opened Mississippi River trade to the United States, provided tax-free markets in New Orleans, settled Florida border issues, and guaranteed Spanish help against Indians who wanted to block U.S. settlers from expanding. The U.S. Senate unanimously ratified the new treaty in 1796, and it seemed for a moment that the United States might have stabilized threats from Indian and European powers.

STUDY QUESTIONS FOR THE UNITED STATES IN THE AGE OF THE FRENCH REVOLUTION

1. In what ways did domestic and international events influence partisan conflict during Washington's presidency?

quiz **2.** How did the development of political parties influence American government in the 1790s?

PARTY CONFLICT INTENSIFIES

George Washington, battered by his critics but sure that he had successfully stabilized the new republic, decided not to serve a third term as president—setting a precedent that would stand for over 100 years. Despite controversies during his second term, Washington's personal prestige, reputation, and leadership had helped to ensure the smooth beginnings of the federal government. Many Americans worried about what would follow after his retirement. As he left office in 1796, Washington published a "Farewell Address" warning "against the insidious wiles of foreign influence." He urged Americans to trade with Europe but to guard against involvement in European politics and "to steer clear of permanent alliances with any portion of the foreign world." Washington wanted the United States to chart its own course in the world and avoid being pushed around by more powerful nations. Washington also warned against factionalism in U.S. politics, but it soon became clear that the United States could avoid neither international problems nor party politics.

Adams in Power

John Adams won the presidential election of 1796, despite opposition from fellow Federalist Alexander Hamilton, who thought him insufficiently conservative. States chose members of the electoral college in a patch-work of methods ranging from popular voting to selection by state legislatures, and the electors did not have to reflect popular opinion in their votes. Prior to the ratification of the Twelfth Amendment in 1804, the candidate who received the second-highest number of votes in the electoral college was elected vice president. Neither the Federalists nor the Democratic-Republicans yet formally nominated candidates for the presidency, and several electors split their votes for a variety of Federalist and Democratic-Republican candidates. As a result, Thomas Jefferson received the second-highest vote total and was elected vice president. The fact that the president and vice president led opposing political parties showed how the parties themselves were not yet solidly organized, disciplined entities.

President Adams had to navigate between Jefferson's Democratic-Republican Party on the one hand and Hamilton's conservative wing of his own party on the other. In 1796, Federalists also won a slim majority in Congress, and they moved quickly to fill the federal judiciary with their allies. Although Adams handled crises well, he was never able to match Washington's popularity or to unite the country around Federalist politics.

THE DEATH OF WASHINGTON George Washington's death in 1799 evoked an outpouring of public grief. In this print, funerary symbols (an urn and obelisk) are topped with a portrait of Washington, attended by mourning women representing "Columbia" (left) and "Justice" (right). An angel representing "fame" blows a trumpet in Washington's honor overhead.

Adams assumed that reverence for the presidency would continue during his service. George Washington's birthday had been celebrated widely as a holiday, but similar Adams celebrations never caught on outside his native New England. John Adams found constant personal and political support from his wife Abigail, who was particularly suspicious of French influence over Jefferson and the Democratic-Republicans.

John and Abigail were the first presidential couple to take up residence in the White House as the planned city of Washington, DC, became the new U.S. capital in 1799. John prayed in a letter to Abigail, "May none but honest and wise Men ever rule under this roof." French planner Pierre L'Enfant, English architects Benjamin Henry Latrobe and William Thornton, and a variety of Irish and African American surveyors and builders worked throughout the 1790s to build a capital city whose design reflected American reverence for Greek and Roman classical ideals. Americans also reflected their political ideas in their taste for neoclassical designs of furniture, silver, glassware, pottery, and china—much of it imported from England. French style also continued to be popular, even as the Anglo-French wars accelerated.

Quasi-War with France

As the United States got caught up in the war between Britain and France, President Adams faced pressure to declare war on France. Adams wrote in a 1796 letter, "I dread

JOHN AND ABIGAIL ADAMS John Adams and Abigail Adams had a close relationship nurtured by frequent correspondence when they had to be apart. Abigail was one of John's strongest supporters when he was vice president and president, and she resented political criticism of her husband. Both John and Abigail remained strong supporters of Federalist causes for the remainder of their lives.

PATRIOTIC DECORATING
Girandole mirrors like this, made from wood or plaster covered in gold leaf, became popular among wealthy, fashionable Americans in the 1790s. Decorating one's home with furniture featuring the bald eagle, a symbol of the United States, was a way to display patriotism and a taste for lavish material goods.

image analysis

not a War, with France or England, if either forces it upon Us, but will make no Aggression upon either, with my free Will, without just and necessary Cause and Provocation." Adams pursued a balancing act of nonaggression throughout his term, despite diplomatic and military crises with France and the persistent urging of some other Federalists. In mid-1796, the French decreed that neutral trade ships would be subject to capture just as British ships were. The British also continued to harass U.S. traders. Tensions rose further during Adams's first few months in office when the French rejected American envoy Charles Cotesworth Pinckney, one of the negotiators of Jay's Treaty with Britain.

Over the objection of many fellow Federalists, and with little consultation with Vice President Jefferson or other Democratic-Republicans, Adams decided to send Elbridge Gerry and John Marshall to join Pinckney in a new diplomatic delegation to France. Emboldened by Napoleon Bonaparte's military victories in western Europe,

QUASI-WAR WITH FRANCE   This cartoon, "Property Protected à la Françoise," lampoons the Quasi-War between the United States and France and the XYZ Affair. In the image, menacing French figures threaten America, represented by the woman dressed in fashionable clothing with a Native American feathered headdress. The "French Directors" demand private plunder to put in their sack at the point of a sword labeled "French Argument." Meanwhile, John Bull, a character representing Great Britain, sits atop a mountain in the background laughing at the conflict.

the French were openly hostile to the Americans when they arrived in October of 1797. In what became dubbed the "**XYZ Affair**," French officials, identified to Congress and in the American press only by those initials, humiliated the American diplomats by demanding bribes that insulted U.S. sovereignty. The chairman of the House Ways and Means Committee famously expressed American resistance to French demands when he declared, "Millions for defense, but not one cent for tribute!" Henrietta Liston, the wife of the British minister to the United States, commented that public opinion seemed suddenly to shift and flow "with violence against the French party" as anti-French petitions flooded into Washington.

Controversy raged throughout 1798, and the Federalist Congress verged on declaring war. Congress fortified the U.S. Navy, and Adams ordered Hamilton to strengthen the still-small U.S. Army. French and U.S. ships skirmished in the Caribbean. In early 1799, as French ships hovered off the coast of America, the two countries seemed to be involved in an undeclared Quasi-War. To deflate tensions, Adams decided to send a new team of diplomats to France in October. Although he managed to avoid all-out war, he faced criticism from political opponents and from fellow Federalists, who thought he was weak on France.

Alien and Sedition Acts

President Adams was less successful at balancing domestic political tensions during the Quasi-War with France. Believing that he had public support, Adams and his allies in

Congress passed a series of **Alien and Sedition Acts** during the summer of 1798. These acts only aggravated political and social conflicts around the country. The three "Alien" acts severely restricted immigration into the United States and gave the president power to deport anyone thought to be dangerous—even for spreading radical political ideas. The Sedition Law imposed steep fines and prison sentences on anyone found guilty of conspiring to "oppose any measure or measures of the government of the United States" or anyone who spoke or wrote maliciously against the government or the president. Both sets of measures targeted Democratic-Republicans, who found support among immigrants from Ireland, France, and the Caribbean as well as from radical newspaper editors. Many Federalists thought they were imitating successful measures the Pitt government in England had imposed to suppress opposition, but the Alien and Sedition Acts backfired.

Unlike many French revolutionaries, most Americans did not really wish to overthrow the social order, and the Sedition Act seemed like an unconstitutional overreaction to political opposition. Several high-profile newspaper editors convicted of sedition and imprisoned for writing against the Adams administration became martyrs who galvanized public support against the Sedition Act. In August 1798, Vice President Jefferson secretly drafted resolutions, passed by the Democratic-Republican–controlled Kentucky legislature, denouncing the laws as unconstitutional and arguing that states need not comply with them. James Madison drafted a similar set of resolutions for Virginia. Other state legislatures, including Massachusetts and Maryland, denounced the Kentucky and Virginia resolutions as dangerous precedents for state nullification of federal law. Americans entered the election year of 1800 barely at peace with France and fraught with internal division over the practice of political opposition.

Slave Rebellions: Saint-Domingue and Virginia

Anxieties among American elites in the late 1790s also increased because of revolutionary upheaval close to home—especially in the form of slave revolts. In 1791, black slaves in the French colony of Saint-Domingue (now the nation of Haiti) on the Caribbean island of Hispaniola revolted against their masters, whom they drastically outnumbered. The rebel slaves joined forces with pro-monarchical Spanish army forces to fight the French colonial government on the island, the richest European colony in the Western Hemisphere. Led by charismatic former slave Toussaint Louverture, the rebels switched to the French revolutionary cause in 1794 after the French government abolished slavery. Louverture, now the governor general of Saint-Domingue, bested Spanish and English forces and took over the entire island of Hispaniola for the French; he also pacified the large mixed-race population on the island. By the end of the decade, Toussaint ruled a Saint-Domingue that seemed headed for independence (Map 8.1).

Toussaint Louverture's constitution for Haiti (1801)

The fears of white U.S. slave owners, like Thomas Jefferson, who worried that the rebellious spirit would spread, seemed justified when a Virginia slave named **Gabriel**, emboldened by the Saint-Domingue revolt and the political divisions he witnessed in his state, planned a large-scale revolt to coincide with the 1800 presidential election. Gabriel's master, Thomas Prosser, hired him out, which enabled Gabriel to build a network of associates in Richmond that included other slaves and radical French émigrés. Gabriel believed that free blacks and white artisans would join his cause, and he planned to carry a banner reading "death or Liberty," a play on Patrick Henry's phrase from the

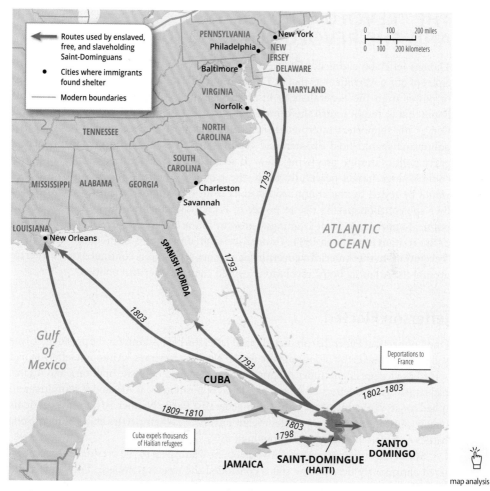

Routes used by enslaved, free, and slaveholding Saint-Dominguans

● Cities where immigrants found shelter

Modern boundaries

PENNSYLVANIA

● New York

Philadelphia ●

NEW JERSEY

● Baltimore

DELAWARE

MARYLAND

VIRGINIA

Norfolk ●

0   100   200 miles

0   100   200 kilometers

TENNESSEE

NORTH CAROLINA

SOUTH CAROLINA

MISSISSIPPI   ALABAMA   GEORGIA

● Charleston

● Savannah

1793

LOUISIANA

● New Orleans

SPANISH FLORIDA

ATLANTIC OCEAN

1793

Gulf of Mexico

1803

Deportations to France

1793

CUBA

1802–1803

1809–1810

Cuba expels thousands of Haitian refugees

1803

1798

SANTO DOMINGO

JAMAICA   SAINT-DOMINGUE (HAITI)

map analysis

MAP 8.1 Migration out of Saint-Domingue/Haiti, 1793–1809 Thousands of people fled or were forcibly removed from the island of Saint-Domingue during the Haitian Revolution. Many, including slave owners, slaves, and free people of color, ended up in U.S. cities.

American Revolution, when he marched on the capital at Richmond. Instead, Gabriel and his compatriots were betrayed, and he was tried and executed in October 1800. Virginia legislators imposed harsher slave codes in the aftermath of the rebellion to crack down on any rebellious slaves who might be inspired by Saint-Domingue.

STUDY QUESTIONS FOR PARTY CONFLICT INTENSIFIES

1. What diplomatic challenges (both with Europe and with Indian nations) faced the United States during the 1790s?

2. How did the Alien and Sedition Acts expose fundamental differences between Democratic-Republicans and Federalists?

quiz

◉ THE "REVOLUTION" OF 1800 AND THE REVOLUTION OF 1804

Thomas Jefferson claimed, "The election of 1800 was as real a revolution in the principles of our government as that of 1776 was in its form." Jefferson referred to the shift in power from the Federalists to his own Democratic-Republican Party and to his hopes that he might return the United States to the principles of the American Revolution as his supporters interpreted them. Because most Americans still believed that politicians should hold disinterested republican values, they did not openly accept party politics despite practicing them. It seemed remarkable that presidential power could change hands peacefully from one party to another. Jefferson's own power would be tested by the continued tensions from the Anglo-French wars, now fueled by Napoleon Bonaparte's rise to power in France. Meanwhile, the radical social and political upheaval in Saint-Domingue grew until the colony declared its independence as the Haitian republic in 1804. Thomas Jefferson brought his Democratic-Republican "revolution" to the American government as other revolutions continued to reverberate around the Atlantic. Both "revolutions" would change American politics.

Jefferson Elected

One Connecticut Federalist predicted that if Jefferson beat Adams for the presidency, "the soil will be soaked with blood, and the nation black with crimes." Although Jefferson had served as vice president under Adams, the two men held opposite opinions, and Adams had largely ignored Jefferson. Adams also faced opposition from Alexander Hamilton and other conservative members of his own Federalist Party. Neither Jefferson nor Adams openly campaigned for the presidency, but members of their parties engaged in vitriolic battles on a state-by-state basis throughout 1800.

State campaigning and legislative elections leading up to the presidential race mattered enormously because the states controlled the electoral college. Voters exercised little direct choice in the presidential election. In 10 of 16 states, the presidential electors were chosen by the state legislature, and the remaining 6 used a patchwork system in which only some of the presidential electors were chosen by popular vote.

By the time each state had chosen its members of the electoral college, in early December, it was clear that the election would be deadlocked. When the electoral college votes were officially tallied, Adams was defeated for president, but neither Aaron Burr nor Jefferson could be declared the winner. Thomas Jefferson and Aaron Burr tied with 73 votes each, and John Adams received 65. The Constitution provided that the candidate with the most votes would become president, while the runner-up would assume the vice presidency, but the Democratic-Republicans had failed to plan their electoral voting well enough to have their intended vice presidential candidate, Aaron Burr, come in second. With Burr and Jefferson tied, the Constitution stipulated that the House of Representatives, still ruled by a Federalist majority, would decide the election.

In February 1801, during a driving snowstorm, the House met in continuous session to decide the election. Although he had earlier agreed to take the vice presidency, Burr refused to concede, and he even considered striking a deal with Federalists to become president. Ultimately, however, after 36 rounds of balloting, Jefferson prevailed, and Burr was elected vice president. Constitutional crisis was averted as the Federalists ceded the presidency to the Democratic-Republicans.

Democracy: Limits and Conflicts

As they transitioned into power, the Democratic-Republicans wished to erase the Federalist influence in politics: the use of centralized federal power, the turn toward Britain, the public debt, and the excise taxes. As the Democratic-Republicans believed in a democracy built on the power of free, white, property-holding men, they limited the political voice of women and free African Americans, both of whom had made some limited advances under the Federalists. In 1807, for example, the New Jersey legislature disenfranchised property-holding women and free African Americans who had voted for decades, largely because they supported the Federalist Party. The writer Judith Sargent Murray claimed that intelligent women of means should share some equality with men, but even such elite white women lost out to the "common" white man in Jeffersonian America.

The Democratic-Republicans exercised power in Congress and the executive branch during the first decade of the 19th century, but they still had to battle the Federalists in state politics and in the federal judiciary. Among his last presidential acts, John Adams appointed Federalists to the federal courts and other offices and nominated moderate Virginia Federalist John Marshall as chief justice of the Supreme Court. Marshall became a strong opponent of the Democratic-Republicans as he put his imprint on the Court. In the landmark 1803 case of *Marbury v. Madison*, Marshall's opinion established the principle of "judicial review," the right of the U.S. Supreme Court to rule on the constitutionality of legislation and executive actions—especially important because Marshall declared that "a law repugnant to the Constitution is void." The case concerned a battle between one of Adams's Federalist appointees and Democratic-Republican secretary of state James Madison, but in the long run, the particulars mattered far less than Marshall's assertion of judicial authority. The Democratic-Republicans tried to counter Federalist judicial power using their impeachment powers, but with little effect.

Excerpt from the majority opinion in *Marbury v. Madison* (1803)

The divide between the parties in the United States remained bitter, not the least because neither one was yet convinced of the legitimacy of party politics. In 1801, John Adams called the Democratic-Republicans "a group of foreign liars, encouraged by a few ambitious native gentlemen," while most Democratic-Republicans held Federalists in no higher regard. Unless personal honor became intertwined with electoral matters—as was the case in 1804 when Vice President Burr killed Alexander Hamilton in a duel over perceived personal insults during the New York governor's race—most battles took place in the realm of politics. Unlike the French or Haitians, Americans in the 1790s did not resort to widespread violence or turmoil to work out their ideological differences.

Haitian Revolution

Slave rebellion and colonial unrest in Saint-Domingue spread into a national revolution by 1804. Although the nation of Haiti declared its independence from France, and Haitians pledged to "live free and independent" in terms familiar to the American Revolution, the new republic did not receive U.S. government support. The 1805 Haitian constitution's permanent abolition of slavery and declaration that "no white

Revolutionary Migrations

Thousands of people moved around the Atlantic world as a result of the French and Haitian revolutions—making migration one of the most important influences of the Atlantic revolutions. Free and slave migrants to the United States from France and Haiti brought with them food, clothing, language, and other traditions that influenced and changed American society.

Tens of thousands of people fled France during the early years of the revolution there, many of whom were clergy and aristocrats, but the ranks of émigrés (as they were known) also included soldiers, peasants, and even workers and middle-class bourgeois radicals whose enemies had expelled them. Among the thousands who spent time in the United States was the former British radical and American Revolutionary pamphleteer Thomas Paine, who assumed French citizenship in 1792 (the year he published *The Rights of Man*) only to flee Napoleon back to the United States in 1802. Most French émigrés did not have the choice to return home until at least the 1820s because the French government confiscated and sold their property and condemned many of them.

Philadelphia, the capital of the United States during the 1790s, became the center of French culture in America during that decade, as scores of French émigrés settled there. Louis Philippe, the future king of France, took part in Philadelphia high society and romanced several American women. One émigré, the Comte de Moré, referred to Philadelphia in the 1790s as "the Ark of Noah full of refugees." French émigrés in Philadelphia established political clubs, fraternal lodges, cultural societies, and businesses ranging from bakeries to wig shops to bookstores and newspapers.

The slave rebellion in Saint-Domingue that became the Haitian Revolution prompted even more migration to the United States: between 1793 and 1809, at least 15,000

man" would "ever be able to acquire any property" struck most white Americans as far too radical.

Toussaint Louverture fought off a French invasion early in 1802. But later that year, French troops arrested him and deported him to France, where he died in prison. Napoleon Bonaparte, the recently declared emperor of France, vowed to suppress Louverture because he was a rival political leader and because he represented, in Bonaparte's opinion, the "black barbarism that was on the rise" in the Caribbean. The French probably planned to reimpose slavery if they could control Saint-Domingue. **Jean-Jacques Dessalines**, another former slave and a skilled military commander, took over leadership of the black revolt. In 1802, after a bloody campaign, Dessalines captured the French stronghold of Le Cap Français. He then expelled French troops and most of the remaining white residents who had not already fled or been executed. On January 1, 1804, Dessalines declared Haitian independence.

The new Haitian republic found little support with President Jefferson, the author of the U.S. Declaration of Independence. Napoleon correctly asserted that "the slaves, white French colonists, and free people of color fled from the island to America. Most Saint-Dominguan refugees, about two-thirds of them white and one-third of them black, ended up in American port cities (Philadelphia, New Orleans, New York, Boston, Baltimore, and Charleston) because they often escaped on French merchant ships.

The thousands of white slave masters who managed to force their slaves to accompany them from Saint-Domingue presented a dilemma for the United States. Slave masters sought loopholes, for example, to the Pennsylvania manumission law that promised freedom after six months to any slave brought to the state. In 1809, Congress voted an exemption to the recent prohibition on international importation of slaves when it allowed white masters to bring more than 3,000 slaves with them to Louisiana from Cuba, where they had taken refuge after the Haitian Revolution. In 1811, Charles Deslondes, a slave brought to Louisiana, led one of the bloodiest and largest slave rebellions in American history.

The United States also influenced Saint-Domingue. Haitian leader Jean-Jacques Dessalines was an admirer of the American Revolution, and future Haitian president and king Henri Christophe had very possibly served among hundreds of mixed-race Saint-Dominguans alongside French troops at the Siege of Savannah during the American Revolution. In later decades, hundreds of African Americans would emigrate to Haiti, viewing the island as a bastion of black power and freedom. Their journey formed just part of the complex story of migration across the Caribbean.

- How do you think the migration of tens of thousands of people across the Atlantic and the Caribbean shaped the relationship between the United States and the revolutions in France and Saint-Domingue?
- How significant was the decision by Congress to allow Saint-Dominguan slaveholders to bring slaves into the United States after the international slave trade had been outlawed?

Spanish, the English, and the Americans . . . are dismayed by the existence of this black Republic." The 1805 Haitian constitution defined all citizens of the Haitian republic as "Black" regardless of their origin, a radical notion to most Americans. White politicians were concerned that American slaves would be encouraged by the successful slave revolt and national revolution in Haiti. Moreover, Jefferson sought good relations with Napoleon. Several southern states extended repressive laws they had passed in the aftermath of Gabriel's rebellion. These laws further restricted the rights of free blacks, imposed harsher slave discipline, and forbade slave owners from freeing slaves and slaves from purchasing their own freedom. Jefferson refused to recognize the independent Haitian republic.

Haitian Declaration of Independence and Abjuration of the French Nation (1804)

The Louisiana Purchase

Although Thomas Jefferson supported the limitation of federal government power, as president he exercised great authority in expanding the territory of the United States.

In the October 1800 Treaty of San Ildefonso, Spain secretly ceded the entire Louisiana territory, including New Orleans, back to France. More than one-half-million Americans living west of the Appalachian Mountains relied on the Mississippi River for their growing agricultural trade, and they worried when Spain closed New Orleans as a precursor to the transfer of power. Jefferson was convinced that development of land by American small farmers held the key to the country's future, and he wanted to prevent Napoleon from pursuing an empire in North America. Although Jefferson had long favored France, he wrote to Robert Livingston in April 1802, "The day that France takes possession of New Orleans, we must marry ourselves to the British fleet and nation."

Instead, Jefferson found a surprising solution to the crisis. Napoleon, preoccupied with troubles in Haiti and a recent military defeat in Egypt, sought to rebuild strength for the next round of war against Great Britain. As a result, when Jefferson sent Robert Livingston and James Monroe to France to attempt to purchase New Orleans and a portion of West Florida, Napoleon's foreign minister Talleyrand instead offered to sell the entire Louisiana territory.

Letter from Thomas Jefferson to John Breckenridge on the constitutionality of the Louisiana Purchase (1803)

The Constitution did not directly address whether the federal government could purchase new territory, but after some agonizing, Jefferson concluded that the "laws of necessity, of self-preservation, of saving our country when in danger" authorized the purchase. In April 1803, he paid $15 million to purchase the vast Louisiana territory, which almost doubled the size of the United States. Jefferson argued that this strong use of federal power fit with his Democratic-Republican vision because it opened so much land for farming. The Louisiana Purchase was hailed as a glorious triumph when it was announced on July 4, 1803, but the reactions of Indian nations who would be brought into contact with the United States remained to be seen.

STUDY QUESTIONS FOR THE "REVOLUTION" OF 1800 AND THE REVOLUTION OF 1804

1. How "revolutionary" was Jefferson's election in the "revolution" of 1800?
2. Why did slave revolts and the Haitian Revolution scare Americans?

quiz

⬥ TRADE, CONFLICT, WARFARE

Jefferson hoped the Louisiana territory could develop U.S. economic growth in agriculture and trade. Between the 1790s and 1807, the United States increasingly defined itself as a commercial nation with a role in the world economy. International trade energized the American economy, but it also led the nation into conflict and war in North Africa and Europe. Trade offered economic benefits, but they came with diplomatic entanglements and military conflict.

Transatlantic and Caribbean Trade

The Anglo-French wars and Caribbean upheaval presented both opportunities and obstacles. Following the Revolutionary War, France, Britain, and Spain all opened new avenues of trade to Americans, who in the 1790s sought to expand opportunities even further. During the first Anglo-French War (1793–1801), American neutral traders had caused international friction, but commerce nonetheless increased. Americans continued to try to expand trade during the European Peace of Amiens (1801–1803), although it proved difficult. When the Napoleonic Wars resumed in 1803, Americans continued their enterprise, but they also increasingly found themselves lured into naval conflict.

When the French Revolution first spread into European warfare, the United States benefited because the French and British allowed Americans limited neutral trading rights that undermined previous Spanish and Portuguese monopolies. American exports grew from $20.2 million in 1793 to $94 million in 1801. Much of that growth came as the United States became the main trade intermediary between European nations and their Caribbean colonies. Both France and Britain allowed U.S. traders to carry goods to their rival colonies in the Caribbean by way of the United States. The Caribbean also absorbed great quantities of American products such as lumber, fish, livestock, corn, and wheat. American shipowners steadily increased their share of European and Caribbean trade.

During the period of European peace from 1801 to 1803, American exports again declined to $54 million; at the same time, however, U.S. traders increased their percentage share of the Caribbean re-export trade. Once the Europeans resumed warfare in 1803, U.S. trade in the Caribbean and Latin America again skyrocketed to its highest level ever. Exports peaked at $108 million in 1807. Imports increased even more, from $33 million in 1793 to $146 million in 1807—an indication of the growing appetite for European goods. Americans were increasingly connected to Europe and Caribbean societies through the goods they exchanged (Figure 8.1).

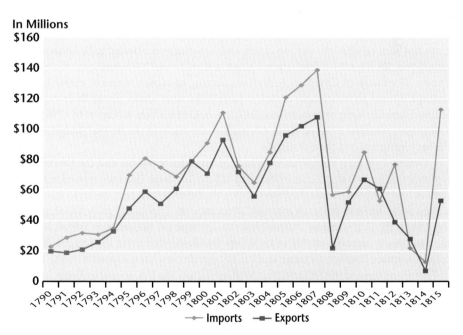

FIGURE 8.1 Total U.S. imports and exports, 1790–1815 Use this graph to think about the causes and effects of the Barbary conflicts and the War of 1812.

Americans curtailed one area of international exchange in this period—the international slave trade. Although the U.S. Constitution forbade Congress to outlaw the international trade before the year 1808, legislative debate on how to halt the international traffic in slaves began in 1806. Congressional representatives from slave and free states disagreed bitterly over the status of illegally imported slaves and punishments for slave smugglers. The British outlawed their slave trade in 1807, and the U.S. Congress followed by passing a law in March of that year banning the international slave trade as of January 1, 1808. The law was significant, although it did nothing to curtail the growing internal slave trade, and the U.S. population of slaves would skyrocket in coming decades even without legal international imports.

One contemporary economic commentator remarked that "the most adventurous became the most wealthy" during the rise in European trade, but those adventurers also exposed themselves and the United States to great risk. Although European states periodically recognized U.S. neutral trading rights, they also regularly interfered with U.S. shipping. After their 1805 victory over Napoleon at the Battle of Trafalgar, the British denied the United States the right to engage in re-export trade with France and began seizing scores of U.S. ships and their cargo. Between 1803 and 1812, the British also detained an estimated 6,000 U.S. sailors and impressed them into the Royal Navy.

Mediterranean Trade: Barbary Wars

The United States also faced conflict in the Mediterranean. In the 17th and 18th centuries, ships from the Barbary states of Algeria, Morocco, Tunis, and Tripoli harassed traders in the Mediterranean and captured foreign hostages. Lacking European protection after the Revolutionary War, the United States sought to contain the Barbary privateers—or pirates, as Europeans and Americans called them—by concluding a series of treaties in the 1780s and 1790s and paying tribute to Barbary rulers. Congress had been reluctant to pay too much, and Americans continued to be harassed and kidnapped. By the mid-1790s, Algiers alone had sold over 100 American citizens into slavery. The image of Christian Americans serving as captive slaves in exotic Muslim settings, spread by newspaper articles, pamphlets, and books about their captivity, aroused American opposition. When Congress paid $1 million to Algiers in 1796 to free American captives—a figure equal to roughly one-sixth of the federal budget—other Barbary leaders raised their demands.

Hand-to-hand combat between American and Tripolitan forces (1804)

Despite President Jefferson's reduction of the defense budget and the Democratic-Republicans' general skepticism of building U.S. naval power, Jefferson proved willing to fight in North Africa. When the Pasha of Tripoli, **Yusuf Qaramanli**, declared war on the United States in 1801, Jefferson imposed a blockade on Tripoli and endorsed shipbuilding. When the U.S. warship *Philadelphia* ran aground off the coast of Tripoli in 1803, the Tripolitans captured all 307 of its sailors and demanded more than $1.5 million in tribute. Captain **Stephen Decatur** and his *Enterprise* crew then slipped into the harbor of Tripoli and burned the *Philadelphia*. **William Eaton**, the U.S. consul to Tunis, invaded the Tripolitan city of Derna with the help of Yusuf Qaramanli's rival, his brother Ahmed. In June 1805, the United States and Tripoli reached a peace agreement that included a new U.S. payment of $60,000 in tribute to ransom the captured American sailors.

Later, Algiers declared war on the United States, but it agreed to a peace treaty after Captain Decatur captured the flagship of the Algerian fleet in June 1815. Despite creative military action, the ongoing Barbary conflicts exposed how weak the United States remained in the world. Only after 1815, when the nation proved it could wage war against Great Britain, did the Barbary states agree to stop demanding tribute payments and allow freer Mediterranean trade.

Western Discontents

Although the Louisiana Purchase had blunted the influence of France inside North America, many U.S. citizens still clashed with Spanish, British, and Indian interests. Several Americans conspired to seize Spanish territory in East Florida and Mexico. After Vice President Burr was not reelected for a second term, he sought to aggrandize himself with a set of convoluted imperial maneuvers. By 1805, Burr had organized western settlers and planned an attack to wrest control of Mexico from Spain. One of his coconspirators, James Wilkinson, who was both the highest-ranking U.S. Army general and a paid Spanish secret agent, revealed the plot to Thomas Jefferson. Burr was captured and tried for treason in 1807, but Chief Justice John Marshall's narrow constitutional interpretation led to Burr's acquittal. Burr fled to England in 1808.

After the 1795 Treaty of Greenville, white American settlers poured into the Northwest Territory, which occupied roughly the area of modern-day Ohio, Indiana, Michigan, and Wisconsin. Population increased so quickly that Ohio reached 60,000 residents and became a state in 1803. This status placed additional pressure on Shawnee and other Northwest Indians who had resisted American expansion and worked with the British after the Revolution. By 1810, there were 230,000 whites in Ohio, and Indian peoples felt constant pressure from this expansion. **Tecumseh**, who had helped lead Shawnee warriors against the United States in the 1790s, moved farther west to the White River in Indiana, where he established Prophetstown. Tecumseh's brother, **Tenskwatawa**, who was known as "The Prophet," preached a nativist religious revitalization that urged Indian peoples to reject the adaptation embraced by tribes like the Cherokee and, instead, to return to traditional ways of life. According to Tenskwatawa, Indians could continue to deal diplomatically and trade with the Spanish, French, and English, but Americans should be avoided because a revelation told him that they were "the children of the Evil Spirit."

Tecumseh gathered a coalition of warriors from several Indian tribes, including Osage, Winnebago (Ho-Chunk), Kickapoo, and Creek, as he used his personal magnetism to build a pan-Indian movement among tribes who all faced American encroachment on their lands. Tecumseh rejected the notion of private landownership, and he urged other leaders to repudiate past American treaties and to refuse new ones. While Tecumseh was away gathering allies, Indiana territorial governor **William Henry Harrison** attacked Prophetstown and defeated Shawnee warriors at the Battle of Tippecanoe on November 7, 1811. Tecumseh aligned with the British in Canada and awaited further confrontation.

Tecumseh's speech to William Henry Harrison on Indian relations with white American settlers (1810)

European Wars and Commercial Sanctions

American tensions with Britain, and to a lesser degree France, built after 1805. Britain and France moved to restrict trade and to impose naval blockades on one another. The British agreed to new trade relations with the United States in the Monroe-Pinckney

Treaty of 1806, but the Democratic-Republican–controlled U.S. Senate refused to ratify the treaty. In the summer of 1807, the British ship *Leopard* fired on the U.S. warship *Chesapeake* and impressed several of her sailors—an action that outraged the American public. Britain declared in the November 1807 Orders in Council that U.S. ships would have to stop in British ports for licensing and inspection before they could trade with France or French colonies or else they would be seized. The French countered later that year with the Milan Decree, which stated ships would be seized if they complied with the British orders.

The Democratic-Republicans controlled large majorities in both houses of Congress, and they tried to avoid war by imposing commercial sanctions on Britain and France. Thomas Jefferson claimed that instead of war, "our commerce . . . if properly managed, will be a better instrument for obliging the interested nations of Europe to treat us with justice." Congress approved the Embargo Act in December 1807, which cut off all foreign trade. The act hurt European economies, but it did far more damage to the United States: the gross domestic product fell by 8 percent. James Madison, Jefferson's Democratic-Republican successor as president, continued to support the notion of controlling international relations through trade sanctions, even though the embargo seemed largely ineffective. In the **Non-Intercourse Act of 1809**, Congress reopened trade with countries other than Britain and France. All restrictions were lifted in May 1810 because they were too difficult to enforce.

France exploited the terms of the legislation that replaced the Non-Intercourse Act, known as Macon's Bill No. 2, to shift American hostilities decisively toward Great Britain in 1811. Macon's Bill No. 2 reopened trade with France and Britain but promised to reimpose sanctions on one side if the other agreed to stop harassing ships and recognize U.S. neutral trading rights. In July, the French foreign minister, the Duc de Cadore, agreed to withdraw sanctions against U.S. shipping, although Napoleon's government only slowly abided by the agreement. U.S. political opinion then turned against Britain.

STUDY QUESTIONS FOR TRADE, CONFLICT, WARFARE

1. How did American policies toward naval interference by the Barbary states differ from those they applied to Britain and France?

quiz **2.** What were the effects of European warfare on American commerce?

❤ THE WAR OF 1812

More than a decade of trying to remain neutral in the wars between France and England had not worked for the United States, and trade sanctions had failed. By 1812, American political ire focused on Great Britain. Especially now that the French were set to allow Americans free trade, how could the British be allowed to continue interfering with American ships and kidnapping American sailors? If the United States refused to fight Britain, would that not compromise its independence won in the American Revolution? Perhaps only warfare would give the United States a chance to be taken seriously on the world stage.

War Declared

President Madison and the belligerent Democratic-Republicans in control of Congress, known as the War Hawks, agitated for war against Britain. Kentuckian Henry Clay, the Speaker of the House, and South Carolinian John C. Calhoun led the charge for war. They faced stiff opposition from Federalists, who feared that their largely New England constituents would be hurt by a cessation of trade. The British continued to harass American ships, although they repealed the Orders in Council and pledged to stop impressment. Just two days before the repeal, unaware that Britain had acted, the U.S. Congress narrowly voted to declare war.

The United States entered the War of 1812 on June 18, despite the resistance of Federalists and many residents of New England and the mid-Atlantic states (Map 8.2). The War Hawks hoped to guarantee "free trade and sailors' rights," to expel Britain from North America, and to pacify Indian nations who they felt stood in the way of American expansion in the West. Shawnee and many other Indians aligned themselves

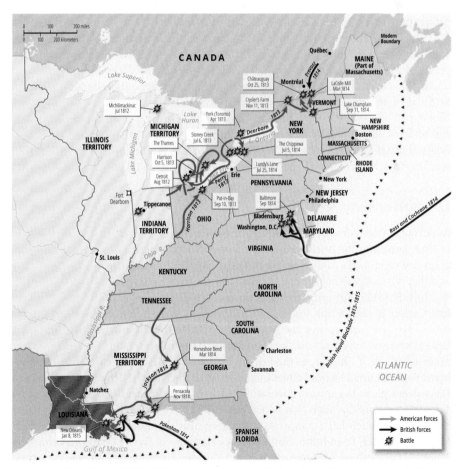

MAP 8.2 The War of 1812 This map depicts the major battles and campaigns in the War of 1812.

with the British, who promised to halt U.S. expansionism. Democratic-Republicans, who had long opposed the British, welcomed the chance to prove that the United States was a force to be reckoned with in the world.

Opposition

Federalist New Englanders, on the other hand, had friendlier relations with the British and saw the war as unnecessary, and they spearheaded opposition to the war. Washington, DC, resident Julia Hieronymous Tevis commented that during the war, "the political animosity existing between the two parties ... was bitter beyond expression." In the week after Congress declared war, the severity of internal conflict became apparent as rioting broke out in Baltimore, a politically divided city. Alexander Hanson, a Federalist newspaper editor, denounced the war in print as "unnecessary, inexpedient" and as driven by Democratic-Republican personal grudges. In return, a pro-war mob demolished his printing office and destroyed other Federalists' property. Hanson was taken into protective custody, but a mob rushed the jail, savagely beat Hanson, and killed former Revolutionary War officer James Lingan, who was trying to protect him. City officials did little to stop the violence.

Despite the chilling effect of the Baltimore riots and accusations of disloyalty, Federalists maintained political resistance throughout the war. Some Federalist ministers preached against the war, and wealthy Federalist merchants declined to finance war bonds. New England Federalists were free to push their opposition because they still held state majorities. Federalist governors in Rhode Island, Massachusetts, and Connecticut all initially refused to mobilize state militias or have them controlled by federal officers, but eventually most militias did participate. In 1814, delegates from New England states gathered in secret at the Hartford Convention, where they discussed seceding from the union and endorsed the idea that states could nullify federal laws.

Excerpt from the Hartford Convention (1814)

U.S. Offensives in Canada

As during the Revolutionary War, Americans unsuccessfully invaded Canada in the War of 1812. Expelling the British from their largest North American colony would surely grant new land to the United States and deny support to Indian enemies. Henry Clay said that "Canada was not the end but the means" by which to strike against the British.

In July 1812, Michigan territorial governor William Hull and his troops crossed into Canada at the Detroit River, but their progress stalled, and British general Isaac Brock then laid siege against the American fort at Detroit. By August, the Americans had surrendered Fort Mackinac and had delivered both Detroit and Fort Dearborn, the present-day site of Chicago, to the British. In October 1812, American forces outnumbered British, Canadian, and allied Indian forces at the Niagara River, but Stephen Van Rensselaer's plans to capture Queenstown Heights failed because he could not figure out a way to cross the river. Van Rensselaer, called "Van Bladder" by his men because he spewed so much hot air in useless speeches, also abandoned plans to attack Fort Erie in November. In addition, commanding army general Henry Dearborn's attack on Montreal failed. Coordinating army and militia troops proved difficult, and on several occasions militiamen refused to cross the border into Canada because they claimed their commissions were null on foreign soil.

Secretary of War John Armstrong focused on Canada again in 1813, as Britain and the United States battled for control of the Great Lakes. In April, an American force under Zebulon Pike inflicted a bloody defeat on the city of York, present-day Toronto. Pike's men looted houses and burned government buildings. In the West, British general Henry Proctor, bolstered by Tecumseh's Indian forces, pushed back the Americans by invading Ohio and attacking Fort Meigs. Proctor failed to stop Indian forces from slaughtering American prisoners along the River Raisin, and "Remember the Raisin!" became a rallying cry among American troops.

Tecumseh and Pan-Indian Resistance

General Proctor's second attack into Ohio in July 1813 was planned by Tecumseh, the Shawnee leader who had continued building alliances with Indians and the British since his forces' defeat by the American military at Tippecanoe in 1811. Proctor and Tecumseh unsuccessfully attacked Fort Meigs a second time and then went after Fort Stephenson, a small fortification on the Sandusky River expertly defended by Kentucky sharpshooters. When Proctor's men lost the engagement, the general blamed Tecumseh and returned his force to Canada. Tecumseh urged the British to continue the offensive against the United States, and he compared Proctor to "a fat animal" that puts its tail "between its legs and runs off." Some of Tecumseh's allies grew disillusioned with the British, and the great warrior fought to hold together his coalition.

TECUMSEH AT THE BATTLE OF THE THAMES This 1833 engraving by William Emmons shows how Americans continued to be fascinated by the death of Tecumseh at the Battle of the Thames long after the battle in 1813. Richard Mentor Johnson, who claimed to be the man who shot Tecumseh, was elected vice president in part because of that reputation. Tecumseh was revered as a brave enemy whose tragic death nonetheless proved American superiority to Indians.

An American army and militia force commanded by former Indiana territorial governor William Henry Harrison and **Richard Mentor Johnson**, a Kentucky congressman, pursued Proctor as he pulled his forces back into Canada. On October 5, 1813, they clashed with Proctor and Tecumseh at the Battle of the Thames near Moraviantown. The American troops routed the British, and although the Indian fighters held out longer, they lost heart when word spread that Tecumseh had been killed. Some of Johnson's militia troops claimed to have cut off pieces of Tecumseh's skin as souvenirs after the battle. It is more likely that Tecumseh's men removed him from the field. Mutilated or not, Tecumseh's death also meant the death of his pan-Indian resistance movement against the United States.

Although some of Tecumseh's allies immediately ended their British alliance and began to make terms with the United States, others continued to resist. Among those who fought in Canada were Little Warrior and other members of the "Red Stick" faction of the Creek Nation, named after the traditional war clubs they used in battle. Since the 1780s, some Creeks had resisted the Creek government's moves toward accommodation and its grants of land rights to the United States in Georgia and Alabama. After returning from fighting with Tecumseh in the summer of 1812, the Red Sticks, armed by the Spanish, ignited a Creek civil war. After Red Sticks destroyed Fort Mims in August, U.S. Army troops joined the fight, and General **Andrew Jackson** pursued the hostile Creeks with a vengeance. In November 1813, Jackson defeated the Red Sticks at Tallushatchee and Talladega and then delivered a crippling blow at the Battle of Horseshoe Bend in March 1814. The United States used the opportunity of the War of 1812 to tamp down Indian resistance.

Naval War

When it entered the War of 1812, no one thought that the United States could match the Royal Navy, the world's most impressive naval fighting force. Both at sea and on the Great Lakes, the U.S. Navy did better than expected and initially outperformed U.S. ground troops. Britain's navy was absorbed in the final struggle against Napoleon, and the United States fielded some skilled commanders. The Democratic-Republicans swallowed their long opposition to naval warfare and endorsed a quick program of shipbuilding. Two impressive early victories came when Captain Isaac Hull's fast USS *Constitution* bested the HMS *Guerriere* off the coast of Boston in August 1812 and when Captain Stephen Decatur's USS *United States* captured the British frigate HMS *Macedonian* as a prize near the Canary Islands in October. In December, the USS *Constitution* outmaneuvered the HMS *Java* near Brazil. American privateers also captured British ships to aid the cause.

Early in 1813, Americans controlled Lake Ontario and repelled a British attack on their naval base at Sackets Harbor. Even more impressive was the September 10, 1813, victory at the Battle of Lake Erie, where **Oliver Hazard Perry** first commanded the *Lawrence* and then, when it became incapacitated, took the helm of the *Niagara* to beat a British fleet of six ships. After the thrilling victory, Perry wrote to William Henry Harrison, "We have met the enemy, and they are ours." Perry felt that his victory partly avenged his friend Captain James Lawrence, who had been killed in a battle between the USS *Chesapeake* and the HMS *Shannon* off the coast of Boston the previous June. Later in 1813, U.S. naval victories slowed once the British imposed a stronger blockade on the United States.

PERRY AND THE WAR OF 1812
Oliver Hazard Perry rose to fame as a naval commander in the War of 1812. His decisive victory over the British at the Battle of Lake Erie and his smart leadership of the naval campaigns in the Great Lakes made him into a popular hero. He went on to collect more accolades against Algeria in the Barbary Wars.

British Offensive

After Napoleon's October 1813 defeat, the British turned attention and resources on the United States. The U.S. troops faced more experienced, better supplied, and better commanded British soldiers.

In the North, the British and Americans traded the advantage in 1814. The governor-general of Canada, Sir George Prevost, planned an offensive at Plattsburgh, New York, in September, but he retreated after American naval forces won a decisive victory on Lake Champlain and cut off his supply route. American General James Wilkinson failed in his effort to attack Montreal in October 1813, but fighting continued on the Niagara the following year. American troops won impressive victories at Chippewa and Lundy's Lane and twice attacked Fort Erie before blowing it up on November 8. The British occupied northern Maine and found the American locals largely sympathetic.

The major British offensive on the Chesapeake was more successful. Congress was slow to fortify Washington while the British blockaded the coast and invaded Maryland in August. On August 24, British forces defeated U.S. troops at Bladensburg, across the Potomac from the capital. Most of the inhabitants of the capital had been evacuated, and congressional clerks and First Lady **Dolley Madison** saved government property and records. The British entered Washington on the evening of August 24 and burned almost every government building, including the White House, before leaving the next day. Then they captured Alexandria, Virginia, without a fight.

The British were stopped when they reached Baltimore in early September. Francis Scott Key wrote the poem "The Star-Spangled Banner" after watching the battle of Fort McHenry on September 13. For 25 hours, the British fired over 1,500 rounds, including exploding shells and screaming Congreve rockets, at Fort McHenry. But American

interactive timeline

TIMELINE 1789–1815

AMERICA	YEAR	THE WORLD
Apr George Washington inaugurated first U.S. president	**1789**	**Jul 14** Crowds storm Bastille in Paris, beginning French Revolution
Dec Philadelphia becomes U.S. capital city as Washington, DC, is built	**1790**	
Dec Bill of Rights ratified	**1791**	**Aug** Saint-Domingue slave rebellion begins
Apr Washington issues Neutrality Proclamation	**1793**	**Jan** French King Louis XVI executed **Mar** France declares war on Spain
Aug Battle of Fallen Timbers **Sep** Washington orders federal military power to put down Whiskey Rebellion **Nov** U.S. and British diplomats secretly sign Jay's Treaty	**1794**	**Feb** France outlaws slavery in its colonies **May** Toussaint Louverture switches allegiance from Spanish to French
Jun U.S. Senate ratifies Jay's Treaty with Great Britain **Aug** United States signs Treaty of Greenville with representatives from 12 Northwest Indian nations **Oct** Pinckney's Treaty (Treaty of San Lorenzo) opens trade on the Mississippi to United States	**1795**	**May** France and Holland ally in Treaty of the Hague **Jul** France and Spain sign peace agreement **Nov** Napoleon Bonaparte and four other "directors" take power in France
Nov John Adams elected president; Thomas Jefferson elected vice president	**1796**	**Feb** France revokes all U.S. treaties **Aug** Spain secretly cedes Louisiana territory to France
Apr President Adams publicizes "XYZ Affair" **Jun–Jul** Congress passes Alien and Sedition Acts **Nov** Kentucky legislature passes Thomas Jefferson's "Kentucky Resolutions" **Dec** Virginia legislature passes James Madison's "Virginia Resolutions"	**1798**	**Jul** Napoleon Bonaparte wins Battle of the Pyramids in Cairo, Egypt
Feb USS *Constellation* captures the French frigate *L'Insurgente* in Caribbean **Feb** President Adams invokes "Toussaint's Clause" and aids Toussaint Louverture **Oct** President Adams sends new diplomatic mission to France to avoid open war	**1799**	**Dec** Napoleon Bonaparte named First Consul of France
Aug Gabriel's rebellion betrayed in Richmond, Virginia **Sep** United States and France agree to end Quasi-War	**1800**	**Aug** Act of Union between Great Britain and Ireland
Jan President Adams appoints John Marshall chief justice of the Supreme Court	**1801**	**Jul** Toussaint Louverture appointed Saint-Domingue governor for life

forces survived the bombardment with their arms intact, and they repelled the British, who retreated from Baltimore on September 15. When the British left Maryland, they took with them 2,000 runaway slaves who later resettled in Canada.

The War Ends

Despite the intense fighting around Washington, DC, the British were anxious to negotiate an end to the American war now that they were at peace with France. Negotiators for both

AMERICA	YEAR	THE WORLD
	1802	France re-establishes slavery on the island of Guadalupe
Feb Supreme Court establishes judicial review in *Marbury v. Madison* **May** United States and France agree on Louisiana Purchase	**1803**	**May** Britain declares war on France
Nov Thomas Jefferson reelected president	**1804**	**Jan** Jacques Dessalines declares independence of Haiti **Dec** Napoleon crowned emperor of France
Jun United States negotiates end to Tripolitan War	**1805**	**Oct** British defeat combined French/Spanish fleet at Battle of Trafalgar
Feb Aaron Burr is arrested for plotting against Spain in American West	**1807**	**Nov** British Orders in Council mandate licensing for all neutral traders **Dec** France's Milan Decree extends blockades to neutral powers
Jan Legislation outlawing the international slave trade becomes U.S. law **Dec** James Madison elected president **Dec** President Jefferson signs Embargo Act	**1808**	Revolutionary movements begin in Mexico
Mar Congress replaces Embargo Act with Non-Intercourse Act	**1809**	Dominican Republic declares independence
May Congress replaces Non-Intercourse Act with Macon's Bill No. 2 **Nov** President Madison opens trade with France and imposes sanctions on Great Britain	**1810**	
Jan Charles Deslondes leads 150–500 slaves and runaways in a violent rebellion outside of New Orleans **Nov** William Henry Harrison defeats Shawnee troops at Battle of Tippecanoe	**1811**	
Jun United States declares war on Great Britain **Dec** James Madison reelected president; Elbridge Gerry elected vice president	**1812**	**Sep** Napoleon Bonaparte invades Russia
Aug The Red Sticks rebellion ignites Creek War	**1813**	**Aug** Austria breaks from France, declares war
Mar Andrew Jackson puts down Red Sticks rebellion at Battle of Horseshoe Bend **Aug** Washington, DC, burned by British **Dec** Treaty of Ghent is signed, ending War of 1812	**1814**	**Apr** Napoleon abdicates power **May** Treaty of Paris ends European war, restores Louis XVIII as king of France
Jan New England Federalists meet in Hartford, Connecticut, to discuss their opposition to War of 1812 **Jan** British defeated at the Battle of New Orleans	**1815**	**Nov** Treaty of Paris ends Napoleonic Wars

sides met in Ghent, Belgium, in the summer of 1814, and talks proceeded through the fall as fighting continued. The United States and Britain signed the Treaty of Ghent, which ended the War of 1812, on Christmas Eve 1814. Britain agreed to evacuate American territory, both sides pledged to make peace with Indian nations, and each side agreed to settle Canadian border issues by future negotiation. Ironically, the treaty made no mention of the prewar naval or trade conflicts that had led to war. The United States ignored Article IX of the treaty, which bound them to restore Native lands taken during the war, and instead treated Indian nations as conquered foes, forcing them to cede millions of acres.

JACKSON'S VICTORY AT THE BATTLE OF NEW ORLEANS   Paintings like this one, which glorified Andrew Jackson's victory at the Battle of New Orleans, helped to propel him into politics and to enhance his reputation for heroism. The image also shows in the foreground Kentucky "hunters"—rustic backwoodsmen who fought with Jackson and were revered in popular culture for their deft use of rifles and noted for their buckskin clothing.

Despite the fact that the treaty restored things to a prewar status quo, the United States claimed victory. In part, the Americans' claim was based on their most glorious battle, fought at New Orleans just days after the peace treaty had been signed, but before anyone in North America had learned of it. On January 8, 1815, Andrew Jackson, helped by a group of international privateers known as the Baratarian pirates, foiled a British attack on New Orleans. British commander Sir Edward Packenham's assault dissolved in the swamps and fog of the Gulf Coast, and Packenham himself was killed as Jackson skillfully defended the city. Jackson seemed to prove that Americans could best a well-formed European force: the combined British force suffered 2,450 casualties compared to the Americans' 350.

Although the War of 1812 changed little in international politics, the United States emerged with a new set of heroes, including Andrew Jackson and Oliver Hazard Perry. Despite the fact that many of their war plans had failed, the Democratic-Republicans gained luster from the war, and the Federalist Party was all but destroyed by its opposition to the war and by backlash against the Hartford Convention. Simultaneously, the Napoleonic Wars were over, and the United States had proved to its citizens and to the world that it could stand up to Great Britain and survive. The world stage had changed with the defeat of Napoleon, and the United States was poised to try to assume a new role in future international dramas.

STUDY QUESTIONS **FOR THE WAR OF 1812**

1. What caused the War of 1812?

2. How were American politics between 1789 and 1815 influenced by other nations, including Indian nations?

quiz

Summary

- The federal government and the first clash between political parties in the United States took shape against a backdrop of transatlantic revolution and warfare.
- Americans supported the French Revolution at first, but its radicalization after 1793 worsened rifts in American politics.
- The United States was increasingly tied to other parts of the world through trade and migration, but these ties also brought conflict and war with North Africans (the Barbary Wars) and Europeans (the War of 1812).
- Slave revolt in Saint-Domingue, which became the Haitian Revolution, influenced U.S. politics, slave revolts, and legal crackdowns on African Americans.
- Indians, some of whom united in a pan-Indian movement, posed stiff military resistance to the United States.
- As political parties developed, American politics in the 1790s were contentious. The Democratic-Republicans had the political upper hand after 1800, but the Federalists opposed them until after the War of 1812.

Key Terms and People

◁))

audio
flashcards

Alien and Sedition Acts 272
Bill of Rights 264
Decatur, Stephen 280
Dessalines, Jean-Jacques 276
Eaton, William 280
Fenno, John 265
Freneau, Philip 265
Gabriel 272
Genet, Edmund Charles 265
Harrison, William Henry 281
Jackson, Andrew 286
Jay's Treaty 266
Johnson, Richard Mentor 286
Little Turtle 267

Louverture, Toussaint 261
Madison, Dolley 287
Marbury v. Madison 275
Non-Intercourse Act of 1809 282
Perry, Oliver Hazard 286
Pinckney's Treaty 268
Qaramanli, Yusuf 280
St. Clair, Arthur 267
Tecumseh 281
Tenskwatawa 281
Wayne, "Mad" Anthony 267
Whiskey Rebellion 267
XYZ Affair 271

Reviewing Chapter 8

1. How did the movement of people between France, Saint-Domingue, and the United States influence political events in the 1790s?
2. Did the United States successfully use warfare to increase its territory and/or clout in the world between 1789 and 1815?
3. What signs do you see that the citizens of the United States were developing a national identity between 1789 and 1815?

Further Reading

Cotlar, Seth. *Tom Paine's America: The Rise and Fall of Transatlantic Radicalism in the Early American Republic.* Charlottesville: University of Virginia Press, 2011. Cotlar explores how the movement of radical people and ideas between Europe and America in the 1790s influenced U.S. politics. The Democratic-Republicans were less radically democratic than many Europeans.

⌄

Egerton, Douglas R. *Gabriel's Rebellion: The Virginia Slave Conspiracies of 1800 & 1802*. Chapel Hill: University of North Carolina Press, 1993. Egerton argues that the election of 1800 provided the political context and opportunity for slave rebellion in Virginia. Gabriel's rebellion was also influenced by the revolutions in France and Saint-Domingue. Both slave revolts discussed in this work had a great impact on Virginia politics.

White, Ashli. *Encountering Revolution: Haiti and the Making of the Early Republic*. Baltimore: Johns Hopkins University Press, 2010. White's book examines how the Haitian Revolution affected U.S. politics and society during the formative years of party contest in the United States. White pays particular attention to how refugees from Saint-Domingue affected the racial thinking of U.S. citizens.

Zagarri, Rosemarie. *Revolutionary Backlash: Women and Politics in the Early American Republic*. Philadelphia: University of Pennsylvania Press, 2007. Zagarri's book shows how white women participated in the political culture and partisanship of the early American republic and that debates about women's rights started in the late 1780s, even as society at large was moving to restrict women to a more "social" and less political role.

America in the World
GOODS, IDEAS, PEOPLE

CHAPTER 8: A New Nation Facing a Revolutionary World, 1789–1815

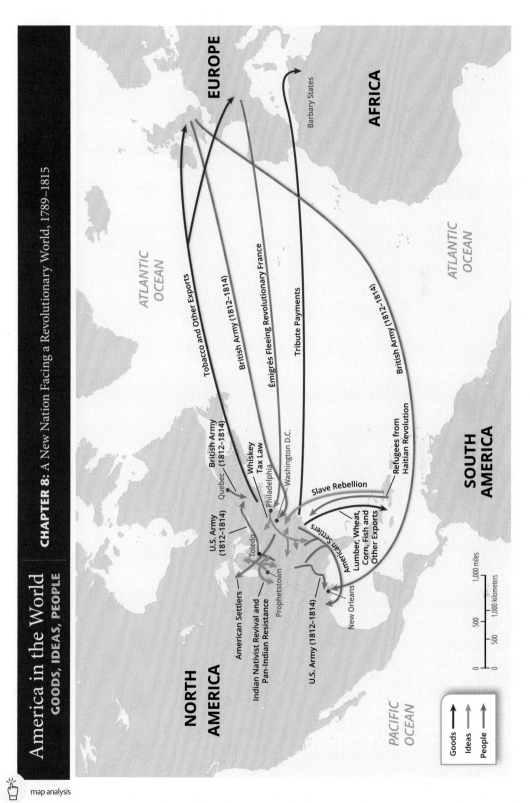

map analysis

This dance blanket was made in the mid-1800s by Anishinaabe/Dakota Indians who were engaged in fur-trading networks. The wool blanket, decorated with silk ribbon and glass beads and owned by relatives of Magdelaine La Framboise, shows a combination of Indian patterns and influences from U.S. quilting techniques.

CHAPTER 9

American Peoples on the Move

1789–1824

Magdelaine Marcot, a woman of mixed Odawa/Dakota and French heritage, married Joseph La Framboise in 1804 in a Catholic ceremony at Michilimackinac (in present-day Michigan). Magdelaine, who became known as Madame La Framboise, had already lived with Joseph since she was 14, and she was raising their two children, also baptized Catholics, among her mother's Odawa kin at Grand Haven, just as she had been raised.

Joseph and Magdelaine La Framboise established a fur trade business that exploited contacts among French traders and Indian kinship networks stretching from Montreal into present-day Michigan and Illinois in the land around Lakes Michigan and Huron. In 1806, when Joseph was killed while embarking on a trade voyage, Magdelaine took over the business. She built a fur-trading empire that made her one of the richest women in North America.

Madame La Framboise made annual journeys between the Grand River valley and the trading post at Fort Michilimackinac, exchanging thousands of pounds of fur for goods that she sold to Indian people and earning as much as £10,000 per year, 10 times the average take of fur traders in that region. She successfully negotiated trade licenses from the British and U.S. governments before and during the War of 1812. La Framboise managed fur suppliers, voyageurs who transported her goods, and two African American slaves.

Her business was so profitable and she exercised so much independent power that La Framboise was seen as a threat by John Jacob Astor's American Fur Company when it moved into the Michilimackinac area in 1818. Eventually, she joined Astor's trade network, which expanded her business contacts as far as present-day Iowa and South Dakota. In 1822, she sold her trading post on the Grand River and entered a genteel retirement.

La Framboise honored the customs of her Indian relatives, dispensing food and supplies to their communities and maintaining Native dress throughout her life. She also established Catholic schools for Indian and Metis children. La Framboise built a house on Mackinac Island, where she became a patron of St. Anne's Catholic Church and where she hosted Frenchman Alexis de Tocqueville in the 1830s during his visit to observe the United States. Her daughter married the commander at Fort Michilimackinac, Captain Benjamin Pierce, the brother of future U.S. president Franklin Pierce.

Magdelaine La Framboise was an exceptional success, but her story of trade, family, travel, and political negotiation typifies the movement and energy that many people experienced around North America between 1789 and 1824.

⊙ EXPLORATION AND ENCOUNTER

At the turn of the 19th century, people and goods moved across the spaces of North America at an ever faster pace. Governments on the North American continent sized up natural resources and prospects for future expansion beyond their areas of permanent settlement. The United States and Spain sent out expeditions to probe the boundaries of North America, to establish ties with Indian peoples, and to survey the natural world. Traders and merchants also encouraged contacts between peoples on different parts of the continent. Competition emerged as explorers and traders crisscrossed the continent.

Lewis and Clark Expedition

Even before he finalized the Louisiana Purchase in April 1803 (see Chapter 8), President Thomas Jefferson asked Congress to fund a mission to explore beyond the Missouri River to claim territory and to establish trade relations with Indian nations. Jefferson appointed his private secretary, **Meriwether Lewis**, commander of the expedition. Lewis chose as his fellow "captain" **William Clark**, a retired army officer who was an excellent backwoodsman and cartographer. Lewis and Clark spent almost a year preparing for their journey, and when they set off on May 14, 1804, they took with them 29 men in what they called their "Corps of Discovery." The Corps included Kentucky hunters, soldiers, French Canadian boatmen, an interpreter, and Clark's African American slave, York.

Jefferson charged Lewis and Clark to communicate to Indian nations that the United States was now in control of the Louisiana territory, to observe plants and animals, to make maps, and to explore routes for future trade to the Pacific. In 1804, the Corps traveled up the Missouri River and met with powerful Indian groups: Teton Sioux (Lakota), Arikara, and Yankton Sioux. Much of the area the Corps surveyed beyond the Missouri River was as yet unexplored by Europeans and Americans, and Lewis and Clark relied on local Indian knowledge. They wintered at the Mandan villages—in present-day North Dakota—where they were joined by French Canadian trader Toussaint Charbonneau and his wife, the Shoshone war captive **Sacagawea**, whom Charbonneau had purchased from Minitari people. Sacagawea remained with the expedition, even after she gave birth to a son. Sacagawea added essential linguistic and geographic skills to the Corps.

Setting out from the Mandan villages in April 1805, the Corps traveled up the Missouri alternately by foot and by canoe until August, when they struggled across the Rockies and the Bitterroot Mountains. The party reached the Pacific in November 1805 and established winter quarters at the Columbia River. Setting out again in the spring of 1806, the group split into smaller parties to attempt to find an easier crossing over the Rockies, but by the time they rejoined at the confluence of

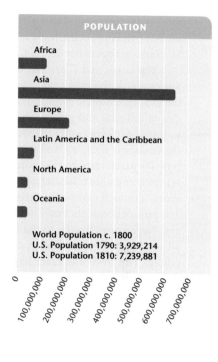

POPULATION

Africa

Asia

Europe

Latin America and the Caribbean

North America

Oceania

World Population c. 1800
U.S. Population 1790: 3,929,214
U.S. Population 1810: 7,239,881

0   100,000,000   200,000,000   300,000,000   400,000,000   500,000,000   600,000,000   700,000,000

Captains Lewis & Clark holding a Council with the Indians

LEWIS AND CLARK This idealized illustration of Lewis and Clark holding a council with some of the Indians they encountered on their journey of exploration appeared as an illustration in the 1810 edition of the journal of their travels, a very popular book. The image shows Lewis and Clark as carefully dressed orators who hold the attention of Indian men and women eager to hear what they say.

the Yellowstone and Missouri rivers on August 12, it was clear that they could find no easy overland Pacific trade route. The voyage concluded when the Corps returned to St. Louis on September 23, 1806.

The Lewis and Clark Expedition succeeded in several ways, even though it did not establish the easy trade routes that Thomas Jefferson had hoped would expand the U.S. agricultural empire. The explorers observed and catalogued hundreds of species of animals and plants, and their maps and landscape descriptions were of use to future explorers and settlers. Lewis and Clark solidified U.S. claims over much of the Louisiana territory, and they claimed portions of Oregon—as they avoided several military parties sent by the Spanish to try to intercept them. They also established good relations and solid trade ties with several Indian groups, most notably Mandan and Shoshoni, although many other groups were skeptical of Lewis and Clark's flashy trinkets and pronouncements that Thomas Jefferson was their new "great father." Teton Sioux and Piegan were hostile to the Corps, and the expedition probably narrowly avoided all-out war with these Indian peoples who scorned the United States' "Magnitude & power." The Lewis and Clark Expedition would, nonetheless, feed decades of westward expansion by U.S. citizens.

First published map of the Lewis and Clarke Expedition (1814)

Zebulon Pike

Spain, also skeptical of American power, contested the southwestern boundaries of the Louisiana Purchase. In 1786, the Spanish governor of New Mexico had concluded peace agreements with the powerful Comanche people and had sent explorer Pedro Vial across the southern Plains to St. Louis. Although the Spanish government later ceded the Louisiana territory to France, which sold it to the United States in 1803, neither treaty clearly defined the southwestern territorial border. Beyond New Orleans and St. Louis, as one historian has put it, the United States had merely bought "the right to enter the arena and compete for control of the Indian country stretching westward to the Rockies."

U.S. military commanders sent Captain **Zebulon Pike** to define the U.S. claim to the southwestern part of the Louisiana territory. Between August 1805 and April 1806, Pike journeyed up the Mississippi River to explore the source of the river and to form relationships with northern Indian groups. In 1806, General **James Wilkinson** sent Pike west from St. Louis to establish diplomatic ties with Osage and Comanche peoples; to try to negotiate peace between traditional enemies, the Kansas and Osage; and to explore the Arkansas and Red rivers without antagonizing Spain.

The task proved impossible. Pike survived intrigue and desertion by his Osage and Pawnee guides, but when he tried to negotiate with Pawnee near the Republican River, they revealed their recent contacts with a large Spanish military force under Lieutenant Facundo Melgares. Abandoning most of his plans for Indian treaties, Pike followed Spanish and Indian trails across the Rockies. By January 1807, he was lost, and his expedition strayed all the way to the Rio Grande very near to Spanish settlement. The Spanish captured Pike and his men in February 1807. Pike was taken first to Santa Fe and then to Chihuahua for interrogation, and several of his men were imprisoned for two years. When Pike was allowed to return to St. Louis in July 1807, he published his journals, filled with his observations of the western territory and Mexico. They proved popular, although President Jefferson never considered Pike's military expedition as significant as Lewis and Clark's scientific and trade exploration. Pike's expedition proved that the United States could not take for granted expansion without resistance, even in the Louisiana territory.

Plains Indian Peoples

Despite challenges, stories from the expeditions of Pike and Lewis and Clark made U.S. government officials and settlers increasingly interested in the Great Plains, where the lives of Plains Indian peoples were changing quickly. By the 1790s, the use of horses for transportation, hunting, and warfare had taken hold both west and east of the Rockies. Villages of Mandan, Hidatsa, and Arikara on the upper Missouri River acted as centers for trade networks that stretched from the Great Lakes to the Pacific Ocean. Western Comanche operated another trade center just northeast of the Rio Grande. By the 1820s, Mandan and Arikara people found themselves squeezed between U.S. and British fur-trading companies.

Along with increased trade came diseases, including smallpox, measles, and whooping cough. All the Plains Indians were forced to try to maintain their societies as they faced downward population pressures. In some areas, mortality rates reached as high as 70 percent in the epidemic outbreaks in the first half of the 19th century.

George Catlin's portraits of Pains Indians, early 1830s

Indian people contested for power. Fights between tribal rivals such as Apache and Comanche continued throughout the period. Nomadic Sioux people gained power over village-based groups such as Mandan and Arikara, whose population density caused epidemics to hit them harder. Factions within Osage tribes desired so badly to keep their advantage in the gun trade that they agreed in 1808 to cede "50,000 square miles of excellent country" (in latter-day Oklahoma, Arkansas, and Kansas) to the United States in return for trade goods. Osage lands became a depository for Indians forcibly removed from the East after the War of 1812. Plains peoples remained powerful until after 1824, but they were beginning to feel pressure from exploration across their lands and growth of the white population.

Astor and the Fur Trade

John Jacob Astor sought profit in western North America. After immigrating to the United States from Germany in 1784, Astor founded his North American Fur Company in New York City in 1785. Undaunted by British trade rules that required Canadian goods to travel to London before they could be sold to the United States, Astor began selling furs to New York and Europe. After Jay's Treaty (1794) allowed direct U.S.–Canadian trade, Astor built up his business and increased his inventory. Through the 1790s, most of the fur made into hats and outerwear in the United States still came from Canadian firms, including the Hudson Bay Company and the North West Company, which operated vast networks of semi-independent Indian and mixed-race trappers. Beaver hats became fashionable among all classes of American men in the 1790s as their prices dropped.

By 1808, Astor had extended his business with a bold move into the newly expanding China trade. He wholesaled furs to China and received payment in trade goods such as tea and silks that he could sell in North America and Europe for a great profit. In 1808, hoping to take advantage of disruptions in the fur trade caused by the Napoleonic

NORTH AMERICAN TRADERS AND INDIANS.
Ganthier and Faden's Map of Canada, 1777.

image analysis

FUR TRADERS This 18th-century engraving depicts the fur trade in North America in extremely idealized terms. Fur traders did pursue friendlier relations with Indigenous people compared to many explorers, but the illustration projects an image of leisure and exchange that is likely more salutary than the reality.

Wars in Europe, Astor received a New York state charter and founded the American Fur Company. Astor planned a network of traders, like Magdelaine La Framboise, who would deal across North America directly with Indian hunters and enmesh themselves in Indian culture. He hoped to gain market share by expanding his operation through the Great Lakes and all the way to the Columbia River. In 1810, Astor formed a new joint-stock company, the Pacific Fur Company, and in 1811, he sent two expeditions to found a trading post on the Columbia River. From that post, Astoria, he hoped to challenge the Russian traders who dominated the Oregon territory.

Astor's plans, however, suffered during the War of 1812, when he failed to gain protection from the U.S. government. Under threat from the Royal Navy, Astor sold Astoria to the North West Company in October 1813. The American Fur Company survived, and Astor convinced Congress in 1816 to bar British citizens from fur trading in U.S. territory. Other smaller fur-trading companies thrived in the United States—including the Missouri Fur Company, cofounded by William Clark—but Astor's business skill and the worldwide scale of his efforts made him one of the richest men in America. Later, sensing a shift in tastes away from furs, Astor moved his fur fortune into New York real estate.

Asian Trade

Astor had been among the first Americans to engage in large-scale Chinese trade. In 1784, Philadelphia financier Robert Morris sent the first American vessel, *The Empress of China*, to Asia. Under the command of Captain John Green, it carried a load of ginseng (prized by Chinese men as an aphrodisiac) and other goods. The United States and China did not share diplomatic relations until 1844, but New York, Providence, Boston, Salem, and Philadelphia merchants quickly built up a significant trade, especially with the port of Canton. During the Napoleonic Wars, U.S. traders quickly expanded their exports to and imports from China. As merchant Thomas Hansyard Perkins remarked, "Embargoes and non-intercourse . . . crossed our path; but we kept our trade with China."

Uninhibited by European monopolies that sought to govern the tea trade, U.S. traders developed relationships with Canton's merchants, who controlled the Chinese tea market. After 1802, American merchants also became involved in the growing opium trade into China. Americans adeptly negotiated the complex system of taxes and bribes in Canton, although they had to follow rules that kept them confined to small areas of the territory. The Chinese bought great quantities of American trade products including ginseng, sea otter fur, and seal fur. But Americans bought even more Chinese products: silk, furniture, porcelain, silverware, wallpaper, hand-loomed cloth, and decorative objects of many varieties. Americans thought of China as an exotic and uncivilized "far eastern" place, but Chinese goods shaped their tastes and fashions. Many merchants viewed China as "the first for greatness, richness, and grandeur of any country ever known."

A tea factory in Canton, China (c.1830)

Many U.S. China merchants also spread into the burgeoning trade with India during the same period. As John Adams wrote in 1785, "There is no better advice to be

Salem   Salem

SALEM, MASSACHUSETTS This 18th century engraving shows the port of Salem, Massachusetts, one of the busiest trading ports in New England. In the 18th century, Salem became a home to shipbuilding and cod fishing; and, by the turn of the 19th century, it had become a major hub for American trade with Europe, the West Indies, China, Africa, and Russia.

given to the merchants of the United States, than to push their commerce to the East Indies as fast and as far as it will go." Before 1783, India had been closed to Americans because the British had allowed the East India Company a monopoly over trade. But the 1783 Treaty of Paris opened the way for American trade with India, and during the Napoleonic Wars in Europe, American merchants took advantage of trade disruptions to expand their Indian trade. American merchants focused mainly on Calcutta because the Bay of Bengal was the easiest entry point for small American ships, which had trouble risking the dangerous seas of the Indian Ocean.

By the 1820s, the trade between Calcutta and New England had grown rich and included not only a huge variety of material but also cultural exchanges. Indian cloth, from cotton sheeting to printed chintzes and elaborate silks, was advertised widely in American newspapers as a luxury good. Americans also consumed saltpeter, indigo, ginger, animal hides, and shellac imported from Calcutta. Many Yankee traders paid cash for their goods purchased in India, but they also traded to India a smaller amount of American goods—rum, glassware, books, timber, and cigars. In 1793, Jacob Crowninshield imported a two-year-old live elephant from Bengal, and "Old Bet" was exhibited throughout the Northeastern Seaboard as a curiosity. In the 1830s, New England traders shifted into trading ice to Calcutta after Congress imposed high taxes on imported textiles and once Frederick Tudor perfected the insulated cargo holds necessary to transport ice all the way from the frozen lakes of New England to the Ganges River. From the 1830s to the 1850s, thousands of tons of ice were exported to India.

Unlike the fur trade in North America, American trade in China and India was rarely accompanied by significant exploration or scientific observation. U.S. merchants gained a foothold in the rich countries of Asia with pure profit in mind. Traders' and mariners' reports about the exotic-seeming East informed the American imagination. Asian trade helped fuel American interest in people, goods, and events far outside U.S. borders.

STUDY QUESTIONS FOR EXPLORATION AND ENCOUNTER

1. In what ways were North American trade and exploration interrelated in this period?
2. Describe the balance of power between the United States, Plains Indians peoples, and the Spanish between 1803 and 1815.

quiz

⊙ SHIFTING BORDERS

As nations expanded across North America, political tensions and clashes resulted. The United States expanded south and west as it created new states and struggled to integrate the territory of the Louisiana Purchase. The Spanish pushed north and east, extending the mission system in California and contesting U.S. expansion in the Louisiana territory. The British and Russians expanded their interests on the borders between the United States and Canada. Thousands of Indian groups sought to deal with these developments through both peaceful and warlike means. How could governments

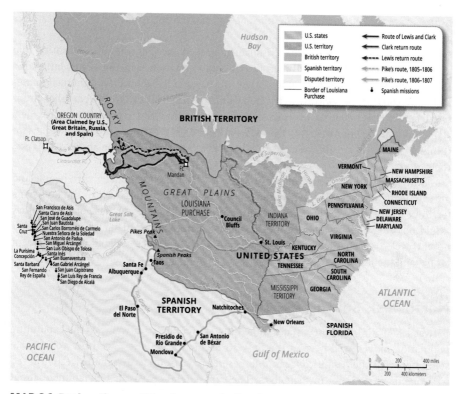

MAP 9.1 Exploration and Development in North America, 1803–1810 During the first decade of the 19th century, both Spain and the United States tried to spread their influence across North America.

best organize efforts to expand as hundreds of thousands of people moved from place to place? Would expansion on the continent bring prosperity, political conflict, or both (Map 9.1)?

Jeffersonian Agrarianism

In the first quarter of the 19th century, an ideology that valued land and farming underlay much of the energetic movement within the United States. Thomas Jefferson called farmers "the chosen people of God" and referred to agriculture as "the most useful of the occupations of man." Jefferson believed that farmers made the most patriotic, hardworking citizens and thought that farming would undergird stable national development and wealth. In Jefferson's vision, independent, white farmers who prized liberty and community sustained the United States. As a prominent Virginian who owned a slave plantation, Jefferson also recognized the role that enslaved black labor would play in creating a class of free and independent white "farmer" plantation owners in slaveholding areas. Others embraced Jefferson's view of agriculture and its contribution to a distinctly American character. Almanacs praised farmers, books such as Hector St. John De Crevecoeur's *Letters from an American Farmer* and George Logan's *Letters*

Addressed to the Yeomanry of the United States sold many copies, and agricultural fairs and competitions were popular.

Hector
St. John
Crèvecoeur,
excerpt
from *Letters
from an
American
Farmer*
(1782)

Although Jeffersonians idolized farming in its own right, they also admitted that agriculture would have to be linked to trade and commerce. In the 1790s, Jefferson's Democratic-Republicans did not wish the United States to become a commercial manufacturing country, in contrast to the beliefs of Alexander Hamilton's Federalist counterparts, but they knew that farmers would have to trade their products to provide a stable national economic base. **Yeomen** and plantation farmers needed at least two things to make this vision of the United States work—land and the ability to market their produce.

Both land and markets brought Jeffersonian farmers into contact with people and governments well beyond their national borders. Jefferson's purchase of the Louisiana territory set the stage for his agrarian ambitions, but the mere purchase of the territory would not guarantee its smooth transition into American farmland. Jefferson himself never traveled west of the Blue Ridge Mountains, but his policies encouraged settlement far beyond them.

Northwest, Southwest, and New States

Between 1789 and 1824, new states joined the United States in waves as the expanding population moved well beyond the Eastern Seaboard. For the first time, not all U.S. states bordered the Atlantic Ocean. Many settlers in frontier areas had already moved west one or more times in their lives. The first federal census in 1790 counted about 4 million inhabitants of the United States, but by 1800 the number had increased to 5.3 million. So many people had moved west that population density barely increased, even though the population was increasing by almost one-third every 10 years. The first new admissions to the union came when western inhabitants broke away from already existing states to form their own political entities: Vermont in 1791, Kentucky in 1792, and Tennessee in 1796.

The 1787 Northwest Ordinance had set out procedures for the Northwest Territory to be surveyed and sold to settlers, who could then apply for statehood. The U.S. victory over Indian nations at the Battle of Fallen Timbers (1794), displacement of Indians during the War of 1812, and postwar treaties signed with Wendat and other northern Indian peoples confining them to reservations opened the way to white settlement. Congress accelerated the settlement process, for example, in the 1802 Ohio Enabling Act that set aside proceeds from land sales to build roads in the territory. Ohio became a state in 1803. Its population soared to over a half a million after 1810, and it emerged as the fourth most populous state by 1820. Indiana and Illinois became states in 1816 and 1818. Settlers tended to move more or less directly west into the Northwest Territory, and these new states reflected a mixture of regional cultures that sometimes conflicted. One U.S. official worried that politics were complicated by people's "attachment to local interests."

As migrants from northeastern states flooded into the Northwest Territory—where slavery was prohibited—many Virginians moved into Kentucky and Tennessee, southern Ohio, Indiana, and Illinois. Other inhabitants of the original southern states moved south and west into Alabama and along the Gulf Coast to Louisiana, Mississippi, and Arkansas. After Massachusetts native Eli Whitney patented an innovative mechanized cotton gin in 1793, cotton processing became easier and more profitable, and settlers moved into many southern areas looking for new land for plantations. Land in Alabama and Georgia produced much better cotton than did land farther north. Cotton production in the United States increased 10-fold between 1800 and 1820. Parts of the Louisiana territory also lured settlers who hoped to make their fortunes on plantations or in the fur trade.

The Missouri Compromise

In 1818, the territory of Missouri applied for admission to the union as a state, the first west of the Mississippi River. Because the number of free and slave states in the union was precariously balanced and because so many slaves lived in Missouri, controversy arose as soon as **Henry Clay** presented resolutions to the House of Representatives to admit Missouri to the union. In February 1819, New York congressman **James Tallmadge, Jr.,** amended the Missouri statehood legislation to ban further introduction of slaves there and to gradually emancipate slaves who already lived in the territory. After vigorous debate, the House of Representatives approved the amendments, but the Senate struck them down. The two houses of Congress could not agree on a Missouri statehood bill, and the matter had to be carried over to the next session of Congress.

Meanwhile, antislavery activists across the mid-Atlantic and New England sent petitions denouncing slavery as an evil that could not be allowed to spread. Several state legislatures adopted competing resolutions for and against the admission of Missouri as a slave state. Congress reconsidered Missouri for statehood in December. Congressmen and President **James Monroe** debated constitutional issues such as whether Congress had the right to place restrictions on new states and whether slaves in the Missouri territory should be immediately counted for representation under the Constitution's three-fifths clause. Some southern congressmen used the relatively uncommon-at-the-time argument that slavery was a positive institution instead of a shameful burden. The spread of cotton agriculture seemed to raise the stakes on slavery's expansion.

Congress reached a complex compromise. Missouri would be admitted as a slave state and Maine would be admitted as a free state—thereby preserving the balance of slave and free states in Congress. Illinois Democratic-Republican senator Jesse B. Thomas also proposed an amendment to define a line on the map to determine future free and slave states that he hoped would avoid future conflict. The line at 36°30' latitude across the Louisiana Purchase territory would permit slavery only to its south. Missouri would stand as the exception because it lay north of the line.

In March 1820, Congress approved the **Missouri Compromise** resolutions. After some additional wrangling when the new Missouri legislature prohibited free blacks from entering the state, Missouri was fully admitted to the union on February 26, 1821. The Missouri Compromise temporarily tamped down the political controversy over slavery, but Thomas Jefferson predicted future trouble when he wrote that the compromise filled him with "terror" because conflict "is hushed, indeed, for the moment. But this is a reprieve only, not a final sentence."

African American Migration and Colonization

The Missouri Compromise emphasized a basic fact of U.S. westward expansion between 1789 and 1824: as a group, black people were even more dramatically affected by demographic change and movement than whites. Both the slave population and the free African American population increased during that time. Over 100,000 slaves were imported into the United States between the end of the Revolution and the abolition of the slave trade in 1808. After 1808, the expansion of U.S. territory and demand for slaves in new plantation areas stimulated the internal market for slaves, and families were regularly broken apart by sales. One historian estimates that "a slave residing in the Upper South after 1815 would have a one-in-three chance of being traded out of state during the first forty years of his or her life." Slaves' living conditions usually deteriorated as they were moved into the Deep South. These conditions were symbolized by the coffle—the method of transportation used to move groups of people on what one slave called "that dreaded and despairing journey to Georgia." Groups of up to 30 people in pairs were chained or tied together by metal halters around their necks and then marched over long distances. Once they arrived at cotton or sugar plantations, most enslaved people faced brutal working conditions (Map 9.2).

The Northwest Ordinance of 1787 had outlawed slavery in the Northwest Territory, but that prohibition did not mean the territories were hospitable to African

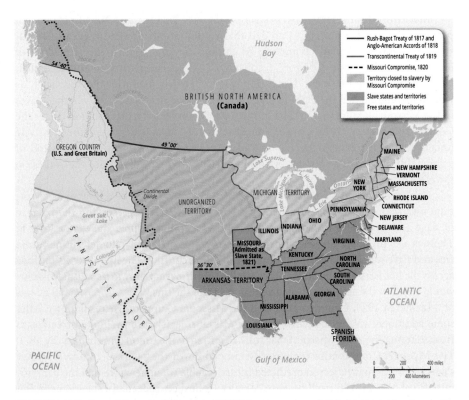

MAP 9.2 U.S. Expansion and Slavery, 1820 The expansion of U.S. territorial borders held great consequences for the development of the institution of slavery and for conflicts over slavery.

Americans. Concerned that slaves might escape to freedom in the territories or to Canada, Congress passed the first federal Fugitive Slave Act in 1793. The act empowered local government officials to help recover runaways and imposed a fine on anyone who helped a "fugitive from justice." Some slave owners who migrated to Indiana and Illinois smuggled slaves with them, and many towns and states governed where and how free African Americans could live and work. In 1813, Illinois forbade free African Americans to settle there, and voters narrowly defeated a proposal to legalize slavery in Illinois in 1824.

Some free African Americans reacted against this kind of animosity by expressing an interest in migrating out of the United States altogether. In 1815, the Quaker sea captain Paul Cuffee, who was of African and Indian heritage, settled a shipload of free African Americans in the African colony of Sierra Leone. Sierra Leone was a British colony backed by private supporters where black British settlers, former American slaves who had fled to Canada, and maroons from Jamaica had all settled since the 1780s. In 1816, Presbyterian minister Robert Finley founded the **American Colonization Society (ACS)**, which counted among its supporters Kentucky congressman Henry Clay, President James Monroe, and others who did not think the races could continue to coexist in North America. In 1821, the ACS transported its first free African American settlers to Liberia, the West African colony that the ACS would govern into the 1830s.

The colonization movement, as it was known, received most of its support from whites who hoped for the opportunity to gradually phase out the institution of slavery by transporting black people to Africa. Many free African Americans rejected the racism expressed by the ACS, even if they were interested in migration themselves. In its first two years, ACS convinced only 22 of the 10,000 free blacks in Philadelphia to embark for Africa. In 1824, some prominent free African Americans in New York and Philadelphia, including minister **Richard Allen** and sailmaker James Forten, founded the Haytian Emigration Society of Coloured People to help African Americans settle in Haiti, whose president Jean-Pierre Boyer offered to pay for their passage. Forten was a great supporter of the black republic in Haiti, although he utterly rejected the white vision of African colonization.

Former president James Madison on the colonization movement (1819)

Spanish Expansion in California

The Spanish empire (independent Mexico after 1822) also pushed its boundaries outward between 1789 and 1824. Although the Spanish had traded with Indians in California since the 1500s, they did not establish colonies there until the 1760s. During the 1780s and 1790s, Spanish officials took steps to expand the colonized area in California to create a buffer between the silver mines in Mexico and Russian and British settlements in Oregon that were moving south.

The main vehicle for Spanish colonial expansion in California was the mission system, which extended government control over territory through a mixture of religious and military means. Franciscan friars, supported by Spanish soldiers, would establish a mission church, baptize nearby Indians, and employ them—sometimes by force—in farming and other trades. Between 1769 and 1821, friars baptized more than 70,000 Indians at the 20 missions that spread across the territory of Alta California. Many Indian people, including Ipai villagers, resisted being colonized, but their defenses were

SAN JUAN DE BAUTISTA, CALIFORNIA The mission of San Juan de Bautista was founded in 1797 by Friar Fermín de Lasuén, the successor to Junípero Serra, the Franciscan friar who spearheaded the spread of the Spanish mission system northward in California. This photo illustrates the church building at the mission that was begun in 1803.

weakened by the population collapse brought on by European diseases. Other Indians, like some Chumash, embraced baptism but retained a syncretic view of the world that maintained their Native beliefs alongside Roman Catholicism. Some Christian Indians later rejected baptism, and Chumash rebelled against the Spanish in 1824.

Severe drought in the 1790s caused many Indians to seek refuge in the missions, where Spanish friars provided food in exchange for labor and conversion. Hispanic settlers called *Californios*, many of them mixed-race Mexicans and descendants of earlier Spanish soldiers and southern Indians, claimed land, and their livestock threatened Native land use. Spanish soldiers compelled Indian laborers to build the system of presidio forts that further consolidated control over California territory. The missions prospered, growing from crude chapels to elaborate adobe towns surrounded by farm fields and trading posts.

STUDY QUESTIONS FOR SHIFTING BORDERS

1. How did Spanish expansion in California compare to efforts of the United States to expand westward between 1789 and 1824?

quiz

2. How did the westward expansion of the United States revive and exacerbate conflicts over slavery?

⊗ SOCIAL AND CULTURAL SHIFTS

The movement of goods, people, and ideas across and beyond North America at the beginning of the 19th century affected the creation of an "American" culture within the United States. The lawyer and future congressman Charles Jared Ingersoll wrote in 1810 that Americans were an "adolescent people . . . dispersed over an immense territory," both attracted to the old culture of Europe and seeking to establish their own identities. Ingersoll's use of the word "adolescent" captured the awkward nature of an American society seeking simultaneously to look backward and forward as it experienced rapid change.

Native Americans and Civilization Policy

In the aftermath of the American Revolution, the United States still confronted powerful Native neighbors. The disastrous campaigns of Harmar and St. Clair demonstrated that Indian nations could fiercely—and effectively—defend their homelands from invasion. George Washington's secretary of war, Henry Knox, sought to develop a more peaceful way of dealing with Native Americans. His solution was called **Civilization Policy.** First deployed in 1795, Civilization Policy sought to remake Indians in the image of Anglo-Americans, using missions, education, and gifts of livestock and farming equipment to change Native languages, religions, economies, and gender roles. Federal officials hoped that acculturated Indians might marry frontier whites and then voluntarily cede land to the United States. Thomas Jefferson wrote, "Let our settlements and theirs meet and blend together, to intermix, and become one people."

Native reactions to Civilization Policy varied. Shawnee brothers Tecumseh and Tenskwatawa led a multitribal nativist movement that rejected Civilization Policy. The Ho-Chunk agreed, saying, "If the Great Spirit had made us like white men, he would have given us a way to be educated like them." Farther south, however, many residents of southern Indian nations—especially Cherokees, Choctaws, Chickasaws, and Creeks— saw value in selectively incorporating aspects of Euro-American culture, a strategy they had already begun to pursue on their own.

Around 1800, the deerskin trade declined, and Native Americans looked for ways to diversify their economies. Many residents of southern Indian nations began to develop profitable ranches and plantations. They welcomed steel plows and other tools offered by the federal government as part of Civilization Policy. By 1820, Choctaw women annually grew, spun, and wove over 10,000 yards of cotton, which they shipped to market. Southern Indian nations also revised governance, vesting increasing power in a centralized government. The Cherokees went the furthest: they developed a repub- lican government in which power was shared among an executive branch, bicameral legislature, and supreme court. Cherokees and many other Native nations welcomed missionaries. While rates of conversion were low, many Indian families valued the schools missionaries established. Potawatomi chief Noonday explained, "I wish our children to be instructed like the whites; then these educated children will become capable of assisting us in the transaction of business with white people."

Constitution of the Cherokee Nation

Ultimately, Civilization Policy proved divisive. Creek Indians disagreed over the policy; some favored culture change, while others promoted nativism. In 1813, this conflict gave rise to the Red Stick War, a Creek civil war. The United States stepped in to aid so-called friendly Creeks, but the conclusion of the war in 1814 imposed a devastating treaty that punished the entire Creek Nation, forcing them to cede 23 million acres. White Americans were eager to seize additional territory, especially the cotton-rich lands owned by southern Indians. Contrary to the aims of Civilization Policy, however, Native Americans used their new skills to defend their remaining homelands.

Gender in Early Republican Society

What it meant to be a white woman changed in this period. Following on the heels of the Revolutionary ideology of republican motherhood, women were expected to help create a better republican society through their ability to raise educated children to be good citizens. As it became clear that a successful republic would be shaped by a virtuous society as well as by correct politics, women also claimed the ability to augment male political virtue by leading benevolent and refined social activities.

Judith Sargent Murray, excerpt from *On the Equality of Sexes* (1790)

White women's educational opportunities expanded dramatically during the early republic, in part as a reaction to the theories of British feminist **Mary Wollstonecraft**, who was read widely in the United States. Women's rights advocate **Judith Sargent Murray** wrote that "women have a talent" and "should be taught to depend on their own efforts." New schools for girls were founded in every region, and girls were included in the growth of, mostly northern, public education. After 1789, women also began to find career opportunities as teachers, and many of the most important girls' academies were founded by women such as **Emma Willard** and Julia Tevis. Most girls were not offered the same education as boys—for example, classical languages were largely off limits. But academic subjects such as math and history joined girls' education in needlework and dancing. Educators differed on whether girls should be educated for their own intellectual fulfillment or more to serve the interests of family and society, but, in either case, greater education meant progress as female literacy rates soared.

Advances in women's legal status proved to be more modest, as state coverture laws continued to define married women as legally under their husbands' control. In the 1790s, however, it became easier for women to obtain divorces. Women petitioned both state and federal legislatures, they participated in political rituals such as Fourth of July celebrations and French Revolutionary festivals, and some wrote for newspapers and magazines. Single women and widows, who could own property, ran businesses such as the Brandywine Ironworks, the successful boilerplate manufactory controlled by Pennsylvania Quaker Rebecca Lukens. Prominent women in Washington, DC, such as

NEEDLEWORK SAMPLER This sampler was sewn by Catharine Ann Speel in Philadelphia when she was 12 or 13 years old, in 1805. Girls often sewed samplers like this to practice stitches and to show off needlework skill, which they learned from family members and at schools. Speel's sampler is typical in showing a house, the alphabet, animals, and a man, and it includes a typical moral poem. Speel identifies herself as her mother's daughter on the sampler, emphasizing female lineage.

congressional wife **Margaret Bayard Smith** and especially First Lady **Dolley Madison**, directly influenced politics by organizing social events that fostered political party organization. The vast majority of poorer women and all black women led less public lives, and changing gender roles affected their daily lives more slowly.

Literature and Popular Culture

Women formed one of the quickest-growing audiences in the United States for the dramatic increase in books, magazines, newspapers, and other kinds of print culture. Historians estimate that by 1790, more than 90 percent of the white population in the United States could read—a figure estimated to be double the rate in Britain. The availability of reading material greatly increased in the following decades. A much smaller percentage of African Americans were literate because many slaves were prohibited from learning. As the postal service expanded, subscription newspapers and magazines made up the majority of mail. By 1822, the United States had more newspaper readers than any other country, and hundreds of papers were printed in small towns in every state and territory. Religious magazines and literary journals, such as the *North American Review*, also attracted wide readership.

Until after 1825, when improvements in printing occurred, most books in the United States remained expensive and were imported from Britain. But publishers such as Philadelphia's Matthew Carey showed interest in producing a truly "American" literature even before then. Many books relied on the American Revolution for plot, and authors such as Mason Locke Weems sought to inspire their readers with biographies such as his *Life of Washington* (1800). **Hugh Henry Brackenridge's** *Modern Chivalry* (1804) satirized the social climbing of Americans on the move. **Susannah Rowson's** bestseller *Charlotte Temple* (1791) appealed to legions of middle-class female readers by transporting the English seduction novel to the United States—it

CHARLOTTE TEMPLE "GRAVE" This photograph from the early 20th century shows the grave at Trinity Church, New York, constructed around 1804, for the fictional character Charlotte Temple. The character created by Susannah Rowson was such a popular figure of tragic romance that after this grave was installed, visitors flocked to leave flowers, pieces of hair, and love letters as tributes to her. Alexander Hamilton is buried nearby.

emphasized the fragility of women's virtue in highly sentimentalized language. More writers—including Rowson, Washington Irving, and James Fenimore Cooper—began to earn their living by publishing. Alongside their fictional works inspired by America's past, histories were very popular. Many cheaper books were plagiarized because copyright enforcement remained quite lax. Transatlantic book culture also nourished American Christianity, as the American Bible Society (1816) and the American Tract Society (1823) grew out of English efforts to spread religious publications.

Americans also amused themselves with traditional sports such as horse racing, cock fighting, and foot races. City dwellers might visit neighbors in taverns or coffeehouses, whereas their rural counterparts met at fairs, dances, or quilting bees. During the 1790s, most state legislatures lifted their colonial prohibitions on theater performances, and by the 1820s, professional companies performed dramas, comedies, and light operas in most cities. Famous English actors made money in the United States, as audiences continued to revere European high culture while also clamoring to watch "true-blue" American plays.

By the time Susannah Rowson died in 1824, young middle- and upper-class white women who avidly read *Charlotte Temple* and other novels had turned her into the first U.S. literary celebrity. They bought, passed around, and discussed her book, and some even made pilgrimages to a gravestone for the character Charlotte Temple in New York's Trinity churchyard. By consuming novels such as *Charlotte Temple*, women showed their influence in American culture, even as religious and literary critics warned that novel reading was a dangerously immoral activity. One critic warned in 1798 that as a young woman reads a novel, "evil steals imperceptibly into her heart."

African American Culture: Slaves and Free People

Even though the institution of slavery denied slaves control of their own lives, African American men and women strengthened black culture between 1789 and 1824. Black culture varied by region and among slave and free populations. The end of the legal slave trade in 1808 meant that blacks could establish their own fully native-born culture, influenced by many different regional African traditions in religion, food, clothing, and funerary and burial practices. Black and white culture continued to be intertwined because many slaves lived with their masters on small farms.

Cultural traditions helped enslaved people to survive the violent reality of day-to-day life, especially on larger plantations. Josiah Henson remembered how he and his fellow slaves balanced misery with the pleasure of family life during his youth in the 1790s: "Along with memories of miry cabins, frosted feet, weary toil under the blazing sun, curses and blows, there flock in others, of jolly Christmas times . . . midnight visits to apple orchards, broiling stray chickens, and first-rate tricks to dodge work." Despite the wide variation in slave life caused by working conditions, the density of the black population, and even the personality of individual slave masters, black people maintained pieces of their own identities despite the institution that controlled them.

"The Old Plantation" (c. 1790)

The free African American population grew in the new republic, especially in the northern states that had abolished or phased out slavery since the end of the American Revolution. The free black population in the United States grew from around 60,000 in 1790 to approximately 235,000 by 1820 (Map 9.3). Both northern and southern

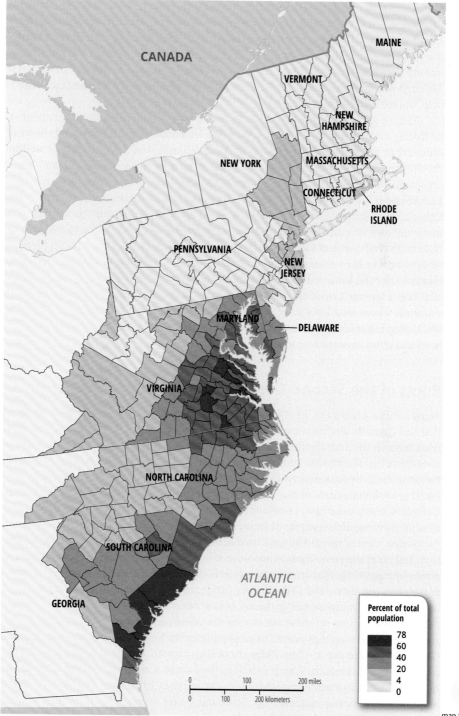

MAP 9.3 African Americans as a Total Percentage of Population, 1790 What is significant about the geographic location of densely populated African American communities?

free African Americans tended to live in cities. In Boston, New York, Philadelphia, Richmond, Charleston, and New Orleans, distinct free African American cultures emerged. Even as the great majority of the African American population continued to live in slavery, both enslaved and free blacks built up family, church, work, and community networks that enriched their lives and fought slavery. As James Forten put it, "Though our faces are black, yet we are men" who seek to enjoy human rights and to help "our afflicted Brethren."

African Americans in cities, often excluded from white institutions, set about establishing their own mutual aid societies, black fraternal lodges, schools, and churches. Most urban black men and women were poor laborers, but a rising class of well-to-do shop owners, hairdressers, doctors, and ministers formed political and social organizations, especially in Philadelphia and Boston. Two former slaves, Richard Allen and **Absalom Jones**, founded the first independent black Protestant church, the Bethel Church, in Philadelphia in 1792. Allen wanted African Americans "to worship God under our own vine and fig tree," and similar congregations sprang up across the North. In 1816, the independent black churches banded together to form the African Methodist Episcopal (AME) denomination. Efforts to found AME churches in the South were blocked after the thwarted 1822 slave revolt plot attributed to Denmark Vesey. Vesey, who was a fervent Christian, was convicted of planning a violent rebellion in South Carolina, whose state legislature promptly forbade separate black churches. Wherever black churches could thrive, however, they nurtured African American cultural aspirations and efforts toward freedom.

Roots of the Second Great Awakening

Many African Americans belonged to Methodist, Baptist, and other Protestant churches that had dramatically increased their membership by the 1790s. The new denominations born in the 18th-century Great Awakening began to experience a new surge of growth, as the Methodists and Baptists quickly grew to be the largest two Protestant denominations by midcentury. Even the more traditional Presbyterian Church experienced growth that outpaced population increase during the early republic. The Roman Catholic Church went from installing John Carroll as its first American bishop in 1789 to administering nine separate dioceses in 1829.

Richard McNemar, excerpt from *The Kentucky Revival* (1808)

A new wave of revivalism took hold across the United States at the turn of the century, and many different kinds of people were swept up in it. Popular preachers held outdoor camp meetings that attracted a mixed audience of whites and blacks, unchurched and church members. The 19th-century camp meeting revivals provided experiential, social occasions when people gathered to hear sermons, meet neighbors, and express religious enthusiasm by speaking in tongues, shouting, weeping, and declaring their salvation. Camp meetings proved most popular in the South and West. The largest and most famous meeting at Cane Ridge, Kentucky, in 1801 attracted as many as 20,000 people to the backwoods. Camp meetings bore some similarity to the informal, and often secret, outdoor gatherings that characterized the Christianity of American slaves, and they also adapted customs from Scots and Ulster revivals. Revivals such as Cane Ridge eventually led to the founding of even more new Protestant denominations such as the Church of Christ, which strayed away from the strict Calvinism of previous centuries. On the other end of the social spectrum, but nonetheless enthusiastic, were the throngs of students who flocked to the Yale College chapel in New Haven, Connecticut, to hear the inspiring sermons of moderate evangelical **Timothy Dwight**, the university president who was Jonathan Edwards's grandson. Dwight converted and educated a generation of ministers including **Lyman Beecher** and Nathaniel Taylor, who became leaders of the **Second Great Awakening** as it grew into a more defined religious movement in the later 1820s and 1830s.

STUDY QUESTIONS FOR SOCIAL AND CULTURAL SHIFTS

1. Did African American survival strategies differ from those of Indians? If so, how? If not, why not?

2. In what ways did printed materials influence the creation of "American" culture from the 1790s to the 1820s? How did print culture affect different groups in different ways?

quiz

FINANCIAL EXPANSION

In the aftermath of the War of 1812, the United States had the chance to capitalize on new trade opportunities and the settlement of new territories brought on by population movement. Enterprising merchants such as John Jacob Astor proved that astronomical profits could be made by people who opened up new avenues of trade and finance, but debates persisted about how much the U.S. government should support business ventures. With the Federalist Party effectively dead in national politics following the War of 1812, leading Democratic-Republican politicians adopted some of the old Federalist embrace of high finance, but not without conflict. Financial expansion helped to contribute to President James Monroe's opinion that the United States was on a "high career of national happiness," but by 1819, good feelings had soured as an economic depression took hold.

Banks and Panics

President James Madison had been convinced by the War of 1812's disruption of foreign trade that the United States must do more to encourage domestic manufacturing. Madison proposed to build roads and canals, to enact tariffs on foreign products, and to reauthorize the charter of the **Bank of the United States (BUS)**. Madison had bitterly opposed the BUS on constitutional grounds when Alexander Hamilton proposed it in 1791, but he now believed that the "expediency and almost necessity" of wartime finance meant that the United States needed a federal bank. Although some "Old Republicans" like Virginian John Randolph opposed the bank and the encouragement of manufacturing, even Thomas Jefferson himself had embraced Madison's vision by 1816 when he wrote, "We must now place the manufacturer by the side of the agriculturalist."

The BUS consisted of a partnership between federal government and private investors, and their intertwined interests became difficult to separate at the end of the War of 1812. Financial speculators, including John Jacob Astor and his fellow merchant

Stephen Girard, bought up bonds and notes, and as their investments fluctuated, so did their commitment to central banking. In January 1815, President Madison vetoed Congress's proposed recharter of the BUS because the bill gave too much private advantage to merchants like Astor and Girard. True to his roots as a strict interpreter of the U.S. Constitution, Madison also vetoed the 1816 "Bonus Bill" that would have funded public transportation because the Constitution did not expressly grant Congress authority to pass such legislation.

Madison still hoped for a central bank, but Congress was contending over a variety of financial issues. Each of the more than 200 private and state banks issued its own bank notes, a practice that drove up inflation. Madison's supporters in Congress, including South Carolinian **John C. Calhoun** and Speaker of the House Henry Clay, proposed a charter for a Second Bank of the United States. The new federal bank, to be based in Philadelphia, would stabilize U.S. currency and would exert control over private investors. President Madison approved the new charter of the Second Bank of the United States in April 1816. In the same month, a 25 percent tariff on foreign wool cloth, cotton, and iron went into effect. Congress also passed legislation authorizing a National Road and other internal improvements advocated by Madison and Henry Clay. But when Congress also raised its own salary rate, voters turned out the majority of representatives in the 1816 election.

In the spring of 1817, newly elected president James Monroe toured the northern states to reach out to disgruntled Federalists, but before he could depart, Monroe had to deal with more controversy over the Second Bank of the United States. A House of Representatives investigation uncovered what one member called "a system of fraud, stock-jobbing, and speculation" that enriched the bank's private directors and threatened public finance. The directors of the Baltimore branch of the BUS alone had embezzled over $1.5 million, an astronomical sum at the time. The public lost confidence in the bank, but a bill to revoke its charter failed in Congress in February 1819.

At the same time, a severe depression halted business expansion. Since the end of the War of 1812, U.S. exports had increased by over 100 percent and agricultural prices had soared. But by the end of 1818, rampant speculation in cotton and land, a

THE SECOND BANK OF THE UNITED STATES
This building in Philadelphia was designed in the Greek revival style by William Strickland and constructed between 1818 and 1824. Between its incorporation in 1816 and the bank war with the Jackson administration that caused it to fold in 1836, the Second Bank of the United States was the most important financial institution in the country.

shortage of gold and silver to back up U.S. currency, and the recovery of the British economy spelled trouble. The plummet of cotton prices in Europe and the United States demonstrated how that product had tightened the links in the transatlantic economy. In 1819, banks and businesses backed by inflated currency began to fail in droves, and the Second Bank of the United States reacted too slowly to prevent a collapse of the economy. The effects were traumatic. Personal bankruptcies soared, land prices plummeted, and the financial crisis even temporarily slowed down the tide of settlers who were willing to uproot and seek new farmland on the frontier.

Corporations and the Supreme Court

Less than two weeks after the Second Bank of the United States survived its challenge in the House of Representatives in 1819, the Supreme Court entered the political debate over federal economic power and issued one of its most important decisions ever. The court unanimously decided in the case of *McCulloch v. Maryland* that central banking was constitutional. Furthermore, Chief Justice John Marshall's opinion supported the idea that the federal government represented the people of one unified United States. According to Marshall, even though the Constitution did not explicitly grant Congress the right to charter national banks, it implied that Congress could do so because it could exercise powers given by the people "for their benefit." The decision struck down a hefty tax that Maryland had imposed on the Baltimore branch of the BUS and declared that federal laws must supersede state action. In the future, the decision would hold power even beyond the issue of banking, as it declared that Congress could use broad powers implied by the Constitution so long as Congress avoided anything expressly forbidden in that document.

Excerpts from Chief Justice Marshall's opinion in *McCulloch v. Maryland* (1819)

John Marshall, an old Federalist whose market ideas matched the new economic climate, led the Supreme Court to deliver several other opinions that buoyed American business and investment. In 1819, the court decided in *Dartmouth College v. Woodward* that New Hampshire could not alter the Dartmouth College charter because Dartmouth was a private corporation whose property the state should not violate. The decision encouraged the development of business corporations, which were just beginning to emerge as a major factor in the U.S. economy and which provided a great advantage to entrepreneurs by limiting their personal liability for business failures. In 1824, the court ruled in a case concerning steamboat monopolies, *Gibbons v. Ogden*, that the Commerce Clause of the Constitution granted the federal government the sole right to regulate interstate commerce. Marshall and the Supreme Court cut through arguments that a "narrow construction" of the Constitution prohibited federal expansion of the economy, and they helped to fuel business development for decades to come.

STUDY QUESTIONS **FOR FINANCIAL EXPANSION**

1. In what ways did the three branches of the federal government each affect the economy during the 1810s?

2. In what ways did the Panic of 1819 reveal the strengths and weaknesses of U.S. economic development?

quiz

POLITICS AND HEMISPHERIC CHANGE

Although financial crisis slowed settlement for a time after 1819, a new wave of political and military engagements would soon again spark frontier movements. In the aftermath of the War of 1812, the United States showed a new confidence in foreign policy. The United States claimed to have no imperial ambitions, but aggressive military action by General Andrew Jackson and assertive diplomacy from Secretary of State **John Quincy Adams** added territory and enhanced the international stature of the nation. The United States linked itself firmly to the rest of the Western Hemisphere when it took an interest in revolutions in Latin America. But how could the United States solidify its new position without igniting more trouble with European nations?

First Seminole War

Since acquiring Louisiana in 1803, U.S. officials had tried various measures to gain Spain's territory in Florida. In 1818, conflict with Seminole Indians gave them new opportunity. Although it is not clear whether Secretary of War John C. Calhoun and Secretary of State John Quincy Adams intended to endorse belligerent action, they nonetheless capitalized on aggressive tactics employed by General Andrew Jackson to gain control of Florida. Seminoles, a coalition of Native peoples and former slaves, encouraged runaways from the United States to seek refuge in their territory in Florida. Seminole groups also harbored Creek refugees who had fled south after the Red Stick War in 1814. In November 1817, U.S. general Edmund Gains burned the Creek village of Fowltown, Georgia, an action that caused reprisals from Florida Creeks and Seminoles against American settlers across the border. Calhoun sent Jackson to protect U.S. settlers and property.

In March 1818, Jackson invaded Spanish territory with a force of Tennessee volunteers, regular army soldiers, and Creek allies hostile to the Red Sticks. Jackson had told President Monroe in January that he wanted to seize "the whole of East Florida," and when he received no reply, he took it as license to act freely. On April 6, Jackson captured the Spanish fort at St. Mark's, and he then attacked Seminole villages on the Suwannee River. In addition to burning property while fighting Indians and African Americans, Jackson also arrested and executed two British citizens whom he accused of helping the Seminoles. On May 28, Jackson occupied the Spanish capitol of Pensacola, expelled governor **José Mascot**, appointed a U.S. territorial governor, and declared that Spain would have to give up Florida if it could not control Seminole people within Spanish territory.

Jackson's actions caused uproar in Washington, DC, where the French, British, and Spanish protested his aggression. Although most of Monroe's cabinet believed that Jackson had exceeded his orders, Secretary of State John Quincy Adams restrained the executive reaction against Jackson. Adams, who had entered treaty negotiations with Spanish diplomat **Luis de Onís**, used the Seminole War as leverage and stressed that Spain had to demonstrate mastery of Seminole people to be trusted. In November 1818, after Onís pulled out of talks, Adams returned control of Pensacola and St. Marks to the Spanish, but controversy over Jackson's actions continued. In January 1819, President Monroe's annual message to Congress disavowed intentions to take over Spanish territory. Congress immediately began to investigate and to debate whether Jackson's actions had been correct. Henry Clay delivered a blistering speech denouncing Jackson,

JAMES MONROE Samuel F. B. Morse painted this portrait of President James Monroe in 1819. Monroe's presidency was marked by the strong influence of cabinet ministers, especially Secretary of State John Quincy Adams, and by nationalist policies that encouraged territorial expansion. The Monroe Doctrine that bore his name warned European countries not to intervene in the affairs of the Western Hemisphere.

but resolutions to censure Jackson were roundly defeated. Mississippi representative George Poindexter declared that Jackson had "fulfilled the measure of his country's glory," and many Americans seemed to agree as they thronged to praise him on a February triumphal tour around the Eastern Seaboard. Early in 1821, Congress reduced the size of the army and removed Andrew Jackson from service.

Transcontinental (Adams–Onís) Treaty

President Monroe, who was quite indecisive, relied heavily on Secretary of State John Quincy Adams to guide him through many different policy decisions. Adams carefully balanced rivalries with other cabinet ministers including Treasury Secretary William H. Crawford and Vice President Daniel D. Tompkins. Adams put his stamp on a whole new era of U.S. foreign policy, and he did much to consolidate the status of the United States as a country to be taken seriously in the world. He had accompanied his father, John Adams, on several diplomatic missions as a young man, and he refined his negotiating skills during the War of 1812 as minister to Russia, where he befriended Czar Alexander I. On taking office, Adams immediately improved U.S. relations with Great Britain. He oversaw the Rush–Bagot Agreement in 1817 in which the British agreed to demilitarize the Great Lakes. In the midst of the diplomatic controversy over the Seminole War, Adams and U.S. minister to Great Britain **Richard Rush** also cemented the Convention of 1818 in which the British agreed to set the border between the United States and Canada at the 49th parallel. After Adams sent a warship to the Oregon coast, the British also agreed to return Astoria to the United States and to recognize some U.S. territorial rights in Oregon.

Shocked by the lack of response from Great Britain to U.S. aggression in Florida and facing growing pressure from the independence movements in Latin America, Spanish officials decided to cut their losses and cede Florida when Luis de Onís returned to his negotiations with Adams in late 1818. Now confident that he could gain Florida, Adams made an even bolder proposal to acquire new territory from the Spanish, who still resisted U.S. claims on the southwestern border of the Louisiana Purchase territory. Adams proposed that Spain cede territory all the way to the Pacific Ocean north of California at the 42nd parallel. This was the first U.S. government bid to extend its territory across the entire continent of North America, a move that Adams wrote in his diary would form "a great epocha in our history." In exchange for Spanish recognition of U.S. rights in Oregon, Adams consented to forgo all claim to Texas. Adams and Onís agreed to these terms in the Transcontinental Treaty (also called the Adams–Onís Treaty) in February 1819.

The United States and Latin American Revolutions

The U.S. Senate ratified the Adams–Onís Treaty just two days after Adams presented it. But Madrid held up final agreement until 1821, in large part because of arguments over U.S. response to the revolutions that had spread across most of Latin America. The United States had proclaimed neutrality in Spain's wars with its colonies in September 1815, but many U.S. traders and private citizens sought to aid Latin American rebels. In August 1817, Washington diplomats turned away an envoy from independence leaders Juan Martín Pueyrredón, Bernardo O'Higgins, and José San Martín, who sought recognition for Argentina, Peru, and Chile. Monroe and Adams reinforced the official position of neutrality despite Henry Clay's legislative efforts and frequent speeches demanding U.S. help to cast off the "despotism" of Spain.

Letter from a South American envoy to John Quincy Adams (1817)

Spain demanded that the United States not aid the Latin American rebels, but public opinion was in the rebels' favor. Many were convinced that these independence movements emulated the American Revolution, and others hoped that the United States might extend its influence south. The successes of Simón Bolívar against Spanish forces in Colombia, Ecuador, and Venezuela between 1819 and 1821; Augustín de Iturbide's securing of Mexican independence in 1821; and San Martín's independence victory in Peru in 1821 helped to convince the Monroe administration to alter its course and propose recognition of the Latin American independence movements in March 1822. By 1826, Congress had agreed to recognize the Republic of Greater Colombia, Mexico, Chile, Argentina, Brazil, the Provinces of Central America, and Peru. Only the black republic of Haiti would have to wait until 1862 for U.S. recognition (Map 9.4).

The Monroe Doctrine

The U.S. recognition of Latin American independence did not end its wrangling with Spain, and, in 1822, other European powers also indicated that they might intervene in the region. Rebellions in Spain and Naples in 1820 had disturbed the Quintuple Alliance powers in Europe (Russia, Austria, Prussia, France, and Britain), who feared that monarchy itself might be threatened by liberal challenges. After the October 1822 Congress of Verona, France restored Spain's King Ferdinand VII to the throne,

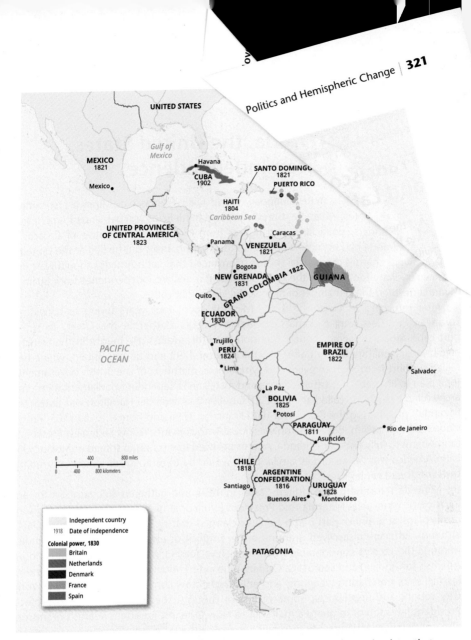

MAP 9.4 Latin America and the Caribbean, c. 1830 This map shows the dates that various Latin American and Caribbean countries attained their colonial independence.

and the United States feared that France, Britain, or other powers might also move on Latin America. By April 1823, Spain retained only Cuba and Puerto Rico as colonies. Although John Quincy Adams agreed to let Spain maintain control there, he warned that the United States would not approve if Spain let any other European power intercede and that the United States might be prepared to invade Cuba if Spain disagreed. Adams also took a hard line in British trade negotiations and objected to a Russian claim on American territory in Oregon. British foreign minister **George Canning** opposed European intervention in Latin America, but American officials

Miranda, the United States,
France, American Independence
and

At the American Revolutionary War in 1783, Francisco de Miranda first came
United States, where he toured cities and battlefields and befriended American
commanders, politicians, and figures from high society. A native of Caracas,
Venezuela, Miranda had become a colonel in the Spanish army, but he fled to the United
States to avoid charges of financial misuse. Convinced that Latin America should walk in
the Revolutionary footsteps of the United States and declare independence from Spain,
Miranda devoted the remainder of his colorful life to that cause.

After returning to Europe in 1785, Miranda spent four years trying to convince
European courtiers and diplomats, including Russia's Catherine the Great, to support Latin America, gaining much attention but little success. He fought in the French
revolutionary military but ran afoul of radicals after 1793 and fled to Britain, where he
rallied support from Spanish exiles and sympathetic members of the British government
for a plan to liberate all of Latin America and install an independent parliamentary monarchy ruled by what he called an "Inca." U.S. politician Alexander Hamilton was drawn to
Miranda's plan during the Quasi-War with France in 1798 and hoped to lead U.S. Army
troops to support him, but Hamilton was not able to convince fellow Federalist President
John Adams to fully endorse Miranda. Adams believed that trying to spread democracy in
Latin America was "as absurd as similar plans would be to establish democracies among
the birds, beasts and fishes."

Miranda returned to the United States in 1805 and gathered U.S. support for an
invasion of Venezuela. Miranda told President Jefferson and Secretary of State Madison
of his plans at a dinner party, and he later claimed that he had their "tacit approval,"
although Jefferson disavowed granting either implicit or explicit blessings to Miranda.
Miranda did receive considerable help from New Yorkers William Stevens Smith (John
Adams's son-in-law) and Samuel G. Ogden, who aided Miranda in outfitting the Leander,
a small ship; purchasing weapons; and enlisting a crew composed mostly of New York
City toughs and apprentices, some of whom thought they were enlisting to protect
President Jefferson or to guard a mail ship to New Orleans. President Adams's grandson
also enlisted with Miranda. Miranda failed to realize that Spanish officials were spying on
him as he prepared for the expedition against their colony.

In February 1806, Miranda embarked from New York City and chartered two additional ships in Santo Domingo. Even though the British navy afforded his vessels some

worried that he would be ignored by other Alliance powers. Canning told U.S. diplomat Richard Rush that he would be willing to issue a joint British–American statement warning Europeans against Latin American intervention. Secretary of State
John Quincy Adams was suspicious of Canning's motives, however, and he decided
the United States should respond alone.

protection, two of Miranda's ships were captured by the Spanish when the party first tried to land in Venezuela. Sixty of Miranda's men were captured and imprisoned in Puerto Cabello, and 10 were sentenced to death. Henry Ingersoll, a former printer's apprentice who had been taken on board to print Miranda's propaganda, wrote in his diary that he and the other prisoners were chained and "marched to the Gallows, where we beheld our companions hanged and beheaded." Ingersoll and the other Americans were imprisoned in Cartagena for years until public outcry and family appeals to European diplomats helped free them. Several resolutions in Congress for the U.S. government to come to their aid failed because federal officials disavowed any responsibility for Miranda's actions.

After the capture, Miranda regrouped at Barbados and invaded the Venezuelan city of Coro in August 1806. He found no support among local residents or clergy, and he eventually fled back to England. Later, when the Venezuelan independence movement began in 1811, Miranda returned, and for a time in 1812 he became the country's ruler. But he quickly lost the faith of Simón Bolívar and other independence leaders, who handed him over to the Spanish. He died in a Spanish prison in 1816, never having gained full support from the United States, a country whose revolution he felt Latin America should "prudently imitate."

PORTRAIT OF FRANCISCO MIRANDA (1750–1816)

Francisco de Miranda, excerpt from a draft constitution for Spanish America (ca. 1795)

- Compare Miranda's 1806 Venezuela invasion to Andrew Jackson's takeover of Florida in the First Seminole War.
- Why do you think neither President Adams nor President Jefferson wanted to support Miranda even though other Americans supported his plans?

Adams took a bold approach and decided to warn Europe in no uncertain terms. Adams drafted Monroe's seventh annual message to Congress, and in it he enunciated what would become known as the **Monroe Doctrine**. In the December 1823 address, Monroe declared that the United States shared common interest with other states in the Western Hemisphere and that the political system in Europe was

interactive timeline

TIMELINE 1789–1823

AMERICA	YEAR	THE WORLD
Mar Pennsylvania lifts ban on theater	1789	Jeremy Bentham publishes *Introduction to the Principles of Morals*
Apr Congress establishes patent office **May** First U.S. copyright law takes effect	1790	France grants Jews recognition of civil rights *The Bounty* mutineers settle on Pitcairn Island
Mar Vermont becomes 14th state	1791	William Wilberforce fails to get Parliament to outlaw slavery in British colonies **Sep** Mozart's *The Magic Flute* first performed in Vienna
May Robert Gray claims Columbia River and part of Oregon territory for United States **Jun** Kentucky admitted to the union	1792	Bubonic plague kills over 750,000 in Egypt Denmark abolishes slavery Mary Wollstonecraft's *A Vindication of the Rights of Woman* is published in London and quickly spreads across Europe and the United States
Apr Scottish fur trader Sir Alexander Mackenzie explores across North America and reaches Pacific Ocean **Oct** Eli Whitney refines his cotton gin design	1793	
Susannah Rowson's novel *Charlotte Temple* is published **Jun** Richard Allen founds Bethel Church in Philadelphia	1794	**Mar** U.S. Revolutionary hero Tadeusz Kosciuszko begins unsuccessful uprising in Poland
Jun Tennessee becomes 16th state	1796	British doctor Edward Jenner invents smallpox vaccine
Eli Whitney contracted to manufacture 10,000 rifles for army using interchangeable parts	1798	Thomas Malthus publishes *Essay on the Principles of Population*
Library of Congress is established	1800	German Alexander von Humboldt maps the South American Orinoco River Ludwig von Beethoven's first symphony first performed in Vienna
Mar Ohio becomes the 17th state in union	1803	Abortion outlawed in Great Britain
May Lewis and Clark Expedition begins **Nov** Lewis and Clark take up winter quarters with Mandan Indians	1804	
Hugh Henry Brackenridge publishes *Modern Chivalry* **Apr** Lewis and Clark Expedition reaches mouth of Yellowstone River **Aug** Zebulon Pike explores for source of Mississippi River **Nov** Lewis and Clark reach Pacific Ocean	1805	
Noah Webster publishes American dictionary **Jul** Lewis and Clark split Corps of Discovery into two parties **Jul** Zebulon Pike sets out to explore southwestern Louisiana territory **Sep** Lewis and Clark Expedition ends in St. Louis	1806	Construction of the Arc de Triomphe begins

AMERICA	YEAR	THE WORLD
	1807	Parliament forbids slave trade in British colonies
Apr John Jacob Astor incorporates American Fur Company **Nov** Osage cede lands in Missouri and Arkansas to United States in treaty signed at Ft. Clark, Kansas	**1808**	Goethe publishes Part I of *Faust*
Campbellite Church of Christ splits from the Presbyterian Church **Jun** John Jacob Astor founds Pacific Fur Company **Oct** President Madison annexes part of West Florida to Louisiana	**1810**	
Jan Congress authorizes President Madison to acquire East Florida	**1811**	British capture Dutch colony of Java
Apr Louisiana becomes 18th state **Jun** Missouri territory is organized	**1812**	**Aug** Swiss archaeologist John Lewis Burckhardt documents ancient city of Petra in current-day Jordan
Emma Willard opens her first school in Middlebury, Vermont	**1814**	Britain buys Cape Colony, South Africa, from Dutch for £20 million
Sep United States declares neutrality in Latin American wars of independence	**1815**	
Indiana admitted to the union **Apr** Congress passes 25 percent trade tariff **Dec** James Monroe elected president	**1816**	
Mar John Quincy Adams becomes secretary of state **Apr** Rush–Bagot Agreement improves relations between United States and Britain	**1817**	
Apr General Andrew Jackson takes control of West Florida in the First Seminole War **Dec** Illinois admitted to the union	**1818**	**Feb** Bernardo O'Higgins and José de San Martín declare independence in Chile
Jan Cotton prices drop, touching off the Panic of 1819 **Feb** Adams–Onís Treaty signed **Feb** Motions of censure against Andrew Jackson fail in Congress	**1819**	**Aug** Manchester protests against Corn Laws result in violence
Mar Missouri Compromise—Missouri and Maine become U.S. states **Dec** President Monroe is reelected	**1820**	**Jan** George III dies; George IV becomes king of England
Adams–Onís Treaty ratified **Feb** Mexico declares independence **Jul** José de San Martín declares Peru's independence **Sep** Mexico cements its independence	**1821**	
Mar President Monroe suggests that United States should recognize Latin American countries	**1822**	First Ashanti War in West Africa begins
Dec Monroe Doctrine articulated in Monroe's annual message to Congress	**1823**	

Excerpt from the Monroe Doctrine (1823), and a rebuttal from a Latin American diplomat

"essentially different" from that of the democratic republics in North and South America. Monroe maintained that the United States would not interfere in European politics or with existing European colonies in the Western Hemisphere, but neither should Europe insert itself any further in the West. Europe could not be allowed to extend its power or monarchical political system in North or South America without, in Monroe's words, "endangering our peace and happiness." European powers should not seek future colonies in the Western Hemisphere and should not seek to reconquer independent states. President Monroe later argued that only Haiti did not earn the right to self-determination because "the establishment of a Government of people of color in the island . . . evinces distinctly the idea of a separate interest and a distrust of other nations."

In later decades and centuries, the Monroe Doctrine would be used as a justification of U.S. intervention in Latin American countries, but for the time being it was mostly a bold statement of independence from European influence. Since 1789, the United States had more than tripled the area of its territory, and its growing population was settling larger areas every year. But the United States did not yet have the military power entirely to enforce its grand vision.

STUDY QUESTIONS FOR POLITICS AND HEMISPHERIC CHANGE

quiz

1. In what ways did the Monroe Doctrine indicate that the United States aspired to a new status in the world?
2. John Quincy Adams has been called one of the most talented secretaries of state the United States has ever had. Why?

Summary

- Between 1789 and 1824, the United States, Spain, Great Britain, and Russia expanded on the North American continent through exploration, settlement, and trade.
- Different Indian peoples responded to pressures on their lives through various combinations of warfare, trade, diplomacy, and cultural adaptation.
- The physical expansion of the United States and the expansion of cotton farming led to conflicts over slavery.
- A new "American" culture reflected the changing social roles of women, African Americans, Christians, and others.
- The United States was increasingly connected to the rest of the world through trade even as new foreign policy following the War of 1812 defined a more assertive position for the country.

Key Terms and People

audio
flashcards

Reviewing Chapter 9

1. Both government policies and individual initiative were crucial to the expansion of the United States. Which was more important, and why?
2. How did the movement of people around North America influence political events between 1789 and 1824?
3. What were some of the most important ways that attitudes toward nature shaped actions of U.S. citizens between 1789 and 1824?

Further Reading

Chasteen, John Charles. *Americanos: Latin America's Struggle for Independence.* New York: Oxford University Press, 2008. This book traces Latin American wars for independence starting in 1808 and examines how various Latin American colonies became independent nations. Chasteen shows the interplay between the United States and many Latin American revolutionary nations.

Forbes, Robert Pierce. *The Missouri Compromise and Its Aftermath: Slavery and the Meaning of America.* Chapel Hill: University of North Carolina Press, 2007. Forbes analyzes the complex political history of American expansionism that led to the delicate Missouri Compromise and traces the consequences of the Compromise for U.S. politics and society.

Hackel, Stephen. *Children of Coyote, Missionaries of Saint Francis: Indian-Spanish Relations in Colonial California, 1769–1850.* Chapel Hill: University of North Carolina Press, 2005. In this book, Hackel examines how California Indians coped with and resisted Spanish religious and military colonial control, even as their populations were decimated by disease. The author presents a particularly in-depth case study of the Mission of San Carlos Borromeo.

Howe, Daniel Walker. *What Hath God Wrought: The Transformation of America, 1815–1848.* New York: Oxford University Press, 2007. Howe's sweeping overview of U.S. history from 1815 to 1848 integrates excellent discussion of territorial expansion, slavery, religious revival, and the development of American literature.

Nash, Gary B. *Forging Freedom: The Formation of Philadelphia's Black Community, 1720–1840.* Cambridge, MA: Harvard University Press, 1988. Nash's account of the free black community in Philadelphia shows how ties of kinship, economic activity, and religion provided the means to create the urban center of free black society in the United States. Nash shows how many African Americans succeeded, despite racism and growing segregation.

America in the World
GOODS, IDEAS, PEOPLE

CHAPTER 9: American Peoples on the Move, 1789–1824

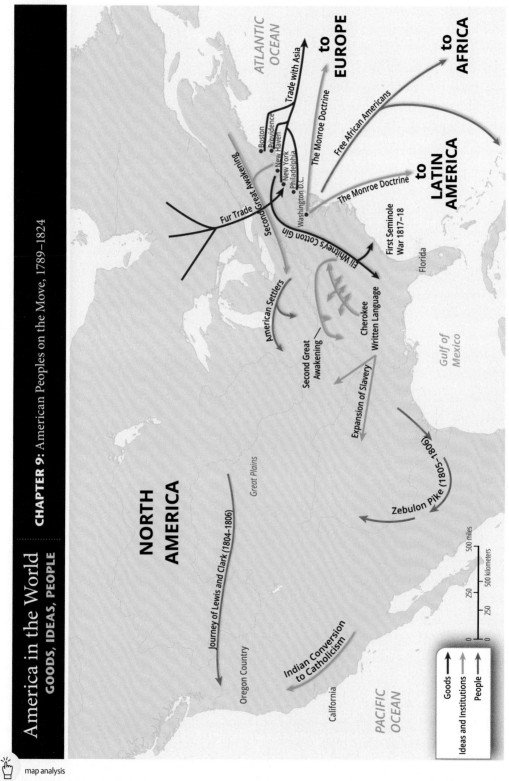

NORTH AMERICA

ATLANTIC OCEAN

to EUROPE

to AFRICA

to LATIN AMERICA

Trade with Asia

The Monroe Doctrine

Free African Americans

The Monroe Doctrine

First Seminole War 1817–18

Florida

Boston
Providence
New Haven
New York
Philadelphia
Washington D.C.

Fur Trade

Second Great Awakening

Eli Whitney's Cotton Gin

American Settlers

Cherokee Written Language

Second Great Awakening

Expansion of Slavery

Zebulon Pike (1805–1806)

Great Plains

Gulf of Mexico

Journey of Lewis and Clark (1804–1806)

Oregon Country

Indian Conversion to Catholicism

California

PACIFIC OCEAN

0   250   500 miles
0   250   500 kilometers

Goods
Ideas and Institutions
People

map analysis

Portrait of Andrew Jackson by Ralph Eleaser Whiteside Earl.

Market Revolutions and the Rise of Democracy

1789–1832

O n July 4, 1830, the residents of Portland, Maine, found themselves bitterly divided by politics. Instead of holding one celebration of Independence Day, Democrats who supported Andrew Jackson held their own separate event, as they no longer wished to celebrate alongside Jackson's opponents, who controlled local government. The two factions were splitting into two parties—the Democrats and the Whigs. Rival newspapers, the Democratic *Eastern Argus* and the *Portland Gazette*, added fuel to the fire of political disagreement in Portland. Both sides used Fourth of July parades, ritual toasting, celebrations, and newspapers to celebrate the nation's birthday and to blast their opponents.

After the rival parades directly passed one another in the center of town, each side adjourned to separate locations where partygoers could enjoy the company of those who agreed with them. The Jacksonian Democrats met at Mr. Attwood's boarding house with elaborate decorations, including a live bald eagle and two miniature commercial sailing ships. The anti-Jacksonians repaired to city hall, which was also "handsomely decorated" for their celebration. The newspaper editors each accused the rival celebrants of being the tools of "vile" party politics instead of engaging in true patriotism, and each party claimed to have hundreds more participants than the other side.

The ritual toasts—long an Independence Day tradition—revealed the bitter partisan divide between Portlanders. The Jacksonians cast President Jackson as the "youngest political son of the late Thomas Jefferson"; "the sincere and untiring friend of the *simple* mechanic"; and a supporter "of the rights of the People, and worthy of their suffrages." Several toasters wished for Democratic electoral success in the fall elections, and Ebenezer Webster threatened the Democrats' electoral opponents: "We will toast them . . . and baste them with democratic butter." Meanwhile, back at city hall, the anti-Jacksonians labeled their opponents "political skunks and other vermin."

Portland's role in the transatlantic economy helped drive political disagreements. Maine grew rapidly between its admission to the union in 1820 and 1830, and its expanding population benefited from thriving agriculture, fishing, lumber, and shipbuilding industries. Maine served as an entry port for cotton, feeding the new textile mills sprouting up throughout New England. Advertisements in local newspapers announced regular commercial and passenger ship traffic between Portland, Boston, and European cities including Belfast and Frankfort. The Cumberland and Oxford Canal opened in 1830 to connect the interior of southern Maine to the port of Portland. Andrew Jackson's supporters in Portland made a clear distinction between their support of this state effort, financed by the locally chartered Canal Bank, and what they considered to be the unconstitutional **"American System"** of Henry Clay that promoted the use of federal government funds for infrastructure projects. The Portland Jacksonians toasted the defeat of the American System and Jackson's veto of the Maysville Road Bill, the most famous federal internal improvement project. The Jacksonian Democrats in Maine drew most of their support from poor fishermen, workingmen, and small merchants, whereas the anti-Jacksonian Whigs attracted wealthier business supporters.

The partisanship displayed in Portland, Maine, characterized the splits in national and local politics taking place all over the United States. Disagreements over how government should best manage the burgeoning capitalist and commercial enterprise in the developing nation would change the character of U.S. politics as the country entered the worldwide Industrial Revolution.

⬇ THE MARKET SYSTEM

Americans had grown used to buying and selling goods since the mid-1700s. The pace and scale of these economic exchanges accelerated, however, and between 1789 and 1832, a fuller market economy took shape in the United States. In a market economy, supply and demand influence the production, distribution, price, and consumption of goods. Before 1789, most rural Americans lived on interdependent family farms, although many, such as southern tobacco planters, sold staple crops and participated in international trade. At the turn of the 19th century, more and more farmers began to produce surplus goods that they could sell locally, regionally, or internationally for cash. Although the vast majority of Americans remained in rural areas, a greater percentage of Americans were moving into towns and cities where manufacturing took place. The greater supply of foreign and domestic manufactured goods that fueled the market system allowed farm families to specialize because they could purchase goods instead of having to produce or trade for everything they needed. The market system intensified economic competition, changed business and labor patterns, and had a profound effect on the lives of everyone in the United States. Technological change, government action, and international exchanges all intensified the development of market capitalism.

Internal and External Markets

The U.S. market economy emerged from the connection of local, regional, national, and international networks of exchange—all of which grew between 1789 and 1832. Although the shifts took place unevenly, by 1800 it was clear that labor markets, capital investment, and prices had converged to create a market system based on currency exchange and commodities. Everyday economic activities were increasingly influenced by market prices and wider economic forces. In a free-market economy, open competition and the exchange of products, credit, and cash balance the optimum production and price of goods. As new kinds of transportation and machinery became available by 1820, many farmers made decisions about what to grow, when to grow it, and how to process it based on market forces.

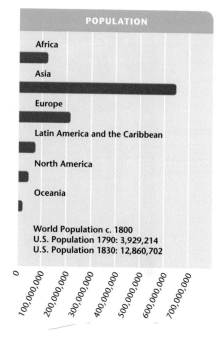

POPULATION

Africa

Asia

Europe

Latin America and the Caribbean

North America

Oceania

World Population c. 1800
U.S. Population 1790: 3,929,214
U.S. Population 1830: 12,860,702

0
100,000,000
200,000,000
300,000,000
400,000,000
500,000,000
600,000,000
700,000,000

As Americans had more opportunities to sell their goods, market connections grew in importance for both agricultural and manufactured products. After the turn of the 19th century, for example, cotton planters in Georgia and Alabama shipped their products to New England textile mills that manufactured and sold cloth across the United States and into the South and West.

European manufacturing could also affect prices and supplies, and international trade played an important role in the market process. Raw materials and trade fluctuated with international disturbances such as the Napoleonic Wars and the War of 1812. The towns and cities inside the United States that grew most rapidly were those—such as Providence, New York, St. Louis, and Philadelphia—that had links both to internal networks of agricultural trade and to external ports that could facilitate international exchange.

Examining one particular product, such as butter, can show how the market transformation worked. Butter went from a product that families produced for themselves to the stuff of international commerce. Mid-Atlantic farm women practiced dairying and butter making widely at the end of the 18th century, and by 1790, surplus butter was traded between farms and sold in Philadelphia. After the War of 1812, more and more women specialized in butter making and started to produce large quantities for sale as a commodity. The stable price for butter, between 17 and 25 cents per pound between the 1790s and 1830s, meant that women could provide income from butter when other farm products fluctuated because of wars or hard economic times. Martha Ogle Forman, a Maryland dairywoman, wrote in her diary in 1824, "We now make more butter than

EARLY CAPITALIST NOSTALGIA This advertisement for butter powder from the 1860s depicts family butter production from earlier decades, as the woman of the house hosts customers while her husband operates a large churn. Linking the commercialized butter powder to the image of fresh butter production evokes nostalgia, which helped small-scale butter producers turn the product into a trade commodity.

we know what to do with." In fact, she did know what to do with the surplus butter: she sold it for profit.

Women like Forman could spend more time making butter because they were able to purchase manufactured cloth instead of spinning and weaving at home. As supplies of store-bought cloth accelerated into the 1830s, so did the production of butter. Farms also adopted new milking methods and new breeds of cows that gave more milk. Butter could be preserved with salt for over a year, and mid-Atlantic butter was sold in markets in Philadelphia, Providence, Annapolis, Charleston, Boston, and other port cities. The international market also grew. Between 1802 and 1835, Americans exported 67 million pounds of dairy products overseas to Europe, the Caribbean, and China. By 1851, men had become more involved with butter making, which began to move into factory production.

The same kind of story could be repeated for scores of other commodities, including cheese, grain, whiskey, pork, and lumber. Homemade and farm goods spread through local, regional, national, and international markets. Individual farmers made decisions based on calculations of price, supply, and demand. The market economy grew through a million single decisions about what to buy, what to produce, and how to sell it.

Technology: Domestic Invention and Global Appropriation

The invention and adoption of new technologies also fueled market activity. Tench Coxe, aide to Treasury Secretary Alexander Hamilton and founder of the Society for Establishing Useful Manufactures, recognized that "machines ingeniously constructed, will give us immense assistance" with economic growth. In the Patent Act of 1790, Congress granted inventors a 14-year monopoly on patented machinery and processes, and patents provided an economic incentive for invention. The federal government went from issuing 3 patents in 1790 to 573 in 1831. The new interest in manufacturing during the War of 1812, when foreign trade was severely restricted, especially spurred domestic invention. The U.S. government issued 244 patents for butter-making equipment alone between 1802 and 1849, and increased butter productivity occurred as women adopted more advanced tools and churns.

Americans invented new technologies to improve both agriculture and manufacturing. By 1792, Delaware inventor Oliver Evans had licensed his designs for continuous-processing flour machinery to more than 100 mills. In 1819, Jethro Wood patented an iron plow constructed from interchangeable parts. After revolutionizing the production of cotton with his mechanized cotton mill in 1793, **Eli Whitney** turned his ingenuity to manufacturing muskets with interchangeable parts. Thomas Blanchard, a mechanic at the Springfield, Massachusetts, armory, invented dozens of machines that allowed for accurate manufacturing of wooden and metal gun parts. In 1831, Illinois inventor **Cyrus McCormick** built his first mechanical reaper, a machine that would revolutionize harvesting in the decades to come.

Design by Oliver Evans for an automated flour mill (1790)

Americans also appropriated some new technologies from abroad—especially from Great Britain. By the early 1780s, British textile mills used mechanized looms and carding machines, but textile workers were discouraged from leaving the country and could be fined if they gave up trade secrets. American agents in New York, Maryland, Pennsylvania, and Massachusetts tried to pay English mechanics to build machinery for them, and they openly advertised in newspapers for men willing to divulge the secrets of British textile inventor **Richard Arkwright**. Trying to stop the smuggling of British machinery into the United States, British consul Phineas Bond, Jr., even inspected cargo in the port of Philadelphia. **Samuel Slater**, a former British textile worker, immigrated to the United States in 1789 and parlayed his knowledge of both machinery and labor management practices into the first successful mechanized mill in the United States. Other British technologies, such as the first steam-powered train locomotives brought to the United States in 1829, were imported legally.

Water and Steam Power

Water power had been harnessed for centuries at saw mills, leather tanneries, and grist mills, but its application in manufacturing grew in the 1790s. The power created by changes in elevation turned water wheels that powered machines with gears and belts. Because of favorable geography, by the early 19th century, Americans were global leaders in harnessing water power for manufacturing. Across the North water power contributed to the growth of textile mills that used machinery to card, spin, and weave cotton and woolen cloth. Thomas Keystone wrote in 1810 that water-powered carding machines "are everywhere established and are rapidly being extended." After the turn of the century, water-powered cotton gins, sugar mills, and rice mills proliferated in the South. Waterwheels drove furnaces and forges essential to ironworks. By 1830, there were an estimated 50,000 water mills in the United States, and the first industrial towns and cities all grew near bodies of water. Location near a water source was so important to all these industries that competition for land near waterways was fierce.

Harnessing steam power from heated water was probably the most important technological innovation in the early market economy. Steam power allowed greater mobility because machinery did not have to be near a waterway. British inventor **James Watt** perfected the first modern steam engine in 1769, although it took several decades of innovation by engineers to make steam power efficient and easy to use. In the first decade of the 19th century, Oliver Evans, the successful American flour mill inventor, patented a high-pressure steam engine that would be used in the first railroad locomotive and in other industrial applications. Steamboats were probably the first significant American contribution to international technology. Steam-powered transportation had the ability to increase the speed of trade dramatically. Pennsylvanian **John Fitch** first used steam to power a boat in August 1787. After several decades of scrambling by various inventors to produce a commercially viable steamboat, **Robert Fulton** perfected a usable high-powered boat engine. Fulton worked with wealthy investor and politician **Robert Livingston** to obtain a monopoly on steamboat traffic in New York waters, and, in August 1807, he launched the *North River Steamboat*—also known as the *Clermont*—the world's first successful commercial steamboat.

Steamboats quickly spread throughout America's inland waterways, and by 1812 they plied waters in the trans-Appalachian West. French engineer Jean Baptiste

STEAMBOATS Robert Fulton's ship *Clermont* was the first commercially viable steamboat in the world. Fulton and Robert Livingston received a monopoly on New York Hudson River steamboat travel and launched the *Clermont* in 1807.

Marestier observed in 1819, "America now possesses several hundred [commercial steamboats] and the people of the New World are already reaping immense benefits." He worried about American "superiority over other nations" in steamboat travel. That same year, the *Savannah*, the first American ship with auxiliary steam power, crossed the Atlantic Ocean. By 1830, hundreds of steamboats, traveling nearly twice as fast as in the 1810s, traded goods on oceans and rivers.

Transportation and Communication

Improvements in transportation—steamboats, roads, canals, and early railroads—played a crucial role in the spread of the market economy throughout the United States in the early decades of the 19th century. Transportation aided a revolution in communications and the movement of commodities. Both federal and state governments invested heavily to speed up and lower the cost of moving goods. Despite political controversy over the use of too much federal power, federal government expenditures on transportation improvements went from less than $100,000 in 1789 to over $1.5 million in 1832. In 1804, **Albert Gallatin**, Thomas Jefferson's treasury secretary, initially proposed the first comprehensive plan for internal improvements.

Henry Clay—who served as a U.S. senator, Speaker of the House of Representatives, and secretary of state between 1809 and 1832—became the leading advocate of publicly funded transportation. Subsidies for roads and canals, in particular, became one of the cornerstones of his "American System"—a group of laws intended to spur domestic economic development that also included **tariffs** and currency regulation. Clay's plans for public improvements, however, ran afoul of several presidents who opposed the overuse of federal power. In 1817, James Madison vetoed the "Bonus Bill" that would have used Bank of the United States funds to pay for roads and canals because he judged it to be unconstitutional. Road building increased exponentially in these decades and proved a key to increased market activity. In the 1790s, turnpikes—roads tailor-made for wagons bearing goods—were constructed up and down the Eastern Seaboard; by the 1820s, they carried hundreds of thousands of tons of freight per year. Many roads, including turnpikes, were built by private companies, encouraged by state subsidies and charters. Congress also took action and authorized the Cumberland Road from Maryland to Ohio in 1806. Efforts to revive funding for a National Road after the War of 1812 were blocked by arguments that road building could not serve a truly "national" interest. In 1822, Congress authorized repairs to the Cumberland Road and extended it to Vandalia, Illinois, but President Monroe, calling the bill unconstitutional, vetoed it. Political controversies over whether roads concentrated too much federal power in one location repeatedly hamstrung a consistent program of federal funding for roads.

Following the War of 1812, several states supplemented road-building projects with early efforts at canal building. Although they would not come into wide use until the later 1820s, canals promised to expand market activity because they mainly aimed to connect inland waters to major avenues of river and oceanic trade. New York authorized construction of the Erie Canal in 1817, but it took almost a decade to be finished. Ohio and Virginia also began major canal projects.

Early railroads also promised to further economic development. In 1830, the Baltimore and Ohio Company founded the first railroad in the United States and opened 13 miles of passenger service between the Baltimore port and Sandy Hook,

Henry Clay, speech in the House of Representatives advocating a tariff (1824)

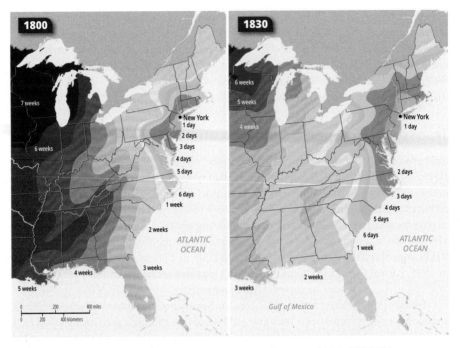

MAP 10.1 Transportation Times Inside the United States, 1800–1830 This map shows how long it took to travel from New York City to other points in the United States. Transportation improvements and technological developments dramatically improved travel time between 1800 and 1830.

Maryland. Between 1830 and 1833, a rail line between Charleston and Hamburg, South Carolina, used steam-powered locomotives to transport hundreds of passengers along the world's longest run of track. These relatively small beginnings would inspire a later era of growth in industry and transportation (Map 10.1).

Transportation advances also improved communication. Congress created the U.S. Postal System in 1789, and by the 1820s it delivered mail along nearly 2,500 postal routes. Increased business activity led to even faster growth: 5,000 post offices opened across the United States between 1819 and 1832. Although Americans used the postal service unevenly in different locations, the mail provided an important means for both private and public communication. A letter could cost as much as 25 cents to mail, but newspapers could be sent for only 1.5 cents. The mails also carried political pamphlets, and advances in papermaking meant that they could be printed more cheaply. Business documents also traveled through the mail and made market connections across great distance possible.

STUDY QUESTIONS FOR THE MARKET SYSTEM

1. In what ways were the market changes in the U.S. economy between 1789 and 1832 revolutionary?

quiz

2. What role did transportation play in U.S. economic development in this period?

MARKETS AND SOCIAL RELATIONSHIPS

In addition to changes in technology and transportation, the transition to a capitalist market economy in the United States also changed the ways that people related to one another in families, workplaces, and neighborhoods. When the magazine *North American Review* considered in 1832 "the influence of machinery . . . and its effects on society" in the market economy, it had to pause to ask, "Is this influence . . . good or evil?" As with any huge change in an economic system, individuals felt the effects unevenly and experienced them in ways that defy simple description. Journeymen or agricultural laborers, who might have once counted on advancing to shop or farm ownership, now often found themselves working permanently for wages. Patterns of labor on farms and in households changed the relationships between husbands and wives, children, and hired help. Enslaved people, who both provided labor and were defined as commodities, also saw themselves subject to market forces.

Manufacturing and the Factory System

The **factory system** of production, one of the biggest economic innovations, radically changed the ways that workers related to business owners and to one another. The factory system referred to the centralization of manufacturing under the ownership of one person or a corporation. Instead of manufacturing goods in homes or in small family-owned workshops, the factory system brought together many unrelated workers under one roof. Instead of working for master craftsmen in a hierarchical system, factory workers labored for wages in defined jobs—usually concentrating on one aspect of production. The factory system did not have to include the widespread use of machines; it was more about ownership and the organization of labor. But as U.S. factories developed, they also became mechanized.

British textile manufacturing firms instituted the factory system in the 1770s, and as Americans turned their attention to domestic production by the 1790s, they became interested in this system. The transition from home work to factory work took place slowly at first, but several early New England industries, including textile mills, shoemaking, and clock making, began to centralize production as they also adopted mechanization. By the 1830s, the factory system had spread to other industries.

In 1790, British immigrant Samuel Slater and wealthy American merchant **Moses Brown** founded the first mechanized cotton mill in the United States in Pawtucket, Rhode Island. By 1793, Slater and Brown had expanded into a larger factory on the Blackstone River, where they housed 1,500 water-powered spindles under one roof. The women wageworkers at Slater's mills used spinning skills they had developed at home and applied them in an industrial setting. The operations also employed children as spinners and men as mechanics. Initially, Slater marketed cloth that was produced partially in workers' homes. Slater and his associates, spreading throughout New England in the 1790s and early 1800s, founded scores of additional mechanized mill operations. By 1810, 31 mechanized mills were operating in the United States, most in Rhode Island or near Philadelphia. The Boston Associates, a corporation formed by wealthy men, including Samuel Cabot Lowell and Nathaniel Appleton, raised the stakes in 1814 when they founded their mill operation in Waltham, Massachusetts. The Boston Associates started their mills with a capital investment of $400,000, almost 10 times Slater and Brown's first

SPINNING MILL   Samuel Slater founded the first successful mechanized spinning mill in North America in Pawtucket, Rhode Island, in 1790. Water-powered mills such as Slater's soon spread across southern New England, changing employment patterns in the region and fueling the Industrial Revolution.

investment, and they centralized all aspects of cloth production under one roof. In an effort to manufacture mass-produced cloth and to capture market share, the Waltham mill owners introduced a labor system that was different from the British model adopted by Slater. They recruited young farm women, who provided the bulk of their mill work and lived in company-controlled boarding houses at the mill. The boarding houses enforced strict rules of conduct both on and off the factory floor. Most of these young "Mill Girls" viewed wage work as temporary, until they could marry and return to farming. The mills paid relatively high wages, but the work was difficult—with one woman in charge of 128 fast-moving spindles or two power looms. The Boston Associates mills were so profitable that they soon established company towns at Lowell, Chicopee, and Lawrence, Massachusetts, and Manchester, New Hampshire. By the mid-1830s, when the "Mill Girls" began to be replaced by a more permanent class of immigrant workers, the boarding houses became less important and relative wages dropped. But the mills continued to influence the character of life in New England into the 20th century.

1851 timetable for the Lowell Mills

Whether in a mill town or in a town like Lynn, Massachusetts, where hundreds of families manufactured shoes, workers saw their lives changed by the advent of the factory system. Working conditions were generally better than they were in British textile cities such as Manchester and Barmen, where poverty, malnutrition, and disease were

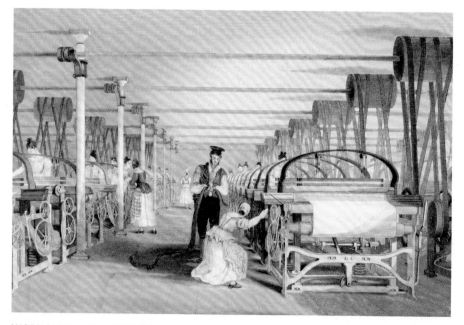

WORK FLOOR OF A COTTON MILL   This engraving of the work floor of a cotton mill shows the power looms at work weaving cloth. Note the gendered division of labor: women operate the looms, while the sole visible man repairs the leather straps that used water power to run the looms. Working on a factory floor like this in the 1830s was a huge change in atmosphere from home textile production.

rampant. Even for people accustomed to hard work, however, labor in mechanized factories posed challenges. As mill worker Lucy Davis explained it, "The work was much harder than I expected and quite new to me." Factory work was often unsafe, and by the 1830s working conditions had deteriorated as work sped up. It is no coincidence that the first widespread strikes and forms of labor resistance accompanied the rise of the factory system. Instead of being defined primarily by family relationships, workers began to see themselves in terms of their labor—now a marketplace commodity as much as butter, clocks, or cloth.

Slavery and Markets

The burgeoning capitalist market economy also held deep consequences for enslaved people, who did not own their own labor and who were regarded as market commodities to be bought, sold, and traded. Slavery had for centuries played a vital role in the transatlantic market economy, and slaves provided the labor for many of the raw materials for factories in the United States and in Great Britain. As cotton agriculture intensified between 1789 and 1832, slaves played an increasing role in the market economy, although some historians argue that the southern economy itself resisted a full integration into capitalism. As commodities, slaves were bought and traded in large open-air slave markets in most southern cities. One master wrote in Louisiana in 1818, "Negroes will yield a much larger income than any Bank dividends" (Map 10.2).

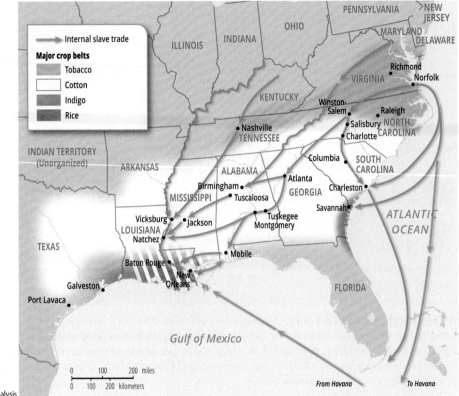

map analysis

MAP 10.2 The Antebellum Slave Economy This map depicts the internal slave trade that continued after Congress outlawed the international trade in 1808 and also depicts some illegal trade that continued with Cuba. Note the location of staple crops that relied on slave labor.

This market logic helped to intensify the racism that increasingly defined all African American lives. Newspapers across the country advertised slaves for sale alongside agricultural produce, manufactured items, luxury goods, and livestock. After the expansion of the cotton economy in Alabama, Mississippi, and Louisiana, the internal slave trade followed the demand for cotton, and in the 1820s, 155,000 slaves were sold into those areas from other states. Some estimates indicate that the domestic slave trade comprised as much as 15 percent of the southern economy. Each sale of an enslaved person represented the rupture of a family and the misery of countless individuals who lived in the slave system. Charles Ball, who escaped from slavery and became an anti-slavery activist, wrote in his autobiography of "the horrors" of being sold away from his family at the age of four. He described how many slaves never recovered from the "shock" of the "sudden and overwhelming ruin" of their families.

Class

Free workers came to be defined as members of a working class. The concept of economic and social class includes a variety of different factors. The relationship of workers

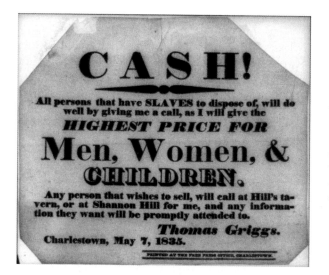

SLAVE TRADER'S ADVERTISEMENT This advertisement for the services of a slave trader in Charlestown, now Charleston, South Carolina, was typical throughout the South up until the 1860s. Enslaved people were advertised for sale and for rent as commodities alongside agricultural and trade goods.

image analysis

to capital helped to create the economic power structures that divided people by class. Social class also contributed to the feelings of affinity and connection that people in different strata of society developed with one another in opposition to those of lower or higher rank. But class never developed in a vacuum apart from race and gender, and people developed multiple identities simultaneously. These identities were shaped by daily activities and relationships.

As the breakdown of the artisan system relegated more Americans to the ranks of permanent wage earners, many workers felt an increasing identification with fellow workers across different trades and industries. Although the United States had a more equal income distribution than Europe, the divide between rich and poor grew significantly.

Wealthy planters, professionals, western landowners, and industrialists all displayed their earnings in the consumption of luxury goods and housing. Emerging middle-class Americans—such as tradesmen, clerks, and housewives—also had access to a growing array of consumer goods such as clothing, furniture, and imported housewares that reinforced their sense of refinement. Middling Americans tended to live in modest-sized houses but to decorate them more elaborately than poorer workers could. If the factory did not provide housing, many factory workers rented rooms in boarding houses, where they might lodge with relatives or other workers.

One sign of working-class identification came when workers began to band together to strike against their employers. After journeyman shoemakers organized one of the first labor protests in American history in 1806, they were prosecuted for conspiracy, but nonetheless strikes became more common. Boarding house life at the Lowell textile mills bred a sense of "sisterhood" among the workers there that reinforced the women's decision to strike in the late 1820s for better working conditions, hours, and pay. Large-scale labor movements would wait for the acceleration of the industrial economy after the Civil War, but they grew from the roots planted by workers who organized during the early years of the factory system.

Urban and Rural Life

The differences among social classes were on display most clearly in the American cities that grew dramatically between 1789 and 1832. The U.S. Census recorded that just 201,655 people lived in cities in 1790—5.1 percent of the population. By 1830, however, the number had grown to 1,127,247—8.8 percent of the population. New York was the largest city in the country in 1830, with just over 200,000 residents, but the next largest city, Baltimore, was less than half that size. No American city was as grand or well developed as London, Amsterdam, Mexico City, Cairo, or Beijing, but American cities were growing fast and assuming a greater role in U.S. culture, politics, and the economy.

Just as in Europe, cities most connected to markets and manufacturing experienced the fastest growth. Cities energized by the market revolution—including New York, Philadelphia, Charleston, Cincinnati, Baltimore, New Orleans, and St. Louis—each developed a flavor of urban culture that mixed popular entertainment, vice, religion, and trade. Social reformers worried that young, unattached men caused upheaval in the city—especially in New York, where young men joined raucous street gangs and fire companies. Writer George Foster wrote that northern cities were "infested with a set of the most graceless vagabonds and unmitigated ruffians." Housing in U.S. cities grew increasingly segregated by class and race, but city streets constituted one of the major sites of social mixing on a day-to-day basis.

Rural economies also expanded, even as family remained the dominant social and economic unit in the experience of the vast majority of Americans. In the first half of the 19th century, economic growth relied on rural agricultural production in both Europe and the United States, and a high rate of rural mobility enhanced economic opportunity. The growth of larger towns also energized rural areas. The trading post and steamboat stop of Madison, Indiana, for example, grew from a few hundred residents in 1812 to well over a thousand by 1830. Towns like Madison housed the mills, markets, and shops that fueled the growth of both rural and urban capitalism. Networks of rural families engaged in trade and, with increasing frequency, market transactions.

STUDY QUESTIONS FOR MARKETS AND SOCIAL RELATIONSHIPS

1. Why did the shift to wage work change the relationship between workers and bosses?
2. How did the market economy affect urban and rural areas differently?

quiz

◎ DEMOCRACY AND THE PUBLIC SPHERE

Alongside the rise in the market economy, by the 1820s, U.S. political life had grown more democratic than ever before. Democratization spread political power to new groups, especially to poor white men who had never held much direct power in American public life. But political rights were also carefully proscribed, and the consolidation of political power in the hands of white men that had begun in the 1790s and that excluded women, African Americans, and Indians picked up speed. The spread of communications and expanded opportunities for participation in political rituals like Fourth of July parades—especially in growing cities—also meant that a wider group of men and women had a chance to influence public life, even if they had little direct power. The ability to debate, celebrate, and influence political life in this expanded "public sphere" developed in the United States just as voting gained importance and politicians had to place new emphasis on persuading the public to support them.

Voting and Politics

The U.S. Constitution guaranteed a representative government, but it had left voting regulation to the states. After 1800, voting took on added importance in U.S. life, and participation in politics became one of the hallmarks of American democracy. At the turn of the 19th century, American leaders still expected deference from common people, and politicians could be criticized for campaigning too vigorously on their own behalf. During the 1800 presidential election, a New York Federalist newspaper sniped that Aaron Burr "stoop[ed] so low as to visit every corner in search of voters"— implying that his electioneering betrayed him as unworthy of political trust and power. The Democratic-Republican victory in that election simultaneously expanded efforts to widen voting rights for white men.

Once the Federalist Party, associated with social elites, died out after the War of 1812, the expansion of white male suffrage took off. No new state admitted to the union after 1815 required property for white men to vote. Even though Congress in the 1780s had set high property-holding requirements for voting in western territories, after the turn of the century Congress removed most impediments to white male voting. A revised Massachusetts state constitution ratified in 1820 removed a religious test and property requirements for white male voters, and New York followed suit in 1821. By 1824, virtually all white men in the United States were eligible to vote, although several states, notably South Carolina and Virginia, resisted removing property requirements until decades later.

Black men saw their voting rights constrict in the same era. The 1821 New York constitution, which expanded white male suffrage, retained property requirements for black male voters. Every state admitted to the union after 1819, with the exception of Maine, disenfranchised black men altogether. By 1830, the Jacksonian Democrats, the chief proponents of universal white male suffrage, had lost the support of propertied African American men who could vote in northern states.

Even though race proscribed voting rights, by 1828 vastly more American men possessed voting rights than men in other countries worldwide. Even France and many countries in Latin America—which had undergone revolutions similar to that in the United States—did not spread the franchise as widely. Great Britain reserved voting for men who held large quantities of property, and even many middle-class white men could not cast ballots there. Even after the Reform Bill of 1832 liberalized British voting rights, far more U.S. men were eligible to vote. The focus on suffrage as a fundamental right and an important factor in U.S. politics also energized voter turnout, which soared to 57 percent in the 1828 presidential election. Voting now also influenced presidential selection more directly than it had previously. In 1800, only two states chose their members of the electoral college by popular vote, but by 1832, only South Carolina did not.

Election of 1824

The emphasis on white men's voting rights changed the character of the 1824 presidential election, as the old Democratic-Republican Party came apart—the victim of its own success. Newly energized local participatory politics led state conventions to nominate presidential candidates—all of whom were Democrats but who differed in political outlook. By the fall of 1824, the four leading candidates were Treasury Secretary **William Crawford**, Secretary of State John Quincy Adams, Speaker of the House Henry Clay, and war hero Andrew Jackson. Crawford and Jackson, from Georgia and Tennessee, respectively, enjoyed strong southern support, whereas Kentuckian Henry Clay drew support from the West. John Quincy Adams locked up New England. Jackson had long clashed with both Adams and Crawford, but he was an even stronger nemesis of Clay's—especially because Clay had criticized Jackson's actions in the Seminole War. Crawford, who had the support of **Martin Van Buren** and his highly organized faction of New York "Bucktail" Democrats, emerged as the early front-runner in the race, but a stroke left his health impaired and hurt his chances.

Andrew Jackson received 42 percent of the popular vote, which was recorded for the first time, as opposed to 33 percent for Adams and 13 percent for both Clay and Crawford. But when the electoral college met, no candidate emerged with the clear majority demanded by the Constitution: Jackson got 99 electoral votes, Adams got 84, Crawford earned 42, and Clay received 37. The Twelfth Amendment to the Constitution (1804) stipulated that the House of Representatives would decide the election from among the top three candidates—and as Crawford's health deteriorated, the race boiled down to Jackson and Adams.

HENRY CLAY Clay, a longtime congressman, was Speaker of the House during the contested presidential election of 1824. Clay's support in the House helped John Quincy Adams win the election, and his rival Andrew Jackson claimed the two men had struck a "corrupt bargain" after Adams appointed Clay as secretary of state in 1825.

Each state delegation in the House received one vote, and Henry Clay—as Speaker of the House—exercised great influence over the election he had just lost. In January, Clay met with Adams. When Congress convened in February, Clay supported Adams, who was then elected president, even though Andrew Jackson had won more popular and more electoral college votes. Jacksonians accused Clay and Adams of striking a "corrupt bargain" to elect Adams. The election splintered the Democratic-Republican Party and set the stage for a dramatic comeback by Jackson in 1828.

John Quincy Adams

John Quincy Adams, who had been a powerful and successful secretary of state under President Monroe, served one largely unsuccessful term as president. In his inaugural address, he announced that "the will of the people" should be the guide "of all legitimate government upon earth," but throughout his term he fell prey to the very "collisions of party spirit" that he pledged to avoid. Adams championed many of Henry Clay's "American System" infrastructure and economic policies, but Congress blocked his proposals for a bankruptcy law and plans to bolster public credit through the Second Bank of the United States. Adams was ridiculed as elitist for proposing to fund scientific education and a national astronomical study. Adams appropriated federal funds for road and canal-building projects, but he had less success when promoting the program of high trade tariffs of Clay's American System. The vote of Vice President **John C. Calhoun** defeated an 1827 bill to raise the trade tax on woolen cloth. Calhoun renounced his previous support of Clay and Adams when he decided trade taxes would hurt his native South Carolina. Calhoun's critique of a broad 1828 trade tax, dubbed the "Tariff of Abominations," helped to solidify his and Jackson's opposition to the "National Republicans," as the Adams–Clay wing of the Democratic Party had become known. Adams even lost the upper hand in foreign policy. He was roundly criticized for his willingness to participate in a Panama conference on North and South American solidarity proposed by Simón Bolívar in 1826.

Andrew Jackson, "The People," and the Election of 1828

Andrew Jackson spent most of John Quincy Adams's term renewing his own campaign for the election of 1828, and Adams's own sitting vice president, John C. Calhoun, became Jackson's running mate. Losing the 1824 election, despite receiving the majority of popular votes, convinced Jackson that democratic suffrage was vital to the health of the republic. In the 1828 campaign, he took his appeal directly to the people. Martin Van Buren, the savvy New York politician who pioneered modern political electioneering, orchestrated a campaign to attract votes, promoting Jackson as a war hero and dubbing him "Old Hickory"—a strong leader who wouldn't break under pressure. The Democrats also organized conventions and public campaign events. Adams and the National Republicans largely rejected the new campaigning, although both sides viciously attacked one another in newspapers. Jackson won the election by a landslide: he got 56 percent of the popular vote and 68 percent of the electoral vote.

Jackson's ascendency benefited from the tensions in society created by the market revolution. Jackson was a wealthy plantation owner by the time he was elected president, but he cultivated the image of a backwoods commoner and expressed commitment to democratic equality, at least among white men. Jackson did not endorse any of the labor-oriented workingmen's (or "Workey") third parties that sprang up in the 1820s and early 1830s, but he did oppose the use of government power to advance the interests of the moneyed few. Much of Jackson's democratic appeal was based on his personal presence, and when he threw open the White House to "the people" for his inauguration in March 1829, hundreds flooded in to greet him. One newspaper wrote, "It was a proud day for the people. . . . General Jackson is *their own* president." In his inaugural address, Jackson thanked the "free people" for choosing him as president and promised them "accountability" as he undertook the "task of reform" of American government.

Jackson and the Veto

Jackson had ample opportunity to put his beliefs in reform, limited government, and direct democracy into action during his first term as president. Many of Jackson's efforts centered around putting men loyal to him in power and alienating those who opposed him. By the middle of his first term, Jackson had gathered around him a "kitchen cabinet" of informal advisors composed of loyal politicians, including Secretary of State Martin Van Buren, Attorney General **Roger B. Taney**, and Senators **Thomas Hart Benton** and **James K. Polk**. Others, including Vice President Calhoun, who secretly worked to bolster South Carolina's opposition to federal trade tariffs, found themselves alienated from Jackson and all but excluded from power. Jackson positioned himself as the protector of "the people" who would wield his presidential veto to protect them from Congress.

As part of this reform program, Jackson challenged the American System both as it had been enacted during Adams's presidency and as it continued to be championed by Henry Clay. In Jackson's first annual message to Congress, he declared, "Every member of the Union . . . will be benefited by the improvement of inland navigation and the construction of highways in the several states," but he also warned that such projects should be funded by the states because federal action may not be "warranted by the Constitution." In the spring of 1830, Congress voted to invest $150,000 in a turnpike company that sought to improve 64 miles of road across Kentucky from Lexington to Maysville. Arguing that he could not allow federal expenditure on a road built within one state, Jackson vetoed the **Maysville Road Bill**. He subsequently vetoed other road-building projects. The Maysville Road and other vetoes hastened the division of national politics into pro- and anti-Jacksonian camps—even as Jackson won the support of an increasing number of average voters, who liked his antielitist tone.

Jackson took an even harder line against the Second Bank of the United States (BUS), the financial source for much of the investment in the American System. Jackson had long been suspicious of centralized banking—indeed, of most banking—and he viewed the BUS as a "hydra of corruption" that manipulated the paper currency market, benefited elites, and suppressed the financial hopes of common Americans. Jackson's position against the BUS gained him support from average people harmed by bank-induced inflation and from many state officials who supported local banks. Jackson feared that the BUS might have "power to control the Government" and that it benefited "a few Monied Capitalists." The bank legitimately raised the credit of the U.S. government and the stability of the U.S. economy, but Jackson styled it as a political enemy.

Although the congressional charter of the BUS did not expire until 1836, its president, **Nicholas Biddle**, applied for renewal in January 1832, and Congress passed a new charter in June of that year. President Jackson quickly vetoed the charter and sent a message to Congress declaring that the BUS was unconstitutional (notwithstanding the Supreme Court's contrary decision decades earlier). Biddle fought back by opposing Jackson's reelection that fall. Jackson installed his staunch supporter Roger B. Taney as treasury secretary. Taney removed federal deposits from the BUS and chose to do federal banking with smaller state banks instead. Biddle continued to fight by contracting credit, but the bank was never rechartered, and it died after 1836. Jackson's strength in the "Bank War" effectively killed centralized federal banking in the United States until the 20th century. Jackson cemented his democratic reputation by declaring, "It is to be regretted that the rich and powerful too often bend the acts of government to their selfish purposes."

STUDY QUESTIONS FOR DEMOCRACY AND THE PUBLIC SPHERE

1. What factors contributed to the expansion of white male suffrage by the 1820s?
2. In what ways and by what means did Andrew Jackson harness anxieties over the market economy to his political advantage?

quiz

ECONOMIC OPPORTUNITY AND TERRITORIAL EXPANSION

The culture of economic growth pushed some U.S. citizens to expand farther into western territories during the era of the market revolution. One settler remembered that when she first came to St. Louis in 1817, "it was a small place, the population not exceeding fifteen hundred, and four brick buildings," but after 1820, "emigrants began to pour in from all parts, . . . bringing with them wealth and enterprise." As U.S. citizens populated western territories in the Louisiana Purchase and beyond, they constantly looked for new resources and new trade opportunities. Some, pushing beyond U.S. boundaries, even sought to establish colonies in Mexico or to conquer Indian territory, bringing greater conflict.

Texas Colonization

Moses Austin was typical of many Americans who saw booms and busts and moved west during the market revolution. In 1798, Austin established the first American settlement in Missouri at Potosi—named after a massive Bolivian silver mine—where he built up a substantial fortune in lead mining and smelting. After losing much of his fortune when the Bank of St. Louis, which he cofounded, failed during the Panic of 1819, Austin decided to seek a new fortune in Spanish territory. Looking for opportunity in Texas—a northern province of Mexico—Austin pushed his business horizons further than most entrepreneurs. Moses, and his son **Stephen Austin**, would become the most important among several founders of private colonies in Texas. Texas colonization set the stage for decades of conflict between the United States and Mexico and eventually led to the Mexican-American War.

Moses Austin died of pneumonia shortly after securing permission to found a settlement in Texas from Spain's royal governor in San Antonio in December 1820. Stephen Austin took up the plan to settle 300 families along the Brazos River. The (now independent) Mexican government of Agustín de Iturbide decided that inviting settlers into sparsely populated Texas would strengthen frontier defenses and provide a bulwark against the United States. Such colonization efforts were common in Latin America during the 19th century, but Mexico's reliance on Anglo-Americans marked a different path.

Over the next several years Stephen Austin received additional grants, and he was the most successful of the *empresarios*, colonization agents who headed private colonies whom the Mexican government had granted permission to start Texas settlements. Austin wanted to integrate his territory into international markets. He attracted over 1,200 families to his lands, and many of them established profitable ranches and farms. Austin and the other *empresarios* remained largely independent throughout the late 1820s, as they appointed their own civil authorities and conducted raids against Krankawa and Tonkawa Indians.

Although Mexican authorities frowned on it, Austin allowed settlers to bring slaves into Texas as long as they were officially classified as indentured servants. When the Mexican government outlawed slavery in Texas in 1830, Austin garnered an exception for his own colonists. Slaves comprised 10–15 percent of the Texas population by 1835. Most of the 10,000 Anglo-American settlers in Texas in 1830 arrived from the southern United States, and they held onto their Protestant religion despite mandatory pledges to become Catholic. Many prominent Tejanos who lived near the Anglo colonies engaged in ranching and trade with the colonists, even though Anglos outnumbered them by 1830. After 1831, when new Mexican governments began to raise taxes and to exert stronger control over Texas, tensions between Mexican officials and Anglo and Tejano settlers quickly rose.

Santa Fe Trail

Texas was not the only contact point between the United States and Mexico that touched the international market economy. Between the 1790s and 1830s, the Santa Fe Trail facilitated the growth of New Mexico as a major outpost of international trade (Map 10.3). By 1810, New Mexico had emerged as an important trade site in northern New Spain after the Spanish subdued Comanche and Apache in the area and a network of Chihuahua merchants established commercial traffic. Following Mexican independence in 1821, Americans entered the New Mexico trade when **William Becknell** led a group of traders from Missouri across Plains Indian trails to Santa Fe. With little investment, Becknell's group realized a 2,000 percent profit by selling cotton cloth, iron hardware, and other manufactured goods to Indian and Spanish inhabitants. In 1822, Becknell began to lead wagon trains between Missouri and New Mexico.

The Santa Fe Trail quickly became a lucrative trade route between the United States and Mexico. By 1825, the U.S. government had surveyed the Santa Fe Trail and secured treaties with Kansas and Osage people, allowing commercial traffic across

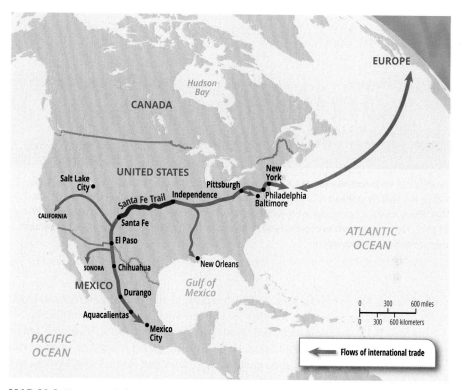

MAP 10.3 Texas and the Santa Fe Trail, c. 1830 In the 1820s, greater numbers of Americans were drawn to the Southwest to trade along the Santa Fe Trail or to settle in the Mexican colonies of Texas. The Santa Fe Trail linked up major international trade networks.

their lands. Plains Indians disagreed about the validity of treaties allowing U.S. trade across their lands, and American traders complained that some Osage were still "lurking about the main pass way—seeking whom they may rob or murder." In 1829, President Jackson authorized U.S. infantry troops to escort shipments of U.S. goods. Despite Indian objections and high Mexican trade tariffs, both Mexican and U.S. traders regularly earned 40–100 percent profits in the Santa Fe trade. Traders' reports published in U.S. newspapers, pamphlets, and magazines piqued American interest in New Mexico and California.

Covered wagons on the Santa Fe Trail

The Black Hawk War

In the Old Northwest, the competition between Indians and Americans for resources was even fiercer, and instead of establishing trade, the United States moved to push Indians off their land. Between 1800 and 1820, American settlers streamed into Illinois, which became a state in 1818. The white population grew to over 55,000. In northwestern Illinois, Sac and Fox Indians retained land where they farmed and mined lead, despite a dubious 1804 treaty in which some representatives agreed that their tribes would move west of the Mississippi River. In the decades following the War of 1812, they were

BATTLE OF BAD AXE RIVER, 1832 This painting depicts the 1832 Battle of Bad Axe River, where Sac and Fox followers of Black Hawk were brutally defeated, ending the Black Hawk War. Black Hawk, a Sac leader who had fought with Tecumseh's multitribal forces in the War of 1812, led a movement to reclaim land in Illinois in 1832, but the defeat and his subsequent capture ended the movement.

pushed across the river into Iowa Indian territory, as the federal government issued leases to lead miners, who then invaded Sac and Fox land in northwestern Illinois.

In May 1832, the Sac leader **Black Hawk**, who had fought with Tecumseh's multitribal forces against the United States in the War of 1812, returned to Illinois with hundreds of Sac, Fox, and Kickapoo people. Black Hawk had clashed with **Keokuk** and other Sac and Fox leaders who favored accommodation to U.S. terms. The governor of Illinois, John Reynolds, called out the militia to drive Black Hawk's people out of the state. When Black Hawk tried to surrender, the militia fired on him, but Indian warriors fought them off. Secretary of War **Lewis Cass** ordered federal troops to reinforce the Illinois militia and some Sioux allies. The combined force, including future national leaders Zachary Taylor, Jefferson Davis, and Abraham Lincoln, pursued Black Hawk into Wisconsin territory. An August battle at the Bad Axe River ended with most of Black Hawk's band (including women and children) being shot, despite the display of a white surrender flag. Black Hawk himself sought refuge with Winnebago Indians, who subsequently turned him over to American authorities.

Excerpt from the Auto-biography of Ma-Ka-Tai-Me-She-Kia-Kiak, or BlackHawk (1833)

The treaties that ended the short Black Hawk War ceded additional Sac, Fox, and Winnebago land to the United States. After serving a year in prison, Black Hawk published a popular autobiography and toured the country, as most observers treated him as a symbol of what they believed to be a defeated and doomed Native American race. In the next decade, many Sac and Fox people would be removed farther west, as their economic prospects diminished.

STUDY QUESTIONS FOR ECONOMIC OPPORTUNITY AND TERRITORIAL EXPANSION

quiz

1. What factors drove Anglo colonization of Texas?

2. How was the market economy different in the West than in the Northeast and the Southeast?

⬇ EXPANDING MARKETS

In the 1820s and 1830s, market activity in the United States expanded even more rapidly than it had in the preceding decades, and the United States played an increasing role in the transoceanic world economy. The market economy that built up in the 1790s entered a new phase of development as it spread and enriched the United States. Although not yet on par with major world economic powers, the United States began to undergo its own version of the Industrial Revolution that was transforming western Europe. Although President Jackson and his opponents disagreed about funding for internal improvements, almost every U.S. politician supported economic development of some kind. Even organizations such as the New York Tract Society that argued against the evils of the market economy spread their message through mass-produced pamphlets and used the roads, mail systems, and technologies promoted by capitalist growth to get their message across. By 1830, the world of markets influenced the everyday lives of more and more Americans.

The Legal Structures of Capitalism

In the 1810s and early 1820s, the U.S. Supreme Court delivered several rulings that encouraged federal involvement in commerce and the rise of the business corporation—one of the major financial tools of capitalist development. John Marshall, a proponent of economic activity, guided decisions that encouraged capitalist development during the last years of his long tenure as chief justice. Between 1825 and 1835, however, Marshall's Supreme Court came under withering attacks by Jacksonian politicians who accused it of "judicial tyranny," claiming that the Court encouraged the same kind of elitist economic power as the Second Bank of the United States. Jackson was able to appoint three associate justices, who took an active role as Chief Justice Marshall became increasingly infirm in his old age. Although on the defensive, Marshall managed to promote the federal control of commerce, which he had advocated in 1824 in *Gibbons v. Ogden*. Marshall also wrote the opinion in *Craig v. Missouri* (1834), which invalidated a law that had allowed Missouri to issue its own paper money.

Excerpts from the majority opinion in *Gibbons v. Ogden*

When John Marshall died in 1835, Andrew Jackson seized the opportunity to put the Supreme Court firmly in the hands of his Democratic supporters. Jackson appointed his Maryland ally, Roger B. Taney, as chief justice in 1836, and the following year he was able to appoint two more justices, leaving the old Marshall nationalists in the minority. Although Taney supported economic development, he favored less federal intervention than Marshall had. Ruling in the 1837 case of *Charles River Bridge v. Warren Bridge*, Taney had the chance to make his legal mark early in his first term as chief justice. Writing for the majority, Taney ruled that the 1785 Massachusetts charter for the private Charles River Bridge had not guaranteed exclusive rights and that courts should not be overly involved in matters of economic development better left to state legislatures. Taney wrote that new technologies and transportation improvements should be allowed to take their course; as "the object and end of all government is to promote the happiness and prosperity of the community by which it is established," local governments would best know how to encourage growth. Taney's rival on the Court, Justice Joseph Story, wrote a blistering dissent charging that the decision allowed interference with sacred corporate rights. But Taney had deftly supported economic modernization while also preserving a narrow interpretation of federal power that pleased Democrats and helped to alienate the newly forming Whig Party.

Whaling

North American Native peoples, such as the Makah, hunted whales and other sea mammals in the Pacific Ocean for thousands of years before European contact. Colonial European settlers hunted Atlantic whales starting in the 17th century, but following the American Revolution, commercial whaling grew in scale. By the 1790s, U.S. vessels sailed all over the world in search of whales, which could be broken down into a variety of trade commodities: oil for lamps, bone stays for corsets and other clothing, and ivory. Between 1794 and 1803, U.S. whaling ships harvested between 3,000 and 12,000 tons of whales per year.

After the War of 1812, the industry began another huge expansion, with more and larger American ships traveling record distances around the world in search of whales. After 1818, American whalers shifted from mainly fishing off the coast of Peru, New Zealand, and Chile to taking advantage of concentrations of sperm whales in the central Pacific Ocean off the coast of Japan and in the Indian Ocean. British whalers dominated the North Atlantic, but Americans controlled other waters, where ice was less of an impediment to profitable fishing. By 1830, very large American whaling ships went to sea for as long as five years at a time and often sailed halfway around the world.

The American whaling industry was based on Nantucket Island, Massachusetts, until the early 1820s, when New Bedford, Massachusetts, became dominant. New Bedford's deeper port accommodated larger ships, and its connection to inland markets helped speed the trade of whale products. Before 1825, most crew members on American ships were American citizens, but after that date more sailors from the areas where whaling occurred began to appear on ship crew lists. New Bedford's population was filled with people from around the world who came to the United States on whaling vessels. By 1835, 35 different U.S. port cities launched whaling ships.

Whaling captains, whose wives often ran family trade businesses in port cities, frequently became wealthy from the products of whaling. Herman Melville, the author of whaling novel *Moby Dick*, wrote that the "lofty mansions" of New Bedford "came from the Atlantic, Pacific, and Indian Oceans. . . . [T]hey were harpooned and dragged up from the bottom of the sea." Average sailors, who performed difficult work breaking down and processing whales while they were still at sea, received wages commensurate to those of most textile workers, although skilled craftsmen might do well on an especially successful voyage. Whaling was very dangerous and financially risky work.

Whaling provided raw materials for scores of trade products and introduced Americans to important parts of the world—including Japan and Hawaii. Hawaiian ports

The Erie Canal

The completion of the Erie Canal indicated just how state governments could invest in the growth of the market economy. When the federal government refused to participate in the project to connect Lake Erie to the Atlantic, New York State funded it entirely. New York governor **DeWitt Clinton** ceremonially broke ground for the project in 1817. Detractors, who doubted the value of the project, dubbed the canal "Clinton's

WHALING   This engraving shows whalers trying to take a whale in the Arctic Ocean and dramatizes the danger, a common theme in visual depictions of whaling. Small parties set out from the main whaling ship to harpoon the whale, but one boat is overturned, plunging the sailors into the icy water. The upended boat flies the American flag.

hosted over 100 whaling ships in 1820 alone. Whaling and its transoceanic reach also influenced American culture, as writers such as Herman Melville and popular-culture depictions of sailors made a mark on the public mind. Whales and their by-products became one of the most important engines of capitalist development—by the middle of the 19th century, whaling was the fifth-largest industry in the United States.

1851 whale chart

- Why do you think American culture was so fascinated with whaling if it was just another capitalist industry?
- Compare and contrast how whaling and butter making contributed to the growth of the market economy.

Big Ditch." Defying critics, the canal was completed in less than 10 years. At the opening of the Erie Canal in 1825, Clinton poured a ceremonial cask of Lake Erie water into the Atlantic Ocean and declared, "May the God of Heavens and the Earth smile . . . and render it subservient to the best interests of the human race."

The Erie Canal was one of the world's largest canals at the time, and it contained several impressive feats of engineering—largely constructed by Irish immigrant

interactive timeline

TIMELINE 1789–1832

AMERICA	YEAR	THE WORLD
Samuel Slater immigrates to United States from England **Jul** Congress passes first tariff in the United States **Sep** Congress creates U.S. Postal Service	**1789**	
Samuel Slater and Moses Brown found the first mechanized cotton mill in United States **Apr** Congress establishes U.S. Patent Office and 14-year monopolies on inventions **Aug** Congress votes to fund the U.S. national debt	**1790**	First rolling mill powered by steam in England
Alexander Hamilton sends report encouraging domestic manufacturing to Congress	**1791**	Paris Academy of Sciences standardizes metric system
Apr Congress establishes U.S. currency system	**1792**	
Jan Eli Whitney demonstrates interchangeable parts by assembling a musket from pieces selected from a pile by President Thomas Jefferson **May** Congress encourages U.S. settlement with favorable sales terms in Harrison Land Act	**1800**	Italian Alessandro Volta invents the electric storage battery
Treasury Secretary Albert Gallatin proposes a comprehensive plan of national canals and roads **Jul** Twelfth Amendment to Constitution is ratified	**1804**	
Frederic Tudor uses insulated ships to begin U.S. ice trade abroad	**1805**	
Aug Robert Fulton begins commercial steamboat service on the Hudson River	**1807**	British colonies of Sierra Leone and Gambia founded **Mar** British ejected from Alexandria, Egypt
Oliver Evans installs first steam-powered flour mill in Pittsburgh **Mar** Supreme Court decides in *Fletcher v. Peck* that contracts are sacred and that Court can overrule state laws	**1810**	Hidalgo's "Grito de Dolores" launches Mexican independence war Frenchman François Appert invents canning process to preserve food
	1811	Workers in the Luddite movement riot and destroy textile machinery British suffrage activists found Hampden Clubs
Boston Associates incorporate their mill business in Waltham, Massachusetts	**1814**	Two-sided cylindrical printing press invented in Germany *London Times* begins publication using steam press

laborers. The 363-mile-long, four-foot-deep canal contained aqueducts and locks that allowed traffic to flow smoothly over ravines and rivers, and it could carry boats each loaded with 50 tons of freight pulled by horses or mules walking alongside the canal. The canal also carried steamboats and passenger traffic. Each of the cities along the canal—Buffalo, Rochester, Syracuse, Utica, and Albany—experienced exponential growth and quickly became a commercial center. Moreover, the canal ensured that New York City would continue to grow as the major U.S. Atlantic trading port. One contemporary commentator noted that what "Europe already begins to admire, America can never forget to acknowledge, that they have built the longest canal in the world in the least time, with the least experience, for the least money, and to the greatest public

AMERICA	YEAR	THE WORLD
Jul Construction on Erie Canal begins	**1817**	British workers riot for higher wages in Derbyshire **Sep** Spain opens West Indies to British trade
May Vessel *Savannah* uses backup steam power to cross Atlantic	**1819**	British establish colony at Singapore Parliament passes maximum 12-hour workday for children in Britain
Congress sets minimum price of $1.25 for sale of public lands	**1820**	
William Becknell opens trade from Missouri to New Mexico on Santa Fe Trail **Sep** Russia claims exclusive settlement rights in Alaska	**1821**	Costa Rica wins independence **Mar** Greek war of independence begins
Mar Supreme Court decides case of *Gibbons v. Ogden* **Dec** When electoral college reveals its votes, no presidential candidate receives a majority	**1824**	Joseph Aspdin patents Portland cement in England
Feb House of Representatives elects John Quincy Adams president **Mar** President Adams appoints Henry Clay as secretary of state, part of what their enemies dub "the corrupt bargain" **Jun** Britain cuts off U.S. trade to its colonies in the West Indies **Oct** Erie Canal is opened with great ceremony	**1825**	**Sep** First ever passenger railroad opens in England
May Congress passes a trade tax, called by opponents the "Tariff of Abominations" **Dec** Andrew Jackson is elected president South Carolina legislature protests "Tariff of Abominations"	**1828**	**Sep** Shaka, Zulu king, is assassinated
	1829	**Sep** Mexico outlaws slavery in Texas but exempts Stephen Austin's colony
Baltimore & Ohio Railroad becomes first U.S. railroad to carry passengers and freight Mexico forbids further colonization of Texas by American citizens	**1830**	English patent for push lawnmower issued
Cyrus McCormick builds first mechanical reaper, making crops much easier to harvest	**1831**	Scotswoman Jane Stewart invents hook-and-eye clothing fastener
Jan Second Bank of the United States president Nicholas Biddle begins the "Bank War" with President Jackson Sac and Fox Indians return to vacated lands in Illinois, touching off Black Hawk War **Aug** Black Hawk's Indians are destroyed in battle on Bad Axe River **Dec** Andrew Jackson reelected president	**1832**	First French passenger railroad opens

benefit." The Erie Canal quickly became a symbol of American economic prosperity and ingenuity.

The Industrial Revolution

Americans declared the Erie Canal to be the greatest in the world because they were increasingly interested in their place in the world economy. Any accomplishment that exceeded those of Europe seemed to be a special point of pride. As the Industrial Revolution in England rapidly expanded textile-producing towns, scores of agricultural workers moved from farm labor into factory work, and for the first time ever England

THE ERIE CANAL CELEBRATION This engraving by John Ludlow Morton and William H. Dougal shows the gathering of boats celebrating the 1825 completion of the Erie Canal, one of the most impressive engineering and transportation achievements in the world at the time. Note the range of international flags represented on the boats assembled to celebrate the connecting of Lake Erie to the Atlantic Ocean.

became a net importer of food products—many of them grown in the United States. In 1830, American workers enjoyed 40 percent higher wages than their counterparts in England. The global labor market seemed to favor colonies and former colonies, with American and Canadian factory workers earning higher wages than many comparable workers in Europe. The total American economy remained smaller than most in western Europe, even though the country expanded rapidly between 1789 and 1832.

As part of the early Industrial Revolution, Americans especially excelled at textile production because it combined their agricultural system, talent for mechanization, and the rapid adoption of new technologies. As one historian explained it, "The cotton industry . . . became in the process of development the great vehicle of a market economy." In 1831, the United States contained almost 700 textile firms that operated 1.2 million cotton spindles and 33,500 mechanized looms. The woolen industry was only one-quarter the size. Before 1830, France and England both consumed large quantities of American cotton, which fed European industrialization. Although working conditions in the United States were generally more comfortable than in England, the high level of child labor and the deteriorating conditions in some mills meant that greater labor woes would soon follow.

Thomas Carlyle, excerpts from "Signs of the Times" (1829)

The Industrial Revolution in England helped to transform world markets and increase the importance of wage labor and technology—and as the United States began an Industrial Revolution of its own, it contributed to the first capitalist global transformation. Both northern and southern American industries were enmeshed in international trade like never before. Southerners, using slave labor, grew cotton that fed mills in the northern United States and Britain, and they participated in systems of international credit, trade, and exchange. One historian has characterized Americans as playing a crucial role in the "pan-hemispheric plantation complex." Agriculture, fueled by market activity, continued to expand in all regions of the United States. Overall, U.S. exports grew from $20 million in 1790 to $82 million in 1832. Americans' role in the market economy also turned their attention to the wider world.

The simultaneous rise of democratic participation in politics by white men in the United States helped to divide political responses to the acceleration of the U.S. market economy. Even as the United States grew more democratic than ever before and was more democratic than most other nations, market forces intensified slavery, and many Americans were left out of democratic politics. Jacksonian Democrats—who walked a fine line between encouraging economic development, as they limited federal government, and touting the rights of the common man—faced a particularly challenging set of political choices as the economy continued to grow after 1830.

STUDY QUESTIONS FOR EXPANDING MARKETS

1. Where and for what reasons did Jacksonian Democrats and their opponents agree and disagree about "internal improvements"?

2. How were changes in the U.S. economy related to changes in U.S. politics between 1815 and 1832?

quiz

Summary

- Between 1789 and 1832, the United States underwent what some historians call a "market revolution," and a capitalist economy took shape.
- Economic changes and mechanization altered American social relationships.
- By the 1820s, U.S. politics were becoming increasingly democratic by opening up suffrage and political participation to almost all white men.
- U.S. citizens had economic interest in western territories—which led to open trade, colonization of Texas, and warfare with several Indian groups.
- By the 1820s and 1830s, the United States was part of a new system of world markets, especially influenced by the early Industrial Revolution in western Europe.

Key Terms and People

American System 332
Arkwright, Richard 335
Austin, Moses 349
Austin, Stephen 349
Becknell, William 350
Benton, Thomas Hart 348
Biddle, Nicholas 349
Black Hawk 352

Brown, Moses 339
Calhoun, John C. 347
Cass, Lewis 352
Clinton, DeWitt 354
Crawford, William 346
factory system 339
Fitch, John 336
Fulton, Robert 336

audio
flashcards

Reviewing Chapter 10

1. How did the market changes in the United States after 1789 continue economic developments that had begun during the colonial period?
2. How did the transformation to a market economy increase tensions between equality and inequality in U.S. society?
3. What were the most important global influences on the U.S. economy?

Further Reading

Beckert, Sven, and Seth Rockman, eds. *Slavery's Capitalism: A New History of American Economic Development*. Philadelphia: University of Pennsylvania Press, 2016. Beckert and Rockman have assembled this anthology of pieces by diverse historians to show the role of slavery in U.S. and global capitalism. Chapters also explore American connections to Brazil and the Caribbean.

Cole, Donald B. *The Presidency of Andrew Jackson*. Lawrence: University of Kansas Press, 1993. Cole argues that Jackson's personal anxieties reflected the anxious attitudes of Americans during the economic and social changes of the time in this very thorough history of Jackson's presidency that provides a lucid narrative of political events.

Deyle, Steven. *Carry Me Back: The Domestic Slave Trade in American Life*. New York: Oxford University Press, 2005. This book is an economic history of the domestic slave trade that developed after Congress outlawed the international slave trade in 1808. It shows how buying and selling slaves became an integral part of the U.S. domestic economy and involved thousands of individual slave owners in transactions that split up black families.

Dolin, Eric Jay. *Leviathan: The History of Whaling in America*. New York: W. W. Norton, 2007. This book charts over three hundred years of the history of American whaling. In addition to presenting gripping tales of whaling voyages, Dolin shows how whaling led to New England's economic growth and helped to connect the United States to the rest of the world through an extensive trade network.

Jensen, Joan. *Loosening the Bonds: Mid-Atlantic Farm Women, 1750–1850*. New Haven, CT: Yale University Press, 1986. This is the classic account of how mid-Atlantic farm women contributed to the growth of the U.S. market economy, especially through their dairying and butter-making activities.

America in the World
GOODS, IDEAS, PEOPLE

CHAPTER 10: Market Revolutions and the Rise of Democracy, 1789–1832

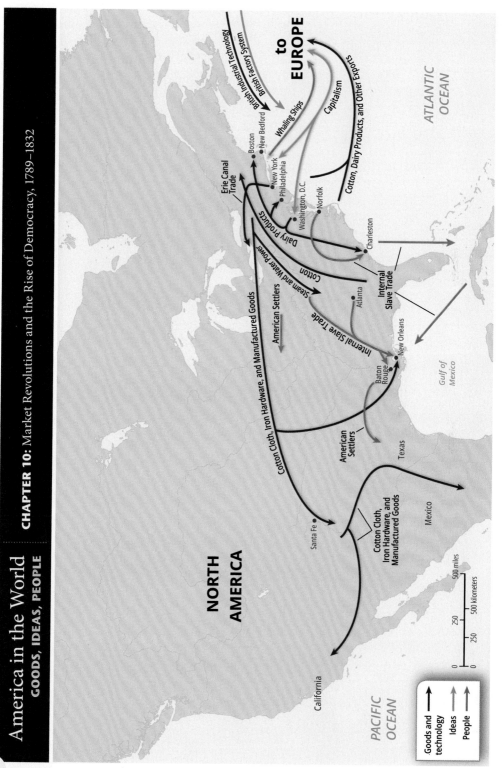

to **EUROPE**

British Industrial Technology

British Factory System

Whaling Ships

Capitalism

Cotton, Dairy Products, and Other Exports

ATLANTIC OCEAN

Boston

New Bedford

New York

Philadelphia

Erie Canal Trade

Washington, D.C.

Norfolk

Dairy Products

Charleston

Cotton

Steam and Water Power

American Settlers

Atlanta

Internal Slave Trade

Internal Slave Trade

New Orleans

Baton Rouge

American Settlers

Texas

Gulf of Mexico

Cotton Cloth, Iron Hardware, and Manufactured Goods

NORTH AMERICA

Santa Fe

Cotton Cloth, Iron Hardware, and Manufactured Goods

Mexico

California

PACIFIC OCEAN

0   250   500 miles

0   250   500 kilometers

Goods and technology

Ideas

People

map analysis

Emigrants Crossing the Plains by Albert Bierstadt, 1867.

New Boundaries, New Roles

n early 1836, reports surfaced in the United States that a mixed band of American and Mexican separatists had been killed down to the last man in the defense of an old mission compound in San Antonio, Texas, called the **Alamo**. Led by the Anglo Sam Houston and the Hispanic Lorenzo de Zavala, the Texas independence movement brought together a diverse group united by their opposition to receiving orders from remote Mexico City. Former Mississippi governor John A. Quitman led some of the many Americans who supported the independence movement. Quitman crossed the Sabine River into Mexico with 17 men and the confidence that he fought for freedom. "If I must die early, let me die with these brave fellows and for such a cause," he proclaimed. Quitman and his band joined Houston's army and helped Texas declare its independence from Mexico. U.S. president Andrew Jackson, serving out the last of his tumultuous eight years, did not interfere with Quitman or the other Americans who crossed the border to fight against Mexico, even though their actions clearly violated American neutrality laws.

Less than a year after Houston and de Zavala helped separate Texas from Mexico, a different American invasion generated a much different presidential response. In the wake of "Patriot Uprisings" in Upper and Lower Canada (today's Ontario and Quebec), Canadian rebels retreated across the U.S. border into northern cities such as Rochester, Buffalo, and Detroit. During 1837, thousands of Americans joined these Canadian separatists fighting the British, just as Americans had joined Texans fighting the Mexicans. In December 1837, the U.S.-born Rensselaer Van Rensselaer led a small group of men across the Niagara River to establish a beachhead for the return of a well-known Canadian rebel, but Jackson's successor as president, Martin Van Buren, dealt aggressively with this group of American adventurers. Van Buren issued a proclamation denouncing the actions, alerted customs agents and U.S. marshals along the border, and eventually sent General Winfield Scott to manage relations in the region. Despite the heavy military presence, Canadian patriots and their American supporters coordinated attacks along the border throughout the year. Pressed by armies on both sides, the men went underground in early 1838, but sporadic attacks occurred into 1841.

Neither the Texas nor the Canadian episodes received official government support, but Jackson's hands-off approach offered implicit support for the former. Mexico had only recently freed itself from Spanish control, and many Americans viewed it as a weak neighbor, ripe for American conquest. Texas independence angered the Mexicans, and America's harboring of Canadian rebels angered the British. In both situations, America negotiated solutions that demonstrated its rising status as a continental power but also one that remained loose at the seams.

AN EXPANDING NATION

In the aftermath of the War of 1812, the United States sought to extend its dominion over the vast western territory ceded by Britain. However, the land was still controlled by Native Americans. Even within Georgia—one of the original 13 colonies—the Cherokee and Creek nations maintained their homelands. West of the Mississippi, the United States claimed only a few military forts strung out across a vast expanse of plains and mountain territory controlled by a variety of Native nations. Other settlers also contested U.S. claims to the region. Mexico claimed the Southwest, which was home to tens of thousands of Spanish-speaking residents. Still, Anglo settlers pushed west, lured by the promise of land and other economic opportunities. At the same time, many other Americans moved against their will, including enslaved people moved from eastern states to the emerging cotton belt and eastern Indians forced to Indian territory. A growing population and a robust economy encouraged the United States to expand, but expansion created new problems. Military conflicts arose as settlers and explorers encountered people with existing claims to the land; political problems developed as leaders wrestled with whether the United States should follow the pattern of previous empires; and cultural conflicts grew as the country sought to incorporate people of widely different backgrounds into an already diverse nation.

The Trail of Tears

Strong Native communities stood opposed to the United States in the East as well. In the Southeast alone, the Cherokee, Choctaw, Chickasaw, Seminole, and Creek counted 75,000 members compared to 330,000 white people and 230,000 black people in the region in 1820. Illinois, Wisconsin, and Michigan likewise included large numbers of Native peoples. The state and federal governments worked sometimes in cooperation and other times at odds with each other to push Indians farther to the west. Andrew

Jackson came to the presidency strongly opposed to the presence of Indians in territory that could be profitably settled by whites and strongly opposed to the practice of the federal government negotiating with Indians as equals. As early as 1817, Jackson said that he had "long viewed treaties with the Indians [as] an absurdity." Born in the Carolina backcountry during the Revolutionary period, when Native peoples contested U.S. borders, Jackson matured in Tennessee when that state was still inhabited by them. From his earliest encounters, he developed a strong antagonism toward those he regarded as "blood thirsty barbarians." Jackson sought "to reclaim them [Indians] from their wandering habits and make them a happy, prosperous people," and as president he used the executive power to force this policy on Indians across the country. Most Anglo-Americans supported his policies.

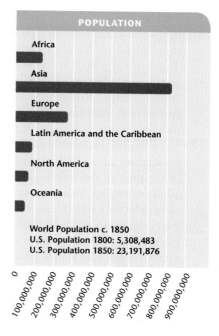

Jackson's most public battle with Indians resulted from the expulsion of Cherokee people from Georgia. According to the treaties passed between the tribe and the federal government, the good faith efforts of Cherokees to live peacefully and productively alongside their American

THE CHEROKEE REMOVAL The forced removal of Indians by the U.S. government created a demographic and historical catastrophe for Indian communities. Cherokee removal, represented here, began in the winter and imposed physical hardships as it alienated Indian people from their ancestral homelands.

neighbors ensured that they could retain their land and their autonomy. Indeed, the Cherokee Nation shared much with their American neighbors: they had a constitutional democracy, high rates of literacy, and an economy based on agriculture and ranching. But as new Anglo settlers generated conflicts, states and the federal government steadily increased pressure on Indians to sell their lands. The government of Georgia, where most Cherokee landholdings lay, harassed the tribe. After gold was discovered on Cherokee-controlled land in 1829, white miners flooded into the region. With their numbers nearing 10,000, they had the clout to convince state leaders to seek the complete expulsion of the tribe.

Following Jackson's lead, Congress passed the **Indian Removal Act of 1830**, which nullified 50 years' worth of treaties between the United States and Indian nations. The law committed the federal government to creating an Indian territory that included all of present-day Oklahoma as well as parts of Kansas and Nebraska and to moving Indians by force into this new region. Cherokees, well-educated and protective of their treaty rights, vigorously resisted. Cherokee leaders sought legal protection against Georgia laws that asserted authority over the tribe. In a series of seminal cases, the Supreme Court, led by Chief Justice John Marshall, declared the Cherokee and all other Indian tribes "domestic dependent nations." Marshall intended this description to establish the sovereignty of tribes over state governments, although still under the umbrella of the federal government. In the 1832 *Worcester v. Georgia* decision, the Court ruled against Georgia's claim that it held authority over the tribe, but the state and federal government ignored the ruling. Without recourse to the army, which could have protected Indian lands from settler encroachment, Marshall could not enforce the decision.

Under Georgia's protection, white settlers continued to move into Cherokee territory in the early 1830s. In 1835, the federal government negotiated a new treaty with a minority group of Cherokee. This new agreement exchanged all Cherokee claims to land in the East for claims in Indian territory and a cash settlement. When U.S. forces arrived in early 1838, few Cherokee had prepared for the trip, and soldiers rounded up and confined people over the summer. Contaminated water, inadequate food, and disease killed many of those restricted in stockades, and many more perished on the 800-mile journey west.

The Cherokees were one of many Indian nations forced to walk the "**Trail of Tears**." With the Indian Removal Act, the Jackson administration sought to force all eastern Indians west of the Mississippi. Most of them came from the Southeast, but there were many northern and midwestern peoples, including Delawares forced from Pennsylvania a century earlier, Potawatomis from the Great Lakes, and the Arkansas valley Osage. Altogether, 100,000 Indians were forced west, though about 20 percent died during removal. Those who survived faced daunting obstacles in Indian territory. The federal government failed to provide many communities with the rations promised in their removal treaties, and Native nations confronted an unfamiliar environment as well as hostile Plains tribes who still contested U.S. claims to the region (Map 11.1).

A Cherokee chief petitions the US government for justice (1840)

The blatant violation of property rights backed by clear title to the land worried many white citizens, even those who disliked Indians. Davy Crockett, the legendary frontiersman, lost his congressional seat for opposing Jackson's policy. The violence and trauma of the forced march to the new western lands created more political enemies for Jackson and a shameful legacy for the American government. Reformers, especially in New England, had protested the Indian Removal Act, and reports of the expulsion and death of so many Native Americans added new urgency to their calls for a more humane Indian policy.

While Jackson and white Georgians were expelling Cherokees from the northern reaches of the state, the Second Seminole War raged farther south. Instead of the

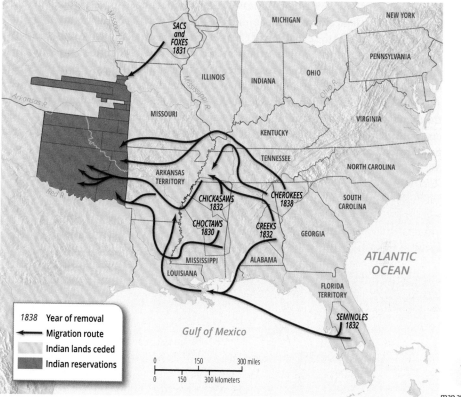

map analysis

MAP 11.1 Indian Removals, 1830s This map shows the routes along which Indians were driven by the U.S. Army during the forced relocations of the 1830s. Jackson's policies moved the last large Indian communities living east of the Mississippi River into the frontier regions of Indian territory.

Cherokee's legal maneuvering, Seminole fighters used their knowledge of the land and ecology to stymie American forces for years. In 1818, Jackson had led the U.S. Army during the First Seminole War, and he eagerly supported efforts to colonize the region at the end of his presidency. Most of the fighting in the second conflict occurred within the Okefenokee Swamp and its hinterlands, a shifting maze of wet and dry ground that disoriented all but the most experienced soldiers. Led by Osceola, a skilled commander, Seminole fighters developed a pattern of attacking and retreating that frustrated and debilitated American troops, who also suffered disease and discomfort in the swamps. The U.S. Army persisted, however, and by 1842, a staggering 90 percent of the Seminole community had been killed or forced to Indian territory. The remaining 600 retreated into southern Florida, where their descendants live today.

Settler Colonialism in the West

In the late 18th and early 19th centuries, settlers moved out of the northeastern region (with a population density of 31 people per square mile) into the midwestern territories (which held only 8 people per square mile) and farther west to the Great Plains. Few people needed to hear New York editor Horace Greeley's injunction "Go west, young man" to know that cheap land awaited them beyond the Mississippi. The result was an emigration stream that paralleled the expulsion of Cherokee and other Indians to the south, with the important difference that Anglo settlers moved voluntarily. Would-be westerners first had to reach the Missouri River. From there, they traveled 2,000 miles to reach the Pacific shore. Between one-quarter and one-half of a million migrants made the trip between 1843 and 1870, when the first transcontinental railroad line opened. Because wagons and the oxen that pulled them required a fairly easy grade and regular access to water, travelers could use only a few routes. Fur traders had pioneered these routes, which California and Oregon promoters began advertising in the mid-1830s (Map 11.2).

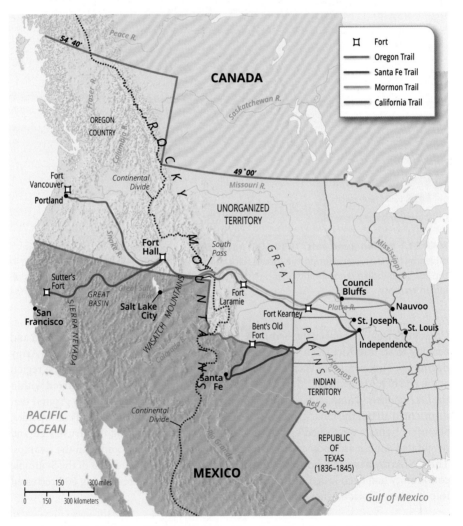

MAP 11.2 Major Overland Trails Western emigrants followed well-established routes across the continent. Starting at the Missouri River, the paths converged in the narrow passes through the Rocky Mountains and then diverged to head toward northern or southern towns on the Pacific coast.

Emigrants moved in earnest after 1842, when news reports heralded the successful journey of a large wagon train of over 100 people. If the trip was not quite the "pleasure excursion" that the *Daily Missouri Republican* claimed, it was at least possible. Most groups traveled about 15 miles per day, leaving Missouri in early May, crossing through the South Pass in early July at 8,000 feet, and only then reaching the hardest part of the trip. The mountains and the wide western rivers made the journey both dangerous and physically demanding; travelers moved quickly to avoid being stuck in the mountains during bad weather. If they survived disease, thirst, and the elements, the settlers might make it to California or Oregon by October.

The rosy advertisements crafted by western boosters rarely conveyed the challenges of living in the West. Mexico nominally controlled most of today's U.S. West, although it paid little attention to the region. Instead, Native peoples dominated the region west of the Mississippi. Indians had long warred with and occasionally allied with the Spanish, but except for those southwestern tribes who had to contend with a persistent Spanish presence, Plains Indians viewed each other as their most important threats. The few French traders who came through the area maintained amicable relations with Native peoples to facilitate business deals. But the American settlers, who started arriving in the 1830s and then increasingly after 1841, posed a threat. Unlike the Spanish or French, these new inhabitants did not come to trade; they built farms and forts and intended to stay. Americans sometimes recognized differences within the larger Native population and even established friendly relations, but generally, settlers' attitudes displayed their ignorance and fear.

In the deeper Southwest, many American settlers regarded the Mexican and Indian residents, whom they rarely distinguished, with a mix of loathing and disgust. At best, settlers treated them as obstacles to the expansion of American power in the region. An 1846 issue of the *Illinois State Register* described Mexicans in the region as "reptiles in the path of progressive democracy . . . and they must either crawl or be crushed." The combination of biology and politics in the paper's explanation reflected contemporary American thinking that certain races might die out because they were "unfit" for the modern world. Few Americans demonstrated much sympathy for Indians or Mexicans displaced by settler encroachment. Ethnographers and scientists such as Harvard's Louis Agassiz added scientific weight to the biological explanation by using skull-size measurements to generate an intellectual hierarchy of the races. Agassiz's methods were hardly scientific—his data were faulty, and he failed to rigorously test and separate evidence from hypothesis—but white Americans accepted his results as natural, even inevitable.

Spanish-speaking residents proved another challenge to U.S. expansion. Mexican independence in 1821 barely affected the northern provinces of New Mexico and California. Living on Mexico's northern edge, far from the administrative center in Mexico City, these settlers maintained their largely pastoral and agricultural economy and Catholic beliefs. In 1834, Mexico reduced the power of the Catholic Church over the country by secularizing the mission lands, but this allowed elite landholders in many places to acquire still more property and social control. In some cases, especially the California territory, the ranchero elite allied themselves with Anglo settlers, but in others they maintained autonomy. In still other cases, the villages created out of mission lands enabled local control and mutual dependency among the Hispanic residents, who retained authority over land and resources into the 1870s despite Americans' efforts.

The Santa Clara mission, California (1849)

Latin American Filibustering and the Texas Independence Movement

As legal settlers ventured into U.S. holdings across the Mississippi, adventurers such as John A. Quitman and Rensselaer Van Rensselaer pushed south and west into the Spanish borderlands or north into Canada. Americans launched some of these expeditions while living outside the United States, but other groups organized within the United States proper and then invaded foreign soil. Between 1800 and 1860, U.S. citizens launched at least 19 separate expeditions into Spanish colonies or Latin American republics. The Spanish themselves offered mixed signals by periodically inviting Anglo settlers who took an oath of allegiance to the Spanish government into the northern reaches of their Mexico territory. Americans described these actions and the people who took them as **filibusters**, from the Spanish *filibustero* and before that, the Dutch term for "freebooter."

Filibusters violated the U.S. Neutrality Act of 1818, which outlawed private warfare. Yet because so many people supported the cause of national expansion, Americans often regarded filibusters as heroes despite their frequent executions as spies and insurrectionaries in the countries they invaded. After tapering off in the 1840s, a new wave of filibusters pushed into Central America in the 1850s. John Quitman and Henry Maury—a southern lawyer and sea captain—recruited men for an expedition to liberate Cuba from the Spanish. William Walker—who invaded Mexico once and Nicaragua three times—became famous across America as the most successful and infamous filibuster of the age. The following poem ran in southern newspapers at the time:

> Success to Maury and his men
> They'll safely cross the water
> Three cheers for Southern enterprise
> Hurrah for General Walker

A Central
American
diplomat
reports on
William
Walker
(1857)

Walker succeeded briefly in Nicaragua, occupying the post of "president" for several months in 1856, only to be expelled and later executed in Honduras. As the poem indicates, southerners led most of the efforts in the 1850s, hoping to add new slaveholding territory to the Union. As a result, filibustering in this decade became embroiled in the larger sectional conflicts over slavery.

Filibusters raised a set of questions related to American expansion and power, although few at the time considered the issue in such systematic detail. Who acted for the United States? Did privately organized ventures represent the interests of the nation? Would American expansion happen violently or peacefully? To what extent would the residents of a place be consulted before American acquisition? Did this style of expansion constitute imperialism? American leaders offered vague and shifting answers to these questions. As filibustering demonstrated, private ventures could sometimes serve as an advance guard for national expansion. Force and persuasion operated simultaneously as Americans expanded their borders.

Some historians argue that Texas should be counted as the grandest filibuster victory because so many Americans poured over the border in 1835–1836 to fight on behalf of the independence movement. But the roots of the Lone Star Republic were more complex. By 1835, two distinct groups in Texas, Tejanos (or Spanish-speaking Texans) and Texians (English-speaking Texans), both criticized Mexican misrule in its northernmost colony. Texians began the movement for Texas's independence, but many Tejanos supported it as well. By early 1836, a small group of English- and Spanish-speaking rebels had retreated to the Alamo. After a pitched battle lasting nearly two weeks, the Spanish forces, led by president and general **Antonio López de Santa Anna**, broke into the compound and killed all the defenders.

Despite this setback, independence forces, rallying to the cry "Remember the Alamo," defeated the main Spanish army and captured Santa Anna in fighting along the San Jacinto River a few months later. The victors issued a Texas Declaration of Independence signed by prominent Texians such as Sam Houston, a former Tennessee congressman who became president of the new republic, and prominent Tejanos, such as Lorenzo de Zavala, who served as vice president. The success of the Texas independence movement built on widespread discontent among settlers over the failures of Spanish administration. Its most immediate changes reflected a desire to mimic its neighbor to the north. Mexico had abolished slavery in 1829, but Texas reinstated it and prohibited free blacks from residing in the new nation. The presence of a new slaveholding nation to the south worried northerners eager to stop the spread of slavery within the union. Even with the exclusion of black men and women, Texas contained a diverse population. Spanish- and English-speaking communities contested for power over the next decade, and after the republic became part of the United States, Protestant Americans worried about the inclusion of so many new Catholics into the country.

Stephen F. Austin justifies Texas independence (1836)

Pacific Explorations

One of the hallmarks of the global ascendancy of western Europeans after 1500 was their use of the sea for warfare and trade. The Portuguese, who perfected a ship that could travel against the wind, used this new technology to begin exploring the West African coast in the mid-1400s. Spanish, English, French, and Dutch explorers soon followed, establishing direct trading links with African and then Asian peoples whose wares had been accessible only via the long overland routes across the Sahara or along the Silk Road connecting China and the Middle East. Military expeditions often followed or accompanied the traders, although Europeans could rarely do more than provide protection to the traders who remained behind. The second wave of European exploration consisted of naturalists and ethnographers who took notes and gathered specimens on voyages across the oceans. The drafting of maps, the exhibition of plants and animals (and sometimes of people), and the use of new ingredients in food and beverages offered evidence of European command of the globe. Americans emulated European powers by making similar expeditions.

In 1838, the U.S. Navy launched the United States South Seas Exploring Expedition. Lieutenant **Charles Wilkes**, a young but domineering sailor (he was court-martialed after the expedition for using excessive force against men under his command), commanded a six-ship flotilla that traveled 87,000 miles over four years of sailing (Map 11.3). Like European expeditions of earlier centuries, the American mission carried a bevy of scholars—including naturalists, botanists, artists, and a linguistics expert—to gather information about parts of the world still quite foreign to most Americans. Wilkes

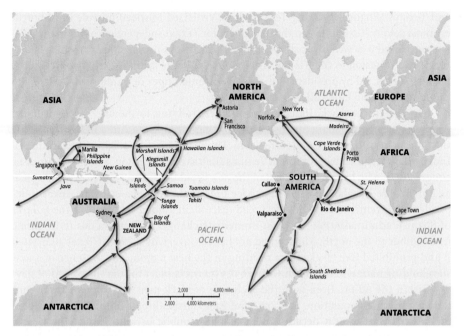

MAP 11.3 Path of the United States Exploring Expedition, 1838–1842 Navy lieutenant Charles Wilkes led the first American circumnavigation of the globe. His flotilla included scientists who sought to map and identify places and products of interest to American traders and politicians.

Alfred
Thomas
Agate's
sketches
of Pacific
islanders
(1838–42)

traversed all the oceans except the Arctic, and naturalists collected samples everywhere the ship stopped. The 60,000 plant and bird specimens collected by scientists during the Wilkes Expedition formed the basis for the Smithsonian Institution when Congress created it a few years later.

Reflecting the growing curiosity among Americans about the rest of the world, Wilkes's reports of the trip detailed both the expedition's travels and also the history of the countries and people encountered along the way. Endorsing the common "civilizational" view, Wilkes described different countries at different levels of development depending on how closely they mirrored European attitudes and institutions. Despite his condescending attitude, especially toward people of the South Pacific, the reports contained a huge amount of descriptive material that helped U.S. residents situate themselves in the larger world. Wilkes's circumnavigation of the globe also put the United States in a small group of modern nations whose explorers could claim to have traveled around the whole world. For Americans, the journey signaled their membership in the exclusive community of nations whose reach extended around the world. It also marked out for American businessmen and traders those places of potential interest for future investment and trade. A midshipman on Wilkes's expedition ominously anticipated the future course of interactions between Americans and those people they encountered in the Pacific: "I could not help thinking, how much better it would be to let them [the indigenes] go their own way, but No, No! We must have all the world like us, if we can."

STUDY QUESTIONS **FOR AN EXPANDING NATION**

1. Compare the various forms of expansion undertaken by Americans in the 1830s and 1840s. What were the similarities and differences among them?
2. What justifications did Americans offer for the dislocation of Native and other long-settled peoples in areas within or adjacent to U.S. borders?

quiz

THE NEW CHALLENGE OF LABOR

Supporters of U.S. expansion drew a sharp distinction between the United States and Europe because they believed that the presence of "free land" ensured there could be no class system in the United States. Such boosters believed that new territory would provide space for future settlers and prevent the consolidation of land that sustained Europe's aristocracies. They worried about the social effects of the increasing economic transformations that threatened to create a working class dependent on the whims of factory owners. Nearly every American visitor to Europe's industrializing cities observed the problem. In 1845, American poet William Cullen Bryant described the poor in Edinburgh, Scotland, as "a throng of sickly-looking, dirty people, . . . [a] wretched and squalid class" that according to his guide comprised more than half the city's population. The Jeffersonian ideal of a republic of free, self-sufficient farmers became even more compelling as Americans watched the changes wracking western Europe. There, industrialization produced an increasingly disaffected class of workers. The influx of new workers and rapid technological and institutional changes in the United States in the 1830s and 1840s threatened to generate the same problems. Despite the vigorous efforts of filibusters and others, land acquisition alone did not solve the problem. The emerging industrial economy demanded workers who sold their labor as a commodity. For these men and women, the prospect of landownership and self-sufficiency stayed forever out of reach. But laboring people in the United States, like those abroad, adopted new forms of politics and economic practice as a way to sustain the egalitarian promise of the country.

White Workers, Unions, and Class Consciousness

Building on an old European tradition, American artisans—such as bookbinders, wheelwrights, and cobblers—owned their own tools, supervised themselves (and often a team of apprentices), and enjoyed lives of respectability and modest comfort. The burgeoning use of steam power and mechanical reproduction in the early 1800s allowed factory owners to underprice and outproduce artisans. This process took several decades, but by 1830, the outlines of a new national economy had emerged. American consumers might have benefited from cheaper and more uniform goods, but skilled

Middlemen Abroad

Europe was not the only destination for interested travelers, and not all travelers toured for pleasure. A growing cadre of American merchants, missionaries, and officials began to circulate in the Pacific in the wake of Charles Wilkes's South Seas Expedition. These men joined a stream of European businessmen eager to trade for Chinese goods. Despite the linguistic and cultural differences within this group, they shared a common orientation as members of the commercial middle class—entrepreneurs from industrializing nations who sought opportunities to buy and sell in the massive and lucrative Chinese market. A marked feature of these new western traders was their willingness to break the law to achieve high returns. One trader noted about his company's new ship that he hoped it would "make us some money. . . . How, I don't care, so it is made." Because the Chinese had little interest in American goods, one of the few ways to accomplish this was through the illegal trade in opium. British merchants pioneered this practice, smuggling the drug from India or Turkey into China against the wishes of Chinese officials. American traders such as Warren Delano (Franklin Delano Roosevelt's grandfather) entered the opium trade alongside them. The British, like the Americans, strongly discouraged the use of opium in their own countries but showed no reluctance to sell it to Asians, and both nations profited handsomely from the early global drug trade.

One of those new businessmen who enriched himself through the opium trade was Augustine Heard, born in 1795 to a prominent trading family in Ipswich, Massachusetts. By the time he was 45, Heard had made a dozen voyages to Indian and Chinese ports and many others in the Atlantic and Mediterranean. One of Heard's partners in China, George Dixwell, also drew on a distinguished New England lineage and counted doctors, businessmen, and teachers among his relatives. Dixwell's aunt cautioned him against the greed that characterized so many New England men who traveled to the Pacific. "I pray you not be over anxious about lucre," she warned him. "Do not [make money] the object of your pursuit. . . . It is unphilosophical, it is unchristian." No doubt Dixwell's aunt condemned the opium trade in even stronger terms, but the profits proved too attractive. Heard's firm, which became one of the largest American trading

workers suffered. The rise of unskilled labor as a major category of work was the most visible symbol of this shift. Between 1820 and 1860, the number of factory workers in the United States increased nearly sevenfold, from 350,000 to two million. This transformation impacted the nation well beyond the economy, shaping politics, social relationships, and the very nature of American cities.

This period saw the rise of machine production; wherever possible, industrialists began substituting machines for the older system of handwork that had dominated production for centuries. In economic terms, artisans became wage laborers. In the process, they began selling their work to employers as they would any other good that could be bought and sold on the market. When workers struck bargains with honest employers who observed the rules of their contracts, the process of selling one's labor could appear normal and even beneficial. Some laborers maneuvered their way up the enterprises in 19th-century China, gained a sure footing through trading opium in the 1840s. The results in China were devastating as addicts multiplied and drug-related crime destabilized the government.

Heard's company formed valuable relationships with opium producers and sellers in India. Kessressung Khooshalchund, a major Bombay trading firm, proved to be an important ally as the Americans contended with varieties in the quality of the drug, storage fees, competition among shippers, and Chinese anger over the drug's impact on their citizens. John Heard, Augustine's nephew, played an active role in soliciting Indian contacts and increasing the firm's commission profits. At the conclusion of a meeting with Kavaldass Luxmichund, an Indian manager for the Kessressung firm, Heard reported that Luxmichund "dipped his thumb into a dish of paint and gave me a mark on the forehead between the eyes, where . . . Hindoos wear the mark of their cast, so that I suppose I may now consider myself a baptized Hindoo. . . . He threw a heavy cashmere shawl over my shoulders, and put a diamond ring on my finger—true Oriental liberality and magnificence." This deep immersion in Asian cultures marked these rising businessmen as members of a cosmopolitan class. Their families bore the marks of their success as well. On his way home, John wondered what to do with Luxmichund's gifts because his mother and aunt already owned Indian cashmere shawls. Heard diversified his company's activities, supplying and selling tea, silk, and other Chinese goods to American companies. Most importantly, the firm established itself as a commission merchant acquiring information about the volume, quality, and price of Chinese goods and selling this information to American buyers. The shrewd diversification of Augustine Heard and Co., its willingness to engage in the drug market, and its appreciation for the global structure of modern capitalism produced real profit for its investors and an expanded sense of American commercial accomplishments for those who read about the firm in American papers.

- How does the importance of the early global drug trade challenge the traditional notion of market exchanges as benevolent or mutually beneficial?
- How would the cultural exchanges (such as the one described previously by John Heard) have shaped a trader's or his family's perceptions of Indians?

income ladder in this period, working, saving, and seizing opportunities when possible, but many more spent their lives as unskilled workers at jobs that did little more than keep them and their families barely alive. When employers did not respect contracts or used the glut of laborers as leverage to exploit the longest workday for the lowest salary, workers suffered terrible deprivation. In New York City, for instance, real wages among the city's major trades declined through the 1830s and 1840s, leaving workers' families earning only half of the $600 per year needed to support a family of four at the time. This decline hit hardest unskilled workers, who typically earned only 60 percent of a skilled worker's wages.

The first decades of the 19th century encompassed such a tangle of growth and decay, of success and failure, that they resist easy summary. But most Americans at the time clearly saw the rise of a distinct American working class. For several decades

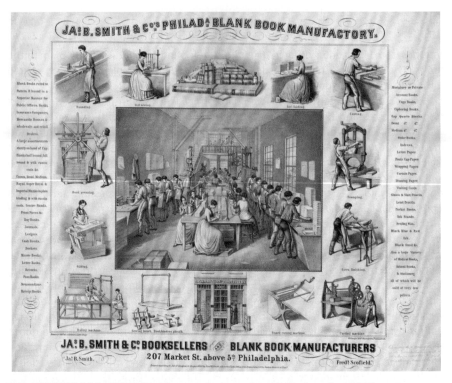

THE GROWTH OF FACTORIES The complexity and sophistication of mid-19th-century factories signaled America's emergence as a growing economic power. Women, usually young and unmarried, made up a significant part of the laboring population in many cities.

after the Revolution, elites and even most artisans believed that America did not have distinct classes, but by the 1830s, few observers confused the absence of a titled aristocracy with the absence of social classes. The change had visible consequences in the northeastern cities with the greatest industrial growth. New York, Philadelphia, and Boston all developed neighborhoods defined by class. As production moved out of the master's home or a home-based workshop, workers had less contact with the owner and his family and more contact with others in their same economic position. They lived in boarding houses and spent their leisure time with other workingmen in their own venues: bars, boxing arenas, and minstrel halls. In the mid-1830s, labor organizing reached a high point in many northeastern cities, particularly among the skilled trades. New York artisans engaged in at least 35 strikes.

Skilled workers used strikes as measures of last resort, but protests over working conditions and wages pushed owners and workers further apart in the 1830s. Over the next two decades, male and female workers initiated more strikes, but usually with little effect, partly because the trade unions organizing among urban residents segregated themselves by gender, race, ethnicity, and craft. The ever-increasing pool of new workers provided a ready supply of strikebreakers for owners. In addition, the depression of 1837 made matters worse for workers. Union membership rolls dropped significantly, and pressure on workers to accept owners' demands—including lower wages—increased.

During the 1830s and 1840s, European workers and their intellectual allies urged increasingly radical solutions to their problems. Most famously, Karl Marx and Friedrich Engels issued the *Manifesto of the Communist Party,* which predicted the abolition of private property and the rise of the industrial working class to a position of political dominance. The *Manifesto,* published in 1848, expressed in print what Americans saw in the streets of Paris, Berlin, Vienna, and Budapest that year as Europe was seized by revolution. Although the 1848 revolutions drew support from a wide range of reformers and sought political changes that Americans had already adopted (such as universal white male suffrage), most U.S. observers saw only violence and destruction. The June Days, when French government forces violently suppressed a mixed force of workers and National Guard troops, epitomized the danger. One French conservative described the June Days as not "a political struggle . . . but a class conflict, a sort of 'servile war,'" and this specter haunted American business and political leaders the way the Haitian Revolution haunted American slaveholders.

American workers, for their part, more closely followed the actions and the writings of English, German, and French reformers than those of revolutionaries. European writers and activists toured American cities in the 1830s, encouraging the formation of class-based political parties. These activists held other surprising ideas as well. Frances Wright, a Scotswoman, emerged as one of the most famous labor leaders of the day. Wright advocated free thought and women's rights, offering a vigorous critique of American inequality to thousands of rapt New Yorkers during her 1829 tour of the city. Her performance, one of the first public addresses on politics by a woman in the United States, scandalized and energized audiences in equal measure. Wright, like fellow activists Robert Dale Owen and George Henry Evans, called on American workers to use their voting power to alleviate the worst effects of industrialization. Born in England, Evans came to the United States in 1820 and published his own papers: first the *Workingman's Advocate* and later *The Man.* His papers, and the intellectual and organizational efforts of Wright, Owen, and others, inspired independent "Workingmen's Parties" in several northeastern cities, but these parties achieved little change at the level of government policy.

1829 cartoon lampooning Frances Wright

Foreign-Born Workers

Some of the people who found their working lives unbearable in their home countries made their way to the United States. Between 1820 and 1860, just over five million immigrants entered the country, with nearly 95 percent coming from northwestern Europe (Figure 11.1). Although immigrants never comprised more than 2 percent of the total population in any given year, their cumulative impact grew considerably during this period. By the Civil War, the foreign born comprised 13.2 percent of the population.

Irish immigrants, mostly Catholic, composed at least a third of all those newcomers to American shores between 1820 and 1860. Many were driven by desperation produced by the "Great Hunger," as the Irish called the famine that plagued their country between 1845 and 1849. But many others came because Protestant English domination of the island's Catholic inhabitants ensured little chance for economic success. Although many immigrants found greater opportunities in the New World, American Protestants displayed strong prejudice against the Irish as well. An 1830 newspaper advertisement for domestic help in New York revealed the routine discrimination faced

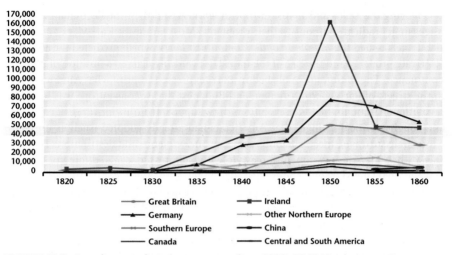

FIGURE 11.1 Immigrants, by country or region, 1820–1860 Northwestern Europe sent the most immigrants to the United States in the 19th century, especially during the famine years in Ireland. By midcentury, however, an increasingly diverse array of immigrants had found their way to the United States.

by many Irish immigrants: "Wanted. A Cook or Chambermaid . . . must be American, Scotch, Swiss or African—no Irish." Irish immigrants tended to settle in the Northeast, and they typically came without the skills to help them succeed. As a result, the Irish took on mostly unskilled positions—as road builders, factory workers, and domestic servants—and formed a substantial part of the poorest class by midcentury. Women comprised a majority of Irish immigrants at this time, which was unique for immigration patterns in the 19th century, and the lower wages paid for women's work further weakened their ability to earn enough to support themselves after the difficult and costly transatlantic journey. The influx of Irish workers allowed managers to push wages down. This economic pressure and the immigrants' Catholic faith stimulated anti-Irish riots led by native workers in the 1830s and, in the 1850s, the virulently anti-immigrant nativist movement.

Anti-Catholic political cartoon (1852)

German immigrants composed another 25 percent of the total immigrant flow between 1830 and 1860, but unlike the Irish, Germans emigrated in larger family groups. They tended to come from rural backgrounds and made the exodus with a strong faith in democracy and opportunity. The men who came tended to have labor skills that ensured they would not remain in unskilled positions for long, and this put them in starker competition with native-born Americans. The German women who emigrated tended to work within their homes or their own communities. Like the Germans, Scandinavian immigrants tended to move in family units, but they pushed even farther west, seeking out open land in the Midwest and Great Plains. Farming became the mainstay for these communities for the next several generations. In these sparsely settled areas in the mid-19th century, immigrants could recreate and maintain their home culture in ways that their families back in Europe could not. In an ironic twist, Scandinavian visitors to the United States in the late 19th century remarked on how traditional their American cousins appeared. America demanded national loyalty from the newcomers but little in the way of cultural assimilation. With each ethnic group free to practice its own traditions, the United States contained an increasingly diverse population as the 19th century progressed.

The New Middle Class

Even as the new immigrants struggled to secure employment, better-established Americans seized opportunities to move up the income ladder. A new middle class emerged in the 1830s and 1840s, partly as a result of the rapid urban growth occurring across the nation (Figure 11.2). Members of this community lacked the wealth to live without working, but they did not perform the physical labor on which most Americans depended. What we now call "white-collar work" emerged at this time. As industrial and other businesses grew larger and more complex, office workers, including clerks and accountants typically attired in cleaner "white" clothes than their working-class peers, were needed to manage the companies' information.

At 312,000 residents, New York City was the largest and wealthiest urban place in the United States in 1840, but the changes that occurred there reappeared in other cities over the next several decades. Cities provided the space for and stimulated the rise of a middle class. The anonymous nature of cities forced residents to identify one another as members of broader social or ethnic communities before they interacted as individuals. American cities, especially northeastern ones, also generated a diversity of living conditions, from the squalid shacks of New York's Bowery to the opulent mansions along Fifth Avenue. Commercial establishments revealed the changes as well. New York, Philadelphia, and Boston soon teemed with retail establishments selling a bewildering array of domestic- and foreign-produced goods. Mass-produced clothing sold best, followed by food, magazines, and books, all components of the increasingly commercialized,

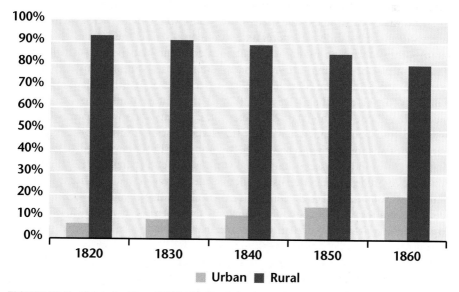

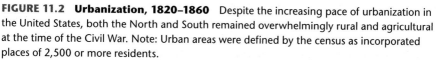

FIGURE 11.2 Urbanization, 1820–1860 Despite the increasing pace of urbanization in the United States, both the North and South remained overwhelmingly rural and agricultural at the time of the Civil War. Note: Urban areas were defined by the census as incorporated places of 2,500 or more residents.

BROADWAY, NEW YORK CITY New York City led the nation in new retail districts, and Broadway epitomized the allure and diversity of products and services that such areas promised the burgeoning consumer class.

increasingly nationalized economy that defined the United States. The shops themselves, often several stories tall and outfitted with the latest light fixtures, paintings, and carpets, presented a new world of purchasing within which burgeoning middle-class Americans could distinguish themselves from those who bought their supplies in the small, single-room, family-run stores more common earlier in the century.

Another way rising middle-class families differentiated themselves from other Americans was by looking to Europe on questions of style in art, music, dress, and literature. Magazines from London and Paris circulated across the Atlantic, allowing Americans to associate themselves with the latest European trends. For the sons (and, much more rarely, daughters) of American elites, no education was complete without a "Grand Tour," an extended journey of travel and education in European cities. The necessity of anchoring themselves to the traditions of Europe revealed the anxieties that beset the middle classes in the period of transition and change in 1830s and 1840s America. At home, these concerns manifested themselves in the injunctions in advice manuals and books to avoid "confidence men and painted women"—the male and female scoundrels who exploited the anonymity and openness of the new urban places to cheat honest people out of their money and their reputations.

The Expansion of Slavery and Slaves as Workers

In contrast to the growing prominence and success of free labor in the North, white southerners made increasingly effective use of slave labor. Thanks to **Eli Whitney**'s cotton gin, which processed picked cotton much faster than human hands could, southern planters doubled the volume of cotton they grew each decade after 1800. As Britain

EVOLVING HOME DESIGN   The layout of homes changed to accommodate the purchasing power of the rising middle class. "Parlors"—private but comfortable rooms in which families could display the furniture, carpets, and chandeliers that signaled their status—started to appear.

and France increased their appetite for the cotton to produce the textiles that they traded around the globe, American investors saw new opportunities in the fertile lands of central Georgia, Alabama, and Mississippi. This region grew rapidly in the 1830s and 1840s, financed by the promise of high returns from cotton. But for African Americans, the cotton gin and the new southwestern settlements promised only more generations of bondage. The high demand for labor in the region encouraged slave owners along the Atlantic Seaboard to sell some of their slaves into an expanding internal slave trade. The route from Virginia and the Carolinas west and south became a second middle passage, marked by the violence and hardship of forced marches and deprivation. In the 1810s, 120,000 slaves marched over the Allegheny Mountains and down the river valleys of the Deep South; by the 1830s, the number had increased to 300,000. Those who remained had to refashion their families, shorn of parents, siblings, or children, under the threat of being sold "down the river."

Many of the planters moving into the new Southwest were the sons of established slaveholders on the Eastern Seaboard. These young men typically moved ahead of their families. Slaves on the new cotton plantations worked under unusually brutal conditions. The young masters, eager to pay off debts incurred in travel and to prove themselves independent men, drove slaves through long hours of clearing land and planting crops. Without their families and the network of social institutions that occasionally checked such behavior, southwestern masters subjected enslaved women to more sexual exploitation and enslaved men to harsher punishments than in the East. Despite the higher mortality rates that accompanied relocation and life in the region, profits remained high, and so more planters flooded the area into the 1850s. William Faulkner's 1936 novel *Absalom, Absalom!*, though written long after this era, captured the violent ambition that characterized this phase of American migration.

▷

The internal
slave trade

In the upper South, most owners organized enslaved laborers as a "gang"—usually a squad of three or four men and women—and set them to work for a specified period of time (typically sunup to sundown). Under the task system, used more often on lower South cotton, sugar, or rice plantations, owners organized work around specific assignments. A group of workers might still function as a unit, but rather than simply laboring all day, they would be assigned a discrete unit of work to complete—so many acres of land to weed or so many pounds of cotton to pick. By allowing workers to use whatever time remained in the day after completing the task for their personal use, the task system built a small measure of incentive into slavery. Owners found the system advantageous for several reasons: slaves worked more efficiently; because slaves typically used extra time gathering or producing supplementary food for their families, owners could reduce the rations they provided; and because most slaves spent extra time with their families, it decreased the likelihood that parents would run away. Even with these mercenary advantages for the owner, most enslaved people preferred the task system because it gave them at least some autonomy. Within the narrow space they carved out, slaves built stronger families and a more resilient and sustaining culture.

Another feature of the slave system provided a similar mix of dangers and opportunities for slaves: the growing rental market. As southern cities and industries developed, urban residents rented slaves; in other cases, corporations dominated the markets, usually because they needed labor but did not want to invest the capital to buy slaves outright (although corporate ownership of slaves also increased in the same period). Rented-out slaves sometimes lived with their temporary owners, in homes or barracks in the case of companies, but in many cases they found their own housing. Owners deducted some portion of a slave's total rental value to be applied to food and housing and gave this to the enslaved person, who remained responsible for arranging for his or her own upkeep. This system benefited slaves by giving them a measure of daily autonomy from their owners, although it also separated family members. It created new problems for city leaders responsible for policing slave behavior in place of absent masters. White workingmen also resented the competition from enslaved laborers.

STUDY QUESTIONS **FOR THE NEW CHALLENGE OF LABOR**

quiz

1. What were the effects of the increasing urbanization and industrialization in 1830s and 1840s America?

2. How did the rise of "free labor" and slavery both stabilize and unsettle the United States in this period?

◈ MEN AND WOMEN IN ANTEBELLUM AMERICA

The economic changes confronting Americans in the decades before the Civil War produced and were shaped by changes in the size and nature of families and gender relations. Drawing on a burgeoning market in parenting advice literature, parents began rethinking how to raise and relate to their children. Love and the open expression of emotion received much more attention in the early 19th century than they had in previous generations. Rather than viewing households as little kingdoms—with a spouse, children, and other dependents recognizing the natural authority of the father as they would the king—parents began emphasizing the affectionate bonds that sustained families. Despite this new emphasis, the lines between men's and women's proper roles within both society and the family began to sharpen. Greater respect between spouses and the mutual obligations of all members of the "domestic" family did not necessarily lead to more liberal values with regard to women's place in the public world.

Gender and Economic Change

Nearly all women in the United States suffered under similar restrictions with regard to their public rights: women could not vote or hold office, could not sue or establish contracts, were barred from positions of leadership in their churches, and were rarely allowed access to higher education or divorce, even from abusive husbands. The law of **coverture** ensured that when a woman married, her property and any wages she might earn became her husband's. These legal constraints clashed with an increasing sense of women as unique individuals who deserved the same moral respect as men. As the nation developed, and especially as the American economy created new opportunities and new situations, states articulated the differences between men and women in law. Differences emerged most noticeably in the North, where the expanding economy drew upper- and middle-class men away from household-based production—principally farming—into paid employment at separate and dedicated work sites. Since the early colonial period, the household had been the basic social and economic unit, the site of both production and reproduction. As the new national and industrial economy took shape, paid work moved outside of the home. For the mostly urban upper classes, this meant that men left the home and women stayed inside it. Alexis de Tocqueville, the famous French visitor to the United States, observed of gender relations in the 1830s that "the inexorable opinion of the public carefully circumscribes [her] within the narrow circle of domestic interests and duties and forbids her to step beyond it."

Those families who experienced this transformation in work increasingly viewed the world outside the household as the "public" space and the domestic space of the home as "private." The men in these households believed that women ruled within the domestic world but should have little presence in the public one. Several factors converged to create this trend. The factories and offices that increasingly employed men outside of the home refused to hire women. Women had traditionally held greater authority in regard to child rearing and the daily household tasks. Finally, Americans regarded the public world of business and government as morally suspect if not corrupt. The market, they believed, functioned as a kind of free-for-all in which participants might engage in any noncriminal behavior in the pursuit of profit, and politics operated according to similar principles. In this world, women's perceived strengths—a highly developed

AN AMERICAN FAMILY, CIRCA 1850 The new emphasis on affectionate relations within families demanded new representations in family portraiture. In addition to individual portraits, families now sat together for paintings or photographs that demonstrated the bonds of love that tied together these domestic worlds.

image
analysis

moral sense and strong sympathies for others—became liabilities. As a result, men sought to exclude women from the public world for their own protection and because they would have been ineffective in the face of male aggression and ruthlessness. This was not a uniquely American practice. Industrial revolutions in England, France, and other parts of western Europe split households as they did across America.

These changes did not occur uniformly across the country. Among families who moved west of the Mississippi River, the household continued to be the center of economic activity, as it was in the South. Men and women in these regions generally spent their days alongside one another. The shared responsibilities in these households appeared as soon as they started on the trek west. Women were responsible for feeding, clothing, child rearing, and doctoring the family if necessary. They also usually participated in the agricultural or pastoral work that sustained most western families. Men were typically responsible for agricultural work, the animals, transportation, and protecting the family. The hardships of the journey ensured that men's and women's duties and needs often overlapped.

The middle-class women who staffed most of the nation's leading reform organizations rejected the intellectual assumptions that divided the genders. The leading female activists in the crusades for temperance, **abolition**, and women's rights drew scorn for their aggression rather than gentle treatment because of their natural sensitivity. Female volunteers performed much of the work done by a wide range of reform associations in the decades up to and through the Civil War. The **Grimké sisters**, Sarah and Angelina, ranked among the best-known abolitionists of the period, and a trio of women—**Susan B. Anthony, Lucretia Mott**, and **Elizabeth Cady Stanton**—led the fight for women's suffrage. Despite this, most men believed that women belonged in the home and not in the office, factory, or store. The separation of space by gender did little to advance modern notions of gender equality, but women could and did use the special protections owed to them under the ideology of separate spheres to educate themselves and to organize the broader movement for full equality. "We are a band of sisters—we must have sympathy for each other's woes," wrote one female activist.

Many Americans knew that the divisions of social and economic labor along gender lines varied within the nation. Class position determined, to a large degree, the extent to which men and women could rigidly separate their duties. Poor families needed the income of their female members and could not afford to remove them from paid work. Slavery, with its identical demands on the labor of black men and women, clearly violated the new norms, as did the many rural white households where production and reproduction remained rooted in the same physical place. Indians, who still controlled most of the western half of the continent, maintained their own gendered divisions of labor. Most importantly, Native women usually controlled the agriculture within their communities. Because early white observers routinely ignored women's work, they often overlooked the importance of farming to Indian economies and inaccurately criticized them for relying too heavily on hunting.

Ladies, Women, and Working Girls

At the same time that state legislatures and churches restricted women's options, women themselves seized new opportunities in the whirl of changes brought on by the market revolution. Some women, of course, pursued paid work out of necessity because their families required the active contributions of all members to survive. In New England, thousands of young women entered schoolhouses as teachers, and many more took employment in the textile mills dotting the region. The mills in Lowell, Massachusetts, in particular, gained renown for their large labor force of young women, who ranged between the ages of 15 and 35. The **Lowell Mill Girls**, as observers called them regardless of age, worked in one of the first large-scale, steam-powered industries in the United States—and one of the most fully globalized. They wove cotton, grown by slaves working on plantations in the southern United States, and shipped the finished products to consumers all across America and around the world. Less well known at the time were the female mill workers of the South. In Georgia, white women comprised a majority of the state's factory workers. In Macon, Columbus, Augusta, and the state capital of Milledgeville, textile factories employed thousands of young, mostly single, women. Like their peers in Massachusetts, these women remained part of their households and returned their often-essential wages to the family.

Harriet Hanson Robinson, excerpt from *Loom and Spindle: Or, Life Among the Early Mill Girls* (1831)

Even in those places without the mechanized mills of Lowell or Augusta, women performed a wide variety of paid work. Most rural women already performed physically demanding and time-consuming household work, and many also engaged in small-scale domestic production. They sold most of the goods produced in town or city markets—from candles and clothing to butter, eggs, and small farm animals. For many of these women, the money they generated was the only cash income a farm family might possess.

Cities presented other working opportunities that women sometimes sought and sometimes were reduced to accepting. As American cities developed in the 1830s and 1840s, more city dwellers with money to spare paid for services that they would have done for themselves in a previous era or a more rural setting. Women filled most of the roles as cooks, cleaners, launderers, seamstresses, and all-purpose domestic help. More ominously, poor women sometimes resorted to prostitution. In the large cities, certain neighborhoods hosted a mix of bars, gambling dens, and brothels that ensured a steady flow of business while creating dangerous work conditions for women.

WORKING WOMEN This cover of a literary journal produced by Lowell Mill workers revealed the awkward position occupied by female workers, poised between the domestic world of home and the mercenary world of factories.

Enslaved women occupied the most ambiguous position within the prevailing visions of women's proper roles. Because of their bondage, enslaved women performed a range of tasks ordinarily undertaken by men. Female slaves in the field worked the same jobs as male slaves. Corporations sometimes owned or rented slave women, just like their male counterparts. In 1810, Virginia's Oxford Iron Works counted nearly one-third of its enslaved workforce as female, some of them cooking and cleaning for the male workers, but others performing regular foundry tasks alongside men. Slave women also contended with a high degree of sexual vulnerability that few free women ever experienced. Despite legal, religious, and social prohibitions, slave owners maintained sexual relationships with enslaved women. The increasing presence of **mulatto**, or mixed-race, people in the United States Census offered physical proof of many of these relationships. Slave mothers educated their adolescent daughters in strategies to protect themselves from this omnipresent danger.

Masculinity on the Trail, in the Cities, and on the Farm

Despite men's dominance in American society in the 1830s and 1840s, notions of manhood changed as unpredictably as those of womanhood. Differences in region and ethnicity produced the sharpest distinctions. In the Northeast, with its concentration of urban areas and highly specialized economies, men found opportunities and incentives to build marriages and families on the basis of affection rather than the older model of hierarchy and authority. Although this transition promised more frequent demonstrations of love among spouses, it also required men to abandon long-held notions of what constituted manly behavior. In earlier decades, affronts to a man's honor demanded an immediate physical, usually violent, response. As new norms of manhood took shape in the increasingly crowded and anonymous northern cities, men placed a premium on self-control, a virtue that diminished conflict while allowing men to retain their

SLAVE LABOR Enslaved women worked alongside men performing long hours of fieldwork on tobacco, cotton, and rice plantations. The lack of gender distinctions in slave labor encouraged many whites to view black women as less feminine than their white counterparts.

honor. Another change was the open expression of emotion, particularly positive emotions, such as love, which took root especially among younger men and reformers. Male abolitionists, for instance, wrote and spoke with each other in extraordinarily intimate and emotional terms, a practice that mirrored the sympathy they strove to generate in the larger public on the issue of slavery. A letter from Charles Sumner, the antislavery Massachusetts senator, to his friend, the poet Henry Wadsworth Longfellow, remarked of their correspondence: "Yr letters seem warm as a lover's heart. I can almost feel the heat when I break the seal."

New attitudes toward manhood took root more slowly in the South, where older and more traditional forms of masculine expression retained favor. The conflict surrounding statehood in the new territory of Florida, brought within the union only in 1819, revealed the importance of expressions of masculinity to political and social authority. As residents built the case for statehood, two political factions coalesced around competing leaders. Men within the territory aligned themselves with one group or the other and zealously guarded the honor and positions of their peers. The southern code of honor, heightened among white men because of the presence of slaves, demanded retaliation for any slight to one's own or one's group's public image or reputation. Floridians gouged eyes, bit off earlobes, and assaulted each other in ways calculated to produce shame by creating a public symbol of one's inferiority. The popular forms of ritualized violence among southerners bonded white men in a shared ethos even as it alienated them from northerners pursuing nonviolent expressions of masculinity. A similar atmosphere prevailed in the emerging Anglo West. The Hispanic West and those areas that received wagon trains included roughly equal numbers of men and women, but the mining towns, the newly formed ranches, and many of the large farms were overwhelmingly male. As a result, the region possessed fewer of the social institutions—churches, schools, and civic groups—that moderated the actions of young men and, consequently, a higher degree of violence and disruptive behavior than the East.

California vaqueros (1849)

At the same time, the growing importance of evangelical Christian values, which stressed charity, humility, and compassion rather than revenge, competed with the system of honor, especially in the South. The shift in emphasis from the public nature of honor, in which men most valued the way their peers viewed them, to Christianity, in which an individual's most important relationship was with God, represented a profound shift in southern culture. As the *Religious Herald* boldly announced in 1837, "A public profession of Christianity is an avowal of our separation from the world, as regards its maxims, pursuits, and pleasures." This transformation happened slowly through the 1830s. As evangelical churches gained influence, the values they represented began to alter southern culture. Northern religious reformers sought similar opportunities to direct the energy and morality of American men. The increasing popularity of bare-knuckle fighting, a sport imported from England complete with foreign fighters, drew scorn from those who emphasized restraint and nonviolence. According to one commentator, boxing was "nothing but brutality, ferociousness, and cowardness," which tended to "debase the mind, deaden the feelings and extinguish every spark of benevolence." Despite such critiques, a wide swath of men from different classes watched, gambled on, and thrilled to matches that could last 50 rounds or two hours of fighting. The popularity of such spectacles revealed the tensions in American culture in the antebellum era—benevolence and sympathy existed alongside violence and aggression.

STUDY QUESTIONS FOR MEN AND WOMEN IN ANTEBELLUM AMERICA

1. How did men's and women's lives differ in the mid-19th century?

2. How did race, region, and class influence changes in masculinity and femininity in the period?

quiz

❂ FREEDOM FOR SOME

The dynamism that characterized gender relations in this period could be seen in the political system as well, where politics developed in two different directions simultaneously. On one hand, Americans broke away from European traditions by liberalizing democracy to include all white men. On the other, Americans increased their commitment to slavery, which created a society based on bonded labor that western Europe had left behind with the end of feudalism in the 1500s. In southern states, these two trends buttressed one another, whereas in the North, they began to generate concern about what kind of country America would become. The tension between liberty and slavery fueled several decades of conflict about the structure and the nature of American democracy. Did individual freedom include the right to enslave other people? Did the federal government have the authority to prohibit slavery? Rather than confront these polarizing issues directly, politicians clashed over apportionment, voting qualifications, and the regional balance of power in the country. The changes they made expanded access to electoral politics and retained an awkward sectional peace, but skeptics wondered whether even the robust American political system could contain the transformations coursing through the country in the 1830s and 1840s.

The Nature of Democracy in the Atlantic World

Americans drew inspiration from a wide variety of sources. The independence movements in Latin America—when various republics broke away from Spain's control between 1810 and 1825—fascinated and encouraged Americans in their own expansion of democracy. Americans found European democratic efforts equally compelling. **Louis Kossuth**, the journalist and political leader in Hungary, attained renown as a freedom fighter throughout the Americas. After his expulsion from Hungary in 1848 by the embattled Hapsburgs (the ruling family of the Austrian Empire), Kossuth toured the United States to great acclaim, receiving a 100-gun salute when his ship reached New Jersey and invitations to the White House and Congress.

Excerpts from Louis Kossuth's speech to Congress (1852)

The liberalization of politics in the United States dovetailed with the market liberalization that occurred at the same time. Despite the conservatism of most Jacksonian Democrats, a faction within the party—known as Young Democrats—began advocating the virtues of markets and global trade over the standard party line, which focused on self-sufficiency and agricultural development. Charles Wilkes's Expedition alerted Americans to the opportunities waiting abroad. Likewise, Young Democrats applauded the British decision in 1846 to repeal their "Corn Laws," high tariffs on imported foodstuffs designed to protect Britain's agricultural sector. Pro–free-trade Americans hoped that the British move would spur the repeal of similar duties around the world and open foreign markets to American products. The same Young Democrats who applauded Wilkes's Pacific explorations and preached free trade celebrated European democratic movements. John O. Sullivan's *Democratic Review*, the unofficial organ of the movement, chronicled the fortunes of Italian, German, and central European rebels, who themselves took inspiration from the American rebels of 1776 against the old aristocracy of Europe.

Americans supported Spanish- or Hungarian-speaking democrats because they seemed to endorse an American idea: that authority should reside in the common people. The great accomplishment of the American Revolution had been to locate the government's sovereignty collectively in the people, not in the divine right of a king. "The people," in this sense, referred to participants in the political order. In Jacksonian America, this still meant native-born white men. The influx of Catholic immigrants, the increasing numbers of free blacks in the North, and the efforts by women to attain the vote challenged assumptions about who could participate in the political process, but white men protected their interests effectively until the Civil War. For several decades after the Revolution, reformers liberalized the political system while at the same time they obstructed efforts by women and racial minorities to gain access to the political system. Changes to the country's economic system followed a similar pattern. The era's prosperity seemed to prove that a decentralized government and open markets could accomplish what Europe's more centralized governments had failed to secure. Such an outlook ignored the active role that government (at all levels) played in stimulating economic development—whether it was the U.S. Army expelling Indians to make way for white farmers or the U.S. Navy establishing trading stations in the Pacific. It also ignored the fact that the profits of economic and political liberalization were not evenly distributed within the population. Enslaved people, Indians, and most women did not enjoy the benefits of limited government and free markets.

LOUIS KOSSUTH The lasting impression of the Hungarian reformer Louis Kossuth can be seen in the monuments erected to honor his contribution to the global democracy movement. This one, in New York City, joined others in Cleveland, Washington, DC, and elsewhere across the United States.

The Second Party System

The practical results of political changes in the United States in the 1830s and 1840s shocked many Europeans, particularly elite Britons who distrusted the wisdom of granting voting rights to all white men. While European politicians and thinkers watched, many gleefully anticipating the imminent collapse of the American republic, Americans pushed ahead. In many states, reformers eliminated two requirements for voting and holding office that had kept the poor out of the political system: property restrictions had required that officeholders and voters own real estate, and poll taxes ensured that only men with disposable income could vote. Most of the millions of immigrants to the country could naturalize themselves as citizens and assume full participation in the political system within a few years of arrival. From our modern perspective, a system in which only white males could vote seems a shallow democracy. But for people at the time, who recalled the legacy of European governance that gave little power to common people, the change was momentous. The addition of transforming previously appointed positions into elected ones, including most local offices such as tax assessor, sheriff, and local judges, produced the most democratic system in the Western world.

Davy Crockett on entering politics in the Jacksonian era (1834)

Another factor that broadened people's access to government was the rise of the Second Party System, organized around Andrew Jackson. Jackson's bold leadership over two terms in the White House generated a host of opposition. Reformers criticized the callousness of his Indian removal, commercial interests condemned his destruction of the bank, and state rights proponents had their own concerns about this slaveholding son of the South who put down South Carolina's attempt to "nullify" the federal tariff. During the 1830s, the **Whig Party** organized around a set of issues that enabled them to build a national coalition; they captured the presidency in 1840 and again in 1848. Whereas the Democrats encouraged the mass immigration of the 1830s and 1840s and welcomed many of these voters into the party, Whig supporters distrusted the largely

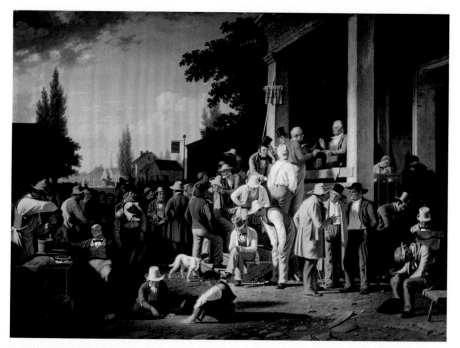

EARLY 19TH-CENTURY VOTING   Caleb Bingham's famous painting captured the social nature of voting in the first half of the 19th century. Men voted publicly, which created the possibility of coercion, intimidation, and fraud but also reinforced the collaborative process of democracy.

Catholic and working-class migrants. Coming largely from the ranks of native-born Protestants, Whigs espoused a vigorous nationalism; supported government investments in infrastructure to stimulate business; and, in some parts of the North, endorsed moderate antislavery politics. In contrast, the Democratic Party preferred state funding and control of development projects, which set them against the federal road, bridge, and river improvements that Whigs promised would energize the American economy. Sociocultural issues, such as closing all government services on the Christian Sabbath and advocacy of temperance, also energized Whig voters.

Democracy in the South

To the surprise of many observers, southern politicians actually liberalized their rules regarding access to the vote and higher office earlier than many northern ones. The southern slaveholders who filled most statehouses rarely initiated change, although the most farsighted among them saw that incorporating nonslaveholding whites into the political order on a more equal footing could ensure the security of the system. By allowing nonslaveholders to have more power in the political system, slaveholders hoped the new voters would be less likely to challenge that system. Henry Wise, a Virginia Democrat who led the state as governor and played a pivotal role in the state's secession from the Union, responded skillfully to challenges within the state for a more inclusive system. Nonslaveholding men living in the western part of Virginia had long complained of unequal treatment by eastern slaveholders—a lament heard throughout the southern states in the 1830s and 1840s. Although late by southern standards, in 1851 Virginia abolished the property requirement for voting and instituted universal white manhood suffrage.

The democracy that evolved in the presence of slavery assumed the mastery and autonomy of white men. The unique characteristics of a democracy based on race emerged several decades before the Civil War. In the nation as a whole, politics knitted the country together, connecting men and women across regions, classes, ethnicities, and religions. But because of the overwhelming endorsement of slavery within the South, neither party could risk being associated with any challenge to it. On this issue, the southern wings of the two parties competed to outdo each other in protecting the South's peculiar institution. This weakness in the party system hastened the political collapse that produced secession and war. In addition, both northern and southern whites showed their preference for white rule. By 1840, free blacks could vote only in Maine, New Hampshire, Vermont, and Massachusetts. New York and Pennsylvania had recently repealed earlier grants of voting rights to black men.

The power of slavery to warp democracy appeared most ominously in South Carolina in 1832. Over the course of that year, politicians in the Palmetto State initiated a conflict with the federal government over the tariff. Beginning during the War of 1812, New Englanders had promoted a tariff—a federal tax on imported (usually finished) goods—as a way to stimulate domestic manufacturing and curb the importing of European products. If European goods became more expensive, tariff supporters argued, Americans would buy more goods made at home. New England manufacturers naturally favored the tariff. Southerners, with little industrial development of their own, complained that the tariff helped the Northeast at their expense. They felt forced to buy either expensive northern-made goods, which seemed to bolster the clout of a region many southerners regarded as a rival, or pay the tariff-elevated prices for European merchandise. When George McDuffie, an Upcountry South Carolina representative, rose to speak about the issue, "his frame came alive with outrage. He shrieked. He kicked. He thumped. He spat. He seemed a revivalist in a death struggle with Satan." In 1828, President Adams supported a high tariff—known as the "Tariff of Abominations" by its enemies—that passed with strong northern support. Southerners in and out of Congress complained vociferously about the legislation, which doubled the tax on many imported goods.

When Jackson came to the White House, many southerners assumed he would push repeal of the tariff. But Jackson's home state of Tennessee benefited from a tariff

ADVANCING THE SOUTHERN ECONOMIC AND POLITICAL AGENDA   Although South Carolina lost the nullification debate, its actions inflamed a sense of injured pride across the South. A decade later, James D. B. DeBow launched his eponymous magazine, *DeBow's Review*, as a platform for advancing the southern economic and political agenda.

Excerpt from *DeBow's Review* (1850)

on hemp imports, and despite his state rights philosophy, Jackson moved slowly against the law. Congress reduced the 1828 tariff in 1832, although it proved too late for the increasingly radical South Carolinians. South Carolina politicians saw only potential gain from denouncing the tariff in stronger and stronger language. By late 1832, John Calhoun—once Jackson's vice president and possible successor—had thrown himself fully against the tariff. He penned an "exposition" against the policy that condemned it as unconstitutional and destructive of the liberty that the union was founded to protect. Building on Calhoun's theory, the South Carolina legislature passed an act "nullifying" the federal law and refusing to collect the tariff at its ports. Carolina politicians hoped to draw support from other southern states, but none followed. President Jackson issued the most famous denunciation of the doctrine of nullification: "I consider, then, the power to annul a law of the United States, assumed by one State, incompatible with the existence of the Union, contradicted expressly by the letter of the Constitution, unauthorized by its spirit, inconsistent with every principle on which It was founded, and destructive of the great object for which it was formed." Congress passed a Force Act and Jackson appeared ready to lead U.S. troops into the South when a compromise was reached. Congress reduced the tariff further, and South Carolina repealed its nullification ordinance. The nation had come dangerously close to secession and war.

Arguments for and against "nullification" by John C. Calhoun and Andrew Jackson (1832, 1833)

Conflicts over Slavery

Southern partisans lost the battle over nullification, but this did not diminish their willingness to defend slavery. Because southern politicians controlled most of the top committee chairmanships and other leadership positions within Congress, they blocked discussion of slavery at the national as well as the state level by imposing the "**gag rule**." On December 13, 1835, a Maine congressman introduced a petition from 172 "ladies" in his district who urged Congress to abolish slavery in the District of Columbia. Similar petitions had been printed in the records of congressional debates, referred to committees, and never touched again. But with abolitionists' opposition to slavery growing more forceful each year, southern representatives protested against the new petition from Maine and insisted that Congress reject it, an unprecedented request. James Henry Hammond of South Carolina, who made the original motion that produced what critics would call the gag rule, asserted that "he could not sit there and see the rights of the southern people assaulted day after day, by the ignorant fanatics from whom these memorials proceeded." Hammond found support among his southern colleagues, many northern allies, and especially party leaders eager to see such a divisive issue removed from debate. For the next nine years, the U.S. Congress refused to consider or even print the memorials and petitions of citizens on the subject of abolition.

Partly owing to the dedicated efforts of former president John Quincy Adams, then representing Massachusetts in the House of Representatives, the House rescinded the rule in 1844. In the meantime, however, the rule underscored the power of pro-slavery southern congressmen to control the institution and transformed the fight over abolition into a fight over free speech as well. Southern power, wielded arrogantly by men like Hammond, probably did more to stimulate antislavery sympathies among white northerners than the work of dozens of dedicated abolitionists.

Only a tiny minority of northerners counted themselves as abolitionists in the years before the Civil War, and even most abolitionists wanted only gradual and peaceful emancipation. The power of persuasion, however, could move millions, and given the North's advantage in population, southerners needed to win—not just stifle—the debate over slavery. Reacting to abolitionist pressure, southerners developed a robust defense of slavery, marshaling history, religion, morality, and economics to demonstrate why Americans had to protect and even extend racial slavery. Ministers such as Virginia's Thornton Stringfellow, political theorists such as George Fitzhugh, economists such as J. D. B. DeBow (publisher of the South's most important business magazine), and politicians such as Hammond and Calhoun together crafted a new defense of slavery that identified it as the one true foundation for white freedom.

Excerpt from George Fitzhugh, *Sociology for the South, Or the Failure of Free Society* (1854)

The **pro-slavery defense**, as it has been called by historians, was built on the idea of racial supremacy espoused by prominent scientists of the day, such as Harvard's Agassiz and the southern physician Josiah Nott. Both men articulated scientific explanations of white racial superiority based on an imputed link between skull size and intellectual ability. Slavery's defenders joined this modern argument to older endorsements of slavery, reaching back to the ancient Greeks and Romans and to the Bible. Many Protestant Christians at the time interpreted the biblical story of Ham as evidence that God had made black people to be the servants of white people. Pro-slavery theorists also built elaborate economic defenses of the institution, pointing to the remarkable wealth produced in southern states through the use of slave labor. James Henry Hammond explained the political defense of slavery in another famous congressional speech that alienated as many northerners as his earlier fight for the gag rule had. According to Hammond, every society required workers who performed the brute labor on which all else rested. He referred to this class as the "**mudsill**" and flatly stated that members of such a class, owing to their constant low-wage labor, could not develop the intellectual capacities to contribute productively to the political life of their society. Hammond condemned northerners for forcing white men—typically immigrants—into this role, whereas he lauded the South for using slaves in this capacity.

James Henry Hammond on the "mudsill" of society (1858)

What could be called the "civilizational" aspect of the pro-slavery argument claimed that slaves could either be held in bondage in America or Africa. And, because America was a Christian nation and Africa was not, slavery in the United States must be better for the slaves. Over time, the argument went, slaves would adopt Christianity, ensuring eternal salvation for their souls. As southerners knew, two awkward facts contradicted this part of the argument: after 1808, international law prohibited the importation of African slaves into the country, so all future slaves were native to the United States. Second, whereas Catholic Spain and Portugal made extensive efforts to convert their slaves to Christianity, Protestant England and later America made no similar effort. Before 1800, very few slaves had adopted Christianity. This failure became one of the chief criticisms of northern opponents of slavery and eventually prompted a slavery reform movement within the South.

STUDY QUESTION FOR FREEDOM FOR SOME

1. Did the changes in American politics in the 1830s and 1840s serve a more liberal or a more conservative social order?

quiz

interactive timeline

TIMELINE 1818–1856

AMERICA	YEAR	THE WORLD
Mar Congress passes Neutrality Act to suppress private warfare	1818	
	1821	Mexico secures independence from Spain Greeks win War of Independence against Ottoman Empire
	1825	Decembrist Revolt in Russia fails
Jul Cherokee Indians ratify tribal constitution modeled on U.S. Constitution	1827	
Frances Wright delivers first public address by an American woman to a mixed-gender audience **Aug** Discovery of gold on Cherokee land in Georgia	1829	
May Congress passes Indian Removal Act	1830	
Alexis de Tocqueville arrives in the United States for a two-year study of the country, resulting in the 1835 publication of *Democracy in America*	1831	Polish revolt against Russian Empire fails
Mar Supreme Court issues decision in *Worcester v. Georgia* holding that Congress has sole authority to regulate relations with Indian tribes **Nov** South Carolina legislature passes "Ordinance of Nullification" intending to nullify federal tariff	1832	
Mar Congress passes "Force Act" giving President Jackson power to suppress South Carolina's refusal to collect federal tariff	1833	
Dec Second Seminole War begins in southern Georgia/ northern Florida	1835	
Mar Mexican forces led by General Santa Anna defeat and kill combined force of Texian and Tejano rebels at the Alamo **Apr** Mexican president and general Santa Anna defeated along San Jacinto River; Texas independence declared **May** U.S. House of Representatives imposes "gag rule" prohibiting introduction or discussion of petitions calling for abolition	1836	

Summary

- The 1830s and 1840s were a key phase in the expansion of the nation. Challenging Spain and Britain for dominance in North America, settlers flooded the landscape west of the Mississippi and dramatically changed the demography and the economy of the region.
- The economic growth spurred by new technology, especially the steam engine, helped drive the rise of a new middle class and of a more clearly defined and self-aware working class, mainly located in the cities.
- The new workplaces, distinguished from older household-based production, were almost entirely all-male places. This change helped generate the growing separation of men's and women's experiences in early America.
- In the South, the West, and among the variety of non-Anglo ethnic communities, men and women worked out different relationships with one another and different expectations of the future.

AMERICA	YEAR	THE WORLD
Dec Rensselaer Van Rensselaer leads American filibusters into Canada	**1837**	
Jan General Winfield Scott sent to Canadian border to suppress violence **May** General Winfield Scott arrives in Georgia and begins confining Cherokee people before their forced march to Indian territory **Aug** Wilkes Expedition sets sail from Hampton Roads, Virginia	**1838**	
Mississippi passes first "Married Women's Property Act," granting married women independent rights to property brought into marriage	**1839**	First Anglo-Chinese War begins
Jun Wilkes Expedition returns **May** First successful large-scale wagon train departs Missouri for the Pacific coast **Aug** Second Seminole War ends; 90% of Seminole killed during conflict	**1842**	First Anglo-Chinese War ends
Dec Congress repeals "gag rule"	**1844**	Treaty of Wanghia between Qing Empire and United States enables first American ambassador to China
Irish famine begins	**1845**	
Jul "Declaration of Sentiments" passed at Seneca Falls, New York, by women's rights advocates calling for equality between men and women	**1848**	Democratic revolutions in Italy, Hungary, Germany, and France
Dec Hungarian democracy activist Louis Kossuth tours United States	**1851**	
William Walker briefly holds office as president of Nicaragua before being executed	**1856**	

- Political elites imposed widespread progressive reforms, creating more democratic political systems across the country. Nevertheless, political power remained securely in the hands of wealthy white men.
- Partly because of the progressive reforms, outsiders of all sorts found ways to influence the political system. These groups, including Native Americans, women, new immigrants, and African Americans, also began using the language of American politics, especially the idea of an egalitarian democracy, to improve their own positions.

Key Terms and People

abolition 384
Alamo 363
Anthony, Susan B. 384
coverture 383
filibuster 370

gag rule 394
Grimké sisters 384
Indian Removal Act of 1830 366
Kossuth, Louis 389
Lowell Mill Girls 385

audio flashcards

Reviewing Chapter 11

1. The most important boundary that changed in this period was the one between men and women. Do you agree with this statement? Why or why not?

Further Reading

Aron, Stephen. *How the West Was Lost: The Transformation of Kentucky from Daniel Boone to Henry Clay*. Baltimore, MD: Johns Hopkins University Press, 1996. An insightful study of land and development politics during the first half of the 19th century.

Berlin, Ira. *Generations of Captivity: A History of African-American Slaves*. Cambridge, MA: Belknap Press, 2003. The best and most concise history of slavery in North America from the early 17th century through emancipation.

Guttierez, Ramon A. *When Jesus Came, the Corn Mothers Went Away: Marriage, Sexuality, and Power in New Mexico, 1500–1846*. Stanford, CA: Stanford University Press, 1991. An analysis of the effects of Spanish invasion and settlement on gender roles and relations in the Southwest.

May, Robert E. *Manifest Destiny's Underworld: Filibustering in Antebellum America*. Chapel Hill: University of North Carolina Press, 2002. An engaging survey of the practice of filibustering in 19th-century America.

Stansell, Christine. *City of Women: Sex and Class in New York, 1789–1860*. Urbana: University of Illinois Press, 1987. An analysis of the changes in family, work, and gender patterns in industrializing America.

Wilentz, Sean. *Chants Democratic: New York City and the Rise of the American Working Class, 1788–1850*. New York: Oxford University Press, 1984. The seminal study of a pivotal moment in the development of a working class in the United States.

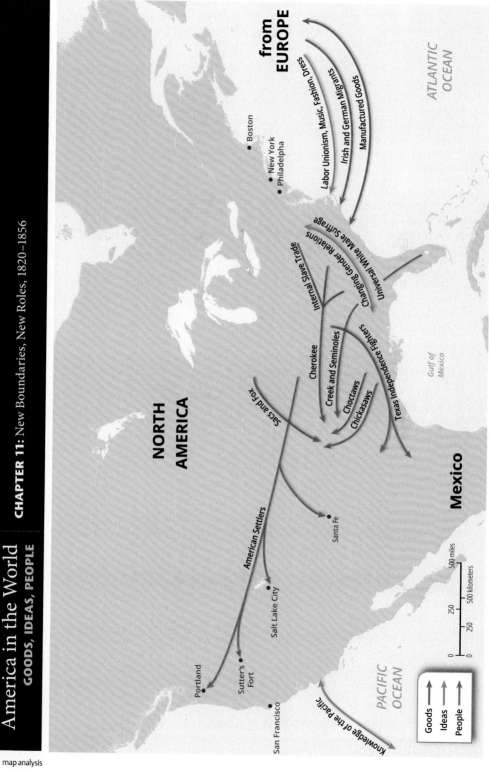

America in the World
GOODS, IDEAS, PEOPLE

CHAPTER 11: New Boundaries, New Roles, 1820–1856

map analysis

from EUROPE

Labor Unionism, Music, Fashion, Dress
Irish and German Migrants
Manufactured Goods

ATLANTIC OCEAN

Boston
New York
Philadelpha

Internal Slave Trade
Changing Gender Relations
Universal White Male Suffrage

Cherokee
Creek and Seminoles
Choctaws
Chickasaws
Texas Independence Fighters

Sacs and Fox

NORTH AMERICA

American Settlers

Santa Fe

Gulf of Mexico

Mexico

Salt Lake City

Portland
Sutter's Fort
San Francisco

Knowledge of the Pacific

PACIFIC OCEAN

500 miles
250
0

500 kilometers
250
0

Goods
Ideas
People

The capture of a still-defiant Nat Turner, leader of a slave rebellion in Southampton County, Virginia.

CHAPTER 12

Religion and Reform

S arah Grimké, born in 1792 to a wealthy Charleston slaveholding family, was prodigiously smart but was denied advanced education by her parents, who preferred her to be trained in the domestic duties of a future plantation mistress. From an early age, Sarah had revolted against the grotesque abuses meted out to slaves at her own and friends' homes. She resisted this stunted future and eventually submerged her ambitions in social pursuits and spiritual practice through the Presbyterian Church in Charleston. Upon discovering the Quaker practice of spiritual and social equality, at the age of 29, she said goodbye to her family and moved to Philadelphia.

Angelina Grimké was Sarah's youngest sister and also her goddaughter. Like Sarah, Angelina found herself repulsed by the ease with which her family and friends accepted the inequities and savagery of slavery. When friends of her mother gathered and criticized their slaves as lazy and dishonest, Angelina asked them, "What made them so depraved?" Rejecting the idea of a biological distinction between the races, Angelina laid blame on the whites who denied enslaved people literacy and the Bible. Walking through Charleston's streets in 1829, she confronted two white boys abusing a slave. The woman appealed to Angelina, which only reinforced her sense of helplessness as a woman opposed to slavery in a state ruled by slaveholding men. "How long, oh lord, wilt thou suffer the foot of the oppressor to stand on the neck of the slave!" she wrote in her diary that night. Angelina longed to help abolish the practice but felt her "hands were bound as with chains of iron." Within the year, she joined her sister in Philadelphia.

Together, the Grimké sisters educated themselves and nursed the radical flame that flickered inside them. They denounced slavery and called for its immediate end, first in print and then through speech. In 1838, Angelina was the first woman to speak to a legislative body in the United States. "I stand before you as a southerner, exiled from the land of my birth by the sound of the lash and the piteous cry of the slave," she proclaimed. The sisters' actions alienated them from their family, but they built a new community among abolitionist activists in the North. Their willingness, as Southerners, to criticize slavery was matched in bravery only by their willingness to challenge the gender norms of the day as well. Together, they personified the radical possibilities of Northern reform at a volatile moment in American history and left a legacy of activism and intellectual work that remains vibrant to this day.

THE SECOND GREAT AWAKENING

In the early decades of the 19th century, a transatlantic revival movement spread from Britain to North America. This **Second Great Awakening**—following the similar religious dynamism of the 1730s—connected evangelical Christians on both sides of the Atlantic who exchanged ideas and strategies that inspired a broad set of social, cultural, and intellectual changes. Participants sought salvation and rebirth inside reenergized churches. The religious ferment of the 1820s and 1830s drew as much on the massive economic and social changes occurring in America as on theology. The increasingly rapid industrialization and urbanization of the country, the rise of a truly national commercial economy, and the surging middle class all spurred both celebration and anxiety (Map 12.1). Earlier generations of Americans had engaged in mostly temporary and localized protest and reform. The evangelical reforms of the 1820s, 1830s, and 1840s, in contrast, drew on broad national support and lasted for decades. The issues they raised—the relationship between religious faith and politics, the responsibility of Christians to improve and uplift their society, and the tension between modernity and tradition—continue to engage us today.

Spreading the Word

In September 1830, **Charles Grandison Finney**, a young man trained in the law but fired with religious zeal, arrived in Rochester, New York. After his conversion, Finney rebuffed a legal client by saying, "I have a retainer from the Lord Jesus Christ to plead his cause, I cannot plead yours." Finney intended to unsettle the complacent and energize the believers. He succeeded magnificently. Preaching every day and three times on Sunday, meeting privately with individuals, and organizing prayer groups, Finney lit the spiritual fire that would consume western New York over the next several years. He spoke directly to people—men and women, rich and poor alike—in their own language. Without a formal pulpit, Finney addressed his listeners as equals. He beseeched them to accept the salvation that he had experienced. "A revival is nothing else than a new beginning of obedience to God," Finney proclaimed. "Just as in the case of a converted sinner, the first step is a deep repentance, a breaking down of heart, a getting down into the dust before God, with deep humility, and forsaking of sin."

As Finney explained, accepting one's sinfulness only began the work of reformed Christians: he exhorted the converted to live every day in accordance with the gospel. Here lay the socially transformative power of the Second Great Awakening. Ministers like Finney encouraged Americans to reform their society, to bring it more clearly into line with God's plan. Despite diverse interpretations of what that world should look like and an uneven embrace of evangelicalism, revivals encouraged massive social action all across the country. As Finney explained, "When mankind become religious, they are not enabled to put forth exertions which they were unable before to put forth. They only exert the powers they had before in a different way, and use them for the glory of God." Finney's religious experiences personified the journey that many converts took.

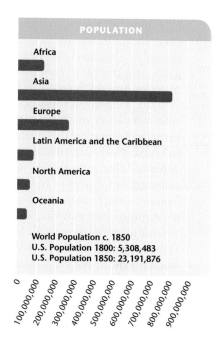

POPULATION

Africa

Asia

Europe

Latin America and the Caribbean

North America

Oceania

World Population c. 1850
U.S. Population 1800: 5,308,483
U.S. Population 1850: 23,191,876

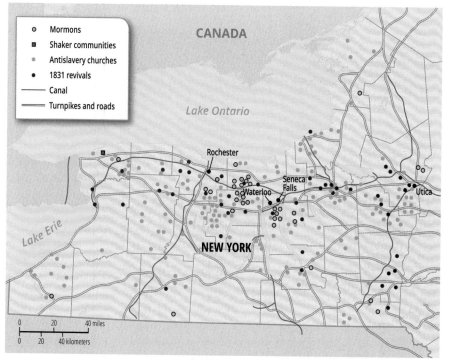

○	Mormons
■	Shaker communities
○	Antislavery churches
●	1831 revivals
——	Canal
==	Turnpikes and roads

CANADA

Lake Ontario

Rochester

Seneca Falls

Waterloo

Utica

Lake Erie

NEW YORK

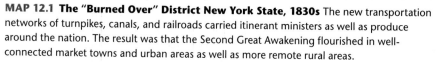

MAP 12.1 The "Burned Over" District New York State, 1830s The new transportation networks of turnpikes, canals, and railroads carried itinerant ministers as well as produce around the nation. The result was that the Second Great Awakening flourished in well-connected market towns and urban areas as well as more remote rural areas.

Excerpt from Charles Grandison Finney, "Instructions to Young Converts" (1835)

He matured within the Presbyterian Church and studied law before turning to the ministry. Convinced that the passive reception of scripture and predestination that he had learned as a boy had failed him, Finney implored his listeners to put the lessons of the gospel into practice in their lives. In the 1820s and 1830s, Finney and other revivalist ministers brought this message to listeners across the United States and overseas.

The "Burned Over" district of upstate New York earned its nickname because the scale and pace of conversions to the new evangelical faith suggested the wildfires that periodically devoured the countryside. Some converts had belonged to more established sects and others came from the ranks of Americans who did not attend church. Finney, and other itinerant ministers who moved from community to community setting up congregations, borrowed from the Methodist practice of camp meetings, outdoor religious events, to develop a new style of open and accessible religion. Whereas their more conservative peers had eschewed public demonstrations of religion, evangelicals stressed the necessity of public revivals as a method of establishing and sustaining faith. Finney argued that "men are so sluggish, there are so many things to lead their minds off from religion . . . that it is necessary to raise an excitement among them, till the tide rises so high as to sweep away the opposing obstacles." This endorsement of public action and of the common sense of average people over the learned wisdom of trained ministers reinforced the accelerating democratization of American politics in the 1830s and 1840s.

Camp Meeting of the Methodists in N. America

METHODIST CAMP MEETING Outdoor revivals served as one of the chief conduits of the new evangelical faiths. Their informality and the mixed audiences—men and women, blacks and whites, slave and free, rich and poor—contributed to the democratic feeling of the movement.

Building a Christian Nation

Between 1820 and 1860 Americans built 40,000 new churches, a vast increase from the 10,000 built in the previous 40 years. Although Protestant sects had dominated the religious life of the British colonies, a majority of citizens did not actively participate in organized religion. At the end of the revival period, probably one-third of all Americans attended church regularly. The evangelical movement spread from New York throughout New England, through Ohio, and through Kentucky into the South. Although many of the early revival preachers embraced a broadly Christian evangelicalism, each sect sought to expand its particular denomination. Because of their resistance to the emotionalism of revivals, neither the Episcopalians (the American version of the Church of England) nor the Presbyterians benefited much from the movement. Instead, Methodists and Baptists established themselves as leading American denominations as a result of the Second Great Awakening (Figure 12.1). The two faiths shared a close affinity with regard to doctrine, but the Baptists benefited from a less centralized network that empowered local ministers and individual churches. In 1831, the year after Finney began his work in Rochester, evangelicals reported over 600 revivals in New York State alone, with most organized by the Methodists and Baptists.

The power of churches in the colonial period came from their official sanction and the prominent role played by ministers and other religious leaders in

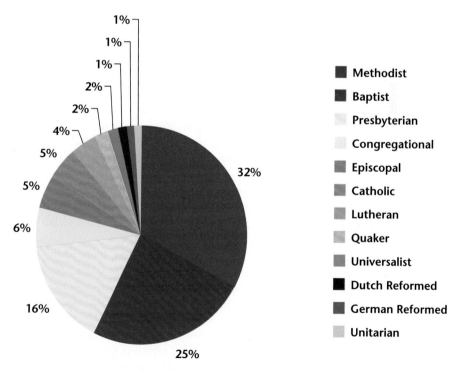

FIGURE 12.1 Church membership, 1850 The results of the Second Great Awakening were clearly visible by 1850, when Baptists and Methodists both counted millions of members, well ahead of other denominations. Note that the numbers are based on aggregate accommodations in churches as counted by the 1850 census.

local communities. The Revolution spurred American Christians to break with the Church of England, and the First Amendment to the Constitution forbade the federal government from "establishing" religion. But the Constitution did not prevent states from maintaining official religions, and several New England states did, with Massachusetts the last to break the connection in 1833. Under the leadership of Thomas Jefferson, Virginia disestablished its official religion just after the Revolution, eliminating the state's financial support for churches and ministers. The circulation of itinerant ministers further decentralized religion. Traveling preachers, often young, single men, adjusted to the physical rigors of long travel on horseback, rough accommodations, and long stretches away from home and family. The youth of most itinerants ensured they held less wealth and were less invested in established ways of thinking. These characteristics meant they might challenge the authority of propertied elites, especially when they did not belong to a specific community and did not suffer the social repercussions of criticizing those in power. Once a critical mass of conversions had occurred, people often organized themselves into a formal church. This process might take months or possibly years.

Mimicking the institutional traditions of the more established sects, evangelicals established colleges at which ministers could be trained. A raft of small colleges built across the Midwest served both denominational and public needs. Charles Grandison Finney assumed the presidency of Oberlin College in 1833, one of the earliest and most influential of these institutions established by evangelical Presbyterians. Southern evangelicals built as well; they founded Wake Forest, Richmond, Furman, Davidson, and Emory in the late 1830s and early 1840s. All told, evangelical reformers built 28 new denominational colleges between 1820 and 1850.

The Second Great Awakening spurred religious growth well beyond the established Protestant sects. The Catholic Church, a presence since the early colonial period, grew on the strength of the immigrant population to whom it ministered. Local, independent churches also sprang up across the nation. In some cases, charismatic charlatans swindled supporters out of money or into bed, while other devout ministers preached and brought their followers to new and meaningful relationships with their God. Ann Lee, a former English Quaker who had moved to the United States, organized followers around a rigid doctrine of gender equality and millennial prophecy. Believers regarded Lee as a second incarnation of Christ and adopted her celibate lifestyle in pursuit of a "heaven on earth." Known as the Shakers for a ritual dance they performed, their asceticism and devotion to high-quality agricultural production and craftwork left a folk art legacy that lived on long beyond Lee.

The most successful of these new sects were the **Mormons**, founded by Joseph Smith in the same upstate New York district in which Finney preached. Smith composed *The Book of Mormon* after receiving what he regarded as divine visions. Preaching a conservative theology of patriarchal authority, Smith drew thousands of followers. But the sect generated fear and anger among other Americans. The Mormons' efforts to build a separate society, their willingness to live under a theocratic hierarchy, and, after 1852, their advocacy of plural marriage spurred mainline Protestant Christians to regard them as a threat. Persecutions followed as they moved from New York to Ohio and then to Missouri and Illinois. A confrontation in Illinois in 1844 left Smith dead and convinced **Brigham Young**, the new leader of the main community, that he must lead his people to a refuge. They chose as their destination the area around the

Extracts from the *History of Joseph Smith, the Prophet* (1838-39)

Great Salt Lake, in today's Utah, then in largely ungoverned territory still belonging to Mexico. Young guided his community—more than 16,000 strong—over the mountains and out of the United States.

Interpreting the Message

Many of the changes proposed by Finney and other revival ministers angered and scared orthodox religious leaders. Traditionalists opposed measures that democratized the churches, especially the use of vernacular language, immediate church membership after conversion, and mixed-sex audiences where both men and women prayed together. Most problematic of all were the doctrinal revisions that Finney preached—revivalists abandoned the Calvinist belief in predestination and advocated a personal engagement with the Bible and their faith. Without denying that God held the power to save souls, Finney demanded that people use their free will to reject sin and pursue a more Christian life. Many of the new evangelicals also endorsed **millennialism**, a belief system organized around an imminent apocalypse, which made salvation all the more urgent.

The religious diversity of the old middle colonies (New York and Pennsylvania) ensured that evangelicals' calls resonated within an already pluralistic atmosphere (Figure 12.2). In New England, the Congregational Church, and to a lesser extent the

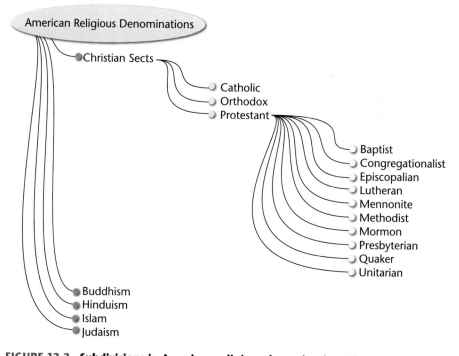

FIGURE 12.2 Subdivisions in American religious denominations The First Amendment's prohibition on state-supported churches and a great tolerance of religious diversity ensured that many sects flourished in the United States. Throughout the 19th century, immigrants brought new faiths to the United States that took root alongside the established denominations.

Presbyterian Church, still reigned as the centers of power in local communities. There, reformers' demands challenged the authority of Congregational ministers and the hierarchy built on the partnership of the church and the Federalist Party. In Northern states generally, the call to act in a more Christian way evolved into an injunction to improve society. The Second Great Awakening targeted sin, both in the actions of individuals and in the effects these actions had on society. The pursuit of a Christian society propelled a host of reform movements including temperance; women's rights; prison, hospital, and asylum reform; better working conditions; and, most significantly, antislavery activism.

Religious reformers took advantage of two unique aspects of America's political system. In Britain, the tight connection between social position and political power ensured that reform efforts proceeded through Parliament. The U.S. system, by contrast, was more decentralized, and the result was that in the early 19th century, American reformers more often went around government rather than through it. Reform movements also benefited from several changes in American law and society. Most importantly, the rapid growth of corporations and a variety of legal opinions establishing the autonomy of private institutions created a public sector and gave reformers the legal right and civic space within which to organize themselves. Reformers also took full advantage of the new print culture. Annual reports connected participants to a world beyond their own, and newspapers spread the language and goals of the movements.

At the same time, the pursuit of perfection created tensions within American life about the role of religious institutions in democracy. Evangelical reform prompted people to ask doctrinal questions about the forces that could or should mediate the relationship between the individual and God and questions about the proper role for religious faith in politics and public policy. One abolitionist responded to fears of "mixing up" politics and religion with the call to "mix them, and mix them, and mix them, and keep mixing, until they cease to be mixed, and politics became religion and religion, politics." Other reformers and many outside the evangelical revival worried that the nation could not endorse particular religious values while ensuring personal liberty, too. Echoing Jefferson's concern, expressed in the Virginia Statute for Religious Freedom, they believed that "our civil rights have no dependence on our religious opinions any more than our opinions in physics or geometry."

STUDY QUESTIONS FOR THE SECOND GREAT AWAKENING

1. What strategies did evangelical ministers use to attract converts?
2. Why did so many people turn to evangelical Christianity in the 1830s and 1840s?

quiz

⊘ NORTHERN REFORM

The most prominent and disruptive reforms concerned temperance, abolition of slavery, and women's rights. These three movements challenged America's political, economic, and social structure. Supporting them required believers to abandon deeply held beliefs about themselves, the natural world, society, and proper relations among each other. Because reform movements represented such a broad and fundamental challenge to American life, they drew on a wide variety of inspirations. In most cases, the Second Great Awakening and religious fervor energized reformers who organized within churches and drew explicitly on Christian doctrine to advocate particular changes. They often received funding from denominational institutions. But other reformers found their calling through secular channels, often by observing the plight of families broken by alcoholism, the slave trade, or domestic violence. Although reform movements appeared all across the country, Northern communities demonstrated greater sympathy for them. The rapid economic changes that characterized this era in the North provided reformers with more projects and weakened the natural opposition to reform expressed by entrenched elites.

Each of the major reform movements contained its own contradictions. Many antislavery activists, for example, worried about the negative effects of slavery on democracy without much regard for slaves as people. Some women's rights advocates used prevailing biological teachings about women's greater sensitivity to argue for their greater voice in public policy, while their opponents used that same information to argue for the exclusion of women from the public sphere. In certain cases, tensions between religious and secular reformers created friction, but generally they worked effectively together. The leadership of women in social reform movements created the greatest challenge. Women's active public role in reshaping American society in the 1830s, 1840s, and 1850s produced a backlash—even some friends of women's rights classified women's public protests as "out of place"—that curtailed many social movements, most noticeably the pursuit of equality between the sexes.

The Temperance Crusade

Most female reformers, and some men too, began their work with a focus on moral reform, especially prohibition of alcohol. In 1826, evangelical ministers formed the **American Temperance Society (ATS)**, which initiated an enormously successful campaign. It was the first major reform effort to grow out of the revivals, and it drew support from ministers of all denominations. The movement did not end the consumption of alcohol in America, but it did help convince millions of people to rethink their relationship to drinking. Temperance also prompted numerous state legislatures to consider legal restrictions on alcohol, no easy feat given the important role alcohol played in American social rituals. Manual laborers, drawing on European traditions, drank alcohol during their morning and afternoon breaks. In 1825, the average American 15 years of age or older consumed seven gallons of alcohol per year, or the equivalent of 110 eight-ounce glasses. By 1850, the per capita consumption rate had fallen to less than two gallons per year. Evangelical clergy argued that alcohol represented a serious threat to the moral order and condemned the social effects of alcohol, mostly on the men who lost jobs, fell away from the church, and abused or abandoned their families. Lyman Beecher, probably the best-known preacher in the country, regarded intemperance as "the sin of our land . . . that river of fire, which is rolling through the land, destroying the vital air, and extending an atmosphere of death" that would "defeat the hopes of the world."

Excerpt from Thomas S. Grimké, "Address on the Patriot Character of the Temperance Reformation," (1833)

Beecher founded the ATS, which called for a total prohibition on alcohol. Evangelicals succeeded in shifting public thinking about drinking by using statistics showing its deleterious effects. By connecting moral reform to scientific analysis and data, reformers broadened the appeal and the argument for their proposals. They needed strong arguments because their appeals demanded a high degree of sacrifice. They insisted that good Christians refrain from all alcoholic beverages, including those used in communion rites, and they even denied church membership to those who drank. These demands helped evangelicals to differentiate themselves clearly from Catholics, most of whom used wine in communion rites and came from cultures where alcohol played an important social role. As a result, temperance rarely had the support of immigrant communities or the Democratic Party, which welcomed them. Other Americans resented the campaign because they perceived it as an attack on individualism and basic freedom.

Lyman Beecher, excerpts from *Six Sermons on the Nature, Occasions, Signs, Evils, and Remedy of Intemperance* (1828)

The desire to purify the body produced a variety of health-reform movements. The first sustained call for vegetarianism in the United States emerged at this time. Sylvester Graham, a pioneer in the field, devised an entire health system emphasizing the moderate intake of stimulants—including tea, coffee, and alcohol—as well as sex, which he advised should be restricted to once a month. His vegetarian diet relied on bread made from Graham flour, which included bran; the flour remains in use today in the United States in the crackers named after him.

The Rising Power of American Abolition

The campaign against slavery grew from humble origins within minority religious communities in England and America. In the 1850s, legislative debates over slavery—especially the 1850 Fugitive Slave Act and the 1854 Kansas–Nebraska Act—pushed many white Northerners into the antislavery camp, but in the 1830s and 1840s, supporters came mostly from within the evangelical world. Quakers and Methodists had historically opposed the institution. John Wesley, Methodism's English founder, hated slavery, and the early American Methodists Thomas Coke and Francis Asbury carried on the fight in the late 18th century when they organized the Methodist Episcopal Church of America. Slavery directly contradicted the egalitarian ethos of much Quaker teaching; although Philadelphia merchants heavily invested in the institution in the 18th century, Pennsylvania hosted the first antislavery organization in the world. Granville Sharp, the early English abolitionist, corresponded with Philadelphia Quakers when he built the British movement. Even in the South, early evangelicals of all denominations often condemned chattel bondage as they pushed their congregants to pursue lives more closely aligned with Jesus's message of universal brotherhood. Still, antislavery work generally remained confined to the churches and schoolhouses of selected Northern hamlets. The key change within the movement came in the early 1830s as antislavery activists transformed into abolitionists and began calling for an immediate end to slavery.

The transition from conservative, gradualist reform to the call for immediate abolition can be seen in the shift of power from the Pennsylvania Abolition Society (PAS), created in 1775 on Quaker principles of pacifism and antislavery, to the New England Anti-Slavery Society (NEASS). The PAS, founded in the inspiring moment of the American Revolution, had pursued a legalistic course seeking individual emancipations

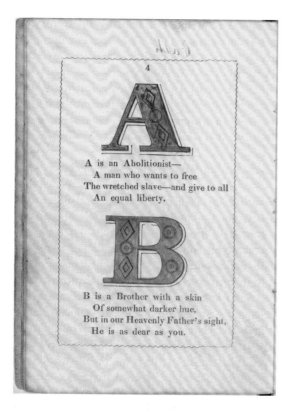

THE ABOLITION MESSAGE Much to the horror of white Southerners, abolitionists printed grammar and spelling textbooks, such as this one, to carry their messages to young people.

of slaves within states and gradual restrictions on slavery through state law. The PAS reflected a conservative faith in elite action. Black people could not join the organization, and lawyers for the PAS made appeals strictly on the basis of reason. By the 1830s, antislavery activists had created a more vigorous and public campaign against the institution. Free African Americans in the North rejected gradual emancipation, and their campaign educated and energized many white activists. In 1841, the black minister Samuel Ringgold Ward, for instance, assumed the pastorship of the South Butler, New York, Congregational Church, and thanks to his efforts his parishioners broke with the main denominational body and pursued independent church reform centered on abolition. In Massachusetts, white activists joined their black peers to create a new model of abolition society. Taking inspiration from the ongoing political liberalization, activists abandoned the older legalistic strategies and appealed directly to the people, often with stirringly emotional appeals. An 1831 edition of the *Abolitionist* included the following poem intended to shame white Northerners into action:

> White Lady, happy, Proud, and Free, Lend awhile, thine ear to me;
> Let the Negro Mother's Wail Turn Thy cheek yet more pale.

Appeals such as these, and the sizeable black membership of the NEASS (nearly a quarter of all members), signaled publicly that abolitionists had shifted both the nature of their critique of slavery and the method by which they explained that critique to the world. "Slavery is a crime," **William Lloyd Garrison** thundered. "Anything which serves as a substitute for the immediate and absolute emancipation of slavery," the NEASS proclaimed, "is delusive, cruel, and dangerous." The NEASS became the model for the national **American Anti-Slavery Society (AASS)**, organized by Garrison in 1833 with immediate abolition as its core message. The AASS organized local chapters, sent speakers around the country preaching against slavery, published narratives of slave life, and eventually appealed directly to Congress for national action on the subject. Garrison, in particular, pursued immediate emancipation with a unique vigor and effectiveness through his newspaper *The Liberator*—initiated in 1831—and his organizing and lecturing on behalf of the cause. By 1837, the AASS counted more than 1,000 chapters with 100,000 members, although abolitionists probably never comprised more than 5 percent of the Northern population. Between 1833 and 1838, Britain ended slavery in its Caribbean colonies, emancipating 800,000 people. Garrison and others drew courage from the British, and French, decision to abandon slavery, and they hoped that American leaders would soon follow course.

Excerpt from the first issue of *The Liberator* (1831)

Garrison's stridency divided the abolition and reform communities as well as the country more broadly. His methods and his message, especially his pursuit of full racial equality for black Americans, frightened even some fellow antislavery activists. Theodore Dwight Weld, a convert to Garrisonian immediatism, initiated a series of discussions about slavery at Lane Theological Seminary in Cincinnati, Ohio, just across the river from Kentucky slavery. Emulating Garrison's racial egalitarianism, Weld and his students took up work in the city's black neighborhoods, where, Weld said, "If I ate in the City it was at *their* tables. If I attended parties it was *theirs—weddings—Funerals—theirs—Religious—meetings—theirs*—Sabbath schools—Bible classes—theirs." After the AASS began advocating immediate abolition, even other antislavery activists turned against them. Catherine Beecher, one of the most prominent reformers in the nation and sister of Henry Ward Beecher, condemned abolitionists as "neither peaceful nor Christian." Beecher, like many others in American society, saw immediate abolition as an attack on the right of property, perhaps the central ideological component of New World capitalism. Beecher argued that calls for immediate abolition increased racism and violence against blacks.

In fact, radical abolitionists more typically brought down a reign of social isolation, expulsion, and violence on themselves. Sarah and Angelina Grimké had been forced to relocate from South Carolina to Pennsylvania as they made their opposition to slavery publicly known, and opponents of abolition continually interrupted their meetings with force. The most notorious incident of violence, although hardly the only one, was the murder of **Elijah Lovejoy**, an abolitionist printer, who had relocated to Illinois in the mid-1830s. Despite warnings and attacks on his shop, Lovejoy continued his work until a mob killed him. Lovejoy's death and other acts like it radicalized many abolitionists. John Brown, whose attempted slave rebellion in Virginia in 1859 served as one of the catalysts to the Civil War, said that Lovejoy's murder convinced him that abolition would not come without violence.

Garrison, Weld, and the Grimké sisters all represented the white face of abolition. Well known and well financed, they demonstrated the ability of 19th-century Americans to see beyond racial differences. But enslaved people themselves proved the most effective opponents of slavery, none more so than **Frederick Douglass**, the most famous and most rhetorically skillful of his generation. Born Frederick Bailey on a Maryland plantation, Douglass learned to read, and in 1838, at the age of 20, he escaped

FREDERICK DOUGLASS The most widely known black abolitionist in the United States, Frederick Douglass campaigned against slavery throughout the North and in the United Kingdom. Born a slave in Maryland, Douglass exhibited skills as a speaker and writer that refuted slaveholder claims that African Americans were suited only for slavery.

image analysis

and made his way to Rochester, New York, where he threw himself into the work of abolition. Articulate in print and speech with a commanding physical presence, Douglass traveled the country lecturing to abolition societies. In Rochester he started his own paper, which circulated across the North. Douglass's narrative of his life sold tens of thousands of copies in the United States and abroad, and like other slave narratives at the time, it introduced readers firsthand to the horrors of slavery.

Excerpt from Frederick Douglass, *Narrative of the Life of Frederick Douglass, an American Slave* (1845)

Black activists targeted the scheme, popular among whites around the country, that slaves should be freed and then deported from the country. This was the platform of the **American Colonization Society (ACS)**, which, since its founding in 1817, continued to attract national leaders to its ranks. During the 1830s and 1840s, the ACS counted among its members the most influential politicians of both regions and parties. Colonization generated intense opposition from black Americans. James McCune Smith, a New York City physician with an interracial practice, led the campaign against the plan. Black opposition to colonization in the 1820s helped drive Garrison and other white abolitionists to support immediate abolition.

Women's Rights

Like the abolitionists and evangelical reformers more generally, advocates of women's rights drew inspiration and legitimacy by connecting their movement with predecessors in Europe. Lydia Maria Child, one of the most influential U.S. women's rights reformers, wrote biographies of an Englishwoman and two French women who provided models of active, virtuous womanhood. German reformers built on the democracy movement of 1848 to call for gender equality as well. In a sentiment with which many American reformers would have agreed, one German activist declared, "The freedom of women is the greatest revolution . . . since it breaks fetters which are as old as the world." American women drew special inspiration from British author Mary Wollstonecraft's *A Vindication of the Rights of Woman* (1792). Wollstonecraft's manifesto rejected the notion of natural differences between men and women and called for full gender equality. Women's efforts to challenge their second-tier status represented as profound a change as abolition. As one historian has noted, "To question sexual hierarchy and distinct spheres of gender was to question a pillar of traditional Christian society more basic and pervasive than the Sabbath."

The confidence to challenge that pillar came from women's success in other reform fields. According to a Boston minister in 1836, "It is to female influence and exertion that many of our best schemes of charity are due." Women played a crucial role in the abolition movement. According to William Lloyd Garrison, "The Anti-Slavery cause cannot stop to estimate where the greatest indebtedness lies, but whenever the account is made up, there can be no doubt that the efforts and sacrifices of WOMEN, who helped it, will hold a most honorable and conspicuous position." Many female reformers toiled first in the abolition movement and then in the 1830s moved into women's rights. This broad title anticipated the feminist movement of the 20th century and, similarly, sought to advance women's interests through political empowerment, economic autonomy, and sexual freedom. Alongside efforts to achieve female suffrage, for instance, female labor leaders agitated for reforms to protect the growing population of women workers in America's industrial cities. In 1844, Sarah Bagley helped found the Lowell Female Labor Reform Association, a group that helped organize thousands of signatures on petitions to the state legislature calling for a 10-hour workday.

Margaret Fuller, excerpt from *Woman in the Nineteenth Century* (1845)

Other women took new roles on themselves and in the process created new possibilities for others. Margaret Fuller, a New England friend of Ralph Waldo Emerson and Henry David Thoreau, edited the transcendentalist magazine the *Dial*, offering insights into U.S. and European philosophy, literature, and art. She wrote *Woman in the Nineteenth Century*, a book that argued for the full equality of men and women. Her journalistic exposés took readers into the almshouse, the asylum, and the prison, demanding reform and improvement. In addition to her religious faith, Fuller drew inspiration from classical and contemporary history and politics. She closely followed the nationalist movements in Germany, Italy, Poland, and Hungary. From 1846 to 1850 she worked, mostly in Italy, as one of America's first war correspondents, as she reported on the civil wars and nationalist movements wracking that country and neighboring states. Although she died tragically at the age of 40, Susan B. Anthony said that Fuller "possessed more influence on the thought of American women than any woman previous to her time."

Women themselves did not agree on reform. A famous debate between Catherine Beecher and Angelina Grimké clarified the challenges facing female reformers. In 1837, Beecher published her *Essay on Slavery and Abolitionism, with Reference to the Duty of American Females*, directed at Grimké's abolition work. In it she declared, "Petitions to congress, in reference to the official duties of legislators, seem, IN ALL CASES, to fall entirely without the sphere of female duty." Grimké responded to Beecher by articulating a strict egalitarian creed: "Whatever it is morally right for man to do . . . it is morally right for women to do." Grimké boldly proclaimed, "I believe it is women's right to have a voice in all the laws and regulations by which she is to be *governed*, whether in Church or State." Beyond participation, she asserted women's rights to rule as well, stating that a woman has "just as much right to sit upon the throne of England, or in the Presidential chair of the United States." Even though a woman had just assumed the English throne—Queen Victoria was crowned in 1837—the active role played by the Grimkés, and other women, generated increasing criticism in the late 1830s and produced deep splits in the reform movement.

Angelina Grimké, excerpts from *Letters to Catherine E. Beecher, in Reply to an Essay on Slavery and Abolitionism* (1838)

Frustrated by the conservative reaction of otherwise reform-minded men, a group of women in western New York organized a convention in 1848 to consider women's rights. The convention's "Declaration of Sentiments," modeled after the Declaration of Independence, listed infringements on women's rights and called for change, including the right to vote. Elizabeth Cady Stanton, one of the convention organizers and one of the most important leaders of the 19th-century women's movement, drafted the declaration. Stanton accepted the need to sacrifice women's exceptionalism to further the causes she advocated, writing in 1842, "I am in favour of political action, & the organization of a third party as the most efficient way of calling forth & directing action." The participation of abolitionists at the convention demonstrated how many worked in both fields. Stanton declared that only Frederick Douglass, 1 of 32 men and the only person of color to attend the Seneca Falls Conference, could really understand what it meant to be disenfranchised. Douglass advocated strongly for women's full rights—his newspaper's masthead boldly declared "All Rights for All!"

Because many white and upper- or middle-class American women believed their responsibility was to raise moral children and preserve domestic space, they regarded female public activism on politically contentious topics as inappropriate. But for other

WOMEN'S RIGHTS This statue, located today in the U.S. Capitol Rotunda, immortalizes three leaders of the fight for women's rights in the United States— Elizabeth Cady Stanton, Susan B. Anthony, and Lucretia Mott—and conveys the as-yet unfinished nature of the struggle.

women the belief that females possessed a stronger innate moral sense compelled them to advocate abolition. They believed that women's greater respect for moral behavior obligated them to address slavery, the chief sin in the nation, even if the act of doing so, which required organizing, fundraising, and petitioning, brought them into fuller participation in the public world of men. The female reformers of this period encountered contradictions that have challenged American women to this day. Embracing women's distinctiveness could both empower and isolate—women used their special position to make real reforms and helped blunt the worst side effects of early industrialization. However, by endorsing women's difference they also ensured that women remained separated from men, especially as more formal politics overtook reform efforts after the Civil War.

Activists' efforts to improve the position and condition of women usually entailed working from within existing institutions—the family, the church, and sometimes electoral politics. In some cases, however, reformers sought to remake society in radical ways, from the ground up. Building what historians now call "utopian communities," these men and women envisioned a new era built on the principles of equality, community engagement, and respect for all people. One of the guiding lights of the movement, Robert Dale Owen, left his native Scotland because the United States offered more promise for the sort of small-scale democratic life he supported. An advocate of abolition and a free school system, and an ardent defender of women's autonomy, Owen founded New Harmony, Indiana, in 1825. Owen took inspiration from socialism, as did other utopian reformers who witnessed the destructive effects of early industrial capitalism. The community lasted only a few years, before lapsing into an individualism that Owen repudiated. He remained a vigorous advocate for progressive causes, writing one of the earliest books advocating birth control in the United States.

An aerial view of New Harmony (1838)

Love and Sex in the Age of Reform

Some of the utopian activists who sought to remake American society in the 1830s and 1840s moved beyond Owen's egalitarianism and called for free love, which meant that love, rather than marriage, should determine the nature of sexual relations between adults. Advocates respected sexual desire in people and espoused a variety of social forms to accommodate individual preferences, including celibacy, polygamy, and group marriage. Due to the strong belief among religious people that sex should occur only within marriage, these reformers drew scorn more often than respect. Although popular memories of the Victorian era conjure images of a loveless and often sexless period, the reality of 19th-century Americans' love lives is much more complicated. Popular advice manuals, for instance, encouraged an erotic life within marriage as a way of celebrating the human and divine spirit. As long as it derived from romantic love, sex within marriage could create an equality between men and women that existed in few other spheres of life, as when one midcentury wife told her husband, "I could *kiss you all over*—and then *eat you up*."

In the 19th century, it was not uncommon for both men and women to share physical intimacy with same-sex friends that differs sharply from the habits of 21st-century Americans. Men, especially those whose occupations required travel, often shared a bed with other men (for warmth and because of sparse options in most rural areas) and, like their female counterparts, exchanged hugs, kisses, and affectionate letters. In the 1830s, when Abraham Lincoln was a young lawyer, he shared a bed with Joshua Fry Speed, and the two developed a deep friendship. As Speed described it, "No two men were ever more intimate." Lincoln's law partner, William Herndon, believed that Lincoln "loved this man more than anyone living or dead."

Distinct from the emotional intimacy common in same-sex friendships, ample evidence exists that 19th-century Americans engaged in same-sex sexual behavior as well. The rise of laws punishing "crimes against nature" in the early 19th century indicates concern among elites that this behavior occurred and that such actions required a legal response, though urban police rarely prosecuted consensual sodomy. Because female sexuality was tied so closely to reproduction, people expressed less concern about female intimacy. Nonetheless, as cities expanded and created new all-male and all-female spaces—workplaces, boarding houses, and bars—opportunities for same-sex sexual relations increased. People who engaged in erotic and physically intimate same-sex relationships did not use modern terms like "gay" to describe themselves, however. We can identify evidence of homosexual behavior in the mid-19th century but not evidence of a homosexual identity, which appeared only late in the century. The term "heterosexual," for instance, was first used in the United States in 1892. This left people who engaged in same-sex relationships without a language to explain it to a public increasingly willing to stigmatize such relationships as deviant. Walt Whitman, the celebrated poet, wrote with great eloquence about the beauty and joy of male love and said about Fred Vaughan, a man with whom he lived for many years, "I have found him who loves me, / as I him, in perfect love," but he still rejected characterizations of himself as homosexual. Other people contented themselves with love seemingly without worry about labels. Charity Bryan and Sylvia Drake enjoyed a relationship "no less sacred to them than the tie of marriage," as a nephew described it. They cherished a long, loving relationship in plain view in a small town in rural Vermont. The crucial roles they played in the community—as skilled tailors who employed a bevy of local women, as active members of their local church, and as aunts who helped raise more than a hundred nieces and nephews—helped sustain a relationship that many neighbors regarded as a marriage.

STUDY QUESTIONS **FOR NORTHERN REFORM**

1. What explains the militancy of abolitionists after 1831?

2. On what grounds did American women argue for greater freedom?

3. How did the various reform movements intersect with one another?

quiz

⊙ SOUTHERN REFORM

Southern evangelicals faced a far greater challenge than their Northern coreligionists. Because slaveholders demanded absolute obedience from their slaves, they built a deeply conservative society. Any challenge to hierarchy and tradition threatened to undermine the foundation of that society. Despite this hurdle, Southern evangelical reformers confronted what they perceived as problems in Southern society. Most evangelicals strongly supported temperance and denounced the personal violence that characterized the system of Southern honor. A handful of brave reformers spoke out against slavery, but opponents often drove them from the region. Southern antislavery reformers were replaced by a new breed of thinkers who advocated for a more Christian slavery. Regardless of the measures they advocated, Southern reformers proceeded more cautiously than their Northern brethren. And, although Southern reformers often corresponded or met with their Northern or European peers, the emerging political culture of sectionalism curtailed cooperation across the regional divide.

Sin, Salvation, and Honor

The dominant value system in the white South prior to the Second Great Awakening emphasized an ethos of honor inherited from ancient models. Through the 1850s, Southerners consumed British Romantic fiction, particularly the courtly chivalry of Sir Walter Scott's novels. With little incentive to scrutinize their society, many white Southerners clung to this secular value system in the face of mounting tensions within their society. The evangelical movement in the South of the 1820s and 1830s expressly challenged prevailing values. Evangelicals sought to replace the standing system in which a person's wealth and status determined one's worth with a system in which one's piety and moral purity determined rank. Attracting followers proved difficult if people had something to lose, as revealed by the response of a Kentucky sheriff who treated his local Methodist preacher well but who refused to commit to the church because, as the preacher explained, "His worldly prospects were good, and he would not give up all for Christ." Southern evangelicals advocated many of the same reforms as their Northern counterparts. Hundreds of Southern communities established local temperance societies, for example. Like Northerners, Southerners feared the effect of alcohol on families and society, but most of all, as one evangelical noted, because it was "one grand hindrance of the success of the gospel." Evangelicals supported Bible and tract societies, Sunday schools, home and foreign missions, and efforts to help prisoners and the disabled.

Southern women played a key role in the evangelical movement and reform, but they rarely extended their work into the broader public women's rights movement found in the North. Southern women tended to focus their efforts on the individual rather than the societal level; they organized locally but not nationally; and increasingly by the 1840s, they sought reforms that promoted the stability of the slaveholding South. For example, in Petersburg, Virginia, a mill town south of Richmond, evangelical women organized Sunday schools, an Education Society, a Young Ladies' Missionary Society, a Married Ladies' Missionary Society, a Tract Distribution Society, and a Ladies' Benevolent Society. They also organized numerous ad hoc committees within the various churches and buttressed reform and benevolence with countless fairs and fundraisers. In addition to real benefits for the community, local and private relief systems allowed community elites to retain control over aid recipients. To receive aid, those in need had to pass the scrutiny of the "ladies." The insistence of Southern evangelicals to pursue reform while respecting the hierarchy of the conservative South reveals how religious revivals and the development of a distinct Southern political identity developed simultaneously throughout the 1830s, 1840s, and 1850s.

Pro-Slavery Reform

The antislavery attitude of early evangelicals in the late 18th and early 19th centuries inhibited the larger reform movement in the South. Early evangelicals sometimes criticized slaveholding, but more often they sought ways to accommodate their religious faith with their racial beliefs. Over time, articulating a pro-slavery Christianity provided one way to claim both piety and respectability. By the 1850s, the central evangelical reform project in the South had become the Mission to the Slaves. Evangelical slaveholders came to regard the act of ministering to slaves as the purest expression of their faith.

Modeling their work on that of West Indian planters who pursued a similar movement in the 1810s, the Mission to the Slaves encouraged masters to improve the physical treatment of slaves with the threat of church or social sanctions for those who failed to do so. In addition, the mission advocated for laws to protect slaves from cruel treatment. As Robert Dabney, one of the foremost Presbyterian ministers of the period, declared, Christians "must be willing to recognize and grant in slaves those rights which are a part of our essential humanity." Owing to the power of slaveholders in Southern society, these reforms could only extend so far. Under Southern law, slaves could not legally marry—although they formed de facto marriages—and evangelicals regarded this as a gross violation of the proper relationship between adult men and women who bore and raised children together. Female evangelicals also advocated protection of female slaves from sexual exploitation. The other main reform of the Mission to the Slaves fulfilled a basic Protestant obligation—ensuring that every person could read the Gospel for himself or herself. Because of the circulation of abolitionist propaganda in the mails and the power of literacy, Southern states made it a crime to teach slaves to read. Evangelical reformers built Sunday schools and worked with individual masters to persuade them that limited literacy posed no threat.

Robert Dabney, excerpt from a letter to his brother on the issue of slavery and Christianity (1851)

As slaveholders increasingly found a home within evangelical churches, they articulated a more individualized and more paternalistic social order. They aimed especially to control those African Americans who converted to Christianity in large numbers for the first time and drew strength from their new faith. Southern evangelicals, by then firmly supporting the morality of slavery, used the occurrence of several major slave rebellions in the 1820s and 1830s to argue for the necessity of conversion. To pacify slaveholders' concerns that evangelical reforms would undermine control of their slaves, evangelicals emphasized that converted slaves would be more obedient. According to Basil Manly, "The dissemination of moral truth will always be found at once the cheapest & most effective support of law & order, the most certain check of incendiarism & turbulence."

Nat Turner and Afro-Christianity

Early Afro-Christianity drew on black folk traditions, many of them African practices. The results of this cultural fusion could be seen in the late 18th century, when Afro-Christians would gather in a circle to proclaim their faith and pray. The "ring" derived from West African traditions but blended easily with the evangelical tradition of small-group public ritual. Other similarities between West African practices and Christianity, including an emphasis on water as a conduit of spirituality, helped draw new worshippers to the faith; rivers, sacred places in African religions, became baptismal

AFRICAN AMERICAN RELIGIOUS PRACTICES The more informal and emotionally expressive religious practices adopted by African Americans alienated some white Christians but gave black Christians a distinctive and rich spiritual practice.

pools. The importance of burial practices and the belief that death brought a "homecoming," as well as a three-part hierarchy of gods that resembled the Christian trinity, made Christianity intelligible to West Africans. Muslim slaves brought to America in the colonial era provided another bridge between faiths. Malinke slaves in Spanish St. Augustine and Sengambians and northern Nigerians in Louisiana left ample evidence that they arrived in the New World already practicing Islam. The close kinship between the two faiths and the syncretic nature of Islam in West Africa ensured that New World Muslims could be expected to understand and perhaps absorb aspects of Christianity without much difficulty.

At least a quarter of all Southern blacks participated in churches by the end of the 1850s (mostly in biracial churches). Although blacks sat in segregated pews, they received egalitarian treatment in many respects. Records reveal that mixed-race churches held blacks to the same moral standards as whites and disciplined them for the same reasons—drunkenness, lying, adultery, and other breaches of the faith. But these same churches never overtly challenged white assumptions of racial superiority. In some cases, masters required slaves to worship with them because they feared the consequences of separate worship. But in other cases, the spiritual sustenance that enslaved people obtained may have outweighed the routine humiliation of separate seating and readings and homilies telling slaves to obey their masters. Certainly the body of Afro-Christian hymns and spirituals that emerged at this period shows a community asserting its solidarity and searching for ways to resist the dehumanization of slavery:

> O brothers, don't get weary,
> O brothers, don't get weary,
> O brothers, don't get weary,
> We're waiting for the Lord.
> We'll land on Canaan's shore,
> We'll land on Canaan's shore,
> When we land on Canaan's shore,
> We'll meet forever more.

Efforts by slaveholders to control African American belief generally failed. By the 1850s, Southern evangelical churches, particularly the Baptists and Methodists, had become major institutions in black American life. Instead of obedience, Afro-Christian theology stressed the equality of all people before God, the necessity of discipline for a people held in bondage, and the promise of eventual deliverance. In their creative use of Christianity, black evangelicals echoed the efforts of enslaved peoples in French and Portuguese colonies, particularly Haiti and Brazil, where a syncretic Afro Catholicism sustained generations of slaves in opposition to French, Portuguese, and later Brazilian slaveholders.

One commonality among all the leaders of slave rebellions in the 1820s and 1830s was their use of religion to radicalize their communities and their positions of religious leadership to mobilize those communities. Denmark Vesey, a free black man in Charleston, South Carolina, drew on these diverse traditions. According to the charges against him, Vesey organized a multiethnic band of slaves and free blacks in 1822 and planned a revolt. Captured before the plan could be sprung, investigators discovered religious leadership throughout the plot, including Morris Brown, an African Methodist Episcopal (AME) pastor. Vesey himself worked as a lay leader in the AME church and used scripture to draw supporters. According to one deposition against him, "His general conversation was about religion which he would apply to slavery, as for instance, he would speak of the creation of the world, in which he would say all men had equal rights, blacks as well as whites." "Gullah" Jack Pritchard surfaced as a leader in the Vesey conspiracy along with another AME member who also maintained a reputation in Charleston as a conjurer.

Evangelical religion's role in spurring resistance to slavery burst into public view with **Nat Turner**'s rebellion in Southampton County, Virginia (Map 12.2). Turner's skills and literacy earned him the respect of local whites, who allowed him to preach to their slaves. Unbeknown to whites, Turner had spent years praying and searching

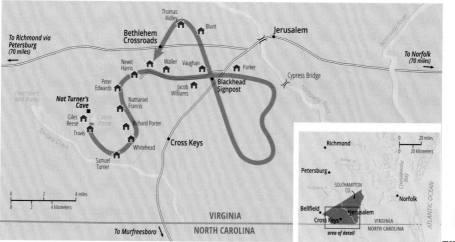

MAP 12.2 Nat Turner's Route in Southampton County, Virginia, 1831 Nat Turner and his band moved from house to house in an attempt to contain news of their rebellion. The violence of their actions marked a trail in blood through Southampton County and seared itself into the mind of the white South.

Celebrating the Black Atlantic

David Walker was not alone in his knowledge of global slavery or his faith in the resiliency of black people, nor was he alone in belonging to the maritime community. Black sailors possessed a unique mobility that exposed them to the diverse experiences and living conditions of people of African descent all around the Atlantic basin. Foremost among those experiences was the Haitian Revolution. Sailors who visited the island offered priceless knowledge about the reality of the hemisphere's only black republic. After watching a military procession, one noted, "They appeared to understand military tactics to perfection. They were elegantly dressed in red frocks and trousers, faced with blue and green. . . . On the whole they were first-rate soldiers." The idea of black soldiers parading would have been particularly impressive to African Americans, who could generally not own weapons and rarely marched in military formation. But Haiti represented more than physical power. Haitians' success at governing themselves proved to American activists that freedom was possible. Despite their pride in Haitians' accomplishments, black people in America (both enslaved and free) expressed great reluctance to speak openly about Haiti because they knew that even a mere mention could inspire panic and violence in whites. What they could and did celebrate openly, after 1834, was emancipation in the British West Indies. Black Americans, like West Indians themselves, enshrined August 1 as Freedom Day. By the 1850s, they held celebrations all across the Northern states, where speakers heralded the nonviolence of British emancipation. "Not by the sword and the bayonet," one Freedom Day participant argued,

Excerpt from *The Confessions of Nat Turner* (1832)

for the right way to fulfill his obligation to God, and he found it in a sacrifice that he likened to Jesus's. In 1831, Turner built a network of loyal men and launched an uprising that killed nearly 60 whites and sent the state into a panic. Although the militia dispersed the rebels and eventually apprehended and executed Turner, the widespread and disciplined organization among slaves on diverse plantations brought home to whites the deepest fears they had harbored since the Haitian Revolution at the end of the 18th century. To fearful whites, he seemed to portend the violence to come if they did not improve their treatment of slaves.

Southern Antislavery Reformers

Angelina Grimké, excerpt from *An Appeal to the Christian Women of the South* (1836)

Nat Turner's rebellion occurred the same year that the abolitionist William Lloyd Garrison began publishing *The Liberator*, a confluence that most white Southerners did not regard as coincidental. Fearing additional slave rebellions, white Southerners quashed all criticism of slavery after 1831. James Henry Hammond's "gag rule" prevented congressional discussion of abolition from 1836 to 1844, and federal postmasters before and after these dates prevented the circulation of abolitionist material in the Southern mails. The Grimké sisters could fully commit to abolition only after they abandoned their family and their region, moving from Charleston to Philadelphia. Angelina Grimké's *An Appeal to the Christian Women of the South* (1836) demanded "but by the force and power of truth." Freedom Day organizers used the ceremonies to unite African Americans with people of color around the hemisphere, but they also understood the political appeal of peaceful emancipation, especially when contrasted with Haiti's violent legacy.

Freedom Day celebrations offered elaborate festivals, with chartered trains to carry participants, parades hosted by civic and charitable groups, and banquets. These events gathered thousands of blacks and whites together, and speakers extolled both the virtue and wisdom of West Indian emancipation. They marshaled statistics to prove the economic superiority of free labor on the islands and celebrated the moral improvement of both free people and whites outside the confines of a slave society. These events offered community leaders an opportunity to combine a proud black identity with a universal uplift of humanity. Frederick Douglass, a frequent speaker at Freedom Day celebrations, asserted that August 1 "belongs . . . to the lovers of Liberty and of mankind the world over." "The sentiment," he noted, "that leads us to celebrate noble deeds . . . is nature and universal. . . . Neither geographical boundaries, nor national restrictions, ought, or shall prevent me from rejoicing over the triumphs of freedom." Like other African Americans, Douglass believed that commemorating West Indian emancipation would help the triumph of freedom in America as well.

Frederick Douglass, excerpt from "West India Emancipation speech" (1857)

- How did black Americans learn about the experiences of other enslaved people in the hemisphere?
- What lessons did they draw from these experiences and how did they shape the struggle against slavery in the United States?

emancipation on the grounds of Christianity and argued that the millennium would come only after slavery had been destroyed. It was probably the only abolitionist tract written by a white Southern woman directed to her peers. The radicalism of her message combined with her personal background brought strong denunciations from conservative ministers in the North and howls of rage from white Southerners who perceived her as a traitor.

David Walker, another exile from the South, proved even more dangerous than the Grimké sisters. Born to an enslaved father and free black mother in North Carolina, Walker remained in the South until the mid-1820s, when he moved to Boston and immersed himself in the abolition movement. After writing briefly for a variety of journals, Walker penned and published *An Appeal to the Coloured Citizens of the World*. Electrifying in its language and vigorous in its argument, the document created a firestorm of criticism in both the North and the South; even many abolitionists found its frank call for resistance too vigorous. Walker, flatly denying the legitimacy of slavery, asserted the universal rights of all people to freedom. He called on the "candid and unprejudiced of the world, to search the pages of history diligently, and see if [any group of people] ever treated a set of human beings, as the white Christians of America do us, the blacks, or Africans."

Walker drafted a brief global history of slavery, running from biblical and classical examples to the role played by European colonizers of the New World who created plantation slavery. Walker's "appeal" sought an international audience. He compared the plight of African Americans to that of other subjugated peoples—Native Americans, the Greeks, the Irish, and the Jews. The range of his learning—from ancient Egypt to the modern Spanish Empire—and his use of these examples proved that black Americans could and did educate themselves to a degree that would have surprised most whites at the time.

In Boston, Walker worked within the larger maritime community. Since the early days of European oceanic exploration, black men had worked as sailors, and they remained, in the 1830s and 1840s, among the most worldly and most important members of the African diasporic community in the Americas. Keen to rebut charges that blacks were incompetent to rule themselves, Walker argued that "the inhuman system of *slavery*, is the *source* from which most of our miseries proceed." Like most antislavery evangelicals, Walker condemned the hypocrisy of Christians holding fellow Christians in bondage. He catalogued the disasters that befell previous slave empires in the hopes of scaring white Southerners into action. Again and again he warned "white Christians" against their continuing sanction of this most diabolical of evils. He closed with an ominous warning: "Americans may be as vigilant as they please, but they cannot be vigilant enough for the Lord, neither can they hide themselves, where he will not find and bring them out."

STUDY QUESTIONS FOR SOUTHERN REFORM

1. In what ways did Southern reform resemble Northern efforts? How were they different?

2. How did black Southerners conceptualize and experience evangelical Christianity?

quiz

CHALLENGES TO THE SPIRIT OF THE AGE

In many respects, the era from the late 1820s to the early 1850s can be defined as much by the role of religion as by economic change, geographic growth, and political development. The growth of evangelical Protestantism preoccupied the lives of many Americans through this period, produced social reforms that changed the lives of millions, and helped propel the sectional divisions that produced the Civil War and emancipation. At the same time, however, the rise of an increasingly secular culture, expressed through novels, newspapers, and the work of mass political parties, matched the spiritual movements of the day. Some of this cultural work faced east, engaged with European questions expressed in largely British and continental idioms. In other cases, authors self-consciously rejected older models and sought to build a uniquely American culture. Much of it was condemned by religious figures because of what they regarded as vulgar content or expression. Most frustrating for the traditionalists was the persistent popularity and wide reach of these new forms of media and communication. Americans were building their first truly national culture.

Emerson, Thoreau, and the American Soul

Ralph Waldo Emerson began his professional life as a Unitarian clergyman but left the ministry in the midst of the tumult in the early 1830s. He wrote essays and criticism

WALDEN;

OR,

LIFE IN THE WOODS.

By HENRY D. THOREAU,

AUTHOR OF "A WEEK ON THE CONCORD AND MERRIMACK RIVERS."

I do not propose to write an ode to dejection, but to brag as lustily as chanticleer in the morning, standing on his roost, if only to wake my neighbors up. — Page 92.

Copy 2

BOSTON:

TICKNOR AND FIELDS.

M DCCC LIV.

THOREAU'S *WALDEN* Thoreau's cabin and the image of man's relation to wildness articulated by *Walden* served for many readers as a counterbalance to the industrializing and urbanizing trends of the early 19th century.

over the next several decades, patronized younger authors such as Henry David Thoreau and Margaret Fuller, and pushed for broad changes in American life. Unlike most of the evangelicals, Emerson sought to reform the American mind. He celebrated a vigorous individualism, articulated most fully in his famous essay "Self-Reliance," in which he encouraged readers to reject tradition. "A foolish consistency is the hobgoblin of little minds, adored by statesmen and philosophers and divines," he wrote famously. Emerson's advice provided reassurance for the new classes that seized opportunities created by industrialization. His call to begin life anew mirrored what many entrepreneurs felt they were doing.

Ralph Waldo Emerson, excerpts from "Self Reliance" (1841)

Henry David Thoreau attempted to live this philosophy when he retreated to a cabin outside Concord, Massachusetts, for two years. Unfortunately, he failed as a farmer and survived through the largesse of friends who stopped by with gifts of food. Although Thoreau could not remove himself entirely from the modernizing world he so distrusted, his volume chronicling the experience, *Walden*, pushed readers to think critically about the costs of the rampant materialism that sustained the dynamic economic growth of the era. *Walden* also represented a challenge to traditional Anglo-American ideas about land use. Thoreau did not seek to maximize the land and encouraged a respectful appreciation for man's dependence on the natural world.

Thoreau and Emerson became associated with the philosophy of **transcendentalism**, an American variant of European Romanticism. Turning away from the rationalism of the Enlightenment, transcendentalists desired to know the world through emotion and intuition. Although it was often expressed in obscure prose, this philosophy, like Emerson's writing in general, proved compatible with trends toward democratization in American society. Transcendentalists put little value on formal education and degrees. Instead, experience and intimate contact with the natural world earned their praise. As Thoreau's experience indicates, their philosophy called for action rather than talk. Both writers supported abolition and other social reforms, but neither appreciated the staid evangelical tone of the movement. Emerson denounced the hypocrisy that blinded would-be reformers from the full implications of their morality, demanding that "goodness must have some edge to it."

The First Mass Culture

Steam power and industrialization, in addition to improving the efficiency of American manufacturing, lowered the price of leisure and recreation items. Printers began producing newspapers in greater volume at a lower cost. In the early 1830s, thousands of "penny presses" sprouted in every city and many small towns throughout the country. These newspapers distinguished themselves from their predecessors because rather than relying on subsidies from political parties, they sought a mass readership. To accomplish this goal, reporters began writing "stories," largely human interest tales about murders, robberies, and assaults. James Gordon Bennett, the editor of the *New York Herald*, the most successful of the new breed of newspaper, realized that the average readers "were more ready to seek six columns of the details of a brutal murder, or the testimony of a divorce case, or the trial of a divine for improprieties of conduct, than the same amount of words poured forth by the genius of the noblest author of the times." Serialized fiction also began to appear, largely stories of romance and duplicity aimed at female readers. Reporters began investigating political news, particularly in Washington, DC, where they gained the scorn of politicians for their willingness to report on their foibles. Even as newspapers helped knit America together with a shared culture, through their focus on conflict they helped exacerbate the disagreements over slavery.

Alongside the theater, which continued to offer performances of Shakespeare and other European classics, arose a much rowdier and uniquely American form of popular entertainment: minstrelsy. Minstrel shows, which began in Northern cities, featured white male performers with blackened faces performing what they imagined to be black behavior. The shows became enormously popular in New York, Boston, and other major cities, with a repertoire of songs and stock characters. Stephen Foster, America's first major songwriter, gained his fame penning minstrel tunes such as "Camptown Races" and "Oh! Susanna," although Foster later wrote songs that celebrated more complex black characters. Minstrel shows succeeded partly because of the way they transgressed boundaries, with whites imitating, celebrating, and lampooning blacks all at once. The all-male audiences and the vigorous physicality of the performances transformed the theaters into showcases for masculine expression. **Walt Whitman**, the bard of the common man, regularly patronized the Bowery Theater, one of New York City's most famous minstrel venues. He described the crowd there

Bryant's
Minstrels,
"Dixie"
(1859)

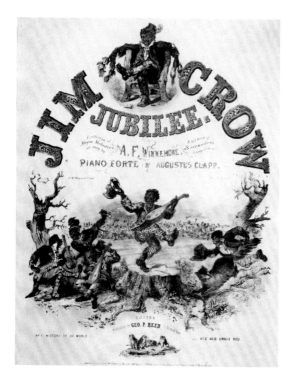

MINSTREL SHOWS The degrading caricatures enacted in minstrel shows drew large white audiences and imprinted on many Northerners erroneous but lasting images of black life.

as "a vast sea of upturned faces and red flannel shirt, extending its roaring and turbid waves close up to the foot-lights on either side, clipping in the orchestra and dashing furiously against the boxes."

The American Renaissance

The emergence of a group of American writers around midcentury—Emerson and Thoreau in essays, Nathaniel Hawthorne and Herman Melville in fiction, Walt Whitman and Emily Dickinson in poetry, and Edgar Allan Poe in all three genres—signaled for many Americans the maturation of their culture. In their settings, their language, and their themes, these authors made the United States a part of world literature. At the same time, however, they engaged in a dialogue with their peers across the Atlantic. They read and wrote with one eye on the European authors in whose traditions they worked—and European authors reciprocated the feeling. British novelist Anthony Trollope referred to Hawthorne as "a brother novelist very much greater than myself."

Hawthorne and Melville, in particular, wrote literature that reflected universal themes. Both men attained their greatest renown for works—*The Scarlet Letter* and *Moby-Dick*, respectively—that achieved little popular success at the time but helped inspire writers and readers in later generations. Melville first gained notoriety for a series of novels, *Typee*, *Omoo*, and *Redjacket*, drawn from his adventures as a young sailor in the Pacific Ocean. The novels blended travelogue and ethnography and provided detailed analyses of the lives of island inhabitants. Melville's most ambitious novel,

WALT WHITMAN Whitman's poetry celebrated the physical and emotional energy unleashed by American growth in the 1840s and 1850s.

Excerpt from *Moby-Dick* (1851)

Moby-Dick, addressed universal questions of power, revenge, and madness. Nonetheless, Melville's work offers insights into mid-19th-century America. The ship that carries the whaling party in *Moby-Dick*, the *Pequod*, carries a remarkably diverse crew, with Indian, African, and South Seas harpooners, white men and black, all bound together by their shared domicile and profession. Melville's imaginary ship mirrored the real-life diversity of America and the difficulty of reconciling so many competing interests and contradictory philosophies in one nation.

Melville's capacious imagination and welcome fictional embrace of diverse ethnic and racial types reflected a broad-mindedness common among this generation of writers. A number of writers, including Whitman, Dickinson, and Poe, took inspiration from what they called Oriental tales, which they read as a "symbol of the unfettered imagination." In many of his poems, Poe adopted the form and message of Asian literature—especially in his use of visionaries and visionary moments—including borrowing from the Koran and Islamic practices. At the same time, this trio of writers pioneered a distinct American poetry.

Whitman advanced this project the furthest. His use of free verse, his frank characterizations of human sexuality, and his vigorous endorsement of a rough and authentic America distinguished his work. In the 20th century, Whitman's work came to be celebrated, particularly his *Calamus* group of poems, which celebrate manly affection and love, as the foundation of gay literature. At the time, *Children of Adam* garnered more critiques because of its explicit celebration of the human body. These led to his being fired from a job with the Department of the Interior. One critic worried that Whitman "sees nothing vulgar in what which is commonly regarded as the grossest obscenity," but this collection included the now classic "I Sing the Body Electric," his famous paean to the vigor and beauty of both men and women. As the collection's title indicates, Whitman saw Americans as an original people. Rather than draw classical parallels or craft aspirational literature, Whitman celebrated the prosaic democracy of America, as in his most famous poem, "Song of Myself," where he writes,

> I am of old and young, of the foolish as much as the wise,
> Regardless of others, even regardful of others,
> Maternal as well as paternal, a child as well as a man,
> Stuff'd with the stuff that is coarse and stuff'd with the stuff
> that is fine,
> One of the Nation of many nations, the smallest the same
> and the largest the same . . .

Emily Dickinson, born in 1830, remained virtually unknown throughout her life. She remained in her parents' home in Amherst, Massachusetts, which she rarely left. She published only a handful of anonymous poems during her lifetime, but the posthumous discovery of her work has inspired fellow writers for the last century and a half. Moving beyond Whitman's experimentation with free verse, Dickinson unshackled every constraint, reimagining meter, rhyme, capitalization, grammar, and punctuation. Her work demonstrated new capacities in language that poets continue to explore. Dickinson professed her understanding of poetry in physical terms, ones that Whitman and Thoreau would well have understood: "If I read a book and it makes my whole body so cold no fire ever can warm me, I know *that* is poetry."

Politics as Gospel

The vitality and diversity of American culture in the 1830s and 1840s could be seen in the political system as well. Senators, congressmen, and presidents recognized the power and importance of the reform movements initiated by evangelicals, but they could not control them. The new issues of the 1830s and 1840s, especially the transformation of artisans into workers and the rapid commercialization of the national economy, spurred the rise of workingmen's parties in northeastern cities, but these lasted only a few years and rarely influenced policy. As slavery began to assume greater national significance, antislavery reformers organized political parties under different names—the Liberty Party in 1840 and 1844 and the Free Soil Party in 1848—that likewise failed to take root. These failures, however, should not obscure the extent to which the nation's political culture reflected the larger dynamism and unpredictability of the era. The promise and the possibilities represented by these short-lived political parties and by the broader rise and fall of the Whig Party encouraged Americans to take politics seriously.

The Whig Party emerged as the main opposition to Democratic dominance. The Whigs coalesced around their shared antipathy for Andrew Jackson—they took their name from the English political party that opposed absolutist kings. By 1840—the first year the Whigs won the White House—the party had emerged with both a guiding ideology and an official organization. The Richmond *Whig* defined its supporters as

interactive timeline

TIMELINE 1801–1855

AMERICA	YEAR	THE WORLD
Aug Cane Ridge, Kentucky, evangelical revival held	**1801**	
Jan American Colonization Society founded	**1817**	
Feb Liberia is founded as a colony for freed American slaves	**1820**	
Jun Denmark Vesey arrested for organizing a slave conspiracy in Charleston, South Carolina	**1822**	
Charles Grandison Finney leads his first revival Robert Dale Owen founds utopian colony in New Harmony, Indiana	**1825**	
American Temperance Society founded	**1826**	
David Walker publishes *An Appeal to the Coloured Citizens of the World* Angelina Grimké joins her sister Sarah in Philadelphia, where they become leading women's rights and antislavery activists	**1829**	
Apr Joseph Smith founds the Mormon Church	**1830**	
William Lloyd Garrison founds *The Liberator*, America's leading abolitionist newspaper Nat Turner leads the deadliest slave rebellion in U.S. history in Southampton County, Virginia	**1831**	
Massachusetts is the last state to disestablish support of an official church Charles Grandison Finney assumes residency of Oberlin College American Anti-Slavery Society is organized under Garrisonian principles	**1833**	Britain begins ending slavery in the British West Indies Ottoman Empire recognizes independence of Egypt
Alexis de Tocqueville publishes Vol. 1 of *Democracy in America* James Gordon Bennett begins publishing the *New York Herald*	**1835**	

those who "prefer liberty to tyranny—who support privilege against prerogative—the rights and immunities of the people . . . against the predominance of the Crown or Executive power." That ideology emphasized republican self-government and an active role for government at all levels to help foster economic development, although Whigs also criticized interference in markets. **Henry Clay** led the party during its two decades in existence, and his "American System" drew the support of Whig businessmen who wanted the federal and state governments to sponsor the construction of the infrastructure—roads, bridges, canals, and railroads—on which private enterprise could build American markets and cities.

The Whig Party also drew in reformers—from humanitarian groups protesting the treatment of Indians to some of the antislavery forces spread around the country. Whigs attracted primarily Protestant voters, often denouncing Catholic immigrants as "dupes" of the Democrats. They drew strength primarily in the North and the upper

AMERICA	YEAR	THE WORLD
Abolitionist printer Elijah Lovejoy murdered in Alton, Illinois, by anti-abolitionist mob Catherine Beecher and Angelina Grimké debate nature of women Severe recession strikes United States	1837	
Frederick Douglass escapes slavery	1838	
Liberty Party nominates James G. Birney for president on an antislavery platform	1840	
Mormon founder Joseph Smith is killed in Illinois; Brigham Young leads Mormons to Utah First telegraph sent between Washington, DC, and Baltimore, Maryland Liberty Party again nominates James G. Birney for president on antislavery platform	1844	
Frederick Douglass publishes first edition of his *Narrative of the Life of Frederick Douglass*	1845	Irish Potato Famine begins, inaugurating a decade of disease that kills 750,000 Irish and drives two million into exile
Lewis Tappan helps found American Missionary Association, which joins antislavery churches	1846	
Lucretia Mott and Elizabeth Cady Stanton lead Seneca Falls Convention, which produces "Declaration of Sentiments" calling for women's rights Free Soil Party nominates Martin Van Buren for president on platform opposing expansion of slavery in western territories	1848	Nationalist movements occur in Italy, Germany, France, and Hungary Karl Marx and Friedrich Engels publish *The Communist Manifesto*
Nathaniel Hawthorne publishes *The Scarlet Letter*	1850	
Herman Melville publishes *Moby-Dick*	1851	
Henry David Thoreau publishes *Walden*	1854	
Walt Whitman publishes first edition of *Leaves of Grass*	1855	

South—Virginia, Kentucky, Tennessee, and North Carolina all saw strong Whig parties. Citizens' enthusiasm for the Democrats, the Whigs, and the smaller third parties made the 1830s, 1840s, and much of the 1850s a period of political dynamism and flux. Men and women invested significant amounts of energy in organizing new parties and advocating new policies. "The spirit of the age," observed the English visitor Fanny Wright, was "to be a little fanatical" (Figure 12.3).

People's willingness to spend time, money, and energy on politics demonstrates a commitment to American democracy that few other nations manifested. England, which saw the beginning of many of the workingmen's parties that inspired American workers of the 1830s, continued to maintain restrictions on voting and office holding that excluded a significant number of even white men from the polls. To international observers, Americans invested more of themselves in their public world. One of the most trenchant observers, the Frenchman Alexis de Tocqueville, expressed some

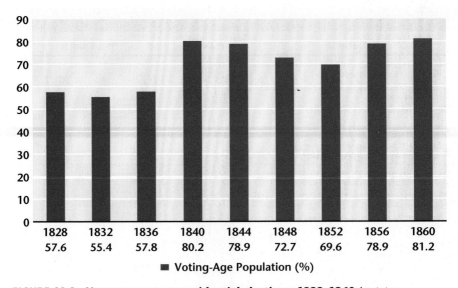

1828	1832	1836	1840	1844	1848	1852	1856	1860
57.6	55.4	57.8	80.2	78.9	72.7	69.6	78.9	81.2

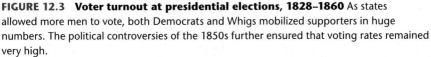

■ **Voting-Age Population (%)**

FIGURE 12.3 Voter turnout at presidential elections, 1828–1860 As states allowed more men to vote, both Democrats and Whigs mobilized supporters in huge numbers. The political controversies of the 1850s further ensured that voting rates remained very high.

skepticism about democratic forms of government. But de Tocqueville also drew inspiration from Americans' enthusiasm for politics and for their public world. He believed that Americans' willingness to create associations and parties would help restore the organic bonds that had once tied together the Old World's societies before the rise of capitalism and democracy. Whereas conservatives feared that the "tyranny of the majority" would overrule reason and liberty in open democracies, de Tocqueville predicted associations of "a thousand different types" would forestall the "tyranny of parties or the arbitrary rule of a prince."

When de Tocqueville observed that Americans were insatiable "joiners," he testified to the emergence of a new civic space in the United States. European countries had official spheres and private spheres and—increasingly after the 16th century—marketplaces, but little room for organized public actions. The reform movements in America in the 1830s and 1840s flourished because a strong evangelical impulse sustained them—many people understood their reform work as saving their own souls as well as that of those they helped—and because of changes in American law. Some of these latter changes—especially the rise of general incorporation laws as a part of the expansion of capitalism during Andrew Jackson's administration—created the opportunity for reformers to organize themselves in ways that would have been impossible in previous years. Social reformers also benefited from the larger process of democratization underway at the same time, which drew new participants into politics and empowered individual citizens to believe that they could solve problems in American life. However, this optimism waned somewhat in the 1850s, as reformers found that some problems resisted easy solution, especially slavery and the continuing growth of poverty among urban residents.

Alexis de Tocqueville on voluntary associations, from Democracy in America (1841)

STUDY QUESTIONS FOR CHALLENGES TO THE SPIRIT OF THE AGE

1. How did transcendentalism relate to the evangelical reform efforts that defined the era?
2. Did the literature of Hawthorne, Melville, Whitman, and Dickinson create a more insular or more open America?

quiz

Summary

- Evangelical Christians on both sides of the Atlantic exchanged ideas and strategies during the Second Great Awakening and inspired a broad set of social, cultural, and intellectual changes in all parts of America.
- Northern women initiated reform efforts—including temperance, women's rights, and abolition—that targeted the same broad range of social ills as did their British counterparts.
- In the South, slaveholders harnessed the power of the Protestant churches to articulate a more individualized and more paternalistic social order, especially as a way to control those African Americans who converted to Christianity in large numbers for the first time and drew strength from their new faith.
- These spiritual movements were matched by the rise of an increasingly secular culture, expressed through novels, newspapers, and the work of mass political parties.

Key Terms and People

American Anti-Slavery Society (AASS) 412
American Colonization Society (ACS) 413
American Temperance Society (ATS) 409
Clay, Henry 430
Douglass, Frederick 412
Finney, Charles Grandison 402
Garrison, William Lloyd 411

Lovejoy, Elijah 412
Millennialism 407
Mormons 406
Second Great Awakening 402
Transcendentalism 426
Turner, Nat 421
Walker, David 423
Whitman, Walt 427
Young, Brigham 406

audio
flashcards

Reviewing Chapter 12

1. How were political democratization and religious awakening related during the antebellum era?
2. What distinguishes the evangelicalism of the 1830s and 1840s from the practice of Christianity in earlier periods?

Further Reading

Carwardine, Richard. *Transatlantic Revivalism: Popular Evangelicalism in Britain and America, 1790–1865.* Westport, CT: Greenwood Press, 1978. This book traces the intellectual and personal links that bound people together across the Atlantic.

Ginzberg, Lori D. *Women and the Work of Benevolence: Morality, Politics, and Class in the Nineteenth-Century United States*. New Haven, CT: Yale University Press, 1990. An analysis of how women's reform work both challenged and reinforced gender conventions in 19th-century America.

Heyrman, Christine Leigh. *Southern Cross: The Beginnings of the Bible Belt*. New York: Knopf, 1997. A study of the origins and maturation of evangelical denominations in the Southern United States through the Second Great Awakening.

Howe, Daniel Walker. *What Hath God Wrought: The Transformation of America, 1815–1848*. New York: Oxford University Press, 2007. A comprehensive history that reveals the intimate relationship between the emergence of new technologies, new ideologies, and new structures of politics in early 19th-century America.

Newman, Richard S. *The Transformation of American Abolitionism: Fighting Slavery in the Early Republic*. Chapel Hill: University of North Carolina Press, 2002. A clear analysis of the shift in strategy and goals from first-generation abolitionists in the 18th century to the more radical 19th-century activists.

Ryan, Mary. *Civic Wars: Democracy and Public Life in the American City During the Nineteenth Century*. Berkeley: University of California Press, 1997. A thoughtful study that chronicles how the development of American cities challenged public and political life.

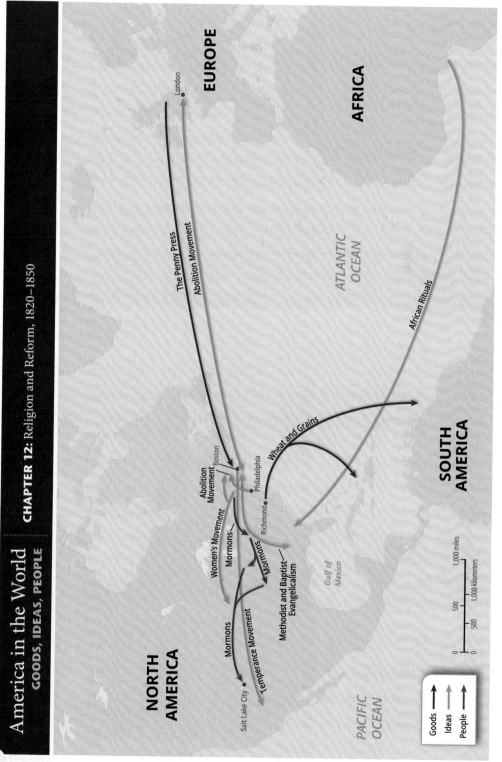

America in the World
GOODS, IDEAS, PEOPLE

CHAPTER 12: Religion and Reform, 1820–1850

EUROPE

AFRICA

London

The Penny Press

Abolition Movement

ATLANTIC
OCEAN

African Rituals

NORTH
AMERICA

Boston

Abolition
Movement

Philadelphia

Women's Movement

Mormons

Richmond

Mormons

Wheat and Grains

Methodist and Baptist
Evangelicalism

Mormons

Salt Lake City

Temperance Movement

Gulf of
Mexico

SOUTH
AMERICA

PACIFIC
OCEAN

0   500   1,000 miles
0   500   1,000 kilometers

Goods

Ideas

People

map analysis

American forces storming the fortress of Chapultepec in Mexico City.

A House Dividing

I n November 1852, U.S. commodore Matthew C. Perry left Norfolk, Virginia, with a fleet of "black ships"—new steam-powered warships. He sailed for the closed society of Japan, which Americans saw as a potential trading partner, a colonial target, and a port and refueling base for whaling ships. Only the Chinese, the Koreans, and the Dutch had limited access to Japan. Britain, which had defeated China in the First Opium War of 1839–1842, opened Western trade to the Pacific Rim, and its success encouraged the United States to approach China and Japan.

The U.S. government instructed Perry to be "courteous and conciliatory, but at the same time, firm and decided." The Japanese should be impressed with "a just sense of the power and greatness" of the Americans. After several months of negotiation, backed by threats that the steam-driven warships would shell the city of Tokyo, Perry secured a meeting with a high-ranking official. Coming ashore in early 1854, nearly 5,000 Japanese greeted the Americans. Cultural and gift exchanges complemented the official business. U.S. soldiers watched a demonstration of sumo wrestling, and U.S. Marines performed a close-order drill exhibition. In one sailor's observation, "there was a curious mélange today here, a function of east and west, railroads and telegraph, boxers and educated athletes, epaulettes and uniforms, shaved pates and night-gowns, soldiers with muskets and drilling in close array, soldiers with petticoats, sandals . . . all these things, and many others, exhibiting the difference between our civilization and usages and those of this secluded, pagan people." The condescension in this statement came mostly from ignorance. The Japanese had insulated themselves from the West, and, as a result, most Westerners knew little about Japanese life. The sailor's perspective also reflected common Anglo-American attitudes about racial and cultural differences that shaped debates in the United States and wherever Americans went abroad.

After he returned to the United States, Perry assured the country that commercial exchange with both Japan and China was imminent, whether compelled by diplomacy or force. Perry described the ascension of America to world power and the acquisition of colonies as inevitable and frankly admitted the likelihood of colonial acquisitions. "In the developments of the future, the destinies of our nation must assume conspicuous attitudes: we cannot expect to be free from the ambitious longings for increased power, which are the natural concomitants of national success." Although few politicians spoke this openly about American interventions overseas, Perry's vision of American power reflected the essence of what both Democrats and Whigs heralded in their campaigns and from the floors of Congress. Outgrowing its status as a recently freed colony, the United States was preparing to become a colonizing power itself.

Japanese
views of
the Perry
expedition

PERRY IN JAPAN   This image of Perry's dinner for Japanese commissioners on one of his fleet's ships emphasizes American power but fails to capture the historical reality. In the 1850s, the United States was only emerging as a naval power and could do little more than ask that the Japanese open their markets to U.S. imports.

THE EXPANSION OF AMERICA

Expansion of trading opportunities in the Pacific was made possible by western expansion during the 1840s. U.S. victory in a war against Mexico brought the territory between the Louisiana Purchase line and the Pacific Ocean under U.S. control. Expansion intensified the conflict between Americans over whether new states should be organized with or without slavery, and these territorial disputes generated sectional animosities. As a result, Northerners fashioned a new political coalition that opposed the expansion of slavery, supported a conservative approach to immigration and naturalization, and promoted federal investment in economic development. Concerned about the threat a sectional party in U.S. politics posed to slavery, Southerners reacted angrily and raised the possibility of leaving the union.

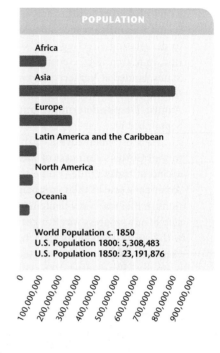

POPULATION

Africa

Asia

Europe

Latin America and the Caribbean

North America

Oceania

World Population c. 1850
U.S. Population 1800: 5,308,483
U.S. Population 1850: 23,191,876

In addition to their predictable differences over economic development, immigration, and slavery, expansion became one of the key issues in the presidential campaign of 1844. In particular, the Democratic candidate James K. Polk advocated the annexation, or territorial incorporation, of Texas. Independent since 1836, the Lone Star Republic had grown from 30,000 residents to 135,000, and its leaders hoped to bring it into the United States as a state. Polk won the election and entered office six days after the United States annexed Texas.

The American Invasion and Conquest of Mexico

The open belligerence of the Polk administration inspired the war party inside Mexico, which took Texas annexation as an affront to the nation's honor. Throughout the period from 1836 to 1847, Mexican officials had contended with rebellions in a host of Mexico's states. People living in the northern region of Mexico had also been subjected to debilitating raids by Indian war parties that stole livestock and sometimes took human captives to enslave or hold for ransom. These problems weakened the Mexican national government at the moment that it entered into war with a more unified and militarily proficient foe. Even as the United States ostensibly pursued diplomatic negotiations in late 1845 and early 1846, Polk created the pretext for war by ordering troops into contested territory south of the Texas border along the Nueces River. When Mexican forces attacked U.S. troops in April, Polk asserted, "American blood has been shed on American soil" and galvanized the country to support war. Most citizens eagerly endorsed the war. Proclaiming "Ho, for the Halls of Montezuma," volunteers flocked to the service. Early Whig opposition to the war crumbled as politicians recalled that Federalist opposition to the War of 1812 had destroyed the party.

The United States launched a three-pronged invasion of Mexico. As General Zachary Taylor and Colonel A. W. Doniphan invaded Mexico's northern territories, Stephen

Kearny led an expedition across New Mexico and into California. The Americans possessed a significant technological advantage with movable artillery, which they used to devastating effect against Mexican forces. But with no sign of Mexican capitulation, in March 1847, General Winfield Scott, the highest-ranking officer in the United States, landed at Veracruz and marched westward toward the capital (Map 13.1). After several clashes with the Mexican army, Scott reached the outskirts of Mexico City in August. Despite determined and bloody resistance, the city fell to the United States on September 14.

As Scott's men advanced through the country, many read a recently published history of Cortés's conquest of Mexico by William Prescott. Prescott's account served as a kind of travel guide—some soldiers read the Spanish version to learn the language. Americans saw in their campaign a historic parallel to the first great clash of civilizations in Mexico. Navy lieutenant Raphael Semmes read the book and observed, "Every step of our progress was fraught with the associations of three hundred years. . . . Time, with his scythe and hourglass, had brought another and a newer race. . . . Nothing could exceed the beauty of this spectacle." Some Mexicans too drew the same analogy, as one politician commented, "The soldiers are telling terrible tales that bring to mind the Conquest."

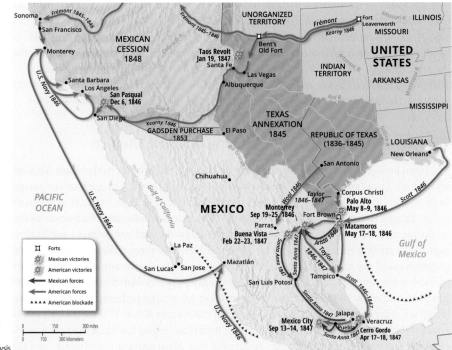

map analysis

MAP 13.1 U.S.–Mexican War The United States launched a three-pronged invasion of Mexico—with Stephen Kearny going into New Mexico, Zachary Taylor securing the southern border of Texas, and Winfield Scott leading the main army on its successful attack on Mexico City. The war added half a million square miles to the United States, more than a third of its prewar territory.

Even though U.S. soldiers prided themselves on liberating the country from the thrall of centuries of Catholic and Spanish tyranny, many chroniclers reflected the long-standing attitudes that had shaped western settlement for decades. Characterizations of Mexican soldiers as "degraded," "hideous," and possessing minds "rather animal than intellectual" flowed back home in letters and newspaper reports. In some cases, the racial differences described by these soldiers were used to justify atrocities committed against Mexican soldiers and civilians. General Taylor, in particular, exercised little restraint over his soldiers. General Scott, by contrast, deplored violence against civilians and managed to occupy Mexico City relatively peacefully. For most of these soldiers, victory in the war demonstrated the superiority of Anglo institutions and provided an opportunity for Mexicans to reform their fractious nation. In describing the conflict, one soldier wrote, "The American eagle seemed to spread his broad pinions and westward bar the principles of Republican government."

Observations of Mexico from a U.S. Army lieutenant (1846)

The war retained its popularity in the United States partly because American forces defeated Mexican forces in every major engagement in the 16-month conflict. Nonetheless, many Whigs and their supporters opposed the war because they feared it would lead America onto the imperial path that had ruined so many European nations. Whig politicians, such as Illinois representative Abraham Lincoln, who maintained their opposition to the war paid a high political price. But enthusiasm from battlefield victories overwhelmed debates over the war's initial legitimacy, and Lincoln lost his reelection to the House to a Democrat. Despite the tactical success that U.S. forces enjoyed during the war, the conflict turned out to be the bloodiest in U.S. history when measured on a per capita basis. The death rate for U.S. servicemen—110 out of every 1,000—remains the highest for any American war. Only a fraction of the soldiers (1,548) died during combat; the vast majority (10,970) died of disease. The war concluded a 20-year history of U.S.–Mexican relations marked by conflict, mistrust, and violence, but the challenge of how to define and police the boundary continued to vex residents of the region.

The Emergence of the New American West

Once the war officially began, President Polk explained his goals: "I declared my purpose to be to acquire for the United States, California, New Mexico, and perhaps some of the Northern Provinces of Mexico." Mr. Polk's War, as critics called it, succeeded spectacularly in this regard. The **Treaty of Guadalupe Hidalgo**, approved by both sides, ceded Texas north of the Rio Grande, California, and New Mexico to the United States for $15 million. It brought 500,000 square miles, nearly 55 percent of prewar Mexico, into U.S. possession and expanded the continental United States by over 40 percent.

Americans coveted California because of its resources and coastal access to the Pacific Ocean and Asian markets. Just as U.S. settlers had poured into Texas in the 1830s, they began streaming into California in the early 1840s. Like the early Texas colonists, these residents pledged nominal allegiance to Mexico but desired independence and annexation to the United States. In 1846, Lieutenant John Frémont, already famous as the "Pathfinder of the West" for his role in exploring the Southwest, reached northern California on a mapping expedition for the U.S. topographical engineers. One month after Frémont supported a settler uprising that declared the "Bear Flag Republic" independent of Mexico, the U.S. Navy arrived off the coast of San Francisco. Although fighting in southern California stretched later into the year, it involved

Making Boundaries

The air was thin and cold on the high desert plateau where the men met in 1851. If they found their view of the ridged and broken terrain of southeastern Arizona majestic, it must also have impressed upon them how difficult a task they faced. Their goal was to identify and mark out the boundary line between the United States and Mexico. Despite years of effort, the senior members of the Joint United States and Mexico Boundary Commission had many more years of work ahead of them. Making the border proved a difficult task. The U.S.–Mexican War concluded in 1848, but it took another decade for the two countries to determine a physical border. The difficulty in mapping a boundary foreshadowed the much greater difficulty both states had in policing a region across which people, ideas, and goods traveled with impunity.

The American surveyor Andrew Gray and the Mexican surveyor José Salazar Ylarregui disagreed about the location of the origin point for the western section of the boundary, along the Rio Grande. As the surveyors marched west, taking readings and measurements, the Mexican and American commissioners searched for provisions to sustain the 100 men who composed the full expedition. They found abandoned settlements and little to sustain them. The region through which they traveled, until recently the northern Mexican province of Nuevo Mexico, had been subjected for decades to predatory raids, primarily by Apaches. These raids had devastated Mexican farming

small numbers and relatively few casualties. In January 1847, the *Californios*, Spanish-speaking Californians, capitulated to the U.S. Navy.

Farther up the coast, Americans were already consolidating new territorial gains. Starting in the late 18th century, British, Spanish, and Russian adventurers had clashed over the right to trade with the Indians along the coast of today's Oregon and Washington. U.S. traders joined the fray in the early 19th century, and by the 1820s, Spain and Russia had abandoned the region. After the American Revolution, the United States and Britain struggled for supremacy in the region.

With the exception of the extreme Pacific Northwest and sections along the eastern front of the Rocky Mountain range, the western regions annexed to the United States in the 1840s possessed a markedly different climate and topography than that of the eastern United States. Early travelers reported on the aridity, giving rise to the label "Great American Desert." Lured by travel pamphlets promising fertile lands and their own experience in the East, settlers moving west brought expectations of profitable farming, but the dry western ecology forced them to modify their plans.

The 1849 discovery of gold in Colorado initiated the settlement of mid-America, which included ranching, freight hauling, and support services for the burgeoning towns in eastern Colorado and western Kansas. The consolidation of the broad middle of North America under U.S. control alleviated security concerns that had troubled Americans since the early 19th century, when a host of European powers remained ensconced on the continent. Even if they did not know what to do with the land and even if, as some Americans feared, organizing the new territories would precipitate political communities in the region, demonstrated the inability of Mexico's central government to protect its northernmost citizens, and enticed the United States to portray its recent war as an effort to bring peace to a troubled region.

Gray's objection, that the boundary line was being drawn too far north, resonated with Southern congressmen, who objected to the commission's conclusion in 1853 and forced the signing of a second treaty that set a new line. Politics were only one factor inhibiting the effort to clearly distinguish the United States and Mexico. Neither country committed the resources to securely control the region in the 19th century. In the absence of a clear national authority, Apache raids continued to endanger residents of the region, a condition that lessened only late in the century when both countries cooperated in joint campaigns against the Indians. Further complicating the situation, residents of the region were now citizens of the United States, but, as mostly Catholic Spanish speakers, they stood apart from the largely Protestant English speakers who populated the eastern reaches of the country. These new Americans maintained their cultural identity and found themselves part of the long-term cross-border traffic that defined the region. Food, music, dance, literature, and goods of all kinds circulated among the people living on both sides of the border that the commissioners labored so hard to draw.

"New map of California, Oregon, Washington, Utah and New Mexico" (1853)

- Why did the United States want a clearly demarcated boundary when none had existed prior to the war?
- What made a clear settlement of a boundary line difficult?

conflicts, most celebrated the accomplishment. Many citizens probably agreed with President Polk when he announced in his 1848 State of the Union, "We are the most favored people on the face of the earth."

Conestogas, Comanches, and Californios

The greatest social conflict in the newly configured American West came from Anglo migrants who regarded Catholic superstition and sin, combined with "cowardly, ignorant, lazy" habits inherited from the Spanish, as the main impediment to fruitful use and development of the region. "If the one half be true that is told of the abomination of the priesthood," one American wrote of the Franciscans, "that order there must be a perfect embodiment of every wicked attribute that darkens the character of corrupt human nature." Anglo settlers believed every outrageous tale of Catholic corruption and depravity. By displacing the native Mexican elite and developing California, Anglos could make money, purify the "American" character, and fulfill their Christian duty.

Not every American shared these views. A long tradition of open trading brought early American travelers together with Mexicans, French, British, and Native peoples. The earliest permanent settlers usually trapped and hunted, intermarried with locals, and spoke both Spanish and English. For these men, and for later emigrants, California represented an escape from the pressures of the East: from dirty cities, tired land, and debts. Americans dreamed of reaching the fantastic new world in the Pacific. Even Henry David Thoreau, the poet of the eastern woods, said, "My needle always settles between west and southwest. The future lies that way to me." Realizing those dreams, in California and the new western territories more generally, proved harder than most settlers imagined.

Controlling the new territory proved nearly as great a challenge as acquiring it. The Conestoga wagons that had already begun carrying Anglo settlers across the Great Plains began heading south in greater numbers, but doing so brought them into the orbit of two powerful Indian nations—Apache and Comanche. Generations of Spanish and then Mexican settlers had tried and failed to pacify these two nations. In 1850, the Apache community probably numbered only 5,000, but its attacks on settler communities had inspired the Mexican government to offer bounties for the scalps of Apache men, women, and children. Comanche represented a more serious threat. More numerous and better organized than Apache, they had lived along the northwestern edges of Texas and in the New Mexico territory since the early 18th century. The Comanche dominated the region well into the second half of the 19th century. They established their authority through military raids on neighbors—Native, Mexican, and American—and sustained their empire through control of markets and regional trade.

Comanche controlled parts of northern Mexico, known as Comanchería, through their ability to reinvent themselves as the Spanish began to push north. Seizing new weapons and tools—especially horses—they wedded these technologies to existing practices such as raiding and slave taking. They created extended networks of kin and dependency across the Southwest. The result was a Native power that existed independently although in connection to the Europeans and later Americans. At almost the same time Anglo settlers began arriving, Comanche society entered a period of internal conflict and decline that weakened it substantially due to the collapse of the bison population. Years of overhunting and a decade-long drought beginning in the mid-1840s destroyed the main source of food, a key commodity, and an essential part of the Comanche spiritual world. These events paved the way for U.S. forces to displace them. In 1852, weakened by starvation, Comanche chiefs appealed to a U.S. Indian agent: "Give us a country we can call our own, where we might bury our people in quiet." The Comanche people did not all die—and although some conceded to U.S. policies that placed Indians on reservations, others resisted and defended their autonomy into the 1870s.

Despite the threats posed by Comanches and others, the prospect of gold drew immigrants to California. Creating a chaotic mix of languages, cultures, and values, 80,000 Anglo settlers, European travelers, and Asian migrants all poured into California in 1849, where, as Mark Twain observed, they "fairly reveled in gold, whiskey, fights, and fandangos." Chinese and Irish migrants ranked at the top of the foreign-born contingent, followed by Germans, English, Welsh, Scottish, French, Chileans, Brazilians, Mexicans, and Canadians. Probably 15 percent of the new residents were from Central or South America, and they labored alongside 6,000–7,000 Miwok Indians. All these new Californians also lived alongside 75,000 Mexican Americans who remained in California after the U.S.–Mexican War. The Treaty of Guadalupe Hidalgo promised them the right to citizenship and respect for their land claims. Even with citizenship, land rights proved hard to maintain, and many Californios lost both status and property to the new arrivals.

Excerpt from Mark Twain, *Roughing It* (1872)

California presented a compelling opportunity—miners dug out more gold in the first decade of California production than had appeared on world markets in the previous 150 years. Chinese, especially Cantonese, migrants came in pursuit of "Gum

Shan" or "Gold Mountain," as the Cantonese referred to California. The Chinese came largely as contract laborers, usually relegated to the service industries that supported mines, and later worked in railroads and construction work. Like the thousands of African American men who came west, Chinese immigrants were segregated in their housing and were offered low-wage jobs with little chance for upward mobility. These men were especially prized by American miners as cooks and cleaners because without them the dramatically unbalanced sex ratios of the gold rush required that men do work that traditionally fell to women. Some fortune seekers abandoned prospecting and made money provisioning the men who were toiling for gold. Levi Strauss was one of these. A 24-year-old German immigrant, Strauss intended to open a dry goods business but responded to the necessity of miners for durable pants. Using a French fabric, denim, Strauss designed a rugged but comfortable pair that became the foundation of his company and the origin of blue jeans in America.

SEEKING GOLD Gold captured the imagination of Americans east and west. Although the popular image of a "gold seeker" was a young, single, white man, the allure of the precious metal drew men and women from all around the globe.

Despite being neither "North" nor "South," California could not escape the sectional controversies that roiled the country throughout the 1850s. Some Southern migrants to the state brought their slaves. Others waited until they received assurances that their property would be safe. Democrats dominated the state, but the party split into pro-slavery and antislavery factions. The violent conflict between these groups in California revealed how deeply the sectional conflict had impressed itself into the fabric of the nation.

STUDY QUESTIONS FOR THE EXPANSION OF AMERICA

1. What were the challenges facing U.S. control of the new western territory?

2. Why did the United States enter war with Mexico, and how did the results transform the nation?

quiz

3. What did the gold rush reveal about the nature of global information and economies in the mid-19th century?

⌄ CONTESTED CITIZENSHIP

As the United States extended its power across the West and over the Pacific, the influx of an increasingly diverse stream of immigrants sparked debate over who could be an American. Native-born Americans, especially Protestants, reacted to the growing diversity by trying to narrowly define citizenship and the rights that came with it. Political and cultural conflicts wrought a massive transformation in the American electorate and partisan alignments. The failure of American politics as a result of these crises eventually helped bring the nation to war in 1861. The first phase of this process saw the collapse of the Whig Party in the face of a challenge from the nativist **Know-Nothing Party**.

The Patterns of Migration

After the conclusion of the U.S.–Mexican War, immigrants flooded the Pacific coast both from the eastern United States and from around the globe. Chinese laborers comprised the largest group of Asian immigrants into America at this time. Between 1840 and 1920, 2.5 million people left China for Hawaii, the United States, Canada, Australia, New Zealand, Southeast Asia, South America, and Africa. Although domestic disturbances and economic hardship compelled these moves, the vast majority of migrants to North America chose their destination. The high cost of travel ensured that many of the Chinese immigrants had to sign contracts agreeing to work for five years at a set wage once they arrived. Despite the potential for exploitation in this scenario, many young men saw it as an opportunity. Especially after the gold rush, news of fortunes circulated

image analysis

ON THE ROAD TO CALIFORNIA   Thousands of Anglo-Americans made the difficult journey across the continent in the 1840s and 1850s seeking land and new opportunities. The mountains in this engraving present a more realistic image than many travelers had of the region, which confounded their expectations of the climate and terrain people they encountered once settled in the West.

widely. One resident in China reported on the effect of the news: "Letters from Chinese in San Francisco and further in the country have been circulated . . . and the accounts of the successful adventurers who have returned would, had the inhabitants possessed the means of paying their own way across, have gone far to depopulate considerable towns." They faced a hard life once they arrived. The California legal system established in 1849 created a rigid binary system of classifying its residents. Laws grouped Chinese, African Americans, and Indians together as "nonwhite" and denied them access to the vote, the state court system, and the schools.

Chinese miners in California, early 1850s.

In contrast to California, the New Mexico territory remained as fluid as it had been under Mexican control, largely because the United States imposed little military control. Instead, the Indian communities—Comanche, Apache, Navajo, Cheyenne, and Kiowa—continued to practice older forms of war making, diplomacy, and trade. But the rapid decline of buffalo herds on the southern Plains, the continued spread of diseases like smallpox, and expansion of the Anglo commercial economy weakened Indian power in the region. American officials worried about the raiding and slave taking among Southwest Indians, a practice Anglos compared to the racial slavery of the Deep South. In 1850, the U.S. territorial governor of the region appealed to the federal government for funds with which he could redeem captives under the old system: "Trading in captives had been so long tolerated in this Territory that it has ceased to be regarded as a wrong; and purchasers are not prepared willingly to release captives without an adequate ransom." The prospect of using federal money to emancipate Indian slaves might well have unsettled Southern Democrats, who would certainly have seen a dangerous precedent in the practice. In any event, the governor received no response, and Native practices ended only with the full military intervention of the United States in the decade after the Civil War.

Although California and the West drew migrants from Mexico and the Pacific, the countries around the Atlantic basin remained the main source of immigrants bound for the United States in this period. As in earlier decades, most immigrants came from German states and Ireland, although the numbers of central and southern Europeans increased. The rate of immigration rose with each passing year, but the destination of most immigrants remained consistent: the North. The ports of Boston, Philadelphia, and New York attracted a majority of the nation's shipping traffic, both for people and for goods. Many immigrants remained in these ports, whereas many others moved westward along the lines laid down—in steel rail, macadamized turnpike, or narrow canal—during the great era of transportation and infrastructural development of the 1840s and 1850s. The combination of free labor policies and a booming economy drew most immigrants to the North. Cities such as Pittsburgh, Cleveland, Detroit, Cincinnati, and Chicago saw their populations explode. These second-tier cities grew at remarkable rates—Chicago increased from 5,000 residents in 1840 to 109,000 in 1860—and achieved a size that the leading coastal ports had required centuries to reach.

But not all of the immigrants went west or north. Some immigrants went south, to such ports as Baltimore, Richmond, Charleston, Mobile, New Orleans, and Galveston. Immigrants who entered Southern ports were more likely to remain in those cities or the surrounding area. Irish migrants established large expatriate communities in many of the southern Atlantic Seaboard cities. These newcomers joined native Southerners, both black and white, who helped develop the urban South. Urban boosters promoted railroads, canals, and banks with the same fervor as their Northern peers. Despite their eagerness to accumulate new technology, however, few white Southerners wanted to replicate the massive urban centers of the Northeast. They anticipated that the anonymity and size of large cities would weaken the ability of masters to control their slaves. Many also resisted the rise of a large community of working-class whites, who might someday see little reason to support slavery. Southern cities also developed more slowly because Southerners invested most of their capital in land and slaves and had little left for the bond-driven commercial development that promoted urban growth in other parts of the country.

New Immigrants and the Invention of Americanism

Among Southern ports, New Orleans was unique for its size, its cultural diversity, and its centrality to dynamic new trade patterns. Occupied by the French and Spanish before entry into the United States through the Louisiana Purchase, the polyglot population consisted of the descendants of various European ethnic groups, an equally wide array of African ethnicities, and a large population of people of mixed descent whom Louisianans referred to generally as "Creole." After the expulsion of French settlers from the Canadian province of Acadia during the Seven Years' War, many relocated to France's colony in southern Louisiana. Here they came to be called "Cajuns" in a corruption of the name of the area from which they came. New Orleans, in particular, invited fusion and cultural mixing. Protestant Americans regarded the city as an exotic and dangerous locale.

The French and Spanish built cathedrals and other public symbols of Catholicism in the city, and most Anglo-Americans continued to regard the faith as both foreign and hostile to democratic life. The entry of millions of new Catholics into the country over the 1840s and 1850s only increased fears about their presence in the country. In addition, native-born Catholics disagreed among themselves about how to respond. A substantial body of English Catholics and French Catholics had migrated south from Canada and established themselves during the colonial era. The influx of Irish Catholics alarmed many American Catholics, who feared that the Irish rejection of Anglo practices and values would further fuel anti-Catholic sentiment (Figure 13.1).

The political conflicts between old Protestants and new Catholic immigrants in the eastern states propelled much of the public policy toward immigration, but western territories possessed their own share of ethnic conflict. The movement of Chinese workers into the West after the U.S–Mexican War generated opposition from native-born workers. Many of the charges leveled at Chinese and other Asian immigrants were similar to the ones used against African Americans: Anglo-Americans accused Chinese men of "lusting" after white women and regarded them as childlike and savage, incapable of functioning as citizens in a republic. According to the *San Francisco Chronicle,* "When the [Chinese] worker arrives here he is as rigidly under the control of the contractor who brought him as ever an African slave was under his master in South Carolina or Louisiana." In 1851, **Hinton Helper**, a leading critic of slavery, told Californians, "I should not wonder at all, if the copper of the Pacific yet becomes as great a subject of discord and dissension as the ebony of the Atlantic." Like his recommendations for freeing the South from slavery—which in his view required deporting African

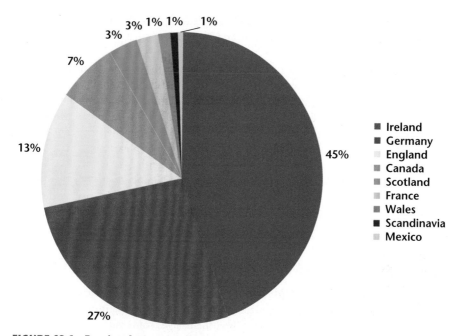

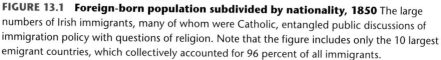

FIGURE 13.1 **Foreign-born population subdivided by nationality, 1850** The large numbers of Irish immigrants, many of whom were Catholic, entangled public discussions of immigration policy with questions of religion. Note that the figure includes only the 10 largest emigrant countries, which collectively accounted for 96 percent of all immigrants.

Americans after ending slavery—Helper thought Asian immigrants had no role to play in settling the West.

The conclusion that Hinton Helper reached reflected one of the most pernicious aspects of mid-19th-century U.S. culture. Helper's conclusion—that black people should be removed from the South and Asian people removed from the West—drew on older traditions, such as those maintained by the American Colonization Society, and the newer science of race. Increasingly, white people in America expressed a harsher and more absolute conception of race and racial difference. Most white members of the Revolutionary generation believed implicitly in the intellectual, physical, and moral superiority of white people over darker-skinned people, but they rarely articulated this idea in their writings. What distinguished the antebellum generation was the centrality of racial thinking. The more diverse America became, the more its white residents emphasized racism as a central aspect of their worldview.

By this time, however, most states had endorsed universal white manhood suffrage; thus, following a short period of residence, new immigrants could participate in the political system. The large numbers of urban immigrants, especially in northeastern cities, raised concerns that these men would corrupt the political system. As one wealthy New York merchant worried, "These Irishmen, strangers among us, without a feeling of patriotism or affection in common with American citizens, decide the elections in the City of New York. They make Presidents and Governors, and they send men to represent us in the councils of the nation." The men who expressed such sentiments supported an increasingly aggressive response to what they perceived as a Catholic disruption of American civic life. A weekly New York journal emerged in the 1830s titled the *American Protestant Vindicator and Defender of Civil and Religious Liberty Against the Inroads of Papacy.*

Public schools became one of the key battlegrounds in the fight over religion and public life. The strong Protestant bias of "nondenominational" schools in Ireland left many Irish Catholics who emigrated with a profound distrust of nonparochial schools. Even native Catholics feared the conforming effects of public schools. In 1843, one American Catholic organization warned parents to guard their heritage: "You must, therefore, use all diligence that your child be instructed at an early age in the saving truths of religion, and be preserved from the contagion of error." Accordingly, Catholics requested that public schools respect Catholic beliefs or simply divert public funds to parochial schools. In 1844, when a Philadelphia bishop criticized the use of the Protestant King James Bible, it incited anti-Catholic riots that left 40 people dead and 60 injured.

The Know-Nothing Movement

New York, long the center of Irish immigrant life in the United States, experienced the most severe and most well-organized **nativist** movement. Beginning in the mid-1840s, different political organizations calling themselves some variant of the "American Party" formed. They shared general goals: to restrict office holding to native-born Americans, to retain the Bible in schools, and to extend the naturalization process from 5 to 21 years. Although these groups had little electoral success, they established the basis for the network of secret fraternal associations known collectively as the Know Nothings that emerged in the 1850s. Nativists feared that the mainstream political parties would not sanction their policies for fear of alienating immigrant voters. If asked about the organization, members answered that they "knew nothing." Outgrowing this fear, however, the organization gradually became more openly political.

Nativists quickly created an opposition party that rivaled and drew strength from the Whigs. The Know-Nothing Party flourished and then disappeared, absorbed by the Republican Party, undone by conflict over slavery just like the Whigs. The brief existence of the party and the fact that it was mostly confined to the North suggests that its appeal was temporary and limited. But the movement tapped into long-standing fears, and nativism did not end with the collapse of the official movement. At the party's height, in the election of 1854, eight governors, more than 100 congressmen, thousands of local officials, and nearly a million citizens proclaimed themselves Know Nothings. In some states, Know Nothings succeeded in restricting public funds for parochial schools, disbanding immigrant militias, imposing literacy tests for voting, and reforming church property ownership rules.

STUDY QUESTIONS **FOR CONTESTED CITIZENSHIP**

quiz

1. How did the entry of new immigrants into the United States in the 1840s and 1850s alter American life?

2. What were the political responses by native-born Americans to this movement?

3. How did the Know-Nothing Party put nativist beliefs into public policy?

◉ SLAVERY AND ANTEBELLUM LIFE

The persistent efforts of enslaved people to escape bondage, to alter the conditions of their slavery, and to assert their own humanity destabilized the system and forced slave-holders to constantly adjust. The increasing defensiveness of slaveholders in the 1840s and 1850s stemmed as much from this internal pressure as from the external pressure applied by abolitionists. The basis of mid-19th-century slavery remained the physical domination that whites could and did exert over slaves, the monopoly on weapons and state power, and the social network supporting slavery that manifested itself in slave patrols and a legal system that oppressed black people at the expense of whites. At the same time, slaves and masters struggled over the psychological, cultural, and social conditions of bondage. The complexity of these relationships, their continuous evolution over time, and the profoundly uneven distribution of power within the system of antebellum slavery taxes the empathetic sensibilities of modern readers, but the importance of understanding the perspectives of the different participants in the system demands that we make the effort.

The Paradox of Slavery and Modernity

The persistence of slavery into the 1850s surprised many Americans. Members of the Revolutionary generation expected that slavery would disappear over time. Most philosophical thought in late 18th- and 19th-century western Europe favored freedom and condemned slavery as inefficient and inhumane. But the United States proved a curious exception within the larger Western world. Defenders of the institution offered increasingly elaborate intellectual and religious justifications, as slavery in North America proved to be a remarkably adaptable economic strategy. When the Scottish thinker Adam Smith denounced slavery in his manifesto of capitalism, *An Inquiry into the Nature and Causes of the Wealth of Nations* (published in 1776), he argued for the greater efficiency of free workers and the necessity of free labor markets within a capitalist system. Smith did not anticipate the ability of slaveholders to adapt their system to an increasingly industrial and urban South. Because Southern cities did not receive the same surge of foreign immigrants as Northern ones, the growth of urban slavery proved vital to Southern cities.

Excerpt from Edmund Ruffin, *The Political Economy of Slavery* (1853)

Enslaved workers, often hired by companies from their rural masters, labored alongside white men in a host of occupations in antebellum cities. The tobacco factories of the upper South used this system extensively. By 1860, hired slaves constituted fully one-half of the tobacco workers in Virginia. Richmond's Tredegar Iron Works, the largest industrial facility in the South, with over 1,000 workers, employed hundreds of enslaved men and women. Masters regarded slave hiring as advantageous because they could sign a contract, receive guaranteed compensation, and dispense with the day-to-day management of slaves. Many of the urban slaves, especially those hired in the 1850s, lived in rented rooms or boarding houses. Masters required them to deduct rent and food expenses from their wages, but enterprising slaves could work overtime or scrimp on necessities and actually set aside money for themselves.

Urban slavery produced other complications as well. With masters absent, enslaved people supervised themselves after working hours. If they congregated in noisy bars and gambling saloons as white workers did, who would oversee them? If they committed

SCENE ON THE LEVEE, AT NEW ORLEANS.

SLAVE LABOR The dynamism of the Southern economy thrived on slave labor, applied to all sorts of farm, urban, and industrial work. Slavery's supporters understood this and fashioned an intellectual defense of the practice to sustain their lifestyle.

crimes, who would be held responsible? The anonymity of growing Southern cities gave slaves a chance to seize an autonomy that few could find on plantations. These problems generated tensions between masters and city officials. The latter understood the necessity of black labor to the operation of their communities but resented having to stand in as masters to supervise and punish enslaved people.

Urban slavery also generated class tensions within the white community and threatened its stability at a time when sectional politics demanded solidarity. In the 1850s, Tredegar's white workers, for instance, went on strike repeatedly over the use of enslaved workers in the factory. Joseph Anderson, the plant's owner, responded aggressively, but most white elites treaded carefully. Worse yet, a handful of Southern advocates of free labor framed a critique of slavery that drew on the class divisions among white Southerners. Hinton Helper, a North Carolinian, issued the most famous attack on slavery from within the South in his book *The Impending Crisis* (1857). Helper called on nonslaveholding whites to overthrow the planter class, destroy slavery, and exile black people from the country. "The lords of the lash are not only absolute masters of the blacks, . . . they are also the oracles and arbiters of all nonslaveholding whites, whose freedom is merely nominal, and whose unparalleled illiteracy and degradation is purposely and fiendishly perpetuated," Helper wrote, setting off a firestorm among Southern elites.

Excerpt from Hinton Helper, *The Impending Crisis* (1857)

Helper and the white strikers at Tredegar raised the central dilemma of protecting white labor inside a slave society. In the North, free labor theorists and politicians argued that white laborers could never be fairly treated in a slave society, whereas in the South, defenders of slavery sought a middle ground. Their precarious position rejected the natural equality of rights that lay at the heart of the American polity and advanced a hierarchical model in its place. South Carolina senator and former vice president **John C. Calhoun** framed the argument clearly: "All men are not created equal. According to the Bible, only two—a man and a woman—ever were—and of those one was pro-nounced subordinate to the other. All others have come into the world by being born, and in no sense . . . either free or equal."

The West Indies, Brazil, and the Future of Slavery

Slaveholders knew from recent history that a false step could collapse the edifice of their power. By 1838, the British government had abolished slavery in its empire, most impor-tantly on the sugar islands of the West Indies. White Southerners carefully studied the events that followed British abolition. What they saw alarmed them. Although British emancipation granted compensation to owners, gave no land to ex-slaves, required a transition period of bonded labor by former slaves, and did not inspire the racial war that many whites had predicted, U.S. slaveholders regarded it as a dramatically un-successful act. Their evidence for the failure of emancipation rested on the decline in West Indian sugar production, which plummeted after the end of the apprenticeship period. Abolitionists, by contrast, hailed the "mighty experiment" as a success. Less concerned with staple crop production, they celebrated the rise of free labor and the self-sufficiency that ex-slaves pursued.

Some Southern slaveholders concluded that the real motive must have been an effort to weaken the United States by undermining slavery. As one South Carolina planter explained, Britain had abolished West Indian slavery to "kindle a flame of fa-natical discontent" that would divide the North from the South. This theory gained ground during the debate on Texas annexation, when Southern congressmen alleged that the United States had to incorporate the state before the British assumed control and emancipated the slaves. At the World Anti-Slavery Convention of 1843, the as-sembled abolitionists encouraged Britain to underwrite the Texans' debt and use that aid as leverage to push for emancipation. When this news reached the United States, it bolstered U.S. support for annexation.

If the West Indies gave white Southerners doubts about the long-term security of slavery, looking farther south buoyed their hopes. Brazilian planters, independent of Portuguese rule since 1822, remained as committed to slavery as did their U.S. peers. Long after the United States outlawed the Atlantic slave trade, Brazil continued to flout international sanctions; between 1835 and 1855 alone, over half a million Africans were smuggled into Brazil, many of them on ships captained by Americans. From shipbuild-ing to sailing to the commerce itself, Americans played a key role in the importation of Africans into Brazil long after the trade had been closed. The fervent dedication to slavery displayed by Brazilians encouraged John C. Calhoun to remark, "Between her [Brazil] and us there is a strict identity of interest on almost all subjects, without conflict, or even competition." Reflecting American concerns about British antislavery work, which included patrolling the waters off the African and Brazilian coasts with the intention of returning illegally captured Africans, Calhoun said that he supported "our mutual interest in resisting [London's] interference with the relation in either country."

Images of slavery in Cuba and Brazil

Inside the Quarter

By 1860, four million black people were held in bondage in the American South. Viewed in financial terms, they represented the single largest investment of any kind in the

United States, with a total aggregate value of roughly $3 billion. During the 1830s through 1850s, slave ownership contracted even as the slave population expanded: fewer white people owned more and more black people. By 1860, 25 percent of Southern households owned slaves, and of these, 10 percent owned more than 12 individuals.

Most slaveholders owned only one or a few slaves. In these situations, slaves worked alongside family members, slept under the same roof, and remained in close contact with white people throughout their lives. Those slaves who lived on large plantations enjoyed a small measure of distance between themselves and their owners. Slaves on plantations lived in their own "quarter," a collection of small cabins usually apportioned one to a family. Within this space, enslaved people fashioned families, communities, and their culture. Each quarter generated its own musicians, historians, storytellers, and healers. Links—of love, friendship, trade, and rivalry—connected slaves from one plantation to another. Despite the best efforts of whites, news and rumor always traveled faster from quarter to quarter than from big house to big house.

Slaveholders alternated between the stark choices laid out by one master who professed, "The surest and best method of managing negroes, is to love them," and another who advised, "We have to rely more and more on the power of fear." Some adopted both these routines. Bennet Barrow, a notoriously harsh Louisiana master, ordered periodic whippings of all his slaves but also gave them frequent holidays and Christmas presents. Owners had a strong economic incentive to keep slaves healthy and satisfied enough with their material conditions that they did not see flight or revenge as a better option. Capitalist slaveholders saw that better treatment could return more profits in the long run.

Without denying the violence and brutality that underlay American slavery, the evidence also reveals that enslaved people used every opportunity to seek small measures of freedom within the system. These actions did not signal acceptance of slavery, nor were they incompatible with the more public and physical acts of resistance that marked so much of the relationship between masters and slaves in the antebellum South. But these measures gave enslaved African Americans the chance to carve out space for spouses, for children, sometimes for literacy or advanced skills, and most importantly for themselves. Each small victory required enormous sacrifice and discipline to achieve, but the body of evidence that scholars have recovered from all aspects of slaves' lives demonstrates the vitality and richness of that life even within bondage.

SLAVE HOUSING
Owners never spent more than the bare minimum to house slaves, but despite their rough surroundings, enslaved men and women built strong and loving families and protective communities whenever they could.

Because enslaved people could not legally marry, some slaveholders regarded slave marriages as unions of convenience that they could sunder with a sale. Because of the overwhelming importance of family, the sale of enslaved people represented the greatest tragedy they could face. Sales may have disrupted one-third to one-half of enslaved families nationwide. Sales revealed the truly mercenary quality of American slavery.

Slave auction, New Orleans (1853)

One of the largest and most dynamic of such markets was located in New Orleans, where slaves arrived by ship, rail, and on foot before being sold and parceled out to the brutal sugar plantations in the region. The high walls of the slave market, built according to city code, kept these inhumane transactions out of sight.

The Creation of African America

The tremendous diversity of African backgrounds inherited by enslaved people in America complicated and enriched the efforts of African Americans to identify themselves as one people. By the early 19th century, free African Americans felt secure enough to claim Africa as a proud ancestral homeland, a practice that went back at least to the founding of the African Methodist Episcopal (AME) Church in Philadelphia in the 1790s. The standard historical and cultural assessments of Africa by whites at the time regarded the continent as uncivilized and dangerously backward. To assert a positive affiliation with Africa, as increasing numbers of free blacks did in the early 19th century, represented a fundamental challenge to the racist attitudes held by white Americans. Martin Delany, a free black man from Virginia who moved to Pennsylvania and later worked with Frederick Douglass, built on earlier efforts to connect black Americans with Africa in historical, emotional, and physical terms. Before the Civil War, Delany advocated the necessity of a separate black nation in Africa, composed of émigrés from the United States, where they could show their superiority in "the true principles of morals, correctness of thought, religion, and law or civil government." Delaney remained in the United States, serving as a major in the U.S. Army during the Civil War, the first black field officer in the United States; the black nationalist idea of a return to Africa that persisted into the 20th century owed much to the decades of work done by men like Delaney.

Excerpt from Martin Delany, "Political Destiny of the Colored Race on the American Continent" (1854)

Positive images of Africa played a central role in the music and folklore of the enslaved people. By the mid-19th century, black Americans had blended these images and ideas with European and Native American traditions to create a uniquely African American culture. Slave spirituals and songs expressed common goals and a shared identity.

> Hail! all hail! ye Afric clan,
> Hail! ye oppressed, ye Afric band,
> Who toil and sweat in slavery bound
> And when your health and strength are gone
> Are left to hunger and to mourn,
> Let independence be your aim,
> Ever mindful what 'tis worth.
> Pledge your bodies for the prize,
> Pile them even to the skies!

Alongside the folk traditions that have formed a basis for much of the investigation into the lives of American slaves grew a burgeoning Afro-Christianity. Careful studies have documented varying rates of African American participation in the different Protestant denominations, which suggests that enslaved people may have been able to choose the denomination to which they belonged. In Virginia, roughly 40 percent of enslaved Christians joined the Baptist Church. Before Nat Turner's rebellion in 1831, black ministers had played a key role in the leadership of enslaved evangelicals; however, following that event, Southern communities policed such activities more closely. Even without their own ministers, Afro-Christians continued to join churches and profess their faith.

The Afro-Christian faith differed in important ways from white evangelicalism. The nature of African American religion in the post–Civil War period offers some insights into the beliefs of enslaved people before the war. Whereas pro-slavery evangelicals focused on submission to God and to masters, Afro-Christians celebrated the day of jubilee, deliverance from evil, and the salvation that awaited those who believed. As one slave noted, "The idea of a revolution in the condition of whites and blacks, is the corner-stone of the religion of the latter." The prophetic tradition offered enslaved Christians an explanation of their world that recognized suffering but promised redemption. David Walker, author of the incendiary pamphlet *An Appeal to the Coloured Citizens of the World* (1829), took solace from God's omnipotence by quoting the Book of Common Prayer:

> The wicked swell'd with lawless pride,
> Have made the poor their prey;
> O, let them fall by those designs
> Which they for others lay.

STUDY QUESTIONS FOR SLAVERY AND ANTEBELLUM LIFE

1. In what ways did enslaved men and women challenge the system of slavery?
2. How did they create families and lives even while still enslaved?
3. How did slaveholders respond to this challenge?

quiz

THE RISE OF THE REPUBLICANS

The dispute over slavery that consumed Northerners and Southerners in the 1850s rarely recognized the humanity or the suffering of enslaved people that emerged so clearly from their music, stories, and actions. White Northerners opposed slavery—principally the expansion of slavery in the western territories—because it corrupted and weakened the American political and economic system. Abolitionists acknowledged the true horror of slavery—mostly as a result of the role played by black people in the movement after 1830—but they remained a tiny minority. Unlike the social and cultural issues that gave rise to the Know-Nothing Party, this dispute mapped itself along sectional lines and held the potential to fracture the nation (Table 13.1). Northerners emerged from the political turmoil of the second half of the 1850s with a new Republican Party, which brought stability to Northern politics but whose sectional posture ultimately inspired white Southerners to abandon the Union.

Table 13.1 Political Parties, 1830–1860

The mid-19th century was one of the most vibrant and fluid periods in American politics. Different groups formed and dissolved a variety of partisan organizations before the emergence of the Republican Party in the 1850s.

Majority Party

Democrats (1800–): supported state rights, slavery, and immigration

Primary Opposition Parties

Whigs (1830–1850s): supported federal investment in infrastructure and social reforms stemming from Second Great Awakening

American Know Nothings (early to mid-1850s): supported strong nativist platform

Republicans (mid-1850s–): supported antislavery policies in western territories and federal investment in development

Issue-Specific Parties

Workingmen's (1830s): locally organized parties supporting workers' rights

Liberty (1840s): abolition party

Free Soil (1848 to early 1850s): opposed expansion of slavery into western territories

Anti-Masons (1828 to mid-1830s): opposed Freemasonry

Southern Rights (1850s): supported Southern interests, especially protection of slavery

Union (early 1850s): Southern offshoot of the Whig Party

Constitutional Union (1860): conservative compromise party dedicated to preserving the union

Free Soil and Free Labor

Disputes over the expansion of slavery into the western territories stretched back to the Confederation Congress, which adopted the Northwest Ordinance banning slavery in the upper Midwest region. Because the legal restrictions applied only to existing territory and because slavery continued to be profitable, the expansion of U.S. territory forced this problem on each succeeding generation. The 1820 Missouri Compromise settled the conflict that arose regarding the incorporation of the Louisiana Purchase lands by establishing a boundary between slave and free territory along Missouri's southern border. The acquisitions after the U.S.–Mexican War precipitated a new round of conflict when Pennsylvania Democrat David Wilmot proposed that slavery be excluded from any new territory gained during the war. Congress voted repeatedly on the Wilmot Proviso but never passed it. Each vote exacerbated sectional rather than partisan differences. As the *Boston Whig* explained of the Wilmot Proviso, "As if by magic, it brought to a head the great question which is about to divide the American people."

The men who organized the Republican Party in the early 1850s possessed the foresight to wed free soil—territories organized without slavery—to the emerging philosophy of free labor. Building on midcentury discussions about capitalism and labor that were taking place all across the Atlantic world, free labor theorists sought to incorporate propertyless men into the electorate without jeopardizing the stability of law and government. European nations had long restricted voting because they believed that propertyless men might call for land redistribution if given the right to vote. The vast majority of unskilled (and even many skilled) workers in the United States owned no property. But rather than defining these workers negatively by the land they did not own, free labor theorists identified them by what they possessed—their labor to sell. This new understanding of labor prompted a shift in emphasis in the legal foundations of American capitalism from the sanctity of property to the sanctity of contract. This view ensured that workers accepted certain responsibilities when they signed a contract—such as assuming liability for personal harm or death in hazardous jobs. It also meant that employers had to respect contracts as well and could not arbitrarily fire or lower the wages of an employee without risking legal retribution. With this change, laboring men now had an investment in the legal and political status quo. Free labor also relied on continuous upward mobility. Men who entered the workforce laboring for others would save their money, succeed to independence, and employ younger men. This process enriched families and society. This Republican ideology juxtaposed the virtue and efficiency of the North's autonomous workers with the immorality and inefficiency of the South's slave economy.

Whig—and later, Republican—economic policies promoted the expansion of a commercial economy into the new regions of the West. Before companies, creditors, and cash could reach the region, however, the West needed laws and governments. Only with the area securely organized, including the all-important court system to resolve conflicts over land deals, would investors commit resources. Because Northerners and Southerners clashed over whether the territory should be organized as free or slave land, territorial development stalled. As a result, one of the most important legislative initiatives of the era—the Transcontinental Railroad—passed Congress only during the Civil War, when the exit of Southern Democrats from Congress gave Republicans the votes to organize the territories and pass the bill. Conflict over slavery's expansion effectively deadlocked Congress on major legislation for over a decade.

The Politics of Slave Catching

Outside Congress, problems manifested themselves along the border between slavery and freedom where slaveholders complained about the lack of cooperation they received from Northern state and local governments when their slaves escaped. The southern boundaries of Ohio and Pennsylvania emerged as the key battlegrounds. The 1842 Supreme Court case of *Prigg v. Pennsylvania* established federal policy on the issue. Edward Prigg, acting for a Maryland slaveholder, entered Pennsylvania to reclaim a woman and her children who had escaped from bondage five years earlier. Prigg carried them off, and Pennsylvania officials convicted him of kidnapping. A proslavery, Southern majority on the Supreme Court ruled that no state law could "in any way qualify, regulate, control, or restrain" actions taken by slaveholders to reclaim their property, establishing a broad right of recapture. Accordingly, the Court set Prigg free and voided the Pennsylvania statute under which he was arrested. Although the decision contradicted the Southern preference for state action on slavery by locating the protection of slave catchers at the federal level, Southerners strongly backed the decision.

Sectional disputes over slave and free territory manifested themselves in religious institutions. The subject had created controversy at national religious conventions for years, with antislavery forces from Northern churches sponsoring resolutions to prohibit ministers from owning slaves and churches from using slave labor. At the same time, Southern ministers crafted the biblical defense of slavery. After a decade of controversy over whether Christianity sanctioned slaveholding, the Baptist and Methodist churches divided over the issue of slavery in 1845.

The tangled problems of slavery, territories, and economic expansion reached a critical point in 1850. Congress had been under pressure to admit California to statehood. Deadlocked over the question of whether California would be free or slave, Congress extended its session into the summer of 1850, and a mood of apprehension and fear gripped the Capitol. Democrats and Whigs finally agreed to a series of bills called the **Compromise of 1850**. The final legislation admitted California as a free state, organized the remainder of the New Mexico territory, banned the slave trade in the District of Columbia, empowered the U.S. Treasury to assume Texas's debts from its independence struggle, and gave the South a much stronger federal **Fugitive Slave Act**. This last provision proved to be the most controversial. It nationalized the process of slave capture and return by requiring federal judges to appoint "commissioners" to hear cases of accused fugitives and by requiring the active complicity of state officers. Northerners, who assumed that most "slave catchers" simply kidnapped free blacks from the North, were appalled by the legislation, which assumed the guilt of the charged party, refused to allow blacks to testify, obviated the standard rules for evidence that would have been present in a court of law, and provided financial incentives for commissioners to find fugitives guilty ($10 as opposed to $5 for those found innocent).

All across the North, individuals protested passage of the legislation, which they believed made them complicit in slavery: "A filthy law," "an outrage to humanity," proclaimed Northern papers. Anyone who obeyed it ought to be "marked and treated as a moral leper," wrote one, while another advised those who did to "repent before God and ask His forgiveness." Bostonians made the most vigorous response, with abolitionists protesting and blocking the removal of accused fugitives through legal and illegal means. The 1854 rendition of the Virginia fugitive Anthony Burns, which precipitated an attack on federal marshals that left one dead, required President Pierce to mobilize the U.S. Marines to escort Burns from the city, as tens of thousands of Bostonians went out into the streets to protest. Burns, marched to the wharf past buildings hung with black bunting to symbolize residents' shame, was the last fugitive slave returned from Boston.

In the context of the fight over the return of fugitive slaves, Harriet Beecher Stowe published *Uncle Tom's Cabin*, which quickly became the most popular novel of the 19th century. It characterized the central crime of slavery as the destruction of slave families through sale and violence. Stowe, the daughter, sister, and wife of prominent Northern ministers, drew inspiration from her involvement with the evangelical movement. She later explained that the novel came to her in a flash, as though a vision granted by God. Stowe's frank depiction of slaveholders' hypocrisy, the sexual exploitation of enslaved women, and the cruelty inherent in the system aroused violent opposition in the South, where book burnings and mass protests greeted the novel. Spurred by Stowe's novel, which was read around the world, a half-million women in England, Ireland, and Scotland sent a petition calling for emancipation to the U.S. Congress.

Harriet Beecher Stowe, excerpt from *Uncle Tom's Cabin* (1852)

The reality of federal protection for slave catchers rather than fugitive slaves, dramatized so effectively by Stowe, inspired several Northern state legislatures to pass personal liberty laws designed to hinder the implementation of the Fugitive Slave Act. Southerners denounced these statutes as unconstitutional nullifications of federal law. When the federal government opposed slavery, Southerners increasingly used the language of state rights to criticize the actions, but when the federal government supported slavery, white Southerners stood firmly behind its protection.

Western Expansion and the Kansas–Nebraska Act

The sundering of religious ties, the widening cultural differences, and the continuing political conflicts revealed internal tensions that contrasted sharply with the international optimism that the United States projected. As Commodore Perry launched his expedition to Japan, the author James Fenimore Cooper noted that Americans had "a longing to see distant lands" to determine the "differences which exist between the stranger and ourselves." Those global aspirations grew from a rapidly expanding economy and the new continental reach of the country itself even as some Americans worried that western expansion could initiate an internal collapse like those that had beset previous empires.

If that collapse came, it would be on the Great Plains. As disputes over slavery increased in the early 1850s, pro-slavery settlers from Missouri pushed to make Kansas a test. They entered the Kansas territory with slaves or in support of slaveholding to dominate the territorial government so that when it presented Congress with a plan for admission, the state constitution would include slavery. Equally motivated to "win" Kansas, free-state settlers mobilized in the East and headed to the territory to combat the pro-slavery "ruffians." Organized by entities such as the New England Emigrant Aid society, free-state settlers understood themselves as the advance guard in a growing war over slavery within the United States. Armed with "Beecher's Bibles," local slang for the Springfield rifles carried by emigrants and named for abolitionist minister Lyman Ward Beecher, antislavery and pro-slavery forces knew this would not be a war of words.

Stephen Douglas, the Northern leader of the Democratic Party and champion of the Transcontinental Railroad, sought to pacify the conflict by organizing the territory under the banner of what he called "**popular sovereignty**." This would have left the decision for or against slavery up to the people present in a territory when it voted for organization. To allow popular sovereignty, Douglas had to engineer the removal of the Missouri Compromise, which, with its prohibition on slavery in territory north of 36°30', prohibited a slaveholding Kansas. This policy change came in the **Kansas–Nebraska Act**, which Douglas hoped would resolve sectional conflict. Southerners supported the legislation, but the Northern response—overwhelming in its dissatisfaction—ruined Douglas's

FORCING SLAVERY DOWN THE THROAT OF A FREE SOILER The political conflict over whether slavery should be allowed in the western territories only escalated through the 1850s. Free Soil activists in the North presented white settlers as the true victims of this effort to expand slavery.

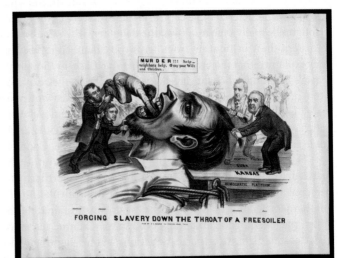

FORCING SLAVERY DOWN THE THROAT OF A FREESOILER

presidential aspirations. Tens of thousands of Northerners protested the act's removal of a 30-year-old policy that had, they argued, successfully curtailed the more violent sectional disagreements that were sure to appear without it. The most well-publicized critique, "The Appeal of the Independent Democrats," arraigned the bill "as a gross violation of a sacred pledge; as a criminal betrayal of precious rights; as part and parcel of an atrocious plot to exclude from a vast unoccupied region immigrants from the Old World and free laborers from our own States, and convert it into a dreary region of despotism, inhabited by masters and slaves." The bill undermined support among Northerners for the Democratic Party and inspired the formation of the Republicans. Concerned about what he regarded as an unwarranted acquiescence to pro-slavery forces, Abraham Lincoln reentered politics in 1854. Lincoln said the repeal of the Missouri Compromise was "wrong in its direct effect, letting slavery into Kansas and Nebraska—and wrong in its prospective principle, allowing it to spread to every other part of the wide world."

Abraham Lincoln's "Peoria Speech" (October 1864)

Rather than stemming the bloodshed, the Kansas–Nebraska Act seemed to exacerbate it (Map 13.2). Newspapers carried weekly reports about bloody attacks and reprisals between free- and slave-state settlers. **John Brown**, an evangelical abolitionist from the East, perpetrated one of the most infamous such episodes when he and his sons attacked a family of pro-slavery settlers along Pottawatomie Creek, hacking them to death with swords. Possibly influenced by revolutionary activists from Europe with whom he collaborated, Brown had abandoned the pacifism and moderate approach of his eastern counterparts. His gang included two Britons energized by the Chartist movement, a Polish revolutionary, a Bavarian, and a Vienna-born Jew who fought under Hungary's Kossuth. After the failures of 1848 to produce liberal states, European radicals may well have seen America as a more hospitable climate. Brown's actions reflected a frustration with the slow pace of change. He and his sons escaped punishment for the massacre, but his infamy preceded him as he headed back east. The violence reached a head with the "Sack of Lawrence" in 1856, when a pro-slavery posse entered the Nebraska capital, destroyed two printing presses, and burned down the Free State Hotel.

In response to the attack on Lawrence, Massachusetts Republican **Charles Sumner**, the first abolitionist senator, took to the Senate floor for a two-day speech titled "The Crime Against Kansas." Because the speech mocked one of South Carolina's senators, Democratic congressman Preston Brooks, the senator's cousin, attacked Sumner in the Senate and beat him into unconsciousness with his walking stick. For Northerners, Sumner was a martyr to the unchecked violence and incapacity for rational action that typified the slaveholding South. Was it any surprise, said Northerners, that men who grew up beating their slaves should turn their whip on those with whom they disagreed? Brooks resigned his seat after a modest censure by the House, and his constituents immediately reelected him. Sumner earned the drubbing he received, Southerners said, and to replace the lost cane, thousands of them sent Brooks new ones, with inscriptions such as "Bully for Brooks!"

Charles Sumner's "Crime Against Kansas" speech (1856)

Rising Sectionalism

The rise of the Republican Party challenged the Democratic supremacy that had reigned since Andrew Jackson's day. Because of the population disparity between the sections, the North possessed more electoral votes and more seats in the House of Representatives. To stay viable at the national level, Democrats had to retain their

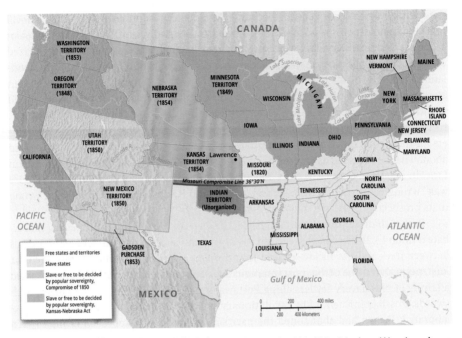

MAP 13.2 Territorial Organization, 1840s–1850s After the U.S.–Mexican War, Americans fought, first rhetorically and then physically, over whether the new territory should be opened to slavery. The 1854 Kansas–Nebraska Act, intended to settle the controversy, only stoked more anger among Northerners, who condemned its repeal of the Missouri Compromise line.

bisectional coalition, and to accomplish this, the party had to respect the wishes of their Southern colleagues. Stephen Douglas observed this rule when he pushed for the repeal of the Missouri Compromise. But doing too much endangered the standing of Northern Democrats with their constituents. Those who sacrificed all to retain the support of Southern slaveholders were called "doughfaces." President Franklin Pierce, who had signed the Kansas–Nebraska Act and then supported an aggressively pro-slavery constitution when the territory petitioned for confirmation as a state, was a doughface. So was **James Buchanan**, a Pennsylvania Democrat elected president in 1856.

Despite the public scorn for men like Buchanan, the Democratic Party remained one of the last truly national institutions in the late 1850s. Gone were the churches, the voluntary associations, and the businessmen's alliances that had operated at the national level. Gone too was the Whig Party, a casualty of the sectional disputes over slavery.

Hoping to finally quell the violence and controversy in Kansas, Presidents Pierce and Buchanan had sided with pro-slavery forces in the state, including forcing through Congress a pro-slavery constitution that a clear majority of Kansas residents opposed. But problems and violence persisted, leading some to argue that the Civil War began on the plains of Kansas long before it started in the East.

Sectional tempers flared higher with the Supreme Court's ***Dred Scott*** **decision** in 1857. Widely regarded as one of the worst decisions of the high court, it was yet another attempt to settle the pressing questions of the day that instead intensified them.

Dred Scott v. Sandford

Scott had been enslaved to an army surgeon who spent years posted to the Illinois and

Wisconsin territory when those areas were under the Northwest Ordinance. Scott's lawyers claimed that he had been illegally held as a slave in free territory. Chief Justice **Roger B. Taney** wrote the majority opinion, ruling that Scott lacked the standing to bring the case and consequently dismissed it. His opinion also included the infamous line that the black man "had no rights which the white man was bound to respect." In direct contravention of the case law on the subject, Taney ruled that black people could not be citizens. On the question of where slaveholders could take their property in safety, Taney issued a broad federal protection of slavery.

This sweeping abolishment of a right that Northerners had exercised for the past 70 years shocked and outraged them. Republicans made the decision a key rhetorical weapon in their arsenal, evidence of a grand conspiracy among slaveholders and their allies in Washington to foist a fully nationalized protection of slavery on Northern states. The *Dred Scott* decision fulfilled Southerners' highest hopes for protecting slavery in the territories, although in doing so through federal rather than state power, it undercut Southern arguments that state rights provided the surest foundation for slavery.

Abraham Lincoln reflected moderate Northern antislavery opinion on the decision, which he condemned strongly as wrong in legal, political, and moral terms but pledged to obey while it stood. Other Americans were not so willing to acquiesce. John Brown, of Kansas fame, came east after the Pottawatomie massacre and planned a more direct response to the problem of slavery. Brown, along with his sons and a handful of black and white supporters, attacked the U.S. arsenal at **Harpers Ferry**, Virginia, in late 1859.

 The Life and Death of John Brown

Funded secretly by six prominent abolitionists, Brown had organized and drilled his men in a small southern Pennsylvania town not far from Harpers Ferry. The plan to seize the town and the arsenal misfired. The first victim was a free black man, a night watchman for the Baltimore & Ohio Railroad. News of the attack reached Washington, DC, and a squadron of U.S. Marines, led by Colonel Robert E. Lee, arrived in Harpers Ferry the next morning. Lee's forces penned Brown's men in a barn, killed several, and captured the rest, including Brown. Brown was charged with attempting to incite a slave insurrection and as expected was found guilty and executed.

Brown retained his composure in jail and on the scaffold. His famous pronouncement at his trial recognized that he could do more as a martyr than as a man: "Now, if it is deemed necessary that I should forfeit my life for the furtherance of the ends of justice, and mingle my blood further with the blood of my children and with the blood of millions in this slave country whose rights are disregarded by wicked, cruel, and unjust enactments, I submit; so let it be done!"

DRED SCOTT Scott's lawsuit made him perhaps the most famous enslaved person in the United States. The decision further inflamed sectional tensions rather than extinguishing them as Chief Justice Roger Taney had hoped.

interactive timeline

TIMELINE 1829–1860

AMERICA	YEAR	THE WORLD
David Walker publishes *An Appeal to the Coloured Citizens of the World*	1829	
	1830	Colombia, Ecuador, and Venezuela established as independent nations
Britain ends slavery in British West Indies	1833	
	1839	Dutch recognize Belgium independence Britain begins First Opium War in China (ends 1842)
William Henry Harrison elected first Whig president but dies after a month in office, succeeded by John Tyler First World Anti-Slavery Convention held	1840	"Act of Union" unites Upper and Lower Canada
	1841	Guatemala, El Salvador, Honduras, Nicaragua, and Costa Rica established as independent nations
Prigg v. Pennsylvania establishes national authority for reclaiming fugitive slaves	1842	
Methodist Episcopal Church forms in dispute over slavery Anti-Catholic riots in Philadelphia **Feb** U.S. Congress passes Texas Annexation Act	1844	Santo Domingo wins independence from Spain
Dec United States formally annexes Texas Baptists divide over slavery	1845	
Apr United States declares war on Mexico **Jun** "Bear Flag" Revolt initiates collapse of Mexican authority in California **Aug** Pennsylvania Democrat David Wilmot proposes amendment to Mexican War appropriations bill outlawing slavery in lands acquired from the war	1846	
Mar General Winfield Scott lands at Veracruz, Mexico, defeats Mexican forces, and begins march toward Mexico City **Sep** U.S. Army captures Mexico City	1847	
Feb Treaty of Guadalupe Hidalgo ends the Mexican War and cedes 500,000 square miles of Mexican territory to United States **Jul** Last U.S. troops leave Mexico **Nov** Whig Zachary Taylor elected president **Dec** Gold discovered near Sutter's Mill in California	1848	

The public reaction in each section to John Brown's raid, like reactions to the caning of Charles Sumner three years before, reflected the gulf between the people of the North and South. For Southerners, Brown was the predictable conclusion of the increasingly radical rhetoric of abolitionists bent on exterminating the Southern people. "Every village bell which tolled its solemn note at the execution of Brown proclaims to the South the approbation of that village of insurrection and servile war," wrote one prominent Southerner. Radicals in the North lionized Brown. Henry David Thoreau eulogized him, saying, "Some eighteen hundred years ago Christ was crucified; this morning, perchance, Captain Brown was hung. These are the two ends of a chain which is not without its links. He is not Old Brown any longer; he is an angel of light."

Most Northerners were less effusive. Democrats and conservatives denounced him in no uncertain terms, and Republicans like Lincoln condemned Brown's method while trying to respect his motive. Any sympathy, no matter how mild, proved too much for

AMERICA	YEAR	THE WORLD
Compromise of 1850 passes, which includes provisions admitting California as a free state; opening New Mexico territory to organization under popular sovereignty; banning slave trade in Washington, DC; and creating strong federal Fugitive Slave Act	**1850**	China's Taiping Rebellion begins
Harriet Beecher Stowe publishes *Uncle Tom's Cabin*, giving expression to Northern antislavery sentiment Election of Democrat Franklin Pierce to presidency	**1852**	Establishment of the Second Empire in France under Napoleon III
Commodore Perry arrives in Tokyo Bay, Japan	**1853**	Gold rush in Australia
Kansas–Nebraska Act passed, abolishing Missouri Compromise Line of 1820 Rendition of fugitive slave Anthony Burns from Boston inflames Northern opposition to Fugitive Slave Act First Republican Party convention held in Jackson, Michigan	**1854**	Crimean War begins—Britain and France oppose Russian expansion into Ottoman territory
American Party formally organizes, linking various nativist parties across the country	**1855**	Henry Bessemer patents more efficient process for steelmaking
May Charles Sumner delivers "Crime Against Kansas" speech in U.S. Senate **May** Preston Brooks beats Charles Sumner in Senate chamber Pro-slavery guerrillas from Missouri lead "Sack of Lawrence" in Kansas territory **Nov** Democrat James Buchanan elected president Whig Party collapses in most states	**1856**	Crimean War ends Second Anglo-Chinese War begins
Dred Scott ruling denies citizenship to African Americans Hinton Helper publishes *The Impending Crisis*, denouncing slavery's effect on the political and economic freedom of poor white men in the South	**1857**	Britain suppresses "Sepoy Mutiny" in India
Gold discovered near Pike's Peak in Colorado **Dec** John Brown leads failed slave insurrection at Harpers Ferry, Virginia	**1859**	**Nov** Charles Darwin publishes *On the Origin of Species*
Black population in the United States reaches four million	**1860**	Second Anglo-Chinese War ends

Southerners. The fire-eaters of the South used Brown's raid, ineffectual as it was, to spur Southerners on to support secession. Brown's plan and timing may have failed at Harpers Ferry, but he could scarcely have chosen a better time. A perfect storm of politics and sectionalism had gathered force throughout the 1850s, before Brown's raid concluded the decade, and sent Americans into the most contentious and important presidential election in U.S. history.

STUDY QUESTIONS FOR THE RISE OF THE REPUBLICANS

1. Why did Northerners and Southerners fight over Kansas, and in what ways did such violence reshape national politics?

2. How did the dispute over slavery (in all parts of the country) escalate in the 1850s?

quiz

Summary

- American expansionists pushed the nation into conflict with Mexico and in the process dramatically changed the ethnic profile of the nation, as they drew within its borders Spanish-speaking residents of California and the Far West.
- Combined with the continuing influx of Irish and German immigrants, this demographic transformation scared Anglo-Americans into a repressive movement, known as nativism, designed to guarantee political control by Protestant elites.
- The acquisition of new territory inspired an escalating battle in Congress among pro-slavery and antislavery forces and mirrored the tensions within the South itself.
- As slaves fought against the system from within, and pro-slavery and pro-free-soil citizens fought each other in Kansas, Republicans coalesced around a policy opposing the expansion of slavery.

Key Terms and People

audio
flashcards

Brown, John 461
Buchanan, James 462
Calhoun, John C. 452
Compromise of 1850 459
Douglas, Stephen 460
Fugitive Slave Act 459
Harpers Ferry 463
Helper, Hinton 448
Kansas–Nebraska Act 460

Know-Nothing Party 446
Nativists 450
popular sovereignty 460
Prigg v. Pennsylvania 458
Dred Scott decision 462
Sumner, Charles 461
Taney, Roger B. 463
Treaty of Guadalupe Hidalgo 441

Reviewing Chapter 13

1. How did the movement of people into and around the United States affect political developments of the period?
2. What was the relationship between slavery and the sectional politics of the 1850s?

Further Reading

Davis, David Brion. *Inhuman Bondage: The Rise and Fall of Slavery in the New World.* New York: Oxford University Press, 2006. A global history of commercial slavery that dominated the Western Hemisphere during the 17th–19th centuries.

Foner, Eric. *Free Soil, Free Labor, Free Men: The Ideology of the Republican Party Before the Civil War,* 2nd ed. New York: Oxford University Press, 1995. The clearest analysis of the various forces that shaped the early Republican Party.

Greenburg, Amy. *A Wicked War: Polk, Clay, Lincoln, and the 1846 U.S. Invasion of Mexico.* New York: Knopf, 2012. A critical history of the U.S.–Mexican War.

Holt, Michael. *The Political Crisis of the 1850s.* New York: Norton, 1978. A concise history of the partisan collapse that prefigured the sectional crisis.

Johnson, Walter. *Soul by Soul: Life Inside the Antebellum Slave Market.* Cambridge, MA: Harvard University Press, 1999. An insightful cultural and economic analysis of the operation of slave markets.

Rugemer, Edward Bartlett. *The Problem of Emancipation: The Caribbean Roots of the American Civil War.* Baton Rouge: Louisiana State University, 2008. A hemispheric history of the relationship between British emancipation and secession and war.

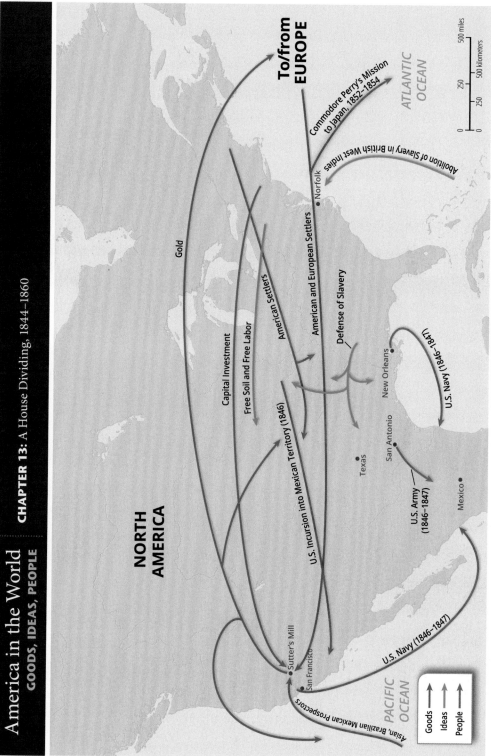

America in the World
GOODS, IDEAS, PEOPLE

CHAPTER 13: A House Dividing, 1844–1860

NORTH
AMERICA

To/from
EUROPE

Commodore Perry's Mission
to Japan, 1852–1854

Abolition of Slavery in British West Indies

Norfolk

ATLANTIC
OCEAN

Gold

American and European Settlers

Capital Investment

Free Soil and Free Labor

American Settlers

Defense of Slavery

New Orleans

U.S. Navy (1846–1847)

San Antonio

Texas

U.S. Incursion into Mexican Territory (1846)

U.S. Army
(1846–1847)

Mexico

Sutter's Mill

San Francisco

U.S. Navy (1846–1847)

PACIFIC
OCEAN

Asian, Brazilian Mexican Prospectors

Goods

Ideas

People

500 miles

500 kilometers

map analysis

President Lincoln confers with generals Ulysses S. Grant (center) and William Tecumseh Sherman (left) near the close of the Civil War.

CHAPTER 14

The Civil War

1860–1865

A single cotton boll weighs less than one-quarter of an ounce. Individual fibers can be carried away by an exhaled breath. But the value of woven cotton to the global powers of the 19th century empowered white Southerners to enslave millions of people and helped convince them that they could win a war of **secession** against the North. Cotton's bonds proved stronger than iron or blood. How did this humble plant wind up implicated in the deadliest episode in American history?

Profits from cotton drove the great expansion of the slave regimes of Alabama, Mississippi, and northern Louisiana, and much of that profit came from overseas buyers. By 1860, British and French mills bought 70 percent of their cotton from the American South. The British textile industry employed nearly one-quarter of the country's workers. Southerners assumed that this dependency guaranteed foreign support in the event of a civil war. Robert Bunch, the British consul at Charleston, explained to London in 1860 that there existed an "almost universal conviction entertained by the South that Great Britain will make any sacrifice, even of principle or of honor to prevent the stoppage of the supply of cotton." Although Britain bought more raw cotton than anyone else, Southerners saw the same trend around the globe. Georgians were cheered by what one noted as the "progressive increase of the consumption of cotton in France, Belgium, Holland, Germany, and Spain."

To explain why wars happen, we need to understand both the underlying causes and those factors that enable people to initiate or wage war. Cotton performs double duty for the Civil War. Profits from the South's staple crops (cotton especially but also sugar and rice) reinforced the importance of slavery and encouraged Southerners to pursue economic and diplomatic strategies at odds with those that Northerners supported.

Second, the global connections that cotton created gave Southerners the confidence to secede. As South Carolina's James Henry Hammond proclaimed, "You dare not make war on cotton. . . . Cotton is King!" Their control of this most important crop emboldened Southerners to perceive themselves as a world power even as their authority within the national community diminished. This paradox was hard to see in 1860, but the Civil War would soon test the durability of King Cotton's throne.

⬇ SECESSION, 1860–1861

In 1860, widespread violence still lay in the future, and adversaries sparred through politics. From the perspective of white Southerners, the rapid growth of the Northern states threatened the balance of power within the United States. Fearful about the future of slavery under a Republican administration, a majority of slaveholding states seceded from the Union. Few anticipated anything more than a short war, if that. Many Southerners assumed that their central place as cotton supplier to French and British textile manufacturers would bring recognition of their new nation before any real war began. For their part, Northerners interpreted secession as a repudiation of self-government, a threat to both America and the future of democracy around the world. Northerners went to war in 1861 to reunify the nation. Determined Southern resistance compelled increasingly severe measures from the North. Over time, a war for union evolved into a war for emancipation, with a twisted legacy of violence, anger, hope, and joy.

The Secession of the Lower South

The battle began with the election of 1860. Democrats convened their party in Charleston, South Carolina, home to the most rabid pro-secession wing of the party. The convention deadlocked over federal protection for slavery in the western territories. Fire-eaters, Deep South advocates of immediate secession, abandoned the meeting rather than accept defeat on this measure. Northern Democrats reconvened in Baltimore several weeks later and nominated Stephen Douglas, whereas Southern Democrats nominated Senator John Breckinridge of Kentucky. Republicans likewise entered their convention in Chicago divided over who should lead the party. Most regarded party leaders William Henry Seward and Samuel Chase as too radical on the question of slavery. Local favorite **Abraham Lincoln** won the nomination because of his strong national showing in the 1858 senatorial campaign against Stephen Douglas and because he did not have a long track record. His moderate stance appealed to Republican Party managers keen to win conservative voters in the North. Lincoln made his personal opposition to slavery clear, but as a strict constitutionalist, he also recognized that neither Congress nor the president had authority over slavery where it already existed. Another group organized itself out of the remnants of the Southern Whigs and nominated Kentuckian John Bell. Calling themselves the Constitutional Union Party, they advocated little beyond a moderate appeal to union in their campaign platform. The four-way contest thus presented voters with the most complex ballot since the election of 1824 (Map 14.1).

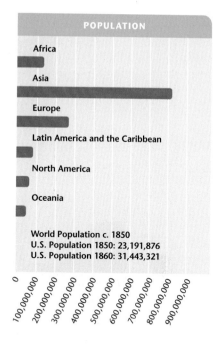

POPULATION

Africa

Asia

Europe

Latin America and the Caribbean

North America

Oceania

World Population c. 1850
U.S. Population 1850: 23,191,876
U.S. Population 1860: 31,443,321

0, 100,000,000, 200,000,000, 300,000,000, 400,000,000, 500,000,000, 600,000,000, 700,000,000, 800,000,000, 900,000,000

The campaign mirrored the deep sectional divisions in the country. Lincoln appeared only before Northern audiences, and many Southern registrars refused to even print his name on ballots. Breckinridge campaigned in the South, and Bell toured mostly the middle of the country. Only Douglas campaigned nationally, reprimanding both Southern and Northern extremists who he believed threatened the Union. Breckinridge never advocated secession, although he was clearly the candidate most sympathetic to the cause of Southern rights. Although Lincoln was not an abolitionist, his firm opposition to the expansion of slavery into the western territories alarmed pro-slavery Southerners. They regarded slavery's expansion as essential to their survival and perceived any restriction as a violation of constitutionally protected property rights. Although he captured only 40 percent of the popular vote, Lincoln won the election by securing a majority in the electoral college.

South Carolina was the first state to respond to Lincoln's election. On December 20, 1860, the state "dissolved" its relationship to the Union. The "Declaration of Causes" issued by the convention began with a stark explanation of slavery's centrality to secession: "Our position is thoroughly identified with the institution of slavery—the greatest material interest of the world." Although Lincoln had not yet assumed office, white South Carolinians believed that Lincoln's administration would try to abolish slavery. Fire-eaters in Mississippi stated the case in equally stark language: "There was no choice left us but submission to the mandates of abolition, or a dissolution of the Union, whose principles had been subverted to work out our ruin." Other slaveholding states shared this sentiment. Over the next six weeks, Alabama, Florida, Georgia, Louisiana, and Texas followed suit, although none demonstrated as much unity as South Carolina. In each of these states, substantial minorities opposed immediate secession. Pro-secession Georgians captured a bare 51 percent in voting for the state's secession convention, whereas in Texas, Governor Sam Houston (the hero of Texas independence) tried to block the legislature from even calling for a convention. Like many conservative Southerners, Houston said he hoped to avoid "the perils of revolution . . . with its attendant horrors of bloodshed, rapine, and devastation." Despite Houston's experience and stature, pro-secession forces in Texas and other states won the day and led their states out

Excerpts from "The Declaration of Causes"

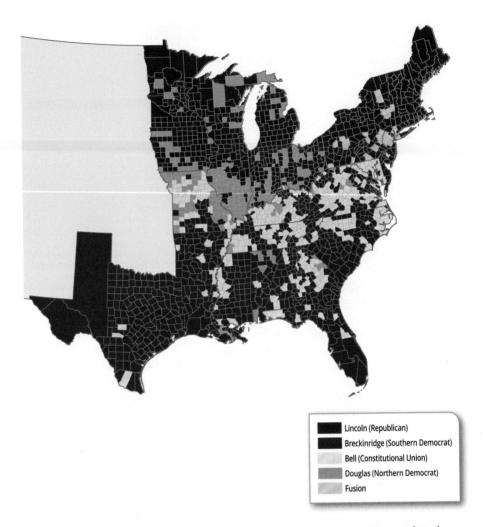

Lincoln (Republican)

Breckinridge (Southern Democrat)

Bell (Constitutional Union)

Douglas (Northern Democrat)

Fusion

MAP 14.1 1860 Presidential Election, by County The four-way contest exacerbated sectional discontent. Abraham Lincoln won the Northern states and enough electoral votes to secure the office, whereas John Breckinridge won the South, and John Bell and Stephen Douglas shared states in the country's middle.

of the Union. On February 4, 1861, representatives of the seven Deep South states assembled in Montgomery, Alabama, and created the Confederate States of America.

Fort Sumter and the Secession of the Upper South

During the long interim between the election and Lincoln's inauguration in March 1861, President James Buchanan did little to address the crisis. Buchanan believed that secession was unconstitutional but that he was powerless to intervene. Buchanan's hands-off policy gave seceding states the false impression that the U.S. government would do nothing to impede their exit. Lincoln waited out the lame-duck period at his home in

"Whew! That Old Hen, Jɛꜰꜰ Dᴀᴠɪꜱ, has been trying to hatch a Rotten Egg."

SECESSION This cartoon reveals Northern scorn for secession and the easy assumption among Northerners that curtailing the process would be quick and painless.

Springfield, Illinois, where he reiterated his oft-stated position that the president had no power over slavery in the states where it already existed but that Congress could regulate or ban slavery in the territories.

Lincoln's inauguration on March 4, 1861, was a solemn affair; it occurred under the cloud of uncertainty about the Union's future that he had pledged to preserve. In his inaugural speech, Lincoln appealed to Southerners to remain loyal—"We are not enemies, but friends"—and to respect the shared history ("the mystic chords of memory") that bound them to the United States. Lincoln's supporters regarded the speech as moderate and conciliatory, but opponents considered his declaration that the Union would "hold, occupy, and possess the property and places belonging to the government" a threat to their peace and security. Both Lincoln and Mississippian **Jefferson Davis**, who resigned from Congress and accepted the presidency of the Confederacy, moved cautiously. Both faced similar challenges—needing to bolster their standing among their own anxious and angry citizens while avoiding war—and for both the momentum of events initiated by others pushed them along. Northerners demanded that Lincoln restore control over federal property—principally, coastal forts and armories in the South—while Southerners pushed Davis to assert Confederate control over the same places.

Even as both sides considered the possibility of war, upper South representatives continued to embrace negotiation. Pro-secession forces knew they represented a minority view in the region, so they inflamed fear of Lincoln. Pro-union forces sought conciliatory agreements from Lincoln and Congress that would reassure Southerners that slavery would be protected. Congress passed and two states ratified a new amendment that would have guaranteed slavery in the states where it existed. But these measures were too little too late. Republicans refused to compromise on the extension of slavery into western

Lincoln's first inaugural address; Jefferson Davis's resignation speech from the Senate territories, recognizing this as a core issue for their supporters. To entice their slaveholding brethren in the upper South to join them, several Deep South states sent commissioners to the region to argue for the necessity of a unified slaveholding South. The Alabama commissioner, Stephen Hale, told Kentuckians that Northerners "had been waging an unrelenting and fanatical war" against slavery since the 1830s. Under a Lincoln administration, whites would "be degraded to a position of equality with free negroes . . . or else there will be an eternal war of races, desolating the land with blood, and utterly wasting and destroying all the resources of the country." Hale's conclusion was clear: "Disunion is inevitable."

The crisis peaked at Fort Sumter, an unfinished earthen fort located in Charleston Harbor. The U.S. commander, Kentuckian Robert Anderson, notified Washington that he could not continue to hold the fort without provisions. Lincoln sent an unarmed ship to restock the food supplies for the small garrison. On April 12, 1861, before the ship reached the harbor, Confederate batteries on neighboring islands opened fire on Fort Sumter. After a lengthy artillery duel, Anderson surrendered the fort. Northerners treated this attack on U.S. property as evidence of an armed rebellion.

Mobilization for War

In the wake of the battle at Fort Sumter, Lincoln called up the militia, requesting 75,000 men enlisted for 90 days to help restore obedience to the law of the United States. Upper South politicians who had resisted secession regarded Lincoln's decision to mobilize an army as an act of betrayal after the months of quiet negotiation. Four more slave states—Virginia, North Carolina, Tennessee, and Arkansas—left the Union for the Confederacy, whereas four others—Missouri, Kentucky, Maryland, and Delaware—remained loyal. A wave of martial enthusiasm swept both the North and the South. George Templeton Strong detailed changes in New York City: "The Northern backbone is much stiffened already. Many who stood up for 'Southern rights' and complained of wrongs done the South now say that, since the South has fired the first gun, they are ready to go to all lengths in supporting the government." At county courthouses, town squares, and city centers, hundreds of thousands of men volunteered for the Union and Confederate armies.

In retrospect, the North's military advantages seem so significant that Southern enthusiasm looks arrogant or rash. At the time, however, most Southerners and many Northerners identified differences more important than manpower and supplies. On paper, the North was much better equipped to fight. It possessed a 5:2 advantage in terms of eligible soldiers, over twice as many draft animals, and a vastly greater industrial capacity. Most importantly, the North had a more commercialized economic system (Figure 14.1). Southerners invested their money in land and slaves, and neither could easily be sold to pay for the war. But the South held both geographic and psychological advantages. The land mass of the Confederacy was three-quarters of a million square miles—larger than the size of continental Europe—with a 3,000-mile coastline; thus, it seemed too large to be conquered by Union forces. Southerners also fought a defensive war—they knew the terrain and took pride and strength in the fact that they were defending their homes against invasion. William Russell, a British journalist traveling through the United States, observed that if Confederate nationalism took root, "it will be difficult indeed for the North to restore the Union. These pieces of bunting [national flags] seem to twine themselves through heart and brain."

Excerpt from William Russell's diary on Southern attitudes toward the North (May 1861)

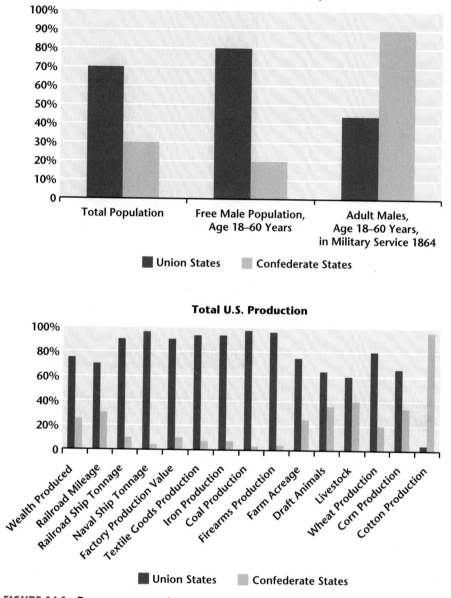

FIGURE 14.1 Resource comparison, United States of America and Confederate States of America The North possessed significant advantages in industrial and agricultural resource production (except cotton), but this became a factor only over time. Confederates entered the conflict aware of their material deficiencies but confident that the war would not last long enough for them to greatly matter.

The U.S. Army contained only 15,000 men in 1860, and nearly one-third of the officers and enlisted men resigned to join the Confederacy. The navy had only three functional vessels in U.S. waters ready for duty. As a result, Northern advantages, especially

NORTHERN VOLUNTEERS SALUTING THE AMERICAN FLAG IN 1861 For soldiers, the flag represented the Union and self-government, the defense of which drew hundreds of thousands into military service in the war's first year.

image analysis

its larger population and greater economic resources, would matter only in a long war. Both sides anticipated a brief struggle—perhaps lasting no longer than the fall of 1861. South Carolina senator James Chesnut famously predicted he would soak up all the blood spilled as a result of secession with his handkerchief, so confident was he that no war would erupt. Washington was unprepared for the influx of men who arrived in the late spring—tens of thousands more than Lincoln's initial call—and without proper facilities, they slept in the Patent Office, the hallways of the Capitol, and any other federal facility that had space. The Confederacy established a training camp outside Richmond to accommodate the influx of troops from around the South.

Even more pressing for the North than space to house soldiers was a vision of the war's purpose. Frederick Douglass and other abolitionists saw the war as an opportunity to destroy slavery. In the May 1861 issue of *Douglass' Monthly*, Douglass began his campaign to forge the link between Union and emancipation. "Fire must be met with water, darkness with light," Douglass wrote, "and war for the destruction of liberty must be met with war for the destruction of slavery. *The simple way then, to put an end to the savage and desolating war now waged by the slaveholders, is to strike down slavery itself*, the primal cause of the war." Democrats and conservative Republicans condemned bloodshed and the destruction of property from other Americans. Lincoln seemed personally aligned with the broad middle of the country. A passionate defender of the Union, he insisted that the first and only goal for the North was the restoration of the rule of law and the obedience of Southern state governments to national law. White Southerners claimed they were defending their autonomy, their independence, as free people. They openly acknowledged that their freedom depended on the preservation of racial slavery. The vice president of the Confederacy, **Alexander Stephens**, famously proclaimed black slavery "the cornerstone" of the new republic.

From the Ballot to the Bullet

An outside observer coming to the United States in 1860 might have had a hard time understanding the source of differences between North and South. Both derived their values from the same historical and religious foundations—western Europe and Protestant Christianity. Both conceived of themselves as democratic and capitalistic. They spoke the same language and shared foodways, fashion, literature, and a developing popular culture of theater, music, and stage entertainment. Both used the American Revolution to justify their way of life. How could two people so similar conceptualize themselves as so different and fight such a catastrophic war? Most people at the time identified slavery as the key difference between the two sections. Despite the absence of the institution in the North, white citizens held racial views similar to those of their Southern peers. Nonetheless, the presence, durability, and dynamism of slavery in the American South produced, over time, sharply different understandings of freedom, citizenship, and the natural rights accorded to all human beings. Lincoln saw his challenge as proving that in democracies, there could be "no appeal from the ballot to the bullet."

The challenge for the North was to compel Southerners back into the Union without alienating them any further. Lincoln believed in the loyalty of most white Southerners, who, he thought, had only been swayed temporarily by fire-eater rhetoric. His optimism proved misplaced; most white Southerners supported the Confederacy in 1861 and still did at the end of the war. The North began the war by treating Southern civilians as American citizens. Union armies were ordered not to confiscate or destroy Southern property. This policy aimed to placate Southerners and their conservative allies in the North and to prove that reunion posed no threat. Radicals in the North lambasted the policy as the "rosewater" strategy and argued that no war could be won by sprinkling perfume on one's opponent. General-in-Chief Winfield Scott, a hero of the War of 1812 and the U.S.–Mexican War, proposed a more vigorous strategy to encircle the Confederacy along the rivers and coastlines and slowly constrict their ability to wage war. Critics who forecast an easy and quick victory lampooned the idea as the "Anaconda plan," arguing that it required too many men and too much time.

Just as public demand for action drove Jefferson Davis to attack Fort Sumter, by midsummer Northern public opinion drove Lincoln to attack the Confederate forces assembled near the railroad junction of Manassas, Virginia, about 20 miles southwest of Washington, DC. The battle attracted curious onlookers hoping to see the rebels retreat. The Battle of Bull Run, named by the North for the creek that flowed through the area, turned out to be far bloodier than anyone on either side had imagined. Although Union forces pushed Confederates back through the morning's fighting, a pause at midday allowed Southern troops to regroup and counterattack. The untrained Union soldiers broke and abandoned the field, scattering the tourists in a hasty retreat back to Washington. By the end of the day, Confederate forces had lost close to 2,000 men and Union forces close to 3,000. Although the Confederate victory embarrassed the North, it inspired greater mobilization and a stronger training regimen through the fall and winter of 1861. Confident that it represented their true superiority, Confederates basked in the victory.

Letter from Union major Sullivan Ballou to his wife before the Battle of Bull Run

WAR IN EARNEST, 1862–1863

In many respects, 1862 proved to be the most important year of the Civil War. As the war continued, it imposed increasing burdens on the populations of both sections. All of these costs—physical, ideological, and psychological—became clear during 1862, yet both sides fought on. As the bloodshed increased, soldiers and civilians on both sides longed for peace. As they moved further from peace, however, they increasingly came to view the other side as a mortal enemy. This prospect worried Abraham Lincoln, who understood the devastating nature of civil wars—the more energetically his commanders pursued Confederate defeat, the harder it became to achieve his goal of rebuilding the Union.

The North Advances

Although Northerners, Southerners, and European observers focused on fighting in the East, the war's center of gravity in early 1862 was in the West. There, Lincoln found the commander who developed a strategy that eventually brought victory to the Union. The general was **Ulysses S. Grant**, a 40-year-old former army officer. Grant first achieved fame by conquering Forts Henry and Donelson, located on the Tennessee and the Cumberland rivers, respectively. Rivers were the one geographic weakness faced by the Confederacy—all the major ones flowed into or through the South, and Union forces used them as avenues of invasion. The capture of the two forts gave federal forces access to all of Tennessee, where they took 14,000 Confederate prisoners and provided a much-needed hero for Northern newspapers. Grant's new nickname—"Unconditional Surrender Grant"—reflected his vigorous prosecution of the war.

By early April 1862, Grant's soldiers had marched to the southern boundary of Tennessee, where they clashed with Confederate forces in a cataclysmic battle around Shiloh Church. Although the battle was a stalemate—with Confederate forces winning the first day and Union forces the next—Northern soldiers retained their position on the battlefield while Confederates retreated into northern Mississippi. The scale of the battle garnered the most attention, with nearly 24,000 total casualties over the two days of fighting. Shiloh was several times worse than anything seen before in North America. Grant grimly noted, "I saw an open field . . . so covered with dead that it would have been possible to walk across the clearing, in any direction, stepping on dead bodies, without a foot touching the ground."

The horrific nature of Civil War battles resulted from the new, more accurate rifled musket with greater range and more powerful and accurate artillery. Officers on both sides failed to adjust the tactics they used in battle despite these new technologies. Trained in grand frontal and flanking (side) attacks, both armies continued to launch assaults against entrenched opponents despite the considerable advantage that the new

The Battle of Shiloh

UNION NAVY EXPANSION   Grant effectively coordinated his movement into Tennessee with naval commanders. The North's rapidly expanding "brown water navy" allowed the Union to bring heavy guns into the range of forts along the Mississippi and Tennessee rivers.

weapons gave to the defensive side. With a few rare exceptions, attacking armies always suffered higher casualties and rarely emerged victorious.

As regular forces engaged in more deadly conflict, civilians experienced the terror and chaos of **guerrilla** conflict. In central Virginia, central Tennessee, Missouri, Arkansas, and much of Kentucky, pro-Confederate civilians spied on, sabotaged, and attacked Union soldiers as they advanced into the region. In some places, guerrillas turned their violence on civilians, targeting black and white Unionists who supported the North. Pro-Confederate women, many with fathers or husbands in military service, often assisted guerrillas with food and information. U.S. soldiers grew increasingly wary of Southern white women. By war's end, some believed their defiance explained why the war lasted so long. Increasingly vigorous methods to curtail guerrilla actions adopted by both governments failed to solve the problem.

The worst violence occurred in those places with the lightest presence of regular troops. Western Virginia, western North Carolina, and nearly all of Missouri were exposed to continuous guerrilla conflict. In these areas, noncombatants—including men, women, and children—used violence to settle old grudges, political resentments, and economic opportunity. Civilians recognized early on that armies ensured their safety, and as a result, increasing numbers of people fled to occupied towns over the course of the war. Cities such as Nashville, Little Rock, and Memphis saw their populations double or triple during the war as a result of the influx of refugees seeking security.

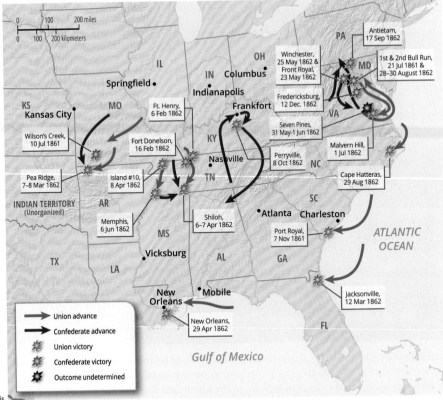

map analysis

MAP 14.2 Major Battles and Campaigns, 1861–1862 Early in the war, Confederate forces established a de facto boundary along the Rapidan–Rappahannock River corridor in Virginia that they maintained through 1862. In the West, the Union experienced more military success, principally along the major rivers leading into the southern interior.

Stalemate in the East

Union forces moved decisively into Confederate strongholds in the West, but they remained stalemated in the East (Map 14.2). After the battle of Bull Run, Lincoln appointed General **George B. McClellan** the new commander of the Army of the Potomac. McClellan spent the winter reorganizing, outfitting, and training his men. The profusion of supplies and the lack of battles endeared him to the soldiers. When the spring weather improved enough to initiate a campaign, McClellan ferried his soldiers down the Chesapeake Bay to Fort Monroe—a Union outpost on the tip of the peninsula between Virginia's York and James rivers. McClellan then squandered his advantage by moving with agonizing slowness up the peninsula toward the Confederate capital of Richmond. From Washington, President Lincoln urged McClellan forward and paced the halls of the telegraph office set up across the street from the White House waiting for news. Unlike Jefferson Davis, Lincoln entered the war with no real knowledge of warfare or the military, but, reading tactical and strategy manuals late into the night, he learned rapidly on the job. Because of his lack of expertise and because of the complexities of Northern politics, Lincoln deferred to his generals early in the war. As they continued to disappoint him, Lincoln assumed an increasingly active role in crafting the overall strategy that led to Union victory. On May 31, after a climactic battle within earshot of Richmond, McClellan pulled his forces back to a base on the York River and gave the Confederates a chance to regroup.

This pause coincided with the elevation of General **Robert E. Lee** to command of Confederate forces in Virginia. Whereas Lee's predecessors had been prone to retreat and delay, Lee favored the offense. His approach to war generated both high casualties for Confederate forces and victories for the South. For many, Lee embodied the spirit of the Confederate nation. Paeans to his religiosity, gentility, and fierceness in battle circulated during the war and long after. Although Lee never became a political figure on the order of Napoleon, his stature helped convince the public to continue fighting. In late June, Lee succeeded in pushing McClellan's troops back to the James River. The campaign, known as the Seven Days, immortalized Lee for saving Richmond and for defeating a much larger Union force. For the North, the Peninsula Campaign was a costly and humiliating defeat.

Abram Joseph Ryan, "The Sword of Robert E. Lee" (ca. 1867)

Another seminal feature of the Peninsula Campaign was the erosion of slavery. Officially, the United States still protected slavery, but the army's disruption of civilian life inevitably weakened the system. With most white men in military service, communities could not muster slave patrols to catch runaways and stop slave conspiracies. As the Union army lumbered up the peninsula, enslaved people seized opportunities to flee. Thus far in the conflict, however, Lincoln insisted the war was about union, not the end of slavery. He hoped to retain the support of the slaveholding border states— Missouri, Kentucky, Maryland, and Delaware—even at the expense of alienating abolitionists in the North. Regardless of official policy or political pronouncements, enslaved people fled by the thousands as the Union army moved through the region.

If Confederates drew dire lessons from the ancillary effects of the Peninsula Campaign, they received great sustenance from the success of their armies in Virginia's Shenandoah valley. In spring 1862, a new hero joined Lee in the pantheon of Confederate history—Thomas Jonathan "Stonewall" Jackson, widely praised for his effective leadership and aggressive approach to warfare. In the valley, Jackson outmaneuvered several Union armies. In a sequence of battles lasting through May, Jackson eluded larger Union forces and prevented them from reinforcing McClellan on the peninsula. When Jackson was killed by friendly fire in mid-1863, he became the Confederacy's best-known martyr and part of the emerging culture of patriotic sacrifice that defined the new nation.

The Union worked to build a culture of national unity as well. Seeking to turn the ethnic diversity of the region into a strength, military recruiters encouraged communities to send regiments with specific ethnic identities into the Northern armies. Irish and German groups led the way in 1861, as they enlisted in the "Irish Rifles" (39th New York Infantry), the "Fighting Irish" (69th New York State Militia), and "Die Neuner" (9th Ohio Infantry). Many of the men who enlisted in these units had been born abroad, and military service offered one way to establish their claim to full citizenship in the United States. Others felt an obligation to defend their new home and the honor of their old ones. As an Irish-American sergeant explained to his relatives in Ireland, "When we are fighting for America we are fighting in the interest of Irland striking a double blow cutting with a two edged sword[.] For while we strike in defence of the rights of Irishmen here we are striking a blow at Irland's enemy and oppressor England. [sic]" Many Irishmen enlisted with the hope of acquiring military training that could be put to use against England in the fight for Irish independence.

Southern and Northern Home Fronts

European national revolutions of the late 1840s demonstrated the tension between liberal social reformers seeking to restructure European society and the unpredictable nature of war. In many countries, revolutions failed and conservative regimes returned to power through violence. In the U.S. Civil War, to some extent, the opposite process occurred. The chaos and unpredictability of war created unintended social consequences that white Southerners who initiated secession did not foresee. Paramount among these was class conflict: some poor and middle-class whites rejected secession partly because they saw it as a policy designed to protect the interests of the wealthy. Every Confederate state witnessed this tension. One of the most articulate spokespersons for this group was Tennessee's William G. "Parson" Brownlow. A journalist and politician, Brownlow made clear the extent and the nature of his opposition to the Confederacy in 1861: "We can never live in a Southern Confederacy, and be made hewers of wood and drawers of water for a set of aristocrats."

Excerpt from the diary of Mary Boykin Chesnut (1862)

The process of military mobilization altered the gender dynamic of Southern society profoundly. Because Southern communities sent such a high proportion of white men to fight, white women had to assume new duties. Beyond the emotional costs for women left alone—one mother wrote to her daughter that she could "hardly endure the sadness of the change, the diminished family circle"—the most problematic new burden was managing slaves, especially the adult male slaves whose labor remained essential. Although women had long directed household slaves, they rarely disciplined male slaves. In Southern cities, women moved into new occupations as well. In Macon and Augusta, Georgia, they staffed textile mills; in Richmond, they worked in munitions factories, and a sizeable number served as clerks in various Confederate departments. Rural women took over virtually all the tasks that were necessary on farms, including making decisions about which crops to raise, how to grow them, and when to sell. By 1863, Michael Raysor, a Floridian serving in Mississippi, finally admitted to his wife that she had bested him as a farmer: "You said that you thought we would have near a hundred head of hogs to fatten this fall. This is doing well, aint it. I think you are a better farmer than I am you have done exceedingly well since I left."

The main push for social change in the North came not in the area of class or gender equality but in racial justice. Abolitionists, long derided as outcasts and denied access to political power, seized opportunities to press their agenda. Frederick Douglass and William Lloyd Garrison remained the leading spokesmen for the movement. From the beginning of the conflict, Douglass worked to frame the conflict as a war of liberty versus slavery. Even as they succeeded in turning the U.S. government away from its cozy relationship with slavery, abolitionists had little luck improving the attitudes of white Northerners toward black people. Discrimination remained commonplace across the North, and whites manifested a much greater passion for punishing slaveholders than they did for helping slaves. The conflict over slavery broke roughly along partisan lines. The Republican Party had already established its opposition to the institution, and the Democratic Party had long harbored slavery's staunchest defenders. The result was that each party, using the issue to press for partisan advantage, complicated an already bloody political landscape.

As the war dragged on, the Democratic Party split into two wings: a pro-war faction that supported the Union while distancing itself from the Lincoln administration, and an antiwar wing known as the "**Copperheads**." Even those Democrats who functioned as a loyal opposition condemned and lampooned Lincoln in the harshest possible language; one asserted that Lincoln was "willing to destroy his country, his party, himself, if he can destroy his opponents." The party gained support from this approach in the congressional elections of 1862, when Democrats reclaimed 28 seats. The Northern war effort was badly stalled in late 1862, and this delay played an important role in Democratic victories. Republican electoral fortunes rose and fell with the successes and failures of the Union army.

Anti-Copperhead cartoon from *Harper's Weekly* (1863)

Despite popular sympathy for the president personally, many elites in the country, including prominent Republicans, regarded Lincoln as an uncouth backwoodsman unfit for higher office. Lincoln enjoyed the coarse popular humor of the day—he often read aloud from his favorite humorists while waiting in the telegraph office for battle reports—but his stories revealed a keen mind. Lincoln's use of language—both grand and commonplace—proved one of the North's greatest assets during the conflict. Democrats responded with fearmongering and openly racist rhetoric. They condemned emancipation and Lincoln for adopting it. "The only true policy for the American government," a Democrat wrote, was "the Constitution as it is, the Union as it was, and the Negroes where they are." This tactic reached a crescendo in the 1864 presidential election, when Democrats argued that Lincoln's policies promoted blacks at the expense of whites and that Lincoln supported interracial sexual relations.

The political landscape of the South was less partisan but no less complex or destructive. One of the Confederate government's first acts was to ban political parties. In the utopian vision of the Confederacy's founders, parties created social conflict where none existed; therefore, by abolishing parties, they could eliminate an important source of friction. This approach ignored the very real divisions—by class, region, religion, and ethnicity—that already existed within Southern communities, and it did little to quell social conflict. Instead of organizing a policy-based critique of Jefferson Davis and other leading officeholders, dissenting politicians targeted their venom directly at Davis. Alexander Stephens, Davis's vice president, became one of the administration's harshest critics, calling Davis "weak and vacillating, timid, petulant, peevish, obstinate, but not firm."

The Struggle for European Support

From the outset of the war, both Lincoln and Davis courted European support for their side—primarily from Europe's two great powers, Great Britain and France. Although Confederate emissaries traveled east, they had little luck, especially in Russia, which maintained a steadfast dedication to the North. France leaned toward the Confederacy but refused to act without Britain, so the two sides primarily struggled to capture British support. Whereas the British aristocracy sympathized with the Confederacy, based on a cultural and intellectual familiarity, the laboring classes supported the Union because of the Republican Party's devotion to the workingman and its opposition to slavery.

The first major international crisis in the Civil War revolved around the seizure of a British ship, the *Trent*, by the U.S. Navy in the Caribbean in late 1861. The U.S. commander, Charles Wilkes, arrested two Confederate commissioners sailing to London and France. The complexities of admiralty law during war clouded the legality of Wilkes's actions, but Britain—responding defiantly—came close to declaring war on

A Global War for Democracy

In the summer of 1861, headlines began announcing the arrival of Giuseppe Garibaldi, the hero of Italian unification, to lead Northern troops. "Garibaldi Coming!" they blared. No more information was needed. Readers knew Garibaldi from his daring exploits in liberation movements around the world and most recently as a leader of the successful campaign to unify Italy into a modern and sovereign nation-state. His name was short-hand for democratic reform and national unity. The prospect of enlisting an Italian revolutionary as a leader of Union forces might seem strange if the Civil War is regarded as a domestic conflict. The fighting occurred within American boundaries (except for a few naval engagements in the world's oceans), and it seemed driven by entirely domestic politics, principally disputes over the expansion of slavery. But the fate of the United States demanded the attention of people around the world.

Reformers and radicals cheered the North, while the forces of political reaction backed the Confederacy. European conservatives balked at the vision advanced by Garibaldi and other liberal reformers. In their view, the Civil War came not because of a lack of democracy but because of an excess. Granting suffrage to poor, propertyless men, as American states had done throughout the antebellum era, invited discord because these were the people mostly easily led astray by a demagogue. Lord Palmerston, the British prime minister, warned that putting "Power in the Hands of the Masses throws the Scum of the Community to the Surface and . . . Truth and Justice are Soon banished from the land." Even if they did not sympathize with the South, some Europeans regarded the war as a necessary corrective and evidence of their own good judgment in restricting the vote to landholding men.

Northerners, for their part, believed they represented the leading edge of the global democratic movement. When Lincoln told Congress that the United States was "the

the United States. Lincoln quietly sought a peaceful resolution, dashing Confederate hopes for a permanent break between the Union and Britain.

Confederate leaders' overconfidence in the persuasive power of cotton produced two deadly blind spots. Pinning their hopes on King Cotton diplomacy, Confederates initiated an embargo on cotton sales to Britain and France in May 1861, as they believed that economic pressure would force them to recognize the Confederacy. But Britain and France both held substantial stockpiles of cotton, which postponed the embargo's impact for well over a year, and for Britain, the volume and substance of Northern trade—especially food—was just as important as the Southern trade in cotton. During the Crimean War of the mid-1850s, U.S. wheat exports to Britain and France had skyrocketed, and these continued after the war. Confederates also failed to recognize the moral values of English textile workers, who derived their livelihood from Southern cotton but supported the Union because of its advocacy of free labor.

Nonetheless, influential members of the British cabinet viewed the U.S. conflict as a net gain for Europe and the division of the country as inevitable given Southern last best hope of man," he meant that only Northern victory would preserve democracy in the eyes of the world. Garibaldi agreed: "The American question is about life for the liberty of the world," he said. His colleague Giuseppe Mazzini—the real leader behind Italy's unification movement—believed that Americans must "be a guiding and instigating force for the good of your own country and that of Humanity." Alongside these Italian revolutionaries, liberal reformers from across Europe cheered on Northern victory. John Bright in England, Édouard Laboulaye in France, and Karl Marx speaking for working people all over the continent endorsed the Northern cause and identified it with the reform movements they championed.

Republicans like Charles Sumner and William Henry Seward, who kept up close correspondence with European observers of the conflict, celebrated this support and drew sustenance especially as Northern war aims broadened to target slavery itself. In the 1830s and 1840s, Garibaldi had fought alongside rebels in Brazil, where he hoped to destroy the slave oligarchy that controlled the country. Like many European liberals, Garibaldi saw American emancipation as an essential component in the broader advancement of democracy and liberty around the world. "You may be sure," he wrote, "that had I accepted to draw my sword for the cause of the United States, it would have been for the abolition of Slavery, full, unconditional," he told a friend. Garibaldi, however, never came to the United States and so never participated directly in the American phase of the great struggle for human freedom that he believed characterized the 19th century. But support from European reformers bolstered the Union cause and demonstrated the global reach of the Civil War. Union victory, when it came, not only brought emancipation and reunion, but inspired reformers around the world to continue their efforts.

Letters from Giuseppe Garibaldi and Giuseppe Mazzini in support of the Union (1865)

- Why were European reformers interested in the U.S. Civil War?
- How did their support matter for the North?

military prowess. Momentum to recognize the Confederacy as a fully independent nation in the eyes of the world peaked in 1862. William Gladstone, the liberal statesman and later prime minister, asserted, "There is no doubt that Jefferson Davis and other leaders of the South have made an Army; they are making, it appears, a Navy; and they have made—what is more than either—they have made a Nation. We may anticipate with certainty the success of the Southern States so far as regards their separation from the North." Gladstone and others had nearly succeeded in convincing Prime Minister Palmerston to recognize the Confederacy when Union forces rebuffed Robert E. Lee's September 1862 invasion of Maryland at Antietam.

After this Confederate defeat, and especially after Lincoln issued the preliminary **Emancipation Proclamation** in its wake, Britain never again came close to recognizing the Confederacy. Emancipation proved to be one of the most useful tools in Lincoln's diplomatic arsenal. In line with his increasingly progressive shift on emancipation, Lincoln initiated diplomatic recognition of Haiti in 1862, a first for the United States since the black republic established its independence from France in 1804. Emancipation also put the United States in synchrony with other global movements toward liberty. In 1861, Czar Alexander II signed the "Emancipation Manifesto," freeing Russia's serfs. Like Lincoln's emancipation of slaves, Russia's change reflected an emerging liberal consensus around the supremacy of individual freedom and of freedom as a precondition for modern economic growth. Karl Marx, who traveled to the United States during the war as a correspondent for the Vienna *Presse*, conflated these events as well, noting, "The biggest things that are happening in the world today are on the one hand the movement of the slaves in America started by the death of John Brown, and on the other the movement of the serfs in Russia."

STUDY QUESTIONS FOR WAR IN EARNEST, 1862–1863

quiz

1. How was the war changing in 1862 in ways that people did not anticipate in 1861?

2. Who was winning the war in 1862?

3. How did international trends and events shape the war's diplomatic struggle?

A NEW BIRTH OF FREEDOM

The centrality of emancipation as a global concern appears obvious in retrospect, but the most revolutionary change of the war came gradually and against the wishes of both Northern and Southern leaders. Although Lincoln had long expressed his personal hatred toward slavery, as president he believed he had little constitutional authority to affect the institution. The action of enslaved people who seized opportunities to escape forced the North to endorse emancipation and destroyed the world's largest and most influential slave society.

Slaves Take Flight

Over the course of the war, at least 500,000 slaves fled to the safety of Union lines. Running away was an especially risky decision before the United States had officially committed itself to emancipation. The United States maintained a contradictory policy. At the top, Lincoln denied any interest in emancipation, largely to ensure the continued loyalty of the border states. In a famous exchange with New York newspaper editor Horace Greeley in August 1862, Lincoln proclaimed, "If there be those who would not save the Union, unless they could at the same time save slavery, I do not agree with them. If there be those who would not save the Union unless they could at the same time destroy slavery, I do not agree with them. My paramount object in this struggle is to save the Union, and is not either to save or to destroy slavery."

Letter from Abraham Lincoln to Horace Greeley, August 22, 1862

Politically conservative generals followed Lincoln's lead and returned slaves to masters who came to Union camps to reclaim runaways. A handful of liberal generals adopted more aggressive policies and refused to return escapees. Abolitionists celebrated two events in particular. In August 1861, General John Frémont, the 1856 Republican presidential candidate, ordered all property of all rebels in Missouri subject to confiscation. Recognizing the damage this action would do to Unionist sympathy in

FLIGHT FROM SLAVERY Eastman Johnson's painting captured the risk and drama of the flight undertaken by over 500,000 enslaved people who sought their freedom in the moments of change produced by the war.

the slaveholding border states, Lincoln immediately revoked the order. In May 1862, General David Hunter, commander of the occupied territories of Low Country South Carolina, Georgia, and Florida, issued an order freeing all the slaves in his department. Again to the great dismay of abolitionists, Lincoln rescinded the order.

Despite the government's resistance, enslaved people continued to flee. Like Northern abolitionists, they recognized that the war grew out of a conflict over slavery. By actively supporting the Union, they could both achieve their own freedom and establish a claim to American citizenship. Once the United States sanctioned emancipation, it faced the challenge of how to handle and where to put the hundreds of thousands of refugees. To facilitate the continued movement of Union armies into the South, those who fled to Union lines lived in supervised facilities know as **contraband** camps. Falling between civilian and military control, the camps were unsanitary and overcrowded. The military also exploited refugees' labor and generally treated them only marginally better than they had been as slaves.

If contraband camps represented the worst of the Union's response to emancipation, the actions of many Union soldiers in the field represented the best. Only a small minority of soldiers came into the army as abolitionists, but over the course of the war, a great number changed their attitudes toward the practice. Exposure to slaves themselves, which few Northerners had experienced before the war, inspired sympathy for their suffering and anger at the abuse they received from masters. Some Northern soldiers used their power to rescue enslaved people and to alleviate the suffering of those who had run away. Sergeant E. C. Hubbard of Illinois entered the war angry that white men were killing one another "all for a detestable black man," but, as he explained to his brother, after seeing how slavery worked in practice, he was "*forced* to change [his] opinion." In early 1864, he wrote home to his staunchly Democratic family that "*slavery is gone*. Peace propositions to Richmond won't save it. . . . The war could never be ended without [slavery's] destruction." African Americans knew this intuitively, and they made vigorous efforts to join the army so they could participate. At the war's start, the U.S. Army excluded black men from service. However, by 1862, black units had been organized in Louisiana and along the South Carolina, Georgia, and Florida Sea Islands. These early regiments were incorporated into the U.S. Army when official black enlistment began in 1863.

From Confiscation to Emancipation

On the issue of emancipation, soldiers were often ahead of both their families at home and politicians across the North. While soldiers grappled with the reality of slavery, most Northerners continued to discuss it in the abstract, as only a piece of the larger political conflict. In 1861, Congress issued the First Confiscation Act, which provided the army with the authority to retain runaway slaves when their labor was being used directly for the Confederate war effort. They expanded this policy in 1862 by declaring free any slave belonging to a rebel owner living in those areas controlled by the Union army. As the war extended into 1862, Northern leaders recognized that by relying on slave labor to produce food supplies and other essentials, the Confederacy could mobilize an enormously high percentage of its military-age men; in most counties, the enlistment rate was well above 60 percent, nearly double that of Northern counties. By attacking slavery directly, the Union weakened the South's ability to fight.

"Dead of the Antietam"

BATTLE OF ANTIETAM Photographer Matthew Brady captured the devastation of the Battle of Antietam when he arrived two days after the fighting. The exhibition of his photos, "The Dead of Antietam," traveled to Northern cities where horrified civilians saw photographic representations of war's costs.

Lincoln came to this conclusion well before he announced it publicly. After watching the hapless retreat of McClellan's army from the gates of Richmond in mid-1862 and the subsequent march of Lee's Confederates through Virginia and into Maryland in the fall of 1862, Lincoln endorsed the use of emancipation as a war policy. Although he risked alienating border state conservatives, Lincoln had given them ample time to see how the war destroyed the institution regardless of policy, and he knew the advantages that would accrue in foreign policy and Union manpower.

In August 1862, Lee's army crashed through a Union force under General John Pope on the fields of Manassas, Virginia, the exact site where they had fought almost a year earlier. The outcome was eerily similar. Despite Pope's loudly proclaimed intention to rid Virginia of Lee, the retreat of Pope's army to Washington allowed Lee to march freely into the North in early September. On September 18, the armies fought again outside the small town of Sharpsburg along the banks of Antietam Creek. The battle proved to be the bloodiest single day of the war, with nearly 23,000 casualties between the two sides. Despite a nearly 2:1 advantage in numbers, the North failed to break Lee's army, and the Confederates retreated safely back across the Potomac River. Although far from the clear-cut victory he had hoped for, Lincoln issued the Emancipation Proclamation on September 22.

Jefferson Davis believed the measure encouraged slaves to murder their masters and condemned the authors of emancipation as "those who have attempted the most execrable measure recorded in the history of guilty man." Lincoln offered a more noble interpretation when he commemorated a national cemetery at Gettysburg. The war heralded a "new birth of freedom," Lincoln said, not just by preserving the Union but by expanding the meaning of freedom to include black Americans as well. The day of jubilee arrived when the proclamation took effect on January 1, 1863. Henry Tuner, a free black minister in Washington, DC, recalled the celebration that evening: "Men squealed, women fainted, dogs barked, white and colored people shook hands, songs were sung, and by this time cannons began to fire at the navy-yard, and follow in the wake of the roar that had for some time been going on behind the White House. . . . Great processions of colored and white men marched to and fro and passed in front of the White House and congratulated President Lincoln on his proclamation. The president came to the window and made responsive bows, and thousands told him, if he would come out of that palace, they would hug him to death. . . . It was indeed a time of times, and a half time, nothing like it will ever be seen again in this life."

Painting by W. T. Carlton, *Watch Meeting-Dec. 31st 1862- Waiting for the Hour* (1863)

Government Centralization in Wartime

Emancipation emerged as the "crown jewel" in the Union's **hard war** policy, which targeted the ability of Confederates to fight by destroying infrastructure, transportation networks, and food supplies for the army. In addition to being a moral act, emancipation allowed the North to seize a vital war resource from the Confederacy. But emancipation also generated criticism in the North because it altered the balance of power between the federal government and the states. Slavery had always been a "domestic institution," that is, one controlled by state law. Before the Civil War, emancipation in the North happened through the mechanism of state constitutional changes. By abolishing slavery through executive order—even in the midst of war—Lincoln reshaped the nature of American federalism. U.S. emancipation also stood out as unique among

TEN-DOLLAR BOND During the Civil War, the Confederacy implemented new taxes, issued loans, and printed currency, which quickly lost its value. Inflation became a serious economic problem and made the purchase of even basic foodstuffs difficult for poor Southerners.

other slaveholding nations, which generally adopted gradual and compensated strategies to end slavery.

Confederate leaders claimed that they had seceded from the Union to protect state rights. In one of the many ironies of the Civil War, the first challenge to state rights came not from Northerners but from those same Confederate leaders. Most Confederate soldiers had enlisted in mid-1861 for one year; thus, their service was slated to end at the start of the 1862 campaign season. With reenlistments stalled, Jefferson Davis deployed both a carrot and a stick. The government offered furloughs and bounties for men who reenlisted, and for those who refused, Davis signed into law a national draft. American authorities had never resorted to a draft before, and Southern soldiers were galled by the policy, especially because the law automatically reenlisted men currently in uniform for an additional three years. Many soldiers believed that exemptions to the law—for certain categories of industrial workers, for state government employees, and for the clergy—amounted to class privilege. Letters of complaint filled newspapers and desertion reached a wartime high. Confederate leaders gradually adopted progressive policies to address concern about unequal sacrifice. Although dissent remained a persistent problem within the Confederacy, civilians and soldiers alike accepted the draft and other policies as necessary measures to help win their independence. The Union also adopted a draft, and it spurred similar resentment and anger among Northern men.

Still, the Confederacy led the way in centralizing measures during wartime. In 1863, the Confederacy adopted two new policies—impressment and a tax-in-kind—that gave significant power to Richmond at the expense of the states. Impressment allowed army quartermasters to seize necessary supplies in exchange for Confederate script. With no gold reserves, Confederate economic policy relied on printed money, rather than on metallic coin, and bonds. The new currency devalued so quickly that most civilians regarded impressment as little more than theft (Figure 14.2). The Confederacy also relied on new taxes. Because these failed to generate the necessary revenue, the Richmond government created a tax-in-kind, which levied 10 percent on all major foodstuffs. Southern civilians complained bitterly about the tax-in-kind and dodged it whenever they could, but the resources gained by the Confederacy were redistributed to

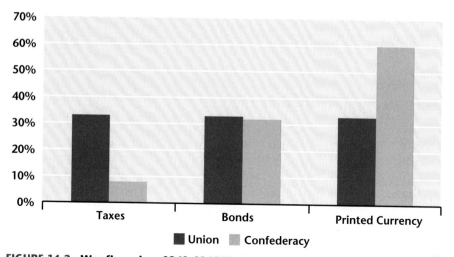

FIGURE 14.2 War financing, 1861–1865 The Union maintained a balanced assortment of funding devices throughout the war. Because most Southerners invested their wealth in land and slaves, they had less capital to shift into war production. Instead, the Confederacy relied more heavily on printed currency, which depreciated rapidly and contributed to a very high inflation rate.

needy families, often the widows of soldiers, in an attempt to equalize the suffering on the Confederate home front. The North imposed its own taxes, and its more dynamic commercial economy produced more revenue.

STUDY QUESTIONS FOR A NEW BIRTH OF FREEDOM

1. Why did the North endorse emancipation in 1862?

2. What role did African Americans play in shaping that change?

quiz

⚆ THE HARD WAR, 1863–1864

The North's economic vitality played a substantial role in helping it wage the war. The Northern commercial economy allowed investors to shift money into war industries with relative ease, and the government created public-private partnerships that enabled rapid innovation and production of war materiel. The Southern economy, although enormously profitable in the antebellum era, was not well suited to financing a capital-intensive modern war. Yet military success eluded the North partly because some Northern commanders were reluctant to engage with the full weight of the region's strength. But that stance changed in late 1863, when Lincoln promoted Ulysses S. Grant, the victor in many western theater battles, to general-in-chief of all Union forces and transferred him to Washington. Grant's approach, implemented by his lieutenants **William T. Sherman** and Philip Sheridan, exploited the North's manpower advantage and aimed directly at the Confederacy's ability to wage war. Grant, however, did not advocate unrestrained warfare. Despite popular memories of the burning of Georgia by Sherman, U.S. troops primarily targeted the public resources and facilities that sustained Confederate troops, not Southern civilians themselves.

Invasion and Occupation

Southerners received their first tastes of the North's hard war policy during the Battle of Fredericksburg, Virginia, in December 1862. After the Battle of Antietam, Lee moved his troops east and Union troops followed. They needed to cross the Rappahannock River to establish a position in the town. Confederate sharpshooters posted in buildings on the south bank fired on Northern engineers trying to build pontoon bridges. Union general Edwin V. Sumner demanded "the surrender of the city . . . at or before 5 o'clock this afternoon." Should the town's mayor refuse, Sumner said he would allow 16 hours for the removal of "women and children, the sick and wounded and aged, &c., which period having expired, I shall proceed to shell the town." The mayor evacuated the town and the Union besieged it. After the Confederates pulled back to a high ridge south of town, Union soldiers entered and, in their frustration, opened private residences and destroyed furniture and household materials. Although Union policy never sanctioned the wanton destruction of private property, the tenacity of Confederate resistance forced a shift in Union policy toward a more destructive war.

Military leaders formulated new strategies as Union armies advanced slowly through the Southern countryside. The Union seized New Orleans and other coastal spots in late 1861 and early 1862, victories that allowed Union troops to move into Louisiana and the Carolinas. In Tennessee and Virginia, the contest between Union and Confederate troops consumed scarce resources and left little for civilians. Southern women were often left to confront Union troops. In some cases they acquiesced, but in many others, they maintained a defiance that landed some in jail.

Despite its manpower advantage, the Union did not have the resources to hold all the territory they seized from Confederates permanently. Instead, they created garrisons in major towns that controlled, to the best of their ability, the regions around them. The result was a three-tiered system, with garrison towns at the center providing the highest degree of security and normal economic and social life. Beyond these were "frontier" regions, where armies provided a looser degree of control. Most dangerous of all were the "no-man's land" regions, places that neither army held but that they frequently raided.

Black Soldiers, Black Flags

In addition to adopting a new hard war policy, after the Emancipation Proclamation took effect on January 1, 1863, the Union began enrolling and organizing units of black soldiers, known as the **U.S. Colored Troops (USCT)**. Some were free black men from the North—Frederick Douglass's sons enlisted early—but many others were former slaves. Enlistment generated controversy in the North, most infamously as one of the causes of the New York City Draft Riots, five days of brutal violence waged by New York's white workingmen against the city's black residents. The riot started at draft offices but quickly turned into an attack on Republican leaders and black New Yorkers. Over 50 deaths, many of them brutal lynchings, shocked the nation and required the services of regular U.S. troops to suppress.

BLACK SAILORS Although black sailors did not receive full equality, they often earned fairer treatment than their land-bound peers. Since the colonial era, trading and military ships had contained racially and ethnically diverse crews, and U.S. naval warships carried on this tradition with black and white seamen working alongside one another throughout the war.

Many white soldiers initially had mixed feelings about black recruits, but they were generally accepted once the new troops proved themselves in battle. The proving grounds came in mid-1863 on the South Carolina coast and in Louisiana. At Fort Wagner, in Charleston Harbor, and at Port Hudson, north of Baton Rouge, black units participated valiantly in bloody attacks on Confederate positions. Northern newspapers reported both battles as evidence that black soldiers could perform as well as white troops. Although discrimination within the army remained—virtually no black men served above the level of sergeant, and black soldiers were paid less than white ones—prejudice against black troops gradually subsided in the North. By war's end, over 180,000 black men had donned the Union blue, and their participation late in the war proved a crucial source of manpower. For black soldiers and their families, military service provided a path to citizenship. As Frederick Douglass made clear, "Once let the black man get upon his person the brass letters US, let him get an eagle on his button, and a musket on his shoulder, and bullets in his pocket, and there is no power on earth or under the earth which can deny that he has earned the right of citizenship in the United States."

Reminisces of a fugitive slave and nurse with the Union Army in South Carolina (1864)

For Confederates, however, black soldiers represented the worst threat that could be imagined. For decades, white Southerners had lived in fear of slave rebellions. Confederates initially responded by classifying black soldiers as slaves in a state of insurrection. State law prescribed death for this action and for the white officers who commanded them. Confederates also threatened to sell black soldiers captured by the South as slaves. The public nature of this debate put U.S. soldiers and their officers on notice, and President Lincoln threatened retaliation against Confederate soldiers if any Northern ones were killed indiscriminately. Although the Confederate policy remained vague, several racial atrocities shocked the Northern public. At Fort Pillow, Tennessee, on the banks of the Mississippi, Confederates under the command of cavalry general Nathan Bedford Forrest killed 300 members of the garrison, many of them black soldiers murdered after they had surrendered. The U.S. House of Representatives formally investigated what came to be known as the Fort Pillow Massacre. Although that event received the most notoriety, similar atrocities occurred in Virginia, Arkansas, Florida, North Carolina, and elsewhere.

The Campaigns of Grant and Sherman

Even without the complicating factor of racial difference, by 1863 the fighting had grown in scale and in violence. The two most important battles of the year concluded on the same day—July 4, 1863. At Gettysburg, Pennsylvania, Union forces defeated Robert E. Lee's Confederates in a three-day battle that produced nearly 50,000 casualties. It marked the first clear defeat of Lee by a Union general. The more strategically significant victory came at Vicksburg, Mississippi, the last major Confederate position on the Mississippi River (Map 14.3). Grant had tried to take the city for six months, and when the city finally fell, he captured a 40,000-man army and the Union won full control of the river. "The father of waters flows unvexed to the sea," Lincoln remarked. The Union had cut the Confederacy in half. Control of water, whether the rivers or the Confederate coastline through the **blockade** imposed by the Union navy, proved essential to the North's eventual victory.

In late 1863, Grant and his lieutenants, pushing back Confederate forces at Chattanooga, Tennessee, effectively reduced the western Confederacy to the Deep South states of Mississippi and Alabama. After Lincoln called Grant east, he made Sherman

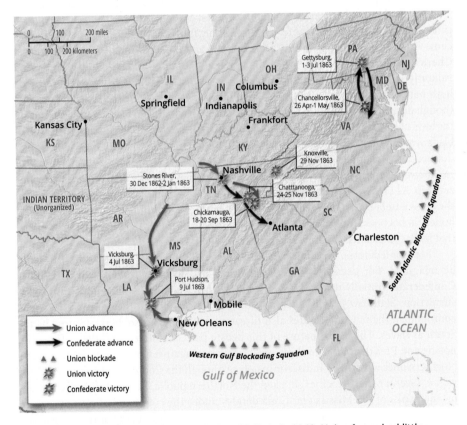

MAP 14.3 Major Battles and Campaigns, 1863 As in 1862, Union forces had little success against Confederates in the East in 1863, although the repulse of Robert E. Lee's army at Gettysburg inspired jubilation. In the West, Union successes were striking. They reclaimed all of Tennessee, took full control of the Mississippi River, and pressed into the northern tier of Deep South states.

commander in the region and gave him instructions to take Atlanta, the second most important Confederate city after Richmond. After several months of hard fighting in 1864, the Confederate army abandoned the city to Sherman and moved north. Sherman reorganized his forces, destroyed the industrial base of the city, and left late in the fall. Sherman instructed his army to live off the land, taking what they needed. Divided into four columns, his men marched to Savannah with little opposition. Soldiers damaged Georgia's infrastructure, liberated thousands of slaves, and terrified the populace. Most of the personal violence and property destruction in the state came at the hand of "bummers"—deserters from both armies—who followed Sherman's troops and took advantage of the chaotic conditions left behind. Sherman reached Savannah in late December—he presented the city "as a Christmas gift" to Lincoln—and then turned north into the Carolinas, intending to enter Virginia from the south and trap Lee's army between his force and Grant's in the north.

Emma LeConte, a college student living in Columbia, South Carolina, witnessed Sherman's invasion of that city. Although Confederates set the fires that consumed much of Columbia, LeConte laid the blame squarely on Sherman: "There is not a house, I believe, in Columbia that has not been pillaged," she wrote. "Those that the flames spared were entered by brutal soldiery and everything wantonly destroyed. The streets were filled with terrified women and children who were offered every insult and indignity short of personal outrage—they were allowed to save nothing but what clothes they wore, and there is now great suffering for food." She concluded, "It would be impossible to describe or even to conceive of the pandemonium and horror." The destruction of Sherman's raid, although confined mostly to public property, caused enormous suffering and hardship for a people already wracked by several years of war.

Excerpt from the diary of Emma LeConte on the destruction of Columbia, SC

In early 1864, when Grant assumed command, his aim was the defeat of Lee's army. Rather than following McClellan's 1862 water route, the Army of the Potomac headed directly to Richmond, and the spring campaign was the bloodiest yet. In six weeks of fighting, Grant lost over 55,000 soldiers and Lee over 30,000, the equivalent of fighting a Battle of Bull Run every day for a month and a half. Grant trapped Lee's army outside Petersburg, a railroad town that served as the conduit for all supplies entering Richmond. The two armies entrenched along ever-lengthening lines stretched between the two cities.

STUDY QUESTIONS **FOR THE HARD WAR, 1863–1864**

1. Why did the level of violence and destruction increase in 1863 and 1864?

2. What role did race play in this process?

quiz

⌄ VICTORY AND DEFEAT, 1865

By late 1864, even staunch Confederates recognized that they were losing the war. Still, the Davis government refused to concede to the two essential terms that Lincoln demanded—reunion and emancipation. As a result, the war stretched into the spring of 1865, with increasing hardship for Confederate civilians facing scarcity imposed by the war and the blockade.

American Nationalism, Southern Nationalism

Given his increasingly untenable position around Petersburg, Lee's main hope in the fall of 1864 was that Lincoln would be defeated by the Democratic candidate, former Union general George McClellan, who had been nominated on a platform committed to ending the war immediately. As late as August, Lincoln himself assumed he would lose, so unpopular was his administration and the course of the war effort, which once again had bogged down. But Sherman's victory in Atlanta, Sheridan's in the Shenandoah valley, and the capture of Mobile Bay reversed his fortunes and Lincoln was reelected. In his second inaugural address, Lincoln set out a beneficent vision for postwar America—"with malice toward none and charity toward all"—but also offered a sobering assessment of responsibility for the war and American slavery. He argued that both the North and the South bore blame for the war's enormous human cost—over 750,000 dead. He did not claim to know God's will but believed the nation's punishment—in which "every drop of blood drawn with the lash shall be paid with one drawn by the sword"—revealed God's displeasure for the wrongs done to generations of enslaved Africans and African Americans.

Abraham
Lincoln's
Second
Inaugural
Address
(1865)

In late March, as Sherman's men tramped through North Carolina, Lee realized that he would have to abandon Petersburg and Richmond. His men's rations had dwindled to virtually nothing, soldiers had left for home in the face of imminent defeat, and Grant nearly surrounded his army (Map 14.4). Lee hoped to move west, resupply his troops, and connect with the small Confederate force in North Carolina, but Union cavalry cut off his retreat. On April 9, 1865, Lee surrendered at the small crossroads town of Appomattox Courthouse. Joseph Johnston's army surrendered to Sherman on April 26 at Durham Station, North Carolina. As cannons tolled across the North, citizens took stock of their victory.

For most white Americans, the reestablishment of the Union was the war's principal accomplishment. When Lincoln issued his "Gettysburg Address," he explained democracy to the world in a way that both ruled out secession and enshrined the truly popular nature of the American experiment. The soldiers buried at Gettysburg, said Lincoln, sacrificed themselves to protect "government of the people, by the people, for the people."

Most Northerners also took pride in emancipation, even if few had supported it at the war's start. Northerners regarded emancipation as further ennobling an already noble victory. John Wesley Powell, who later became the first head of the U.S. Geologic Survey, fought in an Illinois unit during the war. His sweeping vision of victory reflected the thinking of many Northerners: "It was a great thing to destroy slavery, but the integrity of the Union was of no less importance." In Northern victory, Powell foresaw "the ultimate spread of Anglo-Saxon civilisation over the globe." Victory confirmed the sense of a unique destiny that most 19th-century white Americans regarded as theirs alone.

South of the Mason-Dixon Line, Southerners now shared with most of the world's people the experience of having been invaded, occupied, and defeated in a war. The result was a profound rupture in the historical experience of the United States. Despite the Confederacy's internal divisions, the sacrifices of war and the humiliation of defeat provided a common basis for white Southern identity in the postwar era. Rather than solving the problem of sectionalism, in many respects the Civil War created a more distinct and coherent "South" than had ever existed in American history.

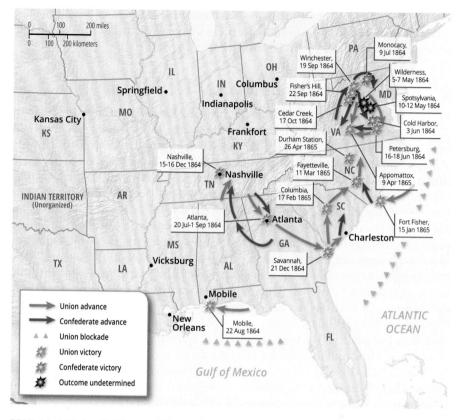

MAP 14.4 Major Battles and Campaigns, 1864–1865 William Sherman's capture of Atlanta and his ensuing march to the coast demonstrated the ability of Union forces to move through the center of the Confederacy. His army eventually moved north to join Ulysses S. Grant to trap the two remaining Confederate armies.

The New Challenge of Race

Another central cause of the war that remained unresolved at its conclusion was the problem of race. The active role played by African Americans on behalf of the Union gave them a claim on the meaning of the conflict. Southern blacks provided crucial military intelligence to Union forces as they entered the region, ranging from basic information such as the location of roads, bridges, and mountain gaps to more detailed intelligence about the movement and size of Confederate forces. The military service performed by black men gave them an even stronger claim to citizenship. In a letter to the Democratic congressman Roscoe Conkling, Lincoln explained the impact of blacks' willingness to fight. After the war, he wrote, "There will be some black men who can remember that, with silent tongue, and clenched teeth, and steady eye, and well-poised bayonet, they have helped mankind on to this great consummation; while, I fear, there will be some white ones, unable to forget that, with malignant heart, and deceitful speech, they strove to hinder it." In many ways, Lincoln's attitudes toward emancipation and black Americans reflected the average white Northerner's. He came reluctantly to emancipation and never adopted a modern conception of full racial equality, but he stood resolutely behind emancipation once it was Union policy, and by the war's end, he advocated limited political rights for black men.

Environmental and Economic Scars of War

As the war rearranged human relations, it also forced a reevaluation of the relationship between people and the environment. Since before the Revolution, Americans had envisioned themselves as developing and enhancing nature. The environmental costs of industrialization and urbanization were already visible in the mid-19th century, and although some citizens felt the costs were too high, most Americans believed that they had a productive and responsible relationship to the land. For four years Federals and Confederates did little but destroy and consume. Sherman's marches through Georgia and the Carolinas left significant environmental devastation. In this region, a conservative estimate puts his destruction at 18,600 mules and horses, 13,300 head of cattle, 19 million pounds of fodder, 22 million pounds of grain and corn, and another 7 million pounds of foodstuffs. Millions of animals were killed and abandoned on the spot. Union general Jacob Cox noted, "From barn, from granary and smoke-house, and from the kitchen gardens of the plantations, isolated foragers would hasten by converging lines, driving before them the laden mule heaped high with vegetables, smoked bacon, fresh meat, and poultry." The wanton slaughter of animals produced a continuous track of rotting flesh and facilitated the spread of disease across the countryside.

The Union's targeting of Southern industrial resources (especially railroad lines) did considerable damage to the landscape as well. After the war, Georgians and South Carolinians, in particular, were confronted with a deeply scarred and damaged land. They also confronted a deeply depressed regional economy. The infrastructural and environmental damage, the destruction of fencing, the inability to tend farmland during

LASTING EFFECT OF WAR The war's physical impact on the South marked the region as distinctive. Although the detritus of conflict was soon removed or repaired, the psychological impact and memories of the conflict lasted for generations.

the war, the loss of capital as a result of emancipation, and the disorganization of the labor market ensured a slow road to recovery in the South.

In the North the experience was nearly the opposite. Although the North experienced substantial inflation, the war stimulated a boom in many Northern industries. Meat production, oil extraction, and all manner of military supplies, from clothing and tents to weapons and ships, saw rapid technological growth. The war hastened the use of mechanization and standardization in production, especially with regard to shoes and clothes, which had to be supplied to the army in huge volumes and standard sizes. The meatpacking plants of Chicago devised a "disassembly" line along which beef and hog carcasses were taken apart so that the constituent parts could be packaged—usually canned—and sold to the army. The techniques devised by Armour and Swift later became the foundation for Henry Ford's assembly line that revolutionized American manufacturing at the turn of the century.

The Last Best Hope of Man?

Like sectionalism and race, the third of the great causes of the Civil War—the dispute over the proper balance of federal and state authority—was not solved by the war. To be sure, the war established the supremacy of the Union and of the federal government. Congressional Republicans, with Lincoln's support, carved out new areas of federal power—especially with regard to banking and currency, western lands, and development—although these were all initiatives that Republicans had supported before the war. On the larger question of ideology, the war did little to resolve the historical tensions between states and the central government. Northern Democrats maintained a steady criticism of the Lincoln administration for the measures it adopted, especially those that altered the traditional balance of American federalism.

At the same time, the war demonstrated that political movements inspired by a strong sense of nationalism could sustain liberal politics. In western Europe, in the years after 1848, nationalist movements often aligned themselves with conservative or reactionary politics, most famously in Germany. Lincoln's frequent exhortations for Americans to identify themselves with the nation—the "mystic chords of memory"—and his rhetorical efforts to place equality and justice at the center of American national identity, a "new birth of freedom," tied American nationalism to a liberalizing political agenda that sundered the government's long embrace of slavery and advocated development policies designed to support the homesteader as well as the speculator. Observers outside the United States affirmed Lincoln's sense of the liberal progress as a consequence of the war and saw how the Union's triumph could help them in their own reforms. The British statesman John Morley drew the connection: "The triumph of the North . . . was the force that made English liberalism powerful enough to enfranchise the workmen, depose official Christianity in Ireland, and deal the first blow at the landlords."

STUDY QUESTIONS FOR VICTORY AND DEFEAT, 1865

1. How did Americans (of all sorts) understand the meaning of the Civil War when it ended?

2. How does the history of the Civil War portrayed here compare to popular and/or family stories about the war?

quiz

interactive timeline

TIMELINE 1861–1865

AMERICA	YEAR	THE WORLD
Dec 1860 to Feb 1861 Secession of lower South (Texas, Louisiana, Mississippi, Alabama, Florida, Georgia, South Carolina) **Apr 12** Confederates open fire on Fort Sumter in Charleston Harbor **Apr** Lincoln calls up 75,000 militia, precipitating secession of upper South (Virginia, North Carolina, Arkansas, Tennessee) **May** Benjamin Butler, Union commander at Fort Monroe on York peninsula, declares three slaves who enter his camp "contraband" and refuses to return them to their owners **Jul** Confederates win Battle of Bull Run (Virginia) and drive Union army back to Washington, DC **Aug** U.S. Congress passes First Confiscation Act, which provides U.S. Army with authority to confiscate slaves whose owners employ them in direct support of Confederate military	**1861**	Kingdom of Italy proclaimed at Turin Czar Alexander II abolishes serfdom in Russia
Feb Union forces capture Forts Henry and Donelson (Tennessee), giving the North control of the Tennessee and Cumberland rivers **Apr** Union wins Battle of Shiloh (Tennessee), forcing Confederates back to Corinth, Mississippi **Apr** President Lincoln signs legislation abolishing slavery in DC, with compensation for the owners **Jun** U.S. Congress outlaws slavery in U.S. territories **Jul** U.S. Congress passes Second Confiscation Act that frees the slaves of any rebel in areas of the Confederacy controlled by Union army and gives Lincoln authority to use contrabands as soldiers **Jun–Jul** Lee repulses McClellan's advance on Richmond during Seven Days' Battle (Virginia) **Aug** Confederates win Second Battle of Bull Run (Virginia) and drive Union forces back toward Washington, DC **Sep** McClellan claims victory in Battle of Antietam (Maryland) after forcing retreat of Lee's army back across the Potomac **Sep** Lincoln issues preliminary Emancipation Proclamation **Oct** Battle of Perryville (Kentucky) forces Braxton Bragg to abandon Confederate invasion of Kentucky **Dec** Confederates win Battle of Fredericksburg (Virginia) with heavy Union casualties	**1862**	

Summary

- The rapid growth of the Northern states, built on immigration from northwestern Europe and increasingly extensive economic ties with that part of the globe, threatened the balance of power within the United States.
- Conflicts over the future of slavery in the West propelled a majority of slaveholding states to secede, a decision buttressed by Southerners' assumption that their central place as cotton supplier to the burgeoning French and British empires would bring recognition of their new nation before any real war began.
- The North interpreted secession as a repudiation of the essence of self-government, a threat to both America and the future of democracy around the world.

AMERICA	YEAR	THE WORLD
Jan Lincoln signs final Emancipation Proclamation, freeing all slaves held in Confederate-controlled territory **May** Confederates win Battle of Chancellorsville (Virginia) **Jul** Union wins Battle of Gettysburg (Pennsylvania) **Jul** Union captures Vicksburg, Mississippi, and gains control of the Mississippi River **Sep** Confederates win Battle of Chickamauga (Tennessee), forcing Union troops back into Chattanooga **Nov** Union wins Battle of Chattanooga (Tennessee), forcing Confederates back into Georgia	1863	"January Uprising" of Poles against Russia begins
May Battle of Spotsylvania (Virginia) **May** Battle of the Wilderness (Virginia) **Jun** Confederates win Battle of Cold Harbor (Virginia) but Union forces push south toward Petersburg **Mid-Jun** Siege of Petersburg, Virginia, begins **Sep** Fall of Atlanta, Georgia **Nov** Sherman's forces leave Atlanta for Savannah **Late Sep–Oct** Union wins decisive victories in battles of Winchester, Fisher's Hill, and Cedar Creek, Virginia, giving Federals control of lower Shenandoah valley **Nov–Dec** Union wins decisive victories in battles of Franklin and Nashville, completing Union control of western theater **Dec** Sherman occupies Savannah, Georgia	1864	First Geneva Convention established to regulate treatment of injured soldiers End of Taiping Rebellion in China, which leaves 20 million dead over 14 years of fighting War of the Triple Alliance—Paraguay against Argentina, Brazil, and Uruguay—begins
Feb Fall of Columbia, South Caroline **Mar** Confederate Congress passes legislation providing for the enlistment of black men into Confederate military units **Apr** Petersburg and Richmond evacuated **Apr** Lee surrenders to Grant at Appomattox Courthouse, Virginia **Apr** Joseph Johnston surrenders to William T. Sherman at Durham Station, North Carolina **Dec** 13th Amendment ratified, abolishing slavery in United States	1865	

- The most revolutionary change of the war came as enslaved peoples seized opportunities to escape, forced the North to endorse emancipation, and destroyed the world's largest and most influential slave society.
- The war spurred the development of new military technologies and new rules about the relationship between soldiers and noncombatants in wartime that circulated within the Western world, raised concerns about America's emboldened and expansionist spirit, and alerted the globe to a new world power.
- Like similar nationalist struggles in Europe at the same time, the U.S. Civil War strengthened the central government but also created new problems of sectionalism and race, as an embittered white South sought to subjugate and control the 3.5 million African Americans freed during the war.

Key Terms and People

blockade 494
contraband 487
Copperheads 483
Davis, Jefferson 473
Emancipation Proclamation 485
Grant, Ulysses S. 478
guerrilla 479
hard war 490

Lee, Robert E. 481
Lincoln, Abraham 470
McClellan, George B. 480
secession 469
Sherman, William T. 491
Stephens, Alexander 477
U.S. Colored Troops (USCT) 492

Reviewing Chapter 14

1. Why did the North win the Civil War?
2. How does the U.S. Civil War compare to other civil conflicts in the 19th and 20th centuries?

Further Reading

Ash, Stephen V. *When the Yankees Came: Conflict and Chaos in the Occupied South.* Chapel Hill: University of North Carolina Press, 1995. The clearest analysis of the nature and experience of occupation for both Southern civilians and Northern soldiers.

Gallagher, Gary W. *The Confederate War.* Cambridge, MA: Harvard University Press, 1997. A probing book that argues for the durability and resiliency of Confederate nationalism.

Grimsley, Mark. *The Hard Hand of War: Union Military Policy Toward Southern Civilians, 1861–1865.* Cambridge, UK: Cambridge University Press, 1995. The most compelling explanation of the shift in Union policy toward a more destructive conflict.

McCurry, Stephanie. *Confederate Reckoning: Power and Politics in the Civil War South.* Cambridge, MA: Harvard University Press, 2010. A vigorous reinterpretation of the Confederate political experience, focusing on the challenges presented by white women and enslaved people.

Rable, George C. *The Confederate Republic: A Revolution Against Politics.* Chapel Hill: University of North Carolina Press, 1994. The best analysis of the political tension between nationalists and libertarians in the Confederacy.

Whites, LeeAnn. *The Civil War as a Crisis in Gender: Augusta, Georgia, 1860–1890.* Athens: University of Georgia Press, 1995. An insightful study of the dynamic relationship between gender conventions and war in the South.

America in the World
GOODS, IDEAS, PEOPLE

CHAPTER 14: The Civil War, 1860–1865

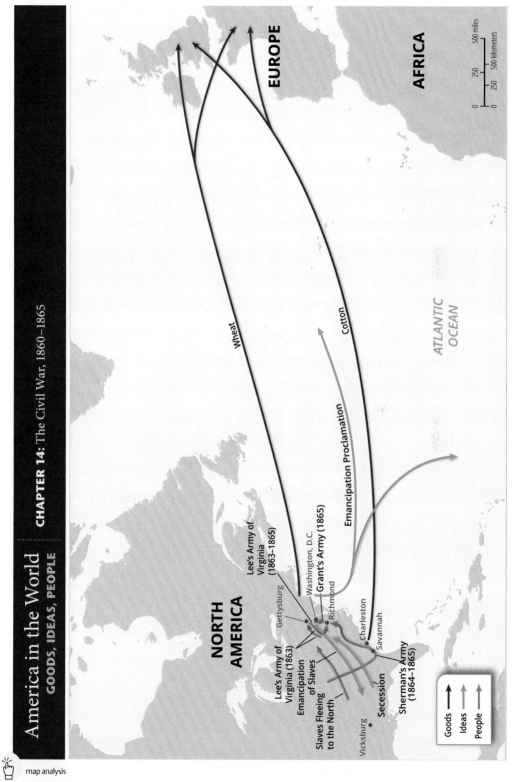

NORTH AMERICA

EUROPE

AFRICA

Wheat

Cotton

Emancipation Proclamation

ATLANTIC OCEAN

Lee's Army of Virginia (1863–1865)

Washington, D.C.

Grant's Army (1865)

Gettysburg

Richmond

Charleston

Savannah

Lee's Army of Virginia (1863)

Emancipation of Slaves

Slaves Fleeing to the North

Secession

Sherman's Army (1864–1865)

Vicksburg

Goods
Ideas
People

0   250   500 miles
0   250   500 kilometers

map analysis

East shakes hands with West at the laying of the last rail that joined the Central Pacific and Union Pacific Railroads on May 10, 1869.

Reconstructing America

Cato, Stepney, Jane, Porter, Patience, and Peggy were among many enslaved black Southerners who lived on plantations in Liberty County, Georgia. In early 1865, they watched as the first wave of deserters from Sherman's Union army came through the county. The Union "bummers" raided plantation houses and slave cabins alike, taking everything edible (and much that was not) and shooting animals they could not carry away. One Confederate described the raiders as "lost in the world of eternal woe. Their throats were open sepulchers, their mouths filled with cursing and bitterness and lies." Despite the hardship they suffered, enslaved people living in the region did nothing to obstruct the Union army. Cato and Stepney, who both organized and managed slave labor under the eye of a white overseer, effectively supported the Union by their inaction. Their stature in the community surely influenced others. They behaved, in the bitter but accurate words of a local slaveholder, as though they "now believe themselves perfectly free." In Liberty County, and throughout the rural South, whites and blacks shared a world based in the hierarchy of slavery and racial dominance and organized around the production schedules of staple crops. As Cato and the others observed the Yankee conquest of Georgia, they saw the dawning of a new era and began to work out what freedom meant. A wide range of choices, opportunities, and perils awaited black Southerners across the region.

Cato and his wife Jane, who lived on a nearby plantation, bided their time through the collapse of the Confederacy. Cato's long experience working the land and managing workers led him to reject the authority of a new overseer hired in late summer 1865. Cato's former owner denounced him as "a most insolent, indolent, and dishonest man." In response, Cato and his wife exercised their freedom in the most fundamental sense—they left Liberty County altogether, moving to nearby Savannah. No longer able to control her former slaves, Cato's ex-owner lashed out by asserting that black people would not last: "With their emancipation must come their extermination."

Despite the rising anger among whites, many freedmen and freedwomen remained in Liberty and set about making contracts for their work. Porter and Patience stayed in the area, and in spite of the fluctuating labor agreements with area planters, they managed to buy their own farm outright. Patience's brother Stepney resided on Arcadia, a coastal plantation that supported two lucrative crops: rice and Sea Island cotton. He began to manage much of the former plantation land at Arcadia and helped coordinate the rental and purchase of land by freed people. The close family networks established among the Gullah people, as the black Southerners in this region were known, undoubtedly aided many in their transition to freedom.

Unfortunately, few freed people experienced the success they did. Peggy, who had lived on the same plantation as Cato, moved to Savannah but contracted smallpox and died. Some freed people began to labor for wages on the plantations that they had once farmed as slaves, but this rarely brought them the financial independence they desired. Others rented land or farmed on shares, splitting the proceeds from the yearly crop with the landlord. The sharecropper system, adopted widely across the South, trapped tenant farmers in cycles of debt and prevented the Southern agricultural sector from diversifying as the world cotton market collapsed. In Liberty County, as elsewhere in the South, the reintegration of the Southern economy into the larger global market reflected the efforts Southerners and Northerners made to reconstruct the nation. But Southerners' failure to build a sustainable and humane economy or a just social and political system represented one of the worst legacies of Reconstruction.

⌵ THE YEAR OF JUBILEE, 1865

The dramatic changes underway in the South and the nation produced surprising outcomes. At the end of the Civil War, white Southerners were defeated and resentful, whereas black Southerners celebrated **Jubilee**, their deliverance from bondage. Northerners likewise celebrated because they had preserved the Union and extinguished slavery in the United States. But great questions remained: What role would recently freed slaves play in American life? What rights would they possess? What obligations did the federal government have to ensure a meaningful freedom? For Washington, the first order of business was re-establishing loyal governments in the South and bringing the region back into a normal relationship with the nation. No precedents guided this process, and grand constitutional questions about the nature of the Union and the meaning of republican government acquired real political weight. Republicans and Democrats, Northerners and Southerners, and blacks and whites divided over the answers to these questions. The wartime task of reunion gave way to the postwar task of Reconstruction, which entailed reorganizing the Southern political system and rebuilding shattered public and private institutions.

African American Families

Of the nearly four million enslaved people in the South before the Civil War, approximately 500,000 fled to freedom during the war and the rest claimed their freedom at the war's conclusion. The most important task confronting freed people was re-establishing families broken by slavery. White Southerners wanted to restore what they considered normal labor relations, but for black Southerners the desire to reunite displaced family members outweighed even the desire for a steady wage. Sales had often dispersed family members across states or even abroad, but in many cases, parents or siblings retained enough information to track down relatives.

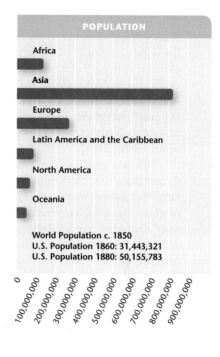

POPULATION

Africa

Asia

Europe

Latin America and the Caribbean

North America

Oceania

World Population c. 1850
U.S. Population 1860: 31,443,321
U.S. Population 1880: 50,155,783

0 100,000,000 200,000,000 300,000,000 400,000,000 500,000,000 600,000,000 700,000,000 800,000,000 900,000,000

Through the late spring and summer of 1865, as white Southern soldiers headed home in defeat, black Southerners took to the road, following letters, reports, and rumors to track the exodus of children, parents, siblings, and loved ones as a result of slave sales. Black Union soldiers had a harder time than most freedmen because they were kept in the service occupying Southern towns into 1866, thus prolonging their reunions with

VICTORY FOR THE NORTH
After four long years, Northerners celebrated Union victory in the Civil War and the end of slavery. But the war's conclusion only began the struggle to define what freedom would mean in practice.

family members. As a South Carolina unit wrote to Union general Daniel Sickles, "The Biggest Majority of our mens never had a Home Science this late War Commence . . . the Greatist majority of them had Runaway from Rebels master & leave they wives & old mother & old Father & all they parent. . . . But General now to see that the war is over . . . we hadent nothing atall & our wifes & mother most all of them is aperishing. [sic]" The army eventually released these soldiers from service, and they quickly sought out family members. This movement added to the uncertainty of the postwar period and alarmed whites who expected blacks to stay and continue the work they had done before emancipation.

The next question that confronted freed people was what work they would do. Across the South, black Southerners faced several choices: wage labor, renting land to farm themselves, sharecropping, or some combination of the three. But the question of where that work happened often took precedence. "If I stay here, I'll never know I'm free," explained one freedwoman as she left the plantation on which she had labored as a slave. Many thousands made the same choice, leaving behind farms and plantations on which they had been raised in favor of a new, if uncertain, life somewhere else. Often, they moved to cities, most overcrowded from the influx of refugees during the war (Map 15.1). Memphis and Nashville both grew by more than a third between 1860 and 1870, while Atlanta's population more than doubled. The movement of freed people into Southern cities created a labor glut, and the problem of unemployment exacerbated white fears of black criminality.

In rural areas, labor contracts and work were the most pressing priorities. Because they did not own land, most freed people had to work for wages. The main challenge

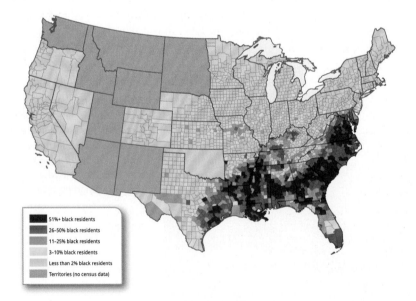

51%+ black residents
26–50% black residents
11–25% black residents
3–10% black residents
Less than 2% black residents
Territories (no census data)

map analysis

MAP 15.1 Black Population of the United States, 1880 Despite the opportunities for movement created by emancipation, few former slaves had the resources to make a full relocation out of the region. As a result, black Americans continued to live predominantly in the South until the second and third decades of the 20th century.

was working out fair and enforceable contracts with former masters or other whites. The Bureau of Refugees, Freedmen, and Abandoned Land (usually called the **Freedmen's Bureau**), established within the U.S. Army in early 1865, helped adjudicate labor disputes in the summer and fall of 1865. Led by former Union general Oliver Otis Howard, the bureau also distributed food rations to blacks and whites during the hard winter that followed and initiated the building of schools, hospitals, and other communal institutions. Despite this important work, elite Southerners resented the intrusion of the federal government and joined with Northern Democrats to denounce the bureau as an unnecessary federal imposition on states' rights. Even moderate Northerners expressed concerns about the freed people's work ethic. Because slaves had labored without incentive, whites did not expect them to understand paid work. In fact, most African Americans adjusted quickly, even when they could not rely on landowners to fairly fulfill the terms of labor contracts. One man, who had relocated to Ohio at the war's end, responded to a request from his former master to return to Tennessee with a request of his own: "We . . . [are] asking you to send us our wages for the time we served you. . . . Here I draw my wages every Saturday night," wrote Jourdan Anderson, "but in Tennessee there was never any pay day for the negroes any more than for the horses and the cows. Surely there will be a day of reckoning for those who defraud the laborer of his hire."

Advice from a Freedmen's Bureau officer to recently freed slaves (1866)

Southern Whites and the Problem of Defeat

The spring and summer of 1865 exhilarated and bewildered Americans throughout the country. The most shocking event was the assassination of Abraham Lincoln. After celebrating the official surrender of Lee's Army of Northern Virginia on April 12, 1865, Lincoln attended a play on the evening of the 14th, Good Friday. John Wilkes Booth, a member of America's most famous acting family, organized a conspiracy to kill Lincoln and several cabinet members. Booth shot Lincoln in his box at Ford's Theater while a conspirator attacked Secretary of State William Seward in his home. Lincoln, unconscious but still alive, was taken to a house across the street from the theater, where doctors tried to save him. Cabinet members, generals, and other officials visited the room where he lay. Lincoln died just after dawn. Secretary of War Edwin Stanton summarized the grim morning and its effect on America's memory of Lincoln: "Now he belongs to the ages." Booth escaped into Maryland before being killed by U.S. troops. Grief and anger flooded across the North, with many citizens blaming the conspiracy on Jefferson Davis, who fled south after evacuating Richmond in early April. Despite the controversies he stoked as president, Lincoln earned the deep appreciation of Northerners by steering the country through the crisis of disunion. Walt Whitman, who had seen Lincoln on his melancholy early morning walks around Washington, spoke for many when he lamented:

Abraham Lincoln, the Martyr, Victorious by John Sartain (1866)

O the bleeding drops of red,
Where on the deck my Captain lies,
Fallen cold and dead.

Some Southerners, Robert E. Lee among them, recognized Lincoln's generosity late in the war and regarded his murder as damaging to their interest. Others, however, could not help but exalt this final turn of events. "Hurrah! Old Abe Lincoln has been assassinated!" a South Carolina woman wrote in her diary. "Our hated enemy has met the just reward of his life." Northerners could not comprehend such an attitude. For them, the restoration of the Union brought relief and confirmation of God's favor over their society. Even as Southerners struggled to reconcile their religious understanding of defeat—many believed it was another test offered by God for his chosen people—they resisted the political consequences of Union victory. Some refused to accept the outcome and abandoned the United States rather than live under what they considered an enemy government. A number of high-ranking Confederate military officers fled to South America, fearful of punishment they might receive from the Union government. Edward Porter Alexander, Lee's chief of artillery, laid his plans on the retreat to Appomattox: "I had made up my mind that if ever a white flag was raised I would take to the bushes. And, somehow, I would manage to get out of the country & go to Brazil. Brazil was just going to war with Paraguay & I could doubtless get a place in their artillery. . . . [T]hen for once I would be on the winning side." Several thousand white Southerners relocated to Brazil (although not Alexander), where they created an expatriate community in one of the last two major slave societies remaining in the Western Hemisphere. More than 10,000 Confederates exiled themselves after the war. This exodus carried men, and sometimes their families, around the world. Many ended up serving as military advisors to foreign governments—including Britain, France, and Germany—and several were employed by the Khedive of Egypt.

Even as white Southerners lamented the war's outcome, they sought the easiest path toward readmission to the Union in hopes of restoring some measure of normality in the South and because it might allow them to retain authority over the freed people. So, despite their vigorous pursuit of independence and their wartime insistence that the Confederacy was a separate nation, many Southerners assumed that they could quickly and easily resume their old position within the United States. Northern Democrats largely agreed. They had long believed that Southerners could not leave the Union, so restoration of rights, especially property rights for Southern whites, would be a simple matter of affirming their future loyalty. Republicans resisted these easy terms but fought among themselves about the proper way to rebuild the nation's political system.

White Southerners also grappled with restoring order in their communities and explaining defeat to themselves. This proved particularly challenging for Southern men. In the prewar era, white men had claimed authority by promising to protect and care for members of Southern society they viewed as inferior to them, including women, children, and black people. Confederate defeat revealed the failure of paternalism. Southern women, in particular, had been forced to assume new burdens and responsibilities during the war. Some had worked in male occupations, including industrial enterprises, and others had managed plantations and household budgets. Would these wartime changes carry over to a new social order in the postwar period? On Virginia plantations, for instance, the economic consequences of defeat and emancipation forced men and women to share tasks and roles that had been distinct before the war. The ethic of mutuality that developed in some rural communities around the South came more from necessity than ideology, but it still challenged one of the core aspects of prewar gender relations. In other places, the effects of the war compelled some women to reaffirm hierarchy rather than press forward with changes. To do this, white women relinquished their wartime responsibilities and advocated traditional gender relationships. As one editorial in a Georgia newspaper noted, "A married man falling into misfortunes is more

"The Conquered Banner" by Fr. Abram Joseph Ryan (1865)

apt to retrieve his situation in the world than a single one, chiefly because . . . although abroad may be darkness and humiliation, yet there is still a little world of love at home of which he is monarch."

Emancipation in Comparative Perspective

Americans followed neither an inevitable nor an entirely distinct path after emancipation. Both Jamaica and South Africa experienced similarly sudden and disruptive emancipation moments in the mid-19th century. Although both places functioned as British colonies when they freed their slaves, in all three societies, whites responded to emancipation by championing racial supremacy. This pursuit took different forms. In Jamaica, white elites used the emerging scientific consensus behind racial hierarchy to abdicate local control to London. As a consequence, white property holders on the island were protected at the expense of black workers. In South Africa, local whites achieved greater autonomy from the colonial office, and although they allowed black voting, whites retained economic and social power. Unlike Jamaica, which had a society sharply divided between a small number of white elites and a high number of landless blacks, South Africa possessed a sizeable rural white population. Like its Southern counterpart in the United States, rural whites joined with elites to resist emancipation and, when resistance proved futile, worked to establish white supremacy.

A pivotal moment in Jamaican emancipation came 30 years after the start of the process. In the fall of 1865, as Americans struggled to devise the rules and goals of their own post-emancipation Reconstruction, word spread through the hemisphere of a rebellion of black farmworkers in Jamaica. The Morant Bay Rebellion stemmed from inequities in post-emancipation Jamaica. The black laboring class continued to be denied access to land and political power, a consequence of policies designed by white leaders that restricted blacks to working as agricultural laborers. The rebellion consumed the eastern half of the island and left hundreds of black laborers dead and hundreds more beaten by state militia forces. American newspapers tracked the event and filtered it through the perspectives of the ongoing struggle over the role of the freedmen in American life. A Southern newspaper described "terrible massacres of the whites" by bands of deranged blacks. They "shuddered to think of what would be the effect of these incendiary teachings in the lately populous slave regions of the South." In contrast, American abolitionists used the event as an object lesson in why full equality and political rights were necessary for all Southerners. According to Senator Charles Sumner, the freedmen of the South "were not unlike the freedmen of San Domingo or Jamaica . . . and have the same sense of wrong."

Excerpt from speech by Senator Charles Sumner (February 1866)

The United States avoided a Morant Bay Rebellion, although it did not grant freed people the degree of freedom Sumner recommended. A key distinction between the three experiments in Reconstruction proved to be the nature of political change in each society. In Jamaica, a mulatto elite, composed mostly of the descendents of slaveholders and their slaves, entered into the political system, but they mostly sided with the white elite. When legislators granted blacks the right to vote in South Africa, they also enacted a property restriction that ensured white domination. In contrast, black Southern men received the vote without restriction. This helped make American Reconstruction the most radical of those slave societies that experienced emancipation in the 19th century.

STUDY QUESTIONS **FOR THE YEAR OF JUBILEE, 1865**

1. How did white and black Southerners respond to the end of the Civil War?

2. What did each group want for the postwar world?

quiz

SHAPING RECONSTRUCTION, 1865–1868

In 1865, a small group of Republican congressmen and senators had high hopes for a vigorous Reconstruction plan. These men—and a substantially more diverse body of black and white male and female reformers who urged them on—foresaw not just the expansion of free labor but a redistribution of Southern wealth and an egalitarian political order that included black male suffrage. Between 1865 and 1866, this group—known as the "radical Republicans"—went from the margins to the center of the political debate, and they did so largely because Northerners perceived President Andrew Johnson as currying favor with an unrepentant South. The fight that erupted between Johnson and his own party in Congress opened strange new rifts in American politics and propelled Republicans toward a surprising and dramatic shift in Reconstruction. In a series of clashes with Johnson, congressional Republicans adopted increasingly radical measures meant to secure the fruits of Union victory in the war and protect the rights of the freed people.

Andrew Johnson's Reconstruction

As the uncertainty of spring gave way to summer, Southern whites confidently assumed they would be allowed to continue with "self-reconstruction." Under this theory, white Southerners reaffirmed their loyalty to the United States through existing political systems. With Congress out of session, Andrew Johnson, the Tennessee Unionist who had become president after Lincoln's assassination, set the terms. Despite radicals' hopes that Johnson would impose strict conditions on the reentry of Southern states, he set the bar low. He required Southerners only to repudiate secession and state debts incurred during the war and confirm emancipation by ratifying the **Thirteenth Amendment**, which outlawed slavery in the United States. Johnson also extended amnesty to most of the high-ranking military and civilian officials of the Confederacy. Over the summer of 1865, Johnson restored voting and property rights to thousands of these men. In some cases, this process divested black families of land they had been given by the U.S. Army during the war. Before the war, Johnson had been a bitter enemy of the plantation elite, championing the cause of the white artisans and nonslaveholding farmers of East Tennessee. But in his efforts to keep pace with the shifting political alignments of the postwar era, Johnson became a staunch defender of white supremacy and recast himself as the defender of embattled white elites.

In fall 1865, Southern states held new state elections. In the upper South, a significant number of former Whigs and Unionists won, but voters in the lower South largely reelected Democratic Party elites who had led the region during the war. Alexander Stephens, the former vice president of the Confederacy, was elected U.S. senator from

Georgia. Most Northerners, and even some Democrats, reacted with shock and anger. Did Southerners really imagine they could send the very men who had led a bloody rebellion against the United States to serve in Congress? Andrew Johnson accepted the results as a product of the democratic process, and radical Republicans grew increasingly uneasy with Johnson's leniency.

Forced to accept emancipation, reconstituted state governments across the region adopted a series of laws known collectively as the "**black codes**" in the fall of 1865, which proscribed both the extent and the limits of freedom for black residents in the region. The rights granted to freed people included the right to marry, to own property, and to participate in the judicial process through suing and being sued and giving testimony in court cases, but the legislators paid much more attention to restrictions on black freedom. The most nefarious of these were the "apprenticeship" laws, which gave county courts the authority to take children away from parents if local judges decided those parents were not capable of providing for them. Children would be assigned a place to work by the court, with the "former master" having priority. Black Southerners and many Northerners perceived this as a blatant attempt to reimpose slavery. The codes also focused not just on ex-slaves but on "all freedpeople, free negroes, and mulattoes," effectively creating a new legal designation in Southern law that singled out black people, whereas previously status (free or slave) had been the key distinction among residents.

Selected statutes from the Mississippi Black Code (1865)

For Northerners, the second half of 1865 proved nearly as disorienting as the first half. Just as they experienced the elation of victory and anguish over Lincoln's assassination, Northerners moved from supporting Johnson's initial measures to reconstruct the South quickly to anger at Johnson's capitulation to Southern arrogance. Carl Schurz, a prominent Civil War general and radical Republican, had been sent on a tour of the South by Johnson in late 1865 to assess the situation, but his findings undercut support for Johnson's policies. White Southerners did not think of themselves as Americans and did not trust black Southerners to work in a new free labor economy. Schurz concluded, "It is not only the political machinery of the States and their constitutional relations to the general government, but the whole organism of southern society that must be reconstructed, or rather constructed anew, so as to bring it into harmony with the rest of American society." As Congress reconvened in December 1865, its members weighed the merits and methods of reconstructing the South. After much debate, Congress slowed down the process of Reconstruction by refusing to seat the delegations recently elected from Southern states. As one constituent wrote to his congressmen, "Let these rebellious states know and feel that there is a power left that can reach and punish treason."

Excerpt from Carl Schurz, *Report on the Condition of the South* (1865)

The Fight over Reconstruction

The desire to punish the South for its refusal to accept the verdict of war manifested itself in the first session of the 39th Congress. These were the men elected in fall 1864, at the moment of the Union's triumph at Atlanta, Mobile Bay, and the Shenandoah valley. They came into office on Lincoln's coattails, and they were overwhelmingly Republican. They held more than a 2:1 advantage in the House of Representatives and a 3:1 advantage in the Senate. Further, as Johnson alienated himself from moderate Republicans, the balance of power in the party shifted toward the radicals. So it was with relative ease that Republicans overcame Democratic objections and refused to seat the congressional delegations sent to Washington by the former Confederate states. Doing so amounted to a public challenge to Johnson's leadership and slowed down Reconstruction. Although Republicans would never have a free hand from their constituents, who worried about Reconstruction's costs and duration, a majority of Northerners and many Southern unionists wanted to reevaluate the purpose and direction of Reconstruction policy in late 1865 and early 1866.

Republican congressmen worried about the economic state of the former Confederacy. In the spring and summer, many freed people signed work contracts with former masters and others. Some of these promised weekly paydays, others by the month, and still others only once a year after harvest. Even if the contracts had been fairly conceived, conflict would have been likely. Union and Confederate forces alike had destroyed huge swathes of the Southern landscape, tearing down fence rails for firewood and tearing up railroads to weaken the Confederates' ability to fight. Most economically damaging of all was emancipation, which represented a capital loss of at least $3 billion for white Southerners. By one estimate, slave property comprised 60 percent of the wealth of the Deep South cotton states. The results of the Civil War in per capita terms were striking: the average total wealth of all Southern farm operators dropped from $22,819 in 1860 to $3,168 a decade later. Freed people thus entered the labor market during a period of severe economic contraction, with most farmers possessing little cash with which to pay workers.

Photographs of destruction in the South

Because of the immediate necessity for freed people to sign a contract of some sort and begin earning money, they were in a poor position to negotiate with landowners. Agents of the Freedmen's Bureau served as the only check on exploitative labor agreements. Freedmen's Bureau agents settled labor disputes when they arose, but the bureau fielded only 900 agents in the whole South, which rarely amounted to more than 1 per county. Despite the importance of their work, Johnson and congressional Democrats denounced the Freedmen's Bureau as an unwarranted extension of federal power. A typical political cartoon condemned the bureau as "an agency to keep the negro in idleness at the expense of the white man." White Southerners were much less subtle in their critique. Josiah Nott, an Alabamian and prominent prewar doctor, fumed against the reorganization of Mobile's public space to accommodate African Americans. "See how the damd Military, the nigger troops, the Freemen's Bureau spit upon us and rub it in." Republicans remained committed to a limited government, and many were concerned about the constitutional issues raised by the Freedmen's Bureau, but most regarded the work as too important to abandon. In 1866, Congress approved a one-year renewal of the bureau. Johnson vetoed the bill and, in a sign of growing Republican solidarity, Congress overrode his veto.

Partisan politics played a large role in shaping the nature of Reconstruction. The Republican Party was only a decade old and had yet to establish any presence in the Southern United States, which it needed if it was to remain a viable entity. Democrats had alienated Northern voters by their opposition to Lincoln's policies during the war. Reconstruction occurred in this moment of partisan fluidity. Republicans sought to build a coalition of "loyal" voters—drawing on former Unionists in the South and African Americans if they were enfranchised, along with their core base in the North. A key component of their rhetoric in the period focused on the "bloody shirt," a patriotic appeal to reward Republicans for steering the country through the Civil War.

They condemned Democrats as traitors who had abetted the Confederacy. Republicans benefited from the rise of the veteran as an American icon during this period. In previous wars, veterans had been honored, but only after the Civil War was military service promoted as the purest expression of civic pride. Veterans themselves played a key role in promulgating this idea. As the head of the Grand Army of the Republic, the Union veteran's association, Major General John Logan advocated this idea most forcefully. According to Logan, "It is wholly safe to say that in his [the veteran's] character of defender of right and justice, with no features of the despoiler and oppressor, and in his attributes of lofty patriotism, of unselfish, inflexible, and enduring courage, of patience under suffering, and of moderation under victory, . . . he has no faithful counterpart in any age of the world."

Memorabilia of the Grand Army of the Republic

Fresh from his defeat over the renewal of the Freedmen's Bureau, Johnson picked another fight with Congress, this time over the 1866 Civil Rights Act. The first instance of federal law designed expressly to protect the rights of citizens, rather than prohibiting the actions of government, the bill was authored by moderate Republican Lyman Trumbull of Illinois and was intended as a middle ground between radicals who wanted strong intervention in Southern states and conservatives who feared the centralizing nature of such action. The bill established a common national citizenship for all people born in the United States and promised the "full and equal benefit of all laws and proceedings for the security of person and property." It also empowered federal courts to hear violations of rights, but the bill principally protected people against state rather than private action. Johnson refused to accept even this moderate measure and vetoed the bill. Johnson's explanation, as with his earlier veto of the Freedmen's Bureau, conveyed his refusal to accept the "centralization" of power initiated by the bill. Johnson also made white supremacy an important part of his veto, arguing that by granting black Americans equal access to the law, it denied rights to whites. To Johnson's horror, the bill seemed to grant "a perfect equality of the white and colored races." Congress again overrode Johnson and passed the legislation. Johnson's opposition to these two central measures and his intemperate veto messages isolated him politically and pushed the sizeable body of moderate Republicans closer to the radicals.

The Civil War Amendments and American Citizenship

After the Civil Rights Act passed, Republicans began debating what would become the **Fourteenth Amendment**. Again, Republicans quarreled among themselves about the propriety of creating federal safeguards for individual rights. And again, moderates won the day, this time crafting a broad guarantee of national citizenship and equality before the law but offering no specific protection of freed people's political rights. The second section of the amendment punished states that denied the vote to black men by reducing their representation in Congress. Under the prewar constitution, enslaved people counted as three-fifths of a free person for the purposes of apportionment; under the Fourteenth Amendment, if not enfranchised, they would effectively count as zero-fifths. This feature might compel Southern states to enfranchise black men, but it put little pressure on Northern states to do the same because ignoring their small black populations did not substantially reduce Northern representation in Congress. The amendment also repudiated the debt accumulated by the Confederate and Southern state governments, leaving the millions of dollars issued during the war in bonds and currency worthless.

EMANCIPATION DAY African Americans held Emancipation Day ceremonies, like the one pictured at the center of this image, to commemorate Union victory and their deliverance from bondage. Despite the opposition of Southern whites, Southern blacks continued to celebrate Emancipation Day and the Fourth of July well into the 20th century.

Lord Glenelg on emancipation and social transformation in the British colonies (1837)

A comparative framework is again useful. In post-emancipation Jamaica, the British had pursued a similarly bold plan for full civil equality, although imposed through the policies of the colonial secretary, Lord Glenelg, rather than through a constitution. In 1837, Glenelg explained that the "great cardinal principle of the law for the abolition of slavery is, that the apprenticeship of the emancipated slaves is to be immediately succeeded by personal freedom, in the full and unlimited sense of the term in which it is used in reference to the other subjects of the British Crown." Glenelg's policies held for a decade, but by the late 1840s, the government had imposed restrictions on the right to vote and eventually suspended Jamaican self-government entirely. In Jamaica and the United States, the central governments issued broad grants of civil equality to recently freed slaves only to back away from these to give landholders more control over their labor force and to prevent black people from entering the political system.

The issue of black voting lurked just beneath the surface of the disputes among Southerners, Johnson, and congressional Republicans. Radicals and even some moderates had long believed in the wisdom and justice of the measure. In 1864, as loyal representatives of Louisiana considered a new state constitution, Abraham Lincoln had suggested voting privileges for the men of color, "especially the intelligent and former soldiers." A partisan imperative was at work as well. Republicans knew that the end of slavery also meant the end of the three-fifths principle in the Constitution, where five enslaved people were counted as three free people for the purposes of enumeration. If unmodified, emancipation would increase the South's representation in the House of Representatives and the electoral college. Enfranchising black men would give Republicans the means to defend themselves and also ensure that the party could build a base of support in the South. Participants in the struggle to adapt political and civil frameworks in a post-emancipation world understood their effort in a global context. Henry Turner, a leading black minister, equated emancipation and the postwar amendments with "the almost instantaneous liberation of the Russian serfs, and their immediate investiture with citizens' immunities." Even as the amendment expanded rights for some, it contracted rights for others. Article I of the constitution refers only to "people" in sections on voting, but the Fourteenth Amendment set the minimum requirements as "male inhabitants" at least 21 years of age.

Shortly after passage of the Fourteenth Amendment, Republicans began work on the **Fifteenth Amendment**. Ratified in 1870, the amendment issued a blanket prohibition against denying the right to vote on the basis of race. The amendment's failure to enfranchise women incensed women's suffrage advocates, who had been working since the 1830s to win women the right to vote. Leading suffrage activists, such as Susan B. Anthony and Elizabeth Cady Stanton, had essentially paused their work on this project during the war to help further emancipation. Congress's failure to consider women's suffrage created deep bitterness and led to tensions within the movement along racial lines. Elizabeth Cady Stanton railed, "Think of Patrick and Sambo and Hans and Ung Tung who do not know the difference between a Monarchy and a Republic, who never read the Declaration of Independence . . . making laws for Lydia Maria Child, Lucretia Mott, or Fanny Kemble." Stanton's angry comparison of immigrants with the leaders of the women's rights movement underscored how personally she resented the missed opportunity in constitutional reform. Despite the setback, women's suffrage activists pressed their efforts at the state level, where 14 state constitutional conventions considered women's suffrage between 1867 and 1879.

Excerpts from the Fourteenth and Fifteenth Amendments (1868, 1870)

The Fifteenth Amendment also completed a fundamental shift in the language of the Constitution and American conceptions of freedom. The first 10 amendments to the Constitution all deny the ability of Congress to legislate on certain topics—they provide a "negative liberty" by protecting the people from government action. The Thirteenth, Fourteenth, and Fifteenth Amendments all conclude with the language "Congress shall have the power to enforce this provision." The postwar amendments rely on the idea of "positive liberty"—grants of power to Congress for it to protect the freedom of certain aspects of Americans' lives.

The fighting between the radicals and the president had long-term significance. It empowered Congress to act decisively when the president would not. Georges Clemenceau, the future prime minister of France, came to the United States in 1865 as a journalist. Clemenceau, an ardent liberal who had come to the United States to study democracy after the war, approved. "Congress may, when it pleases, take the President by the ear and lead him down from his high seat, and he can do nothing about it except to struggle and shout. . . . At each session they add a shackle to his bonds, tighten the bit in a different place, file a claw or tooth, and then when he is well bound up, fastened, and caught in an inextricable net of laws and decrees, more or less contradicting each other, they tie him to the stake of the Constitution and take a good look at him."

Irish Americans and the Fenian Struggle

Many of the Irish Americans who participated in the Civil War believed it was part of a broader liberal movement toward self-determination and democracy for all the world's people. In particular, they supported the Fenians, who aimed to end British control of Ireland. Not long after the South fell to defeat, the Fenians attacked the empire. In May 1866, an army of 800 men invaded Canada and captured Fort Erie. "We have taken up the sword to strike down the oppressor's rod," declared the army's leader, General John O'Neil, "to deliver Ireland from the tyrant, the despoiler, the robber." Although O'Neil's invasion soon faltered and casualties were few (less than a dozen), the attempt revealed Irish Americans as earnest foes of Britain, complicating the already strained diplomatic relations between the United Kingdom and the United States and demonstrating the revolutionary energy generated by the Civil War.

Within a few years of Appomattox, Fenians had organized hundreds of groups in 18 states and 3 territories, comprising perhaps 45,000 members. These men drew on their military training in the Civil War to design plans for emancipating Ireland. They were also emboldened by a change in American immigration law. During the debate over the Fourteenth Amendment, Maine senator William Pitt Fessenden inserted two words into the first section. His change, adopted without a vote, granted citizenship to "naturalized" residents. This provision promised a conflict with Britain, which adhered to the idea of "perpetual allegiance," in which people owed loyalty to the sovereign under whom they were born for their entire life.

Congressional Reconstruction

Thaddeus Stevens
on racial
equality
and
suffrage
(1867)

Thaddeus Stevens, a Pennsylvania Republican, played a key role in the conflict with Johnson and the creation of federal protections for individual rights. Stevens helped lead the radical Republicans in Congress and served as perhaps the ablest and most dedicated white proponent of meaningful freedom for African Americans. Stevens owned a forge in Pennsylvania where he employed and paid equally both black and white workers. In Congress, Stevens used logic, rhetoric, and strong-arm parliamentary tactics to advance his agenda. Like other radicals, Stevens regarded the Southern states as having actually left the Union. He believed that Southern states could now be subjected to specific terms before they were granted reentry into the Union. For Stevens, the most important change—one compelled by humanity and justice as well as political necessity—was to diminish the clout of the white elites in Southern life and elevate the freed people. Stevens believed that this could be accomplished only if the government broke up the great landholdings of the prewar era and distributed the land to former slaves, but President Johnson killed a brief experiment with resettlement undertaken by General William T. Sherman in early 1865. Despite Stevens's urging, Republicans could not bring themselves to advocate the redistribution of property.

In early 1867, the British arrested 28 Fenians in Ireland, including two former Union army officers. Secretary of State Seward reminded the American ambassador, Charles Francis Adams, that "faithful service in the armies or navy of the United States during the rebellion constituted an enhanced claim of persons so serving to the consideration of the Government which they have helped to perpetuate." Irish Americans in the United States inflamed the situation with massive rallies that called on Congress and the president to defend its naturalized citizens abroad. Seward pushed Adams more, noting that Britain's claim to perpetual allegiance "awakened a general feeling of resentment and deeply wounded our pride of sovereignty." As the two nations neared war over the matter, Congress passed a law (along with the Fourteenth Amendment) guaranteeing the right of immigrants to naturalize and of the government to protect them as it would native-born citizens. The veterans and a host of Fenians were eventually released from jails in England, Ireland, and Canada in 1870 when Parliament passed a law allowing British citizens to renounce their native citizenship and naturalize abroad. The liberalization in American and British law stemmed from a most unlikely constituency—nativists in the United States had targeted Irish immigrants in the 1850s as unworthy of citizenship, but the Civil War and Reconstruction spurred a profound rethinking of the meaning and weight of citizenship.

- Why did the U.S. government protect American Fenians even when they took up arms against the British Empire?
- How did the naturalization of Irish immigrants as Americans relate to making freed people citizens at the same time?

For Stevens, the Southern reaction to the Fourteenth Amendment proved the necessity of radically reordering Southern politics. After quick passage by Congress, white Southerners overwhelmingly rejected the measure. The boldness of the Southern refusal to consider the Fourteenth Amendment and the increasingly violent racial politics of the region—whites killed dozens of African Americans in Memphis and New Orleans during riots in the summer of 1866—pushed Congress to seize control of Reconstruction completely. In March 1867, Congress passed the first of a series of Reconstruction Acts. Dramatic in their scope, the legislation consolidated the ex-Confederate states into five military districts, with former Union generals acting as military governors (Map 15.2). To return to the Union, Congress required states to ratify the Fourteenth Amendment and revise their constitutions to provide for black male voting.

The legislative changes of 1867 signaled the decisive shift of power within Washington to Capitol Hill. Angry Republicans hamstrung Johnson with laws of bewildering intricacy in the hopes of creating a pretext for impeaching him. After clashing with Congress over the constitutionality of these laws in mid-1867, the House of Representatives impeached Johnson. The first U.S. president to ever be impeached, Johnson remained in office because the Senate failed to convict him by one vote. However,

ANDREW JOHNSON'S SENATE TRIAL
The impeachment of Andrew Johnson and his subsequent trial in the Senate (pictured here) established the clear dominance of Congress over the process and politics of Reconstruction.

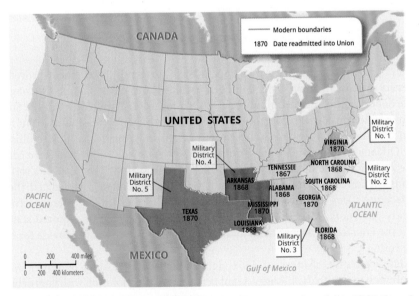

MAP 15.2 Military Districts Established by the Reconstruction Acts, 1867 One of the most radical pieces of legislation passed by the Reconstruction Congresses, these acts divided the South into five districts commanded by a military governor (usually a former Union army general). States had to revise their own constitutions to provide for universal manhood suffrage and ratify the Fourteenth Amendment before being returned to state status.

politically he was powerless. By the end of the year, Republicans turned with relief to selecting Johnson's successor, choosing the enormously popular Union general Ulysses S. Grant. Grant won the election easily in 1868, running on a platform of sectional reconciliation under the slogan "Let Us Have Peace." Despite his optimism, little sectional peace prevailed during Grant's presidency. White Southerners resented the changes forced on them through the Reconstruction Acts, but with no voice in Congress besides a few ideologically sympathetic Northern Democrats, they had little choice but to submit.

The first charge to the military governors now administering the Southern states was to hold elections to select delegates for state constitutional conventions. Black men participated in the election and helped produce a strong Republican victory, including the election of a majority of black delegates in South Carolina and Louisiana. In other Southern states, black delegates comprised only a small percent of the delegates, but even that small number invalidated the entire process for most white Southerners. The victories in the South confirmed that the Republican Party would stay competitive in the region as long as it could maintain the support of African American voters.

STUDY QUESTIONS FOR SHAPING RECONSTRUCTION, 1865–1868

1. Why did Republicans endorse a more radical Reconstruction policy than Andrew Johnson?
2. How did the changes made by Congress reshape the relationship between state and federal power?

quiz

RECONSTRUCTION IN THE SOUTH, 1866–1876

Even as Congress and the president fashioned and refashioned Reconstruction in Washington, black and white Southerners shaped the postwar world on the ground. They disputed the terms of work, housing, property, politics, and social relationships. For black Southerners, the first order of business was to create autonomous lives. True emancipation required not just free individuals but communities dedicated to uplifting and supporting their members. Politically, Reconstruction entailed creating Republican governments that would implement the policies articulated by Congress. Politics monopolized the public's attention, but the success of Reconstruction, and the ability of African Americans to make their freedom real, hinged on rebuilding the Southern economy.

African American Life in the Postwar South

The efforts that black Southerners made to reconstitute their families in the wake of emancipation laid the foundation for their postwar communities. The neighborhoods that defined the life of enslaved men and women in the plantation districts became the basis for new free communities. Churches occupied the heart of these new communities. In some cases, they were new congregations; in others, they were biracial parishes

image
analysis

"SHALL I TRUST THESE MEN, AND NOT THIS MAN?" Republicans hoped to leverage public sympathy for black veterans, who had sacrificed for the Union, into support for black male suffrage. In this illustration featured in *Harper's Weekly*, Columbia, personifying the United States, debates pardoning Confederate soldiers (left) when the African American Union soldier (right) is still denied suffrage.

from before the war that split into separate white and black churches after the war. By 1866, 62 percent of black Methodists had left their prewar churches. But more people came to the independent black churches after the war, and those who did joined a community that played a key role in reconstructing the South. As one Freedmen's Bureau agent noted in his survey of influential black leaders in his area, "Gibbons, a mulatto, is a farmer, and was formerly a slave. He, too, is a Baptist preacher. . . . As a preacher he is very popular, and has a large influence."

Another key change came with the Freedmen's Bureau and its drive to build schools. Before the Civil War, no Southern state maintained a public education system. Northerners viewed education as essential to both political and economic progress. Many Northerners believed that nonslaveholding whites supported secession because they could not see through the misleading rhetoric of slaveholding elites. African Americans, in particular, viewed education as essential. Beginning in contraband camps during the war, freed people sought out literacy. Denied to them as slaves, literacy and higher education promised a life beyond the fields and satisfied many people's desire to read the Bible themselves. People of all ages lined up at churches and schools where instruction was available throughout the day and usually well into the evening. Despite complaints from white Southerners about the cost, public education proved one of the lasting accomplishments of Reconstruction-era governments.

Excerpt
from
Frances
Ellen
Watkins
Harper,
"Coloured
Women of
America"
(1878)

The eagerness with which black Americans embraced their new lives as full citizens of the United States manifested itself in public celebrations of Emancipation Day and the Fourth of July. The first of these events began during the war itself, in Union-occupied territory on the Sea Islands of South Carolina where Union general Thomas Wentworth Higginson listened to a crowd of freed people spontaneously burst into the national anthem when the flag was raised. "I never saw anything so electric; it made all other words cheap; it seemed the choked voice of a race at last unloosed." Higginson captured the people's awareness of their fuller lives as free men and women. "Just think of it; the first day they had ever had a country, the first flag they had ever seen which promised anything to their people." Such celebrations formed the bedrock of an emerging black culture. The most enduring of these events, "Juneteenth," began in Texas as a commemoration of the war's end and evolved into a celebration of African American freedom that continues today.

The parades and festivals that accompanied these events provided an opportunity for community leaders—teachers, ministers, and politicians—to speak on themes both historical and contemporary. The messages they broadcast varied by place, gender, class position, and political ideology. Some emphasized cooperation with whites, whereas others preached self-help. **Martin Delany**, the highest-ranking black officer during the Civil War, told a South Carolina audience in 1865, "I tell you slavery is over, and shall never return again. We have now 200,000 of our men well drilled in arms and used to War fare and I tell you it is with you and them that slavery shall not come back again." Some spoke through the language of religion and salvation, whereas others used the secular language of rights and law. Regardless of their differences, all of the speakers emphasized that black people would remain a permanent and progressive force for change and democracy within America. Rather than distancing themselves from the past, Southern African Americans proudly remembered the perseverance of their ancestors through generations of slavery. Later, anthropologists such as Zora Neale Hurston collected the stories that emerged in this era, a blending of old African motifs and legends in New World settings. The rabbit trickster so central to West African stories played a key role in the legends of the antebellum and postbellum South as "Brer Rabbit" before being incorporated into American culture as Bugs Bunny in the 20th century.

Photographs of former slaves, early 20th century

The festivals through which black Americans celebrated emancipation and Union victory also provided an opportunity for political organization. The Union League emerged as the most important institutional support for black politics. Started during the war by the Republican Party, Union League clubs became social and political centers in many of the North's largest cities. After the war, the Leagues transformed into a grassroots movement that helped black Southerners organize themselves politically. Albion Tourgée, a Northern lawyer who lived in North Carolina during Reconstruction, wrote a famous novel, *A Fool's Errand*, that chronicled his experiences with Reconstruction. He described the Union Leagues as organizations that cultivated "an unbounded devotion for the flag in the hearts of the embryonic citizens, and kept alive the fire of patriotism in the hearts of the old Union element." The "fool" of the novel's title fails to appreciate the depth of hostility manifested by white Southerners against both their black neighbors and Northerners who come south. As Tourgée noted, a more farsighted man might have seen the organization of black citizens and voters as a "grim portent" of the conflict to come.

Even though the Civil War ended the split in the U.S. economy between free and slave labor, it did not equalize wages between the two sections or between the races. The South replaced slavery with a low-wage, free labor system; within that, African Americans consistently received lower pay for equivalent work done by white workers. Most black Southerners remained agricultural workers, but very few worked their own land. Instead, Southerners expanded a prewar practice called sharecropping in which landless workers signed contracts to take up residence and farm plots of land, often on property belonging to former slaveholders. In exchange for leasing land, property owners claimed 50 percent or more of the profits at harvest time. When sharecropping first came into use, it met the needs of property owners who required labor to farm the land but had no money with which to pay wages and workers who wanted more autonomy. **Sharecroppers** set their own schedules and supervised themselves in the field, but crucially it was usually landowners who chose the crop.

A share-cropping contract (1886)

All across the Deep South and much of Arkansas, Tennessee, and North Carolina, that choice was cotton. Merchants, among the few actors in the postwar Southern economic system with access to credit, insisted on receiving cotton. The changes in the global cotton market, however, produced price fluctuations and great uncertainty for growers. Adding to the structural problems, white landowners exploited their laborers and merchants squeezed them on prices for goods and supplies. Egypt and India entered the global cotton market during the Civil War, adding competition and uncertainty for U.S. producers. As a result, sharecropping quickly trapped farmers in cycles of debt. Most signed the contracts hoping to produce enough to clear a surplus and over time accumulate the money to buy their own land. This rarely happened, and tenant farming dominated the South for the next 50 years. The results ensured overuse and poor treatment of Southern lands, a stunted regional economy, and little progress for African American farmers. As Georges Clemenceau, who toured the country in the late 1860s, observed, "The real misfortune of the negro race is in owning no land of its own. There cannot be real emancipation for men who do not possess at least a small portion of the soil."

RECONSTRUCTION OPPORTUNITIES The political opportunities African Americans experienced during Reconstruction were not matched by economic opportunities. Across much of the Deep South, the only work available to black men and women continued to be agricultural labor in cotton fields.

Republican Governments in the Postwar South

The Republican state governments established after the constitutional conventions in 1867–1868 were fragile and awkward alliances between groups with widely divergent interests. Black Southerners represented by far the largest component of the party. They wanted to receive a genuinely fair opportunity to perform work, buy land, gain an education, and live independent lives. White Northern Republicans, labeled "**carpetbaggers**" by conservatives because they assumed Northerners were coming South only to make quick money, focused on economic development. As the national party shifted to support black voting, its Southern wing did so as well, although this was never a priority for the leaders who represented the region in Congress and statehouses. Native white Southerners proved the most troublesome part of the coalition. They had to brave the scorn of fellow whites when they joined the party. Usually prewar Whigs or wartime Unionists, white Southerners rarely came to the party with any interest in black voting or civil rights. Instead, they rejected the Democrats as the party that had led the region into secession and war and hoped that a Republican commitment to free labor would create a firm foundation for the new South. Democrats eagerly exploited the tensions within the Republican Party.

In those states with well-established free black communities before the Civil War, black voters demonstrated a diversity of political opinion. Charleston, Savannah, and New Orleans all included independent, educated, and prosperous communities of free people of color, many of whom carried into the postwar world conservative values on economics and community leadership. The split within black communities can be seen clearly in the case of Mobile, Alabama. After the Union navy captured the port city in August 1864, enslaved people flooded into it seeking freedom. Following the initial flush of enthusiasm in the late 1860s, a deep division opened within the black community. On one hand, well-educated, middle-class blacks pursued a moderate politics focused mostly on economic recovery and the protection of property. To achieve these goals, they advocated cooperation with white Southerners who worked with the Republicans. A larger group, mostly freed people, pushed more aggressively for the protection of civil rights and education, and they did so without white allies. At a volatile moment in summer 1866, a group of black leaders of "the better class," according to the city's conservative paper, approached the mayor to "place themselves on record as good law abiding citizens" and commit themselves to helping suppress any disturbances caused by "either Yankee agitators or New Orleans negroes."

In many places, white conservatives initially boycotted elections that resulted from the constitutional conventions of 1867–1868. Hoping to undermine the legitimacy of these new governments, they succeeded only in hastening Republican dominance. In other states, some conservatives made alliances with Republicans to create coalition governments. But the 1872 national elections, in which Ulysses S. Grant was reelected despite substantial opposition within his own party, revealed a weakness that Democrats longed to exploit. Beginning in 1873, white conservatives returned to the political system and used charges of corruption and profligacy to defeat the Republicans. Both charges contained some merit—Republican legislators in the South, like those of both parties in state governments all across the country, were susceptible to the bribes and favors of the rich and well connected. The wide scale of corruption within Grant's administration had even threatened his reelection. Also, the policies that Republicans implemented—especially public education—required new taxes. Before the war, slaveholders and large property owners had shouldered most of the tax burden, but with no slave property to tax, postwar state governments imposed property taxes on a much broader range of people. Even though the children of white property owners benefited from public education, they condemned the taxes required to pay for them. Democrats capitalized on these policy disputes and campaigned vigorously on the platform of white supremacy to retake state governments. In Virginia, the leaders of the "straight-out" ticket, which refused to compromise with moderate Republicans, explained that "to save the state, we must make the issue *White and Black* race against race and canvass red hot—the position must be made so odious that no decent white man can support the radical ticket and look a gentleman in the face." In Louisiana, Alabama, and other Southern states, this approach yielded electoral victories for Democrats in 1874, 1875, and 1876.

Cotton, Merchants, and the Lien

In 1865, the Southern United States was part of a region, extending south through Central America and the Caribbean and into northeastern Brazil, where plantation agriculture predominated. In the United States, cotton predominated; in the Caribbean, sugar; and in Brazil, coffee (Figure 15.1). Staple crop agriculture required huge plots of land, a large labor force, and high volumes of capital and credit. The plantation system changed but did not disappear after the Civil War. The major change entailed the use of tenant labor or sharecropping in place of the gang labor used under slavery, but land continued to be owned in large allotments and management functioned as it had before the war. Even though many sharecroppers worked with some autonomy, landowners determined crop choices, fertilizer use, and harvest dates.

COTTON PRODUCTION PROSPERED Despite the numerous obstacles to cotton production, Southern river and ocean ports looked much as they had before the Civil War, with bales of cotton stacked and ready for transport, only now into an increasingly competitive global market.

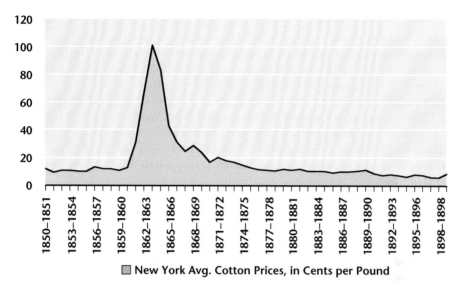

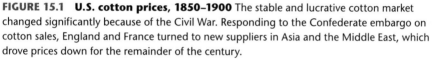

■ New York Avg. Cotton Prices, in Cents per Pound

FIGURE 15.1 U.S. cotton prices, 1850–1900 The stable and lucrative cotton market changed significantly because of the Civil War. Responding to the Confederate embargo on cotton sales, England and France turned to new suppliers in Asia and the Middle East, which drove prices down for the remainder of the century.

Even with the scattered residential pattern typical of the postwar era and the substantial effort made by sharecroppers to claim ownership of the crop, landowning planters continued to dominate Southern agriculture. They did so partly through the effective control of the **crop lien**, which represented farmworkers' claim to ownership of the crops they raised. In Georgia, North Carolina, and Tennessee, the state supreme courts all ruled that the portion of crops given to a sharecropper constituted a wage. This removed from the sharecroppers any legal claim over the crops that they planted, raised, and harvested.

One of the few groups of workers to exercise some control over labor conditions and wages were sugar workers. Sugar's value had spurred Europeans' initial effort to import millions of Africans to the New World. Sugar growing and especially the process of harvesting earned an infamous reputation as the most deadly agricultural work in the Americas. It also required significant skill. Because the sugar cane had to be harvested at exactly the right moment and quickly processed, those workers with knowledge of the crop possessed more leverage to negotiate better terms with their employers. In the decade after emancipation, sugar workers—mostly in Louisiana's southern parishes—used politics and collective action to halt wage cuts and pursued the right to produce garden plots. Even after the Democrats regained power in the states, black sugar workers stayed their ground. Several large strikes in the early 1880s, some with white and black workers cooperating, laid the ground for the broader organization of workers under the **Knights of Labor** at the end of the decade. A white supremacist regime gained power in the state in the 1880s and used violence to crush black resistance. In the other major sugar-producing country in the hemisphere—Cuba—the post-emancipation story evolved differently. By the 1880s, when Cuba's emancipation took full effect, sugar work was not done exclusively by people of African descent. Black Cubans, mixed-race Cubans, and more recent Spanish immigrants all labored together, and their solidarity as workers undercut the use of racism that had been so effective in Louisiana. The comparatively stronger and more diverse community of Cuban sugar workers revealed another route that emancipation could take in the Americas.

Because sharecropping allowed white property owners to make their money from land and related merchant work, it discouraged them from investing in industrial development. Nonetheless, between 1860 and 1880, the number of manufacturing establishments in the South increased from 30,000 to 50,000; from 1880 to 1900, they grew from 50,000 to nearly 120,000, although this was still significantly lower than the Northern total from 1860. The failure to build factories in the Reconstruction-era South was not for lack of trying. The Republicans who assumed power in Southern states in the late 1860s and 1870s set economic development as their number one goal. The most important vital element of this plan was the railroad. Northern Republicans especially had a mystical faith in the railroad's ability to spur development of all sorts. As a Tennessee Republican asserted, "A free and living Republic [will] spring up in the track of the railroad as inevitably, as surely as grass and flowers follow in the spring." Unfortunately, Southern states and Southern investors could not meet the capital demands of new railroad construction. Northern and foreign investors found more lucrative and less risky places to put their money, and despite significant public attention, few new lines were built. What the fever for railroad construction did spur was corruption in state governments. Having perfected their skills on Northern legislatures in the prewar and wartime era—an old saying noted that the Pennsylvania Railroad could do anything with that state's legislature that it wanted except refine it—the lobbyists and agents who came south gained support among legislators by distributing discounted company stock. Frequent charges of corruption weakened Republicans at the polls. Other Republican policies did more to earn the support of their constituents, most importantly Republican efforts to give sharecroppers and tenant farmers control over crop liens.

STUDY QUESTIONS FOR RECONSTRUCTION IN THE SOUTH, 1866–1876

quiz

1. What was the experience of Reconstruction like for freed people in the South?
2. How did freed people in the South protect their interests? How did whites seek to subvert those interests?

THE END OF RECONSTRUCTION, 1877

For most of the 100 years following the end of Reconstruction, historians described the period as its contemporary white critics did—as the unconscionable elevation of blacks to positions of power from which they deprived whites of their rights. Sympathetic to Southern whites and grounded in openly racist assumptions about the moral and intellectual inferiority of black people, these historians promoted a factually inaccurate and deeply compromised view of the era as one that attempted too much and failed. Thanks to a fundamentally different attitude about the meaning of race and a generation of research, historians today hold a nearly opposite view. They regard congressional Reconstruction as well intentioned and appropriate to the situation. In their view, Reconstruction failed because the federal government did not persevere against Southern white resistance. The demise of Reconstruction—defined as the end of Republican governments in the region—came because of forces both internal and external to the South. The changes in how historians have accounted for that end and the meanings they have attached to it reveal how long it took America to outgrow the racial and political values of the era.

The Ku Klux Klan and Reconstruction Violence

The bitterest and most violent opponents of Reconstruction, and black freedom more generally, emerged at the very start of the era. In late 1865, a small group of men gathered in Pulaski, Tennessee, and organized the **Ku Klux Klan (KKK)**. Membership in the group spread by word of mouth across the state and soon through the region. Klan members sought to deny African Americans any legitimate role in the public sphere. As a white newspaper enthusiastically reported about the Memphis chapter in 1868, "It is rapidly organizing wherever the insolent negro, the malignant white traitor to his race and the infamous squatter are plotting to make the South utterly unfit for the residence of the decent white man. . . . It is purely defensive, and for the protection of the white race. . . . It will arrest the progress of that secret negro conspiracy which has for its object the establishment of negro domination." They also targeted white Republicans— especially native white Southerners who cooperated with the party—for their efforts to build an interracial democracy in the South. Klan members whipped, beat, burned, and

Affidavit from a black woman regarding Klan violence in Georgia (September 1866)

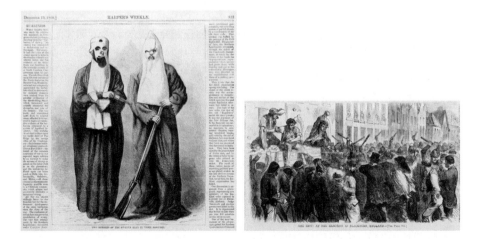

KU KLUX KLAN The Ku Klux Klan, a terrorist group bent on re-establishing white supremacy after the end of slavery, came to dominate many regions of the South. Klansmen pursued black leaders of all stripes—politicians, ministers, businessmen, and teachers—and their white allies with brutal violence.

killed all manner of community leaders through the South. They targeted ministers, teachers, political leaders, and successful businessmen and farmers. The high point of Klan-related violence came in response to the Reconstruction Acts and to the prominent role played by Africans Americans in the reorganization of Southern life between 1868 and 1871.

Excerpt from the testimony of a black voter about Klan violence in South Carolina (1871)

Klan violence grew so public and so extreme that Congress finally took action. In 1870–1871, Republicans passed a series of laws, collectively known as the Force Acts, designed to impede the operation of the Ku Klux Klan. They did this by punishing as a federal crime any attempt to obstruct a person in the practice of a designated civil right. One of the Klan's most effective weapons was intimidation of black voters. The Enforcement Acts targeted this practice directly by designating as conspiracies any attempts to coerce black men at the polls or deny them access to the vote. Congress created the Department of Justice and tasked it with bringing cases against those men who used violence to enforce white supremacy. Finally, in 1871, Congress held hearings at which both victims and alleged members of the Klan told their stories to a national audience. Although the Justice Department was underfunded and less energetic in its prosecutions than Southern Republicans wished, it initiated thousands of prosecutions and secured hundreds of convictions across the South, driving the Klan underground.

Even with their success against the Klan, Northerners did not eradicate violence in Southern life. Klan members became, in effect, an arm of the Democratic Party. In Louisiana, the Knights of the White Camellia and the White League superseded the Klan. Mississippi saw the creation of "rifle clubs." Regardless of the terminology, after 1871, Southern whites reorganized their attack on Republican governments in the states. Louisiana saw a particularly bitter struggle. White conservatives in the state opposed the election as governor of Henry Warmoth, a Northern lawyer and Civil War officer who operated mostly as a party of one, appointing men loyal to him alone and throwing the state into chaos. He was succeeded by William Kellogg, a radical Republican even more noxious to Louisiana Democrats. Kellogg was aided by a sizeable body of white Southerners, including James Longstreet, Lee's beloved corps commander and the most famous ex-Confederate Republican. Louisiana Democrats contested the election of Kellogg in 1872, setting up a rival government, and when the federal government recognized Kellogg as the duly elected state leader, they turned to violence as the means to unseat him.

All across Louisiana in 1873, conservatives began organizing themselves and forcing Republicans out of office. Sometimes they simply intimidated the local sheriffs, judges, and tax assessors who comprised the body of local government in the state. Other times they committed violence against officeholders or their families. The most notorious episode involved an attack on the northern parish town of Colfax. Residents of the town learned of the plan in advance, and perhaps 200 black men from the area converged on the courthouse on the morning of Easter Sunday, 1873. Armed with a variety of weapons, they came to protect the men they had elected. A white militia composed of several hundred men organized nearby, rode into town, and drove the defenders back into the courthouse, which they set afire. The attackers shot men as they escaped and captured more, executing 37 that evening. By nightfall, they had killed probably 150 people in the worst racial massacre in U.S. history. The lesson to Republicans around the state was clear—white Democrats would stop at nothing to

THE LOUISIANA MURDERS—GATHERING THE DEAD AND WOUNDED.—[SEE PAGE 396.]

COLFAX MASSACRE The Colfax Massacre embodied the ultimately successful strategy used in Louisiana, Mississippi, and South Carolina to drive the last Republicans from the region. The failure of local, state, and federal authorities to find any justice for the victims stands as one of the worst tragedies of Reconstruction.

purge them from office. Although Kellogg hung on until 1876, Republican government around the state slowly gave way in the face of this terrorism. Whites in other Southern states observed the success of Louisiana conservatives, and many adopted the same strategy.

Northern Weariness and Northern Conservatism

Governor Kellogg's metropolitan police force helped keep order in New Orleans, but without the support of the federal government, he could do little to protect fellow Republicans in outlying parishes. In a few isolated instances, President Grant sent U.S. troops back into the South to help quell disorder. Interventions such as these exposed Grant to the charge that his administration had failed to secure the peace he had promised in 1868. It opened Republicans to criticism from fiscal conservatives about the continuing expense of Reconstruction and, more cynically, from those who felt that black Southerners needed to defend themselves from whites or suffer the consequences. White Southerners also mastered the art of spreading misinformation;

they convinced many Northerners that black people could not be trusted to participate in democratic governance. The violence in Mississippi in 1875 drove the governor, a young white Northerner named Adelbert Ames, to request federal troops. Grant had responded positively in 1874, sending a small contingent of troops to Vicksburg. The situation deteriorated even more the following year. Ames's telegram to the White House explained the dire situation: "I am in great danger of losing my life. Not only that, all the leading Republicans, who have not run away, in danger. . . . The [White] league here have adopted a new policy, which is to kill the leaders and spare the colored people, unless they 'rise.'" This time Grant worried more about weakening Republicans at the polls in the North than about defending Republicans in the South. "The whole public are tired out with these annual autumnal outbreaks in the South . . . [and] are ready now to condemn any interference on the part of the Government," he told his attorney general. Grant, who had conquered Vicksburg for the Union in 1863, sent no troops this time.

Federal courts likewise reflected Northern impatience with the duration and expense of Reconstruction in their increasing reluctance to support black or Republican plaintiffs. The most important of these cases revolved around the defendants arrested for leading the Colfax Massacre. Unable to secure justice in local courts, federal prosecutors sought a conviction on charges of violating the civil rights of the murdered officeholders. In *United States v. Cruikshank*, the Supreme Court ruled that the Fourteenth Amendment protected citizens against only official state actions and not private violence. Because the massacre's ringleader, William Cruikshank, had operated without state sanction, the amendment offered no protection. Cruikshank went free, and in the process, the court dramatically narrowed the scope of protection offered by the Fourteenth Amendment. The *Cruikshank* case was decided in 1876, the same year that a new Republican won the presidency. Rutherford B. Hayes, a Union general like his predecessor Ulysses S. Grant, entered office under a storm of controversy. He secured the office after the contested election of 1876, when Republicans and Democrats clashed over the returns from Louisiana, Florida, and South Carolina (Map 15.3). Both sides agreed to count the presidential ballots for Hayes but gave Democrats control at the state level. This ended the last three Republican state governments in the South and initiated an era of Democratic dominance that lasted for most of the next century. Shortly after his inauguration, Hayes recalled the last few thousand U.S. troops out of the South, officially ending the period of Reconstruction.

Northerners' fatigue with Reconstruction also resulted from their preoccupation with the rapid changes happening in other parts of the country. The wave of city building in the 1840s and 1850s that had developed during the technological boom of that era increased after the war. Immigrants continued to pour into Northern cities, where their rapid incorporation changed the political contours of the region. Legislation passed by the dynamic wartime Congress also began to bear fruit. The most important of these was the **Homestead Act**, which allowed families to claim 160 acres of land if they improved it over five years of residence. The bill opened the western United States—mostly land gained in the Mexican War or through the Louisiana Purchase—to white settlement. Accompanying settlers in the movement west was the nation's first Transcontinental Railroad, which had also been authorized by the 37th Congress. Congressmen, land developers, and businessmen regarded the railroad line, which reduced

Excerpts from majority opinion in *United States v. Cruikshank*

MAP 15.3 1876 Presidential Election, by State Although the Republican presidential candidate, Rutherford B. Hayes, was credited with the electoral votes of Louisiana, South Carolina, and Florida, these states all elected Democratic governors and legislatures. This ended the presence of statewide Republican rule in the South and marked the end of political Reconstruction.

travel time between the Atlantic and Pacific coasts from months to days, as the nation's most important economic development measure.

As the Union Pacific laid track, Indian communities of the West resisted. During the Civil War, Indians had exploited the opportunity of a distracted United States and

WESTERN MIGRATION By settling the long-standing political conflicts over the future of slavery, the Civil War set in motion massive white migration into the western states and territories. This process brought white Americans into more intimate contact, both benign and malignant, with Native peoples all across the western landscape.

interactive timeline

TIMELINE 1865–1888

AMERICA	YEAR	THE WORLD
Jan Congress proposes Thirteenth Amendment **Mar** Congress establishes Bureau of Refugees, Freedmen, and Abandoned Lands **Apr** Robert E. Lee's army surrenders to Ulysses S. Grant at Appomattox, Virginia **Apr** Abraham Lincoln assassinated by John Wilkes Booth **Apr** Joseph Johnston's army surrenders to William T. Sherman at Durham, North Carolina **Oct** Morant Bay Rebellion in Jamaica **Dec** Ratification of Thirteenth Amendment abolishes slavery in United States Southern state legislatures pass "black codes" Ku Klux Klan organized in Pulaski, Tennessee	**1865**	
Feb President Andrew Johnson vetoes Freedmen's Bureau reauthorization bill **Mar** President Andrew Johnson vetoes 1866 Civil Rights Act **May** Memphis race riot **Jun** Congress proposes Fourteenth Amendment **Jul** Congress overrides Johnson's veto of Freedmen's Bureau Act and Civil Rights Act **Jul** New Orleans race riot	**1866**	Austro–Prussian War
Mar Congress passes Reconstruction Acts Southern state constitutional conventions begin across the South with mixed-race delegates	**1867**	Karl Marx publishes *Das Kapital* Russia sells Alaska to United States Dominion of Canada established
Feb House of Representatives votes to impeach Andrew Johnson **Apr** Senate votes not to convict Andrew Johnson **Jun** Ratification of Fourteenth Amendment establishes rights and due process for citizens **Nov** Republican Ulysses S. Grant elected president	**1868**	Meiji Restoration in Japan begins rapid modernization
Feb Congress proposes Fifteenth Amendment **May** Transcontinental Railroad completed	**1869**	Suez Canal, built by French, opens in Egypt
Feb Ratification of Fifteenth Amendment prohibits discrimination in voting on the basis of race or previous condition of servitude **May** U.S. Congress passes "Force Act" giving it power to crack down on the Ku Klux Klan (followed by complementary legislation later in 1870 and 1871)	**1870**	Franco–Prussian War begins War of the Triple Alliance ends with at least 60 percent of Paraguayan population dead

undermanned forts to re-establish a position of strength. With the coming of peace in 1865, a newly expanded, trained, and disciplined U.S. Army moved west. The Sioux, in particular, had challenged U.S. authority during the war, culminating in a wide-scale uprising in Minnesota that was violently suppressed by the army. Military tribunals had originally sentenced 303 men to death for crimes against settlers during the Minnesota conflicts, but Lincoln commuted the death sentences for 264 prisoners and allowed the execution of 39 others. After the war, western Indians faced an emboldened army without the aid of a sympathetic executive. The shift away from Indians' hunting and low-impact farming practices to the more intensive style of American agriculture caused significant change throughout the Great Plains and the West, and within a few decades spurred a preservation movement aimed at balancing the development of the region and conserving its natural beauty.

AMERICA	YEAR	THE WORLD
Congress holds Ku Klux Klan hearings to assess and publicize violence against freed people and their white allies in the South	1871	Brazil passes gradual emancipation law Rome declared capital of unified Italy Franco–Prussian War ends, Napoleon III overthrown, and Third Republic of France established Rising of the Paris Commune Germany victory in Franco–Prussian War yields unified Germany
Nov Republican Ulysses S. Grant reelected president First national park created at Yellowstone in Wyoming territory	1872	
Apr Colfax Massacre in northern Louisiana kills approximately 150 people	1873	
Nov Democrats gain control of U.S. House of Representatives	1874	
Mar Congress passes 1875 Civil Rights Act	1875	
Mar Supreme Court issues *United States v. Cruikshank* verdict, which restricts meaning of Fourteenth Amendment to protection against actions taken by state actors George Armstrong Custer and his forces are defeated at Battle of Little Bighorn	1876	
Mar Rutherford B. Hayes inaugurated president; recalls last U.S. troops from the South Democrats seize control of last three Southern states (Florida, South Carolina, and Louisiana)	1877	
Albion Tourgée publishes *A Fool's Errand*	1879	
	1886	Cuba abolishes slavery
	1888	Brazil abolishes slavery

Legacies of Reconstruction

Before John Muir, one of the most important environmental activists of the era, gained fame as a protector and champion of the American West, he toured the South during Reconstruction. Leaving his home in Indianapolis in early 1867, Muir walked south to Florida, observing flora, fauna, and the human wildlife along the way. In addition to wry observations about the "long-haired ex-guerillas" of the Tennessee and North Carolina mountains, Muir chronicled the attitudes of the white and black citizens with whom he interacted on his trip. In Georgia, he observed, "The traces of war are not only apparent on the broken fields, burnt fences, mills, and woods ruthlessly slaughtered, but also on the countenances of the people. A few years after a forest has been burned, another generation of bright and happy trees arises. . . . So with the people of this war-field. Happy, unscarred, and unclouded youth is growing up around the aged, half-consumed, and fallen parents, who bear in sad measure the ineffaceable marks of the farthest-reaching and most infernal of all civilized calamities." The sadness that Muir observed in 1867 had changed to anger a decade later. Southern whites ended Reconstruction embittered against African Americans for the efforts they had made to claim civil rights; contemptuous of the federal government for assistance—however meager—they had given that effort; and deeply suspicious of the open, bipartisan politics that had flourished briefly in the 1870s. All three of these attitudes weakened the South over time and encouraged whites to regard the most important political and social goal for their communities as the violent protection of white supremacy.

The unwillingness of federal authorities to enforce the civil rights laws and especially the Fourteenth and Fifteenth Amendments left Southern African Americans isolated, but blacks were never solely victims. From the earliest days of North American slavery, they had resisted the institution, and their actions during and after Reconstruction reveal a similar refusal to be defined by white actions. In early 1866, a group of "colored citizens" in Florida complained to then Secretary of War Grant that "the Civil authoritys here are taking from the Colord People all the fire arms that they find in their Persesion, including Dubble barrel Shot Guns, Pistols of any kind." Without the means of self-defense, they would be reliant on the government for their protection. Years before, Frederick Douglass had observed of black Americans, "It is enough to say, that if a knowledge of the use of arms is desirable in any people, it is desirable in us." As the Florida men who petitioned Ulysses Grant made clear, it remained desirable and, sadly, imperative after the war as well. Perhaps anticipating the day when Northerners would abandon the effort, they closed by noting, "If Congress Do not Stand Squarely up for us, and Make Laws that Will Protect us, over the heads of the States, We are Nothing More than Searfs." Congress did not stand up "squarely," but Southern African Americans forged ahead on their own. They pursued an egalitarian politics through the Republican Party, and many protected and used that vote until the end of the century. They also built communities, churches, schools, and businesses. These institutions and the networks of support and self-improvement that developed among them sustained black Southerners until another struggle against Southern violence produced America's Second Reconstruction—the civil rights movement of the 1950s and 1960s—and the nation finally stood square.

STUDY QUESTIONS FOR THE END OF RECONSTRUCTION, 1877

1. Why did Reconstruction end in 1877?

2. What explains the Northern willingness to abandon the policies they initiated in 1867?

quiz

Summary

- In common with Brazil and Cuba, the two other major slave societies in the hemisphere, the American South struggled to reorganize its labor and landholding systems in the wake of emancipation.
- Unlike in those two nations, in America, blacks gained the vote and helped build new systems of public education over the opposition of Southern whites.
- Southerners needed money to rebuild and modernize the region's infrastructure, but stripped of capital by war and relying primarily on agricultural enterprises, they had little success attracting American or European funds.
- Conservative Southern whites used both voting and violence, the latter formalized in the Ku Klux Klan and white militias, to defeat the Republican governments that represented such a sharp break with the region's past and end Reconstruction.
- Northerners, eager to develop the West and extend American influence within the Caribbean and across the oceans and weary of the expense and trouble of the South, consented to a return to Democratic rule, but the community building and education already enacted by African Americans created the networks that sustained them through the years of Jim Crow.

Key Terms and People

◁))

audio
flashcards

black codes 513	Homestead Act 532
carpetbaggers 525	Jubilee 506
crop lien 527	Knights of Labor 527
Delany, Martin 523	Ku Klux Klan (KKK) 529
Fifteenth Amendment 517	sharecroppers 524
Fourteenth Amendment 515	Stevens, Thaddeus 518
Freedmen's Bureau 509	Thirteenth Amendment 512

Reviewing Chapter 15

1. How did the United States' experience of emancipation and nation building compare to that of other countries in the mid-19th century?
2. Was the Civil War and Reconstruction a "watershed" in American life? Explain what changed and what remained consistent.

Further Reading

Blight, David W. *Race and Reunion: The Civil War in American Memory.* Cambridge, MA: Belknap Press, 2001. The fullest account of changes in the memory of the Civil War, especially the willingness of white Northerners to marginalize the history of slavery and emancipation in the conflict.

Foner, Eric. *Reconstruction: America's Unfinished Revolution, 1863–1877.* New York: Harper and Row, 1988. A comprehensive history of Reconstruction with particular attention to labor and emancipation in the South.

Litwack, Leon F. *Been in the Storm So Long: The Aftermath of Slavery.* New York: Vintage, 1980. A vivid chronicle of the experience of emancipation for black Southerners.

Perman, Michel. *The Road to Redemption: Southern Politics, 1869–1879.* Chapel Hill: University of North Carolina Press, 1984. The clearest analysis of the national- and state-level politics that produced the end of Reconstruction.

Ransom, Roger L. and Richard Sutch. *One Kind of Freedom: The Economic Consequences of Emancipation*. Cambridge, UK: Cambridge University Press, 1977. A comprehensive economic analysis of the effects of the Civil War on the South.

Silber, Nina. *The Romance of Reunion: Northerners and the South, 1865–1900*. Chapel Hill: University of North Carolina Press, 1993. An elegant study that emphasizes the cultural dimensions of the Northern shift toward reconciliation after the Civil War.

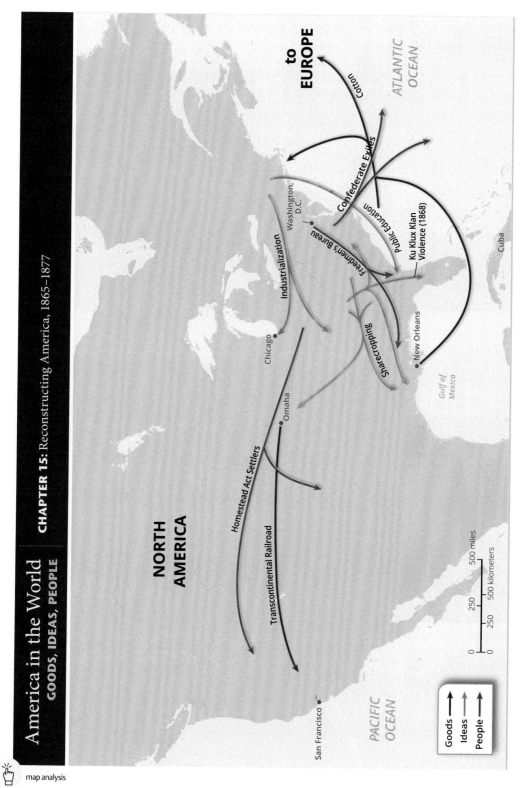

America in the World
GOODS, IDEAS, PEOPLE

CHAPTER 15: Reconstructing America, 1865–1877

to EUROPE

Cotton

ATLANTIC OCEAN

Confederate Exiles

Public Education

Freedmen's Bureau

Washington, D.C.

Industrialization

Ku Klux Klan Violence (1868)

Chicago

Sharecropping

New Orleans

Cuba

Gulf of Mexico

Omaha

Homestead Act Settlers

Transcontinental Railroad

NORTH AMERICA

San Francisco

PACIFIC OCEAN

Goods
Ideas
People

0   250   500 miles
0   250   500 kilometers

map analysis

APPENDIX A

HISTORICAL DOCUMENTS

The Declaration of Independence

When in the course of human events, it becomes necessary for one people to dissolve the political bands which have connected them with another, and to assume, among the powers of the earth, the separate and equal station to which the Laws of Nature and of Nature's God entitle them, a decent respect to the opinions of mankind requires that they should declare the causes which impel them to the separation.

We hold these truths to be self-evident, that all men are created equal, that they are endowed by their Creator with certain unalienable Rights, that among these are life, liberty and the pursuit of happiness. That to secure these rights, governments are instituted among men, deriving their just powers from the consent of the governed; that whenever any form of government becomes destructive of these ends, it is the right of the people to alter or to abolish it, and to institute new Government, laying its foundation on such principles and organizing its powers in such form, as to them shall seem most likely to effect their safety and happiness. Prudence, indeed, will dictate that Governments long established should not be changed for light and transient causes; and, accordingly, all experience hath shown, that mankind are more disposed to suffer, while evils are sufferable, than to right themselves by abolishing the forms to which they are accustomed. But when a long train of abuses and usurpations, pursuing invariably the same object evinces a design to reduce them under absolute despotism, it is their right, it is their duty, to throw off such government, and to provide new guards for their future security. Such has been the patient sufferance of these colonies; and such is now the necessity which constrains them to alter their former systems of government. The history of the present King of Great Britain is a history of repeated injuries and usurpations, all having in direct object the establishment of an absolute tyranny over these States. To prove this, let facts be submitted to a candid world:

He has refused his assent to laws, the most wholesome and necessary for the public good.

He has forbidden his governors to pass laws of immediate and pressing importance, unless suspended in their operation till his assent should be obtained; and, when so suspended, he has utterly neglected to attend to them.

He has refused to pass other laws for the accommodation of large districts of people, unless those people would relinquish the right of representation in the legislature, a right inestimable to them and formidable to tyrants only.

He has called together legislative bodies at places unusual, uncomfortable, and distant from the depository of their public records, for the sole purpose of fatiguing them into compliance with his measures.

He has dissolved representative houses repeatedly, for opposing with manly firmness his invasions on the rights of the people.

He has refused for a long time, after such dissolutions, to cause others to be elected; whereby the legislative powers, incapable of annihilation, have returned to the People at large for their exercise; the State remaining in the mean time exposed to all the dangers of invasion from without, and convulsions within.

He has endeavored to prevent the population of these States; for that purpose obstructing the laws for naturalization of foreigners; refusing to pass others to encourage their migrations hither, and raising the conditions of new appropriations of lands.

He has obstructed the administration of justice, by refusing his assent to laws for establishing judiciary powers.

He has made judges dependent on his will alone, for the tenure of their offices, and the amount and payment of their salaries.

He has erected a multitude of new offices, and sent hither swarms of officers to harass our people, and eat out their substance.

He has kept among us, in times of peace, standing armies without the consent of our legislatures.

He has affected to render the Military independent of, and superior to, the civil power.

He has combined with others to subject us to a jurisdiction foreign to our constitution and unacknowledged by our laws; giving his assent to their acts of pretended legislation:

For quartering large bodies of armed troops among us;

For protecting them, by a mock trial, from punishment for any murders which they should commit on the inhabitants of these States;

For cutting off our trade with all parts of the world;

For imposing taxes on us without our Consent;

For depriving us, in many cases, of the benefits of Trial by Jury;

For transporting us beyond Seas to be tried for pretended offences;

For abolishing the free System of English Laws in a neighbouring Province, establishing therein an Arbitrary government, and enlarging its Boundaries so as to render it at once an example and fit instrument for introducing the same absolute rule into these colonies;

For taking away our charters, abolishing our most valuable laws, and altering fundamentally the forms of our governments;

For suspending our own legislatures, and declaring themselves invested with power to legislate for us in all cases whatsoever.

He has abdicated government here, by declaring us out of his protection and waging war against us.

He has plundered our seas, ravaged our coasts, burnt our towns, and destroyed the lives of our people.

He is at this time transporting large armies of foreign mercenaries to complete the works of death, desolation and tyranny, already begun with circumstances of cruelty and perfidy scarcely paralleled in the most barbarous ages, and totally unworthy the head of a civilized nation.

He has constrained our fellow citizens taken captive on the high seas to bear arms against their country, to become the executioners of their friends and brethren, or to fall themselves by their hands.

He has excited domestic insurrections amongst us, and has endeavored to bring on the inhabitants of our frontiers, the merciless Indian savages, whose known rule of warfare, is an undistinguished destruction of all ages, sexes and conditions.

In every stage of these oppressions we have petitioned for redress in the most humble terms; our repeated petitions have been answered only by repeated injury. A prince whose character is thus marked by every act which may define a tyrant, is unfit to be the ruler of a free people.

Nor have we been wanting in attentions to our British brethren. We have warned them from time to time of attempts by their legislature to extend an unwarrantable jurisdiction over us. We have reminded them of the circumstances of our emigration and settlement here. We have appealed to their native justice and magnanimity, and we have conjured them by the ties of our common kindred to disavow these usurpations, which, would inevitably interrupt our connections and correspondence. They, too, have been deaf to the voice of justice and of consanguinity. We must, therefore, acquiesce in the necessity, which denounces our separation, and hold them, as we hold the rest of mankind, enemies in war, in peace friends.

We, therefore, the representatives of the United States of America, in general Congress, assembled, appealing to the Supreme Judge of the world for the rectitude of our intentions, do, in the name, and by the authority of the good people of these colonies, solemnly publish and declare, that these united colonies are, and of right ought to be free and independent states; that they are absolved from all allegiance to the British Crown, and that all political connection between them and the state of Great Britain, is and ought to be totally dissolved; and that, as free and independent states, they have full power to levy war, conclude peace, contract alliances, establish commerce, and to do all other acts and things which independent states may of right do. And for the support of this declaration, with a firm reliance on the protection of Divine Providence, we mutually pledge to each other our lives, our fortunes and our sacred honor.

The Constitution of the United States of America

We the People of the United States, in Order to form a more perfect Union, establish Justice, insure domestic Tranquility, provide for the common defence, promote the general Welfare, and secure the Blessings of Liberty to ourselves and our Posterity, do ordain and establish this Constitution for the United States of America.

ARTICLE I

Section 1.

All legislative Powers herein granted shall be vested in a Congress of the United States, which shall consist of a Senate and House of Representatives.

Section 2.

The House of Representatives shall be composed of Members chosen every second Year by the People of the several States, and the Electors in each State shall have the Qualifications requisite for Electors of the most numerous Branch of the State Legislature.

No Person shall be a Representative who shall not have attained to the Age of twenty five Years, and been seven Years a Citizen of the United States, and who shall not, when elected, be an Inhabitant of that State in which he shall be chosen.

Representatives and direct Taxes shall be apportioned among the several States which may be included within this Union, according to their respective Numbers, which shall be determined by adding to the whole Number of free Persons, including those bound to Service for a Term of Years, and excluding Indians not taxed, three fifths of all other Persons. The actual Enumeration shall be made within three Years after the first Meeting of the Congress of the United States, and within every subsequent Term of ten Years, in such Manner as they shall by Law direct. The Number of Representatives shall not exceed one for every thirty Thousand, but each State shall have at Least one Representative; and until such enumeration shall be made, the State of New Hampshire shall be entitled to choose three, Massachusetts eight, Rhode-Island and Providence Plantations one, Connecticut five, New York six, New Jersey four, Pennsylvania eight, Delaware one, Maryland six, Virginia ten, North Carolina five, South Carolina five, and Georgia three.

When vacancies happen in the Representation from any State, the Executive Authority thereof shall issue Writs of Election to fill such Vacancies.

The House of Representatives shall choose their Speaker and other Officers; and shall have the sole Power of Impeachment.

Section 3.

The Senate of the United States shall be composed of two Senators from each State, chosen by the Legislature thereof for six Years; and each Senator shall have one Vote.

Immediately after they shall be assembled in Consequence of the first Election, they shall be divided as equally as may be into three Classes. The Seats of the Senators of the first Class shall be vacated at the Expiration of the second Year, of the second Class at the Expiration of the fourth Year, and of the third Class at the Expiration of the sixth Year, so that one third may be chosen every second Year; and if Vacancies happen by Resignation, or otherwise, during the Recess of the Legislature of any State, the Executive thereof may make temporary Appointments until the next Meeting of the Legislature, which shall then fill such Vacancies.

No Person shall be a Senator who shall not have attained to the Age of thirty Years, and been nine Years a Citizen of the United States, and who shall not, when elected, be an Inhabitant of that State for which he shall be chosen.

The Vice President of the United States shall be President of the Senate, but shall have no Vote, unless they be equally divided.

The Senate shall choose their other Officers, and also a President pro tempore, in the Absence of the Vice President, or when he shall exercise the Office of President of the United States.

The Senate shall have the sole Power to try all Impeachments. When sitting for that Purpose, they shall be on Oath or Affirmation. When the President of the United States is tried, the Chief Justice shall preside: And no Person shall be convicted without the Concurrence of two thirds of the Members present.

Judgment in Cases of Impeachment shall not extend further than to removal from Office, and disqualification to hold and enjoy any Office of honor, Trust or Profit under the United States: but the Party convicted shall nevertheless be liable and subject to Indictment, Trial, Judgment and Punishment, according to Law.

Section 4.

The Times, Places and Manner of holding Elections for Senators and Representatives, shall be prescribed in each State by the Legislature thereof; but the Congress may at any time by Law make or alter such Regulations, except as to the Places of chusing Senators.

The Congress shall assemble at least once in every Year, and such Meeting shall be on the first Monday in December, unless they shall by Law appoint a different Day.

Section 5.

Each House shall be the Judge of the Elections, Returns and Qualifications of its own Members, and a Majority of each shall constitute a Quorum to do Business; but a smaller Number may adjourn from day to day, and may be authorized to compel the Attendance of absent Members, in such Manner, and under such Penalties as each House may provide.

Each House may determine the Rules of its Proceedings, punish its Members for disorderly Behaviour, and, with the Concurrence of two thirds, expel a Member.

Each House shall keep a Journal of its Proceedings, and from time to time publish the same, excepting such Parts as may in their Judgment require Secrecy; and the Yeas and Nays of the Members of either House on any question shall, at the Desire of one fifth of those Present, be entered on the Journal.

Neither House, during the Session of Congress, shall, without the Consent of the other, adjourn for more than three days, nor to any other Place than that in which the two Houses shall be sitting.

Section 6.

The Senators and Representatives shall receive a Compensation for their Services, to be ascertained by Law, and paid out of the Treasury of the United States. They shall in all Cases, except Treason, Felony and Breach of the Peace, be privileged from Arrest during their Attendance at the Session of their respective Houses, and in going to and returning from the same; and for any Speech or Debate in either House, they shall not be questioned in any other Place.

No Senator or Representative shall, during the Time for which he was elected, be appointed to any civil Office under the Authority of the United States, which shall have been created, or the Emoluments whereof shall have been increased during such time; and no Person holding any Office under the United States, shall be a Member of either House during his Continuance in Office.

Section 7.

All Bills for raising Revenue shall originate in the House of Representatives; but the Senate may propose or concur with Amendments as on other Bills.

Every Bill which shall have passed the House of Representatives and the Senate, shall, before it become a Law, be presented to the President of the United States: If he approve he shall sign it, but if not he shall return it, with his Objections to that House in which it shall have originated, who shall enter the Objections at large on their Journal, and proceed to reconsider it. If after such Reconsideration two thirds of that House shall agree to pass the Bill, it shall be sent, together with the Objections, to the other House, by which it shall likewise be reconsidered, and if approved by two thirds of that House, it shall become a Law. But in all such Cases the Votes of both Houses shall be determined by yeas and Nays, and the Names of the Persons voting for and against the Bill shall be entered on the Journal of each House respectively. If any Bill shall not be returned by the President within ten Days (Sundays excepted) after it shall have been presented to him, the Same shall be a Law, in like Manner as if he had signed it, unless the Congress by their Adjournment prevent its Return, in which Case it shall not be a Law.

Every Order, Resolution, or Vote to which the Concurrence of the Senate and House of Representatives may be necessary (except on a question of Adjournment) shall be presented to the President of the United States; and before the Same shall take Effect, shall be approved by him, or being disapproved by him, shall be repassed by two thirds of the Senate and House of Representatives, according to the Rules and Limitations prescribed in the Case of a Bill.

Section 8.

The Congress shall have Power

To lay and collect Taxes, Duties, Imposts and Excises, to pay the Debts and provide for the common Defence and general Welfare of the United States; but all Duties, Imposts and Excises shall be uniform throughout the United States;

To borrow Money on the credit of the United States;

To regulate Commerce with foreign Nations, and among the several States, and with the Indian Tribes;

To establish an uniform Rule of Naturalization, and uniform Laws on the subject of Bankruptcies throughout the United States;

To coin Money, regulate the Value thereof, and of foreign Coin, and fix the Standard of Weights and Measures;

To provide for the Punishment of counterfeiting the Securities and current Coin of the United States;

To establish Post Offices and post Roads;

To promote the Progress of Science and useful Arts, by securing for limited Times to Authors and Inventors the exclusive Right to their respective Writings and Discoveries;

To constitute Tribunals inferior to the supreme Court;

To define and punish Piracies and Felonies committed on the high Seas, and Offences against the Law of Nations;

To declare War, grant Letters of Marque and Reprisal, and make Rules concerning Captures on Land and Water;

To raise and support Armies, but no Appropriation of Money to that Use shall be for a longer Term than two Years;

To provide and maintain a Navy;

To make Rules for the Government and Regulation of the land and naval Forces;

To provide for calling forth the Militia to execute the Laws of the Union, suppress Insurrections and repel Invasions;

To provide for organizing, arming, and disciplining the Militia, and for governing such Part of them as may be employed in the Service of the United States, reserving to the States respectively, the Appointment of the Officers, and the Authority of training the Militia according to the discipline prescribed by Congress;

To exercise exclusive Legislation in all Cases whatsoever, over such District (not exceeding ten Miles square) as may, by Cession of particular States, and the Acceptance of Congress, become the Seat of the Government of the United States, and to exercise like Authority over all Places purchased by the Consent of the Legislature of the State in which the Same shall be, for the Erection of Forts, Magazines, Arsenals, dock-Yards, and other needful Buildings;—And

To make all Laws which shall be necessary and proper for carrying into Execution the foregoing Powers, and all other Powers vested by this Constitution in the Government of the United States, or in any Department or Officer thereof.

Section 9.

The Migration or Importation of such Persons as any of the States now existing shall think proper to admit, shall not be prohibited by the Congress prior to the Year one thousand eight hundred and eight, but a Tax or duty may be imposed on such Importation, not exceeding ten dollars for each Person.

The Privilege of the Writ of Habeas Corpus shall not be suspended, unless when in Cases of Rebellion or Invasion the public Safety may require it.

No Bill of Attainder or ex post facto Law shall be passed.

No Capitation, or other direct, Tax shall be laid, unless in Proportion to the Census or enumeration herein before directed to be taken.

No Tax or Duty shall be laid on Articles exported from any State.

No Preference shall be given by any Regulation of Commerce or Revenue to the Ports of one State over those of another; nor shall Vessels bound to, or from, one State, be obliged to enter, clear, or pay Duties in another.

No Money shall be drawn from the Treasury, but in Consequence of Appropriations made by Law; and a regular Statement and Account of the Receipts and Expenditures of all public Money shall be published from time to time.

No Title of Nobility shall be granted by the United States: And no Person holding any Office of Profit or Trust under them, shall, without the Consent of the Congress, accept of any present, Emolument, Office, or Title, of any kind whatever, from any King, Prince, or foreign State.

Section 10.

No State shall enter into any Treaty, Alliance, or Confederation; grant Letters of Marque and Reprisal; coin Money; emit Bills of Credit; make any Thing but gold and silver Coin a Tender in Payment of Debts; pass any Bill of Attainder, ex post facto Law, or Law impairing the Obligation of Contracts, or grant any Title of Nobility.

No State shall, without the Consent of the Congress, lay any Imposts or Duties on Imports or Exports, except what may be absolutely necessary for executing it's inspection Laws: and the net Produce of all Duties and Imposts, laid by any State on Imports or Exports, shall be for the Use of the Treasury of the United States; and all such Laws shall be subject to the Revision and Control of the Congress.

No State shall, without the Consent of Congress, lay any Duty of Tonnage, keep Troops, or Ships of War in time of Peace, enter into any Agreement or Compact with another State, or with a foreign Power, or engage in War, unless actually invaded, or in such imminent Danger as will not admit of delay.

ARTICLE II

Section 1.

The executive Power shall be vested in a President of the United States of America. He shall hold his Office during the Term of four Years, and, together with the Vice President, chosen for the same Term, be elected, as follows:

Each State shall appoint, in such Manner as the Legislature thereof may direct, a Number of Electors, equal to the whole Number of Senators and Representatives to which the State may be entitled in the Congress: but no Senator or Representative, or Person holding an Office of Trust or Profit under the United States, shall be appointed an Elector.

The Electors shall meet in their respective States, and vote by Ballot for two Persons, of whom one at least shall not be an Inhabitant of the same State with themselves. And they shall make a List of all the Persons voted for, and of the Number of Votes for each; which List they shall sign and certify, and transmit sealed to the Seat of the Government of the United States, directed to the President of the Senate. The President of the Senate shall, in the Presence of the Senate and House of Representatives, open all the Certificates, and the Votes shall then be counted. The Person having the greatest Number of Votes shall be the President, if such Number be a Majority of the whole Number of Electors appointed; and if there be more than one who have such Majority, and have an equal Number of Votes, then the House of Representatives shall immediately choose by Ballot one of them for President; and if no Person have a Majority, then from the five highest on the List the said House shall in like Manner choose the President. But in choosing the President, the Votes shall be taken by States, the Representation from each State having one Vote; A quorum for this purpose shall consist of a Member or Members from two thirds of the States, and a Majority of all the States shall be necessary to a Choice. In every Case, after the Choice of the President, the Person having the greatest Number of Votes of the Electors shall be the Vice President. But if there should remain two or more who have equal Votes, the Senate shall choose from them by Ballot the Vice President.

The Congress may determine the Time of choosing the Electors, and the Day on which they shall give their Votes; which Day shall be the same throughout the United States.

No Person except a natural born Citizen, or a Citizen of the United States, at the time of the Adoption of this Constitution, shall be eligible to the Office of President; neither shall any Person be eligible to that Office who shall not have attained to the Age of thirty five Years, and been fourteen Years a Resident within the United States.

In Case of the Removal of the President from Office, or of his Death, Resignation, or Inability to discharge the Powers and Duties of the said Office, the Same shall devolve on the Vice President, and the Congress may by Law provide for the Case of Removal, Death, Resignation or Inability, both of the President and Vice President, declaring what Officer shall then act as President, and such Officer shall act accordingly, until the Disability be removed, or a President shall be elected.

The President shall, at stated Times, receive for his Services, a Compensation, which shall neither be increased nor diminished during the Period for which he shall have been elected, and he shall not receive within that Period any other Emolument from the United States, or any of them.

Before he enter on the Execution of his Office, he shall take the following Oath or Affirmation:—"I do solemnly swear (or affirm) that I will faithfully execute the Office of President of the United States, and will to the best of my Ability, preserve, protect and defend the Constitution of the United States."

Section 2.

The President shall be Commander in Chief of the Army and Navy of the United States, and of the Militia of the several States, when called into the actual Service of the United States; he may require the Opinion, in writing, of the principal Officer in each of the executive Departments, upon any Subject relating to the Duties of their respective Offices, and he shall have Power to grant Reprieves and Pardons for Offences against the United States, except in Cases of Impeachment.

He shall have Power, by and with the Advice and Consent of the Senate, to make Treaties, provided two thirds of the Senators present concur; and he shall nominate, and by and with the Advice and Consent of the Senate, shall appoint Ambassadors, other public Ministers and Consuls, Judges of the supreme Court, and all other Officers of the United States, whose Appointments are not herein otherwise provided for, and which shall be established by Law: but the Congress may by Law vest the Appointment of such inferior Officers, as they think proper, in the President alone, in the Courts of Law, or in the Heads of Departments.

The President shall have Power to fill up all Vacancies that may happen during the Recess of the Senate, by granting Commissions which shall expire at the End of their next Session.

Section 3.

He shall from time to time give to the Congress Information of the State of the Union, and recommend to their Consideration such Measures as he shall judge necessary and expedient; he may, on extraordinary Occasions, convene both Houses, or either of them, and in Case of Disagreement between them, with Respect to the Time of Adjournment, he may adjourn them to such Time as he shall think proper; he shall receive Ambassadors and other public Ministers; he shall take Care that the Laws be faithfully executed, and shall Commission all the Officers of the United States.

Section 4.

The President, Vice President and all civil Officers of the United States, shall be removed from Office on Impeachment for, and Conviction of, Treason, Bribery, or other high Crimes and Misdemeanors.

ARTICLE III

Section 1.

The judicial Power of the United States shall be vested in one supreme Court, and in such inferior Courts as the Congress may from time to time ordain and establish. The Judges, both of the supreme and inferior Courts, shall hold their Offices during good Behaviour, and shall, at stated Times, receive for their Services a Compensation, which shall not be diminished during their Continuance in Office.

Section 2.

The judicial Power shall extend to all Cases, in Law and Equity, arising under this Constitution, the Laws of the United States, and Treaties made, or which shall be made, under their Authority;—to all Cases affecting Ambassadors, other public Ministers and Consuls;—to all Cases of admiralty and maritime Jurisdiction;—to Controversies to which the United States shall be a Party;—to Controversies between two or more States;—between a State and Citizens of another State;—between Citizens of different States;—between Citizens of the same State claiming Lands under Grants of different States, and between a State, or the Citizens thereof, and foreign States, Citizens or Subjects.

In all Cases affecting Ambassadors, other public Ministers and Consuls, and those in which a State shall be Party, the supreme Court shall have original Jurisdiction. In all the other Cases before mentioned, the supreme Court shall have appellate Jurisdiction, both as to Law and Fact, with such Exceptions, and under such Regulations as the Congress shall make.

The Trial of all Crimes, except in Cases of Impeachment, shall be by Jury; and such Trial shall be held in the State where the said Crimes shall have been committed; but when not committed within any State, the Trial shall be at such Place or Places as the Congress may by Law have directed.

Section 3.

Treason against the United States, shall consist only in levying War against them, or in adhering to their Enemies, giving them Aid and Comfort. No Person shall be convicted of Treason unless on the Testimony of two Witnesses to the same overt Act, or on Confession in open Court.

The Congress shall have Power to declare the Punishment of Treason, but no Attainder of Treason shall work Corruption of Blood, or Forfeiture except during the Life of the Person attainted.

ARTICLE IV

Section 1.

Full Faith and Credit shall be given in each State to the public Acts, Records, and judicial Proceedings of every other State. And the Congress may by general Laws prescribe the Manner in which such Acts, Records and Proceedings shall be proved, and the Effect thereof.

Section 2.

The Citizens of each State shall be entitled to all Privileges and Immunities of Citizens in the several States.

A Person charged in any State with Treason, Felony, or other Crime, who shall flee from Justice, and be found in another State, shall on Demand of the executive Authority of the State from which he fled, be delivered up, to be removed to the State having Jurisdiction of the Crime.

No Person held to Service or Labour in one State, under the Laws thereof, escaping into another, shall, in Consequence of any Law or Regulation therein, be discharged from such Service or Labour, but shall be delivered up on Claim of the Party to whom such Service or Labour may be due.

Section 3.

New States may be admitted by the Congress into this Union; but no new State shall be formed or erected within the Jurisdiction of any other State; nor any State be formed by the Junction of two or more States, or Parts of States, without the Consent of the Legislatures of the States concerned as well as of the Congress.

The Congress shall have Power to dispose of and make all needful Rules and Regulations respecting the Territory or other Property belonging to the United States; and nothing in this Constitution shall be so construed as to Prejudice any Claims of the United States, or of any particular State.

Section 4.

The United States shall guarantee to every State in this Union a Republican Form of Government, and shall protect each of them against Invasion; and on Application of the Legislature, or of the Executive (when the Legislature cannot be convened), against domestic Violence.

ARTICLE V

The Congress, whenever two thirds of both Houses shall deem it necessary, shall propose Amendments to this Constitution, or, on the Application of the Legislatures of two thirds of the several States, shall call a Convention for proposing Amendments, which, in either Case, shall be valid to all Intents and Purposes, as Part of this Constitution, when ratified by the Legislatures of three fourths of the several States, or by Conventions in three fourths thereof, as the one or the other Mode of Ratification may be proposed by the Congress; Provided that no Amendment which may be made prior to the Year One thousand eight hundred and eight shall in any Manner affect the first and fourth Clauses in the Ninth Section of the first Article; and that no State, without its Consent, shall be deprived of its equal Suffrage in the Senate.

ARTICLE VI

All Debts contracted and Engagements entered into, before the Adoption of this Constitution, shall be as valid against the United States under this Constitution, as under the Confederation.

This Constitution, and the Laws of the United States which shall be made in Pursuance thereof; and all Treaties made, or which shall be made, under the Authority of the United States, shall be the supreme Law of the Land; and the Judges in every State shall be bound thereby, any Thing in the Constitution or Laws of any State to the Contrary notwithstanding.

The Senators and Representatives before mentioned, and the Members of the several State Legislatures, and all executive and judicial Officers, both of the United States and of the several States, shall be bound by Oath or Affirmation, to support this Constitution; but no religious Test shall ever be required as a Qualification to any Office or public Trust under the United States.

ARTICLE VII

The Ratification of the Conventions of nine States, shall be sufficient for the Establishment of this Constitution between the States so ratifying the Same.

The Word, "the," being interlined between the seventh and eighth Lines of the first Page, the Word "Thirty" being partly written on an Erazure in the fifteenth Line of the first Page, The Words "is tried" being interlined between the thirty second and thirty third Lines of the first Page and the Word "the" being interlined between the forty third and forty fourth Lines of the second Page.

Attest William Jackson Secretary

Done in Convention by the Unanimous Consent of the States present the Seventeenth Day of September in the Year of our Lord one thousand seven hundred and Eighty seven and of the Independence of the United States of America the Twelfth. In witness whereof We have hereunto subscribed our Names,

G°. Washington
Presidt and deputy from Virginia

Delaware
George Read
Gunning Bedford Junior
John Dickinson
Richard Bassett
Jacob Broom

Maryland
James McHenry
Daniel of St Thomas
   Jenifer
Daniel Carroll

Virginia
John Blair
James Madison

North Carolina
William Blount
Richard Dobbs Spaight
Hugh Williamson

South Carolina
John Rutledge
Charles Cotesworth
   Pinckney
Charles Pinckney
Pierce Butler

Georgia
William Few
Abraham Baldwin

New Hampshire
John Langdon
Nicholas Gilman

Massachusetts
Nathaniel Gorham
Rufus King

Connecticut
William Samuel Johnson
Roger Sherman

New York
Alexander Hamilton

New Jersey
William Livingston
David Brearley
William Paterson
Jonathan Dayton

Pennsylvania
Benjamin Franklin
Thomas Mifflin
Robert Morris
George Clymer
Thomas FitzSimons
Jared Ingersoll
James Wilson
Gouverneur Morris

Articles

In addition to, and Amendment of the Constitution of the United States of America, proposed by Congress, and ratified by the Legislatures of the several States, pursuant to the fifth Article of the original Constitution.

   [The first 10 amendments to the U.S. Constitution were ratified December 15, 1791, and form what is known as the "Bill of Rights."]

AMENDMENT I

Congress shall make no law respecting an establishment of religion, or prohibiting the free exercise thereof; or abridging the freedom of speech, or of the press; or the right of the people peaceably to assemble, and to petition the Government for a redress of grievances.

AMENDMENT II

A well regulated Militia, being necessary to the security of a free State, the right of the people to keep and bear Arms, shall not be infringed.

AMENDMENT III

No Soldier shall, in time of peace be quartered in any house, without the consent of the Owner, nor in time of war, but in a manner to be prescribed by law.

AMENDMENT IV

The right of the people to be secure in their persons, houses, papers, and effects, against unreasonable searches and seizures, shall not be violated, and no Warrants shall issue, but upon probable cause, supported by Oath or affirmation, and particularly describing the place to be searched, and the persons or things to be seized.

AMENDMENT V

No person shall be held to answer for a capital, or otherwise infamous crime, unless on a presentment or indictment of a Grand Jury, except in cases arising in the land or naval forces, or in the Militia, when in actual service in time of War or public danger; nor shall any person be subject for the same offence to be twice put in jeopardy of life or limb; nor shall be compelled in any criminal case to be a witness against himself, nor be deprived of life, liberty, or property, without due process of law; nor shall private property be taken for public use, without just compensation.

AMENDMENT VI

In all criminal prosecutions, the accused shall enjoy the right to a speedy and public trial, by an impartial jury of the State and district wherein the crime shall have been committed, which district shall have been previously ascertained by law, and to be informed of the nature and cause of the accusation; to be confronted with the witnesses against him; to have compulsory process for obtaining witnesses in his favor, and to have the Assistance of Counsel for his defence.

AMENDMENT VII

In Suits at common law, where the value in controversy shall exceed twenty dollars, the right of trial by jury shall be preserved, and no fact tried by a jury, shall be otherwise reexamined in any Court of the United States, than according to the rules of the common law.

AMENDMENT VIII

Excessive bail shall not be required, nor excessive fines imposed, nor cruel and unusual punishments inflicted.

AMENDMENT IX

The enumeration in the Constitution, of certain rights, shall not be construed to deny or disparage others retained by the people.

AMENDMENT X

The powers not delegated to the United States by the Constitution, nor prohibited by it to the States, are reserved to the States respectively, or to the people.

AMENDMENT XI

Passed by Congress March 4, 1794. Ratified February 7, 1795.

Note: Article III, Section 2, of the Constitution was modified by Amendment XI.

The Judicial power of the United States shall not be construed to extend to any suit in law or equity, commenced or prosecuted against one of the United States by Citizens of another State, or by Citizens or Subjects of any Foreign State.

AMENDMENT XII

Passed by Congress December 9, 1803. Ratified June 15, 1804.

Note: A portion of Article II, Section 1, of the Constitution was superseded by the Twelfth Amendment.

The Electors shall meet in their respective states and vote by ballot for President and Vice-President, one of whom, at least, shall not be an inhabitant of the same state with themselves; they shall name in their ballots the person voted for as President, and in distinct ballots the person voted for as Vice-President, and they shall make distinct lists of all persons voted for as President, and of all persons voted for as Vice-President, and of the number of votes for each, which lists they shall sign and certify, and transmit sealed to the seat of the government of the United States, directed to the President of the Senate;—the President of the Senate shall, in the presence of the Senate and House of Representatives, open all the certificates and the votes shall then be counted;—The person having the greatest number of votes for President, shall be the President, if such number be a majority of the whole number of Electors appointed; and if no person have such majority, then from the persons having the highest numbers not exceeding three on the list of those voted for as President, the House of Representatives shall choose immediately, by ballot, the President. But in choosing the President, the votes shall be taken by states, the representation from each state having one vote; a quorum for this purpose shall consist of a member or members from two-thirds of the states, and a majority of all the states shall be necessary to a choice. [And if the House of Representatives shall not choose a President whenever the right of choice shall devolve upon them, before the fourth day of March next following, then the Vice-President shall act as President, as in case of the death or other constitutional disability of the President.—]* The person having the greatest number of votes as Vice-President, shall be the Vice-President, if such number be a majority of the whole number of Electors appointed, and if no person have a majority, then from the two highest numbers on the list, the Senate shall choose the Vice-President; a quorum for the purpose shall consist of two-thirds of the whole number of Senators, and a majority of the whole number shall be necessary to a choice. But no person constitutionally ineligible to the office of President shall be eligible to that of Vice-President of the United States.

AMENDMENT XIII

Passed by Congress January 31, 1865. Ratified December 6, 1865.

Note: A portion of Article IV, Section 2, of the Constitution was superseded by the Thirteenth Amendment.

*Superseded by Section 3 of the Twentieth Amendment.

Section 1.

Neither slavery nor involuntary servitude, except as a punishment for crime whereof the party shall have been duly convicted, shall exist within the United States, or any place subject to their jurisdiction.

Section 2.

Congress shall have power to enforce this article by appropriate legislation.

AMENDMENT XIV

Passed by Congress June 13, 1866. Ratified July 9, 1868.

Note: Article I, Section 2, of the Constitution was modified by Section 2 of the Fourteenth Amendment.

Section 1.

All persons born or naturalized in the United States, and subject to the jurisdiction thereof, are citizens of the United States and of the State wherein they reside. No State shall make or enforce any law which shall abridge the privileges or immunities of citizens of the United States; nor shall any State deprive any person of life, liberty, or property, without due process of law; nor deny to any person within its jurisdiction the equal protection of the laws.

Section 2.

Representatives shall be apportioned among the several States according to their respective numbers, counting the whole number of persons in each State, excluding Indians not taxed. But when the right to vote at any election for the choice of electors for President and Vice-President of the United States, Representatives in Congress, the Executive and Judicial officers of a State, or the members of the Legislature thereof, is denied to any of the male inhabitants of such State, being twenty-one years of age,* and citizens of the United States, or in any way abridged, except for participation in rebellion, or other crime, the basis of representation therein shall be reduced in the proportion which the number of such male citizens shall bear to the whole number of male citizens twenty-one years of age in such State.

Section 3.

No person shall be a Senator or Representative in Congress, or elector of President and Vice-President, or hold any office, civil or military, under the United States, or under any State, who, having previously taken an oath, as a member of Congress, or as an officer of the United States, or as a member of any State legislature, or as an executive or judicial officer of any State, to support the Constitution of the United States, shall have engaged in insurrection or rebellion against the same, or given aid or comfort to the enemies thereof. But Congress may by a vote of two-thirds of each House, remove such disability.

Section 4.

The validity of the public debt of the United States, authorized by law, including debts incurred for payment of pensions and bounties for services in suppressing insurrection

*Changed by Section 1 of the Twenty-sixth Amendment.

or rebellion, shall not be questioned. But neither the United States nor any State shall assume or pay any debt or obligation incurred in aid of insurrection or rebellion against the United States, or any claim for the loss or emancipation of any slave; but all such debts, obligations and claims shall be held illegal and void.

Section 5.

The Congress shall have the power to enforce, by appropriate legislation, the provisions of this article.

AMENDMENT XV

Passed by Congress February 26, 1869. Ratified February 3, 1870.

Section 1.

The right of citizens of the United States to vote shall not be denied or abridged by the United States or by any State on account of race, color, or previous condition of servitude.

Section 2.

The Congress shall have the power to enforce this article by appropriate legislation.

AMENDMENT XVI

Passed by Congress July 2, 1909. Ratified February 3, 1913.
Note: Article I, Section 9, of the Constitution was modified by Amendment XVI.
The Congress shall have power to lay and collect taxes on incomes, from whatever source derived, without apportionment among the several States, and without regard to any census or enumeration.

AMENDMENT XVII

Passed by Congress May 13, 1912. Ratified April 8, 1913.
Note: Article I, Section 3, of the Constitution was modified by the Seventeenth Amendment.
The Senate of the United States shall be composed of two Senators from each State, elected by the people thereof, for six years; and each Senator shall have one vote. The electors in each State shall have the qualifications requisite for electors of the most numerous branch of the State legislatures.

When vacancies happen in the representation of any State in the Senate, the executive authority of such State shall issue writs of election to fill such vacancies: *Provided*, That the legislature of any State may empower the executive thereof to make temporary appointments until the people fill the vacancies by election as the legislature may direct.

This amendment shall not be so construed as to affect the election or term of any Senator chosen before it becomes valid as part of the Constitution.

AMENDMENT XVIII

Passed by Congress December 18, 1917. Ratified January 16, 1919. Repealed by Amendment XXI.

Section 1.

After one year from the ratification of this article the manufacture, sale, or transportation of intoxicating liquors within, the importation thereof into, or the exportation thereof from the United States and all territory subject to the jurisdiction thereof for beverage purposes is hereby prohibited.

Section 2.

The Congress and the several States shall have concurrent power to enforce this article by appropriate legislation.

Section 3.

This article shall be inoperative unless it shall have been ratified as an amendment to the Constitution by the legislatures of the several States, as provided in the Constitution, within seven years from the date of the submission hereof to the States by the Congress.

AMENDMENT XIX

Passed by Congress June 4, 1919. Ratified August 18, 1920.

The right of citizens of the United States to vote shall not be denied or abridged by the United States or by any State on account of sex.

Congress shall have power to enforce this article by appropriate legislation.

AMENDMENT XX

Passed by Congress March 2, 1932. Ratified January 23, 1933.

Note: Article I, Section 4, of the Constitution was modified by Section 2 of this amendment. In addition, a portion of the Twelfth Amendment was superseded by Section 3.

Section 1.

The terms of the President and the Vice President shall end at noon on the 20th day of January, and the terms of Senators and Representatives at noon on the 3d day of January, of the years in which such terms would have ended if this article had not been ratified; and the terms of their successors shall then begin.

Section 2.

The Congress shall assemble at least once in every year, and such meeting shall begin at noon on the 3d day of January, unless they shall by law appoint a different day.

Section 3.

If, at the time fixed for the beginning of the term of the President, the President elect shall have died, the Vice President elect shall become President. If a President shall not have been chosen before the time fixed for the beginning of his term, or if the President elect shall have failed to qualify, then the Vice President elect shall act as President until a President shall have qualified; and the Congress may by law provide for the case wherein neither a President elect nor a Vice President shall have qualified, declaring who shall then act as President, or the manner in which one who is to act shall be selected, and such person shall act accordingly until a President or Vice President shall have qualified.

Section 4.

The Congress may by law provide for the case of the death of any of the persons from whom the House of Representatives may choose a President whenever the right of choice shall have devolved upon them, and for the case of the death of any of the persons from whom the Senate may choose a Vice President whenever the right of choice shall have devolved upon them.

Section 5.

Sections 1 and 2 shall take effect on the 15th day of October following the ratification of this article.

Section 6.

This article shall be inoperative unless it shall have been ratified as an amendment to the Constitution by the legislatures of three-fourths of the several States within seven years from the date of its submission.

AMENDMENT XXI

Passed by Congress February 20, 1933. Ratified December 5, 1933.

Section 1.

The eighteenth article of amendment to the Constitution of the United States is hereby repealed.

Section 2.

The transportation or importation into any State, Territory, or Possession of the United States for delivery or use therein of intoxicating liquors, in violation of the laws thereof, is hereby prohibited.

Section 3.

This article shall be inoperative unless it shall have been ratified as an amendment to the Constitution by conventions in the several States, as provided in the Constitution, within seven years from the date of the submission hereof to the States by the Congress.

AMENDMENT XXII

Passed by Congress March 21, 1947. Ratified February 27, 1951.

Section 1.

No person shall be elected to the office of the President more than twice, and no person who has held the office of President, or acted as President, for more than two years of a term to which some other person was elected President shall be elected to the office of President more than once. But this Article shall not apply to any person holding the office of President when this Article was proposed by Congress, and shall not prevent any person who may be holding the office of President, or acting as President, during the term within which this Article becomes operative from holding the office of President or acting as President during the remainder of such term.

Section 2.

This article shall be inoperative unless it shall have been ratified as an amendment to the Constitution by the legislatures of three-fourths of the several States within seven years from the date of its submission to the States by the Congress.

AMENDMENT XXIII

Passed by Congress June 16, 1960. Ratified March 29, 1961.

Section 1.

The District constituting the seat of Government of the United States shall appoint in such manner as Congress may direct:

A number of electors of President and Vice President equal to the whole number of Senators and Representatives in Congress to which the District would be entitled if it were a State, but in no event more than the least populous State; they shall be in addition to those appointed by the States, but they shall be considered, for the purposes of the election of President and Vice President, to be electors appointed by a State; and they shall meet in the District and perform such duties as provided by the twelfth article of amendment.

Section 2.

The Congress shall have power to enforce this article by appropriate legislation.

AMENDMENT XXIV

Passed by Congress August 27, 1962. Ratified January 23, 1964.

Section 1.

The right of citizens of the United States to vote in any primary or other election for President or Vice President, for electors for President or Vice President, or for Senator or Representative in Congress, shall not be denied or abridged by the United States or any State by reason of failure to pay poll tax or other tax.

Section 2.

The Congress shall have power to enforce this article by appropriate legislation.

AMENDMENT XXV

Passed by Congress July 6, 1965. Ratified February 10, 1967.

Note: Article II, Section 1, of the Constitution was affected by the Twenty-fifth Amendment.

Section 1.

In case of the removal of the President from office or of his death or resignation, the Vice President shall become President.

Section 2.

Whenever there is a vacancy in the office of the Vice President, the President shall nominate a Vice President who shall take office upon confirmation by a majority vote of both Houses of Congress.

Section 3.

Whenever the President transmits to the President pro tempore of the Senate and the Speaker of the House of Representatives his written declaration that he is unable to discharge the powers and duties of his office, and until he transmits to them a written declaration to the contrary, such powers and duties shall be discharged by the Vice President as Acting President.

Section 4.

Whenever the Vice President and a majority of either the principal officers of the executive departments or of such other body as Congress may by law provide, transmit to the President pro tempore of the Senate and the Speaker of the House of Representatives their written declaration that the President is unable to discharge the powers and duties of his office, the Vice President shall immediately assume the powers and duties of the office as Acting President.

Thereafter, when the President transmits to the President pro tempore of the Senate and the Speaker of the House of Representatives his written declaration that no inability exists, he shall resume the powers and duties of his office unless the Vice President and a majority of either the principal officers of the executive department or of such other body as Congress may by law provide, transmit within four days to the President pro tempore of the Senate and the Speaker of the House of Representatives their written declaration that the President is unable to discharge the powers and duties of his office. Thereupon Congress shall decide the issue, assembling within forty-eight hours for that purpose if not in session. If the Congress, within twenty-one days after receipt of the latter written declaration, or, if Congress is not in session, within twenty-one days after Congress is required to assemble, determines by two-thirds vote of both Houses that the President is unable to discharge the powers and duties of his office, the Vice President shall continue to discharge the same as Acting President; otherwise, the President shall resume the powers and duties of his office.

AMENDMENT XXVI

Passed by Congress March 23, 1971. Ratified July 1, 1971.

Note: Amendment XIV, Section 2, of the Constitution was modified by Section 1 of the Twenty-sixth Amendment.

Section 1.

The right of citizens of the United States, who are eighteen years of age or older, to vote shall not be denied or abridged by the United States or by any State on account of age.

Section 2.

The Congress shall have power to enforce this article by appropriate legislation.

AMENDMENT XXVII

Originally proposed September 25, 1789. Ratified May 7, 1992.

No law, varying the compensation for the services of the Senators and Representatives, shall take effect, until an election of representatives shall have intervened.

Lincoln's Gettysburg Address

Four score and seven years ago our fathers brought forth on this continent, a new nation, conceived in Liberty, and dedicated to the proposition that all men are created equal.

Now we are engaged in a great civil war, testing whether that nation, or any nation so conceived and so dedicated, can long endure. We are met on a great battle-field of that war. We have come to dedicate a portion of that field, as a final resting place for those who here gave their lives that that nation might live. It is altogether fitting and proper that we should do this.

But, in a larger sense, we can not dedicate—we can not consecrate—we can not hallow—this ground. The brave men, living and dead, who struggled here, have consecrated it, far above our poor power to add or detract. The world will little note, nor long remember what we say here, but it can never forget what they did here. It is for us the living, rather, to be dedicated here to the unfinished work which they who fought here have thus far so nobly advanced. It is rather for us to be here dedicated to the great task remaining before us—that from these honored dead we take increased devotion to that cause for which they gave the last full measure of devotion—that we here highly resolve that these dead shall not have died in vain—that this nation, under God, shall have a new birth of freedom—and that government of the people, by the people, for the people, shall not perish from the earth.

APPENDIX B

HISTORICAL FACTS AND DATA

U.S. Presidents and Vice Presidents

	PRESIDENT	VICE PRESIDENT	POLITICAL PARTY	TERM
1	George Washington	John Adams	No party designation	1789–1797
2	John Adams	Thomas Jefferson	Federalist	1797–1801
3	Thomas Jefferson	Aaron Burr George Clinton	Democratic-Republican	1801–1809
4	James Madison	George Clinton Elbridge Gerry	Democratic-Republican	1809–1817
5	James Monroe	Daniel D. Tompkins	Democratic-Republican	1817–1825
6	John Quincy Adams	John C. Calhoun	Democratic-Republican	1825–1829
7	Andrew Jackson	John C. Calhoun Martin Van Buren	Democratic	1829–1837
8	Martin Van Buren	Richard M. Johnson	Democratic	1837–1841
9	William Henry Harrison	John Tyler	Whig	1841
10	John Tyler	None	Whig	1841–1845
11	James Knox Polk	George M. Dallas	Democratic	1845–1849
12	Zachary Taylor	Millard Fillmore	Whig	1849–1850
13	Millard Fillmore	None	Whig	1850–1853
14	Franklin Pierce	William R. King	Democratic	1853–1857
15	James Buchanan	John C. Breckinridge	Democratic	1857–1861
16	Abraham Lincoln	Hannibal Hamlin Andrew Johnson	Union	1861–1865
17	Andrew Johnson	None	Union	1865–1869
18	Ulysses Simpson Grant	Schuyler Colfax Henry Wilson	Republican	1869–1877
19	Rutherford Birchard Hayes	William A. Wheeler	Republican	1877–1881
20	James Abram Garfield	Chester Alan Arthur	Republican	1881

	PRESIDENT	VICE PRESIDENT	POLITICAL PARTY	TERM
21	Chester Alan Arthur	None	Republican	1881–1885
22	Stephen Grover Cleveland	Thomas Hendricks	Democratic	1885–1889
23	Benjamin Harrison	Levi P. Morton	Republican	1889–1893
24	Chester Alan Arthur	Adlai E. Stevenson	Democratic	1893–1897
25	William McKinley	Garret A. Hobart Theodore Roosevelt	Republican	1897–1901
26	Theodore Roosevelt	Charles W. Fairbanks	Republican	1901–1909
27	William Howard Taft	James S. Sherman	Republican	1909–1913
28	Woodrow Wilson	Thomas R. Marshall	Democratic	1913–1921
29	Warren Gamaliel Harding	Calvin Coolidge	Republican	1921–1923
30	Calvin Coolidge	Charles G. Dawes	Republican	1923–1929
31	Herbert Clark Hoover	Charles Curtis	Republican	1929–1933
32	Franklin Delano Roosevelt	John Nance Garner Henry A. Wallace Harry S. Truman	Democratic	1933–1945
33	Harry S. Truman	Alben W. Barkley	Democratic	1945–1953
34	Dwight David Eisenhower	Richard M. Nixon	Republican	1953–1961
35	John Fitzgerald Kennedy	Lyndon B. Johnson	Democratic	1961–1963
36	Lyndon Baines Johnson	Hubert H. Humphrey	Democratic	1963–1969
37	Richard Milhous Nixon	Spiro T. Agnew Gerald R. Ford	Republican	1969–1974
38	Gerald Rudolph Ford	Nelson Rockefeller	Republican	1974–1977
39	James Earl Carter, Jr.	Walter Mondale	Democratic	1977–1981
40	Ronald Wilson Reagan	George H.W. Bush	Republican	1981–1989
41	George Herbert Walker Bush	J. Danforth Quayle	Republican	1989–1993
42	William Jefferson Clinton	Albert Gore, Jr.	Democratic	1993–2001
43	George Walker Bush	Richard Cheney	Republican	2001–2009
44	Barack Hussein Obama	Joseph Biden	Democratic	2009–2017
45	Donald J. Trump	Michael R. Pence	Republican	2017–

Admission of States into the Union

	STATE	DATE OF ADMISSION		STATE	DATE OF ADMISSION
1	Delaware	December 7, 1787	28	Texas	December 29, 1845
2	Pennsylvania	December 12, 1787	29	Iowa	December 28, 1846
3	New Jersey	December 18, 1787	30	Wisconsin	May 29, 1848
			31	California	September 9, 1850
4	Georgia	January 2, 1788			
5	Connecticut	January 9, 1788	32	Minnesota	May 11, 1858
6	Massachusetts	February 6, 1788	33	Oregon	February 14, 1859
7	Maryland	April 28, 1788			
8	South Carolina	May 23, 1788	34	Kansas	January 29, 1861
9	New Hampshire	June 21, 1788	35	West Virginia	June 20, 1863
10	Virginia	June 25, 1788	36	Nevada	October 31, 1864
11	New York	July 26, 1788	37	Nebraska	March 1, 1867
12	North Carolina	November 21, 1789	38	Colorado	August 1, 1876
			39	North Dakota	November 2, 1889
13	Rhode Island	May 29, 1790			
14	Vermont	March 4, 1791	40	South Dakota	November 2, 1889
15	Kentucky	June 1, 1792			
16	Tennessee	June 1, 1796	41	Montana	November 11, 1889
17	Ohio	March 1, 1803			
18	Louisiana	April 30, 1812	42	Washington	November 11, 1889
19	Indiana	December 11, 1816	43	Idaho	July 3, 1890
			44	Wyoming	July 10, 1890
20	Mississippi	December 10, 1817	45	Utah	January 4, 1896
21	Illinois	December 3, 1818	46	Oklahoma	November 16, 1907
22	Alabama	December 14, 1819	47	New Mexico	January 6, 1912
			48	Arizona	February 14, 1912
23	Maine	March 15, 1820			
24	Missouri	August 10, 1821	49	Alaska	January 3, 1959
25	Arkansas	June 15, 1836	50	Hawaii	August 21, 1959
27	Florida	March 3, 1845			

GLOSSARY

Abolition A pre–Civil War social movement devoted to the emancipation of slaves and their inclusion in American society as citizens with equal rights. (11)

Abu Ghraib Iraqi correctional facility near Baghdad that was widely publicized in 2004 for abuses of Iraqi prisoners of war by the U.S. military and CIA operatives. (31)

Acadians A group of nearly 7,000 French-speaking colonists in Nova Scotia forced to leave Canada by invading British troops during the French and Indian War (also known as the Seven Years' War). Many emigrated to French Louisiana, where they became known as "Cajuns." (5)

Act of Supremacy (1534) English parliamentary act that abolished papal authority over England, making King Henry VIII the head of the Church of England. (1)

Acts of Union (1707) Parliamentary acts that created the United Kingdom by merging the kingdoms and parliaments of England and Scotland. (4)

Adamson Act (1916) Congressional act that granted railroad workers an eight-hour workday and overtime pay. (21)

Affordable Care Act (2010) Health insurance reform legislation designed to cover millions of uninsured Americans. (31)

Agricultural Adjustment Administration (AAA, 1933) U.S. government agency created by the Agricultural Adjustment Act to provide credit, loans, and other subsidies to farmers. (23)

Alamo A mission outpost in San Antonio, Texas, that was defended down to the last man by American and Mexican separatists in the Texas War for Independence of 1836. (11)

Albany Congress (1754) A conference of representatives of seven British North American colonies, held in Albany, New York, to consider strategies for diplomacy with the Indians and dissuade Iroquois from becoming French allies. (5)

Alianza Federal de Mercedes (1962) Organization founded by New Mexico civil rights activist Reies Lopez Tijerina to demand that the government respect land rights granted by the 1848 Treaty of Guadalupe Hidalgo. (27)

Alien and Sedition Acts (1798) Four congressional acts that severely restricted immigration into the United States, gave the president power to deport anyone thought to be dangerous, and restricted speech critical of the federal government. (8)

Alliance for Progress (1961) A multibillion-dollar aid program for Latin America aimed at establishing economic cooperation between the United States and South America. (27)

al-Qaeda A global militant Islamist organization founded by Osama bin Laden around 1989. (31)

American Anti-Slavery Society (AASS) An abolitionist society organized by William Lloyd Garrison in 1833 with immediate abolition as its core objective. (12)

American Colonization Society (ACS) A society of antislavery whites, founded in 1817, which advocated the return of freed slaves to Africa. (9)

American Expeditionary Force (AEF) American armed forces, commanded by General John J. Pershing, sent to Europe during World War I to fight alongside British and French allied units. (21)

American Federation of Labor (AFL) A collective of craft unions, founded in 1886 and headed by Samuel Gompers, that comprised skilled workers and excluded most immigrants and women. (17, 26)

American Indian Movement (AIM) An activist organization devoted formed in Minneapolis in 1968 that was to protecting Indian rights and to upholding established treaties, particularly over land, with federal, state, and local governments. (27)

American Philosophical Society (APS) Scholarly organization founded in Philadelphia in 1743 to promote the dissemination of knowledge in the science and humanities. (5)

American Protective Association (APA) An anti-Catholic nativist organization founded in 1887. The APA advocated strict immigration laws and spread conspiracy theories about Roman Catholics. (18)

American Protective League (APL) Organization of private American citizens who worked with law enforcement agencies during World War I to identify and counteract the activities of German sympathizers and other antiwar advocates. (21)

American Railway Union (ARU) One of the first industrial unions in the United States, founded in 1893 by Eugene V. Debs. The ARU aimed to increase the power of railroad workers by organizing one industry-wide union. (17)

American Recovery and Reinvestment Act (2009) Congressional act allocating $787 billion in economic stimulus funds. The package combined government spending on infrastructure, unemployment benefits, and food stamps with tax cuts. (31)

American System Senator Henry Clay's proposal of 1824 intended to spur domestic economic development as well as tariffs and currency regulation. The System also propounded recognition of Latin American independence movements. (10)

American Temperance Society (ATS) Organization established in 1826 to advocate abstinence from distilled beverages. The movement did not end the consumption of alcohol in America, but it did help convince millions of people to rethink their relationship with drinking. (12)

Americans with Disabilities Act (ADA) Congressional act of 1990 that provided equal rights for people with disabilities. (30)

Anglo-Saxonism As the United States and Great Britain emerged as the world's leading industrial powers in the late 19th century, many began to believe that the English-speaking nations shared common racial characteristics that accounted for their preeminent world standing. Anglo-Saxons, they believed, possessed superior intelligence, were industrious, and had a special talent for spreading freedom and their advanced culture around the world, (19)

Anti-Comintern Pact Agreement signed in 1936 between Nazi Germany and imperial Japan (later joined by Italy) to oppose the Soviet Union and other perceived threats. (24)

Anti-Imperial League American organization formed in 1898 by those who opposed American colonization of the Philippines. (19)

Articles of Capitulation (1664) English policies regarding Dutch residents of New Amsterdam, which granted them religious liberty, freedom from military conscription, property rights, the ability to leave New York within 18 months, and free trade and freedom of movement within the English Empire. (3)

Articles of Confederation The first written framework for a government of the United States, drafted by Congress and in effect from 1781 to 1788. (7)

Astrolabe A navigation instrument used to pinpoint and predict the location of the stars, Sun, Moon, and planets for determining longitude and latitude while sailing at sea. (1)

Atlantic Charter (1941) A joint policy statement issued by the United States and Great Britain that defined the goals and objectives of their alliance at the beginning of World War II. The charter called for disarming defeated aggressors and establishing a permanent system of general security. (24)

Atlantic slave trade The enslavement, trade, and transport of African people to Europe and the Americas, begun by the Portuguese in the early 1440s. (1)

Atlantic world Name given to the area of exploration bordering the Atlantic Ocean and including the five continents of North America, South America, Antarctica, Africa, and Europe. (1)

Baby boom The temporary but noteworthy increase in birth rate in the United States, Great Britain, and Europe in the years immediately following World War II. (26)

Bacon's Rebellion (1676) An uprising of poor white men, free blacks, and some enslaved people led by the English aristocrat Nathaniel Bacon that temporarily drove colonial governor William Berkeley from Jamestown. Participants opposed the government's moderate policy toward local Indians and the concentration of landholding in elite hands. (3)

Balance of powers A model of governance in which authority is distributed to several different branches of government, providing checks and balances against one another. Also known as the separation of powers. (7)

Bank of the United States (BUS) The first federal bank, founded in 1791, that operated until 1811 and provided for the issuance of a national currency and centralization of federal tax collection. (9)

Barbados slave code (1661) English America's first slave code; it prescribed different treatment and contrasting levels of legal protection for enslaved Africans and white servants. (3)

Battle of Bunker Hill The first significant battle of the American Revolution. It actually took place on Breed's Hill, where colonial forces claimed victory and demonstrated that they could resist larger British forces. (6)

Battle of the Bulge The last major offensive by the German army in World War II, fought in Belgium in 1944. (24)

Bay of Pigs invasion Failed operation approved by President Kennedy to invade Cuba with a small CIA-led military force of political Cuban exiles with hopes of liberating the country and removing Fidel Castro from power. (27)

Beaver Wars Seventy-year conflict among Iroquois and their neighbors driven by Iroquois demands for hunting territory and captives. The peak came between 1648 and 1657 with the dispersal of the Huron (also called Wyndat or Wyandotte) Confederacy. (3)

Berlin Airlift A military operation carried out between June 24, 1948, and May 12, 1949, in which U.S. and UK "Candy Bombers" supplied the entire city of West Berlin with 5,000 pounds of food and supplies per day during a critical early Cold War standoff with the Soviets. (25)

Bill of Rights The first 10 amendments to the United States Constitution, ratified by the states in 1791. (8)

Black codes (1865–1866) Laws enacted by southern state legislatures after the Civil War that granted limited rights to former slaves, including the right to marry, own land, and participate in the judicial process, but that also singled out black people under the law and imposed severe restraints on their occupations, mobility, and rights as parents. (15)

Black Legend Politically motivated, factually exploitative conviction that the Spaniards indiscriminately slaughtered Indians, tyrannized them, and imposed Catholicism on them during their 16th-century conquests in the Americas. (2)

Black Panther Party A radical civil rights organization founded in Oakland in 1966 by Huey Newton and Bobby Seale. Members of the Black Panthers advocated black self-determination and armed self-defense against police brutality. (27)

Black Power Ideology that advocated a combination of racial pride and forceful, even violent resistance to anti-black violence during the 1960s and early 1970s. Led by the Student Non-Violent Coordinating Committee (SNCC) and the Black Panther Party, Black Power split the civil rights coalition of the 1960s. It also produced and intensified the white backlash against political, social, and economic gains by African Americans. (27)

Black Tuesday (October 29, 1929) The day that marked the start of the Great Depression, precipitated by a calamitous crash of the stock market. (22)

Blockade Military policy of preventing an enemy from engaging in naval commerce by blocking ports and intercepting ships. (14)

Board of Trade (1696) An advisory council created by King William III of England that was charged with overseeing colonial matters. The act testified to the colonies' growing significance to England's economy. (4)

Boston Massacre (1770) An altercation between occupying British troops and a Boston mob resulting in the death of five colonists. This was a significant incident in the buildup of tensions between Britain and the colonies in the years leading up to the American Revolution. (6)

Boston Tea Party (1773) An act of defiance on the part of Boston colonists to protest the British Tea Act of 1773, a new tax on imported tea, during which 30 to 60 men disguised as Mohawk Indians stormed British tea ships and dumped 90,000 pounds of tea into Boston Harbor. (6)

Bracero Program (1942) Agreement between the governments of Mexico and the United States that granted annual entry to hundreds of thousands of seasonal agricultural workers. Control of the border was generally loosened, and hundreds of thousands of other Mexicans were drawn north by growing opportunities in the greatly expanding U.S. economy. (24)

Bretton Woods agreements (1944) Multinational agreements that established a system for international trade and monetary values to promote economic recovery following World War II. (24)

Brown v. Board of Education of Topeka, Kansas (1954) U.S. Supreme Court decision that outlawed racial segregation in public schools. (26)

Bush Doctrine Foreign policy principles of President George W. Bush, the centerpiece of which was a policy wherein the United States had the right to engage in preemptive war to secure itself against terrorist groups and countries that harbored them. (31)

Bush v. Gore (2000) U.S. Supreme Court decision that determined the winner of the 2000 presidential race between Al Gore and George W. Bush. (30)

Cahokia Once the largest Indian city north of Mexico, located just east of modern-day St. Louis. Peaking around 1100 CE, Cahokia was the capital of a Mississippian chiefdom that extended influence over much of the mid-continent. (1)

Calvinism A Protestant religion that followed the teachings of theologian John Calvin and was practiced by European and American Puritans. (1)

carpetbaggers A person from the northern states who went to the South after the Civil War to profit from Reconstruction. (15)

Central Powers Name given during World War I to the alliance of Germany, Austria-Hungary, and Ottoman Turkey. (21)

Charter of Freedoms and Exemptions (1640) A Dutch West India Company policy that granted 200 acres to whoever brought five adults to New Netherland and promised prospective colonists religious freedom and local self-governance; these offers attracted English Puritans from Massachusetts to eastern Long Island. (2)

Chicano Originally viewed negatively, the term became widely used during the Chicano Movement by Mexican Americans to express pride in a shared cultural, ethnic and community identity.(27)

Chinese Exclusion Act (1882) Congressional act that barred the immigration of Chinese laborers. This law all but ended Chinese immigration and remained in effect until 1943. (16, 18)

Church of England (Anglican Church) English Christian church established by King Henry VIII after his break from papal authority in 1534. (1)

Civil Rights Act of 1964 Congressional act that prohibited discrimination in employment or the use of public places on the basis of race, sex, religion, or national origin. (27)

Civilization Policy First deployed in 1795, Civilization Policy sought to remake Indians in the image of Anglo-Americans, using missions, education, and gifts of livestock and farming equipment to change Native languages, religions, economies, and gender roles. (9)

Code Noir (1685) Slave code mandated by imperial France governing the rights and treatment of African slaves in its colonial territories from the French West Indies to Louisiana. (4)

Coercive Acts/Intolerable Acts (1774) Four British parliamentary decrees enacted in response to unrest and protests in Boston. The acts reorganized the Massachusetts government and placed more authority in the hands of royal appointees. They also imposed royal control over local courts and authorized troops to be forcibly housed in private homes and buildings. (6)

Coinage Act (1873) Congressional act that made gold the nation's monetary standard and halted the making of silver dollars, later referred to by Populists, who wished to expand the nation's money supply with silver, as "the crime of 1873." (18)

Cold War Term given to the political, economic, and military tensions that existed between the United States and its allies and the Soviet Union between 1945 and the dissolution of the Soviet Union in 1991. (25)

Columbian exchange The historic movement of people, plants, animals, culture, and pathogens between the Americas and the rest of the world that began during the time of Columbus. (1)

Committee on Public Information Government agency created during World War I to promote war aims and distribute propaganda. (21)

Committee to Reelect the President (CREEP) Group organized by the Nixon White House to both promote the president's reelection and collect illegal funds to engage in "dirty tricks." (28)

Common law Law based on decisions previously made by judges and courts, as opposed to statutory, or written, laws and statutes; the common law system was rooted in English legal practices. (2)

Commons Lands open to all residents. (2)

Compromise of 1850 Congressional measures created to resolve a series of regional tensions in the United States. The measures admitted California as a free state, organized the remainder of the New Mexico territory, banned the slave trade in the District of Columbia, empowered the U.S. Treasury to assume Texas's debts from its independence struggle with Mexico, and gave the South a much stronger federal Fugitive Slave Law. (13)

Comstock Act Passed by Congress in 1874, this law banned "obscene, lewd, or lascivious material" from the U.S. mail, including anatomy books and information regarding birth control and sex education. (18)

Congress of Industrial Organizations (CIO) Umbrella group of labor unions, formed in 1935, to represent semiskilled workers in major industrial sectors. Unions within the Congress accepted black and other minority workers. (23, 26)

Containment Name given to the foundation of U.S. foreign policy during the Cold War. George F. Kennan argued that Soviet communism was "impervious to the logic of reason," inherently expansionist, and controllable only through "long-term, patient but firm and vigilant containment." (25)

Contraband Legal term denoting war materials that can be seized from an enemy during wartime. During the Civil War, Northern leaders used the term to refer to enslaved people who fled to Union lines seeking freedom. (14)

Contract with America A document conceived by Republican congressman Newt Gingrich in 1993 that promised to make Congress more accountable, balance the federal budget, reverse the tax increases passed in 1993, and reduce the capital gains tax. (30)

Contras Anti-Communist guerrillas funded by the CIA to attack the Sandinista regime in Nicaragua in the 1980s. (29)

Conversion test An exercise developed by Massachusetts Bay Puritans to test prospective church members for membership in their congregation; prospects had to testify to their relationship with God and offer proof that God had saved them. (2)

Copper borderlands Region in southwest United States and northern Mexico where trade and labor networks transcended national borders. (16)

Copperheads Civil War–era nickname for the faction of the Democratic Party that opposed the war. (14)

Counterculture In the 1960s and early 1970s, the name given to the subculture of college-age young Americans who developed distinctively liberal beliefs and practices regarding sexuality, race, gender, politics, and culture; these values stood in contrast to those of the dominant culture of their parents. (27)

Court packing scheme Abortive effort by President Roosevelt in 1937 to increase the number of justices on the Supreme Court. (23)

Covenant As practiced by New England Puritans, an agreement with God that required them to translate their faith into actions that obeyed God's will as revealed in the Bible. (2)

Coverture A principle of British and American law wherein a married woman lost her legal identity as an individual and in which her economic resources would be controlled by her husband. This law prevented married women from owning property. (7, 11)

Crop lien A credit system widely used by southern farmers from the 1860s to the 1920s. This was a way for farmers to get credit before the planting season by borrowing against the value of anticipated harvests. (15)

Cuban missile crisis A tense standoff between the United States and Soviet Union in October 1962 when the United States discovered that the Soviets had begun installing nuclear missiles in Cuba. The incident was the most dramatic nuclear standoff of the Cold War. (27)

Culture war Period of intense secular or religious conflict resulting in political conflict, inability to reach compromise, and polarization of opinion. (25)

Dawes Act (1887) Congressional act that divided two-thirds of Indian tribal lands to be sold off or confiscated. Many Indians who had lived on reservations became essentially landless. (16)

Dawes Plan (1924) A foreign policy that provided a loan from U.S. banks to Germany to stabilize its economy and reduce its reparations burden. (22)

D-Day Code name for the massive Allied invasion of France on June 6, 1944. (24)

Declaration of Independence (1776) American Revolutionary document that declared that the United States was free and independent of the British Empire and sought international recognition for the United States. (6)

Defense Advanced Research Projects Agency (DARPA) U.S. defense agency that created the Internet, originally founded in 1958 to counter Soviet advances in space science. (30)

Defense of Marriage Act (DOMA, 1996) Congressional act that decreed that no state would be compelled to recognize a same-sex marriage conducted in another state, nor would the federal government recognize the existence of such a marriage even if it were performed legally in a state. (31)

Desert Land Act (1877) Congressional act, applicable in 11 western states, that allowed for homesteading on 640-acre parcels of arid land at 25 cents per acre and provided title within three years for a dollar an acre for settled, irrigated land. (16)

Détente Term given to the U.S. relaxation of tension with the Soviets during the 1970s. (28)

Dollar diplomacy Effort by Taft administration to encourage U.S. bankers and businesses to expand into Latin America. (19)

Dominion of New England (1685–1689) A union of English colonies imposed by the English monarchy; it comprised eight contiguous colonies, from New England to New Jersey, under one governor, Edmond

Andros, who dissolved representative assemblies, jailed dissidents, and imposed taxes on lands already owned outright. (3)

***Dred Scott* decision (1857)** U.S. Supreme Court ruling that slaves were not citizens of the United States and were therefore unable to sue in a federal court of law. As a consequence, the federal government had no authority to outlaw slavery in the territories, leaving that choice up to the states. (13)

Dust Bowl Area in the West and Midwest plagued by drought and dust storms in the 1930s. (23)

Dutch West India Company (DWIC) Dutch trading company whose merchants were granted trade monopolies in parts of the New World, and whose activities included the acquisition of territories in the Hudson River valley in New York. (2)

Earthrise First photo of Earth from space captured by *Apollo 8* astronauts on Christmas Eve 1968. (27)

East India Company (EIC) Monopoly trading company of English merchants chartered in 1600 to trade in Asia and India. The company was influential in global British imperial policy into the 19th century. (4)

Edict of Nantes (1598) Proclamation by King Henry IV of France granting rights to Huguenots (French Calvinist Protestants). (2)

Eighteenth Amendment (1919) Constitutional amendment that barred the manufacture and sale of alcohol in the United States. It was repealed in 1933. (20)

Emancipation Proclamation (1863) Proclamation by Abraham Lincoln that freed the slaves living in Confederate states. (14)

Emergency Banking Relief Act (1933) Congressional act that followed the market crash of 1929; it reopened banks and restored bank solvency under Treasury Department supervision. The act also removed U.S. currency from the gold standard. (23)

Emergency Economic Stabilization Act (2008) Congressional act that authorized the U.S. Treasury to budget up to $700 billion to bail out banks and other financial institutions affected by a crisis in subprime mortgage values. (31)

Emergency Immigration Act of 1921 Congressional act that created specific immigration limitations based on national origin. The act banned all immigration from Asia but allowed free immigration from the Western Hemisphere, as the Southwest depended on Mexican and Central American labor. (22)

Encomienda System whereby the Spanish government granted land, villages, and indigenous people to military leaders who conquered land in the Americas. (1)

Equal Rights Amendment (ERA) Proposed amendment to the U.S. Constitution that banned the denial or abridgment of rights on the basis of gender. (29)

Espionage Act (1917) Congressional act passed on the eve of America's entrance into World War I that expanded the definition of treason and defined a variety of acts deemed to comprise espionage. This law was enacted to fight sabotage, spying, and interference with the war effort. (20)

Ethnic cleansing The effort by government or private groups to remove or kill groups of people from land they have traditionally occupied. (30)

Eugenics A popular movement in the first decades of the twentieth century, eugenics aimed to "improve" the human race by genetic engineering, including encouraging the selective breeding of those deemed superior. (22)

Executive Order 9981 (1948) Order by President Truman that established equality in the armed services on the basis of race, color, religion, and national origin. (25)

Exodusters Freed slaves who fled the South in search of better opportunities and treatment in the West after the Civil War. (16)

Factory system The factory system radically changed the ways that workers related to business owners and to one another. It refers to the centralization of manufacturing under the ownership of one person or a corporation. Instead of manufacturing goods in homes or in small family-owned workshops, the factory system brought together many unrelated workers under one roof. (10)

Fair Deal Domestic programs for social reform proposed by the Truman administration. The 21-point program called for an increase in the minimum wage, comprehensive housing legislation for returning veterans, full employment and expanded unemployment benefits, permanent federal farm subsidies, expanded public works projects, and expanded environmental conservation programs. (25)

Fair Labor Standards Act Federal law passed in 1938 that guaranteed workers a minimum wage, overtime pay, and other benefits. (23)

Farmers' Alliance An umbrella movement of agricultural organizations, founded in Texas in 1876, that encouraged men and women to cooperate in running their households and their farms. The Alliance provided the foundation for what would become the Populist Party. (17, 18)

Federalism A system of government that divides powers between a centralized national administration and state governments. (7)

Federalist Papers A series of anonymously authored essays, published in newspapers, supporting ratification of the U.S. Constitution of 1787 by James Madison, Alexander Hamilton, and John Jay. (7)

Feitoria Portuguese name for a fortified trading post, early examples of which were first established in Africa in the 15th century during the early years of the Atlantic slave trade. (1)

Fifteenth Amendment (1870) Constitutional amendment that prohibited the denial of voting rights on the basis of race. (15)

Filibuster A person engaging in unauthorized warfare against a foreign country. (11)

Fireside chats Weekly radio addresses by President Franklin Roosevelt in which he explained his proposals, policies, and actions to the American people. (23)

First Anglo-Dutch War (1652–1654) A naval conflict between England and the United Provinces of the Netherlands that stemmed from trade disputes. England prevailed and secured a trade monopoly with English colonies. Still, English settlers in North America and elsewhere often preferred Dutch goods and continued to trade with the Dutch in defiance of the English monopoly. (3)

First Continental Congress Representatives of the colonies (except Georgia) who met in Philadelphia for the first time in 1774 to articulate their positions and form policies against grievous British laws and regulations. The group charged committees in each colony with vigorously enforcing boycotts; endorsed a declaration of rights and grievances on October 14, 1774; and then adjourned, hoping that the king would change the course of imperial policy. (6)

First Hundred Days President Franklin Roosevelt's first days in office, during which he prevailed on Congress to pass 14 major pieces of legislation including bills to raise agricultural prices, put the unemployed to work, regulate the stock market, reform banking practices, and assist homeowners and farmers in paying mortgages. (23)

Flapper The youthful new woman of the 1920s who, rebelling against her mother's generation, celebrated her freedom by wearing short skirts, bobbing her hair, and smoking and drinking openly. (22)

Four Freedoms Global goals set out by President Franklin D. Roosevelt in January 1941 pledging U.S. support for freedom of speech, freedom of religion, freedom from hunger, and freedom from fear. (24)

Fourteen Points Plan for peace and postwar order proclaimed by President Woodrow Wilson in 1918. (21)

Fourteenth Amendment (1868) Constitutional amendment that guaranteed national citizenship and equality to former slaves and, detailed changes related to the former Confederate states but offered no specific protection of freed people's voting rights. (15)

Fox Wars (1712–1735) A series of wars over slavery and trade in the Great Lakes region that pitted the French and their Indian allies against the Fox (or Meskwaki), Sauk, Mascouten, and Kickapoo nations. (4)

Franciscans A Roman Catholic religious order active in establishing Spanish missions in southwestern North America in the 18th and 19th centuries. (1)

Freedmen's Bureau Shortened name for the Bureau of Refugees, Freedmen, and Abandoned Land, established by the U.S. Army in early 1865 to adjudicate labor disputes in the summer and fall of 1865. (15)

French and Indian War (1756–1763) Also known as the Seven Years' War, a conflict between Britain and France and their respective Indian allies in colonial America. This was largely a conflict between empires for territorial and economic control of the colonies and related trade routes. (5)

Fugitive Slave Act (1850) Congressional act that nationalized the process of slave capture and return by requiring federal judges to appoint "commissioners" to hear cases of accused fugitives and by requiring the active complicity of state officers. (13)

Fundamentalists Christians who interpreted the Bible literally and rejected the notion that traditional faith should enter a dialogue with science and popular culture. (22).

Fur trade The trading of furs, primarily through the St. Lawrence River region, that served as the primary gateway for European goods into North America into the 1600s. (2)

Gag rule Rule adopted by Congress in 1836 to block the discussion of slavery at the national as well as the state level. The rule was repealed in 1844. (11)

Gang system One of two general types of division of labor of plantation slaves, the other being the task system. The gang system involved the work of coordinated groups, supervised by a driver, to maintain an even level of productivity during the workday. (5)

General Allotment Act (1887) Congressional act that divided Indian reservation land into smaller parcels of property. (16)

Gentlemen's agreement (1907) Agreement reached by President Theodore Roosevelt and the Japanese government that stated that the United States would no longer exclude Japanese immigrants if the Japanese promised to voluntarily limit the number of its immigrants to the United States, primarily adult male laborers. (19)

Gilded Age Coined by Mark Twain and Charles Dudley Warner in 1873 to describe how the United States seemed to be gilded, covered with the gold generated for millionaire industrialists. But the gold covering often proved to be a thin veneer, masking a world of greed, exploitation, and poverty. (17)

Ghost Dance Originating among the Paiute Indians around 1870, The Ghost Dance religion was a response to the subjugation of Native Americans by the U.S. government. It was an attempt to revitalize traditional culture in the face of eroding tribal sovereignty. (16)

Glass–Steagall Banking Act (1933) Congressional act that established strict guidelines for banking operations and expanded the power of the Federal Reserve System. The act also founded the Federal Deposit Insurance Corporation. Some regulations associated with the original act were repealed in 1999, leading to mismanagement and scandals in the banking and finance industries and the recession beginning around 2009. (23)

Globalization A term that was popularized in the 1990s to refer to the knitting together of the world's economies through new information technology and the end of the artificial political barrier of the Cold War. (30)

Glorious Revolution (1688) Uprising of the English Parliament against King James II that transformed the English system of government from an absolute monarchy to a constitutional monarchy and the rule of Parliament. (3)

Good Neighbor Policy Policy adopted by the Franklin D. Roosevelt administration after 1933 that pledged the United States would not interfere militarily in Latin America. (24)

Gospel of Wealth A philosophy popularized by Andrew Carnegie that called upon the wealthy few in the Gilded Age to benefit society through philanthropy. (17)

Grand Settlement of 1701 A pair of treaties between Iroquois and the French that stabilized relations between the two in the Great Lakes and northeast parts of North America. (4)

Grandfather clause Allowance created by southern state constitutions in the 1890s permitting any person who had voted before 1867 or had a father or grandfather who had voted to be exempt from the literacy test or other restrictions. The aim of this law was to increase the number of eligible white male voters while eliminating black voters. (20)

Great Depression International economic depression and the United States' worst economic downturn to date. Beginning at the end of 1929 and lasting for 10 years, the catastrophe spread to every corner of the country, wrecking lives and leaving people homeless, hungry, and desperate for work. (22)

Great Migration The large-scale movement of African Americans during and after World War I from the South to the North, where jobs were more plentiful. (21)

Great Railroad Strike of 1877 The first and largest general strike in U.S. history, sparked by wage and hour cuts of railroad workers in the midst of an economic depression. The strike was marked by violence as well as nonviolent sympathetic strikes by workers across the nation. President Rutherford B. Hayes used federal troops to help break the strike after roughly a month. (17)

Great Recession The international economic collapse of 2008 in which credit markets around the world froze and banks stopped lending to one another. Businesses dependent on lending began to downsize and fail. The meltdown affected financial institutions and governments throughout the world. (31)

Great Society President Lyndon Johnson's name for a series of social and economic reforms, begun in 1965, to end racial discrimination, expand educational opportunities, end hunger and poverty, and make health care available for all. (27)

Gulf of Tonkin Resolution Congressional authorization requested by President Lyndon Johnson in 1964 that gave him the power to escalate military action in Vietnam without additional congressional approval. (28)

Guerrillas Irregular combatants who acted locally and outside the laws of war, sometimes attacking soldiers and other times civilians. (14)

Hamdan v. Rumsfeld Supreme Court ruling in 2006 restricting the Bush administration's use of military commissions to try accused terrorist detainees at Guantanamo Bay. (31)

Hard war Union's policy during the American Civil War that targeted the ability of Confederates to fight by destroying infrastructure, transportation networks, and food supplies for the army. (14)

Harlem Renaissance An African American cultural and arts movement of the 1920s centered in the Harlem neighborhood of New York City. (22)

Harpers Ferry (1859) Failed raid led by abolitionist John Brown on the U.S. arsenal in Harpers Ferry, Virginia. Brown's capture and execution led to greater regional tensions leading up to the Civil War. (13)

Haymarket Affair A violent conflict between protesting workers and police in Chicago's Haymarket Square in 1886 that created antiunion hysteria and brought about the demise of the Knights of Labor. (17)

Helsinki Accords A set of principles that accepted the post-1945 division of Europe into East–West spheres. The accords recognized the right of all Europeans to seek peaceful change, and the Soviets agreed in a general way to respect human rights in their sphere. (29)

Holden v. Hardy (1898) U.S. Supreme Court decision that upheld Utah's law limiting the working hours of miners to eight hours per day. (20)

Homestead Act (1862) Congressional act that allowed families to claim 160 acres of land if they improved it over five years of residence. The act opened the western United States to settlement. (15, 16)

Homestead Lockout An 1892 incident in which Carnegie partner Henry Clay Frick locked out workers at the Carnegie steel works in Homestead, Pennsylvania, when they refused a new contract, leading to violence and the destruction of their powerful union. (17)

Horizontal integration An innovation of the modern corporation aimed at eliminating destructive aspects of competition by purchasing competitors or establishing agreements among them to share profits. (17)

House of Burgesses The first representative government assembly and ruling body established in the English settlements in America; founded by the Virginia Company in 1619, this assembly replaced martial law with English common law, setting in motion the development of the county court system. (2)

House Committee on Un-American Activities (HCUA) Congressional committee formed in 1938 to search for Communists and conspiracies within the United States including penetration into the labor movement and federal agencies. Although discredited during the 1950s for its investigations of entertainment and media figures, the committee was not abandoned until 1975. (25)

Hudson's Bay Company English trading company, formed in England in 1670, that competed with the French in North America. (3)

Huguenots Name given to the French followers of Calvinism, a Protestant religion founded by theologian John Calvin. (1)

Immigration Restriction League An anti-immigration organization founded in Boston in 1894 that promoted legislation to restrict the immigration of southern and eastern Europeans. (18)

Indentured servitude An arrangement offered by various English enterprises to attract English people to the colonies, exchanging free passage by ship to America for up to seven years of labor. (2)

Indian Removal Act (1830) Federal law that nullified 50 years' worth of treaties between the United States and many tribes. The law resulted in the relocation of more than 45,000 Indians living east of the Mississippi to points farther west, opening up lands for white settlers. The law committed the federal government to creating an Indian territory west of the Mississippi. (11)

Indian Reorganization Act (1934) Congressional act that slowed the division of reservation land into small plots, encouraged tribal self-government, and established Indian-run corporations to control communal land and resources. (23)

Industrial Workers of the World (IWW) Radical labor union, also known as "Wobblies," founded in 1905. The union embraced all workers in "one big union," called for the overthrow of capitalism, and advocated industrial sabotage. It was especially active in the West up to World War I. (20)

Industrious revolution Preindustrialization period associated with 18th-century British North America during which there was a diversification of labor, development of a market-oriented society, and a labor shift from services to marketable goods. (4)

Initiative, referendum, and recall First proposed by Populists in the 1890s, the initiative and referendum, adopted originally in Oregon, made it possible for voters to place legislation directly before the electorate for a vote in general elections; the referendum allowed voters to repeal state legislation with which they disagreed; the recall gave voters the power to remove any public official who did not, in their view, act for the public good. (20)

Instant cities Urban areas such as San Francisco and Denver that grew rapidly from frontier outposts to major regional cities during the settlement of the West. (16)

Insular Cases (1901–1954) A series of U.S. Supreme Court cases that were applied to all of the new territories added to the United States in which it was ruled that American constitutional rights and liberties did not extend to all lands under U.S. control. (19)

Interstate and Defense Highways Act (1956) The largest public works program in American history, approved by President Dwight Eisenhower, that facilitated the growth of suburban America and the businesses and industries that sustained it. (26)

Iran-Contra scandal Scandalous effort by Reagan administration that involved ransoming hostages in Lebanon, selling arms to Iran, and illegally funding the Contras in Nicaragua. (29)

Jacobite Rebellion (1715) One of a series of attempts to restore James II to the throne of England. England's last Catholic monarch, James II, was deposed by Parliament during the Glorious Revolution of 1688. Thereafter, rebels in England, Ireland, and Scotland launched serial uprisings but were not successful. Many of these rebels—some voluntarily, others by force—resettled in North America. (4)

Jamestown The first permanent English settlement in America, founded in 1607 and located in what is today coastal Virginia. (2)

Jay's Treaty (1794) Treaty with Britain granting the United States trade rights on the Mississippi and in the British East Indies and removing remaining British forts on American territory. (8)

Jesuits (Society of Jesus) A Catholic male religious order, founded in Spain in 1534, that was active in winning converts overseas. (1)

Jim Crow laws State and local laws that originated in the South in the mid-1880s and legally separated people according to race. These laws spread to many public facilities and established a policy of racial segregation that favored white citizens. (20)

Johnson–O'Malley Act of 1934 Congressional act that provided federal aid to improve health care and education for Indian tribes. (23)

Joint-stock companies An early form of shareholding company that was used by the British to finance development of the colonies. (2)

Jubilee In the context of the Civil War, Jubilees were celebrations by black Southerners marking their deliverance from bondage. (15)

Kansas–Nebraska Act (1854) Congressional act that repealed the Missouri Compromise. The bill's new policy of "popular sovereignty," intended to allow settlers in a territory to decide the status of slavery, initiated a strenuous debate about the future of slavery in the western territories. (13)

Katsina Ancestral god spirits of Pueblo peoples. (3)

Keating–Owen Child Labor Act (1916) Law that banned interstate commerce in goods produced by child labor. Struck down by U.S. Supreme Court as unconstitutional in 1918. (20)

Kellogg–Briand Pact (1928) Also known as the "Pact of Paris," an agreement signed by 62 nations that agreed not to use war as an instrument of national policy. The pact was initiated by the United States and France. (22)

Kent State The campus where the Ohio National Guard in the spring of 1970 killed and wounded antiwar demonstrators. (28)

Keynesian economics The idea that the government can boost the economy and counter recessions by increasing deficit spending on public projects. (23)

King Philip's War (1675–1676) Conflict between Indian inhabitants of the New England region, the English colonists, and their Indian allies. Named after the Indian leader Metacom, known to the English as King Philip. (3)

King William's War (1689–1697) The first of several colonial wars between English and French colonists in North America and their Indian allies. (3)

Kiva An underground chamber used by Pueblo Indians for religious ceremonies. (2)

Knights of Labor The first national labor union, founded in Baltimore in 1869. The Knights aimed to organize all laboring people into one large, national union, offering membership regardless of race, gender, or national origin. The organization rejected capitalism and wage labor and demanded a fair share of wealth for workers who produced it. (15, 17)

Know-Nothing Party Antiforeign, anti-Catholic political organization established in 1854 and consisting of a network of secret fraternal associations. The party was largely a nativist reaction against large-scale European immigration. The organization's name stemmed from its secrecy; if asked about the organization, members would essentially deny any knowledge of it, saying that they "knew nothing." (13)

Ku Klux Klan (KKK) An organization associated with the bitterest and most violent opponents of Reconstruction and black freedom. Formed in Pulaski, Tennessee, in late 1865, Klan members devoted themselves to denying African Americans any legitimate role in the public sphere, stressing the superiority of white, Protestant, Anglo-Saxon citizens. The Klan was revived in the 1920s as an anti-immigrant, anti-Catholic, and anti-Jewish organization. (15, 22, 26)

Lady of Cofitachequi A Native American woman who ruled a vast chiefdom in the Carolinas during the 1500s. She was a paramount chief, meaning that she had gained control over other chiefdoms through warfare and diplomacy. (1)

Laissez-faire economics An economic doctrine that insisted that government should not interfere with businesses or the market. The term is from the French, meaning "leave it alone." (17)

Lawrence v. Texas (2003) U.S. Supreme Court decision that overturned most state anti-sodomy laws used to criminalize homosexual behavior. (31)

League of Nations Organization created after World War I to promote global peace and cooperation (21)

Lend-Lease Act (1941) Massive military and economic aid program to assist nations fighting Germany and Japan in World War II. (24)

Levittown First massive planned subdivision, created in the New York suburbs on Long Island, constructed after World War II. (26)

Limited Test Ban Treaty (1963) An agreement between the United States and the Soviet Union that ended aboveground atomic weapon testing but permitted continued testing underground. (27)

Linen Act of 1705 British parliamentary act that encouraged the export of Irish linen to North America. In turn, the act increased the demand in northern Ireland for colonial flaxseed, the source of linen. (4)

Literacy Act (1917) Clause of the U.S. Immigration Act of 1917 that barred the entry of any persons unable to read in their own language on the grounds that this lack demonstrated their ignorance. (21)

Lochner v. New York (1905) U.S. Supreme Court decision that struck down a New York law limiting the hours that male bakers could work. In the Court's opinion, the state had no right to regulate their hours. (20)

Lowell Mill Girls Female workers associated with the textile mills in Lowell, Massachusetts. The mills had a large labor force of young women, who ranged between the ages of 15 and 35 and worked in one of the first large-scale steam-powered industries in the United States. (11)

Ludlow Massacre (1914) An attack by local deputies and state militia on striking United Mine Workers members in Ludlow, Colorado. At the request of mine owners, the militia attacked a camp of striking miners who had been evicted from company-owned housing, killing 14 people, including 11 children. Soon labeled the Ludlow Massacre, the killings sparked violent retaliation by the miners. (20)

Lusitania British passenger liner torpedoed by a German submarine in 1915 while sailing between New York and England. The attack killed 1,200 of the 2,000 passengers and crew, including 128 Americans. (21)

Lynching The murder of African American individuals by a mob, often by hanging, shooting, or burning, that was especially prevalent in the 1890s South. (20)

Malintzín A native Nahua woman from the Gulf Coast of Mexico who figured importantly in the Spanish conquest of Mexico by acting as the translator and advisor to Hernán Cortés, leader of a Spanish expedition. (1)

Maine (battleship) A U.S. battleship that exploded on February 15, 1898, killing 260 American sailors. Americans blamed Spain for the explosion, drawing the United States closer to war with Spain, which was declared two months later. (19)

Manhattan Project Secret U.S. scientific and military program during World War II dedicated to the development of an atomic bomb. The project was led by J. Robert Oppenheimer and employed 150,000 workers at numerous secret sites, including Los Alamos, New Mexico. (24)

Mann Act (1910) Congressional act that outlawed the transport of women across state lines for "immoral purposes." (20)

Manumission The freeing of slaves by their owners. (4)

Marbury v. Madison (1803) U.S. Supreme Court decision that firmly established the principle of "judicial review," the right of the U.S. Supreme Court to rule on the constitutionality of legislation and executive actions. (8)

March on Washington (1963) Civil rights demonstration in which Martin Luther King, Jr., delivered the "I Have a Dream" speech. (27)

Maroons Groups of people who escaped slavery and formed independent communities, usually in inaccessible places. Such communities existed in the Caribbean as well as North and South America. (4, 5)

Marshall Plan (European Recovery Plan, 1948 A massive foreign aid program approved following World War II that called for aid packages to help western Europe, including West Germany, and Japan rapidly rebuild their devastated economies, restore industries and trade, and rejoin the free world. (25)

Massachusetts Bay Company A business enterprise founded by English Puritans and merchants in 1629 that founded the Massachusetts Bay Colony, resulting in a swell of English emigration to the colonies. (2)

Matrilineal A society in which social identity is based on kinship and descendency from the mother. (2)

Maysville Road Bill (1830) A bill authorizing federal investment in a private turnpike company that was vetoed by President Andrew Jackson because he opposed using central power for infrastructure improvement. (10)

McCarran International Security Act (1950) Congressional act requiring the registration of American Communist Party members; the act reinforced perceptions of immigrants as a source of radicalism during the Cold War and set the tone for a contentious debate about immigration in the coming decade. (25)

McCarthyism Term named for Wisconsin senator who engaged in "witch hunts" against real and mostly imagined Communists inside the United States. (26)

McKinley Tariff (1890) Congressional act that ended the practice of allowing Hawaiian sugar to enter the United States duty free, ending Hawaii's favored status and threatening its sugar industry. (19)

McNary–Haugen Acts (1927–1928) Congressional acts that required the government to support crop prices by buying basic farm commodities. (22)

Meat Inspection Act (1906) Congressional act that required federal inspectors from the U.S. Department of Agriculture to inspect livestock in slaughterhouses and to guarantee sanitary standards. (20)

Medicaid A health care plan that originated with President Lyndon Johnson's Great Society programs in which the federal government provided states matching grants to pay for medical costs of poor people of all ages. (27)

Medicare A health plan that originated with President Lyndon Johnson's Great Society programs that provided universal hospital insurance for Americans over 65. (27)

Medicare Modernization Act (2003) Congressional act that subsidized the cost of some, but not all, medication taken by seniors. (31)

Mercantilism An economic philosophy of English and French governments founded on the belief that control of foreign trade—including the acquisition of raw materials from their colonies—was key to securing the kingdom that ruled them. (3)

Methodists A Protestant evangelical sect, rooted in the 18th-century Anglican revival movement, that accepted slaves and freed blacks and opposed government intervention in religion. (5)

Millennialism A belief system organized around an imminent apocalypse, which makes salvation all the more urgent. (12)

Minutemen In Revolutionary War times, local militias in Massachusetts and Connecticut that went on alert in response to pending British military action. (6)

Miranda v. Arizona (1966) Supreme Court decision that required police to tell suspects of their right to remain silent and to have access to legal counsel. (27)

Mississippian societies Name given to Indian societies of the Mississippi valley formed around 700 CE and peaking between 1100 and 1300. (1)

Missouri Compromise Legislation passed by Congress in 1820, admitting Missouri as a slave state and Maine as a free state, in an effort to preserve the balance of power between slave and free states. With the exception of Missouri, the law prohibited slavery in the Louisiana Territory north of the 36° 30' latitude line. The Missouri Compromise was repealed by the Kansas-Nebraska Act of 1854. (9)

Model Cities Federal urban aid program created by President Lyndon Johnson to encourage physical and economic revitalization of the nation's poorest urban areas. (27)

Modern corporation A form of corporation pioneered by railroads before the Civil War and then developed in the last quarter of the 19th century distinguished by its organization, massive scale, and forms of management. (17)

Modernists Religious leaders, influenced by the Social Gospel movement of the late 19th century, as well as Darwin's theory of evolution and archaeological discoveries, who believed Christianity should respond positively to new knowledge and social conditions. (22)

Monetarists Proponents of a conservative economic movement that favored a change to tax and spending policies. Led by Milton Friedman, these economists insisted that prosperity and freedom required reduced government spending along with more stringent control of the money supply. (29)

Monroe Doctrine (1823) Policy introduced by President James Monroe, who declared that the United States shared common interest with other states in the Western Hemisphere and that the political system in Europe was "essentially different" from that of the democratic republics in North and South America. (9)

Montgomery Improvement Association (MIA) An organization of black clergy and community leaders formed in 1955 and led by Martin Luther King, Jr., who refined a philosophy of nonviolent protest for boycotters. (26)

Moral Majority Political lobbying movement organized by religious conservatives in 1979. (29)

Moravians (United Brethren) A Protestant religious sect, revived in Germany in 1727 and brought to Georgia in 1735, that sought to create closed, economically autonomous, sex-segregated communities in which Christian liturgical rituals and piety infused daily life. (5)

Mormons A Protestant religious sect founded by Joseph Smith, who preached a conservative theology of patriarchal authority. (12)

Muckraking An early form of investigative journalism. Believing that exposing facts could rouse the public to demand change, "muck-raking" helped bring about major reforms in the late 19th and early 20th centuries. (17)

Mudsill A sociological theory first proposed in 1858 by South Carolina senator James Henry Hammond, who stated that a division of upper and lower classes was the natural order of society, a view that was interpreted by many as a thinly veiled excuse for exploiting slavery. (11)

Mujahideen Islamic-inspired Afghans and foreign guerrillas who fought the occupying Soviets in Afghanistan during the 1980s. They counted among their ranks Saudi fundamentalist Osama bin Laden. (29)

Mulatto A mixed-race person in the United States. (11)

Muller v. Oregon (1908) U.S. Supreme Court decision that upheld an Oregon law limiting the workday of female laundry workers to 10 hours per day. (20)

My Lai Massacre (1968) Massacre by American troops of 504 unarmed Vietnamese villagers during the Vietnam War. (28)

Natchez War (1729–1731) Rebellion staged by Natchez warriors and African slaves against French colonists in Mississippi, suppressed by the French and their Choctaw allies. (4)

National American Woman Suffrage Association (NAWSA) Organization founded in 1890, headed by Carrie Chapman Catt, that sought a constitutional amendment to give women the right to vote. (20)

National Association for the Advancement of Colored People (NAACP) Civil rights organization founded in 1909 that was innovative in establishing legal action as a powerful basis of the fight for African American rights. (20)

National Association of Colored Women (NACW) A group organized in 1896, and made up largely of black middle-class women, that addressed the needs of black neighborhoods by establishing hospitals, day nurseries, and kindergartens and also attacked segregation and lynching. The organization's motto was "Lifting as We Climb." (20)

National Organization for Women (NOW) An organization founded in 1966 that advocated an end to laws that discriminated against women, opportunity to work at any job, and equal pay for equal work. (27)

National Origins Act of 1924 Congressional act that established strict immigration ceilings and quotas favoring northern European immigrants; it served as the basis of immigration policy until 1965. (22)

National Parks Act of 1916 Congressional act that created the National Park Service and aimed, in part, to preserve national park lands and "leave them unimpaired for the enjoyment of future generations." (20)

National Recovery Administration (NRA) Early and unsuccessful New Deal effort to promote industrial recovery from the Great Depression. The NRA wrote "production codes" for each industry that encouraged cooperation among competing businesses to set stable prices and wages. (23)

National Security Act of 1947 Congressional act that consolidated the U.S. military command. Under the new system, a representative from each military branch would advise a newly created secretary of defense and the president through the Joint Chiefs of Staff Office. (25)

National Security League A private patriotic organization founded in 1916 to promote military preparedness and to push for the "Americanization" of recent immigrants. (21)

National Woman's Party (NWP) A party founded in 1916 by Alice Paul and like-minded suffragists that conducted numerous protests to win women the right to vote, including marches and "silent sentinels" picketing outside of the White House. (20)

Native American Graves Protection and Repatriation Act (1990) Congressional act that encourages ethical research by requiring federally funded institutions to share information about human remains as well as sacred and culturally significant items with descendant communities, which may also arrange for repatriation. (1)

Nativism A rejection of foreigners and foreign influence. This term can be applied to followers of the Delaware prophet Neolin, who in the mid-1700s sought to purge Indian country of British settlers as well as ideas and goods from Britain. Later, it became a name given to a strong anti-immigration, anti-Catholic activist movement that flourished in America from the 1830s to the 1850s and the 1890s to the 1920s. The term "nativists" was given to those who strongly opposed the influx of immigrants into American society. (5, 18)

Nativists Political organizations that formed in the mid 1840s, particularly in New York and other northern cities. Nativists shared general goals: to restrict office holding to native-born Americans, to retain the Bible in schools, and to extend the naturalization process from 5 to 21 years. Although these groups had little electoral success, they established the basis for the network of secret fraternal associations known collectively as the Know Nothings that emerged in the 1850s. (13)

Navigation Acts One of a series of English regulations and taxes on colonial trade dating from 1650 to 1775. (3, 4, 6)

Neoconservatives A small but influential coalition of Democrats and Republicans who rejected many of the tenets of liberalism and détente and called for more limited government at home and a more muscular military stance abroad. (29)

Neutrality Acts Series of congressional laws passed between 1935 and 1939 restricting the power of the president and of private citizens and businesses to aid foreign nations at war. (24)

New Deal Collective name given to President Franklin Roosevelt's programs to fight the Great Depression, first articulated during his 1932 presidential campaign. He pledged to use federal power to ensure a more equitable distribution of income and rebuild the economy from the bottom up. (23)

New England Company The first Protestant missionary organization, founded by Puritans in 1649, that focused on Native peoples of the Northeast. Led by a board of prominent New England colonists, the company appointed missionaries and teachers in an attempt to convert and Anglicize Indians. (3)

New Freedom Name given to Woodrow Wilson's 1912 presidential platform, which promised an attack on "bigness" in government and business, and his advocacy for small business and fair competition enforced by only minimal government interference. (20)

New Frontier Name given to President John F. Kennedy's collection of programs to expand economic and social opportunities in the United States. (27)

New Left Counterculture protest movement of the 1960s whose young activists intentionally distanced themselves from the ideological infighting, Marxist leanings, and labor organizing of the Old Left of the 1930s and 1940s. (27)

New Look President Dwight Eisenhower's military reorganization of 1954 that established the central philosophy of the doctrine of "massive retaliation" linked to expanded espionage as more economically feasible than containment alone. (26)

New Nationalism Name given to President Theodore Roosevelt's platform in 1912 that advocated expansive government activism and regulation for the public interest. (20)

New Woman A term first applied to women in the 1890s who defied traditional middle- and upper-class Victorian feminine ideals by emphasizing education, work outside the home, woman suffrage, and vigorous physical activity. (22)

New world order An idea proclaimed by President George H. W. Bush in 1989 in which the United States, the world's preeminent superpower, would lead multinational coalitions to enforce its standards of international behavior. (30)

Nineteenth Amendment (1920) Constitutional amendment granting women the right to vote. (20)

No Child Left Behind (NCLB) Act Program proposed by President George W. Bush in 2001 to improve educational outcomes for poor and minority children. It renewed federal funding for several existing school programs and provided some additional money for reading and math instruction. In return, all states had to implement "standards based educational reform," a term that in practice meant standardized testing of students in reading and math. (31)

Nongovernmental organizations (NGOs) Independent groups that supported foreign relations and political programs and fostered the growth of global capitalism during the Cold War. (25)

Non-Intercourse Act (1809) Congressional act that reopened trade with countries other than Britain and France. (8)

North American Free Trade Agreement (NAFTA) Trade agreement approved by Democrats and Republicans in 1993 during the administration of President Bill Clinton. This agreement lifted barriers to trade between the United States, Mexico, and Canada; nearly all conventional economists believed that it would lift living standards in these countries. (30)

North Atlantic Treaty Organization (NATO) The organization created in 1949 by Western leaders as an alliance for mutual defense against the Soviet Union. (25)

Obergefell v. Hodges Supreme Court decision in 2015 holding that the Fourteenth Amendment guaranteed same-sex couples the right to marry. (31)

Occupy Wall Street Protest movement active in 2011 that criticized predatory banks and corporations. (31)

Ohio Company of Virginia A group of land speculators composed mainly of well-connected British planters to whom the state of Virginia had granted over 300,000 acres by early 1745. They opened the door to British trade in the South, competing with the already established French traders. (5)

Olive Branch Petition (1775) Petition sent by the Continental Congress to King George III of England seeking his intervention in the conflict with Parliament over taxes. (6)

Open Door Policy Principles drafted in 1899 by Secretary of State John Hay requesting that European powers put an end to the further partitioning of China and open up areas of China claimed by each power to allow them to compete fairly for Chinese trade. These policies asked for unhindered access to markets where they could compete successfully against economic rivals. (19)

Organization of Petroleum Exporting Countries (OPEC) Cartel organized by major oil-producing nations to boost prices for crude oil that became effective in the 1970s. (28)

PAC—see Political action committee. (29)

Palmer Raids Series of actions by federal agents in 1919 and 1920 to arrest and deport radical immigrants. (21)

Pan-Africanism An international movement that aimed to unite peoples of African descent around the world to seek equal rights and cast off white supremacy and colonialism. (22)

Panama Canal A canal opened in 1914 linking the Atlantic and Pacific oceans that enhanced access to U.S. colonies in the Pacific as well as trade with Asia but poisoned U.S. relations with Latin American countries because of the questionable way that the United States gained rights to build the canal. (19)

Parliament Legislative body of the British government. (3)

Patient Protection and Affordable Care Act Also known as "Obamacare," law passed in 2010 that mandated broad health insurance coverage for both employees at larger firms and those without health coverage. (31)

Peace Policy An agreement organized by General Ely Samuel Parker in which the Indian commissioners and leaders of various Christian denominations provided Indians with food and clothing in exchange for promises to abandon cultural traditions and to assimilate into American society. (16)

Pendleton Civil Service Act (1883) Congressional act that established the modern civil service and initiated an examination for a classified list of federal jobs, including most government departments, custom house jobs, and post office positions. (18)

Pentagon Papers Popular name given to a collection of classified government documents that were illegally made public in 1971. The documents outlined decision making by the U.S. Defense Department during the period from World War II to the Vietnam War. (28)

People's (Populist) Party A third party made up largely of rural people frustrated with the unresponsiveness of the Republican and Democratic parties to their pressing needs. The People's Party ran candidates for president in 1892 and 1896 on a platform demanding major reforms, including government ownership of railroads, a graduated income tax, and the free coinage of silver. (18)

Pequot War (1636–1638) Conflict between the Pequot Indians of the Connecticut River valley and British colonists and their Indian allies. (2)

Pietism A Protestant religious movement that linked North America, Britain, the Netherlands, and central Europe. Pietists promoted the personal piety of believers and the evangelization of all, includng American Indians and enslaved Africans. (4)

Pinckney's Treaty (1795) A treaty with Spain that fully opened Mississippi River trade to the United States, provided tax-free markets in New Orleans, settled Florida border issues, and guaranteed Spanish help against Southwest Indians who moved to block U.S. settlers from expanding the West. (8)

Plantation Act of 1740 British parliamentary act that allowed non-Catholic aliens who resided for at least seven years in British North America, received communion in a Protestant church, swore allegiance to George II, and paid two shillings to become citizens. (5)

Platt Amendment (1901) Amendment to the new Cuban constitution that gave the United States broad authority to intervene to preserve Cuban independence and required Cuba to sell or lease land for U.S. naval stations and coaling bases. (19)

Plessy v. Ferguson (1896) U.S. Supreme Court decision that upheld the legality of Jim Crow laws by declaring that segregation based on race was constitutional as long as "separate" facilities were "equal." It soon became clear, however, that facilities for black Americans, such as schools, railroad cars, and waiting rooms, were rarely, if ever, equal to those provided for whites. (20)

Political action committee (PAC) A private group dedicated to the election of a given political candidate or to the influencing of a policy decision in government. (29)

Political machines Political organizations established in most major U.S. cities by the late 19th century that offered a variety of services to constituents, especially immigrants, in exchange for votes and party loyalty. (18)

Polygamy A marriage custom of having more than one partner at the same time, such as a man with more than one wife. (4)

Pope's Day Also known as Guy Fawkes Day, an observance named after the rebel who attempted to blow up both houses of Parliament at Westminster in 1605. Fawkes and his coconspirators opposed Protestantism and wished to restore Catholic rule in England. Caught in the act, Fawkes was executed. Thereafter, British subjects, including North American colonists, celebrated the triumph of Protestantism with raucous festivities, including the burning of the pope in effigy. (4)

Popular sovereignty A policy established in the mid-19th century that permitted settlers in newly established western territories to decide on the policy of slavery for themselves. (7, 13)

Prigg v. Pennsylvania (1842) U.S. Supreme Court decision that established federal protection to southerners seeking to reclaim fugitive slaves who had escaped to the North. (13)

Privateer A government-contracted but privately owned warship used to attack foreign ships and disrupt trade. (1)

Proclamation of 1763 An order issued by King George III of England that prohibited settlements beyond a line west of the Appalachians running from the Hudson River south to Florida. (6)

Pro-slavery defense Based on the idea of racial supremacy espoused by prominent scientists of the day, such as Louis Agassiz and Josiah Nott, pro-slavery defenders joined this modern argument to older endorsements of slavery, reaching back to the ancient Greeks and Romans and to the Bible. (11)

Protestantism A Christian reform movement that arose in Europe during the 1500s and denied the authority of the Catholic Church. (1)

Pueblo War for Independence (1680–1696) A revolt by a diverse coalition of Pueblo Indians that succeeded in forcing Spanish colonists out of New Mexico for over a decade. (3)

Pullman Strike A strike led by Eugene V. Debs and the American Railway Union in 1894 in response to massive wage cuts at the Pullman Palace Car Company. The strike and boycott of trains pulling Pullman cars froze rail service in the Midwest and slowed it elsewhere until federal troops helped crush it. (17)

Pure Food and Drug Act (1906) Congressional act that outlawed adulterated or mislabeled food and drugs and gave the federal government the right to seize illegal products and to fine and jail those who manufactured and sold them. (20)

Puritans Europeans who followed the Christian teachings of theologian John Calvin, defied the Catholic Church, and sought to place the governance of church affairs in the hands of local officials, ministers, and elders. (1)

Queen Anne's War (1702–1713) A war fought between the British and French for control of North American colonies, simultaneous with a war in Europe over the Spanish monarchy. (4)

Quitrent A land tax or rent imposed on colonists by their European governing body. (3)

Reaganomics Informal term for policy of cutting taxes on the well-to-do and reducing government regulation of business to promote growth. (29)

Reconquista Expansion of western European Christian nations during the 1400s into Muslim settlements on the Iberian Peninsula. (1)

Reconstruction Finance Corporation (RFC, 1932) Federal program of President Herbert Hoover to loan money to struggling banks, railroads, manufacturers, and mortgage companies during the Great Depression. (23)

Redemptioners In the 18th century, indentured servants who paid for their passage across the Atlantic by selling their services when they landed. (5)

Requerimiento (1513) A Spanish royal decree read by conquistadors to Native groups in the Americas that encouraged them to either submit to Christianity and Spanish rule or face warfare and slavery. (1)

Rerum novarum A papal encyclical from Pope Leo XIII, issued in 1891, condemning the exploitation of laborers and supporting state intervention to promote social justice. (20)

Revivalists Leaders and advocates of various evangelical Protestant campaigns of the First Great Awakening in the 18th century. Revivalists sought to rekindle widespread religious enthusiasm in the American colonies. (5)

Roe v. Wade (1973) U.S. Supreme Court decision upholding a woman's constitutional right to terminate a pregnancy. (29)

Roosevelt Corollary A corollary to the Monroe Doctrine articulated by President Theodore Roosevelt in 1904 that declared that the United States had the right to intervene in the affairs of Latin American nations to ensure order. (19)

Rough Riders Colonel Theodore Roosevelt and his First Volunteer Cavalry Regiment, who became national heroes for their daring exploits during the Spanish-American War. (19)

Royal African Company A British mercantile firm that received the royal monopoly on trade in Africa. Active in the gold trade, by 1663 the company possessed exclusive rights to buy and transport slaves across the Atlantic for sale in British colonies. (3)

Royal Orders for New Discoveries (1573) Decree by King Philip II of Spain that missionaries should play the principal role in exploring, pacifying, and colonizing new territories; it also mandated that baptized Indians should live on missions, learn to speak Spanish, keep livestock, cultivate European crops, and use European tools to master European crafts. (2)

Royal Society An elite organization founded in London that connected colonists and residents of the capital in the pursuit of scientific evidence and investigation. (3)

Russo-Japanese War A 1904 war between Russia and Japan sparked by rival imperial claims in Asia. President Theodore Roosevelt brokered a peace treaty between the two countries in 1905, earning him the Nobel Peace Prize. (19)

St. Augustine First Spanish settlement in North America, founded in 1565. (1)

Salutary neglect Name given to the practice of colonists to defy or ignore British laws that they found onerous, often with the complicity of those charged with enforcing them. (4)

Science lag Term used to describe the perceived disparity between U.S. and Soviet education programs during the Cold War. (26)

Scopes Trial Highly publicized 1925 trial of Tennessee high school science teacher John Scopes, who was found guilty of teaching the theory of evolution in violation of state law. (22)

Secession The act of withdrawing formally from an existing union with another political state. (14)

Second Anglo-Dutch War (1664-67) Fought between England and the United Provinces for control over the seas and trade routes. (3)

Second Bill of Rights List of "economic bill of rights," proposed by President Franklin D. Roosevelt in 1944, that guaranteed every citizen a job, a living wage, decent housing, adequate medical care, educational opportunity, and protection against unemployment in postwar America. (24)

Second Great Awakening Religious revivalist movement of the early 19th century that echoed the Great Awakening of the 1730s. The movement linked evangelical Christians on both sides of the Atlantic to exchange ideas and strategies that inspired a broad set of social, cultural, and intellectual changes. (9, 12)

Securities Act of 1933 Congressional act that required companies selling stock to the public to register with a federal agency and provide accurate information on what was being sold. (23)

Securities Exchange Act of 1934 Congressional act that created the Securities and Exchange Commission to regulate stock markets and activities by brokers. (23)

Sedition Act (1918) Amendments to the Espionage Act of 1917 that added a variety of offenses to the list of prohibited acts, including the use of "disloyal, profane, scurrilous, or abusive language about the form of government of the United States, or the Constitution of the United States." (20)

Separation of powers Political concept articulated by French Enlightenment philosopher the Baron de Montesquieu that each state should establish a balance between executive, legislative, and judicial powers. (7)

September 11 Shorthand for attacks on the World Trade Center and Pentagon that took place on September 11, 2001. (31)

Settler colonialism A distinctive colonizing strategy (different from trade- or mission-based colonialism) whereby collections of immigrants from foreign places used their numbers to gain control of territory and resources from indigenous peoples. (5)

Seventeenth Amendment (1913) Constitutional amendment that mandated the direct election of U.S. senators. (20)

Sharecroppers Farmers who rented land or farmed on shares, splitting the proceeds from the yearly crop with the landlord. (15)

Shays' Rebellion (1786–1787) An armed insurrection by indebted Massachusetts farmers, led by Daniel Shays, to prevent the state government from seizing their property. (7)

***Shelly v. Kraemer* (1948)** U.S. Supreme Court case outlawing racial housing covenants. (26)

Sherman Antitrust Act (1890) Congressional act aimed at dismantling combinations and trusts that restrained trade. It was the first U.S. law to restrict business monopolies, but loopholes and court decisions rendered it largely ineffective. (17)

Sixteenth Amendment (1913) Constitutional amendment that authorized a federal income tax on both personal and corporate income. (20)

Smoot–Hawley Tariff of 1930 A tariff passed in 1930 at the onset of the Great Depression that made it especially difficult for international manufacturers to sell their products in the United States, resulting in retaliatory tariffs that worsened the international economy. (22)

Social Darwinism A theory, popularized by Herbert Spencer, that purported that Charles Darwin's theory of evolution could be applied to human society as well. This belief that society evolved and improved through competition in which the "fittest" survived justified noninterference by the government in the economy and workplace as well as the massive fortunes amassed by industrialists. (16, 17)

Social Gospel A broad, multidimensional, and international movement among Protestants in the late 19th and early 20th centuries that insisted that Christian principles needed to be applied to social problems. (18)

Social Security Act (1935) Congressional act that established a federally administered retirement system for workers at age 65, funded primarily by contributions—payroll taxes—from workers and employers, not general tax revenues. (23)

Society for the Propagation of the Gospel in Foreign Parts (SPG) Anglican reform organization founded in 1701 for sending missionaries to North America and the West Indies. (4)

Society of Friends ("Quakers") A Christian religious sect that broke from the Church of England and established itself in America during the 17th century. (3)

Soft power The use of marketing and selling of culture products in support of political and military policies. During the Cold War the selling of American culture and ideology through global marketing of everything from Levi's jeans and Coca-Cola to music and movies played a central role in Cold War foreign policy. (25)

Sons of Liberty Groups of colonial protestors, originating with the 1765 Stamp Act, who spread anti-British sentiment between colonies. (6)

Spanish Civil War Successful revolt by the Spanish army, with assistance from Germany and Italy, to overthrow the democratic government of Spain. (24)

Stagflation A slowly growing economy with high rates of unemployment and inflation. (28)

Stamp Act (1765) British parliamentary act that required that many forms of colonial printed materials and products be affixed with revenue stamps, or taxes, paid to the British. (6)

Stono Rebellion (1739) The largest uprising of enslaved Africans in mainland North America during the 18th century in which 80 or more slaves burned South Carolina plantations as they marched toward Spanish Florida. (5)

Subprime mortgages Home loans offered to buyers with poor credit histories. Fees made these profitable to lenders but often resulted in defaults and foreclosures. (31)

Sunbelt Band of warm-climate states of the southern and southwest United States that grew in political, cultural, and economic significance after massive post–World War II migrations. (27)

Tariff A tax on imported goods. (10, 18)

Task system One of two general types of division of labor of plantation slaves, the other being the gang system. The task system assigned individuals specific tasks. Rather than being part of a group that worked continuously to the day's end, the task system allowed individuals to end their workday when their task was done and thus granted them more autonomy. (5)

Tax Act of 1916 A revenue law that substantially raised taxes on high-income Americans and expanded the estate tax on inherited wealth. (21)

Tea Party Grassroots conservative movement active from 2010 that called for limited government. (31)

Teapot Dome Scandal Bribery scandal, uncovered in 1924, implicating Secretary of the Interior Albert Fall, a member of President Warren Harding's cabinet who took bribes in return for lucrative leases to drill for oil on government-owned land. (22)

Teller Amendment (1898) An amendment to Congress's declaration of war in April 1898 that stated that the United States would not colonize Cuba. (19)

Tennessee Valley Authority (TVA) Federal agency created in 1933 to construct a network of dams and hydroelectric projects to control floods, generate power, and promote growth in a chronically poor area of the South. (23)

Third World Term used to classify mostly nonwhite nations considered inferior to "First World" nations such as the United States and its Western allies. (25)

Thirteenth Amendment (1865) Constitutional amendment that outlawed slavery in the United States. (15)

Timucua Revolt (1656) A rebellion that exposed tensions in colonial Florida under Spanish rule. The Timucua, a diverse group of Florida Indians, accepted Catholic missions but rebelled against abusive labor and military policies enforced by Florida's Spanish governor, Diego de Rebolledo. Ultimately, the Timucua lost the conflict and were forced to resettle, but their actions forced Rebolledo to stand trial in Spain. (3)

Townshend Acts (1767) British parliamentary acts that taxed common goods in the colonies such as tea and other commodities.

The acts represented Britain's resolve to control and regulate the colonies. (6)

Trail of Tears Cherokee name for the United States' forced removal of their people from the Southeast to other lands. In early 1838, few Cherokee had prepared for the trip; contaminated water, inadequate food, and disease killed many of those restricted in stockades, and many more perished on the 800-mile journey west. (11)

Transcendentalism An American variant of European Romanticism which turned away from the ratioof the Enlightenment. Transcendentalists desired to know the world through emotion and intuition. (12)

Transportation Act (1718) British parliamentary act that mandated the exile of convicted criminals to North America, mostly those who had committed property crimes such as theft. (4)

Treaty of Guadalupe Hidalgo Treaty between the United States and Mexico that ended the Mexican-American War, signed on February 2nd, 1848. In exchange for $15 million, Mexico ceded to the United States Texas, and all of the land west of Texas stretching up to Oregon, including California. (13)

Treaty of Paris (1763) The treaty ending the French and Indian War. The terms of the treaty transformed eastern North America's political geography. France surrendered North America, swapping Canada for the return of Guadeloupe. France ceded Louisiana to Spain, and Spain traded Florida to the British to regain control of Havana. The British Empire claimed almost all of North America east of the Mississippi. (5)

Treaty of Tordesillas (1494) Treaty signed by Spain and Portugal that divided newly discovered lands between them, specifically those in Africa (to Portugal) and those associated with Columbus (to Spain). (1)

Treaty of Versailles (1919) The treaty that ended World War I and created independent Poland, Czechoslovakia, Yugoslavia, Hungary, Finland, and the Baltic states of Latvia, Lithuania, and Estonia. (20)

Triangle fire A raging fire that in March 1911 swept through the Triangle Shirtwaist Company in New York City, killing 146 workers, mostly young women, and leading to a series of workplace reforms. (20)

Truman Doctrine Policy announced by President Harry Truman in 1947 whereby the United States pledged to defend allies against Communist threats. (25)

Tuscarora War (1711–1715) A revolt by Tuscarora Indians against colonists in North America sparked by grievances over the Indian slave trade and land theft. (4)

U.S. Colored Troops (USCT) Black troops consisting of freed black men and former slaves who enlisted in the Union Army after the Emancipation Proclamation of January 1, 1863. (14)

United Colonies of New England (1643) Union of the Massachusetts Bay, Plymouth, Connecticut, and New Haven colonies to bolster their mutual defenses and negotiations with Indians. (2)

United Fruit Company A Boston-based company originally established for importing bananas to the United States from Latin America. It was known as "the Octopus" for its involvement and influence in the affairs of Honduras, Guatemala, and Costa Rica. (19)

United Mine Workers (UMW) An industry-wide union for mine workers founded in 1890. (17)

United Nations (UN) An organization open to all nations, established in 1945, for maintaining world peace. It is headquartered in New York. (24)

United Nations Security Council A 15-member council tasked under the UN Charter signed on October 24, 1945, with "maintenance of international peace and security." Member nations of the Security Council were obligated under the Charter to comply with Council decisions and resolutions. (25)

United States v. E. C. Knight Co. (1895) U.S. Supreme Court decision that weakened the Sherman Antitrust Act by declaring that the federal government could regulate only monopolies engaged in interstate commerce. (17)

Universal Negro Improvement Association (UNIA) Pan-African organization founded by black nationalist leader Marcus Garvey that emphasized black separatism and "Africa for Africans." (22)

USA PATRIOT Act (2001) Congressional act that expanded the Justice Department's powers to conduct surveillance on terrorist suspects at home abroad. (31)

Vertical integration A hallmark of the modern corporation that cut costs and guaranteed a flow of raw materials by controlling both the production and distribution processes. (17)

Vice-admiralty courts Colonial courts established by the English Board of Trade to enforce the Navigation Act of 1696. (4)

Virginia Company of London English joint-stock company established in 1606 by a royal charter that gave it exclusive rights to colonize from New England south to Virginia. (2)

Voting Rights Act (1965) Congressional act that outlawed literacy tests to vote and gave the Justice Department the power directly to register voters in districts where discrimination existed. (27)

War of Jenkins' Ear (1739–1742) A conflict sparked by an imperial rivalry between Britain and Spain that ensured British primacy in the Southeast and led to the legalization of African slavery in Georgia. (5)

Watergate scandal Composite term for illegal political acts by Nixon administration that culminated in the 1972 burglary of the Democratic Party headquarters and subsequent cover-up. (28)

Whig Party American political party formed in 1834 that supported government investments in infrastructure to stimulate business and, in some parts of the North, endorsed moderate antislavery politics. (6, 11)

Whiskey Rebellion (1794) Violent uprising in western Pennsylvania by farmers who refused to pay a federal tax on liquor. (8)

Williams v. Mississippi (1898) The U.S. Supreme Court decision that upheld Mississippi's disfranchisement amendment aimed at eliminating the black vote. (20)

Women's Christian Temperance Union (WCTU) The nation's largest female reform organization of the 19th century, formed in 1874, specifically dedicated to the banning of intoxicating beverages. The WCTU also sought the vote for women. (18)

Works Progress Administration (WPA) The largest and most ambitious New Deal relief and recovery program. Created in 1935, it employed millions of workers and built much of the nation's public infrastructure. (23)

XYZ Affair (1797–1998) Name given to a scandal caused by French diplomats demanding bribes from American diplomats, leading to a rise in tensions between the United States and France. (8)

Yamasee War (1715–1717) A multinational uprising of Native Americans in the Southeast that challenged colonialism in South Carolina and led to the decline of the Indian slave trade in that region. (4)

Yellow journalism Name given to sensationalist newspaper journalism of the late 19th century. This type of journalism provoked widespread public support for the Cuban rebels. (19)

Yeomen The term applied in the 18th and early 19th centuries to self-sufficient farmers who owned small plots of land, an idealized type. (9)

CREDITS

MAP, FIGURE, AND TABLE SOURCES

Maps by International Mapping.

America in the World (Population) Source(s): United States Population Division; United Nations, Department of Economic and Social Affairs, Population Division (2011). *World Population Prospects: The 2010 Revision*; Massimo Livi Bacci, *A Concise History of World Population* (Wiley-Blackwell, 2001).

CHAPTER 1

Map 1.1   Source(s): Helen Hornbeck Tanner, ed., *The Settling of North America: The Atlas of the Great Migrations into North America from the Ice Age to the Present* (New York: MacMillan, 1995), 29; Mark C. Carnes, ed., *Historical Atlas of the United States* (New York: Routledge, 2003), 20–21.

Map 1.2   Source(s): Michael Coe et al., *Atlas of Ancient North America* (New York: Facts on File, 1986), 44–45.

Map 1.3   Source(s): Mark Kishlansky et al., *Societies and Culture in World History* (New York: Harper Collins, 1995), 414; *The Oxford Atlas of Exploration*, 2nd edition (New York: Oxford University Press, 2008), 34; Patrick K. O'Brien, gen. ed., *The Oxford Atlas of World History*, concise ed. (New York: Oxford University Press, 2002), 116–17.

Map 1.4   Source(s): D. W. Meinig, *The Shaping of America: A Geographic Perspective on 500 Years of History: Volume 1: Atlantic America, 1492–1800* (New Haven: Yale University Press, 1986), 5; Alfred W. Crosby, *Ecological Imperialism: The Biological Expansion of Europe, 900–1900* (New York: Cambridge University Press, 1985), 110; Albert C. Jensen, *The Cod* (New York: Thomas Y. Crowell, 1972), 3; Patrick K. O'Brien, gen. ed., *The Oxford Atlas of World History*, concise ed. (New York: Oxford University Press, 2002), 116–17.

Map 1.6   Source(s): Peter Bakewell, *A History of Latin America*, 2nd edition (Malden, Mass.: Blackwell, 2004), xxii.

Map 1.7   Source(s): *The Oxford Atlas of Exploration*, 2nd edition (New York: Oxford University Press, 2008), 34, 124; Patrick K. O'Brien, gen. ed., *The Oxford Atlas of World History*, concise ed. (New York: Oxford University Press, 2002), 120.

CHAPTER 2

Map 2.1   Source(s): *The Cambridge History of the Native Peoples of the Americas: Volume 1: North America: Part I*, eds. Bruce G. Trigger and Wilcomb E. Washburn (New York: Cambridge University Press, 1996), 345, 346; *The Oxford Atlas of Exploration*, 2nd edition (New York: Oxford University Press, 2008), 124.

Map 2.2   Source(s): *The Cambridge History of the Native Peoples of the Americas: Volume 1: North America: Part I*, ed. Bruce G. Trigger and Wilcomb E. Washburn (New York: Cambridge University Press, 1996), 341.

Map 2.3 Source(s): *The Cambridge History of the Native Peoples of the Americas: Volume 1: North America: Part I*, ed. Bruce G. Trigger and Wilcomb E. Washburn (New York: Cambridge University Press, 1996), 405; *The Settling of North America: The Atlas of the Great Migration into North America from the Ice Age to the Present*, ed. Helen Hornbeck Tanner (New York: MacMillan, 1995), 42; James Oakes et al., *Of the People: A History of the United States* (New York, Oxford: Oxford University Press, 2010), 77.

Map 2.4 Source(s): Jenny Hale Pulsipher, *Subjects unto the Same King: Indians, English, and the Contest for Authority in Colonial New England* (Philadelphia: University of Pennsylvania Press, 2005), 78.

CHAPTER 3

Map 3.1 Source(s): *The Historical Atlas of Canada*, ed. R. Cole Harris (Toronto: University of Toronto Press, 1987), Volume 1, Plate 35.

Map 3.2 Source(s): David Eltis and David Richardson, *Atlas of the Transatlantic Slave Trade* (New Haven: Yale University Press, 2010), 18–19; Assessing the Slave Trade. 2009. *Voyages: The Trans-Atlantic Slave Trade Database.* http://www.slavevoyages.org (accessed November 29, 2011); Gregory O'Malley, "Beyond the Middle Passage: Slave Migration from the Caribbean to North America, 1619–1807," *The William and Mary Quarterly*, 3rd Series, 66 (January 2009), 141–42, 146, 160–61, 163.

Map 3.3 Source(s): Mark C. Carnes, ed., *Historical Atlas of the United States* (New York: Routledge, 2003), 48.

Map 3.4 Source(s): *The Cambridge History of the Native Peoples of the Americas: Volume 1: North America: Part I*, ed. Bruce G. Trigger and Wilcomb E. Washburn (New York: Cambridge University Press, 1996), 416, 426; Andrew K. Frank, ed., *The Routledge Historical Atlas of the American South* (New York: Routledge, 1999), 20.

Figure 3.1 Source(s): Assessing the Slave Trade. 2009. *Voyages: The Trans-Atlantic Slave Trade Database.* http://www.slavevoyages.org (accessed November 29, 2011).

Figure 3.2 Source(s): David Eltis, *The Rise of African Slavery in the Americas* (New York: Cambridge University Press, 2000), 9.

Figure 3.3 Source(s): David W. Galenson, *White Servitude in Colonial America: An Economic Analysis* (New York: Cambridge University Press, 1981), 83, 84.

Table 3.1 Source(s): Assessing the Slave Trade. 2009. *Voyages: The Trans-Atlantic Slave Trade Database.* http://www.slavevoyages .org (accessed November 29, 2011).

Table 3.2 Source(s): Richard Middleton, *Colonial America: A History*, 3rd edition (Oxford, England: Blackwell, 2002); Charles M. Andrews, *The Colonial Period of American History*, *Volume 4: England's Commercial and Colonial Policy* (New Haven: Yale University Press, 1938).

CHAPTER 4

Map 4.1 Source(s): Carl Waldman, *Atlas of the North American Indian*, 3rd edition (New York: Facts on File, 2009), 79; Colin G. Calloway, *First Peoples: A Documentary Survey of American Indian History*, 3rd edition (Boston: Bedford/St. Martin's, 2008), 295.

Map 4.2 Source(s): Paul Kelton, *Epidemics and Enslavement: Biological Catastrophe in the Native Southeast, 1492–1715* (Lincoln: University of Nebraska Press, 2007), 201.

Map 4.3 Source(s): David Eltis and David Richardson, *Atlas of the Transatlantic Slave Trade* (New Haven: Yale University Press, 2010), 18–19; Assessing the Slave Trade. 2009. *Voyages: The Trans-Atlantic Slave Trade Database.* http://www.slavevoyages .org (accessed November 29, 2011).

Map 4.4 Source(s): Mark C. Carnes, ed., *Historical Atlas of the United States* (New York: Routledge, 2003), 73.

Figure 4.1   Source(s): Assessing the Slave Trade. 2009. *Voyages: The Trans-Atlantic Slave Trade Database.* http://www.slavevoyages.org (accessed November 29, 2011).

Table 4.1   Source(s): Aaron S. Fogleman, "Migrations to the Thirteen British North American Colonies, 1700–1775: New Estimates," *Journal of Interdisciplinary History* 22 (1992), 691–709; Assessing the Slave Trade. 2009. *Voyages: The Trans-Atlantic Slave Trade Database.* http://www.slavevoyages.org (accessed November 29, 2011).

CHAPTER 5

Map 5.1   Source(s): David Eltis and David Richardson, *Atlas of the Transatlantic Slave Trade* (New Haven: Yale University Press, 2010), 18–19; Assessing the Slave Trade. 2009. *Voyages: The Trans-Atlantic Slave Trade Database.* http://www.slavevoyages.org (accessed November 29, 2011).

Map 5.2   Source(s): Mark C. Carnes, ed., *Historical Atlas of the United States* (New York: Routledge, 2003), 59.

Map 5.3   Source(s): Mark C. Carnes, ed., *Historical Atlas of the United States* (New York: Routledge, 2003), 58; Andrew K. Frank, ed., *The Routledge Historical Atlas of the American South* (New York: Routledge, 1999), 20.

Map 5.4   Source(s): Robert H. Ferrell and Richard Natkiel, *Atlas of American History* (New York: Facts on File, 1987, 1993), 30; Mark C. Carnes, ed., *Historical Atlas of the United States* (New York: Routledge, 2003), 58.

Map 5.6   Source(s): Robert H. Ferrell and Richard Natkiel, *Atlas of American History* (New York: Facts on File, 1987, 1993), 16; *Historical Atlas of Canada*, R. Cole Harris, ed. (Toronto: University of Toronto Press, 1987), Volume 1, Plate 30.

Map 5.7   Source(s): *Historical Atlas of Canada*, R. Cole Harris, ed. (Toronto: University of Toronto Press, 1987), Volume 1, Plate 30.

Figure 5.1   Source(s): Assessing the Slave Trade. 2009. *Voyages: The Trans- Atlantic Slave Trade Database.* http://www.slavevoyages.org (accessed November 29, 2011).

Figure 5.2   Source(s): Jay Coughtry, *The Notorious Triangle: Rhode Island and the African Slave Trade, 1700–1807* (Philadelphia: Temple University Press, 1981), 34.

Figure 5.3   Source(s): Jacob Cooke, ed., *Encyclopedia of North American Colonies* (New York: Scribner's, 1993), 1, 470.

Table 5.1   Source(s): Aaron S. Fogleman, "Migrations to the Thirteen British North American Colonies, 1700–1775: New Estimates," *Journal of Interdisciplinary History* 22 (1992), 691–709; Assessing the Slave Trade. 2009. *Voyages: The Trans-Atlantic Slave Trade Database.* http://www.slavevoyages .org (accessed November 29, 2011).

Table 5.2   Source(s): Richard Middleton, *Colonial America: A History*, 3rd edition (Oxford: Blackwell, 2002); Jack P. Greene, ed., *Settlements to Society: A Documentary History of Colonial America* (New York: W.W. Norton, 1975).

CHAPTER 8

Figure 8.1   Source(s): *Historical Statistics of the United States Millennial Edition Online*, eds. Susan B. Carter, Scott Sigmund Gartner, Michael R. Haines, Alan L. Olmstead, Richard Sutch, and Gavin Wright (Cambridge University Press, 2011).

CHAPTER 10

Map 10.2   Source(s): Steven Dutch, University of Wisconsin–Green Bay; C.O. Paullin, *Atlas of the Historical Geography of the United States* (Carnegie Institute, 1932, reproduced in facsimile by Greenwood Press, 1975).

CHAPTER 11

Map 11.3   Source(s): Nathanial Philbrick, *Sea of Glory: America's Voyage of Discovery, the U.S. Exploring Expedition, 1838–1842* (New York: Viking, 2003).

Figure 11.1 Source(s): *Historical Statistics of the United States, 1789–1945*. Dept. of the Census, 1949. Series B 304–330—Immigration— Immigrants by Country: 1820 to 1945.

Figure 11.2 Source(s): *Historical Statistics of the United States, 1789–1945*. Dept. of the Census, 1949. Series B 13–23: Population, Decennial Summary—Sex, Urban- Rural Residence, and Race: 1790 to 1940.

CHAPTER 12

Map 12.1   Source(s): John H. Thompson, *Geography of New York State* (New York: Syracuse University Press, 1966).

Map 12.2   Source(s): Kenneth Greenberg, *The Confessions of Nat Turner* (Bedford/St. Martins, 1996).

Figure 12.1 Source(s): Eighth U.S. Census. Schedule 1.

Figure 12.3 Source(s): Lyn Ragsdale, *Vital Statistics on the Presidency* (Washington, DC: Congressional Quarterly Press, 1998), 132–38.

CHAPTER 13

Figure 13.1 Source(s): Campbell J. Gibson and Emily Lennon, "Historical Census Statistics on the Foreign-Born Population of the United States: 1850–1990." Population Division, U.S. Bureau of the Census, Washington, DC 20233–8800. February 1999, POPULATION DIVISION WORKING PAPER NO. 29, Table 4. Region and Country or Area of Birth of the Foreign-Born Population.

CHAPTER 14

Map 14.1   Source(s): Aaron Sheehan-Dean, *Concise Historical Atlas of the U.S. Civil War* (New York: Oxford University Press, 2008).

Map 14.2   Source(s): Aaron Sheehan-Dean, *Concise Historical Atlas of the U.S. Civil War* (New York: Oxford University Press, 2008).

Map 14.3   Source(s): Aaron Sheehan-Dean, *Concise Historical Atlas of the U.S. Civil War* (New York: Oxford University Press, 2008).

Map 14.4   Source(s): Aaron Sheehan-Dean, *Concise Historical Atlas of the U.S. Civil War* (New York: Oxford University Press, 2008).

Figure 14.2 Source(s): Douglas B. Ball, *Financial Failure and Confederate Defeat* (Urbana: University of Illinois Press, 1991); J. G. Randall, *The Civil War and Reconstruction* (Boston: D.C. Heath, 1937); Richard Cecil Todd, *Confederate Finance* (Athens: University of Georgia Press, 1954).

CHAPTER 15

Map 15.1   Source(s): Aaron Sheehan-Dean, *Concise Historical Atlas of the U.S. Civil War* (New York: Oxford University Press, 2008).

Map 15.2   Source(s): Aaron Sheehan-Dean, *Concise Historical Atlas of the U.S. Civil War* (New York: Oxford University Press, 2008).

Map 15.3   Source(s): Aaron Sheehan-Dean, *Concise Historical Atlas of the U.S. Civil War* (New York: Oxford University Press, 2008).

Figure 15.1 Source(s): James L. Watkins, *King Cotton: A Historical and Statistical Review, 1790–1908* (New York: James L. Watkins and Sons, 1908).

PHOTO CREDITS

9.3: Courtesy of the Library of Congress

9.4: Courtesy of the Library of Congress, HABS CAL, 35-SAJUB, 1—4

9.7: Courtesy of the Library of Congress, HABS PA, 51-PHILA, 223—1

9.9: DeAgostini Picture Library/M. Seemuller/Bridgeman Images

Chapter 10

10.1: Courtesy of the Library of Congress, LC-USZ62-20478

10.3: Private Collection Photo © Christie's Images/Bridgeman Images

10.4: Private Collection Ken Welsh/Bridgeman Images

10.5: Courtesy of the Library of Congress

10.7: New York Public Library, USA/Bridgeman Images

Chapter 11

11.2: Courtesy of the Library of Congress, LC-DIG-ppmsca-24871

11.3: Granger NYC, All Rights Reserved

11.6: Granger NYC, All Rights Reserved

11.7: Granger NYC, All Rights Reserved

11.9: Saint Louis Art Museum, Missouri, USA Gift of Bank of America/Bridgeman Images

Chapter 12

12.1: Courtesy of the Library of Congress, LC-USZC4-772

12.5: Granger, NYC, All Rights Reserved

12.6: Library of Congress/Corbis/VCG via Getty Images

12.7: Granger NYC, All Rights Reserved.

Chapter 13

13.3: Courtesy of the Library of Congress, LC-DIG-ppmsca-02887

13.7: Wikimedia Commons, uncredited photo circa 1857

Chapter 14

14.5: Brooklyn Museum of Art, New York, USA Gift of Gwendolyn O.L. Conkling/Bridgeman Images

Chapter 15

15.3: Private Collection Peter Newark American Pictures/Bridgeman Images

15.4: Courtesy of the Library of Congress, LC-DIG-ds-07129

15.6: Courtesy of the Library of Congress, LC-DIG-det-4a26992

INDEX

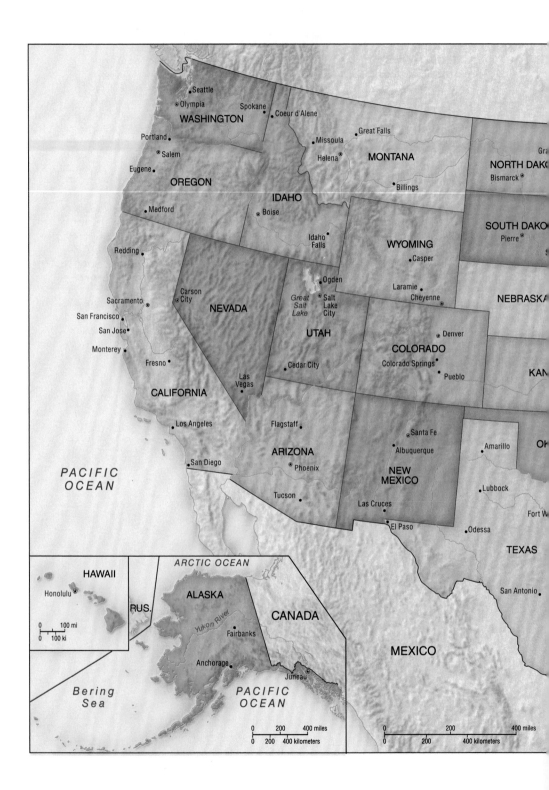

Seattle
Olympia
Spokane
Coeur d'Alene
WASHINGTON
Portland
Salem
Eugene
OREGON
Medford

Missoula
Great Falls
Helena
MONTANA
Billings

Gra
NORTH DAKO
Bismarck

IDAHO
Boise

Idaho
Falls

WYOMING
Casper

SOUTH DAKO
Pierre

S

Redding

Carson
City
Sacramento
San Francisco
San Jose
Monterey
Fresno
CALIFORNIA
Los Angeles

San Diego

PACIFIC
OCEAN

NEVADA

Ogden
Great
Salt
Lake
Salt
Lake
City
UTAH
Cedar City
Las
Vegas

Laramie
Cheyenne
NEBRASKA

Denver
COLORADO
Colorado Springs
Pueblo
KAN

Flagstaff

ARIZONA
Phoenix
Tucson

Santa Fe
Albuquerque
NEW
MEXICO
Las Cruces
El Paso

Amarillo
OK

Lubbock

Fort W
Odessa
TEXAS

San Antonio

HAWAII
Honolulu

ARCTIC OCEAN

ALASKA
RUS.

CANADA

Yukon River
Fairbanks

MEXICO

0   100 mi
0   100 ki

Anchorage

Juneau

Bering
Sea

PACIFIC
OCEAN

0   200   400 miles
0   200   400 kilometers

0   200   400 miles
0   200   400 kilometers

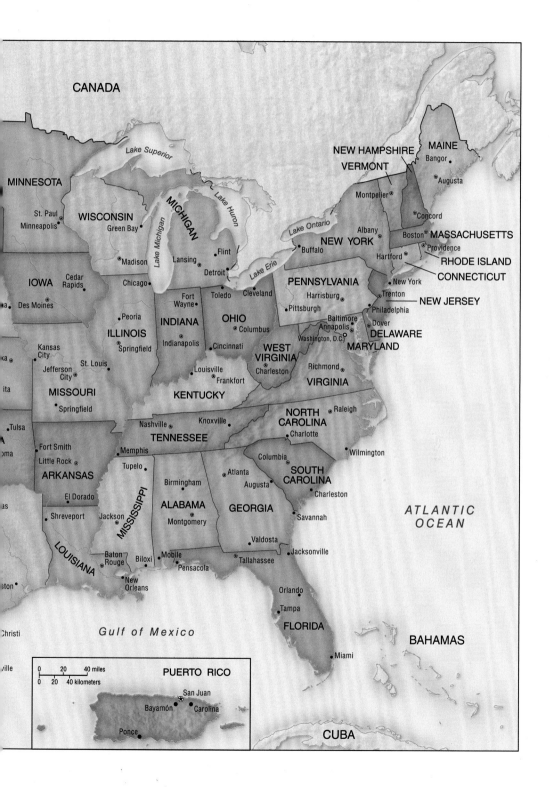

CANADA

MINNESOTA

Lake Superior

St. Paul
Minneapolis

WISCONSIN
Green Bay

MICHIGAN

Lake Huron

Lake Michigan

Madison

Lansing
Flint

IOWA
Cedar
Rapids

Chicago

Detroit

Lake Erie

Cleveland

NEW HAMPSHIRE
VERMONT

MAINE
Bangor

Augusta

Montpelier

Concord

Albany

Boston
MASSACHUSETTS
Providence

NEW YORK
Buffalo

Hartford
RHODE ISLAND
CONNECTICUT

Des Moines

Peoria

Fort
Wayne

Toledo

PENNSYLVANIA

New York

ILLINOIS

INDIANA

OHIO
Columbus

Harrisburg

Pittsburgh

Trenton
NEW JERSEY
Philadelphia

Kansas
City

Springfield

Indianapolis

Cincinnati

WEST
VIRGINIA

Baltimore
Annapolis

Dover
DELAWARE

Jefferson
City
St. Louis

Louisville

Charleston

Washington, D.C.

MARYLAND

MISSOURI
Springfield

Frankfort

KENTUCKY

Richmond

VIRGINIA

Tulsa

Nashville
Knoxville

NORTH
CAROLINA

Raleigh

Fort Smith
Little Rock

Memphis

TENNESSEE

Charlotte

Columbia

Wilmington

ARKANSAS

El Dorado

Shreveport

Tupelo

Jackson

Birmingham

Atlanta

Augusta

SOUTH
CAROLINA

Charleston

LOUISIANA

MISSISSIPPI

ALABAMA
Montgomery

GEORGIA

Savannah

ATLANTIC
OCEAN

Baton
Rouge

Biloxi
Mobile

Valdosta

New
Orleans

Pensacola

Tallahassee

Jacksonville

ston

Orlando

Tampa

BAHAMAS

Gulf of Mexico

FLORIDA

Miami

Christi

0   20   40 miles

0   20   40 kilometers

PUERTO RICO

ville

San Juan

Bayamón
Carolina

Ponce

CUBA

ARCTIC OCEAN

Beaufort
Sea

Baffin
Bay

Greenland
(DENMARK)

Greenland
Sea

Davis Strait

ICELAND

Hudson
Bay

Labrador
Sea

Bering Sea

Gulf of
Alaska

CANADA

IRELAND

UNITED
KINGDOM

BELGIUM
FRAN
SW

NORTH PACIFIC
OCEAN

UNITED STATES

NORTH ATLANTIC
OCEAN

PORTUGAL   SPAIN

30°N

MEXICO

Gulf of
Mexico

BAHAMAS

MOROCCO

ALGER

WESTERN
SAHARA
(Morocco)

CUBA
JAMAICA
BELIZE HONDURAS
GUATEMALA
EL SALVADOR NICARAGUA

HAITI

DOMINICAN
REPUBLIC

ANTIGUA & BARBUDA

DOMINICA
ST. LUCIA
BARBADOS
GRENADA
TRINIDAD AND TOBAGO

MAURITANIA

MALI

ST. KITTS & NEVIS

Caribbean
Sea

ST. VINCENT &
THE GRENADINES

CAPE VERDE

SENEGAL

GAMBIA
GUINEA BISSAU

BURKINA
FASO

GUIN

BE

COSTA RICA

VENEZUELA

GUYANA
SURINAME

SIERRA LEONE

IVORY
COAST

GHAN

PANAMA

COLOMBIA

FRENCH GUIANA (Fr.)

LIBERIA

TOGO
EQUA

0°   Equator

ECUADOR

Gulf of
Guinea

SAO T
& PRI

PERU

BRAZIL

BOLIVIA

PARAGUAY

SOUTH ATLANTIC
OCEAN

30°S

SOUTH PACIFIC
OCEAN

URUGUAY

CHILE

ARGENTINA

60°S

Weddell
Sea

AN

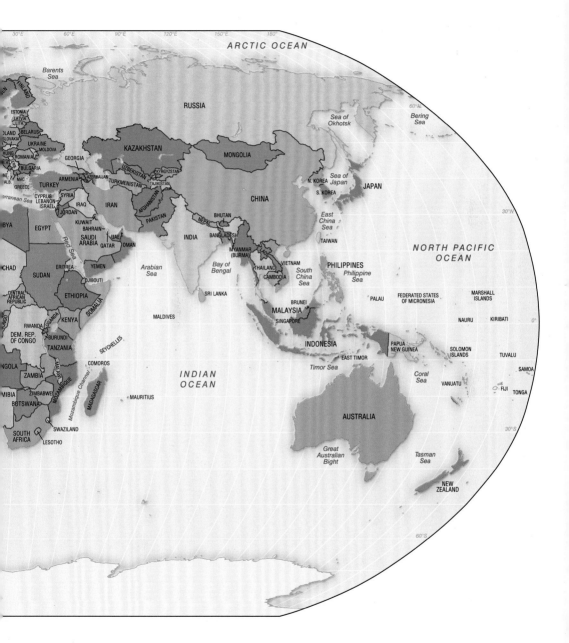